How Taxes Affect
Economic Behavior

Studies of Government Finance: Second Series

TITLES PUBLISHED

How Taxes Affect Economic Behavior

HENRY J. AARON
JOSEPH A. PECHMAN
Editors

Studies of Government Finance

THE BROOKINGS INSTITUTION

WASHINGTON, D.C.

Library of Congress Cataloging in Publication Data:

Main entry under title:

How taxes affect economic behavior.

   (Studies of government finance. Second series)
   Includes index.
   1. Taxation—United States—Addresses, essays,
lectures. 2. Fiscal policy—United States—
Addresses, essays, lectures. 3. United States—
Economic policy—1961– —Addresses, essays,
lectures. I. Aaron, Henry J. II. Pechman,
Joseph A., 1918– . III. Brookings Institution.
IV. Series.

HJ2381.H68   336.2'00973   81-1040
                                               AACR2

ISBN 0-8157-0012-1
ISBN 0-8157-0011-3 (pbk.)

9 8 7 6 5 4 3 2 1

THE BROOKINGS INSTITUTION is an independent organization devoted to nonpartisan research, education, and publication in economics, government, foreign policy, and the social sciences generally. Its principal purposes are to aid in the development of sound public policies and to promote public understanding of issues of national importance.

The Institution was founded on December 8, 1927, to merge the activities of the Institute for Government Research, founded in 1916, the Institute of Economics, founded in 1922, and the Robert Brookings Graduate School of Economics and Government, founded in 1924.

The Board of Trustees is responsible for the general administration of the Institution, while the immediate direction of the policies, program, and staff is vested in the President, assisted by an advisory committee of the officers and staff. The by-laws of the Institution state: "It is the function of the Trustees to make possible the conduct of scientific research, and publication, under the most favorable conditions, and to safeguard the independence of the research staff in the pursuit of their studies and in the publication of the results of such studies. It is not a part of their function to determine, control, or influence the conduct of particular investigations or the conclusions reached."

The President bears final responsibility for the decision to publish a manuscript as a Brookings book. In reaching his judgment on the competence, accuracy, and objectivity of each study, the President is advised by the director of the appropriate research program and weighs the views of a panel of expert outside readers who report to him in confidence on the quality of the work. Publication of a work signifies that it is deemed a competent treatment worthy of public consideration but does not imply endorsement of conclusions or recommendations.

The Institution maintains its position of neutrality on issues of public policy in order to safeguard the intellectual freedom of the staff. Hence interpretations or conclusions in Brookings publications should be understood to be solely those of the authors and should not be attributed to the Institution, to its trustees, officers, or other staff members, or to the organizations that support its research.

Foreword

THE POOR PERFORMANCE of the American economy in recent years has generated considerable interest in the use of tax policy to stimulate economic growth. Opinions regarding the possible effectiveness of tax policy in achieving this objective differ sharply. Some believe that changes in tax rates and in key structural features of the tax system would increase work, saving, and investment and boost the growth of productivity dramatically. Others believe that these claims are exaggerated.

Although public finance economists have always accepted the idea that taxation can have significant effects on incentives, it is only recently that they have turned to making quantitative estimates of these effects. Much of this research has been reported in professional journals not read by the public. Since the issues are important as well as complex, the Brookings Institution convened a conference of experts on October 18–19, 1979, to evaluate competing claims and to arrive at the best quantitative estimates of alternative tax policies.

The papers presented and discussed at the conference were prepared by scholars trained in modern econometric techniques. The areas covered include labor supply, business investment, corporate financial policy, the stock market, capital gains, residential construction, saving, and charitable contributions. Each author was asked to review previous estimates of the effects of tax policy in the particular area assigned to him and to prepare his own estimates on the basis of the most recent data available to him. This volume contains the papers presented at the conference, revised to take into account the comments and suggestions of the conference participants, and the comments of the formal discussants of each paper. The introductory chapter provides a summary of the papers and of the major points raised in the conference discussions.

The editors, Henry J. Aaron and Joseph A. Pechman, are, respectively, a senior fellow in and director of the Brookings Economic Studies program. The manuscript was edited by Elizabeth H. Cross and the index was prepared by Florence Robinson. The project was supported with funds provided by the Ford Foundation and the National Science Foundation. This is the fourteenth volume in the second series of Brookings Studies of Government Finance. Both series are devoted to examining issues of taxation and public policy.

The views expressed in this book are those of the authors and the conference discussants and should not be ascribed to the Ford Foundation, the National Science Foundation, or to the trustees, officers, or other staff members of the Brookings Institution.

BRUCE K. MAC LAURY
President

January 1981
Washington, D.C.

Contents

ix

Tables

Figures

Contents

HENRY J. AARON *and* JOSEPH A. PECHMAN

Introduction and Summary

TAXES divert resources from private to public use. But they also influence how private agents use resources, and Congress has used the tax laws aggressively to influence private behavior. The study of the intended and unintended effects of taxes on private consumption, investment, financial structure, and labor supply has been a major preoccupation of public finance economists for decades. For many years the public seemed to be interested more in the way taxes affect the level of economic activity than in how they influence the character of that activity. But popular attention is increasingly being devoted to a subject that has long absorbed the economics profession—how taxes affect the supply and allocation of resources.

The papers in this volume report on the state of economic research into the effects of taxes on labor supply, business equipment investment, corporate financial structure, the prices of common stock, capital gains, housing investment and prices, saving, and charitable giving. They do not purport to encompass all the ways taxes influence economic behavior. Nor do they tie together in a single framework the simultaneous influence of taxes on decisions that in fact influence one another. The difficult problem of relating the simultaneous effect of taxes on each of these important aspects of economic behavior must still be solved. But these papers do report important areas of progress in identifying the economic effects of taxes and they suggest how our understanding can be further improved.

Labor Supply

Taxes on labor income raise more than half of all federal revenues. They are among the more prominent instruments of income redistribu-

1

tion. Also, they change various kinds of economic behavior, including decisions by people about how much they should work—how many hours a year, how many years during their lives, how hard, and at what tasks.

Jerry Hausman reexamines one aspect of this question—how taxes affect the annual number of hours worked. His findings contrast sharply with the results of earlier research. Economists have held previously that the labor supply of prime-age males is quite insensitive to variations in income or wage rates, that the labor supply of wives is sensitive to both wage rates and other family income, and that the sensitivity of the labor supply of female heads of household is somewhere in between. These findings led immediately to the inference that income taxes could not seriously distort the labor supply of prime-age males, but that they did distort the labor supply decision of wives and, to a considerably lesser extent, of female household heads.

Hausman begins his paper with a critique of the methods previous investigators used. Most failed to adequately specify the variety of taxes and transfers that workers face and hence the complexity of the schedule of net wages they can earn as they increase the number of hours worked. Such net wages may rise or fall as the hours of work increase, depending on the worker's place of residence, sex, age, and other factors. These variations in net wages create difficult problems in economic theory that have not been incorporated explicitly in most previous research. Once these complications are incorporated into models of economic behavior, however, new and difficult problems of how to measure behavioral responses to earnings opportunities arise.

These difficulties led Hausman to the second innovative feature of his paper, the application of recently developed econometric methods to the estimation of labor supply functions. His estimation technique explicitly allows for differences among workers in the degree to which taxes change the number of hours they work. Hausman finds that the combination of federal and state income taxes and the payroll tax leads husbands to reduce the amount they work significantly—about 8 percent for men who earned between $8,000 and $12,000 in 1975—and imposes significant inefficiencies as measured by "deadweight loss." Deadweight loss is the dollar value of the distortions that result as taxpayers seek to avoid paying all the taxes they would have to pay if they behaved as they would if taxes were collected as lump-sum payments. The deadweight loss for a worker earning $6.18 an hour, the average wage in 1975, is 22 percent of revenue collected. For a worker earning $10.00 an hour the deadweight loss is 54 percent of revenue collected.

Hausman's results raise important questions about the structure of income taxation in the United States. Replacement of the present mix of progressive personal income taxes and payroll taxes with a proportional income tax or an income-type value-added tax would reduce the deadweight loss from taxes on prime-age males by about 45 percent for the worker earning $6.18 and 53 percent for the $10 worker. The results for wives and female household heads are similar, but these findings do not clash with the accepted findings of other investigators.

Both the formal discussants of Hausman's paper praised its innovativeness. One pointed out that the study deals with only one of the ways in which workers can alter their labor supply in response to taxes. In addition to varying hours worked, they may change their decisions about how much training or education to acquire or about what occupations to pursue. Available information does not permit analysis of these effects, although in the view of a number of the participants in the conference they may be quite important. This discussant also pointed out that simulations based on optimal tax theory and previously available estimates of labor supply suggested that the need to balance economic efficiency with distributional equity implied that only limited progressivity is optimal. Hausman's findings would lead to even lower estimates of optimal progressivity.

The other formal discussant warned that care should be exercised in interpreting Hausman's results because they depend to an important degree on the variability in the income elasticity of labor supply that is one of the distinguishing features of the model. He pointed out that the particular functional form of the distribution of the preferences used in the study may have influenced the estimates. In particular, some workers may increase labor supply when their incomes rise. In addition, the model adopted by Hausman permits some workers to reduce labor supply by large and possibly unrealistic amounts in response to increases in income. Permitting labor supply to increase when income rises and not permitting large negative responses might alter the results significantly.

The consensus of most conference participants was that Hausman's findings emerged from sound theoretical and careful and imaginative empirical work. Nevertheless, a number of doubts and questions emerged. One participant stressed that the handling of preferences for work and leisure was simplistic. For example, the model not only did not allow for the impact of taxes on career choice and the acquisition of human capital, but also did not allow for the interaction between the labor supply choices of husbands and those of wives. In some cases decisions by wives to increase work and earnings might induce husbands, conscious of intra-family status, to work and to earn more themselves, a possibility not allowed for in Hausman's model.

Some concern was expressed about the quality of the data used in the study, particularly those relating to assets. One participant stressed that the official benefit-reduction rate in the aid to families with dependent children program was misleadingly high because of the prevalence of special allowances and deductions. Another participant suggested that workers in 1975, the year to which Hausman's data referred, were probably unable to work the number of hours they would have preferred because of high unemployment and relatively short workweeks during that recession year.

A number of participants questioned the importance to public policy of the estimates of deadweight loss. They stressed the interest of the public in the effects of taxes on labor supply. They recognized that Hausman's estimate that taxes reduced the labor supply of husbands by about 8 percent was higher than previous estimates, but they suggested that this response was relatively modest and would be unlikely to perturb policy-makers; in any event, it was at least a more relevant number, given active political concerns, than the estimates of deadweight loss. Other conferees disputed this position and defended the importance of the concept of deadweight loss in thinking about improvements in the tax structure. Despite its abstraction, this concept provides a better measure of the losses from tax-induced distortions than changes in the number of hours worked do, according to these participants.

One discussant raised the question of whether Hausman's findings bore on the relative attractiveness of income and consumption taxation. Hausman expressed the view that his conclusions related more to the costs and benefits of progressivity than to the relative advantages of different tax bases.

Private Business Investment

For many years economists have debated whether changes in the cost of capital or in expected sales explained more of the variation of business fixed investment. Patric Hendershott and Sheng-Cheng Hu take up this question again in their paper. The cost of capital is the full cost of hiring or renting a capital good, taking account of depreciation, interest, inflation, and taxes.

Previous investigators have shown that the relative importance of these two possible determinants of investment depends on several factors. The first is the degree to which the optimal mix of capital and labor used in production depends on the relative price of capital and labor. If the mix is insensitive to variations in relative factor prices, variations in the desired capital stock and hence in investment undertaken to achieve that capital stock depend only on expected sales. If the mix is sensitive to variations in relative prices, variations in investment depend on both expected sales and, through relative prices, on such influences as changes in interest rates, inflation, and tax policies.

Even if it becomes clear that both factor prices and expected sales affect the ultimately desired capital stock, the speed of such effects still depends on a second crucial aspect of the capital stock, the degree to which methods of production using existing capital goods can be modified when the cost of capital and thus the optimal capital–labor ratio in production change. The more readily the capital–labor ratio can be altered, the more rapid will be the effect on investment of changes in the user cost of capital. Hendershott and Hu find that factor proportions of newly purchased equipment respond to changes both in expected sales and in the cost of capital. Once capital has been put in place, however, they find some evidence that factor proportions are not quickly altered in response to changes in the user cost of capital. The alteration occurs only gradually as capital depreciates; it therefore derives from the difference between the current user cost of capital and those of previous periods when orders were placed.

When either the cost of capital or expected sales change, businesses cannot immediately adjust the capital stock to its new, desired level. As a result, both the ratio of the market value of a firm's debt and equity to the replacement cost of its nonfinancial assets and the rate of capacity utilization may fluctuate. Hendershott and Hu find that the first of these variables explains little of the variation in equipment investment, but that this investment is sensitive to the rate of capacity utilization. Because the lag between orders and deliveries is uncertain and the investor has only limited control over it, they restrict their analysis to orders. Hendershott and Hu do not explain orders for structures with the same model because an adequate order series is not available and because the user costs during the periods when this long-lived capital was initially ordered cannot readily be computed. The results presented here apply only to equipment investment.

Changes in taxes—tax rates, depreciable lives, and tax credits—have a sizable effect on investment through their impact on the user cost of capital. For example, Hendershott and Hu estimate that, if no other variable changed, cutting the tax service life of equipment in half would have increased the desired equipment stock in 1978 from $800 billion to $910 billion, or almost 14 percent. Half of the adjustment would occur within four years; three-quarters, within eight. The authors note that these estimates overstate the actual increase in investment because other variables would probably change in an offsetting manner; in particular, interest rates would rise unless capital were available in unlimited quantities at a constant interest rate (for example, from borrowing abroad). Because interest rates would rise, the increase in the stock of equipment would be less than 14 percent, and some of that smaller increase would come at the expense of other types of investment.

The discussion ranged over several topics. A number of participants stressed the importance of the point made by Hendershott and Hu that a model of equipment investment should be fitted into a larger framework that included equations explaining other types of investment and savings. Only in such a framework could the impact on investment in equipment of interest rates, the supply of savings, and other forms of investment be explicitly considered.

One discussant held that the effect of changes in the cost of capital on investment is probably more important than Hendershott and Hu's unconstrained estimates suggest. He argued that when investment is high, in part because the user cost of capital is low, capacity utilization tends to be high. Thus part of the correlation between capacity utilization and investment is spurious and part of the influence on investment attributed to the rate of capacity utilization should in fact be attributed to the cost of capital. He preferred Hendershott and Hu's constrained estimates, which attributed a much smaller role to capacity utilization.

Some discussion centered on the specific measure for the cost of capital that Hendershott and Hu developed. One discussant argued that the conceptually correct measure is not the weighted average of the bond rate and equity yield they used, but rather the marginal cost of capital to investing firms. While holding that a measure of marginal cost is theoretically preferable, this discussant acknowledged the great difficulty of developing one in practice.

Corporation Finance

The effect of taxation on the financial policy of corporations has puzzled economists for a long time. The classical analysis of this subject by Franco Modigliani and Merton H. Miller published about twenty years ago concluded that investors would be indifferent to the debt–equity ratio and the dividend payout rate if there were no taxes and no costs of bankruptcy. Their capital-asset pricing model assumes that shareholders can borrow just as easily as corporations and at the same rate. Shareholders can therefore offset any financial actions taken by the firm not to their liking; if the firm does not borrow enough, they can borrow more, and vice versa.

If bankruptcy is introduced into the model but no account is taken of taxes, debt finance raises costs because lenders will require a higher interest rate to compensate them for the added risk. Consequently, debt finance will be more expensive than equity finance and firms will issue no debt. Personal and business taxes work in the other direction. If there is no bankruptcy or if bankruptcy is costless, investors pay lower taxes by owning debt (because firms can deduct interest on debt but not dividends) and firms have an incentive to increase their debt–equity ratios without limit. When both bankruptcy and taxes are taken into account, there is an equilibrium debt–equity ratio at which the firm is indifferent between debt and equity finance. Each firm has its own optimal debt–equity ratio, and individuals will hold diversified portfolios of debt and equity. However, taxes affect the choice of assets held by different people (for instance, high-income people will prefer capital gains to dividends). As a result, risk will be spread inefficiently among investors. The inefficient allocation of risk is the welfare cost of having a tax system that treats the returns from different assets differently.

Although progress has been made in explaining why firms issue both equity and debt, economists have yet to explain the size and stability of dividends. Since capital gains are taxed at a lower rate than dividends, firms are encouraged to avoid paying out their earnings. However, on the average, the stock market seems to value capital gains and dividends about equally. One explanation of the existence of dividends and the stability of dividend payments may be that they are signals to investors concerning the relative strength of different firms. Nevertheless, economists have not yet satisfactorily explained the dividend policies of corporations.

In their paper, Gordon and Malkiel summarize the implications of the capital-asset pricing model, with particular emphasis on how the possibility of bankruptcy affects the financial decisions of corporations. Their figures suggest that the costs of the threat of bankruptcy are high and that these costs have not been fully appreciated by previous investigators. On the assumption that the difference between the after-tax rates of return on equity and debt are equal to the expected marginal bankruptcy costs, they estimate that the distortion in debt–equity ratios resulting from the tax system generated a deadweight loss of $3.2 billion in 1975. They also estimate that the loss arising from inefficient risk-taking is small. They do not attempt to calculate the loss from any possible distortion in dividend payout rates because of the unsatisfactory state of theory regarding corporate dividend policy. Since the major source of inefficiency from the present tax system is too much debt in corporate finance, they conclude that any of several ways of reducing the tax distortion favoring debt finance would produce significant welfare gains.

Much of the discussion centered on another cost the tax on corporate profits is alleged to impose on the private economy. Gordon and Malkiel as well as others have pointed out that, if bankruptcy cannot occur, firms will invest until the marginal rate of return on new investments is the same as the interest rate they must pay on borrowed money. Such projects will produce cash flow just sufficient to pay off a loan adequate to finance the whole project and will not generate any tax liability. Because interest is deductible, the rate of return to the firm at the margin would appear to be independent of the corporation tax. On these assumptions, the corporation tax does not induce a misallocation of real capital in the private economy if all investments are financed by debt.

A number of participants, including Gordon and Malkiel, argued that these assumptions are unrealistic. In the first place, firms cannot borrow without limit because the risk of bankruptcy rises as the fraction of debt in the firm's total liabilities rises, other things being held constant. Thus firms must have recourse to equity markets where the distorting effects of the corporation income tax are generally acknowledged. When the potential costs of bankruptcy are recognized, the relevant interest rate that equates the return on real investment and new debt includes expected bankruptcy costs. The present expected value of potential bankruptcy costs forms a wedge between the marginal return on corporate capital and the market interest rate. This cost reduces corporate investment below the level that would be optimal in the absence of the tax. Second, the corporation tax may be especially burdensome for small businesses because they cannot borrow as large a fraction of their capital as established businesses can. Third, the analysis does not take into account the effect of inflation on corporate tax liabilities. Firms using borrowed capital have been better protected from the increase in the real tax burden caused by inflation than those relying heavily on equity capital.

Another question that arose concerns the distinction between the social costs of bankruptcy and the private costs affecting the financial decisions of business firms. Several of the participants held that the social costs exceeded the private costs of bankruptcy; as a result, they believed that the Gordon-Malkiel cost measurements understated total costs. Others interpreted Gordon and Malkiel as saying that the private costs are the only social costs; if this is the case, they may have overstated total costs because some of the private costs are matched by private gains (for example, purchasers of bankrupt firms gain at the expense of the original holders of the equity and debt of such firms). Gordon and Malkiel agreed that, because of the many uncertainties, it is not clear whether their estimates understate or overstate total costs.

One participant asked why Gordon and Malkiel's estimates of the costs of bankruptcy were so much higher than previous estimates. They replied that previous estimates, which relied on the records of trustees' fees reported to the Securities and Exchange Commission, identified only a small portion of the direct costs. Many costs other than trustees' fees arise in bankruptcy proceedings, however, such as costs in time of the firm's managers, costs from the uncertainty of the outcome, disruption of the firm's operations, and inefficient incentives to liquidate instead of reorganize the firm. And even when bankruptcy proceedings are avoided, costs arise from reduced investment incentives, negotiation and monitoring activity of the lenders, and perhaps informal reorganizations. The indirect technique of estimating total bankruptcy-related costs used by Gordon and Malkiel, based on the difference between the rates of return on debt and equity capital, ought to include all the above types of costs.

The existence of dividend payments despite the additional tax that must be paid by shareholders was also discussed. Gordon and Malkiel emphasized that dividends signal the market regarding the financial potential of firms. However, it was pointed out that this signal is rather costly—the additional tax is probably on the order of $15 billion annually. It was generally agreed that the explanation of why firms persist in paying dividends despite such a large penalty remains a puzzle.

Stock Prices

Economists used to speculate that stock prices would perform particularly well during inflation because, unlike bonds, dividends and retained earnings tend to rise with prices. Stocks, it was asserted, would act as a hedge against inflation, but bonds would not.

Not much has been heard of this line of argument lately. At about the same time that inflation began to be troublesome, the steep rise in stock prices that had stretched with few interruptions from the late 1940s through the late 1960s abruptly stopped. By 1979 nominal stock prices in the aggregate had not risen for a decade, and real stock prices—adjusted for the decline in the purchasing power of the dollar—stood at more than 40 percent below their level in 1972 and slightly below the low point reached during the recession year of 1975.

The economics profession has adapted to the stubborn refusal of events to follow its predictions by trying to explain the stock market's perversity. It is pointed out, for example, that inadequate depreciation allowances depress real business profits below book profits and that the tax advantages of homeownership lead investors to put more of their portfolios into owned homes and less into other investments. Others have cited rising personal income tax rates in general, and less favorable tax treatment of capital gains in particular, as stock market depressants. These explanations rest on factors that make stocks genuinely less attractive as investments.

Another line of argument holds that much of the poor performance of the stock market derives not from real factors, but from the apprehension of investors about business prospects or from the inability of investors to estimate the prospective value of equity investment in a period of persistent inflation.

Roger Brinner and Stephen Brooks examine these hypotheses. They find a number of underlying factors that would have led one to expect current stock prices to be considerably higher than they are today. Their statistical analysis attributes the difference to investors' loss of confidence resulting from economic instability and misperceptions about prospective corporate earnings during inflation.

In their empirical appraisal, the authors begin with a careful estimate of the expected present value of anticipated dividends and capital gains on equities held for a representative period. Each of the components of the return is appropriately measured on an after-tax basis. Brinner and Brooks find that 70 percent of the *variation* in stock prices is explained by *variations* in this present expected value. Based on this variable alone, however, stock market prices in 1978 would have been nearly twice as high as they were, reflecting an enormous discount compared to the 15 percent average discount that prevailed from 1955 to 1970. This discount, and hence most of the remaining variation in stock prices, is found to be due to two phenomena. First, investors' confidence in the economy (as measured by the University of Michigan Index of Consumer Sentiment) and perceptions of money market conditions have significant impacts. For example, the 1974 turmoil associated with Watergate and tight credit conditions are estimated to have depressed the market by slightly more than 20 percent. Second, inflation has so distorted corporate balance sheets in which physical assets are recorded at book value rather than replacement cost that investors are systematically underestimating the net worth of corporations. From the mid-1950s through the late 1960s corporate net worth measured on a replacement-value basis closely tracked the book value; each measure doubled in the period 1955–67. But from 1967 to 1978 replacement net worth increased by a factor of three though book value increased by a factor of only two, and Brinner and Brooks's analysis indicates that stock market participants only partially appreciated the true value of the increase that had occurred. This failure produced an average equity price in 1978 approximately 20 percent below the legitimate value. Recognition of this illusion increases the explanatory power of the model by an amount comparable to the confidence and credit variables.

Brinner and Brooks also devote considerable attention to the impact of taxes on equity values. Taxes levied only on capital gains will depress market values in predictable ways based on the present value of the tax burden. But the authors also note that general increases in personal taxes have conflicting effects on equity prices; other things being equal, a rise in income tax rates cuts both the after-tax stream of dividends and capital gains and the discount rate applied to these future streams. Through their analysis the authors conclude that, while tax changes over the past two decades have had significant impacts on equity prices (when the statistical definition of significance is used), the actual size of the tax effect has been relatively small. The tax reductions of the early 1960s did provide a boost to the market, but this effect has been almost fully offset by the upward creep in personal rates since then.

Discussion of the Brinner-Brooks paper raised a number of questions about the methods they used and suggested alternative explanations for the poor performance of the stock market. One discussant claimed that the tax rate the authors had used in calculating an after-tax discount rate was improperly estimated and that the assumptions regarding the future paths of dividends and earnings were inconsistent, leading to implausible implicit estimates of retained earnings. According to this discussant, rather than calculating the average tax rate of dividend recipients, the authors should have used the tax rate implicit in the relative yields on taxable and tax-exempt bonds.

One participant suggested that much of the divergence between the continued rapid growth of the present expected value of dividends and sale proceeds and the sluggish performance of stock prices could be attributed to inflation-induced fears—about the greater swings in relative prices that can be expected during inflation, about the threat of controls, or about government policies undertaken to curb inflation that incidentally cause recession and declining profits. This view drew support from several conference participants, but provoked the comment that while such fears might be important there is no way to quantify them and hence to measure their importance.

Capital Gains

The taxation of capital gains has been a controversial issue since the federal income tax was enacted in 1913. Until 1921 capital gains were taxed as ordinary income. Capital losses were not deductible in 1913–15, deductible only from capital gains in 1916–17, and deductible in full from income of any kind in 1918–21. Beginning in 1922, special low rates were adopted for capital gains and various restrictions were placed on the deductibility of losses. From 1942 to 1969 capital gains on assets held for more than six months were taxed at half the ordinary rates, with a maximum of 25 percent; capital losses were offsettable against capital gains plus $1,000 of ordinary income. The holding period distinguishing short- from long-term capital gains was lengthened to nine months in 1977 and twelve months beginning in 1978. From the beginning of 1970 to October 31, 1978, the maximum tax rate on long-term capital gains was set at 25 percent on gains of less than $50,000 and 35 percent on gains of $50,000 or more; and the excluded portion of capital gains was subject to a special "minimum tax on tax preferences," which increased the maximum tax rate on capital gains to about 40 percent for taxpayers subject to the minimum tax and to as much as 49 percent for a few taxpayers who were subject to both the minimum tax and the maximum tax rate of 50 percent on earned income. The maximum offset of capital losses against ordinary income was raised to $2,000 in 1977 and to $3,000 beginning in 1978.

The Revenue Act of 1978 reduced the tax rates on long-term capital gains to 40 percent of the tax rates on ordinary income. With a maximum ordinary income tax rate of 70 percent, the maximum tax rate on capital gains became 28 percent. This reduction in the capital gains tax rates was justified on the ground that the rates imposed throughout most of the 1970s were discouraging risk-taking and capital investment. Some estimates made before enactment of the 1978 act suggested that rate reductions of the magnitude adopted would greatly increase the number of capital gains transactions from the sale of corporate stock and actually raise rather than lower tax collections from capital gains.

Joseph J. Minarik addresses these questions, using data from the Treasury Capital Assets file for 1973, which contains detailed information on the sources of capital gains of income tax payers. He found that the effect of the capital gains tax rates is mitigated by the ability of taxpayers to time their realizations of capital gains so as to take advantage of offsetting losses. High-income taxpayers with diversified portfolios, in particular, can realize losses sufficient to greatly reduce or even eliminate the tax on their gains. Such transactions were not confined to shares of stock; indeed, there was a striking tendency for stock losses to be used to offset gains from real estate and other assets.

To measure the lock-in effect of the capital gains tax, Minarik provides estimates of the realized long-term capital gains from the sale of stock based on a regression equation that captures a number of the characteristics of taxpayers that are likely to affect the decision to sell assets. These characteristics include the size of the taxpayer's portfolio (represented by the amount of dividends received), income from other sources, gains and losses on other assets, itemized deductions, business losses, and the marginal tax rate on capital gains. In this equation, the existence of large business losses or large itemized deductions is associated with larger realizations of capital gains, suggesting that taxpayers take advantage of their low marginal tax rates to realize capital gains.

Like previous investigators, Minarik found that for the entire tax return population there was no apparent relationship between the capital gains tax rates and realizations. He was more successful, however, when tax returns reporting dividends of less than $3,000 were omitted from the analysis. The elasticity of realizations with respect to the capital gains tax rate turns out to be negative, but less than one in absolute value, for tax-payers with portfolios between $90,000 and $600,000 and more than one in absolute value for those with portfolios of $600,000 or more, with an average between −0.44 and −0.79. In other words, a reduction in capital gains tax rates from, say, 28 to 21 percent (a 25 percent reduction) would increase realizations by 11 to 20 percent. On the basis of this analysis, Minarik concludes that the Revenue Act of 1978 did not generate enough new capital gains realizations to offset the revenue loss from reducing the tax rates on capital gains.

A major question raised in the discussion was that an analysis of cross-section data is likely to reveal only the short-term effects of a change in the capital gains tax rate. In an analysis of capital gains reported by a randomly chosen panel of identical taxpayers over the period 1967–73, Gerald Auten and Charles Clotfelter found that the long-term response to the capital gains tax rate is larger than the short-term response. Unfortunately, because the sample was randomly chosen, the panel did not include many wealthy taxpayers. Furthermore, the data included capital gains from all sources, and it is impossible to isolate gains from stock transactions.

A question was also raised about the tax variable used by Minarik in his analysis. Ideally, what is needed is an estimate of the marginal rate faced by taxpayers when they are deciding whether to realize a capital gain or not. Minarik argued that the marginal capital gains rates on the first or last dollar of capital gains on stock are subject to distortion resulting from carry-overs and losses on other assets. Instead, he used the average effective tax rate on a predicted amount of stock gains for fifty-six subpopulations (based on a cross-classification of dividends and adjusted gross income net of stock gains). It was agreed that the choice of the proper tax rate variable remains a difficult problem in this type of analysis.

The conferees also debated whether the regression estimates should be based on the actual sample cases without weights or whether weights should be assigned to them on the basis of the sampling procedure. The data file Minarik used is a stratified sample of tax returns, with the sampling rates increasing with adjusted gross income (which includes capital gains). One conferee argued that the correct practice would be the usual one of running the regressions without weights. Another defended Minarik's use of the weights, arguing that the positive correlation between the sampling rates and realized capital gains would bias the coefficients in any regression with gains as the independent variable unless the weights were used.

Several of the participants commented that the emphasis placed on the impact of the capital gains rates on investment incentives does not take into account the important role of loss offsets. Three decades ago, Musgrave and Domar demonstrated that a progressive income tax with full loss offsets would result in increased risk-taking. It was generally agreed that the effect of the tax structure on investment depends on the treatment of losses as well as gains.

Housing

For more than a decade prices of owner-occupied housing have risen faster than the general price level. This robust performance contrasts with the sluggish movement of the prices of common stocks and with the price trends for rental housing. A number of authors have speculated that the differences in these price trends may be related to the interaction between various personal and business tax provisions and the increases in inflation that have been characteristic of the U.S. economy since 1965.

Frank de Leeuw and Larry Ozanne demonstrate that these hypotheses are consistent with the facts. They develop a model of the value of an investment related to the value of the services that investment generates, operating costs, depreciation, the probable period of ownership, scrap or sales value, and tax provisions. Their analysis measures the size of a number of well-known qualitative findings on the tax advantages owner-occupants enjoy; but they go further and calculate the effect on the "demand price," or present discounted value of the investment. Thus disallowing the deductibility of mortgage interest would reduce the price of a hypothetical representative house by 9.2 percent; if net imputed rent (gross rental value less all expenses) were taxed too, the price of the same house would drop by 14.3 percent. The price of a hypothetical rental housing project would decline 7.2 percent if owners could not deduct more than economic depreciation in calculating their tax liabilities.

When inflation occurs, the value of housing tends to rise unless mortgage rates rise by considerably more than one percentage point for each percentage point of inflation. The fact that interest is fully deductible against ordinary income, while the added value at the time of sale is taxed only at capital gains rates, if at all, assures this result despite the limitation of depreciation on rental housing to historical costs.

The effect of inflation on the relative price of various assets is dramatic. At 12 percent inflation, if interest rates are twelve percentage points higher than they were when prices were stable, the value of owner-occupied housing will be about 22 percent higher, the value of rental housing about 12 percent higher, and the value of plant and equipment investment about 22 percent lower than they would be if prices were stable and no other characteristics of the investment changed. In other terms, owner-occupied housing worth the same as plant and equipment when prices were stable would be worth over 50 percent more at 12 percent inflation, purely because of tax factors, if interest rates rose the same number of percentage points as the inflation rate. Such tax-induced distortions in relative values can be expected to cause major shifts in investment patterns and generate serious inefficiencies.

De Leeuw and Ozanne suggest the magnitude of some of these changes by calculating not only the short-run effect of changes in tax laws or in the rate of inflation on the demand price of assets, but also the long-run effect of such changes on rental price, housing stocks, and tenure choice. For example, under present tax laws, they estimate that a rise in the rate of inflation from 0 to 12 percent causes a long-run drop of 15 percent in the implicit rental price of owner-occupied housing, and a long-run drop of 12 percent in the price of rental housing.

To reduce distortions in investment patterns caused by inflation, de Leeuw and Ozanne recommend two changes in tax laws affecting housing investment. First, they argue in favor of putting a cap on the maximum allowable amount of mortgage interest that homeowners can deduct. They would place the limit high enough so that few homeowners would be affected by it now. But as prices rose, increasing numbers of homeowners would feel the limit. Second, if interest develops in indexing the base used in calculating depreciation on rental housing, de Leeuw and Ozanne propose that such a move be combined with the establishment of realistic rates of true economic depreciation.

In discussing their paper, one discussant pointed out a number of different inefficiencies that flow from the tax-induced distortions in values estimated by de Leeuw and Ozanne. The most obvious is the overconsumption of housing. Others include reductions in personal saving caused by the perceived rise in home equity and the unequal distribution of these gains within metropolitan areas, which could distort patterns of development between city and suburb.

Another discussant presented information showing that, despite the evidence adduced by de Leeuw and Ozanne, the owner-occupancy rate rose negligibly in the period 1973–77, less than 0.3 percent over the five years. He pointed out that investors could not know at time of purchase whether prices would continue to rise sufficiently to justify interest commitments and that transition costs for renters wishing to become homeowners were considerable.

Two of the conference participants disagreed about whether inflation had or had not increased the cost of capital to corporations. If it had, this strengthened the conclusions of de Leeuw and Ozanne.

There was considerable discussion about whether the value of housing would tend to rise if interest rates rose more than one percentage point for each percentage point of inflation. One participant held that if interest rates rose by $1/(1 - t)$ percentage point for each point of inflation, where t is the tax rate of the marginal investor, housing prices would be unaffected by inflation. The revised paper by de Leeuw and Ozanne shows that this conjecture is almost correct for owner-occupied housing but argues that the assumption that a rise in mortgage rates of $1/(1-t)$ for each percentage point of inflation is unrealistic historically and not necessarily appropriate theoretically. Small effects on the prices of houses remain because of other tax provisions.

One discussant suggested that recent increases in the standard deduction (or zero-bracket amount) had denied some inflation-related tax advantages that taxpayers who itemized would have enjoyed previously. Another discussant acknowledged the validity of this observation but pointed out that even nonitemizers benefit from the nontaxability of net imputed rent.

Several participants explored the policy implications of the findings reported by de Leeuw and Ozanne. One observed that, to the extent that the value of current tax provisions has been capitalized and sold, changing the tax laws would create inequities for current owners who expected such provisions to continue. Another discussant suggested that one can correct the undertaxation of housing investment relative to other investment just as easily by according tax advantages to other investments as by curtailing privileges now enjoyed by owner-occupants. Not only would the course of extending tax advantages have better political prospects, but it would also produce superior allocative results if, as some participants held, income from capital in general is overtaxed.

Saving

One of the more elusive problems for economists and econometricians has been to explain the behavior of saving in the United States. A quarter of a century ago, Edward F. Denison observed that, since the 1920s, the ratio of total *gross private* saving (the sum of household and corporate saving) to the gross national product was constant when the economy was operating at or close to full employment. Paul David and John Scadding later confirmed that this relationship has probably held since 1898. These observations suggest that increases in retained earnings of corporations are perceived by households as increases in their own saving and that increased taxes may be associated by households with increased government consumption that they regard as equivalent to personal consumption. Such ultrarational behavior is possible, but many economists have been unwilling to accept it as plausible. Other attempts to explain the saving behavior of households directly on the basis of rates of return on saving and other variables have yielded widely varying results.

George von Furstenberg attempts to explain saving behavior in the United States in the period 1955–78 by identifying the factors that account for the three major components of national saving: government, personal, and corporate saving. The novel features of his analysis are, first, the introduction of a "fiscal surprise" variable to explain personal saving and, second, the identification of the way in which the three sectoral saving rates interact. The fiscal surprise variable is the deviation of the government saving rate (that is, the surplus or deficit of all units of government) from the rate implied by past fiscal experience. The explanatory variables for corporate saving include real net national product, the gap between actual and potential output, the inventory valuation and capital consumption allowance adjustments, and the effective tax rate on corporate profits. The explanatory variables for personal saving include the gap between actual and potential output, government taxes and transfers, consumer durable goods, and—to allow for the dependence of personal saving on the other sectors—the fiscal surprise variable and corporate saving. All the variables in the analysis are expressed as ratios to the net national product to reduce the risk of simultaneity bias.

Von Furstenberg finds that, although the gross national saving rate is relatively constant, its components are not. The corporate saving rate is reduced when the government increases its saving by raising corporate taxes. Personal saving is negatively related to corporate saving. This result confirms the findings of others that individuals "pierce the corporate veil," so that an increase in corporate saving is reflected in a reduction of personal saving, and vice versa. On the other hand, von Furstenberg denies that personal saving is invariant to government saving. Fiscal surprises generated through personal taxes or transfers have little effect on personal consumption or national saving, because households save or dissave in the expectation that aberrations from the government's normal policies will be reversed. However, changes in the rate of government purchases of goods and services have a powerful effect on national saving. On the average, according to von Furstenberg, the national saving rate is raised by 90 percent of a reduction in government purchases, but by only 10 percent of an unanticipated tax increase or reduction in transfer payment.

Since government purchases generally reflect long-run policies and variations in transfer rates do not have much effect on household saving, it is clearly difficult to change national saving by government policy. Von Furstenberg believes that it may be possible to do so by substituting one tax for another, even without changing the ratio of taxes to net national product. For example, reduced taxes on corporations—say, through higher depreciation allowances—offset by increased taxation of labor income could increase business investment. He agrees, however, that the timing of the effect of such substitutions on the supply of saving is uncertain.

Most of the discussion was directed at the validity of the specifications used by von Furstenberg in designing his behavioral relationships. His contention that the government saving rate can be described by a stable reaction function was questioned. Several of the discussants argued that the government surplus or deficit is not the best instrument for determining the reaction of households to government fiscal policy. They suggested that household behavior depends on the size and type of taxes and governmental expenditures, rather than on the difference between total taxes and total expenditures. It was also pointed out that von Furstenberg in the end lumps together all levels of government, even though the determinants of fiscal policy at the federal level are significantly different from those at the state and local levels.

Doubts were also expressed about the specifications used by von Furstenberg in explaining personal and corporate saving. Essentially, his saving rates depend on the level of business activity, the gap between potential and actual gross national product, and a few variables that are appropriate to each sector. Several participants asserted that there are additional complexities in the relations that determine personal and corporate saving that were not captured in these equations.

Von Furstenberg attempted to include after-tax real rates of return on household net worth in the personal saving equation, but these variables seemed to have no significant effect on the sectoral saving rates or produced doubtful results. For example, the real interest rate variables in one of the personal saving equations has a negative sign, suggesting that an increase in the real interest rate reduces the personal saving rate. Some discussants argued that, because the rate of return affects both the numerator and the denominator of the personal saving rate, there is no reason to suppose that the net effect will necessarily be positive. Others suggested that von Furstenberg's inability to find a statistically significant relationship between rates of return and sectoral saving rates reflects the inappropriateness of the specifications used in his analysis.

The general conclusion of the discussion seemed to be that more explicit modeling of the household and corporate sectors will be needed to identify the factors that explain sectoral saving rates. More work is also needed to determine how anticipated and unanticipated government fiscal policy actions affect consumer and business behavior.

Charitable Contributions

The federal income tax deduction for charitable contributions was enacted in 1917, when tax rates were raised sharply to help pay for World War I. The purpose of the deduction was to encourage continued charitable giving in the face of the high wartime tax rates. Until recently, no one had studied the effectiveness of the deduction in promoting this objective. The first econometric study was by Michael K. Taussig in 1967, who analyzed the contributions of itemizers in the 1962 Treasury federal income tax file. He found that the elasticities of contributions with respect to income were significantly larger than one but the elasticities with respect to price (or one minus the tax rate) were not significantly different from zero for income classes below $100,000. Above $100,000, the price elasticities were slightly negative but significant. Robert A. Schwartz, who performed a similar exercise in 1970 on the basis of time series data for various income classes, found that the income elasticities were much lower than one in all income classes and the price elasticities for incomes above $10,000 were significant but also less than one in absolute value.

A flurry of new estimates began to appear in the late 1970s as a result of the work of Martin Feldstein and various associates, some of which was sponsored by the Commission on Private Philanthropy and Public Needs. Many of the calculations were based on cross-section data obtained from Treasury tax files for various years. In general, the price elasticities in these calculations turned out to be larger in absolute value than one and the income elasticities to be less than one. In some cases, the price elasticities in lower income classes were found to be higher than in upper income classes. Since a price elasticity with absolute value of more than one means that charitable contributions increase by more than the revenue lost as a result of the deduction, supporters of private charities and foundations have used these results to justify even more generous deductions or tax credits than the law now provides for charitable contributions.

In this volume, Charles T. Clotfelter and C. Eugene Steuerle provide new estimates of the price and income elasticities of charitable giving, using principally two new sources. The first, the 1975 Treasury tax file, is similar to the tax files used by previous investigators; the second is a Treasury file for a 1-in-5,000 random sample of federal tax returns filed for the years 1967–73. When specifications were similar to those in previous studies, the 1975 data yielded roughly the same results as those obtained for previous years. When the authors estimated separate price equations for each income class, they found large price elasticities, none significantly smaller than one in absolute value. However, following a suggestion by John A. Brittain, Clotfelter and Steuerle also calculated the elasticities on the assumption that there is an interaction between the price and income elasticities. This modification alters the previous results significantly. The price elasticities are now found to be small at lower income (or higher price) levels and to exceed one in absolute value only at the highest income levels. Emil Sunley obtained similar results with this specification when he used it for an analysis of the contributions in the 1973 Treasury tax file.

Clotfelter and Steuerle also examined time series data on charitable contributions. Using aggregate data for constant-real-income groups, they found that price elasticities were significantly smaller for 1970–75 and 1962–75 than previously reported estimates for the years 1962–70. Using a panel file, they obtained price elasticities for the 1967–73 period that are also less than one in absolute value. However, this randomly selected sample is more accurate for middle-income than for high-income taxpayers, and standard errors are larger than those derived from time series data. Clotfelter and Steuerle point out that these estimates may understate the long-run price elasticity of charitable giving because of possible lags between adjustments to the tax incentive and changes in behavior.

Clotfelter and Steuerle conclude that the price elasticity of charitable giving is significantly different from zero, but not the same in all income classes. Most of their estimates suggest that the price elasticity increases as income increases, so that the tax incentive for charitable giving is most effective in the higher income classes.

The two formal discussants of the Clotfelter-Steuerle paper focused their comments primarily on the differences among the price elasticities of charitable giving by income classes. Both were persuaded by the Clotfelter-Steuerle results that the price elasticity is low at the lower income levels and exceeds one for only a small proportion of the population, those at relatively high incomes (above $30,000 in 1975 prices). Under the circumstances, a single measure of price elasticity for all income groups is not adequate to predict the revenues lost as a result of contribution deductions (or any alternative plan). To make such an estimate, the elasticity at each income level must be weighted by the amount of the contributions made at that level. One discussant attempted such a weighting for the year 1975; he found that the revenue loss exceeded the contributions reported on returns with itemized deductions for income classes below $25,000 and that contributions exceeded the revenue loss above $25,000. For all classes combined, because of the stimulus in the top brackets, total contributions exceeded the revenues lost by a small amount.

During the general discussion, considerable attention was devoted to the meaning of the price elasticities calculated for the lowest income classes. The introduction of a term allowing for the interaction between income and marginal tax rates led to estimates of some positive price elasticities for those at the very lowest end of the income scale, suggesting that the deduction discourages charitable giving at these levels, a result that cannot be rationalized. Clotfelter and Steuerle also note that this paradoxical result can be applied by extrapolation to itemizers excluded from the samples on which the estimates were based. However, there was general agreement that itemizers with very low incomes are atypical. Some of the conference participants pointed out that this group must include many persons who have sustained losses or are temporarily in these income classes for other reasons. Thus their charitable contributions are high relative to their incomes. Several participants argued that the Clotfelter-Steuerle results showing increasing elasticities as incomes rise should be accepted for all income brackets except the lowest.

One discussant also pointed out that the revenue effect is only one of the considerations that should be taken into account in evaluating the deduction for charitable contributions under present law. He suggested that the welfare implications of a rise in contributions associated with an equal decline in revenues needs to be investigated. Clotfelter and Steuerle noted that contributions to private organizations may or may not be adequate substitutes for public expenditures of the same amount, nor is it clear that the types of organizations fostered promote the public interest in all cases. Along with a number of other participants in the conference, they emphasized that the merit of the tax incentive for charitable giving must be judged on broader criteria than the differences between decreased revenues and increased contributions.

Concluding Observations

The conference concluded with a discussion of issues that spanned several of the papers. A number of participants noted the need for a broad framework that takes account of the interdependence among variables treated in various papers. For example, changes in the rate of inflation would have direct effects on saving, the stock market, homeownership, and investment in corporate equipment. But the inflation-induced change in, say, demand for owner-occupied homes would affect interest rates, which, in turn, would affect saving, other forms of investment, and stock prices; the change in stock prices might then affect business investment plans. None of the papers took such general equilibrium effects into account, because each was limited to only one sector. A fully satisfactory treatment of the impact of taxes on each of these quantities, however, would require a framework that simultaneously calculated the effect on all. All agreed that achievement of this objective lay in the future.

One participant commented that most of the papers dwelled at some length on inflation. He suggested that taxes had observable effects on savings, investment, labor supply, and other economic quantities when prices were stable and that it was important to understand these influences; taxes had additional, and sometimes quite different, effects when inflation occurred, and these effects should be analyzed separately. Without challenging the theoretical validity of this distinction, other participants applauded the emphasis on inflation in the conference papers. During a period when inflation was increasing, they held, inattention to the effects it generates by interacting with the tax system would exclude from analysis the most important effects of the tax system on the allocation of resources.

One conference participant strongly challenged the emphasis of a number of the papers on calculating the excess burden, or efficiency loss, attributable to taxes. He stated that he did not think that the public, Congress, or policymakers had the slightest interest in welfare costs as measured by excess burden, and he questioned whether they should. With respect to labor supply, for example, most people were interested in whether taxes increased or decreased the number of hours worked and the acquisition of human capital, but they would be quite uninterested in estimates of the excess burden as a percentage of revenues collected. He subsequently elaborated on the reasons why people do not and should not place much weight on such estimates. Apart from the econometric uncertainties, such estimates presume that resources would be efficiently allocated without the tax provisions under study. In the presence of other distortions, the excess burden from a tax provision may be either more or less than the conventional estimates. Also, citizens and politicians may have values—the promotion of economic growth, changes in the distribution of income, or the promotion of certain types of expenditures—that are not comprehended in the normal utility-maximizing model used for calculating excess burden. In contrast, people can directly conclude whether they think a change in taxes that raises labor supply is a move in the right or the wrong direction.

While a few other participants endorsed this position, many defended the usefulness and value of the calculations of the efficiency losses resulting from taxation. One participant pointed out that in the particular case of the effect of taxes on labor supply the reforms discussed by Hausman would both increase labor supply (which all agreed would be popular) and reduce excess burden. Another participant acknowledged that he could imagine the problem that might arise if some change in taxes was shown to increase labor supply and to reduce economic efficiency; in such a case policymakers might be encouraged to adopt the change because they liked the increase in labor supply and did not care about the estimates of the detrimental effects on efficiency. But such conflicting signals were not present in any example presented at the conference. Furthermore, he stressed the value of calculations of excess burden in appraising the value of tax changes affecting the supply of factors of production other than labor. Congress should pay attention to estimates of the excess burden of alternative taxes on energy, for example. He summarized his position by stating that "if Congress is not going to listen to economists about excess burdens, we might as well all go home, because that is basically what economics is about."

During the concluding comments many of the participants praised the advances in theory, data, and econometric techniques embodied in the papers presented at the conference. However, they also stressed that research to date has produced only tentative results and that policymakers should not treat them as conclusive. While progress is being made toward an understanding of the impact of taxes on saving, investment and other private spending decisions, asset valuation, and financial behavior, considerable work remains to be done. One participant, taking exception to this optimistic appraisal, judged that "we still do not know much about the economic effects of taxation, but we are learning better what the questions are."

JERRY A. HAUSMAN

Labor Supply

ALTHOUGH income and payroll taxes account for 75 percent of federal revenues, most economists have concluded that they cause little reduction in the supply of labor and do little harm to economic efficiency. The results of this study contradict that comforting view. Direct taxes on income and earnings significantly reduce labor supply and economic efficiency. Moreover, the replacement of the present tax structure by a rate structure that proportionally taxes income above an exempt amount would eliminate nearly all of the distortion of labor supply and more than half of the economic waste caused by tax-induced distortions.

Income taxes, in principle, can cause people to work either more or less. Taxes lower the net wage and reduce the labor supply through the compensated substitution effect. But taxes also reduce income, causing people to consume less of all normal goods, including leisure. Thus taxation of labor income can well lead to either more work effort or less. Besides the direction of change, of interest is the size of the effect. One task of this paper is to measure the effect of the existing tax system and of alternative tax systems on the supply of labor.

This paper also reports estimates of the effect of the current tax system on individual welfare. It is a common misconception to assume that a tax is not distortionary if it has little or no effect on market behavior. On the contrary, taxes affect economic efficiency through the compensated substitution effect. If the income effect and the substitution effect offset each other exactly, a tax could still leave individuals much worse off than

I am grateful to Henry Aaron, Cary Brown, Peter Diamond, and Dan Holland for helpful suggestions; to Margaret Tsang, John Hamilton, and Paul Ruud for research assistance; and to the National Science Foundation for research support.

another tax that altered market behavior would. To measure the effect of taxes on economic efficiency, I use the concept of "deadweight loss." When people are taxed they are made worse off, an effect measurable as a loss of consumer's surplus.[1] The difference between the loss people suffer from an actual tax, such as an income or payroll tax, and the loss they would suffer from a lump-sum tax of the same amount—that is, one with no compensated substitution effect—is the deadweight loss, a measure of the distortion created by the tax. The change in individual welfare, the additional money the individual would have to receive to be as well off as he was before the imposition of the tax, is thus equal to the sum of the revenue collected plus the deadweight loss.

This paper presents estimates of changes in labor supply and dead-weight loss for three groups: husbands, wives, and female heads of household. The estimates come from an econometric model of labor supply that takes account of federal and state income taxes as well as the payroll tax.

In brief these results show that the current tax system does significantly reduce labor supply. Husbands work about 8 percent less than they would in the absence of taxes. The reduction in work by wives and female household heads is even greater because they generally face higher tax rates than husbands do.[2] My results confirm the repeated finding of other studies that the tax-induced change in the net wage does not greatly affect the hours worked by husbands, but unlike previous studies, I find an important income effect. As a result deadweight loss is a substantial proportion of tax revenues raised. Because the ratio of deadweight loss to revenue collected increases with the progressivity of the tax, an important trade-off exists between the objectives of reducing inequality and the goal of economic efficiency. The economic cost of a progressive income tax is higher than most previous studies have indicated. Both conclusions hold if the current tax system is compared with a proportional tax system containing exemptions for low-income families that yields the same revenue. A proportional tax system with initial exemptions can still be quite progressive in the lower range of earnings, but not in the higher range. I find

---

1. It is crucial in this area to use the correct theoretical notion of consumer's surplus based on the compensated rather than the market demand or supply curve. I will refer to this issue later. For some calculations that demonstrate the importance of using the correct measure, see Jerry A. Hausman, "Exact Consumer's Surplus" (Massachusetts Institute of Technology, June 1979).

2. I assume that wives respond to the marginal tax rate based on total family income and husbands respond to marginal tax rates based only on their own earnings and the family's nonlabor income.

that a proportional tax with exemptions causes less reduction in labor supply than the current system—1 percent instead of 8 percent. Deadweight loss falls from an average of about 29 percent of tax revenue under the current system to 7 percent with no exemptions under the alternative system. Not only is the economic cost of the current tax system substantial but various tax reform proposals could significantly reduce them.

While these results are straightforward, the analytic methods necessary to reach them are not. Most of this paper is devoted to explaining the problems of economic theory and econometrics that must be overcome to reach reliable conclusions. The next section shows how taxation confronts workers with choices different from those assumed in most previous studies. Most theory of consumer behavior and labor supply is based on constant market prices and wages that are independent of quantity purchased or of the number of hours of labor supplied. However, these theoretical notions need to be modified to take account of the progressive rates of the personal income tax, of such other provisions of the tax code as the earned income credit, the standard deduction, and social security payroll taxes, and of transfer programs such as aid to families with dependent children, all of which cause the net wage to vary, depending on the number of hours worked. Little definite knowledge can be gained by a theoretical analysis of the effect of taxes and transfers. One cannot usually deduce whether a change in tax rates, other tax provisions, or transfers will increase or decrease hours worked. Only empirical investigation can determine the sign and magnitude of the effect of taxation. The second section describes the econometric techniques needed to measure the effect of taxation when tax laws create nonlinearities in the budget sets. The third and fourth sections describe the federal and state taxes and transfers applicable to labor earnings, present detailed results of estimates of the effects of taxes and transfers on labor supply for husbands, wives, and female heads of household, and show the effects of various tax reform proposals, which seem superior to the current tax system, given my model estimates.

A Model of Labor Supply and Taxes

In a world without taxes, the traditional theory of labor supply is closely related to the theory of consumer demand. That is, the individual faces an exogenously determined market wage along with prices of other goods. He may also receive nonlabor income. Given the existence of a

Jerry A. Hausman

Figure 1. Proportional Tax on Labor Income

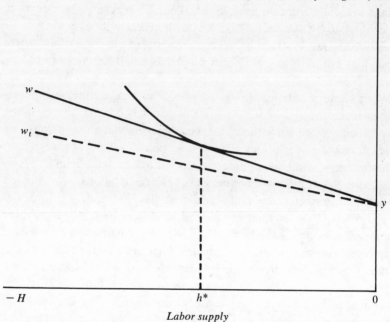

utility function, defined over hours of work and consumption of other goods, the individual decides how many hours to work and how much of each consumer good to buy. Alternatively, think of the consumer as demanding leisure instead of supplying hours of work.[3] But the matter is no longer so simple when taxes are introduced.

The Proportional Tax Case

Figure 1 illustrates the rather straightforward extension to a proportional tax on labor earnings. Households can consume a composite good, representing all goods other than leisure, measured on the vertical axis, and leisure measured on the horizontal axis (leisure is at a maximum when labor supply is zero). Nonlabor income is denoted by y. The original pretax market wage is represented by the solid line, w, and the labor

3. In fact, many theories of labor supply use the concept of full-time hours and leisure demand. However, I do not use it here since it raises unnecessary complications in estimation while adding nothing essential to the theory. For an example of its use, see Robert E. Hall, "Wages, Income, and Hours of Work in the U.S. Labor Force," in Glen G. Cain and Harold W. Watts, eds., *Income Maintenance and Labor Supply* (Rand McNally, 1973), p. 102.

supply by h^*. The effect of a proportional tax is then to lower the net after-tax wage to $w_t = w(1-t)$, represented by the dashed line in the figure. Depending on preferences, desired hours of work may be higher or lower when the net wage is w_t than when it is w. Theory cannot determine whether the compensated substitution effect, which lowers preferred hours of work, or the income effect, which raises them, would dominate. Thus even in the simplest case of proportional taxation, econometric estimates are necessary to determine whether the income or substitution effect is stronger. So long as there is only a single net wage, however, there are no serious econometric problems.

What makes this case so special is that nonlabor income is unaffected by the tax, which falls only on labor income. If nonlabor income were also subject to tax, another income effect, which would cause labor supply to rise, would have to be taken into account. The total effect of taxation on labor supply is still indeterminate.

Nonproportional Taxes and Transfers

If tax rates are progressive or there are transfer programs, both the net wage and nonlabor income are affected.

THE PROGRESSIVE TAX CASE. The simplest case, that of a progressive tax on labor income, is shown in figure 2. Three marginal tax rates, t_1, t_2, t_3, lead to three after-tax wages, w_1, w_2, w_3, respectively. The transition between tax rates t_1 and t_2 occurs at H_1 hours of work, that between t_2 and t_3 at H_2 hours. Associated with each tax rate is a measure of "virtual" income, the intercept on the axis measuring nonlabor income that arises if the net wage line is extended to the vertical axis. Assume that, faced with the progressive tax schedule shown in figure 2, the individual would choose to work a particular number of hours (such as h^* in figure 2), earning a net wage of w_2. He would then choose to work the same number of hours if he had nonlabor income of y_2 and could earn a net wage of w_2 however many hours he worked; hence y_2 is called virtual income. Each budget segment is defined by its net after-tax wage and its virtual income along with the hours of work that define the limits of the segment.[4]

4. I borrow the terminology of virtual income from the idea of a virtual light source in physics. The individual behaves "as if" his nonlabor income is y_i when he is in budget segment i even though his actual nonlabor income is y_1. The virtual income term for the effect of taxes was first used by Gary Burtless and Jerry A. Hausman, "The Effect of Taxation on Labor Supply: Evaluating the Gary Negative Income Tax Experiment," *Journal of Political Economy*, vol. 86 (December 1978), pp. 1103–30.

Figure 2. Progressive Tax on Labor Income

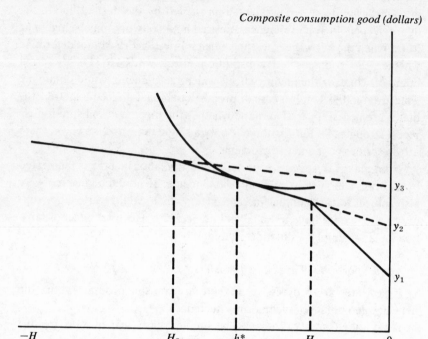

Composite consumption good (dollars)

Once again, it would be convenient to be able to state on the basis of theory whether a change in tax rates or a change in before-tax wage rates will increase or decrease labor supply. It is not possible, in general, to do so. Again, a change in a progressive tax introduces offsetting income and substitution effects so that desired hours of work may either rise or fall. If the market wage increases, the budget set rotates clockwise, increasing all net-wage rates and leaving all virtual incomes unchanged. Therefore, so long as the individual's preferred hours of work remain on the same budget segment, the effect of a wage change can be analyzed by considering the income and substitution along that budget segment alone. However, the individual can change to either a higher or a lower budget segment when the market wage changes, so this effect would also need to be taken into account. Likewise, when tax rates change, individuals may want to shift from one budget segment to another. Thus both movements along a given budget segment and movements between budget segments

Figure 3. Labor Supply with a Nonconvex Budget Set

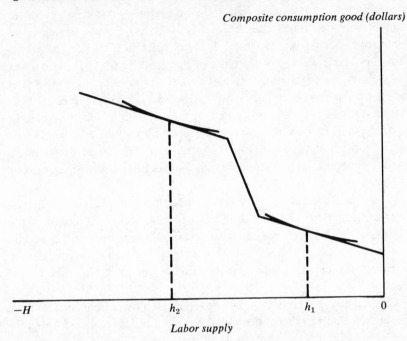

Composite consumption good (dollars)

$-H$ h_2 h_1 0

Labor supply

must be considered. The values of the income and substitution effects at a point do not supply sufficient information to permit reliable estimates of the effects of taxation on labor supply. To make such estimates, one must know the individual's preferences or, equivalently, his utility function. I shall show how knowledge of the worker's utility function arises in the process of estimating his or her labor supply function.

THE NONPROGRESSIVE TAX CASE. When tax rates are not uniformly progressive, matters become more complex since the budget set is no longer convex.[5] As a result, it is possible for there to be two (or more) tangencies of the indifference curves with the budget set (h_1 and h_2 in figure 3). One of these tangencies is preferred to the others. But the usual methods of analysis employed in most previous studies are inadequate for identifying these various local optimums or determining which one is best.

5. As will be discussed subsequently, even the federal tax system is not truly convex because of the effect of social security tax payments, the earned income credit, and the standard deduction. However, it may well be that treating taxes in a convex budget set is a sufficiently good approximation for empirical work.

Nonconvex budget sets arise from the presence of government transfer programs.[6] The three most important programs of this type are aid to families with dependent children (AFDC), social security benefits, and a negative income tax program. The tax rates and transfer payments shown in figure 3 are characteristic of the majority of AFDC programs (as well as the negative income tax experiments). Nonlabor income is raised by the governmental transfer. The individual then faces a high marginal tax rate, usually 40 percent or higher, until he reaches a certain income (the break-even point), corresponding to a certain number of hours worked, at which all benefits have been taxed away. Beyond the break-even point, the individual rejoins the federal tax system, here taken to be progressive.

Almost nothing can be said a priori about the effect of the kind of taxes and transfers shown in figure 3 on labor supply. The possibility of multiple tangencies between indifference curves and the budget set (h_1 and h_2 in figure 3) does not arise in the case of consistently progressive schedules. To determine the global optimum one must know the utility function.

Consistently progressive schedules always have a tangency that is unique and that represents the global optimum if desired hours are positive.[7] Furthermore, the effect on labor supply of a change in the market wage, taxes, or the earnings limits is "smooth" in the appropriate mathematical sense that the change is continuous. In cases such as the one shown in figure 3, this reasoning no longer follows. A small change in taxes or transfers may cause a large and discontinuous jump in labor supply. Thus it seems that no general propositions hold about the effect of taxes in the presence of a nonconvex budget set.

The Fixed Costs of Working

The fixed costs associated with working also create nonconvex budget sets which require knowledge of the utility function to determine labor

6. A nonconvexity may also arise, not from the tax system but from fixed costs of working. See, for example, Jerry A. Hausman, "The Effect of Wages, Taxes, and Fixed Costs on Women's Labor Force Participation," paper presented at the National Bureau of Economic Research–Social Science Research Council Conference on Taxation, June 1979, forthcoming in the *Journal of Public Economics*.

7. See Jerry A. Hausman, "The Econometrics of Labor Supply on Convex Budget Sets," *Economic Letters*, vol. 3 (1979), pp. 171–74, for further analysis and implications of this case.

Figure 4. Budget Set with Fixed Costs Included

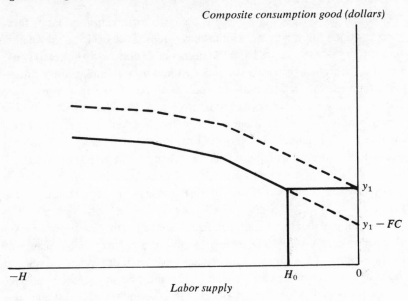

Composite consumption good (dollars)

y_1

$y_1 - FC$

$-H$ H_0 0

Labor supply

supply. Fixed costs—for transportation, child care, and job search—are particularly important for women because they earn lower wages, work fewer hours, and enter and leave the labor force more than men do. Figure 4 shows how fixed costs affect the decision about how many hours to work. When fixed costs are ignored, nonlabor income is y_1 and wages and taxes are similar to those in figure 2. However, the presence of fixed costs, FC, lowers the effective budget set to the point $y_1 - FC$. Under no circumstances would the individual choose to work between zero and H_0 hours because she would have more income and more free time if she did not work at all.[8] The importance of fixed costs could explain the often noted empirical fact that few people are observed working less than ten or fifteen hours a week.[9]

8. This nonconvexity invalidates the simple reservation wage theory of labor force participation since hours also must be accounted for. In a labor force participation study of welfare mothers, I found average fixed costs to be on the order of $100 a month. Hausman, "Effect of Wages, Taxes, and Fixed Costs."

9. Giora Hanoch, in "A Multivariate Model of Labor Supply: Methodology for Estimation" (Rand Corp., September 1976), took fixed costs into account and also found them to be an important influence on labor force participation. However, he ignored the effect of taxes.

Labor Force Participation

Another issue to be considered is the effect of taxation on labor force participation. Some previous studies have treated the decision on whether or not to work as separate from the decision on how many hours to work, but the theoretical grounds for this distinction are implausible. Thus I treat them together. In situations such as those shown in figure 1 (the convex cases) the analysis is straightforward. Whether to work or not depends only on the net wage in the lowest bracket, w_1, and on virtual income, y_1. An increase in taxes that lowers w_1, but leaves y_1 alone, reduces labor force participation. A tax change that reduces y_1, for example, taxation of a spouse's income, increases participation. No effect is created by tax changes that alter the net wage in any bracket except the first.

In situations like those shown in figures 3 and 4 (the nonconvex cases) changes in any tax rate may affect labor force participation because of the possibility of two or more tangencies between indifference curves and the budget set. Thus the complete budget set must be considered in analyzing the participation decision.[10] Because the tax and transfer systems raise nonlabor income and lower the net wage, a further increase in first-bracket tax rates or transfers always lowers the labor force participation of the population. Changes in taxes or transfers above the bottom bracket are not easily analyzed, and their effect cannot be predicted on the basis of theory alone.

Other Issues

Lewis has emphasized that the market wage may depend on hours worked.[11] For example, hourly wages on part-time jobs may be lower than those on full-time jobs because of fixed costs in the production process.[12] This possibility may be represented by an earnings curve like that shown in figure 3.

The possibility that people may not be able to work as many hours as they would like raises harder problems than the possibility that hourly wages may depend on the number of hours worked. "Involuntary" un-

10. I have developed a model for this case and discuss the various possibilities in "Effect of Wages, Taxes, and Fixed Costs."

11. H. G. Lewis, "Hours of Work and Hours of Leisure," Industrial Relations Research Association, *Proceedings, 9,* 1956.

12. The necessity of paying fringe benefits, except for social security payments, is not a sufficient reason when total compensation is taken into account. Of course, most studies neglect fringe benefits because of lack of data.

employment and the necessity to work full time because part-time work is unavailable fall into this category. In the next section I shall show how to handle this problem if one knows it exists. But a more difficult problem is to ascertain if individuals are actually constrained. There have been protracted debates about the possible existence of involuntary unemployment. Unfortunately, answers to survey questions on preferred hours of work cannot be trusted. Because data are poor, I make no attempt in practice to build quantity constraints into my empirical work.

The labor supply theory presented here does not take adequate account of the types of jobs people take or how intensely they work while on the job.[13] Taxes make nonpecuniary rewards more attractive because they are not taxable, so that money earnings may seriously misrepresent the relative full remuneration of different jobs. In principle such perquisites can be assigned a money value and included in earnings. But it is not possible in practice to measure adequately the value of certain types of nonmonetary rewards of jobs. Data are lacking even on such well-known facts as the tendency of full-time jobs to provide better health benefits or better pension benefits than part-time jobs do. A person would certainly consider these factors in deciding whether, for whom, and how much to work. But until better data exist, fringe benefits must be ignored.

One final characteristic of the model presented here deserves emphasis. This model is static. It ignores such phenomena as on-the-job training or the eighty-hour weeks put in by young lawyers whose hoped-for reward is future income, not current earnings. In both cases current compensation is an inadequate measure of earnings. I try to minimize such problems by restricting my sample to certain age groups and types of jobs. A complete theory and other econometric techniques will be required to measure the effect of taxes when these intertemporal considerations are also brought into the analysis. My feeling is that estimates of the distortions caused by taxation are likely to be increased when intertemporal considerations are incorporated.

Summary

The traditional model of the effect of taxes on labor supply must be changed because it incorrectly assumes a constant market wage; in fact, net after-tax wages depend on total labor income. Progressive taxation, transfer payments, and the fixed costs of working result in a schedule of

13. To the extent that wages reflect intensity of work, this problem may not be too serious. However, for many jobs wages may be only loosely related to current effort and longer run goals more important.

net wages that may rise and fall repeatedly. Except in a few cases, the effect of a change in the tax rate on labor supply cannot be determined on a priori grounds. The econometric problems encountered in attempts to take these nonconvexities into account are formidable. The next section examines these problems and describes my solutions to them. Nontechnical readers may wish to skip it and go to page 44, where I describe the data I used and my empirical estimates of the effect of taxes and transfers on the supply of labor and on economic efficiency.

The Econometrics of Labor Supply with Taxes

The essential feature that distinguishes econometric models of labor supply with taxes from traditional demand models is the nonconstancy of the net after-tax wage.[14] Except in the case of a proportional tax system, the net wage rate depends on hours worked because of the operation of the tax system. Thus econometric techniques need to be devised that can treat the nonlinearity of the budget set. However, it is important to note at the outset that a simultaneous equation problem does not really exist, even though the net wage received depends on hours worked. Given a market wage that is constant over hours worked and a tax system, the nonlinear budget set faced by the individual in deciding on his preferred hours of work is determined exogenously.[15] An econometric model ought to take the exogenous, nonlinear budget set and explain the individual choice of desired hours. I first describe such a model for convex and nonconvex budget sets. As expected, the convex case is simpler to deal with. I then turn to other issues: model specification when tastes vary, the fixed costs of working, and quantity constraints on available labor supply.

The Traditional Model

Traditional econometric models of labor supply have estimated specifications such as

(1) $$h = g'(w, y, z, \beta) + \epsilon = h^* + \epsilon,$$

where w is the market wage, y is nonlabor income, z is a vector of personal characteristics, and β is a vector of unknown coefficients represent-

14. Nonconstant prices do exist in the demand for other goods, for example, electricity with a declining block rate. The situation is very similar to my analysis of the nonconvex budget set.

15. If the market wage depends on hours worked, the same reasoning holds because the budget set is still exogenous.

ing individual tastes assumed to be constant in the population. The parameters are estimated by minimizing the sum of squares between observed hours, h, and desired hours, h^*, where ϵ is a stochastic term with mean zero. If the labor supply function is linear, ordinary least squares regression techniques are used. To deal with taxes, this model must be made more general because taxes convert the single market wage each worker faces into a vector of net after-tax wages and corresponding virtual incomes. As demonstrated in the preceding section, desired hours usually depend on the complete vectors of both net wages and virtual incomes. If one used the observed net wage and virtual income that corresponded to actual hours, one would create a simultaneous equations bias because the particular net wage, w_i, and virtual income, y_i, chosen would be correlated with ϵ. Alternatively, if one put all the net wages and virtual incomes into equation 1, estimated parameters would depend on the particular budget sets faced by the individuals in the sample. Thus one would not have a structural econometric model that could be used to assess the behavioral response to an altered tax system. Instead, a labor supply model should include individual maximization of utility over the nonlinear budget set and account properly for the multiplicity of net wages and virtual incomes.

Econometric estimation is quite straightforward in the case of a convex budget set. Because a unique tangency or a corner solution at zero hours will determine desired hours of work, one need only ascertain where the tangency occurs. The problem to be solved is to find desired hours of work, h^*, when the individual is faced with the convex budget set, with m linear segments, B_i, for $i = 1, \ldots, m$.[16] To find h^*, the specification of desired hours on a given budget segment, B_i, is taken:

$$(2) \qquad h_i^* = g(w_i, y_i, z, \beta).$$

Calculate h^* and if $0 \le h_i^* \le H_1$, where H_1 represents the first kink-point hours in figure 2, h_1^* is feasible and represents the unique tangency of the indifference curves and the budget set. If h_1^* is less than or equal to zero, desired hours of work are zero. However, if $H_1 \ge h_1^*$, then h_1^* is not feasible and one moves to the next budget segment.

If $H_1 \le h_2^* \le H_2$, this would be the unique optimum. If $h_1^* > H_1$ and $h_2^* < H_1$, then $h^* = H_1$, so that desired hours fall at the kink point. Otherwise one goes on and calculates h_3^*. By trying out all the segments one

16. The technique used here is more fully explained in Hausman, "Econometrics of Labor Supply on Convex Budget Sets."

finds (1) a unique tangency; (2) that $h_i^* = 0$, meaning that a person does not work at all; or (3) that $h_i^* > H_i^*$ for all i, which means that people work some number of hours, H, which represents a physical maximum of hours worked. Then a nonlinear least squares procedure or Tobit procedure to take account of minimum hours at zero should be used to compute the unknown taste parameters.[17]

The Model with Nonconvexities

The case of the nonconvex budget set, as in figure 3, is more complicated because equation 2 can lead to more than one feasible tangency, which leads to many potential desired hours of work. One can decide which of these feasible h_i^*'s is best of all by working backward from the labor supply specification of equation 2 to the underlying preferences, which can be represented by a utility function.[18] The basic idea is to make use of Roy's identity-from-duality theory; this generates the labor supply function from the indirect utility function, $v(w_i, y_i)$, which corresponds to the direct utility function defined over hours of work and the composite good, $u(h, x)$. That is, individual preferences are equally well represented as a function of consumption and as a function of prices and income. The latter specification is more convenient for econometric work because it is linked directly with market demand by a mathematical equation.[19]

17. The statistical procedure would basically minimize the sum of

$$\sum_{j=1}^{N} (h_j - h_j^*)^2,$$

where j represents individuals in the sample. Perhaps a better technique would be to use Tobit, which enforces the constraint that $h_j \geq 0$.

18. Burtless and Hausman, "Effect of Taxation on Labor Supply." That work was done in the framework of labor supply and a composite consumption good. The techniques can also be used in the many-goods case although it is more difficult to apply. Alternatively, one can begin with a utility function specification and derive the labor supply function as do T. J. Wales and A. D. Woodland, "Labour Supply and Progressive Taxes," *Review of Economic Studies,* vol. 46 (January 1979), pp. 83–95.

19. Roy's identity gives market demand as the ratio of the derivative of the indirect utility function with respect to the wage divided by the marginal utility of income,

$$(3) \qquad \frac{\partial v(w_i, y_i)}{\partial w_i} \Bigg/ \frac{\partial v(w_i, y_i)}{\partial y_i} = h_i^* = g(w_i, y_i, z, \beta),$$

along a given budget segment. So long as the Slutsky condition, which ensures concave preference, holds, $v(w_i, y_i)$ can always be recovered by solving the differential equation 3. In fact, $v(\cdot)$ often has a simple closed form for commonly used labor supply specifications.

I assume that desired hours of work is a linear function of net wages, w_i, virtual incomes, y_i, and personal characteristics, z. Given the equation $h_i^* = \alpha w_i + \beta y_i + z\gamma$, the indirect utility function is

$$(4) \qquad v(w_i, y_i) = e^{\beta w}i \left(y + \frac{\alpha}{\beta} w_i - \frac{\alpha}{\beta^2} + \frac{z\gamma}{\beta} \right).$$

Given the indirect utility function, all of the feasible tangencies can be compared, and the tangency with highest utility is chosen as the preferred hours of work, h^*.[20] Then, as with the convex budget set case, either nonlinear least squares or a Tobit procedure can be used to estimate the unknown coefficients.

While some people resist using a specific parameterization of the utility function, it should be realized that writing down a labor supply function as in equation 2 is equivalent to writing down a utility function under the assumption of utility maximization. To the extent that the labor supply specification yields a robust approximation to the data, the associated utility function will also provide a good approximation to the underlying preferences. The utility function allows global comparisons to determine the preferred hours of labor supply. The convex case needs only local comparisons, but the nonconvex case requires global comparisons because of the possibility of multiple tangencies of indifference curves with the budget set.

I next introduce the possibility that people differ in their tastes for work. In the labor supply specification of equation 1, all individuals respond in the same way to variations in virtual income. In other words, they are assumed to have identical β's so that the variation in labor supply of observationally equivalent individuals must arise solely from ϵ. However, empirical studies constrained by that assumption inadequately explain observed hours of work. Greenberg and Kosters were the first to allow a dispersion of preferences to affect their model in an important way.[21] Burtless and Hausman allowed for variation in preferences by

20. The indirect utility function can be used to evaluate tangencies on both budget segments and at kink points so that the direct utility function is unnecessary. As figure 3 shows, a tangency will not occur at a nonconvex kink point, but it may occur later on a convex portion of the budget set.

21. David H. Greenberg and Marvin Kosters, "Income Guarantees and the Working Poor: The Effect of Income Maintenance Programs on the Hours of Work of Male Family Heads," in Cain and Watts, eds., *Income Maintenance and Labor Supply*, pp. 14–101. For many linear regression specifications where the effect of

permitting β to be randomly distributed in the population.[22] Their results indicated that variation in the response to differences in virtual income seemed more important than variation in the response to differences in net wages.[23] The basic idea behind the taste variation specification is that individuals' preferences differ in ways not captured by variations in background and family characteristics represented by the vector z.[24] Perhaps an example will help clarify the specification. A sample of wives whose husbands earn approximately the same income can illustrate such variation in tastes. Family characteristics such as the number and ages of their children will affect their work decisions. The net wage they will receive is also important. Yet even with similar families and similar market wages, some wives will work full time, others part time, and many not at all. The traditional model of equation 1 with identical tastes produces estimates that all wives prefer to work the same number of hours (h^* is the same) and attributes all variation to random causes, represented by ϵ. My specification gives an alternative explanation for why h^* varies among the wives—differences in the income-leisure trade-off. The mathematical specification that permits estimation of the parameters is set forth in appendix A to this chapter.

Quantity Constraints

Quantity constraints can enter labor supply models in two ways. First, a person might have the choice of working either full time—say, forty hours a week—or not working at all. It is still possible to estimate the

---

taxes is not accounted for, variations in preferences lead only to an efficiency issue for the econometric estimator. However, taxes create an essential nonlinearity in the problem because of the multiplicity of net wages and virtual incomes, so variation in preferences can be important. A similar issue arises in the specification of discrete-choice models. See, for example, Jerry A. Hausman and David A. Wise, "A Conditional Probit Model for Qualitative Choice: Discrete Decisions Recognizing Interdependence and Heterogeneous Preference," *Econometrica*, vol. 46 (March 1978), pp. 403–26.

22. Burtless and Hausman, "Effect of Taxation on Labor Supply."

23. It is interesting to note that Greenberg and Kosters allowed for a similar type of variation in preferences. However, they did not allow for the effect of taxes, so the results cannot be compared.

24. A preferable specification would permit all coefficients to vary in the population, but the mathematical complexity of the approach, given the essential nonlinearity of the problem, seems beyond current computer techniques that can be used at reasonable cost.

parameters of a labor supply function by discrete-choice models that allow a distribution of preferences.[25]

A second kind of quantity constraint arises if each job carries a given wage and a particular number of hours that must be worked. Again, a discrete-choice framework seems appropriate to model this situation.[26] I do not allow for quantity constraints in my empirical estimation because their empirical importance is unclear. The standard deviation of hours worked for prime-age males who actually worked is around fourteen hours a week. Thus the model of flexible labor supply with fixed costs may provide a reasonably good approximation to reality, especially in the long run.

Summary

This section and appendix A demonstrate how the nonlinearity of the budget set that taxes create can be accounted for in an econometric

25. Hausman and Wise, "Conditional Probit Model." For example, one can begin with the linear labor supply specification $h_i^* = \alpha w_i + \beta y_i + z\gamma$, along with the associated indirect utility function of equation 3. To compare indirect utility at zero and forty hours, one needs to specify the w_i and y_i that would lead to the appropriate number of hours being chosen in an unconstrained setting. But w_i and y_i can be solved by using the desired hours supply equation and the linear equation through the point that gives net after-tax earnings for that number of hours of work. For forty hours the equation is $E_{40} = w_i \cdot 40 + y_i$, where E_{40} arises from the budget set. One can solve the two equations in two unknowns for w_i and y_i and use the values for the required utility comparison so that α, β, and γ can be estimated. It turns out that this procedure is equivalent to solving for the direct utility function where only quantities appear so that quantity constraints enter in a straightforward manner. For instance, the direct utility function for my example is

$$(5) \qquad u(h, x) = \frac{1}{\beta}\left(h - \frac{\alpha}{\beta}\right)\exp\left\{\left[-1 - \beta\left(x + \frac{z\gamma}{\beta} - \frac{\alpha}{\beta^2}\right)\right] \Big/ \left(\frac{\alpha}{\beta} - h\right)\right\},$$

where x is consumption of the composite commodity. However, for general labor supply specifications, the direct utility function need not exist in closed form, in which case the previous solution procedure can be used with the indirect utility function. Of course, specification of a direct utility function could be done *ab initio*, but it might not be easily combined with the labor supply functions of unconstrained individuals. Thus using a labor supply specification together with the associated direct and indirect utility functions would allow incorporation of quantity constraints into a model of labor supply.

26. Use of either the indirect or the direct utility function would allow the appropriate utility comparisons to be made. The range of choices that a given individual faces would need to be known. But the choice set might be either established by survey questions or estimated from a data set of the choices of similiar individuals.

model. The labor supply (leisure demand) curves are still the focus of model specification. If the budget set is convex, the only new complication is the need to search for the budget segment on which h^* falls. When the budget set is nonconvex, it is necessary to solve for the indirect utility function associated with the labor supply specification. Then the multiple tangencies of the budget set and indifference curves can be compared to find the h^* that corresponds to maximum utility. I have joined previous analysts in emphasizing the importance of allowing for variation in preferences and the fixed costs of working.

Federal Income Taxes, State Income Taxes, and AFDC

The pattern of net wage rates and virtual incomes created by federal and state income taxes and by the welfare system is extremely complex. Because the estimates presented in the next section are based on a 1975 sample, I shall describe taxes and transfers as they existed in that year and note any significant changes since then. The sample used below does not contain actual tax returns, which necessitates assumptions about the type and amount of deductions people actually claimed. These assumptions are unlikely to be seriously erroneous because all federal tax brackets but the first few were $4,000 wide for joint returns in 1975.

Income and Payroll Taxes

I represent the basic federal income tax system in 1975 by twelve brackets.[27] The first bracket is $1,000 wide with succeeding brackets (after $4,000) falling at intervals of $4,000. Because I am interested in the effect of taxes on labor supply, I consider only taxes on earned income. Table 1 lists the brackets along with the marginal tax rates and average tax rates at the midpoint of the bracket. The average tax rate is significantly below the marginal tax rate in all brackets above the lowest ones until earned income is well above $50,000. Thus if people react to average, rather than marginal, after-tax income, estimates of behavior may differ considerably from those presented below. In another sense, however, the theory used in this paper involves both the marginal net wage and the appropriate virtual income reflecting average tax rates up to

27. The text describes my procedure for joint returns. I followed similar procedures for single persons and heads of household but do not report the details here.

Table 1. Basic Federal Tax Rates on Earned Income for Married Couples Filing Joint Returns, 1975

Taxable income[a] (dollars)	Marginal rate	Average rate at midpoint
0–1,000	0.14	0.140
1,000–4,000	0.16	0.148
4,000–8,000	0.19	0.167
8,000–12,000	0.22	0.182
12,000–16,000	0.25	0.197
16,000–20,000	0.28	0.212
20,000–24,000	0.32	0.228
24,000–28,000	0.36	0.245
28,000–32,000	0.39	0.263
32,000–36,000	0.42	0.279
36,000–40,000	0.45	0.296
40,000–44,000	0.48	0.312
44,000 and over	0.50	...

a. These brackets are exactly according to the internal revenue code except for the $1,000–$4,000 bracket, where I averaged the three $1,000 brackets into a single $3,000-wide bracket.

the current tax bracket. In that sense, all characteristics of the tax system are accounted for.

I assumed that all married couples filed jointly, that individuals used personal exemptions, and that married couples filing jointly used the standard deduction up to the maximum amount of $2,600 when income was $16,250 or higher. The peculiar structure of the standard deduction creates a nonconvexity.[28] I assumed that people with incomes of $20,000 or more claimed itemized deductions equal to the average for joint returns in each tax bracket, as reported in *Statistics of Income*. The earned income credit causes additional fluctuations in tax rates. It equaled 10 percent of earnings below $4,000 of gross income, less 10 percent of adjusted gross income above $4,000. For a person with income exclusively from earnings, the credit would reach a maximum of $400 at income of $4,000 and would vanish at $8,000. The credit creates a nonconvexity at the break-even point ($8,000 if all income is from earnings) because the tax rate falls by ten percentage points. Social security (FICA) contribu-

28. In 1975, for income below $11,875, the standard deduction for married couples filing jointly was $1,900, but between $11,875 and $16,250, it was 16 percent of income. Thus at approximately $12,000 of taxable income the marginal tax rate falls to 84 percent of its previous value, creating a nonconvexity since the net wage rises at this point. The standard deduction was used on approximately two-thirds of all tax returns in 1975.

tions were 5.85 percent up to a limit of $14,100 for 1975, causing the marginal tax rate at that income level to fall from about 0.28 to about 0.22.[29] I investigated the importance of these nonconvexities by comparing results based on actual tax rates with other estimates derived from a convex approximation of the actual tax schedule.[30] As indicated in the next section, I found that nonconvexities were important for female heads of household and wives but not for husbands.

Forty states and the District of Columbia imposed either progressive or proportional taxes on earned income in 1975. Sixteen states permit taxpayers to deduct federal income taxes in calculating taxable income.[31] To avoid an inordinate number of tax brackets, I matched state tax brackets with the federal tax brackets and averaged the state tax rates within the federal tax brackets. This procedure may cause minor problems. First, I could not include city taxes on income or wages because data on residence or job location were unavailable. Also, a resident of one state who works in another may pay a higher rate; for example, a resident of New Hampshire, which has no income tax, pays Massachusetts state taxes on his Massachusetts earnings. Again, lack of data prevents the appropriate adjustments. It is unlikely that these approximations cause large errors.

Welfare

For female heads of household, aid to families with dependent children may have more influence on labor supply than the tax system. It has often been contended that AFDC discourages work and that its re-

29. Additional tax brackets have been added to table 1 to account for the effect of the standard deduction, earned income credit, and FICA contributions. Both the percentage tax and the limit on FICA have risen markedly since 1975.

30. To form the convex approximation, I join kink points by a new budget segment when the kink points initially enclose a nonconvex section of the budget set. A more precise mathematical description is that I form the convex hull of the budget set. Thus I smooth out the nonconvexities by an averaging procedure that results in a convex budget set.

31. Delaware has the highest overall marginal tax rate, 19.8 percent. At $15,000 after personal exemptions, California, Hawaii, and Oregon all have marginal tax rates of 10 percent; Wisconsin's is 11.4 percent, Minnesota's is 14 percent. Nebraska, Rhode Island, and Vermont are the only states that take a constant percentage from the federal taxes paid. Vermont takes the highest proportion, 25 percent. Among states with proportional rates after personal exemptions, Illinois has a rate of 2.5 percent, Massachusetts has a rate of 5 percent, and Indiana and Pennsylvania have rates of 2 percent. Details of state income taxes can be found in Advisory Commission on Intergovernmental Relations, *Significant Features of Fiscal Federalism: 1976–1977 Edition* (Government Printing Office, 1977).

placement by a negative income tax could significantly decrease the work disincentive.[32] AFDC benefits differ from state to state, but, in general, benefits depend on family size and are reduced by 67 percent of earnings of more than $30 a month until the break-even point is reached. States reimburse recipients for work-related expenses, including taxes, if any.[33] This system creates a sizable nonconvexity because the marginal tax rate decreases from 67 percent to approximately 16 percent at the break-even point. Figure 5 illustrates the basic outline of the AFDC budget set. The number of hours yielding earnings at which the 67 percent rate of benefit reduction begins is represented by H_1. Break-even hours, $\tilde{H}$, may not be reached even by women who work full time. For example, if the transfer payment is $300 a month for a family with three members, for a forty-hour week $\tilde{H}$ is reached only if the wage exceeds $2.80 an hour.[34]

The fact that states reimburse AFDC recipients for work-related expenses is a potentially important problem. To the extent that such expenses rise with income, the effective tax rates are below 67 percent. Since I do not know how far the effective tax rates are below statutory rates, I must use the latter. To the extent that work-related expenses are fixed costs and do not depend on actual hours worked (for example, transportation costs), the procedure I have adopted accommodates them by the simple expedient of reducing the net fixed costs of working. Hourly expenses such as child care that can be deducted are omitted. In previous work I have found that the size of the transfer payment from welfare has

32. However, for a sample in Gary, I found that the income effect overwhelmed the substitution effect, making the sample of black women on the negative income tax less likely to work than women on AFDC. Hausman, "Effect of Wages, Taxes, and Fixed Costs."

33. However, if fixed costs of working are important, this $30 exemption will have only a minor effect on labor supply.

34. Three states modify the system by establishing need standards. They reduce both the transfer payment amount and the marginal tax rate by a fraction ranging from 0.54 in South Carolina to 0.86 in New Mexico. Eight states have maximum payment amounts. They set a maximum payment for a two-recipient family of from 15 percent in Mississippi to nearly 100 percent in other states of the basic need level of the family. (The incredibly low level of AFDC in Mississippi is well known but certainly deserves mention. Maximum monthly payments for families of two, three, and four recipients were $30, $48, and $60, respectively, in July 1975.) Labor income does not then reach the 0.67 tax rate until total income reaches the need level. For instance, in Missouri the need level for a three-recipient family is $325 but the maximum payment is only $120. According to my calculations, until earnings reach $205 (at a $2.25 wage rate, when the person works about ninety hours a month), only federal taxes would be paid.

Figure 5. AFDC Budget Set

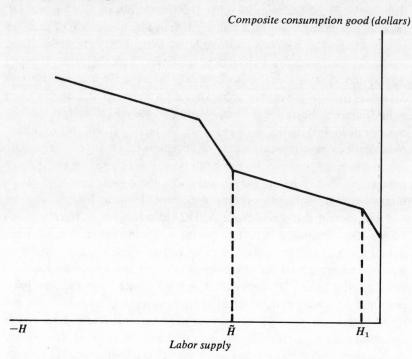

a significantly larger effect on work response than the tax rate does.[35] Although further refinements are desirable, the procedure used here is unlikely to introduce large errors.[36]

Estimation Results

This section presents estimates of the effect of taxation and transfers on the labor supply of a sample of husbands, wives, and female family heads drawn from the University of Michigan Panel Survey on Income

35. Hausman, "Effect of Wages, Taxes, and Fixed Costs."
36. Several studies of effective tax rates for AFDC fail to distinguish between fixed-cost expenses like transportation and hourly expenses. Their finding of approximately a 50 percent effective rate is thus downward biased. Only hourly work expense deductions should enter the effective rate calculation. Also, I do account for some deductions, such as FICA and federal taxes, that lead to a lowering of the effective AFDC tax rate.

Dynamics.[37] At the current stage of model development the labor supply of each family member must be estimated independently. I have treated the husband as the primary worker in a family and the wife as the secondary worker, an assumption made in all previous empirical research on the effect of taxes on labor supply.[38] My results can thus be compared with the findings of previous research. The obvious next goal of research is a model that allows for joint family labor supply decisions.

For both husbands and wives I consider each of two cases: a tax and transfer schedule based on actual law (the nonconvex case) and a smoothed tax schedule where the effects of FICA, the earned income credit, and the standard deduction are approximated by a consistently progressive convex budget set. Because the latter case is much simpler, it is interesting to know if the results differ much in the convex and nonconvex cases. For female heads of household I consider only the nonconvex case because AFDC introduces a large initial nonconvexity, as figure 5 indicates. The model permits people to work or not to work, it allows for a distribution of preferences, and it encompasses fixed costs of working. Thus it treats the considerations raised in earlier sections except quantity constraints on the number of hours worked.

After estimating the unknown parameters, I use the model to calculate the effect of taxes on labor supply. I begin with the traditional calculation of deadweight loss to compare the effect of the current tax system with that of a system where taxes are raised in a nondistorting lump-sum manner. While the nondistorting case is imaginary, it does set an upper bound on possible improvement from an altered tax system. If the upper bound was small, extensive research on gains from altering the tax system would promise little return. My initial calculations of deadweight loss focus on the individual with average tastes and average characteristics in the population.[39] This calculation then answers the hypothetical question: after

37. I used the part of the sample not covered by the Survey of Economic Activity so as not to overweight low-income earners. Specific sample considerations will be discussed when the results for each group are presented. Other population groups such as unmarried male heads of household could not be estimated because of insufficient data.

38. Orley Ashenfelter, and James Heckman, "The Estimation of Income and Substitution Effects in a Model of Family Labor Supply," *Econometrica,* vol. 42 (January 1974), pp. 73–85, consider a joint family labor supply but do not attempt to account for the effect of taxation.

39. Since I allow for a distribution of tastes in the population, I look at individuals for whom I only know the probability of their having a given set of taste parameters.

one accounts for taxes raised and hypothetically returned to the individual as a lump-sum payment, how much additional income would the taxpayer require to be as well off as he would be in a no-tax world? In other words, the deadweight loss measures the economic loss attributable to the distortion created by the tax.[40]

After calculating the deadweight loss and labor supply effect for the average individual in each of the three groups, I turn to the question of tax reform. I consider, as an alternative to the current tax system, a proportional tax system with an initial exemption. The overall tax system continues to be progressive for low-income individuals, but as labor income rises, net after-tax wage does not decrease as fast as it does under the current system. Because of time and cost considerations, I do the calculations only for husbands. I find the proportional tax rate necessary to raise the same revenue from husbands as the current tax system does. I then measure the effect of a shift from the present tax system to a proportional tax system on deadweight loss and labor supply. I find the effect of such a change to be substantial.

Results for Husbands

The estimated results for husbands are presented in table 2. They are based on data for a sample of 1,085 married men constructed from part of the University of Michigan Panel Study on Income Dynamics data for 1975. Men in the study were excluded if they had been part of a previous

---

40. To calculate deadweight loss, I use the correct theoretical notion based on the compensated labor supply curve. I take the indirect utility function of equation 4 and compute the corresponding expenditure function

$$(6) \qquad e(w_i, u) = e^{-\beta w_i} u - \frac{\alpha}{\beta} w_i + \frac{\alpha}{\beta^2} - \frac{z\gamma}{\beta}.$$

This equation tells the amount of income required for a person with net wage w_i to reach utility level u. When the pretax market wage w is reduced by taxes, equation 6 shows how much additional income the person needs to be as well off as in the lump-sum tax world. This estimate is Hicks's measure of consumer's surplus. Further details of this measure along with associated index number considerations are contained in my "Exact Consumer's Surplus." I then subtract taxes raised from consumer's surplus to measure deadweight loss. While deadweight loss is the correct theoretical measure for the welfare effect of taxation, I also measure the effect on desired hours of work from the current tax system. Since there is considerable current interest in "supply side" effects from taxation, I calculate how labor supply might change if the distortionary effect of taxation were removed. The supply side calculations neglect the labor demand aspect that would be used in a full general equilibrium calculation.

Table 2. Annual Hours of Work of Husbands[a]

	Coefficient	
Variable	*Convex*	*Nonconvex*
Virtual income–nonlabor income		
(thousands of dollars)[b]	2.037	1.061
	(0.0729)	(0.245)
Standard deviation of virtual income co-		
efficient (reflecting taste differences)[b]	0.6242	0.4541
	(0.0234)	(0.0570)
Mean of β (truncated distribution)	−0.166	−0.153
Median of β (truncated distribution)	−0.120	−0.113
Wage	0.0002	0.0113
	(0.0090)	(0.0106)
Constant	2.4195	2.366
	(0.0589)	(0.153)
Children under 6	−0.0039	0.0113
	(0.0255)	(0.0635)
Family size	0.0341	0.0657
	(−0.170)	(0.0310)
Age variable (age 45 = 0)	−0.0011	−0.0055
	(0.0108)	(0.0235)
House equity (thousands of dollars)	0.0026	0.0036
	(0.0009)	(0.0008)
Bad health	−0.1387	−0.0520
	(0.1436)	(0.564)
Standard deviation of residual (σ_η)	0.2794	0.2862
	(0.0178)	(0.0540)

a. The equation estimated is:

$$h_{ij} = \alpha w_{ij} + \beta y_{ij} + z_j\gamma + \eta_j,$$

where $j = 1, \ldots, N$. Asymptotic standard errors are given in parentheses below each estimated coefficient.
   b. The coefficient of virtual income is the mean of the truncated normal distribution of values of β ($\bar\beta_T$ in the figure below). As noted in the text, however, I assume that β cannot take on positive values, so the relevant part of the distribution is the part to the left of zero. Hence the mean and median of β in the table (shown as $\bar\beta_T$ and $\tilde\beta_T$ in the figure) are based only on the truncated distribution of β.

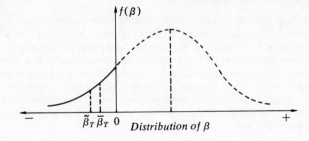

Distribution of β

Survey of Economic Opportunity. The sample was restricted to prime-age males, from twenty-five to fifty-five years old. Farmers, the self-employed, and the severely disabled were excluded. Annual hours of work is the dependent variable. Approximately 0.5 percent of the sample did not work in 1975. Nonlabor income was formed by attributing an 8 percent return to financial assets, and house equity was treated as a separate variable because of its special untaxed character.[41] Age was treated by including a variable equal to zero if a person was forty-five or under and equal to the person's age minus forty-five if he was older. The bad health variable was set to one if the person responded affirmatively to a question asking whether his health limited the type or amount of work he could do. Federal and state taxes were calculated according to the conventions described in the last section.

Most of the coefficients shown in table 2 are estimated quite precisely, in the sense that plausible variations of the coefficients, suggested by the standard errors, are behaviorally unimportant. The wage and nonlabor income coefficients especially are precise in this sense. The socioeconomic variables have coefficients of reasonable magnitude, except for house equity, which perhaps reflects factors in the mortgage credit market and the special tax treatment of houses.

I note first that the uncompensated wage coefficient is essentially zero. Not only is the estimate close to zero, but the estimated standard error is quite small. If the coefficient, in fact, is two standard deviations larger than estimated for the nonconvex case, an increase in the net wage of $1.00 along a budget segment leads to an increase of desired work of 32.5 hours a year, or less than 2 percent of the sample mean. The best guess of the effect on desired hours of such a wage change (based on the most likely value of the wage elasticity) is 11.3 hours for the nonconvex case and 0.2 hour for the convex case. The finding of an extremely small uncompensated wage effect accords with previous empirical findings. Thus the reduction in the net wage alone by the income tax has almost no effect on hours worked by husbands.

41. While it is difficult to construct a measure of nonlabor income, the use of virtual incomes reduces the attendant errors-in-variables problem along all but the first budget segment (see figure 2). Because the tax system creates a large variance in virtual income for each person, econometric analysis indicates that for most individuals errors of measurement in nonlabor income should not be particularly serious. The treatment of virtual incomes may well explain why the coefficient of nonlabor income is substantially larger than previous studies have found. If taxes are not accounted for, errors in measurement can lead to a substantial downward bias in the estimated coefficient.

However, the results in table 2 do differ from previous studies in indicating a significant income effect. Remember that I allow the sensitivity of desired hours of work to differences in virtual income to vary across the population, but I assume that increases in income never raise desired hours of work. Consequently, the distribution is substantially skewed, as it is the extreme left tail of a truncated normal distribution.[42] I find substantial variation in tastes in the population, which indicates the imporance of not assuming identical tastes, as past studies of labor supply have done.

The wage and income variables from the convex and nonconvex budget sets are similar, with the mean of the income coefficients differing by 8 percent. The most substantial differences arise from the effects of family size and bad health.[43] On balance, it is probably safe to conclude that the nonconvexities introduced by the earned income credit, social security taxes, and the standard deduction can be smoothed to produce a convex budget set for estimation purposes.

LABOR SUPPLY. Taxation has important effects on labor supply. Federal taxes cause a person with average tastes in the $8,000–$12,000 federal tax bracket to work 187.6 hours, or 8 percent *less* than he would choose to work in the no-tax case.[44] As indicated below, tax reform could significantly reduce these effects on labor supply.

DEADWEIGHT LOSS. The deadweight loss of the present tax system also is large. The fact that the substitution effect is about as large as the income effect, though of opposite sign, suggests that welfare loss may be substantial. The results are given in table 3 for persons with average tastes and other socioeconomic variables and a mean wage of either $6.18 an hour or $10 an hour. The deadweight loss calculations replace only federal taxes with lump-sum taxes and leave state income taxes in place. For the average person who earns $6.18 an hour, the deadweight loss is $235, which is 2.4 percent of his net income and 21.8 percent of the tax reve-

42. Note that in table 2 the mean β for the convex case is estimated to be −0.166, with the median estimated as −0.120, a difference of 32 percent. For this case the twenty-fifth percentile is reached at −0.234 and the seventy-fifth percentile is reached at −0.050.

43. The addition of one member to the family increases desired work by sixty-five hours a year in the nonconvex case, but only thirty-four hours in the convex case. The difference between the two cases in the estimated effect of bad health is eighty-seven hours a year.

44. For these calculations I used the mean β of −0.153 from table 2. Mean non-labor income is 1.266, and $z\gamma$ from equation 7 (in appendix A, below) is estimated at 2.59. The mean wage is $6.18 an hour.

Table 3. Deadweight Loss Calculation for the Average Individual[a]

Dollars unless otherwise specified

Average wage (dollars)	Before-tax income	Tax paid	Dead-weight loss	Dead-weight loss as percent of net income	Dead-weight loss as percent of taxes	Dead-weight loss with pro-portional tax
6.18 an hour	10,976	1,078	235	2.4	21.8	129
10.00 an hour	19,662	3,474	1,883	11.7	54.2	885

a. Based on nonconvex estimates from table 2. Mean data: $z\gamma$ = 2.593, y_1 = 1.266, w = $6.18, β = −0.153. Actual mean hours = 2,123; predicted mean hours = 2,181.

nues collected from him. The fact that the deadweight loss for a person earning $10 an hour is $1,883, which is 11.7 percent of net income and 54.2 percent of tax revenues, illustrates the impact of progressivity. The deadweight loss is much reduced if the same revenue is collected from a proportional tax. The deadweight loss for the person earning $6.18 an hour is $129, or 59.9 percent less than that from the progressive tax case. For the person earning $10 an hour deadweight loss for a proportional tax is $885, 75.5 percent less than that from the progressive tax. These estimates roughly approximate the deadweight loss from a comprehensive income-type value-added tax or a proportional consumption tax. The effect of an income tax that is proportional on income over an exempt amount is examined below.

The finding of a significant income effect and concomitant welfare cost for male heads of household is contrary to the received knowledge in the field.[45] The finding that taxes cut labor supply by 8 percent also contradicts previous research, which claimed it was near zero. Progressivity enlarges the reduction in labor supply. Because most earlier studies treated the tax system "as if" it were proportional, they did not find the income effect found here.[46] To the extent that my findings are substantiated in

45. Joseph A. Pechman, *Federal Tax Policy*, 3d ed. (Brookings Institution, 1977), chap. 4.

46. Robert Hall derived results from the Survey of Economic Opportunity that also indicate the presence of an income effect for males; see his "Wages, Income and Hours of Work." However, his results are difficult to compare with the findings presented here because of his method of treating nonlabor income in the presence of taxes. But it is interesting that Hall's is the only other study I know of that attempts to account for taxes and does not constrain the income effect to a preassigned value. Thus my study and Hall's results confirm the hypothesis that an income effect for males appears when the effect of progressive taxes is entered into the model of labor supply. Burtless and Hausman, "Effect of Taxation on Labor Supply," also found an important income effect for black male heads of household in the Gary negative income tax experiment.

future research, the previous presumption that progressive taxes have little effect on the labor supply and little deadweight loss needs to be revised.

Results for Wives

Previous findings that the labor supply decisions of married women are sensitive to the gross wage suggest that the reduction in net wages caused by taxes as well as the income effect will affect the number of hours these women want to work. I follow other researchers in assuming that the labor supply decisions of wives are made as if the labor supply and earnings of their husbands were given and unaffected by their own labor supply. Wives are therefore considered secondary workers, an assumption that may be inaccurate for some households. The fact that only half of the wives in my sample are in the labor force suggests that treating wives' earnings as conditional on husbands' earnings is reasonable. The crucial question is whether husbands' earnings should influence wives' labor supply as exogenous nonlabor income. It is probable that some husbands adjust their hours of work to their wives' earnings, but I have not taken account of such interactions.

The results presented below are based on data about the wives of the men used in the preceding section. They indicate that the wage rate of wives is relatively insensitive to the number of hours worked.[47] Thus to estimate the labor supply model, I assumed each person faces a constant market wage, regardless of the number of hours supplied. Another problem is how to predict the market wage for those in the sample who do not work. It is possible that women who do not work would be offered different wages from women with the same characteristics who do work. I address the possibility of such selection bias in appendix B and find that it is not important.[48]

The estimates of the wives' labor supply equations are presented in table 4. The nonconvex and convex cases are analogous to those for husbands in table 2. Also included is another nonconvex case where explicit account is taken of the fixed costs of working. First, note the sub-

47. The evidence for this statement appears in appendix B to this chapter.
48. That is, wives who work may not provide an appropriate sample to estimate a wage equation because their average market wage might be higher than that of nonworking wives with identical family and individual backgrounds. These findings agree with previous studies when the sample selection estimation is done correctly. The issue of sample selection bias for wives' wages is first discussed in Reuben Gronau, "The Effect of Children on the Housewife's Value of Time," *Journal of Political Economy*, vol. 81 (March–April 1973), pt. 2, pp. S168–69.

Table 4. Annual Hours of Work of Wives[a]

Thousands

Variable	Coefficient		
	Convex	Nonconvex	Nonconvex with fixed costs
Virtual income (thousands of dollars)[b]	2.0958	1.7519	2.0216
	(0.1389)	(0.1475)	(0.1186)
Standard deviation of virtual income coefficient (reflecting taste differences)[b]	0.5390	0.4836	0.5262
	(0.0460)	(0.0490)	(0.0711)
Mean of β (truncated distribution)[b]	−0.125	−0.118	−0.123
Median of β (truncated distribution)[b]	−0.089	−0.085	−0.088
Wage	0.4951	0.5058	0.4608
	(0.2310)	(0.0932)	(0.1062)
Intercept	0.5790	0.3501	0.6234
	(0.9517)	(0.4907)	(0.5766)
Family size	0.2387	0.2202	0.2144
	(0.1270)	(0.0773)	(0.1259)
Children under 6	−0.1695	−0.1123	0.1472
	(0.3426)	(0.2239)	(0.1576)
College education	0.7851	−0.7205	0.6903
	(0.4216)	(0.2390)	(0.4389)
Age			
34–45	0.0233	0.0733	0.0824
	(0.0110)	(0.0349)	(0.0436)
45 and over	−0.1066	−0.1043	−0.1989
	(0.0644)	(0.0539)	(0.0660)
Health	−0.4771	−0.3139	−0.3581
	(0.7274)	(0.4753)	(0.4647)
House equity	−0.0221	−0.0150	−0.0210
	(0.0172)	(0.0039)	(0.0113)
Fixed costs			
Intercept	...	...	1.2125
			(0.3570)
Children under 6	...	...	0.1720
			(0.9541)
Family size	...	...	−0.2118
			(1.6106)
Standard deviation of residual (σ_η)	0.3086	0.2907	0.2801
	(0.2388)	(0.2099)	(0.2386)

a. The equation estimated is:
$$h_{ij} = \alpha w_{ij} + \beta y_{ij} + z_j \gamma + \eta_j,$$
where $j = 1, \ldots, N$, or
$$h_{ij} = \alpha w_{ij} + \beta(y_{ij} - FC_j) + z_j \gamma + \eta_j,$$
where FC_j = fixed costs. Asymptotic standard errors are given in parentheses below each estimated coefficient.

b. See footnote b, table 2.

stantial uncompensated wage and income elasticities. For the average woman who is working full time, the uncompensated wage elasticity is 0.995 for the nonconvex results and 0.978 for the convex results; when fixed costs are added the uncompensated wage elasticity falls to 0.906.[49] Fixed costs of working are an estimated $105 a month for the mean in the sample.[50] All three estimates indicate that the income tax reduces wives' labor supply in large part by decreasing the net after-tax wage. To the extent that a wife is a "secondary" worker, she faces a "marriage tax" because the first dollar of her earnings is taxed at the rate applicable to the last dollar of her husband's earnings. For that reason the tax effect may be much greater than it would be if wives' earnings were not added to husbands' earnings for tax purposes.

The three estimates of the effects of virtual income—the husband's earnings, which are regarded as independent of the wife's, labor supply, and the additional effect of the progressive tax structure—are similar. The mean β is around -0.12 and the median is -0.09. It is important to realize that, while the tax effect on the net wage and the tax effect on nonlabor and virtual income offset one another, the deadweight loss of the two effects is cumulative. For example, a wife who works full time at $4 an hour, whose husband earns $10,000 a year, and who files jointly faces a marginal tax rate of 28 percent. She will pay $2,080 in federal income taxes on her earnings after deductions.[51]

Deadweight loss is calculated to be $1,208, or 58.1 percent of tax revenue. The tax treatment of married persons thus creates substantial deadweight loss for working wives. If the wife were taxed as a single person not eligible for the earned income credit, standard deductions, or exemptions her husband used, federal taxes on her earnings would fall from $2,080 to $1,250, a decrease of 50.9 percent, and deadweight loss

49. This estimate may be derived as follows: I take the estimated wage coefficient from table 4, use the mean wage for wives who work, $4.15 an hour, and taking taxes into account, compute the wage elasticity at mean hours of work for full-time workers—1,925 hours a year. Harvey S. Rosen, "Taxes in a Labor Supply Model with Joint Wage-Hours Determination," *Econometrica,* vol. 44 (May 1976), pp. 485–507, finds an elasticity that exceeds 2.0, but this estimate seems distinctly high. It may result from incorrect adjustment for virtual incomes or not taking account of the limited dependent variable.

50. These results for fixed costs are quite close to ones I found in an entirely different sample; "Effect of Wages, Taxes, and Fixed Costs."

51. The calculations are somewhat more difficult to interpret for wives than for husbands. Low β wives are much more likely to work than high β wives are. By doing this calculation at sample means, I am probably underestimating deadweight loss for working wives and overestimating deadweight loss for nonworking wives.

would fall almost proportionately, from $1,208 to $731, a decrease of 50.2 percent. The appropriate policy question would be to decide whether other tax proposals, such as a proportional tax, would decrease the dead-weight loss proportionately more than revenue.

Another way of looking at the same point is to compare the increase in revenue generated by moving from taxing the woman as an individual to taxing her jointly with her husband, which is $830, with the increase in the deadweight loss, which is $477. The ratio of deadweight loss to the difference in tax revenue is 57 percent. This last comparison demonstrates the large cost in economic efficiency of moving from one tax system to another. Each extra dollar raised in tax revenue is accompanied by approximately 57 cents lost as excess burden.

Female Heads of Families

The last set of empirical results on which I report is a labor supply model for prime-age female heads of household with children under eighteen living at home. The sample consists of 119 females, each of whom is eligible for AFDC payments if her income is low enough.[52] Consequently, the budget set for each woman reflects the welfare provisions of her state. Of the 119 women, 22 did not work at all in 1975, 6 worked fewer than 500 hours, 16 worked 500 to 1,000 hours, and 75 worked more than 1,000 hours. Only the nonconvex labor supply model with fixed costs of working is plausible, as the AFDC tax and transfer system introduces a very large nonconvexity into the budget set. Fixed costs turn out to be an important element of the model as they did for the results for wives.[53]

The results for the labor supply of female family heads are given in table 5.[54] Taxes influence the labor supply through their effects on virtual

52. It is important not to forget that I used the part of the Panel Study on Income Dynamics that had not been included in the Survey of Economic Opportunity; the result is a rather small sample. However, inclusion of SEO individuals would have raised problems of sample selection bias because they earn less, other things being equal.

53. Fixed costs also are an important influence on decisions to enter the labor force. See Hausman, "Effect of Wages, Taxes, and Fixed Costs."

54. Hourly wages of female heads of household, like those of wives, appear not to be affected by hours worked. Nor did I find any significant evidence of sample selection in the wage equation used to predict wages for the 22 women who did not report a wage in 1975. The least squares results for the wage equation are virtually identical to the maximum likelihood results when the possibility of sample selection bias is allowed for.

Table 5. Annual Hours of Work of Female Heads of Household[a]

Variable	Coefficient
Virtual income (thousands of dollars)[b]	2.0617
	(0.1154)
Standard deviation of virtual income coefficient (reflecting taste differences)[b]	0.5359
	(0.0448)
Mean of β (truncated distribution)[b]	−0.122
Median of β (truncated distribution)[b]	−0.086
Wage	0.3509
	(0.0249)
Intercept	0.4557
	(0.0825)
Family size	0.1753
	(0.0395)
Children under 6	0.2500
	(0.0839)
College education	0.2848
	(0.1559)
Age	
35–45	0.1138
	(0.0470)
45 and over	−0.1912
	(0.1160)
Health	−0.1202
	(0.0510)
House equity	−0.0194
	(0.0130)
Fixed costs	
Intercept	1.3449
	(0.3857)
Children under 6	0.6596
	(0.3224)
Family size	−0.6544
	(0.1254)
Standard deviation of residual (σ_η)	0.419
	(0.0943)

a. The equation estimated is:
$$h_{ij} = \alpha w_{ij} + \beta(y_{ij} - FC_j) + z_j\gamma + \eta_j,$$
where $j = 1, \ldots, N$. Asymptotic standard errors are given in parentheses below each estimated coefficient.
b. See footnote b, table 2.

income and on net wages. The uncompensated wage elasticity of the average woman who is working full time and is earning too much to be eligible for AFDC is 0.526. The uncompensated wage elasticity of the average woman working 1,000 hours and subject to the 67 percent AFDC marginal tax rate is 0.463.[55] The wage elasticities of female household heads are midway between those of husbands and those of wives. This finding is plausible; many wives may be secondary earners, but husbands do not have AFDC or any other program that would permit significant withdrawal from the labor force. On the other hand, female household heads on the average respond to changes in virtual income about the same as wives.[56]

I made no attempt to calculate deadweight loss from the mixture of taxes and transfers female household heads have because no lump-sum counterpart to this mixture would provide a meaningful comparison. It is possible to estimate how female household heads would respond to changes in this system and how deadweight loss would change. For example, a woman with a market wage of $3.00 an hour who is receiving AFDC and faces the 67 percent marginal tax rate would increase her labor supply by 78.9 hours a year if the tax rate were lowered to 50 percent. If she was initially working 1,200 hours a year, tax revenue would fall $344, but her consumer's surplus would rise $707, a decrease in excess burden of $363. Such a change in AFDC rules would not affect most women working full time because their income is too high for AFDC eligibility and would continue to be so after the tax change. Estimation of the full effects of a drop in the AFDC tax rate on the tax revenue and consumer's surplus requires a full-scale simulation of changes in the AFDC system. The modest wage elasticities make clear that commonly discussed decreases in the AFDC tax rate will increase the cost of AFDC because the rise in labor supply would be too small to offset increased entitlements. However, AFDC budget increases would be counterbalanced by even larger gains in consumer's surplus. Thus a real trade-off exists in considering reform of AFDC tax rates as well as income guarantees.

55. These wage elasticities are significantly higher than those I found in my study of black households headed by females in the Gary negative income tax sample. See "Effect of Wages, Taxes, and Fixed Costs." In my study of Gary females, labor force participation was about 28 percent; in this sample labor force participation is 81 percent. The samples represent two different populations and cannot be strictly compared.

56. The mean value of β is -0.122, with a median of -0.086 for female family heads, so the distribution of preference is significantly skewed.

For female household heads whose incomes are above the limits for AFDC, the progressive tax system entails deadweight loss of the same order of magnitude as that for husbands. Again a switch to a proportional tax significantly lowers deadweight loss.

Directions for Tax Reform

In this section I present estimates of the effect of taxes on labor supply and on deadweight loss of the full sample rather than of only the illustrative individuals described in the preceding section. Because preferences for work vary in the population and the progressive tax system is nonlinear, calculations for illustrative individuals may not accurately indicate the effects of the tax system on the entire sample. To deal with this problem I have simulated the effects of alternative tax systems over a representative sample of approximately 1,000 husbands to assess the effects of tax reform.[57] I consider the effect of changes in the federal tax system only. I first compare the current tax system with a nondistortionary lump-sum tax system yielding the same revenue and calculate the effects on labor supply, welfare, and income distribution of the current progressive tax.

RESULTS FOR THE FULL SAMPLE. The results for the full sample resemble the illustrations presented earlier. The current tax system significantly reduces desired hours by an average of 197.5 a year, 8.6 percent of total desired hours. This result emphasizes the importance of the effects of the income tax on labor supply. The average expected deadweight loss is $634, 28.7 percent of tax revenues raised, 3.5 percent of pretax earnings, and 4.3 percent of net earnings after tax.[58] The elasticity of utility to tax revenues raised is 2.99. Thus small changes in the tax system can lead to large changes in individuals' welfare.

It is important to know not only the average deadweight loss but also

---

57. I consider here the effect of tax reform only on husbands. Similar computations could be done for wives and female heads of household.

58. This estimate of deadweight loss is based on the exact *equivalent variation* corresponding to my desired hours of work supply function. I use the equivalent variation rather than the compensating variation because for tax reform purposes the current situation is the basis for comparison. The compensating variation measure uses the nondistortionary tax level of utility. The equivalent variation measure uses the level of utility resulting from the current tax system. The equivalent variation seems preferable in discussions of tax reform because the nondistortionary lump-sum tax is impossible to achieve. Thus the equivalent variation measures welfare improvement relative to the current tax system.

Table 6. Market Wage and Deadweight Loss

Wage quintile	Wage (dollars an hour)	Mean deadweight loss (dollars)
1	2.25–4.23	78
2	4.23–5.45	217
3	5.45–6.30	362
4	6.30–7.58	498
5	7.58 and over	1,032

its distribution. Table 6 displays the range of market wages and the mean deadweight loss in each of five wage quintiles of the sample. Deadweight loss rises sharply with the market wage and associated tax rates. For example, the mean wage in the fourth quintile is 36.0 percent higher than in the second quintile, but the mean deadweight loss is 83.1 percent higher. Such a more-than-proportional rise in deadweight loss is the expected result of a progressive income tax, since deadweight loss should increase approximately as the square of the marginal tax rate. It indicates that the distribution of tax burdens is far different from the distribution of tax payments. One cannot say how fast deadweight loss should rise in a progressive tax system, but the large proportion of the excess burden of the tax borne by recipients of high wages may be a reason for tax reform.

ALTERNATIVE TAXES. The revenue that the present system generates could be obtained by a proportional tax imposed on income over an exempt amount. Table 7 presents estimates of the impact on labor supply and of the deadweight loss from four such alternatives. The first alternative is a proportional tax on all income with no personal exemptions; a 14.6 percent rate raises revenue equal to that from the current progressive tax system in the sample. Such a tax would reduce desired hours of work 27.5 hours a year from the no-tax case, less than one-seventh of the desired reduction caused by the current tax system. The average deadweight loss is 7.1 percent of taxes collected, one-fourth of the 28.7 percent under the present system. Table 7 also shows the effect of three other taxes yielding the same revenue as the present system. One taxes income over an exemption of $1,000 per family at 15.4 percent; the second taxes income over an exemption of $2,000 per family at 16.9 percent; and the third taxes income over an exemption of $4,000 per family at 20.7 percent. The stub and the first column of the table give the exemption level and the marginal tax rate needed to raise the same revenue as the current tax system. As the exempt amount and the proportional tax rate necessary to yield constant revenue rise, the effect of the tax on desired hours of work changes little. The third column shows that the ratio of deadweight loss to taxes begins to rise rapidly as the tax rate increases. But even with an exemption of $4,000 per family and a proportional tax rate of 20.7 percent, deadweight loss is a little less than half of that from the present system. Last, note that a proportional tax with an initial exemption leads to a good deal of progressivity at low levels of earnings. The proportional tax systems with an initial exemption of $2,000 or more have a lower average tax rate for husbands earning less than $8,000 a year than the present system does. But note also that the increase in the average tax rate slows considerably after $16,000. These results might be expected to lead to a sharp reduction in deadweight loss since, as a very rough approximation, excess burden rises with the square of the tax rate.

The structural model of labor supply developed here casts light on the effect of possible tax reform. Most of the findings arise from the significant compensated substitution effect present in individuals' labor supply decisions. Thus tax reform proposals that lower the marginal tax rate may substantially decrease deadweight from income taxation. However, I would like to reemphasize the important point that all my calculations are necessarily based on a partial equilibrium analysis. Changes in the market wage are certainly a possible outcome of wide-ranging income tax reform. But with market wages fixed, my estimates indicate that desired hours of work would increase by between 5 and 10 percent if the present tax system were replaced by a proportional tax. This increase in labor supply permits lower average tax rates than the current internal revenue code even when a positive exemption exists. "Supply-side effect" thus allows for greater progressivity at low income levels and smaller average tax rates at higher levels of income. Distributional issues become important in assessing these proposals, but the results indicate that the progressive income tax system may be a costly way to seek income redistribution. Other, more cost-effective means of income redistribution may well exist.

Table 7. Effects of a Proportional Tax with Initial Exemption

Exemption level (dollars)	Tax rate (percent)	Effect on desired annual hours of work	Deadweight loss as a percent of taxes	Tax rate on annual income of			
				$4,000	$8,000	$16,000	$24,000
0	14.6	−27.5	7.1	0.146	0.146	0.146	0.146
1,000	15.4	−28.2	8.3	0.116	0.135	0.144	0.148
2,000	16.9	−29.9	9.8	0.085	0.127	0.148	0.155
4,000	20.7	−34.5	14.5	0.000	0.104	0.155	0.172
Current tax system	Internal revenue code	−197.5	28.7	0.119	0.147	0.173	0.188

Appendix A: Mathematical Specification of Estimation Procedure

Along each segment of the budget constraint there is a preferred number of hours of work, h_i^*:

(7) $$h_i^* = \alpha w_i + \beta y_i + z\gamma,$$

where w_i is the net wage on segment i, y_i is virtual income for segment i, z represents socioeconomic variables, and α, β, and γ are the parameters to be estimated. For fixed α, β, and γ, desired hours, h_i^*, may not be feasible, because h_i^* may be greater or less than the hours at the end points of the budget segment H_{i-1} and H_i. If desired hours are feasible, the indifference curve and the budget segment are tangent. If the budget set is convex, this tangency is unique, and I then use the stochastic specification for the deviation of actual hours from desired hours for person j as

(8) $$h_j = h_{ij}^* + \eta_j.$$

Because observed hours $h_j \geq 0$, the stochastic term η_j is assumed to be independent truncated normal across individuals in the population. This assumption yields a Tobit specification for the hours-worked variable. However, if $h_j^* = 0$, I assume that the individuals choose not to work and set $h_j = 0$. Because the final model has two sources of stochastic variation, the interpretation of η_j differs from that of the error term in standard models. Here the individual chooses, among jobs that differ in normal (long-run) hours worked, the one with working hours closest to his h_j^*. But observed h_j may differ because of unexpected layoffs, short time, overtime, or the worker's poor health together with measurement error. As an empirical matter, the standard deviation of η_j is reasonably small, indicating that people successfully match jobs to their desired hours of work.

If the budget set is nonconvex, h_i^* is not necessarily unique because multiple tangencies can occur between the indifference curves and the budget set. Then the particular h_{ij}^* is chosen that leads to maximum utility, which is determined by the use of the corresponding indirect utility function from equation 4. Again I use the stochastic specification of equation 6 to express the deviation of actual hours from desired hours of work. It is interesting to note that, although certain kink points such as $\tilde{H}$ in figure 5 in the nonconvex case cannot correspond to desired hours, one might still observe them as actual hours of work because of the stochastic term η_j in the model.

The second source of stochastic variation in the model arises from a distribution of tastes in the population that is assumed to be independent of η_j. In line with my previous research, I specify β to be a truncated normal random variable in the interval $(-\infty, 0)$.[59] I specify an upper limit of zero because I assume that leisure is a normal good. As β ranges over the permissible interval, there is a certain probability that any amount of hours corresponds to desired hours h^*. Other things being equal, individuals with greater β have more desired hours of work. But rather than estimate a particular person's β, I estimate the probability distribution for possible values of β in the population and choose the value most likely to generate the distribution of hours of work actually observed.

To develop the appropriate likelihood function, I first note that any budget set can be described as a collection of budget segments and kink points. For each budget segment or kink point, I determine the values of β that will make the desired hours fall on that budget segment or at the kink. First, consider those whose observed hours of work equal zero. An individual works zero hours either because his β is so negative that $h^* = 0$ or because η_j was sufficiently negative in equation 8 to cause $h_j = 0$ even though $h_j^* > 0$. Therefore, the probability of zero hours[60] is

$$(9) \quad pr(h_j = 0) = \int_{-\infty}^{\beta_j^*} f(\beta)\, d\beta + \sum_{i=1}^{m} \left[\int_{\beta_{i-1,j}}^{\beta_{ij}} \int_{\infty}^{q_{ij}} f(\beta) g(v_{ij})\, dv_{ij}\, d\beta \right]$$
$$+ \sum_{i=1}^{m-1} \left\{ \int_{\infty}^{q_{ij}} [F(\beta_{ij}) - F(\beta_{i-1,j})] g(v_{ij})\, dv_{ij} \right\}.$$

The minimum β that causes desired hours to be positive for person j is β_j^*, so that the first terms in equation 9 correspond to zero desired hours. The middle term is the probability that desired hours fall along one of the m budget segments, but that the stochastic term η_j is so negative that actual

59. If β is not truncated, similar qualitative results are found, but the parameters are estimated with considerably less precision. In my "Effect of Wages, Taxes, and Fixed Costs," other distributions than the normal are tried with very similar results. The truncation restriction that makes leisure a normal good seems well supported by previous work.

60. The probability of some of the terms in the sums of equation 9 may well be zero, especially in the nonconvex case, where whole budget segments may be skipped and nonconvex kink points cannot correspond to desired hours.

hours are zero. Here $v_{ij} = \eta_j + \beta y_{ij}$, so that v_{ij} is distributed normally as $N(\bar{\beta} y_{ij}, \sigma_\beta^2 y_{ij}^2 + \sigma_\eta^2)$ and $q_{ij} = -\alpha w_{ij} - z_j \gamma$. The joint probability density of this term is bivariate normal. The last term in equation 9 corresponds to desired hours falling at one of the $m - 1$ kink points but actual hours are zero due to η_j. For those observed to be working, the probability of actual hours of work is similar but simpler because the first term is absent and only univariate probability densities are required since truncation of hours worked does not take place. Thus the probability that individual j works h_j hours is

(10) $$pr(h_j) = \sum_{i=1}^{m} \left[\int_{\beta_{i-1,j}}^{\beta_{ij}} d(h_j - h_{ij}^*) f(\beta) \, d\beta \right]$$
$$+ \sum_{i=1}^{m-1} \{ [F(\beta_{ij}) - F(\beta_{i-1,j})] \, d(h_j - h_{ij}^*) \}.$$

The first term corresponds to the budget segments and the second term to kink points, so that h_{ij}^* corresponds to kink hours H_{ij}. Then over the n sample observations the log likelihood function takes the form

$$L(\alpha, \beta, \gamma, \sigma_\beta^2, \sigma_\eta^2) = \sum_{j=1}^{n} \{ (1 - D_j) \log [pr(h_j = 0)] + D_j \log [pr(h_j)] \},$$

where D_j is an indicator variable with $D_j = 0$ if person j does not work and $D_j = 1$ otherwise. The parameters are estimated by maximum likelihood techniques.[61] Thus the estimated parameters are chosen by the criterion of maximizing the likelihood of the model of equations 9 and 10 explaining the observed hours of work in the sample h_j over the n individuals. Since my sample sizes are typically about 1,000 individuals, the optimal large-sample properties of maximum likelihood estimation should apply in this case.

Appendix B: Econometric Issues and Techniques

Female Labor Supply

I briefly consider two econometric issues that arise in female labor supply. First, I consider the possibility that the market wage rate may depend

61. I used the algorithm by E. K. Berndt, B. H. Hall, R. E. Hall, and J. A. Hausman, "Estimation and Inference in Nonlinear Structural Models," *Annals of Economic and Social Measurement*, vol. 3 (October 1974), pp. 653–65. Starting values were obtained by instrumental variable estimates.

68

Jerry A. Hausman

Table 8. Logarithmic Wage Regression[a]
Sample size: 574

Variable	Ordinary least squares	Linear	Polynomial	Piecewise linear
1. Hours	...	0.00353 (0.00459)	0.0768 (0.0869)	...
2. Hours^2	...	...	−0.00160 (0.00173)	...
3. Hours from 0 to 20	...	...	...	0.00456 (0.01964)
4. Hours from 20 to 35	...	...	...	−0.00689 (0.0313)
5. Hours, 35 and up, minus 35	...	...	...	0.0108 (0.0569)
Standard error	0.348	0.343	0.328	0.384
$\bar{R}^2$	0.332	...	...	...

a. Numbers in parentheses are asymptotic standard errors.

on hours of work. Rosen found marginal evidence of a wage-hours locus, but the empirical magnitude of the relationship was not large.[62] However, my results do not reveal a statistically significant market wage-hours locus in the sample. Nor do I find a large economic effect, even when questions of statistical significance are disregarded. Various specifications were tried where hours entered as a regressor for the market wage equation, either in piecewise linear form or as a polynomial. An instrumental variable procedure was used to estimate the coefficients since hours are an endogenous variable.

Table 8 presents some of the results for the market wage equations where the log of the market wage is the left-hand-side variable. Other variables used as regressors are tenure with employer, tenure in position, race, union status, education, and college graduation. I do not present the estimated coefficients for these variables because my main focus is on the market wage and hours relationship. The results in table 8 reveal no significant market wage-hours locus. Every asymptotic standard error exceeds the size of its estimated coefficient. Furthermore, the empirical magnitudes are not especially large. For instance, the linear relationship predicts that a thirty-five-hour worker's wage would be 5.3 percent higher than the market for a twenty-hour worker. At the mean of the sample this

62. Rosen, "Taxes in a Labor Supply Model."

difference corresponds to about 20 cents an hour. When one turns to the polynomial regression presented in the third column, one finds that the wage difference that corresponds to going from a twenty-hour week to a thirty-five-hour week is about 4 percent, so that again no important difference is found. Last, the piecewise linear regression also does not reveal evidence of wage-hours locus although the coefficients are very imprecisely estimated. I conclude that working wives in my sample do not face a market wage-hours relationship.[63] I therefore use a constant market wage in my labor supply estimates.

The next problem to be resolved is how to predict the market wage for those who do not work. The usual missing data procedure is to fit a least squares regression on those wives who work, say, $w_j = z_j \delta + \epsilon_j$, and then to use the estimated coefficients to predict the market wage for nonworking wives. But as Gronau pointed out, sample selection bias may be present to cause ϵ_j on the average to be positive for working wives and negative for nonworking wives.[64] Thus least squares estimates and forecasts would be biased. To test for this possibility, I used a sample selection model that jointly considers the decision to work and the market wage.[65] The crucial parameter is then the estimated correlation between the stochastic term in the decision-to-work equation and the market wage equation. The finding of significant correlation between the stochastic disturbances of the two equations would indicate that sample selection bias is present. My estimate of this correlation is quite small, 0.132, with an asymptotic standard error of 0.182. Furthermore, the estimated coefficients of the wage equation are virtually identical to the coefficients estimated from least squares on the subsample of working women. I therefore find no evidence whatsoever of sample selection bias. These findings agree with previous studies in which the sample selection model for female labor supply has been used correctly.

63. My finding of the effect of hours on wages is much less than that of Rosen. Ibid.

64. Gronau, "Effect of Children."

65. This model specification was first used by Hanoch, "Multivariate Model of Labor Supply," and by James J. Heckman, "The Common Structure of Statistical Models of Truncation, Sample Selection and Limited Dependent Variables and a Simple Estimator for Such Models," *Annals of Economic and Social Measurement,* vol. 5 (Fall 1976), pp. 475–92. The exact maximum likelihood procedure used is given in Zvi Griliches, Bronwyn H. Hall, and Jerry A. Hausman, "Missing Data and Self-Selection in Large Panels," *Annales de l'Insee,* vol. 30, no. 31 (1978), pp. 137–76.

Previous Empirical Research

Empirical research that allows for taxation's effect on labor supply is quite recent. The older labor supply literature allowed for an effect of a gross market wage on labor supply and sometimes used nonlabor income as a regressor too. However, the effect of taxes was not explicitly introduced. In fact, in the Cain and Watts volume, which concentrated on the effect of a negative income tax on labor supply, almost all the papers used the market wage in estimating labor supply functions, so taxes were not accounted for.[66] Kosters did introduce taxes into a labor supply model but used average tax rates to stay within a linear budget-set framework. In his reported empirical work, he too used the market wage.[67] The previous literature was thus estimating labor supply curves without taking account of taxes.

Initial attempts to account for the effect of taxes was made by Diewert, Hall, and Wales.[68] The authors of these three papers all considered the case of a progressive tax system, so the budget set is convex. A linear approximation to the budget set was used to account for taxes. That is, observed hours of work were used along with the market wage to establish the marginal tax bracket and the net after-tax wage. This observed net wage along with the corresponding observed virtual income was then used in the estimation of the labor supply function. Accounting for taxes by linearizing the budget segment marked an important advance over the "reduced form" approach that had been previously used. In a nonstochastic model it is strictly correct, since the individual would make the same choice over the linearized budget constraint as he would over the full nonlinear budget set. However, in a stochastic model, where hours worked is a random variable, problems arise. Correlation between the right-hand-side variables and the stochastic disturbance is introduced by this technique. The net after-tax wage now is a nonlinear function of the left-hand-side variable. Virtual income is similarly correlated with the stochastic disturbance. While the size and direction of the bias are diffi-

---

66. Cain and Watts, eds., *Income Maintenance and Labor Supply.*

67. Marvin H. Kosters, "Income and Substitution Effects in a Family Labor Supply Model," Report P-3339 (Rand Corp., December 1966).

68. W. Erwin Diewert, "Choice on Labour Markets and the Theory of the Allocation of Time" (University of British Columbia, 1971); Hall, "Wages, Income and Hours of Work"; and Terence J. Wales, "Estimation of a Labor Supply Curve for Self-Employed Business Proprietors," *International Economic Review,* vol. 14 (February 1973), pp. 69–80.

cult to calculate because of the nonlinearity of the budget set, linear approximations indicate that the wage coefficient is likely to be downward biased and the income coefficient to be upward biased. The size of the bias depends on the relative size of the variance of the stochastic disturbance versus the variance of net wages and virtual income. But since the variance of the stochastic disturbance is typically found to be substantial in empirical work, the bias is potentially large.

An instrumental variable procedure that accounts for the simultaneous equation bias of the linear approximation method was first used by Hausman-Wise and Rosen.[69] Here a nonlinear reduced-form equation that excludes the net wage and virtual income is used to arrive at a conditional expectation of hours worked for each individual. Then the net wage and virtual income that correspond to the *predicted* budget segment are used as instruments for the *observed* net wage and virtual income from the linear approximation.[70] In his paper Rosen employed an interesting test of tax perception by testing to see whether the coefficients of the market wage variable and the tax variable were the same. He could not reject the hypothesis of equality, leading to the conclusion that individuals do perceive the effect of taxes and react to the net after-tax wage rather than the market wage.

While the instrumental-variable procedure does offer a simple computational approach, it is not totally satisfactory. The linear approximation uses only local budget-set information while the individual is maximizing over a global budget set. For instance, the conditional expectation of the labor supply equation may have hours that lie off the budget segment whose net wage and virtual income appear on the right-hand side. Forecast hours are then inconsistent with the budget segments that are used to form the forecasts. Thus potentially important information is neglected and inconsistencies are not accounted for. More important, the approach does not adequately account for the corners of the budget set that occur at kink points. Preferred hours are more likely to occur at kink points for a given family of indifference curves, but the instrumental-variable approach neglects this fact. Finally, nonconvex budget sets cannot be ade-

69. Jerry A. Hausman and David A. Wise, "The Evaluation of Results from Truncated Samples: The New Jersey Income Maintenance Experiment," *Annals of Economic and Social Measurement,* vol. 5 (Fall 1976); and Rosen, "Taxes in a Labor Supply Model."

70. Because of the nonlinearity it is important to do actual instrumental variable estimation, not two-stage least squares estimation. The latter estimator leads to inconsistent results.

quately treated. The instrumental-variable procedure cannot account for parts of budget segments that are not utility-maximizing points. The most recent techniques can account for these additional factors although only at the expense of more complicated nonlinear estimation techniques. But given the nonlinearity of the budget set, the requirement for more complicated statistical techniques should not be surprising.

The latest techniques to take taxes into account have been developed by Burtless-Hausman, Wales-Woodland, and Hausman.[71] These approaches consider the complete budget set in computing preferred hours rather than using only a local approximation. Wales and Woodland begin with a constant elasticity of substitution (CES) utility specification and consider the case of a convex budget set only.[72] Burtless-Hausman and Hausman consider both convex and nonconvex budget sets. They begin with a specification of labor supply and derive the associated indirect utility function by using Roy's identity. The nonconvex budget sets may arise from nonconvexities in the tax system or from the presence of fixed costs of working. These papers also allow for a distribution of preferences in the population. I will not describe the models in more detail since they are discussed at length in foregoing sections of this paper. The shortcomings of the local methods seem to be overcome with these more sophisticated models. The main drawback is computational. However, further research in the area should allow for more general specifications with less computational burden. By requiring that the conditional expectation of preferred hours be consistent with the associated net wage and virtual income, an important element of specification consistency is introduced. I see this consistency aspect as perhaps the most important advance of the global models over the local approximations. The results can also then be used to forecast what the effect of an altered budget set would be, such as a projected change from one tax system to another.

Comments by Michael J. Boskin

I plan to do three things in commenting on Jerry Hausman's paper: first, to describe what he did and some of his important results; second, to dis-

71. Burtless and Hausman, "Effect of Taxation on Labor Supply"; Wales and Woodland, "Labour Supply and Progressive Taxes"; and Hausman, "Effect of Wages, Taxes, and Fixed Costs."

72. Their model constrains the income effect by their choice of a CES functional form. In fact, they do not reject a Cobb-Douglas specification. Their results thus differ markedly from mine.

cuss some things not in this paper that are relevant to the effects of taxes on the supply of labor; and third, to briefly introduce some important policy issues.

Let me start by saying that Hausman has done several things, and he has done most of them extremely well. He has tried to take account, in a very careful way, of a very large number of problems that arise in trying to look at the labor-leisure choice in a simple, static, one-period two-good model. Among those important factors are the effects of alternative tax features. It would not be unfair to my friends in the labor economics profession to charge that most of them, in previous studies of labor supply, have ignored taxes; and it would do my colleagues in public finance no injustice to suggest that, while they have stressed taxes, they have ignored most of the econometric difficulties in estimating labor supply. These critical comments apply to some of my own earlier work as well.

We usually work within simple one-person, one-period, two-good models with linear prices and proportional taxes. Once upon a time we believed that we could regress measured hours of work on wage rates, income, and background variables, and so estimate wage and income elasticities.

Then we learned that we had to take into account such facts as the piling up at zero labor supply of some groups in the population, especially wives, and we realized that it did not make sense to have estimated labor supply equations that predicted negative labor supply for reasonable values of the independent variables. Moreover, the theoretical upper limit to labor supply requires that eventually the labor supply function be nonpositively sloped at some wage level. Also, we do not observe wages for nonworking wives, for example, who are either temporarily or permanently at home. That list of problems has formed the basis of much work in applied econometrics and labor economics in the last half dozen years.

To those problems are added the problems of nonlinearities caused by progressive income tax rates and nonconvexities caused by other tax provisions and social security benefits, as well as the complexities of AFDC and other means-tested programs. Hausman carefully discusses how the federal income tax, state income tax, social security, AFDC, and negative income tax programs affect the budget constraints facing such consumers.

He then explains the econometric procedures necessary to deal with each of these in turn and several of them in combination. Until quite recently we relied heavily on cross-section data or negative income tax experiments to estimate income, wage, and substitution elasticities of labor supply. In general, we held that prime-age males worked full time regardless of their wage and nonwage income and that their wage and income elasticities were close to zero; that the wage elasticity of wives was substantial; and that the labor supply of the elderly was quite wage-elastic. Only recently have the effects of social security on the labor supply decisions of the elderly been taken into account.

Against this background, Hausman takes a sample of husbands, wives, and female household heads and estimates labor supply on the presupposition that the husband is the primary worker and the wife is the secondary worker. In his model the labor supply decisions of husbands and wives are not jointly made, but the statistical problems are complicated enough even when this interaction is not allowed. He allows for the truncation of hours of work at zero and for the possibility of nonconvex budget sets. He allows for fixed costs in working, a recent innovation in work on labor supply. He assumes a labor supply function that, along each segment, is linear in wages and "virtual income" (virtual income being the extension of the budget line to the vertical axis measuring nonwage income).

He used just over a thousand married men, aged twenty-five to fifty-five, in the part of the 1975 University of Michigan Panel Study on Income Dynamics that had not been included in the Survey of Economic Opportunity. He excluded farmers, the self-employed, and the disabled.

Some of his results differ substantially from those of most other investigators. Like most, he estimates an uncompensated wage elasticity very close to zero. But in sharp contrast, he estimates a nontrivial negative income elasticity of labor supply. Putting these two results together yields a substantial compensated wage effect on labor supply.

These findings lead Hausman to his conclusion that income taxes impose a large deadweight loss because of the substitution effect on the labor supply even of husbands, who had previously been thought to have trivial compensated labor supply elasticities.

Hausman provides a variety of estimates, and he is very careful in doing so. He goes back to a specific utility function, which he derived, again, by working back from the labor supply functions along each segment, to find the excess of lost consumer surplus over taxes collected. For husbands with an hourly wage rate of $6.18, deadweight loss equals 22 percent of their taxes; for those making $10.00 an hour, the deadweight loss is 54 percent of tax revenue. Replacement of the current tax system by a proportional income tax would significantly reduce this loss. Those results are the most striking in the paper.

For wives he estimates an uncompensated wage elasticity of around 1.0 when fixed costs are disregarded and around 0.6 when they are recognized. Also, for wives the income effect is negative and the compensated wage elasticity is large. And again deadweight loss is large, 57 percent of tax revenue.

For female heads of household he gets an uncompensated wage elasticity of about 0.5 and similar deadweight losses.

One aspect of his econometric technique requires comment. He assumes that leisure is a normal good and therefore truncates possible coefficients of the income effect at zero. I do not object to that assumption, as most previous studies have concluded that leisure is not an inferior good.

There are more basic questions, however. Most of the debates about tax policy concern the effects of taxation on human capital formation and investment as well as on work effort. There is little information about the effects of tax policy on the formation of human capital. With even the simplest kind of growth model of the economy, one would be concerned about the rate of growth of the effective labor force, not about the hours of work of a particular component of it. There is substantial evidence from the work of Heckman, Rosen, and others that the proportion of work hours spent on job training is extremely important, say, through the age of thirty-five or forty. If so, the observed current wage rate is not the real hourly wage rate. Currently measured hours of work are a combination of hours spent working and hours spent training. Furthermore, cross-sectional data may compound the effect of taxes not only on current wages but also on future wages.

In summary, Hausman provides an improved set of estimates of the short-term labor supply function. But they should be seen against the backdrop of the larger question of how taxes affect labor supply in the long run when workers can vary not only hours but training and career choice as well.

Taken at face value without consideration of such complications, these results imply a large deadweight loss in the labor supply decisions of the most important group in the labor force—prime-age males. But large differences remain between the labor supply elasticity of husbands and that of wives.

Comments by Gary Burtless

Jerry Hausman's paper makes two valuable contributions to the literature on taxation and work effort. First, it provides important new empirical estimates of the work response to federal, state, and FICA taxation. And second, the paper carefully—though incompletely—assesses the earnings and welfare losses arising from the current American system of progressive taxes. Hausman's estimates of labor supply response, unlike many previous estimates in this area, were based on a random cross section of individuals from the U.S. population. Moreover, his estimates were obtained using a more sophisticated theoretical and statistical apparatus than has been applied in almost any other investigation of taxation and work effort. In spite of their impressive credentials, the results in this paper—particularly those for husbands—will be controversial because they indicate the presence of far more responsiveness to taxation than has generally been suspected. Moreover, because of this finding of substantial tax responsiveness, Hausman's estimates of the excess burden attributable to taxation may greatly exceed some previous estimates.

Before remarking on the credibility of the empirical estimates, I will briefly summarize a few points about the relationship between desired work effort and taxes. The basic relationship posited in the paper is linear:

$$(11) \qquad\qquad h = c + \alpha W + \beta Y$$

and

$$(12) \qquad\qquad h = 2{,}663 + 11.3W - 0.113Y.$$

Desired annual work effort, h, is presumed to be a linear function of the *net* wage rate, W, and some measure of annual family income, Y; c, α, and β are unknown parameters. To fix ideas, in equation 12 I have supplied Hausman's estimates of c, α, and β for the *median* prime-age male in a four-person family.[73] In this study, Y is measured at zero hours of

73. See table 2, "nonconvex" results. To obtain my estimates of c I assume that the family consists of 0.5 child under the age of five and 3.5 other persons. Also, the husband is assumed to have a 0.4 probability of being older than forty-five and a 0.1 probability of having poor health. It is assumed that equity in the home is $10,000 and that taxable unearned income is $500 a year. The median β, or income coefficient, among husbands is -0.113.

work effort and can be thought of as the amount of family disposable income if the breadwinner does not work at all. The definitions of W and Y should cause no difficulty if attention is restricted to linear terms of trade between work effort and family disposable income. For example, consider the budget segment closest to the origin in figure 6, the segment $0A$. The slope of $0A$ is minus the wage, and the intercept, 0, is the family's attainable income in the absence of any earnings by the husband. To see how much the husband will work if he chooses to locate on $0A$, simply solve equation 12 by substituting the wage and income level along $0A$ for W and Y, respectively.

It is fairly easy using equation 12 to compute the work effort response to either a lump-sum tax or a proportional tax on earnings. The former reduces the intercept of $0A$ and the latter reduces the slope (in absolute value). Note from equation 12 that, whereas a lump-sum tax may substantially increase labor supply (by 113 hours per year for every $1,000 in tax), a proportional tax imposed solely on wage earnings will cause only very minor reductions in work effort. For example, a proportional tax that reduces net wages by $2.00 will only reduce work effort by half a week per year (or about 1 percent). It is precisely this finding—that the uncompensated supply curve is vertical—that has often misled analysts into believing that the effects of taxation are trivial. This incorrect inference is sometimes based on an invalid analogy between proportional taxation and the progressive tax system.

In fact, progressive taxation combines some aspects of both proportional taxes and lump-sum transfers. To see this, consider the kinked budget line $0AB$ in figure 6. On the first segment, $0A$, the breadwinner's earnings are not subject to taxation; on the second segment, AB, earnings above a certain limit are subject to a constant marginal tax, t. Consequently, the slope of AB is equal to only $(1 - t) \times 100$ percent of the slope of $0A$. According to Hausman's estimates, this displacement in slope causes only a minor reduction in work effort. Note, however, that the intercept of the taxed budget segment, AB, is much higher than that of the untaxed segment, $0A$. From the point of view of the maximizing consumer who prefers to locate along AB, this situation is no different from one in which the government has given him a lump-sum transfer (in this case equal to y') and levied a constant tax on earnings equal to t. According to Hausman's estimates, *the implicit lump-sum transfer has a substantial effect on desired work effort* even though the marginal tax does not. Thus when both aspects of the progressive tax system are taken into

Jerry A. Hausman

Figure 6. Welfare Comparison of a Progressive Tax and a Lump-Sum Tax

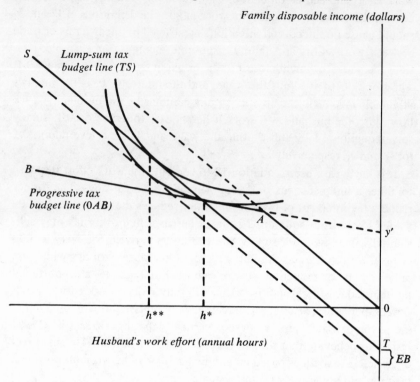

Family disposable income (dollars)

account, the present tax structure may have a substantial impact on the hours and earnings of prime-age husbands.

To make this point clear, I have computed work effort, earnings, and taxes for the median husband whose individual labor supply is given in equation 12.[74] A husband with a gross wage rate of $5.00 an hour and taxable unearned income of $500 a year would choose to work 2,514 hours a year and earn $12,570 in gross wages under the 1975 tax system. At this level of income, his federal and FICA taxes would be $2,320 and his cumulative federal and FICA marginal tax rate would be slightly below 28 percent. While this marginal rate causes his net wage to be $1.40 per hour less than his gross wage, it has only a small direct effect on de-

74. I assume a four-person family and joint filing of federal taxes. Federal and FICA taxes, which are computed according to the schedules provided by Hausman, are taken into account in my computations, but state taxes are assumed to be zero.

sired work effort. On the other hand, the progressive tax also has an effect analogous to giving the worker a $1,200 lump-sum transfer, which causes a much more important reduction in work effort. Taken together, the marginal tax and the implicit lump-sum transfer cause the worker to reduce his work effort by about 6 percent from the amount he would work if there were no taxation.

A more interesting comparison, and one that Hausman stresses, is with a pure lump-sum tax system in which the individual tax levy is exactly equal to the taxes raised in the progressive tax system. For the individual being considered, this lump sum would equal −$2,320. I compute that the individual subject to this lump-sum tax—but to no marginal tax on earnings—would choose to earn $14,625 a year, or about 16 percent more than he would earn under the 1975 progressive tax system. Moreover, the individual would prefer his situation in this pure lump-sum system to his previous utility maximum under the progressive tax system. This point can be seen in figure 6, where h^{**} (desired hours under pure lump-sum taxation) is plainly preferred to h^* (desired hours under the progressive tax).

A customary measure of utility loss arising from tax-induced distortion is excess burden. This is simply the amount of monetary compensation that would be required to make good the utility difference between attainable maxima under pure lump-sum and progressive taxation, respectively. The compensation is usually computed using pretax prices, as may be seen in figure 6, where T is the amount of taxes raised by progressive taxation at h^*; T is also the amount of the lump-sum tax. The measure of excess burden, EB, may be computed by using the indirect utility function, equation 4 in Hausman's paper. The excess burden for the median husband with a gross hourly wage of $5.00 is $302, or about 13 percent of federal and FICA taxes and 3 percent of net wages. (These estimates are not dissimilar to those reported by Rosen for the Stone-Geary utility function;[75] they substantially exceed Rosen's estimates based on the CES utility function, however.)

Another alternative to the progressive tax system is a strictly proportional tax system. For example, if the median husband with a $5 gross hourly wage was subject to a 17.8 percent proportional tax on income, he would pay the same tax on $12,570 in gross earnings under either the pro-

75. Harvey S. Rosen, "The Measurement of Excess Burden with Explicit Utility Functions," *Journal of Political Economy,* vol. 86 (April 1978), pp. S132–33.

Jerry A. Hausman

Figure 7. Welfare Comparison of a Progressive Tax and a Proportional Tax

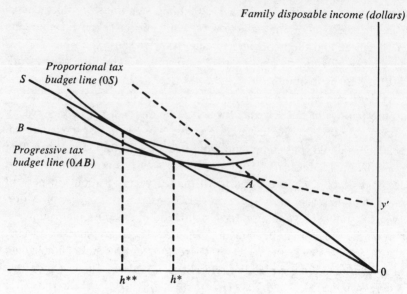

Husband's work effort (annual hours)

portional or the current progressive tax system. As may be seen in figure 7, the proportional tax system will induce greater work effort than the progressive tax. It will also be preferred by the rational consumer. With respect to the progressive tax system, however, the 17.8 percent proportional tax does not increase well-being nearly as much as the lump-sum tax. It would take only $35 to compensate the median husband for the utility difference between the proportional and the progressive tax systems. By contrast, it takes $302 to compensate him for the utility difference between the lump-sum and the progressive tax systems.[76]

In addition to the individual supply curve, I shall consider Hausman's version of the population supply function. A basic difference between Hausman's results and those of his predecessors is that the population supply function consists of individual functions that are quite diverse.

76. One should note, however, that the 17.8 percent proportional tax I have been describing ends up raising more tax revenue than either the progressive tax or the lump-sum tax it is replacing. If the proportional tax rate were reduced so that, taking account of the work effort response, it raised exactly the same revenue as the progressive tax it replaces, the relative utility differences between the proportional and the progressive tax schemes would be greater than $35.

This diversity arises from the presumed diversity of β, the income coefficient. Up to now I have been considering the decisions of the *median* husband, whose labor supply function is written as equation 12 above and whose β is presumed to be -0.113. However, according to Hausman's estimates, about 30 percent of all husbands have an income coefficient that is less than half of this median (that is, $|\beta| \leq 0.056$). For these husbands, responsiveness to progressive taxation is less than half of the response of the median husband. The excess burden attributable to progressive taxation is also far smaller. On the other hand, about a quarter of the population is estimated to have an income coefficient that is at least twice as high as the median (that is $|\beta| \geq 0.226$). For these individuals, the responsiveness to taxation—especially to its lump-sum-transfer aspect—is much greater than that of the median individual; the excess burden is also much greater. Hausman in his paper considers the deadweight loss of an "average" person, but the "average" income coefficient in this skewed distribution is in the highest one-third of the population distribution. Consequently, his estimates of the deadweight loss attributable to taxation are substantially higher than they would be for the median individual, but may come closer to reflecting the "average" deadweight loss attributable to taxation.

One point I would like to stress, then, is that *most* individuals are not very responsive to taxation and suffer very modest reductions in well-being as a consequence of the progressive nature of the tax schedule. In fact, in this respect Hausman's results are similar to some previous findings on tax responsiveness and excess burden. On the other hand, there is an important minority of husbands who are very responsive to the implicit lump-sum-transfer aspect of progressive taxation and who consequently suffer large welfare losses because of the way in which taxes are levied. I feel that Hausman's characterization of the diversity of work preferences provides a far closer approximation to reality than the maintained assumption in most previous research that all individuals have identical preferences except, perhaps, for a random intercept term. Consequently, his finding that an important minority of individuals is responsive to progressive taxation seems to me to be more plausible than the findings of some previous studies, which were based on the unrealistic assumption of identical or virtually identical preferences.

The interesting microsimulation results presented near the end of the paper also deserve comment. These results provide an indication of the national work effort and welfare losses that arise from the progressivity of the income tax system. These losses are substantial. U.S. prime-age husbands reduce their work effort by almost 9 percent in comparison with their behavior in a lump-sum tax world, and the deadweight loss associated with this reduction amounts to 5 percent of pretax earnings. Of course, the computed welfare losses are valid only under the assumption that economic agents derive no satisfaction from their knowledge that the tax system is progressive. Presumably, some agents derive such satisfaction; otherwise, it would be difficult to explain the prevalence of progressive tax schemes in this country and throughout the world.

If the amount of progressivity in the present tax system reflects society's taste for progressivity, then Hausman's results may suggest just how much worth is attached to this social good.[77] There are two reasons to believe that society may have less taste for progressivity than the current tax system reflects. First, the internal revenue code does not reflect a genuine social consensus, but rather represents the product of a particular form of democratic government. Stable majorities in that government may be attracted by the proposition that it is desirable to concentrate the main burden of taxation on as small a number of voters as possible. Progressivity achieves that end. Second, even if voters were completely disinterested, in the sense that they tried to maximize social welfare rather than their private well-being, there is no reason to suppose that a socially desirable level of progressivity would be chosen. As I have tried to make clear using Hausman's empirical estimates, the median voter is not particularly responsive to the lump-sum transfers implicit in progressive taxation. Lacking information about the diversity in responsiveness to taxation, he may erroneously assume that his fellow voters are equally unresponsive. However, an important minority of potential labor force participants is very responsive to taxation, and this minority suffers a disproportionate share of the deadweight loss arising from progressivity. Under these circumstances, it would not be surprising if a disinterested—albeit ill-informed—majority chose "too much" progressivity.

Though the microsimulation results are extremely suggestive, I nevertheless conclude by urging caution in the use of Hausman's estimates for public policy pronouncements. Specifically, I would not let the tail of Hausman's preference distribution wag that dog of public policy, namely, the current tax system. Hausman assumes that preferences are distributed

77. Strictly speaking, the valuation put on progressivity per se should be estimated by computing the apparent welfare loss of the current tax system in comparison with a *proportional* tax system, not a lump-sum tax system.

as a truncated normal random variable, and he empirically estimates a distribution in which most of the observations are found to be reasonably immune to the baleful influence of taxation. As is well known, however, the normal distribution trails off into infinity, and consequently a certain fraction of husbands are found who have an unhealthy appetite for leisure when faced with a progressive tax scheme. It is those in this tail of the preference distribution who cause the larger-than-expected tax response and excess burden in the progressive tax system. Yet there is really little theoretical or empirical basis for accepting or rejecting Hausman's assumed preference distribution function. The data certainly support the notion that preferences differ; they may equally well support the hypothesis of a uniform or a doubly truncated distribution of varying preferences. Either alternative may have substantial implications for *average* tax responsiveness and *average* excess burden in the U.S. economy.[78]

A final point deserves emphasis here. Hausman constrains his preference distribution so that no person in his sample can have a positive earnings response to a lump-sum transfer (in other words, leisure is assumed to be a normal good). This constraint is consistent with economic theory, but one may reasonably ask whether the behavior of every economic agent is equally consistent with theory. By imposing the constraint, Hausman undoubtedly influences the shape of the distribution of preferences and hence may influence the average estimated effects of taxation.

In spite of the limitations of Hausman's empirical estimates, I think they provide a useful and not unreasonable view of workers' response to taxation under the maintained assumption of economic rationality. For the *median* husband in his sample, his findings are not basically dissimilar to those of some earlier analysts. It is the estimated distribution around this median, however, that leads to the unexpected finding of some large responses to progressive taxation. It is also the distribution around the median, rather than the median itself, that is most open to both theoretical and statistical reexamination.

---

78. A related point is that under the current tax system the largest tax response and excess burden arise in the case of persons earning high wages. Yet from a statistical point of view, predictions of hours, earnings, and welfare changes arising from a particular tax change are least reliable precisely for persons at the extreme ends of the wage and income distribution. The predictions are more accurate around the mean in the sample, where the tax responsiveness and excess burden are comparatively small. This is another reason to be cautious in accepting the large economywide estimate of excess burden that may be implied by the empirical estimates reported by Hausman.

PATRIC H. HENDERSHOTT *and* SHENG-CHENG HU

Investment in Producers' Equipment

THE RATES of growth in real output and labor productivity during the most recent economic upswing have been much below those of earlier expansions. Real gross national product grew at an annual rate of 2.5 percent from 1973 to 1978, in contrast to the annual 3.5 percent between 1955 and 1973. Annual growth in productivity in the nonfarm private economy fell from 1.6 percent between 1965 and 1973 to under 1 percent in 1973-78. A contributing factor was a sharp slowdown in the annual growth in the capital–labor ratio from nearly 3 percent in the 1948-73 period to 1.75 percent after 1973.[1] While a consensus has emerged that government actions should be taken to raise the share of capital spending in GNP, there appears to be no agreement on the type of actions to be taken. Some contend that the user cost of capital for nonresidential structures should be reduced through liberalization of depreciation policies, expansions in investment tax credits, or a cut in the corporation income tax rate. Others maintain that the only sure way to increase investment is to keep the rate of capacity utilization high.

In an equilibrium economy, the sensitivity of investment to the user cost of capital depends on the ease with which capital and labor can be substituted for one another in production. If there can be no substitution between capital and labor, then capital acts as "pure clay" in the production function; ex ante as well as ex post net investment is motivated solely

1. *Economic Report of the President, 1980*, pp. 85 and 204; and *Economic Report of the President, 1979*, p. 68.

85

by the expected growth in output. At the other extreme, if the technology allows changes in the capital–labor ratio both before and after the installation of capital, the technology is characterized as "putty-putty"; a reduction in the user cost induces not only greater net investment for any given expected increase in output but also substitution of capital for labor in the production involving previously produced capital goods. Technology in which the desired capital–labor ratio for net or replacement investment depends on the user cost of capital but in which the capital–labor ratio cannot be altered once capital is purchased is called "putty-clay." The greater the ex ante or ex post responsiveness of the desired capital–labor ratio is to changes in the relative costs of capital and labor, the more responsive investment is to the user cost of capital. While the possibility of multiple work shifts suggests some ex post factor substitution, this paper presents weak evidence that technology is largely putty-clay. Strong evidence is provided that the production function is not one of fixed proportions (that is, pure clay). Changes in the rental price of capital affect the character of new and replacement investment, but have little effect on production methods with existing capital.

The user cost of capital and capacity utilization need not affect net and replacement investment in the same way. Net investment is influenced by the *expected* growth in output and the *level* of the user cost of capital. Replacement investment, on the other hand, depends on both the amount of capital to be replaced and changes in the cost of capital since the capital being replaced was initially installed. Given a stable age distribution of capital, replacement investment is directly related to the total capital stock and thus the *existing level* of output. The empirical results are strongly consistent with this newly posited relationship between replacement investment and the ratio of past to current user costs.

The preceding statements rest on the implicit assumption that equilibrium is achieved each period so that the desired and the actual levels of capital are equal, and the rate of capacity utilization is optimal. However, unexpected changes or lags in responses to changes in output and cost of capital could cause the capacity utilization rate to become suboptimal. In such a disequilibrium situation the ratio of the market value of the debt and equity of a firm to the replacement cost of its nonfinancial assets— Tobin's q—would no longer be equal to unity.[2] We have tried to discover whether or not disequilibrium adjustment is important in explaining in-

2. James Tobin, "A General Equilibrium Approach to Monetary Theory," *Journal of Money, Credit, and Banking*, vol. 1 (February 1969), pp. 15–29.

vestment behavior and whether Tobin's q or capacity utilization measures capture this adjustment better. Our evidence suggests that disequilibrium is important and that the capacity utilization rate provides a much superior proxy for this influence on investment.

One must measure the cost of capital accurately to assess its impact on investment correctly. Accurate specification and measurement of income taxes, investment tax credits, tax depreciation, the financing rate, and expected inflation are necessary. Considerable controversy exists regarding the latter two variables. For the financing rate, we employed a weighted average of the long-term bond rate and an estimate of the expected return on equity, with the bond rate receiving a weight of one-quarter. Others advocate using only the bond rate (pure debt finance) or replacing the bond rate with a short-term debt rate.[3] And there will always be debate over how best to estimate the expected rates of inflation and of return on equities. We have not tested alternative formulations. Our estimate of the real after-tax financing rate moves in the plausible range of 4.5 to 6.5 percentage points. One alternative—a constant real financing rate—was tested to determine whether the key tax variables alone significantly affected investment. The evidence supports this proposition.

Among the many measures of investment, we examined the ratio of the real value of orders for equipment (net of an estimate of required pollution control orders) to the real stock of equipment. Orders are preferable to investment outlays as a dependent variable because the length of the lag between orders and outlays varies directly with unfilled orders in the relevant industries. Thus virtually any aggregation of investment outlays will include capital goods with different lags between the placement of orders and their delivery, causing "the" lag to vary over time as the composition of orders changes. Adding technological to expectational lags, as the use of investment outlays would do, complicates both the estimation and the interpretation of the results. The relationship between outlays and orders is best left to a second estimation. Orders for structures are not explained because the model of optimal feasible replacement investment cannot be applied empirically to them.

The remainder of the paper is divided into four sections. The first two present a theory of investment behavior and describe the behavior of the user costs of capital for both equipment and structures over the past

3. Robert E. Hall, in "Investment, Interest Rates, and the Effects of Stabilization Policies," *Brookings Papers on Economic Activity*, 1:1977, pp. 16–121 (hereafter *BPEA*), argues for the use of a short-term rate, but the discussants disagree.

quarter century. The equation estimates are reported in the third section, and a summary concludes the paper. The construction of the user costs is discussed in detail in an appendix.

The Determinants of Business Fixed Investment

We begin with a restatement of the neoclassical theory[4] in a world with putty-clay technology, discuss lagged responses and the role of disequilibrium proxies, and consider the impact of pollution-control legislation.

The Optimal Feasible Rate of Replacement Investment

If the production function is of the Cobb-Douglas form,[5] the marginal productivity conditions imply that in equilibrium

$$(1) \qquad K = \alpha(Y/c),$$

where K is real capital, Y is the real output the capital is expected to produce, c is the user cost of capital, and α is the elasticity of output with respect to capital.

Assume that the depreciation rate of capital is a constant, d, so that depreciation, and thus replacement investment (I_r), equals dK_{-1}. Let ΔK, ΔY, and Δc stand for changes in the stock of real capital, real output, and the user cost of capital from one period to the next, respectively; then real gross investment, I, is as follows:[6]

$$(2) \qquad I = \Delta K + I_r = \alpha(\Delta Y/c) - K_{-1}(\Delta c/c) + dK_{-1}.$$

In equation 2, $\alpha(\Delta Y/c)$ measures the part of investment attributable to

---

4. Estimation based on this approach is widely associated with Dale W. Jorgenson. See his original work, "Capital Theory and Investment Behavior," *American Economic Review*, vol. 53 (May 1963, *Papers and Proceedings, 1962*), pp. 247–59; and his survey of the literature in "Econometric Studies of Investment Behavior: A Survey," *Journal of Economic Literature*, vol. 9 (December 1971), pp. 1111–47.

5. See Albert K. Ando, Franco Modigliani, Robert Rasche, and Stephen J. Turnovsky, "On the Role of Expectations of Price and Technological Change in an Investment Function," *International Economic Review*, vol. 15 (June 1974), p. 412, n. 29.

6. The difference form of equation 1 can be written as

$$\Delta K = \alpha(\Delta Y/c) + \alpha Y_{-1}\Delta(1/c)$$

or, if the lag of 1 is used,

$$\Delta K = \alpha(\Delta Y/c) - K_{-1}(\Delta c/c).$$

The first term denotes the output-growth effect, and the second term the capital/labor-energy substitution effect.

anticipated increases in sales given the cost of capital and the elasticity of output with respect to increased capital. The second term, $K_{-1}(\Delta c/c)$, denotes the change in the quantity of existing capital that would be preferred given a change in the user cost of capital. The third term, dK_{-1}, is simply replacement investment. Equation 2 is correct only if technology is putty-putty (that is, existing capital can be modified when the user cost of capital changes) and there are no lags in adjusting the capital stock to its new optimal level when anticipated sales or the cost of capital changes.

Now consider the case where lags exist solely because of the existence of putty-clay technology. Old capital must be combined with other inputs in fixed proportions, and substitution takes place only when capital is replaced. Thus the second term in equation 2 disappears. Also, the replacement investment term takes a different form. In general, the loss in production owing to depreciation depends on the technology utilized when the investment occurred—the desired output–capital ratio at that time. At any point t periods ago, the desired ratio was c_{-t}/α. If γ_t represents the proportion of the existing capital stock that was ordered t periods ago and thus depended on c_{-t}, then gross investment would be[7]

(2a) $$I = \alpha(\Delta\gamma/c) + dK_{-1}\Sigma\gamma_t(c_{-t}/c).$$

In a world with mixed technology, some putty-putty and some putty-clay, equations 2 and 2a must be combined. With β measuring the fraction of capital that is based on putty-putty technology, the general expression for the gross investment function is given by

(3) $$I = \alpha(\Delta Y/c) - \beta K_{-1}(\Delta c/c) + K_{-1}[\beta + (1 - \beta)\Sigma\gamma_t(c_{-t}/c)]\, d.$$

The last term shall be denoted by $K_{-1}d^f$, where d^f is the optimal feasible

---

7. If all capital depreciates at the yearly rate d, depreciation can be expressed as a function of past gross investments:

$$dK_{-1} = d\sum_{t=1} I_{-t}(1 - d)^{t-1},$$

and the loss of production owing to this depreciation is

$$d\Sigma(c_{-t}/\alpha)I_{-t}(1 - d)^{t-1}.$$

At the current desired output–capital ratio, the real investment necessary to replace the lost production is then

$$I_r = d\Sigma(c_{-t}/c)I_{-t}(1 - d)^{t-1} = dK_{-1}\Sigma\gamma_t(c_{-t}/c),$$

where $\gamma_t = I_{-t}(1 - d)^{t-1}/K_{-1}$ and $\Sigma\gamma_t = 1$. Adding the output growth term, $\alpha(\Delta Y/c)$, gives equation 2a.

replacement investment fraction given the proportion $(0 \leq \beta \leq 1)$ of technology that is putty-putty.

Production and Expectational Lags and Disequilibrium Proxies[8]

The preceding formulation assumes an instantaneous response to changes in output growth and the cost of capital, within the constraint of the form of the technology. But there are time lags in production, so it is useful to replace real gross investment outlays on the left side of equation 3 with the real value of orders; the technological relationship between real gross investment and current and past real values of orders is best obtained in a second estimation.[9] Moreover, given production lags, the capital stock to which current orders are directed is one at some point in the future. Thus it is an expected future level of output (and user cost of capital) that is relevant to the desired capital stock, and it is the change in this expected level that is relevant to current orders. Following Bischoff and Ando and others,[10] we assume that anticipated relative prices are functions of past relative prices and that anticipated capacity requirements are dependent on anticipated output and costs. These are, in turn, a function of past outputs.[11]

8. Hall, "Investment, Interest Rates, and the Effects of Stabilization Policies," provides an illuminating and provocative discussion of lags in investment responses.

9. Von Furstenberg has expressed shipments, S, of equipment as a lagged function of orders:

$$S = \sum_{t=0}^{m} [a_{-t} + b_{-t}(UORD/S)]ORD_{-t},$$

where $\Sigma a_{-t} = 1$, and $\Sigma b_{-t} = 0$. Unfilled orders, denoted by $UORD$, are defined as

$$UORD = UORD_{-1} + ORD - S.$$

The length of the time lag for equipment was estimated by von Furstenberg to be five quarters; the lag would be longer for structures. See George M. von Furstenberg, "Corporate Investment: Does Market Valuation Matter in the Aggregate?" *BPEA*, 2:1977, pp. 347–97.

10. See Charles W. Bischoff, "Hypothesis Testing and the Demand for Capital Goods," *Review of Economics and Statistics*, vol. 59 (August 1969), pp. 354–68; Bischoff, "The Effect of Alternative Lag Distributions," in Gary Fromm, ed., *Tax Incentives and Capital Spending* (Brookings Institution, 1971), pp. 61–130; and Ando and others, "On the Role of Expectations."

11. When this formation of expectations is allowed for, orders can be expressed as

$$ORD = \alpha\Sigma\theta_i^1(\Delta Y_{-t}/c) - \beta K_{-1}\Sigma\theta_i^2(\Delta c/c)_{-t} + K_{-1}d^f,$$

where $\Sigma\theta_i^i = 1$ for all i. The main difference between this equation and those of Bischoff and Ando and others is the second summation and the last term. In the earlier analyses, β was set to equal zero (technology is putty-clay), and thus the sec-

Realism requires us to admit that we are unlikely to get much explanatory power from a distributed lag on the rate of change in the user cost of capital (the second variable in equation 3). We suspect that technology is more putty-clay than not and, more important, that technology varies across industries and possibly over time. Fortunately, alternative approaches to capturing disequilibrium adjustments exist: equation 3, with β equaling 1, implicitly assumes that the actual stock of capital at the beginning of each period equals the desired stock at the end of the preceding period; that is, desired investment is realized. The introduction of time lags does not necessarily invalidate this assumption. So long as the desired increase in capital resulting from growth is expected and time lags are known, firms can always order ahead for capital they may desire in the future. In this case it is still true that desired and actual levels of capital are equalized each period. But if the increased demand for capital is unexpected and time lags are not certain, the desired level of capital will diverge from the actual level. Such discrepancies would cause the capacity utilization rate to deviate from the "optimal" level and the market value of existing capital to deviate from its replacement cost.

Tobin's q theory is an attempt to explain adjustments in the capital stock based on q, the ratio of the market value of a firm's debt and equity to the replacement cost of its existing nonfinancial assets, including land.[12] When the desired and actual levels of capital are equal, q is unity and investment consists of only the replacement component (plus an expected

---

ond summation disappeared. The last term was approximated by $da\Sigma w_t \ (Y/c)_{-t}$, where $\Sigma w_t = 1$.

The first summation in the equation can, of course, be rewritten as a distributed lag on Y/c rather than $\Delta Y/c$, where the lagged coefficients would then sum to zero rather than α. If the approximation for replacement investment were employed, the coefficients on Y/c should sum to αd. Earlier researchers employed a distributed lag on Y/c and obtained coefficients whose sum is far greater than αd. Hall ("Investment, Interest Rates, and the Effects of Stabilization Policies," pp. 83 and 95–98) argues persuasively that this violates the theory of investment to an unacceptable extent. More specifically, the results imply that a permanent fall in the cost of capital makes net investment permanently higher in a nongrowth world.

12. See James Tobin and William C. Brainard, "Asset Markets and the Cost of Capital," in Bela Balassa and Richard Nelson, eds., *Economic Progress, Private Values and Public Policy: Essays in Honor of William Fellner* (Amsterdam: North–Holland, 1977), pp. 235–62; Tobin, "General Equilibrium Approach"; and William C. Brainard and James Tobin, "Pitfalls in Financial Model Building," *American Economic Review*, vol. 58 (May 1968, *Papers and Proceedings, 1967*), pp. 99–122. For a sympathetic empirical test of the theory, see John H. Ciccolo, Jr., "Four Essays on Monetary Policy" (Ph.D. dissertation, Yale University, 1975).   .

growth component in a growing economy).[13] However, if changes in the cost of capital and other exogenous variables are unexpected and there are lags in adjustment, or if the length of lag is uncertain, then q need not be unitary. An excess of q over unity induces further investment and a shortfall stifles such outlays. Similarly, discrepancies between actual (CU) and "normal" (CU_n) capacity utilization rates might reflect divergencies between the desired and actual capital stocks.[14]

Pollution-Control Legislation

Pollution-control legislation has required capital outlays to "purify" both existing capital and new capital. Real outlays for pollution control and abatement increased about 25 percent annually between 1968 and 1973 and have since remained at about the 1973 level (see table 1). As a share of total real outlays on nonresidential fixed capital, pollution-control outlays roughly tripled, from 1.4 percent to over 4 percent, between 1968 and 1973. Pollution-control capital outlays directly raise total capital outlays and thus orders.

Because such investments are required by law, we subtract an estimate of them (PC) from total orders (ORD) before trying to relate orders to sales, the cost of capital, and other influences. The estimate of PC is the product of total orders and the percentage of pollution-control outlays in total nonresidential fixed capital outlays. This percentage is listed in column 2 of table 1 for 1967–78; the 1.4 value for 1967 is assumed to have held for all preceding years. Also, the requirement that pollution-control capital outlays accompany new nonpollution or "productive" capital outlays lowers the desired level of the latter. This indirect effect is accounted for in the construction of the user cost of capital (see the appendix to this chapter).

The Estimation Equation

The basic equation tested is

$$(4) \quad (ORD - PC)/K_{-1} = \Psi + \alpha(\Sigma v_t y_{-t})/c \\ + \lambda(q - 1) + \lambda'(CU - CU_n) + d'.$$

13. In fact, q may be less than unity owing to differences in taxes on dividends and capital gains. See Alan J. Auerbach, "Wealth Maximization and the Cost of Capital," and "Share Valuation and Corporate Equity Policy," National Bureau of Economic Research Working Papers 254 and 255 (Cambridge, Mass.: NBER, July 1978).

14. Von Furstenberg, in "Corporate Investment," finds capacity utilization to be a much stronger determinant of investment than q is. We shall employ the q series calculated by von Furstenberg.

Table 1. Pollution-Control Capital Outlays, 1967–78

Year	Capital outlays, real nonresidential pollution control (billions of 1972 dollars) (1)	Pollution-control outlays as a percent of gross private nonresidential fixed investment (2)	Pollution-control outlays on new capital as a percent of gross private nonresidential fixed investment (3)
1967	1.49	1.4	1.4
1968	1.50	1.4	1.4
1969	2.06	1.8	1.8
1970	2.84	2.6	2.0
1971	3.43	3.2	2.2
1972	4.46	3.8	2.4
1973	5.40	4.1	2.6
1974	5.03	3.9	3.0
1975	5.48	4.8	3.0
1976	5.50	4.6	3.0
1977	5.50	4.2	3.0
1978	5.50	3.9	3.0

Sources: Column 1, 1967–72, McGraw-Hill Economics Department, "12th Annual Survey of Pollution Control Expenditures," press release (New York, May 1979); 1973–77, Gary L. Rutledge, "Pollution Abatement and Control Expenditures in Constant and Current Dollars, 1972–77," *Survey of Current Business* (February 1979), table 2, line 7, less residential systems in table 4, pp. 14–15, 17; 1978, estimated. Column 2, National Income and Product Accounts, *Survey of Current Business*, various issues. Column 3, authors' estimates.

This results from substitution of the disequilibrium proxies, division by K_{-1} to reduce the statistical problem of heteroscedasticity, approximation of $\Sigma\theta^1(\Delta Y_{-t}/K_{-1})$ by $\Sigma v_t y_{-t}$—where $y_{-t} = (\Delta Y/K_{-1})_{-t}$—for computational ease, and introduction of a constant term to allow for possible misspecifications, mismeasurements, or nonlinearities.[15] The coefficients to be estimated are Ψ, α, λ, λ', and the v_t (the combined accelerator–cost-of-capital variable).

We expect that Ψ will be approximately zero, a value consistent with the absence of serious misspecifications, mismeasurements, or nonlinearities. Further, the value of $\alpha = c(K/Y)$ should be within the range of the product of the observed values of the capital–output ratio and the cost of

15. Let $\lambda(q - 1) = (K^* - K_{-1})/K_{-1}$ and $\lambda'(CU - CU_n) = (K^* - K_{-1})/K_{-1}$, where λ denotes the relationship between the percentage deviation of the desired (K^*) and actual (K_{-1}) capital stocks and the deviation of q from unity, and λ' denotes the relationship between this percentage deviation and the deviation between the actual and normal capacity utilization rates. The second summation in footnote 11 can then be approximated as $\lambda K_{-1}(q - 1) + \lambda' K_{-1}(CU - CU_n)$. Subtraction of pollution-control orders and performance of the other steps gives equation 4.

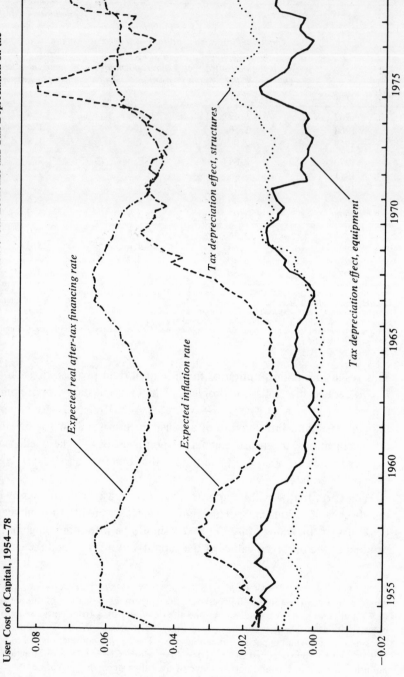

Figure 1. Expected Inflation Rate, Real Rate of Interest, and the Effect of Differences between Economic and Tax Depreciation on the User Cost of Capital, 1954–78

capital over the estimation period. Because K/Y has ranged between 0.33 and 0.44 and our estimates of c lie between 0.22 and 0.32, α should fall within the 0.07 to 0.14 range. We expect both λ and λ' to lie between zero and one. Finally, the v_t should be positive.

The primary purpose of the empirical tests is to measure the sensitivity of equipment orders to the cost of capital, and thus to underlying tax and financial parameters. In the process we shall attempt to shed some light on whether technology is putty-putty or putty-clay and the importance of q and capital utilization in explaining equipment orders.

User Costs of Capital

The user cost of capital is a simple concept in theory; it is the real rental rate that a firm pays to rent a unit of real capital. In a world without taxes and inflation and with perfect capital markets, the user cost would equal "the" rate of interest plus the depreciation rate. In the real world, one must be concerned with debt and equity rates, loan-to-value ratios, tax rates and credits, asset tax service lives and depreciation methods, the formation of expected inflation rates, and pollution-control legislation. The relevance of these is demonstrated in the appendix, where a theoretical expression for the cost of capital is derived. At this point we simply state that the real user cost (c) is given by

$$(5) \qquad c = (P_k/P_y)[(1 - \mu)(r_a - p + d)/(1 - \tau) \\ - \tau d/(1 - \tau) + \tau(d - d^*)/(1 - \tau)] = \rho,$$

where P_k/P_y is the ratio of capital to output prices, μ is the investment tax credit, $r_a - p$ is the expected real after-tax financing rate, τ is the corporate profits tax rate, d is the economic depreciation rate, and $d - d^*$ is the difference between the economic and tax depreciation rates.

The Expected Real After-Tax Financing Rate and Inflation Rate

Figure 1 contains plots of the expected real after-tax financing rate, the expected inflation rate, and two other variables that will be defined below. Specification of these two rates is somewhat complicated and is discussed in the appendix. At this point we simply note their behavior. The expected real after-tax financing rate is a weighted average of the real after-tax bond rate (one-quarter weight) and the real after-tax equity yield (three-quarters). While the former has declined markedly since the early 1960s, the latter has increased.[16] As a result, the expected real after-tax financing rate is a rather stable series. As the top series in figure 1 shows, the real rate stayed within the range of 4.5 to 6.5 percentage points during the 1954–78 period and had no apparent trend. There is cyclical movement in the series; the real rate exceeded 6 percent only in booms in the mid-1950s (1954:4–1957:4), the late 1960s (1966:2–1969:1), and the late 1970s (1978:2–1978:4).

The expected inflation rate has both a strong cyclical movement and an upward trend. The calculated expected inflation rate rose from 1.5 percent to 3 percent in the mid-1950s, fell to nearly 1 percent in the early to middle 1960s, rose into the 4 to 5 percent range in the late 1960s, and jumped to well above 6 percent in 1975 and again in 1978.

Tax and Economic Depreciation

Under present law the service life for tax purposes is usually less than the economic service life, and assets may be depreciated on an accelerated rate schedule that exceeds the actual depreciation rate. Specifically, the double-declining-balance method may be employed to depreciate equipment (only straight-line depreciation was allowed before 1954), and the 150 percent declining-balance method may be used to depreciate structures (200 percent was available between 1954 and 1968, but straight-line was required before 1954).[17] Moreover, the permissible tax service life for structures, on the average, declined from forty-two years in 1952 to thirty-seven years in 1956 and has since remained there; that for equipment fell from an average of seventeen years in the early 1950s to eleven

---

16. The following data indicate these trends (the underlying data are given in the appendix).

	After-tax equity	After-tax debt	Expected inflation	Real equity	Real debt
1962:3–1963:3	7.24	2.05	1.15	6.09	0.86
1978:3–1978:4	16.20	4.44	7.08	9.12	−2.64
Change	8.96	2.39	5.93	3.03	−3.50

17. See Allan H. Young, "Alternative Estimates of Corporate Depreciation and Profits: Part I," *Survey of Current Business,* vol. 48 (April 1968), pp. 17–28; and Young, "New Estimates of Capital Consumption Allowances in the Benchmark Revision of GNP," *Survey of Current Business,* vol. 55 (October 1975), pp. 14–16, 35. The proportion of new investment depreciated via accelerated methods rose rapidly from 31 percent in 1954 to 75 percent in 1959. (This proportion is now over 90 percent.) Another source of rapid depreciation in the early 1950s was the sixty-month amortization of defense facilities reintroduced during the Korean War.

years in the early 1970s.[18] While there is some uncertainty about actual economic depreciation rates, they are surely far less than those allowed under tax law. The most plausible annual percentage rates of depreciation for equipment and structures, in the aggregate, appear to be 0.13 and 0.04, and the most reasonable economic lives are sixteen and fifty years.[19]

A more important source of discrepancies between depreciation deductions and actual depreciation in the current inflationary environment is the tax requirement that the depreciating capital must be valued at historic rather than replacement cost. Given the independence of future expected tax depreciation from expected inflation, an increase in the expected rate of inflation reduces the present value of expected future tax depreciation and thus the value of tax deductions. In fact, the combination of expected inflation and the historic-cost requirement has resulted during the past quarter century in tax depreciation lower than economic depreciation at replacement cost in all years except the early 1960s (1962–66 for structures and 1964–66 for equipment).

Inspection of figure 1 illustrates the powerful impact of changes in the expected inflation rate on *TXDE* and *TXDS,* the respective effects of differences between economic and tax depreciation on the costs of capital for equipment (*E*) and structures (*S*).[20] The plotted series in figure 1 also reflect the major changes in depreciation law discussed above. For example, the sharp reductions in tax service lives for equipment show up as declines in *TXDE* in 1964:1 and 1971:3,[21] and the switch from 200 percent declining-balance depreciation for structures to 150 percent is the source of the rise in *TXDS* in 1969:1.

As can also be seen, *TXDS* rose sharply relative to *TXDE* between 1969 and 1978. At a relatively modest expected inflation rate of 5.5 per-

18. Ibid.

19. See Patric H. Hendershott and Sheng-Cheng Hu, "Government-Induced Biases in the Allocation of the Stock of Fixed Capital in the United States," in George M. von Furstenberg, ed., *Capital, Efficiency, and Growth* (Ballinger, 1980), pp. 323–60. In that paper a 3 percent depreciation rate was assumed for structures. In retrospect this rate seems too low, given the assumed economic life of fifty years.

20. From equation 5 it is clear that the effect of a $d - d^*$ gap on the cost of capital depends on relative prices and the corporation tax rate. That is,

$$TXD = (P_k/P_y)\tau(d - d^*)/(1 - \tau).$$

21. The impact on *TXDE* of the shortening of the tax service lives in 1962:3 does not show up until 1964:1 because the simultaneous introduction of the investment tax credit raised *TXDE* by reducing the depreciable value of equipment. Passage of the Long amendment, which allowed depreciation of the full amount of equipment, removed the impact of the tax credit on *TXDE*.

Table 2. Sources of Change in the User Cost of Capital, 1954–78[a]
Percentage point change

	Equipment						Structures				
		Contribution to change in cost of capital						Contribution to change in cost of capital			
Period	Change in cost of capital	Real interest rate	Economic less tax depreciation	Investment tax credit	Corporation tax rate	Ratio of capital to output prices	Change in cost of capital	Real interest rate	Economic less tax depreciation	Corporation tax rate	Ratio of capital to output prices
1954:1–1957:3	4.80	3.31	−0.03	0.0	0.02	1.50	4.05	3.66	−0.26	0.02	0.63
1957:3–1964:1	−8.49	−1.87	−2.42	−2.44	−0.68	−1.08	−5.71	−2.20	−0.88	−0.60	−2.03
1964:1–1969:2	5.85	2.12	1.94	2.17	0.68	−1.06	5.47	2.38	1.44	0.78	0.87
1969:2–1972:4	−7.37	−1.90	−1.09	−2.28	−1.39	−0.71	−2.59	−3.36	−0.06	−1.37	2.20
1972:4–1975:2	3.72	2.47	1.22	−1.07	0.17	0.93	7.94	2.45	0.68	0.26	4.55
1975:2–1976:4	−1.34	−0.27	−1.30	…	0.05	0.18	−1.32	−0.14	−0.79	0.08	−0.47
1976:4–1978:4	1.80	0.90	0.82	…	0.01	0.07	3.20	1.38	0.50	0.02	1.30

a. The method of calculating the contribution is as follows:
Economic less tax depreciation:

$$d - d^* : \left(\frac{\tau_{-1}}{1 - \tau_{-1}}\right)\left(\frac{P_k}{P_y}\right)_{-1} \Delta(d - d^*)$$

Investment tax credit

$$\mu : \left(\frac{r_a - p + d}{\delta_a(- \tau)}\right)_{-1}\left(\frac{P_k}{P_y}\right)_{-1} \Delta\mu$$

Corporation tax rate

$$\tau : \frac{\Delta\tau}{(1 - \tau)(1 - \tau_{-1})}\left[\frac{(1 - \mu)(r_a - p + d)}{\delta_a} - d^*\right]_{-1}\left(\frac{P_k}{P_y}\right)_{-1}$$

Ratio of capital to output prices

$$P_k/P_y : \left[\left(\frac{P_k}{P_y}\right)\Big/\left(\frac{P_k}{P_y}\right)_{-1} - 1\right]_{C_{-1}}$$

Real interest rate

$r_a - p$: residual

A variable without subscript refers to the end of the period; the −1 subscript refers to the beginning of the period. The levels of the costs of capital are given in the appendix.

cent, the difference between economic and tax depreciation raises the cost of capital for structures by 2 percentage points, but that for equipment by only half a percentage point. The recent relative rise in *TXDS* stems from two factors. First are the above-noted depreciation law changes in 1969 and 1971 against structures and in favor of equipment. Second is the sharp relative rise in the price of structures. The ratio of capital prices to output prices (P_k/P_y) for equipment was the same in 1978 as in 1963, but the ratio for structures rose by over 40 percent. This rise magnified the impact of the increase in the difference between economic and tax depreciation on the cost of capital.

A 1979 legislative proposal (not passed) would have reduced the tax lives of all nonresidential structures and "long-lived" equipment to ten and five years, respectively.[22] Adoption of this proposal would have substantially lowered the costs of capital for business investments. At 1978 values of the variables, the value of tax depreciation would exceed depreciation on equipment by 2.5 percentage points and on structures by 3 percentage points.[23] In contrast, the value of tax depreciation is 1 percentage point less than tax depreciation under current law for equipment and 1.5 percentage points less for structures. In spite of such declines, costs of capital would still be higher for business investments than for investment in owner-occupied housing.[24]

Changes in User Costs, 1954–78

Table 2 contains data on the sizes and sources of "cyclical" swings in the costs of capital for equipment and structures. The divisions of the periods coincide roughly with peaks and troughs in the user costs, which are listed in the appendix. As can be seen, the changes were large, especially before 1975.

Changes in the real rate of interest contribute to all swings, but they account for over half the movement in the user costs in only two of the seven periods: 1954:1–1957:3 and 1972:4–1975:2 for equipment and 1954:1–1957:3 and 1969:2–1972:4 for structures. Because an increase in expected inflation lowers the value of historic-cost depreciation, all

22. Capital Cost Recovery Act of 1979, H.R. 4646.
23. Of course, the reductions would vary within the categories, being greater the longer the economic lives of the capital goods.
24. See Patric H. Hendershott and Sheng-Cheng Hu, "Inflation and Extraordinary Returns on Owner-Occupied Housing: Some Implications for Capital Allocation and Productivity Growth," *Journal of Macroeconomics,* vol. 3 (Spring 1981); and Hendershott and Hu, "Government-Induced Biases."

major changes in the difference between economic and tax depreciation are associated with changes in the expected inflation rate in the same direction. For equipment, more liberal depreciation write-offs increased the value of tax depreciation relative to economic depreciation during the 1957:3–1964:1 and 1969:2–1972:4 periods; for structures, the switch to 150 percent declining-balance depreciation in 1969 produced the same effect. The changing contribution of the investment tax credit reflects its introduction, temporary suspension, reimposition, and increase. The tax rate, too, reflects legislated changes: the tax cut in 1964, the surcharge in 1968, and its removal in 1970–71. The ratio of capital to output prices had little effect on the cost of capital for equipment because the ratio stayed within the 0.92 to 1.06 range. For structures, however, the ratio rose sharply, from 1.05 in early 1969 to 1.40 by the end of 1974, significantly raising the user cost.

Empirical Estimates

Before estimating the strength of the various influences on investment, one must decide on the precise order series to be explained and the period of estimation. It is desirable to explain orders for equipment and structures separately for three reasons. First, the user cost has differed markedly for equipment and structures owing to differences in tax depreciation, application of investment tax credits, and movements in relative prices. Second, one would expect the lag between the placement of orders and the production of capital to be longer for structures than for equipment. Third, calculation of the optimal feasible replacement investment fraction requires user cost data for a period of years equal to the life of the capital good before the start of the estimation period; the long lives of structures effectively limit application of the optimal feasible replacement model to equipment. The Federal Reserve–MIT-Penn (FMP) model builders adjusted the series for real manufacturers' new equipment orders to remove the influence of exports and imports, thereby creating a real equipment order series that is consistent with the real equipment investment and capital stock series produced by the Commerce Department.[25]

The earliest quarter for which data on orders is available is 1953:2, but given the assumed sixteen-year life of equipment and 1950:1 as the first quarter when the user cost of equipment can reasonably be calcu-

25. Ando and others, "On the Role of Expectations."

Figure 2. The Ratio of Equipment Orders to Stock and the Cost of Capital, 1957–78

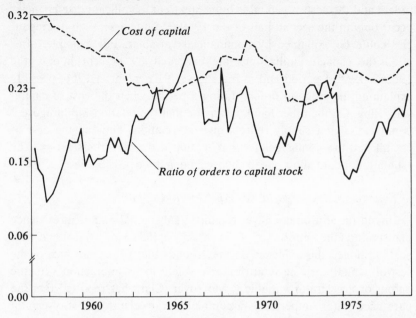

lated, the optimal feasible replacement fraction for equipment is not fully specified until 1966:1. However, the small weights given to discrepancies between the cost of capital many quarters ago and the current value suggest that such discrepancies can be ignored. In effect, we assume that the past user cost of capital equals the current value before 1950:1 in all calculations of the optimal feasible replacement fraction. Thus for equipment this fraction equals the economic depreciation rate, 0.13, before 1950:1. From that point, it declines to 0.115 (if technology is "putty-clay") in 1957:1 and then ranges as high as 0.156 in 1971:4 and drops to 0.122 in 1978:4. The movement is less if capital that is in place can be modified in part to change the capital–labor ratio when the user cost of capital changes. Because the decline in the optimal feasible replacement fraction before 1957 could be spurious, the estimation for equipment begins with 1957:1.[26]

Figure 2 shows the ratio of equipment orders (less those required by pollution legislation) to the equipment stock $[(ORD - PC)/K_{-1}]$ and the

26. A second reason for beginning the estimation after the mid-1950s is the difficulty of accounting for the impact on the tax depreciation rate of the reintroduction of sixty-month amortization for defense facilities in the early 1950s.

real user cost of capital. The expected strong inverse relation between orders and the cost of capital is quite apparent. Significant discrepancies occur only in the second half of the 1960s.[27] Of course, such discrepancies could be explained by nonfinancial variables. For example, after 1953 the capacity utilization rate exceeded 89 percent in only the 1965:2–1966:4 period and averaged over 91 percent in 1966, possibly explaining the surge in orders during a period when the cost of capital was rising. On the other hand, it may be that the relationship in figure 2 is not causal but simply reflects high correlations between the cost of capital and the nonfinancial variables that drive the orders series. The estimation should allow one to choose among these possibilities.

Evidence on the Importance of the Cost of Capital

Jorgenson and others have developed substantial empirical evidence that supports the importance of the cost of capital to investment.[28] Eisner has questioned this evidence on the grounds that the significance of the cost-of-capital variable is attributable solely to its interaction with the output or accelerator variable.[29] Moreover, Clark has reported that the pure accelerator outperforms a combination accelerator–cost-of-capital formulation, and von Furstenberg has argued that the capacity utilization rate is the dominant determinant of business nonresidential fixed in-

27. The outlier in 1968:1 may reflect an error in the orders series. The ratio of the Commerce Department and FMP series fell from 1.41 in 1967:4 to 1.24 in 1968:1 and then rose to 1.52 in 1968:2. A number of preliminary equations were estimated with a dummy variable (1 in 1968:1 and 0 elsewhere) included. The results were similar to those obtained when the dummy was not included.

28. See Jorgenson, "Capital Theory and Investment Behavior," and "Econometric Studies of Investment Behavior"; Robert E. Hall and Dale W. Jorgenson, "Tax Policy and Investment Behavior," *American Economic Review,* vol. 57 (June 1967), pp. 391–414; Bischoff, "Hypothesis Testing and the Demand for Capital Goods," and "Effect of Alternative Lag Distributions"; and Ando and others, "On the Role of Expectations."

29. See Robert Eisner, "Tax Policy and Investment Behavior: Comment," *American Economic Review,* vol. 59 (June 1969), pp. 379–88; and Robert Eisner and M. I. Nadiri, "Neoclassical Theory of Investment Behavior: A Comment," *Review of Economics and Statistics,* vol. 52 (May 1970), pp. 216–22. One piece of evidence on the significance of the cost of capital that is not "suspect" on these grounds is Ernst R. Berndt, "Reconciling Alternative Estimates of the Elasticity of Substitution," *Review of Economics and Statistics,* vol. 58 (February 1976), pp. 59–68. Berndt explains capital–labor and output–capital ratios for U.S. manufacturing over the 1929–68 period with user cost variables.

vestment.[30] Determination of the role, if any, of financial variables in investment decisions is of crucial importance to policymakers and is a principal aim of this paper.

To obtain independent estimates of the importance of the accelerator and cost-of-capital variables, the summation in equation 4 is initially approximated by two separate variables, $(\Sigma v_t y_{-t})/\bar{c}$ and $\bar{y}/c$, where bars over variables denote mean values during the 1957–58 period. Table 3 gives regression coefficients for equations containing these and other variables. Coefficients of determination are not reported for equations beyond the first three because they are not comparable owing to differences in the dependent variables.

Equation 3-1 is the pure accelerator case. Neither the cost of capital nor the optimal feasible replacement rate (d^f, which is heavily dependent on c) appears. Because the latter variable has been excluded, the expected constant term is 0.13, the depreciation rate. As is hardly surprising, the accelerator is a potent, highly significant force. The t-ratio on the sum of the distributed lag weights exceeds 10 and this variable alone explains three-fifths of the movement in the ratio of orders to capital stock.

Equations 3-2 to 3-4 demonstrate the importance of the cost-of-capital variable. In 3-2 the constant depreciation rate implicit in the constant term is replaced by a measure of the optimal feasible replacement fraction specified on the assumption that technology is pure putty-clay. As expected, the constant drops close to zero and the coefficient on the replacement rate is very close to unity. In 3-3, the constant mean value of sales divided by the user cost of capital replaces the optimal feasible replacement fraction.[31] The expected magnitude of this variable is α, or about 0.1. The variable is significant with the expected positive sign, but the coefficient is implausibly large.[32] Obviously $\bar{y}/c$ is capturing the impact of

30. See Peter K. Clark, "Investment in the 1970s: Theory, Performance, and Prediction," *BPEA, 1:1979,* pp. 73–113; and von Furstenberg, "Corporate Investment."

31. Tests for lagged responses to the cost of capital were not successful, the implication being that the current and expected costs of capital are the same. This is not surprising since some components of the user cost—the equity and inflation rates—were constructed as expected variables.

32. This value of the coefficient implies that an increase in the user cost of capital from 0.22 to 0.32 would reduce the ratio of orders to the capital stock by roughly one-third.

Table 3. Preliminary Regressions for Orders for Equipment, 1957:1–1978:4[a]

Equation number	Putty-putty fraction of technology[b]	Coefficient						Summary statistics		
		Pure accelerator[c]	Cost of capital[d]	Tobin's q less unity	Capacity utilization rate less 0.85	Optimal feasible replacement investment fraction[e]	Constant	Standard error	Durbin-Watson	$\bar{R}^2$
3-1	NR	0.160 (0.015)	...	...	...	...	0.130 (0.006)	0.0237	0.74	0.61
3-2	0.0	0.140 (0.015)	...	...	...	0.962 (0.250)	0.010 (0.032)	0.0220	0.89	0.67
3-3	NR	0.139 (0.014)	1.304 (0.284)	...	...	...	0.014 (0.026)	0.0213	0.95	0.69
3-4	0.0	0.136 (0.015)	0.212 (0.292)	...	...	1.0 (const.)	−0.014 (0.027)	0.0219	0.91	...
3-5	0.0	0.022 (0.026)	0.292 (0.253)	0.0037 (0.0198)	0.497 (0.090)	1.0 (const.)	0.032 (0.025)	0.0189	1.26	...
3-6	0.4	0.137 (0.014)	0.645 (0.288)	...	...	1.0 (const.)	−0.054 (0.026)	0.0216	0.93	...
3-7	0.4	0.019 (0.026)	0.733 (0.247)	0.0107 (0.0193)	0.498 (0.088)	1.0 (const.)	−0.006 (0.024)	0.0185	1.31	...
3-8	0.0	0.098 (0.005)	0.212 (const.)	...	0.283 (0.050)	1.0 (const.)	0.0 (const.)	0.0193	1.15	...

a. Orders (net of pollution) are real quarterly flows at annual rates, deflated by the beginning-period stock of equipment, y is measured at annual rates (for example, 0.10), and c, d^f, and CU are in decimals. Standard errors of the coefficients are given in parentheses; standard errors of the equations appear under "summary statistics."
b. NR indicates that β is not relevant (d^f does not appear in the equation).
c. $(\Sigma v y_{-i})/\bar{c}$.
d. Variable d^f, which depends on c and β.
e. Variable $d^f/\bar{c}$.

changes in c on both net new orders and replacement investment.[33] Because the variables measuring the optimal feasible replacement fraction and the user cost of capital are so highly correlated, they will not enter the equation with coefficients of the same sign. To overcome this problem, we imposed a coefficient of 1 on the former in equation 3-4 by subtracting the replacement investment fraction from the ratio of orders to capital before estimation. The result is what would be expected in light of equations 3-2 and 3-3 and is appealing theoretically. The coefficient on $\bar{y}/c$ is now close to that on the accelerator variable, and the constant term is near zero.

The disequilibrium variables, $q - 1$ and the deviation of actual from normal rates of capacity utilization (normal capacity utilization is assumed to be 85 percent), are added in equation 3-5. As can be seen, the former has little impact, but the latter is highly significant. While the reduction in equation standard error is desirable, the effect of the capacity utilization rate on the coefficient on the accelerator variable is not. Obviously the utilization rate is playing a larger part than the disequilibrium role assigned to it.[34]

Equations 3-6 and 3-7 are repeats of 3-4 and 3-5, but with the optimal feasible replacement fraction based on the assumption of 40 percent putty-putty technology. As could be predicted, the main impact of the switch is to raise the coefficient on the cost of capital. Because the assumption that technology is partly putty-putty dampens the movement in the optimal feasible replacement fraction, movements in $\bar{y}/c$ now have a greater effect on orders. The implausibly high coefficients on the cost of capital in equations 3-6 and 3-7, 0.645 and 0.733, respectively, suggest that technology is putty-clay.

33. To illustrate the correlation between d^f and $\bar{y}/c$, the following equations were run (standard errors are in parentheses):

$$d^f = 1.388 \, \bar{y}/c$$
$$(0.005)$$
$$\bar{R}^2 = 0.85$$

and

$$d^f = 0.026 + 1.116 \, \bar{y}/c.$$
$$(0.004) \quad (0.040)$$
$$\bar{R}^2 = 0.90$$

34. Frank de Leeuw has suggested that the larger role could be an intentional "overordering" during periods of high utilization rates to compensate for delays in the filling of orders. Such firms would then anticipate canceling some future orders. In fact, unusually large cancellations apparently occurred in 1970, 1974, and especially in 1975. Whether these were "anticipated" cancellations or simply a response to declining sales is uncertain.

Table 4. Equipment Orders with First-Order Transformation, 1957:2–1978:4[a]

				Coefficient					Summary statistics	
Equation number	Putty-putty fraction of technology	Pure accelerator	Cost of capital	Tobin's q less unity	Capacity utilization rate less 0.85	Optimal feasible replacement investment fraction	Constant	Rho		Standard error	Durbin-Watson
4-1	0.0	0.133 (0.025)	−0.334 (0.551)	...	...	1.0 (const.)	0.041 (0.051)	0.58 (0.09)		0.0184	2.12
4-2	0.0	0.028 (0.035)	0.098 (0.389)	0.0135 (0.0272)	0.440 (0.121)	1.0 (const.)	0.050 (0.037)	0.39 (0.10)		0.0176	2.04
4-3	0.4	0.134 (0.024)	0.163 (0.534)	...	...	1.0 (const.)	−0.006 (0.049)	0.57 (0.09)		0.0183	2.11
4-4	0.4	0.025 (0.034)	0.570 (0.369)	0.0186 (0.0261)	0.446 (0.116)	1.0 (const.)	0.008 (0.035)	0.37 (0.10)		0.0174	2.02
4-5	0.0	0.124 (0.010)	0.098 (const.)	...	0.142 (0.080)	1.0 (const.)	0.0 (const.)	0.50 (0.09)		0.0181	2.08
4-6	0.4	0.113 (0.009)	0.163 (const.)	...	0.199 (0.076)	1.0 (const.)	0.0 (const.)	0.48 (0.09)		0.0177	2.09

a. See table 3 and the text for the measurement of the variables. Standard errors of the coefficients are given in parentheses; standard errors of the equations appear under "summary statistics."

While one obviously cannot accept the low output-capital elasticity implied by the coefficients in the accelerator in equations 3-5 and 3-7, it would be desirable to use at least some of the considerable explanatory power of the utilization rate. With this in mind, equation 3-5 was rerun with the constant term constrained to zero. We hoped that this reduction in the constant would allow the accelerator to have more influence. Regrettably, it was the coefficient on the cost of capital that rose. We then constrained the constant to zero and the coefficient on the cost of capital to that in 3-4. The result is equation 3-8. As can be seen, this experiment returns the coefficient on the accelerator to the acceptable range, and preserves most of the reduction in the equation standard error caused by the inclusion of the utilization rate in 3-5.

All of the equations in table 3 contain autocorrelated residuals (the Durbin-Watson ratios are in the 0.7 to 1.3 range).

The first four equations in table 4 are repeats of equations 3-4 to 3-7, except that the autocorrelation is corrected by the Cochrane-Orcutt semi-difference transformation (the rho values are reported in the table). The primary effect of this transformation is to reduce the coefficient on the cost of capital. Now that in 4-1 is too low and that in 4-4 is too high. The utilization rate continues to destroy the coefficient on the accelerator variable, and the q variable is not working. Equations 4-5 and 4-6 reflect an effort to retain some of the explanatory power of the utilization rate; the effort is more successful if technology is 40 percent putty-putty.

Estimates Assuming a Constant Real Rate of Interest

As noted in the appendix, calculation of the cost of capital is a complex and sometimes subjective matter. Our greatest difficulties were in determining proxies for the expected return on equity and the expected inflation rate. With our proxies, the real after-tax financing rate moves within the range of 4.5 to 6.5 percentage points during the 1954–78 period. While this range strikes us as quite plausible, others might disagree. We also tested the assumption that the real after-tax average financing rate was constant throughout this period.[35]

35. Changes in the cost of capital for various periods between 1954:1 and 1978:4 and sources of the changes are listed in table 2. As can be seen, swings in the real rate contributed to each of the listed changes. Thus the assumption of a constant real rate will dampen movements in c. On average, the absolute changes in c for the periods between 1957 and 1978 listed in table 2 are reduced by one-fourth. The changes in c from the 1957:3–1964:1 period through the 1976:4–1978:4 period are -6.70, 4.63, -5.52, 2.07, -1.27, and 1.18.

Table 5. Regressions with a Constant Real Rate of Interest[a]

Equation number	Putty-putty fraction of technology	Coefficient						Rho	Summary statistics	
		Pure accelerator	Cost of capital	Tobin's q less unity	Capacity utilization rate less 0.85	Optimal feasible replacement investment fraction	Constant		Standard error	Durbin-Watson
3-2a	0.0	0.128 (0.018)	...	...	...	0.963 (0.343)	0.011 (0.042)	...	0.0228	0.82
3-3a	0.0	0.104 (0.019)	1.754 (0.302)	...	...	...	−0.009 (0.023)	...	0.0202	1.03
3-4a	0.0	0.111 (0.015)	0.861 (0.323)	...	...	1.0 (const.)	−0.069 (0.029)	...	0.0219	0.92
3-5a	0.0	0.010 (0.027)	0.692 (0.293)	0.0040 (0.0206)	0.398 (0.093)	1.0 (const.)	−0.005 (0.029)	...	0.0194	1.20
4-3a	0.4	0.120 (0.024)	0.695 (0.563)	...	...	...	−0.054 (0.051)	0.54 (0.09)	0.0183	2.08
4-4a	0.4	0.020 (0.034)	0.870 (0.433)	0.0222 (0.0273)	0.398 (0.120)	1.0 (const.)	−0.021 (0.042)	0.39 (0.10)	0.0175	2.03

a. See table 3 and the text for the measurement of the variables. Standard errors of the coefficients are given in parentheses; standard errors of the equations appear under "summary statistics."

Table 6. Estimates of the Accelerator (*v*)

	Ordinary least squares (equation 3-8)		Autoregressive transformation			
Lag, by quarter			Pure putty-clay (equation 4-5)		Partial putty-putty (equation 4-6)	
	v	*t-ratio*	*v*	*t-ratio*	*v*	*t-ratio*
0	0.081	4.2	0.082	3.2	0.082	3.1
1	0.084	5.9	0.090	5.1	0.091	4.9
2	0.086	7.9	0.096	7.1	0.097	6.9
3	0.086	9.8	0.099	8.0	0.100	7.8
4	0.086	10.5	0.100	7.8	0.102	7.5
5	0.084	10.0	0.098	7.4	0.100	7.1
6	0.080	9.3	0.095	7.2	0.096	7.0
7	0.077	8.7	0.089	7.4	0.090	7.1
8	0.072	8.4	0.081	7.3	0.081	7.0
9	0.066	8.2	0.070	5.9	0.069	5.5
10	0.059	7.7	0.057	3.5	0.054	3.2
11	0.050	6.2	0.042	1.7	0.037	1.5
12	0.041	4.0	...	...	...	...
13	0.031	2.2	...	...	...	...
14	0.018	1.0	...	...	...	...
Addendum:						
Year			*Percent of response*			
1		33.7	36.7		37.0	
2		32.7	38.2		38.8	
3		24.7	25.0		24.1	
4		9.0	...		...	

The results are reported in table 5, where the equation numbers refer to the analogues in tables 3 and 4. Comparison of these equations with the earlier ones modifies the basic story very little. The standard errors for the equations are almost identical and only the coefficients on the cost of capital change perceptibly (the change is an increase of about 0.5). Thus our results on the importance of the cost of capital hold explicitly for its tax and depreciation components.

Combining the Accelerator and Cost-of-Capital Variables

Thus far we have established the importance of the cost of capital and have estimated equations that support the major implications of equation 4; namely, that the coefficient on the optimal feasible replacement fraction is one and the responses to the accelerator and cost-of-capital variables are similar. The remaining task is to combine these variables, as is done in equation 4. To do so, we use the distributed lag weights for the accelerator relation (the v_t) estimated in equations 3-8, 4-5, and 4-6, which are reported in table 6 along with their *t*-ratios. As can be seen, the

Table 7. Equipment Orders with Accelerator and Cost of Capital Combined[a]

		Coefficient							Summary statistics	
Equation number	Putty-putty fraction of technology	Accelerator and cost of capital[b]	Lagged combined variables[c]	Tobin's q less unity	Capacity utilization rate less 0.85	Optimal feasible replacement investment fraction	Constant	Rho	Standard error	Durbin-Watson
7-1	0.0	0.089 (0.050)	0.055 (0.050)	...	...	1.0 (const.)	0.003 (0.005)	...	0.0216	0.89
7-2	0.0	0.003 (0.047)	0.040 (0.044)	−0.007 (0.020)	0.463 (0.083)	1.0 (const.)	0.040 (0.012)	...	0.0187	1.24
7-3	0.0	0.083 (0.049)	0.062 (0.049)	...	0.115 (0.051)	1.0 (const.)	0.0 (const.)	...	0.0210	0.93
7-4	0.2	0.050 (0.042)	0.079 (0.042)	...	...	1.0 (const.)	0.009 (0.009)	0.56 (0.09)	0.0181	2.00
7-5	0.2	−0.027 (0.044)	0.071 (0.038)	0.012 (0.027)	0.396 (0.110)	1.0 (const.)	0.052 (0.015)	0.42 (0.10)	0.0170	2.02
7-6	0.2	0.042 (0.045)	0.099 (0.045)	...	0.110 (0.084)	1.0 (const.)	0.0 (const.)	0.58 (0.09)	0.0180	2.03

a. See table 3 and the text for the measurement of the variables. Standard errors of the coefficients are given in parentheses; standard errors of the equations appear under "summary statistics."

b. Represented by $\Delta Y^*/(K_{-1}c)$.

c. Represented by $[\Delta Y^*/(K_{-1}c)]_{-1}$.

weights are significant both individually and collectively. The weights in 4-5 and 4-6 are quite similar. Two values of the sum of weighted sales divided by the cost of capital, $\Sigma v_t y_{-t}/c = \Delta Y^*/(K_{-1}c)$, are employed in the next set of equations. The first, which is used in equations without the semidifference transformation, is based on the weights from 3-8; the second, which is used in equations with the transformation, is based on the weights from 4-5. The optimal feasible replacement fraction used in the first set of equations reported in table 6 is based on the assumption that technology is 20 percent putty-putty.

The story of table 7 is, not surprisingly, similar in many respects to that told earlier. The q variable still has little impact and the estimated effect of the deviation of actual from normal capacity utilization is very large, raising the constant term to implausible heights and doing the reverse to the coefficient on the combined accelerator–cost-of-capital variable. One difference in these equations is the now apparent one-quarter lagged response to the cost of capital. With the constant term constrained to zero, the capacity utilization rate does contribute to the explanatory power of the equation, although the contribution is small, particularly in the semidifferenced equation (7-6). We prefer equations 7-3 and 7-6 because they have the highest explanatory power of equations with coefficients within the theoretically acceptable range. The correspondence between the coefficients in these equations is exceptionally close. The sums of the coefficients on the combined accelerator–cost-of-capital variables, about 0.14, and the coefficients on the utilization rate, 0.11, are very close. The slightly more lagged response in the semidifferenced equation 7-6 is largely explained by the shorter lag in the construction of the combined accelerator–cost-of-capital variable for that relation.

Comparison of the explanatory power of equations 7-1 and 7-3 with that of 3-1 reinforces our earlier conclusions about the superiority of a model including the cost of capital and the utilization rate (to reflect a disequilibrium response) over the pure accelerator model, 3-1. The adjusted $\bar{R}^2$ of the latter is 0.61. Those of 7-1 and 7-3, with the same dependent variable—$(ORD - PC)/K_{-1}$—are 0.68 and 0.70, a 23 percent reduction in the unexplained variance, $1 - \bar{R}^2$, of equation 3-1.

Figure 3 shows the observed and calculated (on the basis of equation 7-3, after moving the replacement investment fraction to the right-hand side) ratios of orders. While the general ability of the estimated equation to trace out orders is obvious, a number of problems are apparent. For example, both the timing and the amplitude of the calculated series is off

Figure 3. Observed and Calculated Ratios of Orders to the Stock of Equipment, 1957–78

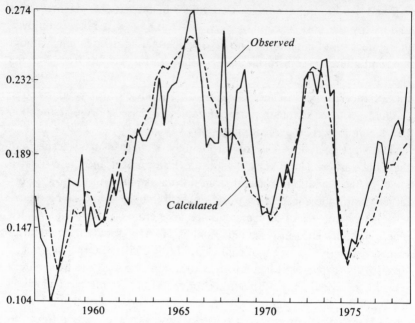

in 1957–59, and the calculated series rises about two quarters too soon in 1962–65 and too late in 1976–78. However, the most glaring error occurs in the 1968:4–1969:3 period, where the observed surge is not captured at all. The surge is surprising since real output was not growing rapidly, the capacity utilization rate was down from its 1966 peak, and the cost of capital was at historically high levels in 1968–69. One possible contributory factor could have been orders in anticipation of the removal of the investment tax credit in April 1969.[36]

The Impact of Changes in the Cost of Capital

Table 8 contains mean values of the observed and calculated ratios of orders during various intervals in the 1957–78 period. The intervals cor-

---

36. At some point in 1968 the existing tax credit probably ceased to be viewed as permanent. As Robert E. Lucas, Jr. ("Econometric Policy Evaluation: A Critique," in Karl Brunner and Allan H. Meltzer, eds., *The Phillips Curve and Labor Markets* [North-Holland, 1976], pp. 19–46), has shown, a credit viewed as temporary will have a much greater stimulative impact than a credit viewed as permanent.

Table 8. The Historic Relation between Cyclical Movements in the Ratio of Orders and in the Cost of Capital, 1957–78

Period	Observed order ratio (1)	Calculated order ratio[a] (2)	Impact of variations in cost of capital[b] (3)	Proportion of change in calculated order ratio attributable to variations in cost of capital[c] (4)
1957:1–1962:3	0.153	0.157	−0.015	...
1962:4–1964:3	0.206	0.219	0.016	0.50
1964:4–1966:4	0.246	0.250	0.017	0.03
1967:1–1968:3	0.193[d]	0.214	−0.001	0.50
1968:4–1969:3	0.227	0.186	−0.012	0.39
1969:4–1972:2	0.172	0.169	0.007	−1.12
1972:3–1974:3	0.231	0.223	0.025	0.33
1974:4–1976:4	0.151	0.143	−0.003	0.35
1977:1–1978:4	0.202	0.181	−0.004	−0.03

a. Based on equation 7-3 with d^f moved to the right-hand side.
b. The difference between the calculated ratio and the calculated ratio with c and d^f set at their mean values of 0.2575 and 0.1326, respectively.
c. The change in column 3 divided by the change in column 2.
d. Excluding 1968:1 (see footnote 27).

respond to periods of high, medium, and low activity in orders. For example, the orders ratio was relatively low from 1957:1 to 1962:3, from 1969:4 to 1972:2, and from 1974:4 to 1976:4, and high from 1964:4 to 1966:4, from 1968:4 to 1969:3, and from 1972:3 to 1974:3.[37] Comparison of columns 1 and 2 reveals the above-noted fact that the equation fits reasonably well in all periods except 1968:4 to 1969:3. Column 3 measures the direct and indirect impact of deviations of the cost of capital from its mean on calculated orders. Column 4 is the proportion of the change in the calculated orders ratio attributable to variations in the user cost of capital. This proportion is one-third or greater in five of eight periods. Only in one period—between 1969 and the early 1970s, when orders declined—did the cost of capital change so as to mitigate the change in the orders ratio that would have otherwise occurred. That is, movements in the cost of capital have generally acted to trigger swings in the orders ratio rather than to dampen accelerator-induced swings.

37. Comparison of the first two columns in table 8 reveals both the general ability of the estimated equation to explain the cyclical movement in the orders ratio and the failure of the equation to capture the 1968:4–1969:3 boom.

Reduction in Tax Service Lives

As noted in the section on the cost of capital, a 1979 legislative proposal would have reduced the average tax service life of equipment from the present eleven years to five. Analysis of this proposal is useful both for its own sake and to illustrate the effect on orders of a reduction in the cost of capital. The precise disturbance is a reduction in the tax service life from thirteen to six years for the period 1962:3–1971:2 and from eleven to five years between 1972:3 and 1978:4. The result is a reduction of 2.5 to 4 percentage points in the cost of capital.[38] A full sixteen years is required for the impact of a reduction in the cost of capital to work its way through the term measuring the optimal feasible replacement fraction, although slightly more than half of the impact is achieved within the first four years and more than three-quarters is achieved within eight years. The direct impact through investment undertaken to expand capacity will, of course, continue as long as real growth occurs. The lowering of the tax life raises the orders ratio (which averaged 0.19 during the 1962–78 period) by 0.026 for 1964–68, 0.014 for 1969–73, and 0.010 for 1974–78. This impact varied with the magnitude of the decline in the cost of capital (see footnote 38), the time since the initial decline in the user cost of capital (the optimal feasible replacement investment fraction), and the amount of investment for expansion. Given the 0.10 average value of the growth in output divided by initial capital and the estimated elasticity of output with respect to the stock-of-equipment coefficient of 0.14, a decline in the user cost of capital from 0.26 to 0.225 would be expected to raise the ratio of orders to the capital stock permanently by about 0.01.

Summary

Estimation of the impact of changes in the user cost of capital on orders for equipment, and thus on equipment investment, requires specification of an orders equation. Our theoretical framework begins with an investment model based on the work of Jorgenson, adds the capacity utilization rate and Tobin's q as disequilibrium proxies, accounts for required pollution-control outlays, and introduces the concept of optimal

38. The impact on the tax depreciation rate of a given change in the tax service life varies positively with the real rate of interest, and the impact of changes in the tax depreciation rate on the cost of capital varies positively with the corporation tax rate and with the ratio of capital goods to output prices.

feasible replacement investment to allow for putty-clay technology. In the final formulation, the cost of capital affects the ratio of orders to the equipment stock through two channels: the ratio of the expected rate of growth in output to the cost of capital and the optimal feasible replacement depreciation fraction. The latter equals the economic depreciation rate if the technology is putty-putty or if the desired factor intensity of replaced capital equals its actual intensity, which is the case if the current and past costs of capital are identical. In general, the value of the optimal feasible replacement fraction is a weighted average of the ratios of lagged to current costs of capital, the weights being the fraction of each vintage of capital in the total existing stock.

Addition of these cost-of-capital effects to an equation including only the accelerator (the expected output growth rate) reduces the unexplained variance by 20 percent. The long-run impact of a permanent decline in the cost of capital of 1 percentage point is a 1 percent increase in the ratio of new orders to the equipment stock. The short-run impact is about two and a half times larger and decays to the long-run effect over a sixteen-year period as the equipment stock is replaced. Weak evidence exists that technology is largely putty-clay; the independent estimate of the effect of the cost of capital becomes *higher* than is consistent with theory when significant putty-putty technology is allowed. There is little doubt that a reduction in the cost of capital (such as would be generated by the proposed lowering of the tax depreciation life of equipment) would significantly increase the stock of equipment.

There is no support for q as a determinant of orders for equipment. In contrast, the estimated impact of the capacity utilization rate tends to be too large and has to be restricted to prevent the accelerator from being weakened to a theoretically unacceptable degree.

Two experiments were run to indicate the effect of changes in tax, depreciation, and financial policies implied by our estimated equation. The first is a comparison of orders calculated (1) with observed values of the cost of capital and the optimal feasible replacement fraction and (2) with these two variables set at their 1957–78 mean values of 0.2575 and 0.1326. This experiment indicates both the quantitative importance of movements in the cost of capital and the tendency of these movements to stabilize or destabilize orders for equipment. Second, the orders ratio was calculated over the 1962–78 period on the assumption that the tax depreciation life of equipment had been lowered in 1961. This gives an indication of the time path of the impact of a specific policy action.

The effect of deviations from the mean in the cost of capital (and thus in the optimal replacement rate) on the orders ratio was significant, lowering that ratio by 0.015 in 1957:1–1962:3, and raising it by 0.017 in 1964:4–1966:4 and by 0.025 in 1972:3–1974:3. Moreover, the effect was not particularly stabilizing. In two of the three periods of booming orders, 1964:4–1966:4 and 1972:3–1974:3, declines in the cost of capital accounted for a third or more of the rise in orders from the previous trough; a rise in the cost of capital occurred only during the short-lived equipment boom of 1968:4–1969:3. Further, the cost of capital was at least as likely to be high during periods of low orders (especially 1957:1–1962:3) as not. In general, movements in the cost of capital generally acted to trigger swings in the orders ratio rather than to dampen accelerator-induced swings.

A halving of the tax service life of equipment was estimated to reduce the cost of capital by 2.5 to 4 percentage points, depending on the values of the corporation tax rate and the ratio of prices on capital and output goods. Such a cut in the tax service life would, other things being equal, raise the desired equipment stock from the end-of-1978 value of $800 billion to about $910 billion. If production lags, which might add a year to the adjustment period, are ignored, half, or $55 billion, of the increase would occur during the first four years, and another quarter would occur in the second four years. Also, normal growth-induced equipment investment would be $6.5 billion more a year in 1978 dollars as a result of the cut in tax service lives.

The decline in the cost of capital resulting from the reduction in tax service life is surely overstated in the above partial equilibrium analysis for two reasons. First, the supply of equipment goods was implicitly assumed to be infinitely elastic, but it is more likely that the price of equipment will rise relative to the general price level, thereby partially offsetting the initial decline in the user cost. Second, the stimulus to outlays on equipment will raise private issues of securities and thus real interest rates (the more the business tax cut is deficit financed, the greater the rise in interest rates will be). This, too, will act as a partial offset to the initial decline in the cost of capital.[39] Analysis of a full model of the investment-saving matrix, relative prices, and financing rates and explicit assump-

---

39. Martin Feldstein and Lawrence Summers, "Inflation, Tax Rules, and the Long-Term Interest Rate," *BPEA, 1:1978,* pp. 61–109.

tions regarding both the response of macroeconomic policy and the method of financing the business tax cut are necessary to obtain a reasonable estimate of the impact of the change in tax lives or of any capital-allocative policy.[40] We hope that future work will be devoted to such a general equilibrium analysis.

With regard to business investment, further experimentation with measurement of the cost of capital is probably in order. Specifically, the effect of possible anticipation of the removal of the investment credit in 1969 should be modeled and, more generally, care should be given to distinguishing between temporary and permanent (in the eyes of businessmen) changes in the components of the cost of capital. Consideration of alternative proxies for the expected cost of equity funds and expected inflation might also be desirable. Finally, experimentation with more general production functions, such as the translog function, is another area for future work.[41]

Appendix: The Real User Cost of Capital

In this appendix we derive a general expression for the real user cost of capital, discuss difficulties in computing expected real after-tax financing rates, and present the data underlying the computed costs of capital for equipment and structures.

Basic Framework

As is well known, the decision to invest depends on whether the present value of the expected future revenue generated by investment, net of direct operating expenses and indirect taxes, exceeds the supply price of capital. In our analysis we assume that inflation is expected to cause the supply price of capital and net revenues to rise at rate p (profit margins are constant). Further, the productivity of the investment and thus real net revenues are expected to decline at the output decay rate of d per year for a finite period N, at which point the capital good is discarded. In

40. See Patric H. Hendershott and Sheng-Cheng Hu, "The Relative Impacts of Various Proposals to Stimulate Business Investment," in George M. von Furstenberg, ed., *The Government and Capital Formation* (Ballinger, 1980), pp. 321–36.

41. See, for example, Ernst R. Berndt and Laurits R. Christensen, "The Translog Function and the Substitution of Equipment, Structures, and Labor in U.S. Manufacturing, 1929–68," *Journal of Econometrics*, vol. 1 (March 1973), pp. 81–113.

the absence of direct taxes we can then write:

(6)
$$P_k = \sum_{t=1}^{N} (1 + p - d)^{t-1}(1 + r)^{-t}P_y\rho,$$

where

P_k = current supply price of capital

$P_y\rho$ = current expected net revenue (ρ is the marginal physical product of capital and P_y is the output price)

r = financing rate (an average of interest rates on debt i and equity e)

p = annual rate of expected inflation in revenues and capital goods prices

d = annual rate of economic depreciation, and

N = the actual or economic service life.

Because $1 - (1 + p - d)^N(1 + r)^{-N} = [1 - (1 + p - d)(1 + r)^{-1}]$ $\times \Sigma(1 + p - d)^{t-1}(1 + r)^{-(t-1)}$,

(7) $\Sigma(1 + p - d)^{t-1}(1 + r)^{-t}$
$$= [1 - (1 + p - d)^N(1 + r)^{-N}](r - p + d)^{-1}.$$

With the use of 7, 6 can be rewritten as

$$P_k = \delta P_y\rho(r - p + d)^{-1},$$

where $\delta = 1 - (1 + p - d)^N(1 + r)^{-N}$ and converts the present value of an infinite stream to that of an N-period stream. The cost of capital is obtained by solving for:

(8) $c = [(r - p + d)P_k]/(\delta P_y) - \rho.$

Equation 6 ignores the existence of income taxes and investment tax credits. Moreover, care must be taken to account for the deductibility of interest and depreciation charges allowed under the tax law. The following assumptions are made:

1. Income is taxed at the rate τ, and the effective rate of the investment tax credit is μ.

2. A portion α of the net investment $(1 - \mu)P_k$ is debt financed (that is, α is the loan-to-value ratio); the debt and equity portions remain constant throughout the life of the asset; and debt financing charges are deductible from the income tax base.

3. Depreciation is deductible from the income tax base. The depreciation allowed for tax purposes in period t is dx_tP_k (in the absence of the Long amendment, tax depreciation is $dx_t(1 - \mu)P_k$).

4. No recapture provisions or capital gains taxes are in effect.

With these assumptions the analogue to equation 6 is:

$$(9) \quad (1 - \mu)P_k = \sum_{t=1}^{N} (1 + r_a)^{-t}\{(1 + p - d)^{t-1}(1 - \tau)P_y\rho$$

$$+ d(1 + p - d)^{t-1}\tau P_k + \tau[dx_t - d(1 + p - d)^{t-1}]P_k\},$$

where r_a is now the after-tax average financing rate used to discount after-tax cash flows:

$$(10) \quad r_a = (1 - \tau)\alpha i + (1 - \alpha)e_a,$$

and e_a is the after-tax return on equity. The second term in the braces in equation 9 captures the tax saving from the depreciation deduction based on true economic depreciation, and the third the tax saving from the difference between the value of the depreciation deduction allowed under the tax law and that consistent with true economic depreciation. Using equation 7 with r_a replacing r gives

$$(11) \quad c = (P_k/P_y)\{(1 - \mu)(r_a - p + d)/[\delta_a(1 - \tau)]$$
$$- \tau d/(1 - \tau) + \tau(d - d^*)/(1 - \tau)\} = \rho,$$

where δ_a is defined as δ but with r_a replacing r, and d^*, the average annual rate of tax depreciation, is

$$(12) \quad d^* = [(r_a - p + d)/\delta_a]\Sigma dx_t(1 + r_a)^{-t}.$$

If tax depreciation were equal to economic depreciation at replacement cost, then $dx_t = d(1 + p - d)^{t-1}$, $d^* = d$ (from equation 12), and thus $TXD = 0$. As noted in the text, such is not the case.

We still must account for the requirement that pollution-control capital outlays accompany nonpollution or "productive" capital outlays. Leahey suggests that such pollution-control outlays be treated analogously to a negative investment tax credit (before the Long amendment).[42] Required pollution-control outlays raise the user cost of productive capital, and deter investment, by raising the effective price of productive capital goods. If required pollution-control outlays accompanying a new facility are v percent of the total cost, the effective price of the productive capital has risen to $1/(1 - v)$ of the market price. Thus P_k in equation 11 is divided by $1 - v$. Annual estimates of v, which equal

42. See M. Cary Leahey, "The Impact of Environmental Controls on Capital Formation," in von Furstenberg, ed., *The Government and Capital Formation*, pp. 383–99.

the share of real nonresidential fixed capital outlays that are pollution-control outlays associated with new (as opposed to existing) capital, are given in column 3 of table 1 for 1967–78. The 0.014 value for 1967 is assumed to have held for all prior years.

Expected Real After-Tax Financing Rates

Calculations of the real after-tax financing rate requires specification of the debt rate (i), loan-to-value ratio (α), tax rate (τ), after-tax equity rate (e_a) and expected inflation rate (p). The first three are easily specified. For i, the rate on Aa-rated utility and industrial bonds is employed; for α, 0.25, the ratio of the market value of corporate debt to the replacement value of corporate real assets, is used.[43] The corporation tax rate should reflect both the marginal federal and state and local income tax rates. The marginal state and local rate is approximated by the average rate (this rate was 0.057 in 1977, giving a total marginal corporation rate of 0.51).

Reasonable proxies for the expected return on equity and expected inflation are more difficult to obtain. In the absence of tax credits, the expected real after-tax rate of return on corporate equity issued to finance an investment project would be

$$(13) \quad e_a - p = [(1 - \tau)(P_y\rho - dP_k - iD) - \tau(d - d^*)P_k + pD]/E,$$

where D is the debt issued to finance the project and equals αP_k, E is the equity issued and equals $(1-\alpha)P_k$, and the pD term reflects the expected real gains accruing to shareholders owing to the expected erosion in the real value of this debt. Substituting for D and E and solving for ρ, we obtain equation 11 with $\mu = 0$ and $\delta_a = 1$.

The problem is the practical one of estimating $e_a - p$ from historical data. In general, the expected real earnings accruing to equity holders from new investment are the sum of expected after-tax operating earnings (EAT) and the expected erosion in the market value of the debt. Thus

$$e_a - p = (EAT + pD)/E.$$

Historically, $D = \alpha RA$, where RA is the investment in real assets. Assuming a marginal q of unity, $E = (1-\alpha)RA$. To substitute and solve,

$$(14) \qquad e_a = EAT/[(1 - \alpha)RA] + p/(1 - \alpha).$$

43. Von Furstenberg has computed this ratio quarterly for 1952–77. His estimates suggest that the ratio has varied little. See von Furstenberg, "Corporate Investment."

The first term is approximated by $q(EAT/E)^*$, where $(EAT/E)^*$ is the average earnings–price ratio during the current and previous eleven quarters. We measure EAT as reported after-tax profits of nonfinancial corporations plus (1) the inventory valuation adjustment, which eliminates inventory capital gains, and (2) the capital consumption adjustment, which eliminates any fictitious profits resulting from underdepreciation by converting tax depreciation allowances to replacement-cost depreciation; the market value of stocks is obtained by dividing dividends on common stock by Standard and Poor's dividend–market-value ratio for common stock. The q multiplication adjusts for the fact that the average q has deviated from unity.[44]

Before we turn to proxies for the expected inflation rate, it is useful to consider the relationship between the real after-tax financing rate, $r_a - p$, and the expected inflation rate. Substitution of equation 14 in equation 10 yields

(15) $$r_a - p = (1 - \tau)\alpha i + EAT/RA.$$

That is, given our proxy for e_a, the real after-tax financing rate is independent of whatever proxy is chosen for the expected inflation rate.[45] As a result, one should not be surprised that $r_a - p$ is rather stable.

In spite of the independence of the calculated $r_a - p$ from p, an estimate of expected inflation is needed because the estimate of d^* is a (negative) function of r_a, which, from equation 15, moves one-for-one with p. The basic inflation rate considered is the deflator for nonfood business products net of energy and the impact of price controls in the 1971–75 period. The adjustments for energy and price controls are those of Gordon.[46] The expected inflation rate is assumed to be a distributed lag on past inflation rates. Not only is the length of the lag uncertain, but there is some evidence that the lag is variable. Apparently changes in observed inflation in the late 1960s and 1970s have been built into expectations more quickly

44. The resultant e_a is roughly consistent with that underlying the analysis of Burton G. Malkiel, "The Capital Formation Problem in the United States," *Journal of Finance*, vol. 39 (May 1979), pp. 291–306.

45. It is worth noting, at a theoretical level, that $r_a - p$ is, at least in a ceteris paribus sense, also independent of i. We can express EAT as $EAT = (1 - \tau)EBIT - \tau(d - d^*)RA - (1 - \tau)iD$, where $EBIT$ is earnings before interest and taxes and RA is real assets. Substituting for EAT in equation 15 and replacing D/RA with α yields $r_a - p = (1 - \tau)EBIT/RA - \tau(d - d^*)$.

46. The price series adjusted for energy and price controls are those of Robert J. Gordon, "Can the Inflation of the 1970s Be Explained?" *BPEA, 1:1977*, pp. 253–79.

Table 9. Data Employed in Computation of User Costs of Capital, 1953–78

Year and quarter	Equipment and structures				Equipment only						Structures only				
	e_a	i	p	τ	P_k/P_y	δ_a	N	$d - d^*$	μ	c	P_k/P_y	δ_a	N	$d - d^*$	c
1953:1	0.0854	0.0325	0.0398	0.5312	0.9832	0.9230	17	0.0302	0.0000	0.2516	1.0772	0.9630	42	0.0168	0.1361
2	0.0893	0.0356	0.0375	0.5315	0.9937	0.9295	17	0.0297	0.0000	0.2639	1.0902	0.9716	42	0.0160	0.1488
3	0.0867	0.0352	0.0305	0.5305	0.9954	0.9359	17	0.0259	0.0000	0.2687	1.0988	0.9781	42	0.0140	0.1581
4	0.0817	0.0325	0.0228	0.5314	0.9933	0.9406	17	0.0211	0.0000	0.2695	1.1029	0.9821	42	0.0115	0.1639
1954:1	0.0810	0.0305	0.0178	0.5310	0.9884	0.9451	17	0.0148	0.0000	0.2684	1.0667	0.9856	42	0.0077	0.1628
2	0.0862	0.0302	0.0172	0.5301	1.0014	0.9488	17	0.0149	0.0000	0.2805	1.0549	0.9884	42	0.0073	0.1702
3	0.0905	0.0302	0.0158	0.5310	1.0023	0.9523	17	0.0144	0.0000	0.2893	1.0557	0.9907	42	0.0066	0.1798
4	0.0949	0.0301	0.0142	0.5300	1.0102	0.9559	17	0.0137	0.0000	0.3000	1.0531	0.9926	42	0.0059	0.1889
1955:1	0.1003	0.0310	0.0183	0.5299	0.9941	0.9554	16	0.0129	0.0000	0.2948	1.0443	0.9925	38	0.0043	0.1857
2	0.1001	0.0313	0.0179	0.5307	0.9914	0.9556	16	0.0123	0.0000	0.2940	1.0507	0.9926	38	0.0039	0.1872
3	0.1039	0.0321	0.0205	0.5307	1.0003	0.9555	16	0.0137	0.0000	0.2992	1.0558	0.9927	38	0.0046	0.1898
4	0.1019	0.0320	0.0189	0.5305	1.0033	0.9558	16	0.0122	0.0000	0.2983	1.0701	0.9927	38	0.0038	0.1914
1956:1	0.1032	0.0316	0.0201	0.5310	1.0081	0.9554	15	0.0092	0.0000	0.2958	1.1051	0.9926	37	0.0032	0.1963
2	0.1070	0.0346	0.0233	0.5322	1.0200	0.9550	15	0.0107	0.0000	0.3019	1.0907	0.9925	37	0.0039	0.1952
3	0.1095	0.0378	0.0258	0.5314	1.0294	0.9544	15	0.0115	0.0000	0.3050	1.1060	0.9923	37	0.0043	0.1976
4	0.1183	0.0405	0.0317	0.5325	1.0444	0.9543	15	0.0145	0.0000	0.3159	1.1034	0.9924	37	0.0056	0.2016
1957:1	0.1157	0.0417	0.0295	0.5320	1.0527	0.9549	15	0.0128	0.0000	0.3169	1.1053	0.9927	37	0.0047	0.2015
2	0.1162	0.0432	0.0300	0.5312	1.0501	0.9548	15	0.0127	0.0000	0.3158	1.1149	0.9927	37	0.0046	0.2031
3	0.1205	0.0483	0.0335	0.5313	1.0441	0.9545	15	0.0145	0.0000	0.3171	1.1093	0.9926	37	0.0055	0.2038
4	0.1191	0.0457	0.0333	0.5311	1.0569	0.9538	15	0.0142	0.0000	0.3181	1.1002	0.9922	37	0.0054	0.1994
1958:1	0.1131	0.0381	0.0308	0.5331	1.0448	0.9522	15	0.0126	0.0000	0.3072	1.0734	0.9912	37	0.0048	0.1879
2	0.1111	0.0386	0.0311	0.5327	1.0493	0.9509	15	0.0125	0.0000	0.3048	1.0747	0.9905	37	0.0049	0.1842
3	0.1074	0.0430	0.0297	0.5325	1.0496	0.9505	15	0.0115	0.0000	0.3017	1.0711	0.9902	37	0.0044	0.1811
4	0.1046	0.0445	0.0288	0.5331	1.0527	0.9499	15	0.0108	0.0000	0.2998	1.0710	0.9898	37	0.0042	0.1786
1959:1	0.1037	0.0448	0.0288	0.5322	1.0461	0.9493	15	0.0107	0.0000	0.2959	1.0588	0.9894	37	0.0041	0.1746
2	0.1018	0.0473	0.0279	0.5319	1.0466	0.9493	15	0.0100	0.0000	0.2947	1.0512	0.9893	37	0.0038	0.1724
3	0.0984	0.0486	0.0261	0.5313	1.0426	0.9492	15	0.0087	0.0000	0.2906	1.0412	0.9892	37	0.0032	0.1687
4	0.0930	0.0497	0.0231	0.5314	1.0372	9.9490	15	0.0067	0.0000	0.2847	1.0397	0.9889	37	0.0022	0.1654
1960:1	0.0897	0.0489	0.0213	0.5332	1.0393	0.9487	15	0.0056	0.0000	0.2828	1.0404	0.9885	37	0.0016	0.1636
2	0.0888	0.0477	0.0212	0.5333	1.0407	0.9481	15	0.0055	0.0000	0.2815	1.0253	0.9881	37	0.0016	0.1596
3	0.0843	0.0450	0.0184	0.5326	1.0445	0.9478	15	0.0036	0.0000	0.2781	1.0206	0.9878	37	0.0007	0.1556
4	0.0827	0.0467	0.0177	0.5323	1.0417	0.9477	15	0.0031	0.0000	0.2759	1.0110	0.9876	37	0.0005	0.1531

1961:1	0.0812	0.0432	0.0167	0.5325	1.0398	0.9474	15	0.0024	0.0000	0.2734	1.0130	0.9874	37	0.0001	0.1519
2	0.0820	0.0462	0.0173	0.5325	1.0368	0.9476	15	0.0028	0.0000	0.2738	1.0091	0.9875	37	0.0003	0.1522
3	0.0814	0.0464	0.0171	0.5331	1.0299	0.9475	15	0.0026	0.0000	0.2716	1.0066	0.9874	37	0.0002	0.1515
4	0.0792	0.0451	0.0159	0.5339	1.0273	0.9472	15	0.0018	0.0000	0.2688	1.0085	0.9871	37	−0.0002	0.1502
1962:1	0.0763	0.0450	0.0141	0.5334	1.0222	0.9472	15	0.0005	0.0000	0.2650	1.0007	0.9870	37	−0.0009	0.1472
2	0.0737	0.0428	0.0130	0.5334	1.0182	0.9464	15	−0.0003	0.0000	0.2606	0.9999	0.9863	37	−0.0013	0.1443
3	0.0722	0.0433	0.0117	0.5332	1.0195	0.9468	13	−0.0007	0.0550	0.2397	0.9975	0.9866	37	−0.0019	0.1438
4	0.0734	0.0425	0.0123	0.5327	1.0189	0.9470	13	0.0010	0.0550	0.2403	0.9975	0.9867	37	−0.0017	0.1445
1963:1	0.0722	0.0424	0.0115	0.5327	1.0154	0.9469	13	0.0006	0.0550	0.2386	0.9956	0.9866	37	−0.0020	0.1435
2	0.0717	0.0433	0.0109	0.5338	1.0123	0.9473	13	0.0002	0.0550	0.2383	0.9970	0.9869	37	−0.0023	0.1443
3	0.0724	0.0435	0.0110	0.5334	1.0093	0.9477	13	0.0002	0.0550	0.2384	0.9953	0.9872	37	−0.0023	0.1449
4	0.0750	0.0442	0.0123	0.5332	1.0066	0.9480	13	0.0009	0.0550	0.2400	0.9948	0.9875	37	−0.0018	0.1468
1964:1	0.0777	0.0444	0.0132	0.5136	1.0084	0.9489	13	−0.0060	0.0550	0.2309	0.9972	0.9882	37	−0.0015	0.1459
2	0.0780	0.0448	0.0126	0.5135	1.0085	0.9498	13	−0.0065	0.0550	0.2322	0.9967	0.9888	37	−0.0018	0.1474
3	0.0791	0.0444	0.0125	0.5139	1.0057	0.9503	13	−0.0065	0.0550	0.2329	0.9989	0.9892	37	−0.0019	0.1493
4	0.0802	0.0448	0.0128	0.5135	1.0000	0.9508	13	−0.0064	0.0550	0.2328	1.0000	0.9895	37	−0.0019	0.1508
1965:1	0.0820	0.0444	0.0132	0.4930	0.9974	0.9515	13	−0.0062	0.0550	0.2306	0.9971	0.9900	37	−0.0018	0.1482
2	0.0831	0.0453	0.0128	0.4934	0.9973	0.9526	13	−0.0065	0.0550	0.2325	1.0006	0.9906	37	−0.0020	0.1510
3	0.0852	0.0463	0.0136	0.4934	0.9926	0.9531	13	−0.0060	0.0550	0.2335	1.0064	0.9910	37	−0.0018	0.1540
4	0.0853	0.0475	0.0127	0.4935	0.9945	0.9540	13	−0.0066	0.0550	0.2353	1.0151	0.9915	37	−0.0022	0.1572
1966:1	0.0891	0.0503	0.0143	0.4944	0.9912	0.9548	13	−0.0057	0.0550	0.2384	1.0172	0.9920	37	−0.0017	0.1614
2	0.0952	0.0531	0.0178	0.4943	0.9853	0.9553	13	−0.0037	0.0550	0.2416	1.0244	0.9924	37	−0.0006	0.1666
3	0.0976	0.0578	0.0184	0.4940	0.9889	0.9563	13	−0.0034	0.0550	0.2456	1.0265	0.9930	37	−0.0005	0.1703
4	0.1007	0.0579	0.0199	0.4940	0.9890	0.9567	13	−0.0026	0.0550	0.2480	1.0270	0.9932	37	−0.0001	0.1727
1967:1	0.1053	0.0538	0.0230	0.4958	0.9837	0.9561	13	−0.0009	0.0550	0.2485	1.0283	0.9930	37	0.0009	0.1738
2	0.1101	0.0570	0.0265	0.4960	0.9882	0.9560	13	−0.0009	0.0550	0.2526	1.0370	0.9931	37	0.0019	0.1775
3	0.1128	0.0607	0.0285	0.4959	0.9853	0.9559	13	0.0020	0.0550	0.2538	1.0393	0.9932	37	0.0024	0.1794
4	0.1200	0.0648	0.0336	0.4966	0.9810	0.9559	13	0.0045	0.0550	0.2570	1.0389	0.9933	37	0.0037	0.1826
1968:1	0.1266	0.0651	0.0390	0.5457	0.9753	0.9543	13	0.0072	0.0550	0.2710	1.0385	0.9927	37	0.0051	0.1972
2	0.1286	0.0680	0.0411	0.5448	0.9761	0.9538	13	0.0082	0.0550	0.2717	1.0400	0.9925	37	0.0056	0.1971
3	0.1250	0.0645	0.0393	0.5448	0.9795	0.9532	13	0.0073	0.0550	0.2692	1.0412	0.9922	37	0.0052	0.1942
4	0.1293	0.0673	0.0436	0.5455	0.9756	0.9521	13	0.0094	0.0550	0.2696	1.0401	0.9917	37	0.0063	0.1938
1969:1	0.1310	0.0717	0.0461	0.5478	0.9676	0.9512	13	0.0106	0.0550	0.2685	1.0484	0.9914	37	0.0114	0.2013
2	0.1337	0.0757	0.0495	0.5476	0.9609	0.9500	13	0.0122	0.0000	0.2909	1.0567	0.9908	37	0.0122	0.2018
3	0.1332	0.0800	0.0509	0.5472	0.9547	0.9489	13	0.0128	0.0000	0.2877	1.0716	0.9903	37	0.0126	0.2024
4	0.1287	0.0859	0.0492	0.5489	0.9532	0.9483	13	0.0121	0.0000	0.2850	1.0851	0.9898	37	0.0123	0.2027

Table 9 (*continued*)

Year and quarter	Equipment and structures						Equipment only				Structures only				
	e_a	i	p	τ	P_k/P_y	δ_a	N	$d - d^*$	μ	c	P_k/P_y	δ_a	N	$d - d^*$	c
1970:1	0.1243	0.0872	0.0477	0.5200	0.9534	0.9479	13	0.0114	0.0000	0.2726	1.0927	0.9895	37	0.0120	0.1915
2	0.1212	0.0909	0.0468	0.5193	0.9514	0.9472	13	0.0110	0.0000	0.2695	1.1012	0.9890	37	0.0119	0.1903
3	0.1145	0.0878	0.0432	0.5198	0.9527	0.9463	13	0.0094	0.0000	0.2649	1.1134	0.9882	37	0.0112	0.1876
4	0.1160	0.0852	0.0462	0.5196	0.9527	0.9441	13	0.0109	0.0000	0.2629	1.1206	0.9868	37	0.0120	0.1850
1971:1	0.1166	0.0751	0.0480	0.5083	0.9569	0.9419	13	0.0119	0.0000	0.2577	1.1215	0.9852	37	0.0125	0.1771
2	0.1173	0.0792	0.0498	0.5075	0.9505	0.9409	13	0.0127	0.0000	0.2555	1.1253	0.9846	37	0.0130	0.1765
3	0.1113	0.0790	0.0462	0.5089	0.9517	0.9408	11	0.0037	0.0250	0.2361	1.1378	0.9842	37	0.0122	0.1759
4	0.1101	0.0754	0.0460	0.5086	0.9446	0.9398	11	0.0037	0.0550	0.2215	1.1543	0.9833	37	0.0122	0.1758
1972:1	0.1129	0.0739	0.0486	0.5082	0.9461	0.9387	11	0.0050	0.0550	0.2221	1.1598	0.9826	37	0.0129	0.1759
2	0.1110	0.0746	0.0475	0.5078	0.9462	0.9387	11	0.0045	0.0550	0.2212	1.1599	0.9825	37	0.0126	0.1750
3	0.1058	0.0754	0.0437	0.5081	0.9482	0.9394	11	0.0027	0.0550	0.2199	1.1671	0.9828	37	0.0117	0.1752
4	0.1066	0.0740	0.0439	0.5089	0.9366	0.9395	11	0.0028	0.0550	0.2180	1.1736	0.9829	37	0.0117	0.1771
1973:1	0.1055	0.0746	0.0421	0.5098	0.9290	0.9407	11	0.0018	0.0550	0.2172	1.1881	0.9838	37	0.0112	0.1815
2	0.1071	0.0764	0.0423	0.5107	0.9269	0.9418	11	0.0017	0.0550	0.2190	1.2008	0.9647	37	0.0112	0.1868
3	0.1128	0.0811	0.0457	0.5098	0.9231	0.9424	11	0.0030	0.0550	0.2220	1.2166	0.9855	37	0.0119	0.1936
4	0.1199	0.0785	0.0498	0.5098	0.9153	0.9425	11	0.0046	0.0550	0.2237	1.2299	0.9859	37	0.0127	0.1994

1974:1	0.1198	0.0827	0.0485	0.5152	0.9160	0.9441	11	0.0038	0.0550	0.2271	1.2732	0.9869	37	0.0123	0.2122
2	0.1245	0.0926	0.0503	0.5192	0.9204	0.9461	11	0.0042	0.0550	0.2343	1.3305	0.9884	37	0.0125	0.2313
3	0.1435	0.1020	0.0623	0.5254	0.9271	0.9466	11	0.0087	0.0550	0.2483	1.3799	0.9894	37	0.0146	0.2549
4	0.1603	0.0858	0.0738	0.5215	0.9456	0.9443	11	0.0131	0.0550	0.2565	1.3956	0.9886	37	0.0164	0.2573
1975:1	0.1689	0.0911	0.0802	0.5202	0.9612	0.9439	11	0.0153	0.0850	0.2521	1.3931	0.9887	37	0.0173	0.2597
2	0.1703	0.0975	0.0810	0.5177	0.9776	0.9445	11	0.0154	0.0850	0.2574	1.3855	0.9891	37	0.0173	0.2599
3	0.1580	0.0966	0.0712	0.5173	0.9823	0.9465	11	0.0117	0.0850	0.2549	1.3890	0.9898	37	0.0158	0.2595
4	0.1527	0.0947	0.0669	0.5187	0.9880	0.9471	11	0.0101	0.0850	0.2547	1.3834	0.9900	37	0.0152	0.2581
1976:1	0.1478	0.0876	0.0632	0.5173	0.9874	0.9471	11	0.0087	0.0850	0.2511	1.3696	0.9898	37	0.0146	0.2518
2	0.1448	0.0888	0.0608	0.5188	0.9793	0.9477	11	0.0076	0.0850	0.2487	1.3694	0.9900	37	0.0141	0.2526
3	0.1361	0.0865	0.0539	0.5180	0.9844	0.9488	11	0.0048	0.0850	0.2463	1.3587	0.9903	37	0.0128	0.2483
4	0.1301	0.0823	0.0494	0.5195	0.9848	0.9491	11	0.0030	0.0850	0.2436	1.3595	0.9903	37	0.0120	0.2463
1977:1	0.1268	0.0827	0.0470	0.5196	0.9859	0.9494	11	0.0019	0.0850	0.2426	1.3752	0.9904	37	0.0114	0.2483
2	0.1346	0.0836	0.0530	0.5184	0.9809	0.9485	11	0.0044	0.0850	0.2440	1.3791	0.9901	37	0.0127	0.2503
3	0.1363	0.0817	0.0549	0.5159	0.9909	0.9476	11	0.0052	0.0850	0.2457	1.3762	0.9897	37	0.0131	0.2473
4	0.1345	0.0842	0.0536	0.5182	0.9984	0.9480	11	0.0046	0.0850	0.2477	1.3939	0.9898	37	0.0128	0.2516
1978:1	0.1354	0.0875	0.0533	0.5208	1.0022	0.9490	11	0.0043	0.0850	0.2512	1.4015	0.9904	37	0.0127	0.2576
2	0.1555	0.0908	0.0670	0.5195	0.9882	0.9483	11	0.0095	0.0850	0.2570	1.4011	0.9906	37	0.0149	0.2659
3	0.1607	0.0910	0.0704	0.5193	0.9905	0.9482	11	0.0106	0.0850	0.2601	1.4238	0.9907	37	0.0154	0.2727
4	0.1633	0.0943	0.0712	0.5200	0.9877	0.9491	11	0.0107	0.0850	0.2621	1.4343	0.9913	37	0.0154	0.2793

than was the case in the 1950s and early 1960s.[47] After examining the "plausibility" of expected rates based on different length lags, the following assumptions were made:

$$\sum_{i=0}^{11} \hat{p}_{t-1}/12 \quad \text{for} \quad 1954:1-1967:1,$$

and

$$\sum_{i=0}^{7} w_i \hat{p}_{t-1} \quad \text{for} \quad 1967:2-1978:4,$$

where $\hat{p}$ is the observed inflation rate and the w_i are $w_0 = 0.23$, $w_1 = 0.20$, $w_2 = 0.16$, $w_3 = 0.13$, $w_4 = 0.11$, $w_5 = 0.08$, $w_6 = 0.06$, $w_7 = 0.04$, and are those estimated by Hendershott and Van Horne.

The Underlying Data

Equation 11, with P_k divided by one less the fraction of real nonresidential capital outlays that are pollution-control outlays on new capital (see table 1), defines the user cost of capital. Data for all the variables in equations 11 and 12 except for d, dx_t, and μ (for structures only, which is equivalent to zero for all periods) are listed in table 9 for the 1953:1–1978:4 period. The data series are divided into three parts, those relevant to both equipment and structures, those relevant to equipment only, and those pertaining to structures only. The symbols above the data series are the same as those used in equation 11. All data are at annual rates.

Recall from the text that $d = 0.13$ for equipment and 0.04 for structures for all quarters. Also $\mu = 0.0$ for structures in all quarters. Tax depreciation in period t, dx_t, is not listed. It is calculated according to the relevant accelerated method and the proportion of total investment that is undertaken by firms that employ accelerated methods (recall that only straight-line depreciation was permitted before 1954). We assume that 27 percent of investment in 1954:1 was depreciated by accelerated methods and that this percentage rose by 3 percentage points per quarter through 1957:4, 1 percentage point per quarter from 1958:1 to 1959:4, and a quarter percentage point per quarter thereafter. By 1978:4 the percentage was 94. The difference between the economic and tax depreciation rates, $d - d^*$ (see equation 11), is listed.

47. See Patric H. Hendershott and James C. Van Horne, "Expected Inflation Implied by Capital Market Rates," *Journal of Finance*, vol. 28 (May 1973), pp. 301–14; and Robert J. Gordon, "Wage-Price Controls and the Shifting Phillips Curve," *BPEA, 2:1972*, pp. 385–421.

Comments by Emil M. Sunley

Hendershott and Hu estimate equations for new orders of machinery and equipment. In the final section of the paper they simulate the increase in orders that might be induced if tax depreciation was further accelerated. They do not, however, embed their estimating equation in a fully specified macromodel. Thus the paper does not trace out the impact that an increase in orders would have on actual investment. The authors explicitly recognize this.

The crucial question about tax incentives for investment is not whether they will stimulate additional demand in the economy and thus, if there is unemployment, more jobs, but whether the tax incentives are effective at tilting the consumption-investment mix of the economy for any given level of output. An answer to this question would require that investment equations such as those estimated by Hendershott and Hu be embedded in a full macromodel. Simulations should be made where tax incentives for investment replace, say, individual tax reductions of the appropriate magnitude to ensure that aggregate demand in the economy is maintained. Only then could one see what effect this substitution had on the split between investment and consumption goods.

Investment incentives also can affect the allocation of investment between structures and equipment and across industries. Single-equation models cannot capture these effects, which may be more important than the overall impact on the investment share. An improved allocation of the capital stock is equivalent to having a larger stock; in fact, it is even better because you do not have to give up current consumption to get it. Tax incentives that distort the allocation of capital can reduce the effective size of the capital stock. For example, the Conable-Jones depreciation proposal simulated in the paper provides a much greater incentive for long-lived assets than for short-lived ones. Conable-Jones thus favors industries such as primary metals and utilities and provides little benefit for textiles and construction.

A discussant, however, should not condemn the authors for failing to write the paper he would have liked to see; he should instead comment on the paper they did write. Hendershott and Hu in the first half of the paper carefully develop the theoretical underpinnings of their investment equation. The last half of the paper presents empirical estimates of alternative specifications of the equation.

Theoretical Model

Hendershott and Hu develop the neoclassical investment model along
lines similar to those followed by Jorgenson. To this they add the accelerator, Tobin's *q*, and the capacity utilization rate. Mandatory pollution-
control investment is excluded from orders.

They follow Leahey[48] in treating mandatory pollution investment as a
negative investment credit before the Long amendment. This treatment is
unsatisfactory because pollution investment itself is eligible for the investment credit and accelerated depreciation. On theoretical grounds it would
be better to treat pollution investment as an increase in the capital–labor
ratio in the production function.

They also assert that the permissible tax service life for buildings has
remained at thirty-seven years since 1956. This is surely in error. Component depreciation clearly has lowered the average tax life of buildings.

Table 2 is most helpful in breaking down the effect of the various components of the user cost of capital on its swings. The real rate of interest is
the most important component, but in this analysis it is estimated as the
residual component. Since 1954 accelerated tax depreciation, the investment tax credit, and tax rate cuts have reduced the user cost of capital for
machinery and equipment by 5.6 percent. Even in the period 1964–78,
these tax changes offset the impact of inflation on effective tax rates.

Empirical Results

I cannot help but feel that Hendershott and Hu, after developing an
elaborate investment equation, must be somewhat disappointed in their
empirical results. The estimated equations for structures were unsatisfactory and were omitted. These equations may only indicate that the data
for orders of new structures, a residual series, are poor. The two most important variables in explaining orders for equipment are the accelerator
and capacity utilization. This must give considerable comfort to acceler-
ationists.

Hendershott and Hu conclude that the cost of capital has a significant
and substantial influence on investment in producers' equipment. This conclusion seems overstated. In the final set of estimated equations (table 7),
the accelerator and cost-of-capital variables are combined so one cannot
say how important the cost-of-capital variable is by itself. The combined

48. Leahey, "The Impact of Environmental Controls on Capital Formation."

variable generally is not statistically significant. In these equations the most important explanatory variable is capacity utilization unless the estimating equation is constrained. In the preliminary regressions presented in table 3, the cost of capital sometimes enters as an independent regressor and sometimes enters indirectly as a determinant of the feasible rate of replacement investment, d^I. These cost-of-capital variables generally lose their statistical significance as soon as capacity utilization is entered as a regressor.

The conclusion that Tobin's q is not a significant determinant of investment may be overstated. Whenever Tobin's q is regressed on investment, capacity utilization is also used as an explanatory variable. One is never able to see how Tobin's q would do by itself.

I fear that the conclusion to be drawn from this paper is essentially the same conclusion that Harberger reached at the 1967 Brookings Conference on Tax Incentives and Capital Spending: "I cannot help reflecting on the disparity of the results."[49]

49. Arnold C. Harberger, "Discussion," in Fromm, ed., *Tax Incentives and Capital Spending*, p. 256.

ROGER H. GORDON *and* BURTON G. MALKIEL

Corporation Finance

ANALYZING the effect of the federal tax structure on corporate financial policy is one of the most complex tasks of tax incidence and financial theory. The corporation tax, the personal income tax, the bankruptcy laws, and the costs of financial reorganization must all be considered simultaneously. Yet much of the early literature on the determination of corporation financial structure, the early contribution by Modigliani and Miller being the prime example,[1] was developed without consideration of taxes. Even the literature that does allow for the effects of taxation has drawbacks. Many of the implications of the models, such as the conclusion that debt–equity ratios will increase without limit and new equity will never be issued, are clearly counterfactual. Also, there has been little theoretical or empirical effort to measure the efficiency costs of the effects of taxation on capital structure.

The first section of this paper explores various models of corporate financial policy with taxation. We find that, unless allowance is made for both uncertainty and costs of bankruptcy, the models have important

The authors thank Daniel Frisch, Daniel Feenberg, Elvira Krespach, James Rauch, and Stephen Williams for assistance in the computational work; Alan Blinder, David Bradford, Jerry Butters, Mervyn King, and Richard Quandt for helpful suggestions on earlier drafts of the paper; and the officers of the two financial corporations and of the Securities and Exchange Commission who made available to us their records dealing with the costs involved and settlement terms for several bankruptcies and reorganizations. Finally, we acknowledge financial support from the National Bureau of Economic Research Project on the Changing Roles of Debt and Equity, and from the John L. Weinberg Foundation.

1. Franco Modigliani and Merton H. Miller, "The Cost of Capital, Corporation Finance, and the Theory of Investment," *American Economic Review*, vol. 48 (June 1958), pp. 261–97.

counterfactual implications, which undermines confidence in other forecasts of these models. We therefore use only a model that allows for uncertainty and costs of bankruptcy in drawing inferences.

Next, a time series for the aggregate debt–equity ratio is developed and
the consistency of the time series and cross-sectional variation in debt–
equity ratios with the implications of the models is explored. In the third
section are estimates of the magnitude of some of the efficiency costs and
the equity implications resulting from the existing tax structure.

In the last section we analyze a variety of possible changes in the tax
structure. In addition to describing how these tax changes are likely to
alter behavior, the efficiency and equity implications of the changes are
examined.

The Theory of Corporate Financial Policy

Though the purpose of this section is to analyze corporate financial
policy with taxation, it is useful to first review the early development of
the theory without taxation. This will provide a basis for comparison
when taxes are introduced.

Capital Structure in a No-Tax World

The classical articles on financial policy are by Modigliani and Miller.[2]
While their arguments were modified somewhat in later articles,[3] their
basic approach is still used. Their main result is that, with no taxation
and no bankruptcy, corporate financial policy is irrelevant—that is, if investment policy is held constant, investors will be indifferent to the debt–
equity ratio or the dividend payout rate. Under any investment policy,
therefore, neither dividend policy nor decisions regarding capital structure affect the value of the firm. And since only stocks are risky and bonds

2. Ibid.; and Merton H. Miller and Franco Modigliani, "Dividend Policy,
Growth, and the Valuation of Shares," *Journal of Business,* vol. 34 (October 1961),
pp. 411–33.

3. See, for example, Eugene F. Fama and Merton H. Miller, *The Theory of Finance* (Holt, Rinehart, and Winston, 1972); Jack Hirshleifer, *Investment, Interest
and Capital* (Prentice-Hall, 1970); Joseph E. Stiglitz, "A Re-Examination of the
Modigliani-Miller Theorem," *American Economic Review,* vol. 59 (December
1969), pp. 784–93; Stiglitz, "Some Aspects of the Pure Theory of Corporate Finance: Bankruptcies and Take-Overs," *Bell Journal of Economics and Management Science,* vol. 3 (Autumn 1972), pp. 458–82; and Stiglitz, "On the Irrelevance
of Corporate Financial Policy," *American Economic Review,* vol. 64 (December
1974), pp. 851–66.

are riskless, risk will be spread efficiently and, under certain assumptions, investment will be efficient.

The argument underlying these conclusions is as follows. Assume that a firm receives $1,000,000 as return on its investments after expenses in each period. The firm has debt of $5,000,000 on which it owes $500,000 in interest payments each period. Stockholders therefore receive $500,000 (assuming all net earnings are paid out as dividends). Suppose the stockholders have borrowed $2,000,000 to purchase their shares, in which case they owe $200,000 in personal interest payments. (The firm and the individual are assumed to face the same 10 percent interest rate.) Stockholders as a group therefore receive a net income of $300,000 each period.

Suppose the firm decides to decrease its debt–equity ratio by selling stock, using the proceeds to retire $1,000,000 of the debt. The firm's interest payments on the remaining $4,000,000 of the debt will be $400,000, leaving $600,000 for dividends. The firm's stockholders then have the option of borrowing $1,000,000 to buy the new issues of stock. If the stockholders employ this personal leverage, they will pay a total of $300,000 in interest on their own debt and will receive net each year the same amount ($600,000 in dividends less $300,000) in interest payments as they received before the change.[4]

Under the assumptions in this model, stockholders could completely undo the effects of any action by the firm to change its debt–equity ratio and so would find the change irrelevant. Since personal borrowing is a perfect substitute for corporate borrowing, the firm cannot profit from additional leverage, and since individuals can undo any degree of corporate leverage by buying bonds and shares of the levered company, the firm is not hurt by a capital structure that is more levered than investors desire. In fact, not only is any one firm's financial policy irrelevant, but the aggregate financial policy of the corporate sector is too.

---

4. Algebraically, let $\tilde{x}$, a random variable, be the rate of return, r the interest rate, D the firm's debt, and B the borrowings of the shareholders. With a 100 percent payout rate, stockholders receive $\tilde{x} - rD - rB$ each period. Suppose the firm sells Δ of stock to retire the same amount of debt and shareholders borrow Δ to buy the new issues of stock. They will then receive:

$$\tilde{x} - r(D - \Delta) - r(B + \Delta) = \tilde{x} - rD - rB,$$

which is the same amount as before. Note that, if the firm borrows, Δ is negative and the debt–equity ratio increases. A glossary of terms is given in appendix A to aid the reader in following the model.

While it has been assumed so far that the entire net return to the firm is paid out as dividends, the same argument leads to the conclusion that the dividend payout rate is also irrelevant. For suppose that the firm chooses to retain some additional portion of its earnings. Given the firm's investment policy, this change implies that the additional retentions will be used to retire securities (or to sell fewer additional securities on the open market to finance its investment program). Suppose the retentions are used to repurchase $1,000,000 of debt. The stockholders can then increase their borrowing by $1,000,000, thereby obtaining funds that will exactly offset the loss in dividends while leaving themselves with the same cash flow in future periods as they would have had before the change. Such individual transactions can be employed to offset any payout changes, thus rendering dividend policy irrelevant.[5]

What are the implications of this simple model for the efficiency of risk-bearing and of real investment? Peter Diamond has demonstrated that, when individuals can bear part of the risk in a firm only by purchasing a proportionate share of the firm's profits, a competitive stock market will spread these risks efficiently across investors (assuming there are no binding constraints on short sales). Efficient risk-spreading exists if at the margin each investor demands the same risk premium to absorb an additional unit of risk. A fully competitive market would achieve this result since all individuals buy lottery tickets until the market price just compensates them for absorbing an additional unit of risk, thereby equating risk premiums for all investors. Diamond also shows that under certain assumptions about competitive securities markets (which rule out any degree of market power for any firm in these markets) real investment will also be efficient.[6]

The above argument on the irrelevance of corporate financial policy depends on a number of assumptions. The chief one is that there is no bankruptcy for the firm or for the individual. Under this assumption, it follows that everyone faces the same interest rate, regardless of the amount borrowed. If bankruptcy is introduced but is assumed neither to

5. Alternatively, when the firm cuts its dividends, it can issue fewer new shares. Shareholders can then offset the lost dividends by selling their own shares and yet retain the same percentage of ownership in the firm as they would have had without the change. The argument here does not depend on the absence of bankruptcy, since the debt–equity ratio remains unchanged.

6. Peter A. Diamond, "The Role of a Stock Market in a General Equilibrium Model with Technological Uncertainty," *American Economic Review,* vol. 57 (September 1967), pp. 759–76.

entail any cost when ownership is transferred to bondholders nor to create any moral hazard, the firm's financial policy will still be irrelevant as long as there are perfect substitutes for the firm's debt and equity in other available securities. Since any subdivision by the firm of its total random return into two securities (debt and equity) is already available to investors through combinations of alternative securities, and since the sum of the prices of these two securities must by competition equal the price of that proportional share in the firm, the firm cannot gain by changing its financial policy.[7]

Under what assumptions would the firm's debt and equity have perfect substitutes among combinations of the other available securities? The assumptions of the simple capital asset pricing model would be sufficient. Here a traded security is characterized completely by its covariance with the return on the market as a whole. No change in the financial policy of a firm with a given investment policy will affect the market return so long as bankruptcy is costless. The value of a firm will therefore depend only on its expected return and the covariance of this return with the market, and not on how this return is divided between debt and equity. Other conditions are (1) the existence of complete contingent commodity markets,[8] and (2) the existence of financial intermediaries willing to repackage without cost the financial structure of the firm whenever it might be profitable.[9] To the degree that these assumptions are realistic, corporate financial policy is irrelevant.

Costs of Bankruptcy

But for many reasons bankruptcy is not costless. First, the process of bankruptcy itself entails significant administrative expenses for lawyers, accountants, appraisers, and others. (The magnitude of these costs is explored later.) The bankruptcy process also creates uncertainty for se-

---

7. However, Auerbach and King deal with a simple case involving one firm, two investors, and two states of the world, where even costless bankruptcy can lead to an optimal capital structure. Their case involves changes in the pattern of returns across states of nature that, in effect, change the set of available securities and so directly affect the utility of investors. See Alan J. Auerbach and Mervyn A. King, "Corporate Financial Policy, Taxes, and Uncertainty: An Integration," National Bureau of Economic Research Working Paper 324 (Cambridge, Mass.: NBER, 1979).

8. Stiglitz, "A Re-Examination of the Modigliani-Miller Theorem."

9. Since by assumption a financial intermediary can create any securities that the firm can create, they can provide perfect substitutes. See also Stiglitz, "On the Irrelevance of Corporate Financial Policy."

curity holders, in addition to the basic uncertainty in the return on the real investments.[10] The courts have not consistently followed legal priorities in determining settlements, and legal costs themselves are unpredictable. Given the uncertain interpretation of the law, any group of security holders might bring suit claiming that they received an insufficient share. Furthermore, as will be seen below, while informal reorganizations may entail lower costs than bankruptcy, they may be difficult or impossible to arrange.

Bondholders may also push for liquidation instead of reorganization even when liquidation is inefficient. This may happen because there is little room for the courts to deviate from the absolute priority of bondholders under liquidation. Also, under liquidation, bondholders could receive up to the par value of their bonds even if the market value of the bonds had fallen substantially because of a general rise in interest rates.

The very possibility of bankruptcy creates opportunities for the firm's managers, acting in the interests of stockholders, to aid stockholders at the expense of existing bondholders through inefficient financial policy and investments. For example, suppose the firm were to issue new debt with equal priority in bankruptcy to old debt, using the proceeds to undertake new investment or to repurchase stock. The previous debt holders would suddenly own a riskier asset, yet the interest payment they receive could not adjust to reflect that increased risk. By financing the debt in several issues rather than all at once, the firm may receive more favorable overall terms. Similarly, if the firm undertakes a new risky investment, implying a higher probability of bankruptcy, existing bondholders are worse off, yet again the interest payment on their securities cannot readjust.[11] Conversely, new safe investments may lower the probability of bankruptcy, aiding existing bondholders. The previous arguments about the irrelevance of the debt–equity ratio and the efficiency of investment assumed that bondholders charged the interest rate appropriate for the risk they absorbed. Clearly, if the firm subsequently changes the amount

10. Such risks could be avoided by purchasing the firm's equity and bonds proportionately. However, there are often incentives (such as institutional constraints and tax incentives) to specialize in only one of the firm's securities, in which case this additional risk becomes important.

11. Bondholders will attempt to prevent such actions through covenants in the initial contract. While they normally require that new debt be subordinate to old debt, the courts may not abide by absolute priority rules. Also, their ability to prevent the firm from shifting toward riskier investments is limited.

of risk they absorb—as illustrated in this example—investment incentives are distorted.[12]

Bondholders are not quite so vulnerable, of course. They may attempt to anticipate these actions by the firm and charge an appropriate interest rate. Investment would still be inefficient, however, since the interest rate on the bonds would still be invariant to the riskiness of the later investment projects chosen by the firm. To obtain lower interest costs, the firm would have to guarantee bondholders initially, through indenture provisions in the bond contract, that it would not engage in activities that harmed existing bondholders. Such guarantees involve substantial negotiation and monitoring costs, and it is most unlikely that the provisions would be foolproof. It is probably impossible to avoid the moral hazard issue completely unless the firm does not issue risky debt.

Without bankruptcy costs and taxes, a firm's financial policy would be irrelevant. However, with bankruptcy costs but no taxes, risky debt entails costs but no compensating benefit. It may therefore be concluded that without taxes the firm would finance itself almost entirely by equity[13] —whatever debt was issued would be essentially riskless. Bankruptcy costs would then be effectively zero. The dividend payout rate would be irrelevant; or if individuals preferred dividends to capital gains, or vice

---

12. For further discussion of these moral hazard problems in debt contracts, see Stewart C. Myers, "Determinants of Corporate Borrowing," *Journal of Financial Economics,* vol. 5 (November 1977), pp. 147–75; and Michael C. Jensen and William H. Meckling, "Theory of the Firm: Managerial Behavior, Agency Costs and Ownership Structure," *Journal of Financial Economics,* vol. 3 (October 1976), pp. 305–60.

13. Such a strategy would also give the firm the most flexibility in acquiring new funds; this was suggested by Myers in "Determinants of Corporate Borrowing." Nevertheless, several other considerations that should lead firms to choose more debt have been suggested in the literature: (1) lower underwriting and selling fees for debt than equity issues (William J. Baumol and Burton G. Malkiel, "The Firm's Optimal Debt-Equity Combination and the Cost of Capital," *Quarterly Journal of Economics,* vol. 81 [November 1967], pp. 547–78); (2) the use of the amount of debt as a signal to investors of management's expectations about bankruptcy risk (Stephen A. Ross, "The Determination of Financial Structure: The Incentive-Signalling Approach," *Bell Journal of Economics,* vol. 8 [Spring 1977], pp. 23–40); (3) moral hazard or agency costs involved with public equity issues on a par with those discussed above with debt issues (Jensen and Meckling, "Theory of the Firm"); (4) moral hazard costs in the individual debt substituted for firm debt (the individual can provide collateral other than the firm's equity, however, so individual borrowing may dominate borrowing by the firm); and (5) the greater flexibility of debt, implying increased borrowing at certain times to meet seasonal and other short-term needs for funds.

versa, the firm would have the incentive to take such preferences into account.[14] With zero probability of bankruptcy and the use of only the stock market in spreading risk, the risk from the investment would be spread efficiently among investors and, subject to certain qualifications, investment incentives would be efficient.

Introduction of Taxes

The two taxes affecting a firm's financial structure are the corporation income tax and the personal income tax. The corporation tax provides a strong incentive to finance through debt—as interest payments are deductible from operating earnings before income taxes are imposed but taxes must be paid on the residual owned by the shareholders. However, interest income is taxed under the personal income tax. While dividends are taxed at the same rate as interest,[15] capital gains are taxed at a lower effective rate because (1) 60 percent of long-term capital gains are excluded from taxable income; (2) the tax is due (without interest penalty) only when the asset is sold or may never be paid if it is part of a bequest; and (3) the individual can selectively realize capital losses sooner than capital gains. Therefore, the personal tax favors equity finance. Whether the total tax system favors the use of debt or equity finance depends on a balancing of the advantages of one tax against the disadvantages of the other.

NO UNCERTAINTY, NO BANKRUPTCY.[16] In the ideal setting where there is neither uncertainty nor bankruptcy, the firm will continue to invest until the pretax marginal return on its investments (after covering depre-

14. When transactions costs are taken into account, for example, the payout rate will be of concern to both investors and issuers. People who need to use the returns from their investments for consumption can avoid the substantial brokerage charges incurred in selling off small pieces of their security holdings if they receive dividends. But they will prefer retention by the firm if they would reinvest their returns anyway. Similarly, by retention, the firm would avoid the underwriting and selling fees involved in new issues. One might therefore expect consumers to prefer firms with little need for funds and reinvestors to prefer firms with a greater need for funds.

15. This is not necessarily the case. For example, $200 of the dividends of married couples ($100 for single persons) may be excluded from taxable income. Moreover, corporate shareholders can exclude 85 percent of dividend receipts from taxable income.

16. The model is basically a formalization of Miller's arguments, though it borrows also from King and Stiglitz. See Merton H. Miller, "Debt and Taxes," *Journal of Finance*, vol. 32 (May 1977), pp. 261–75; Mervyn A. King, "Taxation and the Cost of Capital," *Review of Economic Studies*, vol. 41 (January 1974), pp. 21–35; and Joseph E. Stiglitz, "Taxation, Corporate Financial Policy, and the Cost of Capital," *Journal of Public Economics*, vol. 2 (February 1973), pp. 1–34.

ciation and expenses) has been reduced to the market interest rate. Repurchase of debt and new real investment are alternative uses of funds, so they should earn the same net after-tax rate of return at the margin. Both alternatives receive the same tax treatment (assuming economic depreciation in the tax law and no investment tax credit). The net returns from investment are taxed at regular corporate rates. The net reduction in cash outflow from purchasing debt is taxed at the same rate since deductions from taxable income are reduced. Thus both alternatives must have the same rate of return before tax as well. Unincorporated businesses will also invest until the marginal return on their investment equals the market interest rate, for similar reasons. This implies that in spite of the corporation income tax (if explicit investment incentives are ignored) investment earns the same pretax marginal rate of return in both corporate and noncorporate uses. However, because of the personal income tax, individuals will invest until their after-tax return is equal to their marginal time preference rate.[17] Therefore, even though the investment is allocated efficiently, an inefficient amount of investment results from the distortions in the personal income tax.[18]

The firm's optimal decision rule for equity investments is to finance new investment through new stock issues until the stock market values the returns of a dollar of marginal real investment at just a dollar.[19]

17. If the market interest rate is r and the marginal personal tax rate is m, individuals will invest until their marginal time preference rate is $r(1 - m)$ while the marginal product of capital will equal r.

18. If the investment tax credit and accelerated depreciation are taken into account, however, investment is also allocated inefficiently. David F. Bradford, "Tax Neutrality and the Investment Tax Credit," National Bureau of Economic Research Working Paper 269 (Cambridge, Mass.: NBER, August 1978).

19. This result is analogous to Tobin's q theory of investment as developed in James Tobin, "A General Equilibrium Approach to Monetary Theory," *Journal of Money, Credit, and Banking,* vol. 1 (February 1969), pp. 15–29; John H. Ciccolo, Jr., "Four Essays on Monetary Policy" (Ph.D. dissertation, Yale University, 1975); and George M. von Furstenberg, "Corporate Investment: Does Market Valuation Matter in the Aggregate?" *Brookings Papers on Economic Activity,* 2:1977, pp. 347–97. (Hereafter *BPEA.*) In these papers, q is the ratio of the total market value of the firm (debt and equity) to the replacement cost of the firm's capital stock (without taking obsolescence into account). Here, q is the ratio of the value in the stock market of a marginal investment divided by its purchase cost. Though one advantage of the first definition of q is that it is easier to measure, Gordon and Bradford have estimated a time series for q as defined in this paper. Roger H. Gordon and David F. Bradford, "Taxation and the Stock Market Valuation of Capital Gains and Dividends: Theory and Empirical Results," *Journal of Public Economics,* vol. 14 (October 1980).

Clearly, there would be no new equity issues if the stock market consistently valued a dollar of real investment at less than a dollar. However, the firm would also find it profitable to borrow further, using the funds to repurchase equity—and these repurchases would continue until the stock market valued the firm's marginal real investment at its replacement cost or until there was no more equity outstanding.[20]

If repurchase of equity is forbidden (or very costly), however, the firm will merely issue no new equity as long as the market values the marginal real investment at less than its replacement cost.[21] In fact, repurchase of equity is illegal in Great Britain. In the United States, although repurchases are not illegal as such, complications can arise. For example, if repurchases precisely imitate dividend payments (periodic percentage repurchases from each shareholder), the payments will be taxed as dividends.[22] Bradford, Auerbach, and Stiglitz each explore models in which the market values the marginal real investment at less than its replacement cost as a result of a constraint preventing the repurchase of equity.[23] Any existing equity is left over from the period before the imposition of the corporation tax (when, as argued above, equity finance would have been favored) or from the initial equity established to incorporate the firm. These models all have the counterfactual implication, however, that no *new* equity will be issued.

Since it is difficult to maintain that corporations, even after forty years, would not have taken advantage of these arbitrage profits and since new issues of equity do occur, it will henceforth be assumed that the debt–equity ratio does not deviate systematically from its equilibrium value.

Optimal firm behavior, then, means that, in equilibrium, the firm will

20. For if the firm were to borrow an additional dollar, it would owe r more in interest payments each period. Assume it repurchases q dollars of equity, where q is the value in the stock market of the returns to a dollar of the marginal real investment. The repurchase, by freeing the returns to a dollar of real investment, allows the firm just to cover its additional interest payments, a result implied by optimal debt finance of investment. But since $q < 1$, the firm is left with $1 - q > 0$ in profits. Equity would therefore continue to be repurchased until q equaled 1 or until there was no more equity outstanding.

21. Existing equity will remain, but the amount is a historical accident.

22. Another problem, in principle, is prosecution for trading on inside information.

23. David F. Bradford, "The Incidence and Allocative Effect of a Tax on Corporate Distributions," *Journal of Public Economics,* forthcoming; Alan J. Auerbach, "Wealth Maximization and the Cost of Capital," *Quarterly Journal of Economics,* vol. 93 (August 1979), pp. 433–46; and Stiglitz, "Taxation, Corporate Financial Policy, and the Cost of Capital."

invest until its marginal return equals the market interest rate and the stock market values the marginal real investment at exactly its replacement cost.[24] Assuming that firms satisfy these two equilibrium conditions, the optimal portfolio behavior of investors depends on the dividend policy of the firm and tax rates at both the firm and the individual level. On Miller's assumptions that no dividends are paid and that capital gains are not taxed,[25] the investor is indifferent between bonds and equity if the individual marginal tax rate is equal to the corporation tax rate. If it is less than the corporation rate, he will invest only in bonds; if it is greater than the corporation rate, he will invest only in equity.[26] The equilibrium debt–equity ratio therefore depends on the personal income tax rates and the distribution of wealth across tax brackets. Since the federal corporation tax rate is now 46 percent and the maximum federal marginal personal tax rate is 70 percent, many individuals might do best to invest in equity on these assumptions. Since it is assumed that no dividends are paid, returns to equity come after corporation taxes but then are free of tax; investments in bonds are therefore inferior for all investors with tax rates above the corporation tax rate even though returns to bondholders are not subject to corporation taxes.

When all investors have purchased their preferred security, the marginal investor (for whom the corporation tax rate is the same as his marginal tax rate) will be just indifferent between receiving the returns from a given real investment through debt and receiving them through equity. While returns to equity come after the payment of corporation income taxes, those returns will not be taxed again. On the other hand, bond returns, though not subject to corporation income taxes, will be subject to personal income taxes at the same rate. The firm will therefore be indifferent to how it finances the real investment. In fact, assuming that the firm is small relative to the market so that the firm cannot affect the characteristics of the marginal security holder, it will find irrelevant any change in its financial policy, large or small. The Modigliani-Miller con-

24. If s is the marginal return on real investment, the two conditions are (1) $s = r$ from optimal debt finance, and (2) $q = 1$ from optimal equity finance. Were q greater than 1, the firm would continue to sell new equity to undertake real or financial (bond) investments until q equaled 1.

25. Miller, "Debt and Taxes," pp. 266–67.

26. If the individual can purchase negative quantities of either asset, he will find it profitable to sell the less desirable asset and to invest the proceeds in the other asset. He will continue to do this indefinitely or until his tax rates have evolved to the point where he is indifferent between the two assets.

clusions are thus maintained at the firm level. However, as noted above, the aggregate debt–equity ratio does have a unique optimal value, which depends on the distribution of assets across tax brackets.

How realistic are these assumptions? In particular, is the marginal individual tax rate on the returns to equity effectively zero? Since taxes on capital gains are paid only at realization (with no interest penalty for the postponement), or not at all if the share is still owned when the investor dies, the capital gains tax rate will certainly be very small for many investors. However, empirically the payout ratio is approximately 0.55.[27] Therefore, the individual tax rate on equity is zero only as long as the marginal personal tax rate on dividends is zero. The exclusion of the first $200 of dividends from taxable income for married couples ($100 for single persons) makes it zero for small investors; but for these investors, the personal tax rate is normally lower than the corporate rate, so hardly anyone in this category will own equity.[28] Miller and Scholes point out that for very large investors extra dividends may enable the investor to increase the interest deduction just enough to offset any tax due, which also implies that the tax rate on dividends is zero.[29] For the restriction on interest deductions to be binding, however, the investor must be deducting well over $25,000 in interest.[30] According to a representative cross-section of federal individual tax returns, only 0.02 percent of taxpayers who receive dividends appear to face a binding constraint on interest deductions.[31] For almost all individual investors potentially interested in equity in this context, therefore, the tax rate on dividend and interest income can be expected to be the same.

If the marginal tax rates on dividends and interest are the same, when will an investor be indifferent between debt and equity? Suppose the dividend payout is 55 percent and the individual's effective capital gains rate is about one-fifth of his ordinary marginal tax rate.[32] Investors will then

27. This is the average figure in the national income and product accounts for 1970–75.

28. Nontaxable investors will prefer bonds to equity for the same reason.

29. Merton H. Miller and Myron S. Scholes, "Dividends and Taxes," *Journal of Financial Economics*, vol. 6 (December 1978), pp. 333–64.

30. In 1975 the maximum income tax deduction allowed under the federal individual income tax was $25,000 plus dividend and interest income and other investment income (realized capital gains plus items on schedule E).

31. We are grateful to Daniel Frisch for doing these calculations.

32. This is the case with a 60 percent exclusion and assuming postponement of the tax until realization halves the effective rate.

be indifferent between debt and equity only if their marginal personal tax rate is about 70 percent.[33] Thus, with reasonable values for the parameters, essentially no individual investors will own equity.

This implication of the model is reinforced if tax-free debt is introduced. Appendix A presents evidence that the interest rate on tax-free debt has been approximately 75 percent of the corporate bond rate. Thus the maximum tax rate that individuals have to pay on interest receipts is just 25 percent.[34] While under Miller's assumptions only individuals with a marginal personal tax rate in excess of the 46 percent corporation rate will prefer equity to bonds, no one will actually face a marginal tax rate this high. It may be concluded that nobody will own equity.

Thus when the relative rates of return on debt and equity make firms indifferent between debt and equity finance, essentially all individual investors will prefer owning debt to equity—the equilibrium financial structure under these assumptions will involve only debt. This conclusion is dramatically counterfactual. In a world of certainty and taxes, it does not seem possible to explain an equilibrium financial structure with both debt and equity. An analysis that ignores uncertainty is clearly unsatisfactory.

UNCERTAINTY, NO BANKRUPTCY.[35] In a setting of uncertainty, with no bankruptcy, bonds would remain riskless securities (if inflation is ignored). Whereas without uncertainty the firm invested until the marginal

---

33. Assume that the firm pays out as dividends p percent of its after-tax profits and reinvests the rest. Also assume that the investor with a marginal tax rate of m on interest payments has a marginal tax rate of n on dividends and an effective tax rate of c on capital gains.

When investing a dollar in bonds, the investor receives $r(1 - m) = s(1 - m)$ each period. When investing a dollar in equity, the investor receives as dividends $ps(1 - \tau)(1 - n)$ after tax. The firm has also reinvested $(1 - p)s(1 - \tau)$ per dollar of real investment, implying a capital gain to the shareholder of $(1 - p)s(1 - \tau)$ $(1 - c)$ after personal income tax. Assuming that the investor must buy only nonnegative quantities of either asset, he will invest in the asset giving the higher rate of return and only in that asset. He will be indifferent between the two assets only if

(1) $\qquad r(1 - m) = s(1 - m) = ps(1 - \tau)(1 - n) + (1 - p)s(1 - \tau)(1 - c).$

If $p = 0.55$, $n = m$, $c = 0.2m$, and $\tau = 0.46$, the investor will be indifferent between debt and equity when $m \approx 0.7$.

34. If m is the tax rate on interest income, the model implies that, if $(1 - m) <$ 0.75, the individual would borrow and deduct the interest payments from taxable income in order to invest in tax-free bonds. However, the Internal Revenue Service would disallow the interest deduction in this case, eliminating such incentives.

35. This is the setting used by Modigliani and Miller, "Cost of Capital."

return equaled the interest rate, now the firm invests until the marginal return is just enough above the market interest rate to compensate shareholders for the extra uncertainty.[36] As before, the firm would be indifferent to financing additional investment by issuing new equity when the stock market values the returns from a dollar of real investment at a dollar. (If the stock market consistently values the returns from a dollar of real investment at less than a dollar, the firm can borrow to repurchase equity and make arbitrage profits.)

When these conditions are satisfied, would anyone now choose to purchase equity? Were the return on a particular investment nonstochastic, the firm would still invest until the marginal return just equaled the market interest rate. But by the arguments of the previous section, an investor would be willing to pay a dollar in the equity market for the returns on such an investment only if his marginal tax rate was at least 70 percent, without taking into account the existence of tax-free debt. It can also be shown, however, that even when the investment is risky, so that it must earn above the market rate of interest, only an investor with at least the same 70 percent marginal tax rate would be willing to pay a dollar in the equity market for the return on such an investment.[37] If tax-free debt paid a return of about 75 percent of the (taxable) market interest rate, nobody would pay a dollar in the equity market for the return on the marginal real investment. As long as debt remains riskless, the firm will

---

36. The required expected rate of return, $\bar{s}$, on the marginal dollar investment is $\bar{s} = r + \rho$, where ρ is the risk premium demanded by shareholders, before corporation tax, to compensate for bearing the extra risk.

37. The return on a dollar of real investment before corporation tax can be represented by $s = r + \rho + \xi$. Here ξ represents the random element, with mean zero, in the return on the investment. Optimal debt finance implies that equity holders will be indifferent to the last dollar of debt-financed real investment, so will be just willing to accept the residual $s - r$, which has expected return ρ, as compensation for also accepting the stochastic return ξ. Optimal equity finance implies that equity holders will be willing to pay a dollar for the returns on a dollar of real investment, so they will pay a dollar for an expected return $r + \rho$ along with a stochastic return ξ, all before the corporation tax. With the two results combined, equity holders must be willing to pay one dollar to receive a nonstochastic return r. However, as shown earlier, when the alternative investments are riskless taxable bonds also earning r and tax-free bonds earning $r_f \approx 0.75r$, no individual would invest a dollar in equity to earn a nonstochastic before-corporation-tax rate of return r. With equity, the after-tax return is at best $r(1 - \tau) = 0.54r$, and tax-free debt earns $0.75r$. As long as debt remains riskless, the firm will always have an incentive to increase the debt–equity ratio without limit.

always have an incentive to increase the debt–equity ratio without limit. Thus the model, allowing for uncertainty but not bankruptcy, still has dramatically counterfactual implications.

UNCERTAINTY WITH BANKRUPTCY. We have shown that, with costless bankruptcy and without taxes, the debt–equity ratio would be irrelevant. With taxes, however, investors would pay less tax through owning debt, so firms would increase their debt–equity ratios without limit.[38] Since firms (and their lenders) do tend to limit the extent of financial leverage, it is clear that bankruptcy is sufficiently costly to affect the value of the firm materially.

If bankruptcy is costly, why does the market fail to find some device to avoid such costs? Presumably, avoiding these costs is in the best interests of the various claimants on the firm. However, negotiation with the full set of investors is difficult—especially when there are public bondholders. Bankruptcy costs are due in large part to these difficulties.

While the availability of alternatives to formal bankruptcy puts some upper bound on the costs of bankruptcy,[39] these alternatives are themselves costly. Costs are not avoided by informal reorganization, for the essential problem of negotiating a complicated settlement among parties with different interests and different legal remedies remains. Indeed, the problems are sometimes so complex that informal reorganizations without bankruptcy either are impossible to achieve or can be arranged only with costs as large as those incurred with formal bankruptcy. This is especially true if there are many classes of security holders, all of whom must agree to a reorganization plan and all of whom may take recourse to litigation if they subsequently feel they were treated unfairly.

There is also a potential problem of externalities. When any partial coalition of investors considers preventing the firm from going bankrupt, it ignores the resulting benefits or costs accruing to the remaining investors. But the smaller the coalition, the larger this externality. The benefits to the coalition of avoiding bankruptcy may not be as large as

---

38. The Internal Revenue Service could threaten to reclassify debt as equity for tax purposes if debt finance was used almost exclusively. This threat would create an incentive to maintain enough equity to forestall the danger. It is doubtful, however, that one can rely on this explanation for the amount of equity actually in existence.

39. See Robert A. Haugen and Lemma W. Senbet, "The Insignificance of Bankruptcy Costs to the Theory of Optimal Capital Structure," *Journal of Finance*, vol. 33 (May 1978), pp. 383–93.

the costs of keeping the firm out of bankruptcy even if the benefits to the investors as a whole are large enough.[40]

Another inducement to bankruptcy is that, as the size of debt increases relative to the value of the firm, the management, acting in the interest of stockholders, ignores costs borne by bondholders or bank lenders resulting from an increase in the probability of bankruptcy and finds inefficient investments becoming profitable. Bondholders, unable to prevent such actions, may well stop the erosion in the value of their securities by forcing the firm into bankruptcy in spite of the transactions costs of bankruptcy.

Finally, formal bankruptcy may be the only way a firm in distress can obtain new financing. This is because new loans to the bankrupt firm receive an enforceable first lien on its assets while new loans to a reorganized company cannot receive the same degree of protection.

How should these bankruptcy costs be modeled when studying the firm's debt-equity decision? The covenants with existing bondholders normally require that, unless certain earnings coverage and liquidity ratios are met, any further debt issued have lower priority in bankruptcy than the existing debt. When considering additional debt, the stockholders and the potentially lowest priority debt holder form a coalition. Only the bankruptcy costs that might be borne by this coalition will be considered in the decision to increase the debt of the firm. These costs will depend mainly on the relation of the existing amount of debt to the underlying capital and on the variability of both prior and additional earnings or cash flow (which together make default probable), though the form of dependence will vary by firm. Only part of the total costs of bankruptcy will be borne by this coalition, however, the fraction depending on the priority rules in bankruptcy and the circumstances under which bankruptcy would occur.[41] As will be seen below, "me-first" rules are often not honored in bankruptcy proceedings.

40. Bulow-Shoven and White give examples of a coalition of bank lenders and equity holders that would choose to force bankruptcy in spite of the costs, at the expense of the public bondholders. See Jeremy I. Bulow and John B. Shoven, "The Bankruptcy Decision," *Bell Journal of Economics,* vol. 9 (Autumn 1978), pp. 437–56; and Michelle J. White, "Public Policy Toward Bankruptcy: Me-First and Other Priority Rules," *Bell Journal of Economics,* vol. 11 (Autumn 1980).

41. These decisions will be inefficient to the degree that some of the costs created by a higher debt–equity ratio are ignored in financing decisions, since they are borne by existing bondholders. Increasing the fraction of bankruptcy costs borne by this coalition would therefore improve the efficiency of investment and financial decisions, and revisions in the legal structure of bankruptcy ought to aim at this.

Assume that the firm sells its securities on a market satisfying the assumptions of the capital asset pricing model, derived with taxes, as in Brennan or Gordon-Bradford. Here the equilibrium net-of-tax risk premium on any asset just compensates for the component of that asset's risk that moves with the market as a whole—any other component can be diversified away and merits no risk premium.[42]

At the equilibrium debt–equity ratio, both the outstanding debt and the equity of the firm must satisfy the capital asset pricing equation so that investors are willing to buy them, and the firm must find that after corporation taxes the issuance of either debt or equity is equally costly at the margin. Moreover, when investment is optimal, investors must be willing to pay a dollar to receive the returns from a one-dollar marginal investment, whether the financing was from debt or from equity. What are the implications of these equilibrium conditions?

We explore first the relative profitability of debt and equity finance when the probability or costs of bankruptcy are not affected by the choice.[43] Even for this case, two new complications must be addressed. First, when debt and equity finance are considered, though total bankruptcy costs are assumed to be unchanged, the fraction of the receipts in bankruptcy going to the coalition of equity holders and the possible new bondholder may be affected by the financing decision. However, if the new debt is, in fact, junior in priority to all existing debt, as new equity would be, this may not occur. Second, even if the amount of uncertainty borne by the coalition is the same whether debt or equity finance is used,

42. All securities traded in the market will satisfy the equation:

$$(2) \qquad \bar{g}_i + \alpha(\bar{d}_i - r_z) = \beta_i[\bar{g}_M + \alpha(\bar{d}_M - r_z)].$$

Here, $\bar{g}_i$ is the part of the expected return on the ith security that is given capital gains treatment, $\bar{d}_i$ is the part of the expected return taxed at ordinary rates, and r_z is the return, also taxed at ordinary rates, on the riskless asset. The subscript M refers to the market index, β_i measures the (systematic) riskiness of the ith security, and it is assumed that only g_i and g_M are stochastic; α is a weighted average across investors of the relative value of a dollar of dividends to each investor compared with that of a dollar of capital gains, and is the same for all firms. When only taxes affect the relative values of capital gains and dividends, an investor's relative value of dividends would equal $1 - n/1 - c$. When $m \neq n$ for all investors, however, the weight α_b on bond interest payments would differ from the weight α on dividend receipts. M. J. Brennan, "Taxes, Market Valuation and Corporate Financial Policy," *National Tax Journal*, vol. 23 (December 1970), pp. 417–27; and Gordon and Bradford, "Taxation and the Stock Market Valuation of Capital Gains and Dividends."

43. This setting is essentially the same as that used in the previous section. The conclusions remain unchanged when the capital asset pricing model is used.

the risk premium demanded for the given risk may be affected by the financing decision. But because of the implicit assumption in the Gordon-Bradford model that all stochastic returns are taxed at the capital gains rate, the capital asset pricing model implies that the total risk premium[44] required to compensate investors for bearing all the risk depends only on the covariance of the uncertainty with the market uncertainty, not on how the uncertainty is split between bondholders and equity holders.

Since the total risk borne by the coalition and the price demanded for bearing that risk are unaffected by the financing decision, only the risk premium received[45] must be taken into account in order to decide whether the firm will find debt or equity finance more profitable. As long as the risk premium received is equal under either debt or equity finance of a given investment, the market will value the returns independently of the form of finance, which implies that the firm is also indifferent to the form of finance. However—as before, when the financial decision did not affect bankruptcy risk—the market receives a larger risk premium from debt finance than from equity finance, so the firm will still prefer debt finance.[46]

44. The total risk premium is the right side of equation 2.
45. The risk premium received is the left side of equation 2.
46. When a dollar of investment is financed by equity, the expected receipts to the firm after corporation tax (including expected bankruptcy costs) are $\bar{s}\,(1-\tau)$. With p still representing the percent paid out as dividends, the risk premium received, as valued in the market, is the left side of equation 2:

$$EV(\bar{s}) = (1-p)\bar{s}(1-\tau) + \alpha p\bar{s}(1-\tau) - \alpha r_z,$$

where $EV(\bar{s})$ represents the expected return to equity over the risk-free rate resulting from before-tax return $\bar{s}$. When the same investment is financed by debt, the expected after-tax receipts to the firm are $r + (\bar{s}-r)(1-\tau)$. Where there are zero expected capital gains on bonds and bond finance is used, bondholders would receive an expected risk premium $\alpha_b r - \alpha r_z = BV(r)$, the expected value to bondholders of the return r over the risk-free rate, and equity holders would receive the rest, increasing the risk premium they receive by $EV(\bar{s}-r) + \alpha r_z$. When comparing the expected value to investors in the firm of using equity or debt finance, $EV(\bar{s})$ is compared with $BV(r) + EV(\bar{s}-r) + \alpha r_z$. If they are equivalent,

$$BV(r) + \alpha r_z = EV(\bar{s}) - EV(\bar{s}-r) = EV(r) + \alpha r_z,$$

or
(3) $$\alpha_b r = (1-p)r(1-\tau) + \alpha p r(1-\tau).$$

This comparison is equivalent to that in equation 1 assuming $\alpha = 1 - n/1 - c$ and $\alpha_b = 1 - m/1 - c$, implying that investors prefer bonds except when α_b is extraordinarily small. But of course this should be the case since any effect of the financing decision on the probability of bankruptcy has so far been ignored, so that the situation is basically the same as that of the last section.

A decision to finance an extra dollar with debt instead of equity, however, will increase the probability of bankruptcy and the moral hazard associated with risky debt. These increased costs will be split between the existing bondholders and the equity holders (perhaps in coalition with the new junior bondholders).[47] The component of the costs that will be borne by the existing bondholders will be ignored by the coalition in deciding whether to increase debt. Assume that the other component of the increased costs is itself an increasing function of the ratio of the existing debt to the underlying capital stock. These increased costs include the extra risk premium demanded resulting from the correlation of these bankruptcy costs with the market risk,[48] as well as the decline in expected return directly caused by the increase in expected bankruptcy costs. The existence of bankruptcy costs makes equity finar.ce relatively more attractive. In equilibrium, the tax advantages of an extra dollar of debt would be just offset by the additional bankruptcy and moral hazard costs implied by the replacement of a dollar of equity with debt.[49] Since the bankruptcy costs will vary by firm for many reasons, particularly the variability of the firm's earnings, the equilibrium debt–equity ratio will also vary by firm, and the firm with more variable earnings will choose a lower debt–equity ratio.

The capital asset pricing model can also be used to explain individual investor debt-equity decisions. In choosing the optimal portfolio in this model, the individual invests until the risk premium received on each asset after tax just compensates for that asset's contribution to the riskiness of

47. To the extent that equity also has moral hazard or agency costs, the increased costs described are net of the decrease in agency costs associated with the decrease in equity. See Jensen and Meckling, "Theory of the Firm."

48. This systematic component of bankruptcy costs is often ignored. An important cause for systematic, or market, risk is the sensitivity of corporate returns to general market conditions. But a cyclical downturn is likely to increase the probability of bankruptcy and its associated costs. Firms with high debt–equity ratios are therefore likely to have higher anticipated systematic risk. See Barr Rosenberg and James Guy, "The Prediction of Systematic Risk," Working Paper 33 (University of California at Berkeley, Graduate School of Business Administration, 1975).

49. Call $c(D/K)$ the total increase in bankruptcy costs from financing an extra dollar by debt instead of equity. Now, the firm has chosen an equilibrium amount of debt when:

(4) $$\alpha_b r = (1 - p)r(1 - \tau) + \alpha p r(1 - \tau) + c(D/K)$$

or

(5) $$c(D/K) = r[\tau - (1 - \alpha_b)] + (1 - \alpha)(1 - \tau)pr.$$

his portfolio.[50] Each individual will have an incentive to own every asset, though he might find it profitable to have a short position in some securities.[51] The composition of individual portfolios will vary because marginal tax rates and utility functions differ (if no risk-free asset exists). Those with lower tax rates would normally put smaller shares of their portfolios into equity, but everyone would be active in the market for equities. Unless an individual is completely indifferent to acquiring a share of equity, at the existing price he could profitably buy or sell shares.[52]

Another implication of the model is that risk is distributed inefficiently by the securities market as a result of tax distortions. Risk will be efficiently distributed only if, at the margin, each individual demands the same risk premium (charges the same price) for accepting a given lottery. Because taxes influence portfolio choices, this efficiency condition will not be met.

In equilibrium those in all tax brackets are indifferent between debt and equity at the margin. Any relative tax advantage of equity over debt must therefore be counterbalanced by a larger cost at the margin of bearing the risk in equity—the risk premium on equity ought to be larger in equilibrium for those with a relative tax advantage in equity.[53] Those with a relative tax advantage in equity own relatively more equity. As a result, there will be a higher covariance of the return on new purchases of equity with the return on their portfolios as a whole, leading to a larger risk premium at the margin. Individuals in higher tax brackets will find that

50. For each individual, an equation analogous to 2 will be satisfied for all securities. In the equation, however, α will equal the ratio $1 - n/1 - c$ for that investor, and the subscript M will no longer refer to the market portfolio but to that individual's utility-maximizing portfolio.

51. Negative holdings of assets should occur only when tax rate differences are extremely large. When all persons have the same tax rates, they all own a proportionate share of the market portfolio. Except in degenerate cases (such as in Miller, "Debt and Taxes"), portfolios will change continuously as the tax law moves away from equal rates. Large differences in rates would be necessary before any holdings of equity became negative.

52. This conclusion contrasts with the complete portfolio specialization implied by Miller's 1977 model. Since he ignored uncertainty, he ended up with corner solutions when solving for optimal portfolios. Miller, "Debt and Taxes."

53. The capital asset pricing model implies that, for any given market security, an individual in equilibrium would just be satisfied wth the risk premium he does receive. This premium is:

$$\bar{g}_i + \alpha d_i - \max (r_f/1 - c, \alpha r_z),$$

where $\alpha = 1 - n/1 - c$. The behavior of this expression as a function of α provides the justification for the statements in the text.

equity tends to be relatively more attractive than bonds, because these investors obtain tax advantages from the relatively favorable treatment of capital gains. For those in the highest tax brackets, however, there is a relative tax disadvantage in equity since tax-exempt bonds have such a high return after tax compared with equity. The condition for efficient risk-spreading is thus not achieved. Individuals demand different risk premiums for holding additional amounts of equity at the margin.

In summary, when allowance is made for both uncertainty and costly bankruptcy, the implications for the firm's equilibrium financial policy are the following.

First, each firm will have its own optimal debt–equity ratio, with firms with riskier investments choosing a lower debt–equity ratio. The debt–equity ratio is no longer indeterminate nor is there an incentive to increase it without limit.

Second, individuals will hold diversified portfolios, with those in the lowest tax brackets owning relatively little equity and those in the highest tax brackets specializing in tax-exempt bonds. Unlike the case assumed by Miller, however, there is no specialization of portfolios.

The obvious counterfactual conclusions of the earlier models have therefore been eliminated.

A Note on Dividends

If the firm is allowed to choose an optimal dividend payout rate, what do the models imply? It was shown that, when there are no taxes, the dividend payout rate is irrelevant. Unfortunately, the above models— even those that include bankruptcy—seem to imply that, contrary to fact, no dividends should be paid.[54] While a few attempts have been made to rationalize the payment of dividends, the size and stability of dividends remain puzzling.

When a firm considers the payout of available funds as dividends, it also has the choice of using the funds for the repurchase of equity, new investment, or retirement of debt. Assume that one dollar per share will be paid out by the firm in this period either for dividends or for repurchase. If the firm chooses to pay the dollar as dividends, each shareholder must pay a personal tax on the dollar. If the firm instead decides publicly to repurchase shares, the remaining shareholders experience a capital gain of a dollar, which will be taxed when realized, and the share-

54. Alternatively, the implication is that dividends are more valued relative to capital gains than one would have expected, given their relative tax treatment.

holders who sold out experience a capital gain of the same amount, which is taxable immediately. If transactions costs are sufficiently small, shareholders for whom the capital gains tax is lower than the tax on dividend income would prefer repurchase to dividends, and vice versa.

If, instead of using the dollar per share to repurchase shares, the firm were to retain the money and use it for new investment or for the retirement of debt (equivalent at the margin), the total value of the equity would increase. Optimal finance implies that the stock market should be willing to pay a dollar at the margin for an additional dollar of equity-financed real investment. Each share would therefore experience a capital gain of a dollar, so in equilibrium retentions are equivalent to repurchase.[55]

The presumption that the capital gains tax rate is lower than the tax rate on dividends leads to the conclusion that firms ought not to pay dividends. However, not all investors will favor repurchases. For example, married couples are not taxed on the first $200 of dividends and single persons are not taxed on the first $100, yet they do pay a tax on capital gains. For corporations owning shares in other corporations, 85 percent of dividends received are deductible, so the corporation tax rate on intercorporate dividends is 7.2 percent, assuming a marginal corporation tax rate of 46 percent. The top statutory tax rate on corporate capital gains is 28 percent, so that even with the gain from postponement of the payments until realization one would expect the capital gains rate to be higher than the dividend tax rate for corporations. Also, tax-exempt institutions pay no tax on either dividends or capital gains and are sometimes constrained against spending capital gains; consequently, these institutions may prefer dividends.

What incentives does the firm face, given these differences in the tax treatment of various shareholders? It may be assumed that the firm's objective, and implicitly that of a majority of its shareholders, is to maximize the value of its shares. Under the assumptions of the capital asset pricing model, the market values dividends relative to capital gains by a factor that is simply a weighted average across investors of their own valuations of dividends relative to capital gains.[56] The weight on any investor's valua-

55. If the debt–equity ratio is not in equilibrium, $q \neq 1$. After-tax capital gains on each share are then $q(1 - c)/N$. An investor now prefers retentions if, and only if, $q > 1 - n/1 - c$. However, repurchases continue to dominate dividends as long as $c < n$.

56. For a derivation, see Gordon and Bradford, "Taxation and the Stock Market Valuation of Capital Gains and Dividends."

tion is larger for investors who are less risk averse at the margin (infinite if risk neutral), which probably gives corporations and institutions (each of which value a dollar of dividends more than a dollar of capital gains) more importance in the determination of the market valuation of dividends relative to capital gains.

If in spite of the extra weight on the less risk averse the market values a dollar of capital gains more than a dollar of dividends, the firm can increase the value of its equity by repurchasing shares rather than paying dividends.[57] Fortunately, it is possible to estimate the value of capital gains relative to dividends in the market by comparing the average returns on equity in firms with similar riskiness but different dividend payout rates. Black and Scholes find the relative values of the two forms of return to be statistically indistinguishable, and Gordon and Bradford find that dividends and capital gains tend to be valued equally, although the relative valuation fluctuates.[58]

Since the stock market seems to value dividends and capital gains equally, these empirical results are consistent with firms paying dividends. But with the less favorable tax treatment of dividends, how can the market value dividends and capital gains equally? As already indicated, taxes do not affect all investors in the same way. Moreover, taxes are not the only factor affecting the relative value to investors of dividends and capital gains. Transactions costs, for example, will favor dividends for many shareholders who intend to consume the income. Small investors— for example, those with $5,000 or less invested in a single security— would face transactions costs of well over 10 percent were they to liquidate a small fraction of their investment instead of receiving dividends. Alternatively, investors may have an irrational preference for dividends.[59]

Even if the market tends to value dividends and capital gains equally, however, there is another problem. The firm will find it profitable both to retain earnings or repurchase its stock and to pay dividends only if dividends and capital gains are valued *exactly* equally. If one is valued more than the other, the firm should either retain everything or retain nothing and pay out all it can as dividends. Yet dividend payments are extraordi-

57. The presumption that firms ought not to pay dividends is equivalent to the hypothesis that $\alpha < 1$.

58. Myron Scholes and Fischer Black, "The Effects of Dividend Yield and Dividend Policy on Common Stock Prices and Returns," *Journal of Financial Economics*, vol. 1 (May 1974), pp. 1–22; and Gordon and Bradford, "Taxation and the Stock Market Valuation of Capital Gains and Dividends."

59. See Fischer Black, "The Dividend Puzzle," *Journal of Portfolio Management*, vol. 2 (Winter 1976), pp. 5–8.

narily stable over time. Some factor clearly is being ignored by the models. To the extent that dividend recipients, such as retired people and tax-exempt institutions, use dividends for consumption or current outlays, one can rationalize some desire for stability in payments. However, many recipients do not consume out of dividends, yet virtually all firms have stable dividend payments.

One explanation for the stability of dividend payments is that the level of dividends is used as a signal to investors concerning the financial strength of the firm.[60] This use of dividends is appealing. Since firms have latitude in inventory valuation, depreciation accounting, and expensing or capitalizing certain outlays, it is not always possible to obtain a good estimate of corporate earnings from reported data or from earnings figures adjusted on the basis of publicly available accounting information. A dollar of earnings for one company may not be equivalent to a dollar of earnings for another. No such ambiguity exists with a dollar of dividends, however. Hence the corporation may use dividends to provide the financial community with information about true earnings.

While dividend payments may benefit the firm by creating favorable expectations of future profits, a given dividend payout rate also creates additional costs. In addition to higher personal taxes, dividends increase the firm's need to seek outside funding, or to cut back on investments, to replace the money paid out. The firm itself must pay substantial transactions costs, such as underwriters' fees, to float new issues of debt or equity. Moreover, large new issues can usually be sold only at a discount from prevailing market prices. Presumably the firm trades off these benefits and costs when choosing its dividend payout rate. Everything else being equal, more profitable firms will find any given level of dividends relatively less costly since they will use outside funding less frequently or at lower cost. As a result, they will choose a higher payout rate, which makes dividends useful as a signal.

One implication of this explanation is that the level of dividends is much less sensitive to the relative value of dividends and capital gains in the market—the lower valuation of dividends is only part of the cost of paying dividends. Once dividends are used as a signal of "normal" earning power, firms are reluctant to cut dividends in response to a temporary drop in earnings (or to finance a large investment), since the dividend cut might be misinterpreted by the market.

60. See Sudipto Bhattacharya, "Imperfect Information, Dividend Policy, and 'The Bird in the Hand' Fallacy," *Bell Journal of Economics,* vol. 10 (Spring 1979), pp. 259–70.

For this signaling argument to be convincing, however, several questions must be answered. First, are there cheaper ways to signal profits than paying dividends? For example, commitments to repurchase equity or debt would put the same financial pressure on the firm and provide the same signal, yet they appear to be less expensive to investors since they imply lower tax costs. However, when the tax costs are lower, firms have to signal more aggressively to distinguish themselves from each other, which implies extra costs resulting from a drop in retained earnings. It is not necessarily true that the total costs of the signal are lower when tax costs are lower. Second, increases in dividends that signal higher profits result in an immediate capital gain, yet the costs occur gradually and may extend into the future. There may thus be an incentive for current shareholders to signal falsely to induce an increase in the share price and then to sell out before the costs are recognized by the market. The taxation of capital gains at realization could dampen incentives for such speculation. More important, the threat of legal sanctions is undoubtedly a strong disincentive against such manipulation.

In spite of the progress made, a full explanation of why dividends are paid is still lacking. But, there seem to be enough approaches to explaining the existence of dividends to prevent the fact that they do exist from undermining confidence in the general model of the firm described above.

Incentives for Saving and Investment

With no uncertainty, the firm would invest until the marginal product of capital equaled the market interest rate, since it has the alternative of investing in financial assets that earn the market interest rate yet receive the same tax treatment. When there is uncertainty, however, the marginal investment financed by debt must earn enough both to compensate equity holders for the risk of the investment and to offset the added bankruptcy costs arising from such debt-financed investment.[61]

Alternatively, if the investment is financed by equity, the return after

---

61. In the capital asset pricing model, if $\alpha = 1$ and the return on bonds and on the riskless asset receive the same tax treatment so that the α_b weight on each is the same, a bond-financed investment will be valued at par by the market when

$$(6) \qquad (\bar{s} - r)(1 - \tau) + \alpha_b r = \alpha_b r_z + \beta_i(g_M + d_M - \alpha_b r_z) + C_D.$$

Here r is the interest rate on the bond. The term C_D captures the effect on bankruptcy costs of a dollar of debt-financed investment. Solving for $\bar{s}$ gives

$$(7) \qquad \bar{s} = r - (\alpha_b/1 - \tau)(r - r_z) + (\beta_i/1 - \tau)(g_M + d_M - \alpha_b r_z) + C_D/(1 - \tau).$$

The second term captures the more favorable tax treatment of the risk premium in bonds than in equity.

corporation tax and after personal taxes on dividends and capital gains must earn the risk-free interest rate after tax plus enough to compensate for the risk of the investment. Nevertheless, there is an offsetting gain because of the reduction in bankruptcy costs implied by the decreased debt–equity ratio.[62]

At the optimal debt–equity ratio, both expressions will be equal.[63] The implied marginal product of capital will now exceed the value it would have if there were no taxes but the same market interest rate. However, the tax-induced distortion will not be as large as assumed in many earlier studies.[64] To the extent that debt finance is used and to the extent that the higher personal tax on the returns from debt than on those from equity offsets the effects of the corporation tax, the distortion is reduced.[65]

62. Under the same assumptions as in footnote 61, an equity-financed investment will break even when

(8) $$\bar{s} = \alpha_b r_z (1 - \tau) + [\beta_i(g_M + d_M - \alpha_b r_z)]/(1 - \tau) + C_E/(1 - \tau).$$

Here C_E captures the effect on bankruptcy costs of a dollar of equity-financed investment. (At least the decrease in the debt–equity ratio implied by such an investment would have a negative effect on bankruptcy costs.)

63. At the optimal debt–equity ratio, the firm would not care whether it financed a small investment by debt or by equity, implying that equations 6 and 7 are satisfied simultaneously. Subtracting one equation from the other then implies:

(9) $$r[\alpha_b - (1 - \tau)] = C_D - C_E.$$

But this equation is identical to equation 5, which characterized the optimal amount of debt when $\alpha = 1$. The right side indicates the effect on bankruptcy costs of adding a dollar of debt and subtracting a dollar of equity, holding the capital stock constant, so it is identical to $c(D/K)$.

64. For example, Arnold C. Harberger, *Taxation and Welfare* (Little, Brown, 1974); Martin Feldstein, "The Welfare Cost of Capital Income Taxation," *Journal of Political Economy*, vol. 86 (April 1978), pt. 2, pp. S29–S52; and John B. Shoven and John Whalley, "A General Equilibrium Calculation of the Effects of Differential Taxation of Income from Capital in the U.S.," *Journal of Public Economics*, vol. 1 (November 1972), pp. 281–321.

65. In equilibrium, the firm will finance γ percent of any new investment by debt, where γ is chosen so that the debt–capital ratio will continue to satisfy equation 9. Taking a weighted average of equations 7 and 8, we find:

(10) $$\bar{s} = \alpha_b r_z/1 - \tau - (\gamma r/1 - \tau)[\alpha_b - (1 - \tau)] + (\beta_i/1 - \tau)(g_M + d_M - \alpha_b r_z)$$
$$+ [\gamma C_D + (1 - \gamma)C_E]/1 - \tau.$$

For no distortion to exist, the marginal investment ought to earn the risk-free rate plus an amount just sufficient to compensate for the social costs of the risks and possible bankruptcy costs created by the investment. If the marginal costs of risk-bearing by the government were the same as the marginal costs of risks borne by the private sector (as would be the case if risk was allocated efficiently across investors), the expected bankruptcy costs would measure the social costs of risk-bearing. There is no presumption, however, that the last two terms of equation 10

Debt–Capital Ratios in Practice

In theory, debt–capital ratios are influenced both by taxes and by expected bankruptcy costs: tax implications suggest high debt ratios, and the possibility of costly bankruptcy pushes in the opposite direction. In this section, actual debt ratios are examined to see whether they are consistent with theory.

Construction of a Time Series

To construct a time series of the ratio of debt to total capital, a sample of 2,000 nonfinancial companies was obtained from Standard and Poor's Compustat tapes; the data cover 1957 through 1978. In this series, which is shown in table 1, debt consists of the sum of long-term debt plus current liabilities, total capital equals the sum of debt and equity, and equity consists of the sum of the common and preferred stock and surplus accounts. Ratios were calculated at both book and market values. Since many companies on the Compustat tape did not have data for all years, the ratios given in table 1 are not for the same companies in every year.[66]

---

will properly capture the social costs of increased bankruptcy risk, though the effect of pure expansion of the firm on bankruptcy costs would not be very large. If the expansion does not affect bankruptcy costs, the only distortion is that created by the tax structure. This is measured by the deviation of the first term in equation 10 from r_z. Simple algebra implies that this deviation equals:

$$(11) \qquad [\tau - (1 - \alpha_b)](r_z - \gamma r)/(1 - \tau).$$

The equivalent distortions in Harberger's formulation is $\tau r_z / 1 - \tau$. For reasonable parameter values, the distortion here is less than a third as large.

66. The book values of debt and equity capital were obtained directly from the tapes; the market values were estimated. The market value of common stock of each company was obtained simply by multiplying the number of shares outstanding by the price at the end of each year. Serious estimation problems, however, arose in calculating the value of preferred stock and debt. Fortunately, a study by von Furstenberg, Malkiel, and Watson, sponsored by the American Council of Life Insurance, from which market values could be estimated was available before publication. George M. von Furstenberg, Burton G. Malkiel, and Harry S. Watson, "The Distribution of Investment Between Industries: A Microeconomic Application of the 'q' Ratio," in von Furstenberg, ed., *Capital, Efficiency, and Growth* (Ballinger, 1980), pp. 395–460. In this study, a ratio of market to book value for debt capital was estimated for two-digit industries by means of a sampling of actual bond prices for companies in the year-end editions of *Moody's Bond Record*. Book values were converted to market values by multiplying the book value figures by the ratio for the two-digit industry to which the company belonged. Similar techniques were used to estimate the value of preferred stock. The value of the preferred stock for each of the companies in the sample was estimated by multiplying that company's preferred dividends as recorded on the Compustat tapes by the reciprocal of that year's dividend yield on preferred stock for the industry to which the company belonged.

Table 1. Estimated Ratios of Debt to Total Capital, Nonfinancial Corporations, 1957–78

Year	Unadjusted ratios		Ratios adjusted to common number of firms		Ratios adjusted to common number of firms and including leases and pensions, book value	Ratios with total capital adjusted to replacement cost	
	Book value (1)	Market value (2)	Book value (3)	Market value (4)	(5)	Book value (6)	Market value (7)
1957	0.219	0.158	0.241	0.212	n.a.	0.203	0.187
1958	0.218	0.123	0.243	0.171	n.a.	0.209	0.197
1959	0.213	0.112	0.237	0.156	n.a.	0.208	0.193
1960	0.225	0.124	0.242	0.168	n.a.	0.219	0.205
1961	0.230	0.116	0.244	0.158	n.a.	0.229	0.214
1962	0.234	0.173	0.249	0.180	n.a.	0.237	0.225
1963	0.234	0.160	0.246	0.165	n.a.	0.245	0.233
1964	0.239	0.158	0.247	0.157	n.a.	0.248	0.236
1965	0.258	0.157	0.262	0.159	n.a.	0.256	0.244
1966	0.286	0.191	0.288	0.192	n.a.	0.267	0.247
1967	0.310	0.181	0.311	0.181	n.a.	0.279	0.248
1968	0.328	0.179	0.330	0.179	n.a.	0.279	0.231
1969	0.348	0.213	0.349	0.213	n.a.	0.286	0.233
1970	0.370	0.228	0.372	0.224	n.a.	0.291	0.225
1971	0.367	0.234	0.369	0.234	n.a.	0.300	0.235
1972	0.367	0.227	0.367	0.226	n.a.	0.302	0.249
1973	0.367	0.280	0.367	0.279	0.497	0.307	0.267
1974	0.381	0.363	0.381	0.362	0.511	0.306	0.260
1975	0.375	0.316	0.374	0.316	0.499	0.300	0.248
1976	0.362	0.293	0.362	0.293	0.485	0.286	0.258
1977	0.358	0.321	0.358	0.321	0.473	0.293	0.270
1978	0.350	0.313	0.358	0.325	0.462	0.295	0.255

Source: Based on data in Standard and Poor's Compustat tapes. For an explanation, see George M. von Furstenberg, Burton G. Malkiel, and Harry S. Watson, "The Distribution of Investment Between Industries: A Microeconomic Application of the 'q' Ratio," in von Furstenberg, ed., *Capital, Efficiency, and Growth* (Ballinger, 1980).
n.a. Not available.

The book and market value estimates are shown in columns 1 and 2 of table 1. Since the data in each year are not based on the same numbers of observations, these estimates may be misleading. For example, the sample may include an increasing number of high-debt firms over time,[67] which would lead to an upward bias in the trend of recorded debt ratios. To deal with this problem, an adjusted series—shown in columns 3 and 4—was calculated on the basis of the companies for which data were available in successive years.[68] It appears that the time trend in the original figures did have a slight upward bias.

Column 5 presents adjusted debt to total capitalization ratios that include the values of noncapitalized leases and unfunded pension liabilities in debt figures. These were available on the Compustat tapes only after 1972.

A series of debt ratios that differ in several respects from those in the first five columns is given in columns 6 and 7. First, all nonfinancial corporations are included, rather than only those available on the Compustat tapes. Second, debt is equal to the sum of all short- and long-term interest-bearing liabilities less interest-bearing liquid assets.[69] Third, the ratio is figured against the replacement cost of assets including net fixed capital stock, land, and inventories.[70] Fourth, the debt at market value was obtained by assuming an average maturity of corporate liabilities and imputing a change in market value from recorded changes in market interest rates.

Long-Term Trends of the Aggregate Debt Ratios

Table 1 shows a fairly consistent pattern irrespective of the method by which the debt ratios were measured. Debt ratios rise until the early 1970s and then stabilize or fall. The market value series tends to rise

67. High-debt firms in earlier years would be less likely to survive to 1978, so would be included in the sample less frequently.

68. The levels of book and market debt and total capitalization were measured in the year in which the number of companies with both debt and equity measures was the largest. The growth rates in the two measures between any two consecutive years were estimated from the set of companies with all data available in both years. Columns 3 and 4 report the ratio of the two resulting figures. The adjusted series provides a better estimate of changes in debt–capital ratios since it assumes merely a common rate of change in debt and total capitalization across firms rather than a common value of debt–capital ratios across firms.

69. These data, estimated from the flow-of-funds accounts of the Federal Reserve Board, are from von Furstenberg, "Corporate Investment."

70. The latter figures were obtained from the Bureau of Economic Analysis, Department of Commerce, and were also included in ibid.

somewhat less than the book value series until 1973. In 1974, however, the ratio of debt to market value rises sharply because of the collapse in the equity market. While some of this rise was reversed as equity markets recovered during the late 1970s, aggregate debt ratios at market values were still almost double their 1957 level in 1978. When the series are adjusted to a common number of firms (columns 3, 4, and 5), the rise in debt ratios is slightly smaller; when they are adjusted to replacement costs, the rise is smaller still (columns 6 and 7). This is so because the replacement value of corporate assets rose sharply with the high inflation rates of the 1970s.

The calculations in column 5 deserve special note. When the data are adjusted for leases and pensions, the fall in the debt ratio after 1974 is much sharper than in the other book value series in columns 1 and 3. Apparently, lease financing became far less desirable in the late 1970s following a ruling of the Financial Accounting Standards Board that changed the reporting requirements for leases. As a result, firms tended to cut back leases more than ordinary debt.[71] These ratios suggest that there was a sharper cutback in debt than is revealed by the reported figures, which do not include lease financing.

The data in table 1 are easily reconciled with the predictions of the capital asset pricing model developed in the previous section. We found that the tax incentive to shift a dollar into debt, everything else being constant, was proportional to the nominal interest rate.[72] Therefore, when the nominal interest rate increases, the firm has the incentive to increase its debt–value ratio until, in equilibrium, the effects on bankruptcy costs of any additional switch into debt are equally higher. Historically, the movement of the nominal interest rate has closely paralleled the reported movement in the debt–value ratio, just as the theory predicts.

Expectations about future tax rates could also be expected to alter the equilibrium debt–equity ratios. During the postwar period, it became increasingly clear that corporation tax rates, a legacy of the 1940s, would remain high. As this expectation solidified, the use of debt finance should have increased.

71. This conjecture is confirmed by examining the behavior of the subset of Compustat companies reporting leases. From 1974 to 1978 there was little change in the debt ratio not including leases and pensions: the 1974 ratio was 0.393 and the 1978 ratio was 0.384. When leases and pensions are included, however, the ratio falls sharply, from 0.511 in 1974 to 0.462 in 1978. The chief cause of the decline was the behavior of the lease accounts.

72. See footnote 49, above.

Table 2. Average Annual Default Rates for Corporate Bonds, by Decade, 1900-77[a]
Percent

Period	Default rate
1900–09	0.9
1910–19	2.0
1920–29	1.0
1930–39	3.2
1940–49	0.4
1950–59	0.04
1960–69	0.03
1970–77	0.21

Sources: 1900–65, Thomas R. Atkinson, with Elizabeth T. Simpson, *Trends in Corporate Bond Quality* (National Bureau of Economic Research, 1967); 1966–77, Smith Barney, Harris Upham and Co., "Trends in Corporate Bond Quality" (New York, various issues).

a. The default rates are percentages of the par values of bonds not in default at the beginning of a given year that went into default during the year.

Also, as the degree of uncertainty in the economy declines (increases), we ought to expect an increase (decrease) in debt–value ratios. During the 1950s and early 1960s, it was generally accepted that deep depressions such as that of the 1930s were highly unlikely. Indeed, by the mid-1960s financial analysts probably had become overconfident about the stability of the U.S. economy and the ability of the fiscal and monetary authorities to "fine tune" away even mild recessions. These developments should have increased debt–capital ratios.

The cutback in the debt ratios following the 1973–74 shocks to the economy also seem consistent with the theory. Few people believed in the 1960s that the economy would suffer a 9 percent unemployment rate or that the inflation would rise to double digit rates. Fewer still believed that both could occur simultaneously. The depth of the 1974–75 recession made it clear that the economy was not as stable as had been believed. The higher inflation rates of the 1970s further increased risk perceptions. High levels of inflation are associated with greater variance in the rate of inflation and with a greater dispersion of relative prices.[73]

These conjectures on changes in expectations about the stability of the economy are consistent with data on actual default rates of corporate bonds from 1900 through 1977 (see table 2). In the 1950s and 1960s default rates fell considerably below those recorded early in the century.

73. On both accounts, one would expect that a given debt ratio would carry an increased probability of bankruptcy. Hence it is possible that the debt ratios existing in 1973–74 were considered higher than optimal for the more unstable economic environment.

During the 1970s, however, they rose (though not to the levels of the earlier years), suggesting that bankruptcy costs increased as the performance of the economy deteriorated.

Cross-sectional Examination of Debt Ratios

Our theory suggests that individual companies with the greatest inherent risk of bankruptcy should have the lowest debt ratios. If the theory is correct, companies with the greatest instability of cash flow should experience liquidity problems and thus fail to meet debt-service requirements the most frequently. The hypothesis to be tested is whether the debt ratio of particular companies is directly related to the variance of their cash flows.

To make this test, we again turned to the sample of nonfinancial corporations on Standard and Poor's Compustat tape. Cash flow was defined as earnings available for common equity plus interest plus depreciation and other noncash charges. The variance of cash flow was measured by taking the standard error of the estimate from a regression of cash flow on a constant and a linear time trend fitted to ten or fifteen years of data. The variance of the cash flow was divided by the average capital value of the firm so as to normalize the instability measure. Debt ratios were calculated at both book and market.

Table 3 gives some representative results from this test. In general,

Table 3. Variance of Cash Flow of Nonfinancial Corporations, Selected Periods, 1963–77

Period	Measure of capital value	Number of observations	Coefficient of variance of normalized cash flow[a]	Correlation coefficient
1963–77	Book value	1,501	−0.97 (−3.66)	0.09
1963–77	Market value	1,730	−0.43 (−2.00)	0.05
1963–72	Book value	1,069	−1.02 (−3.91)	0.12
1968–77	Book value	1,299	−2.39 (−6.81)	0.19

Source: Based on data for nonfinancial corporations in Standard and Poor's Compustat tape.
a. Normalized cash flow is the variance of the cash flow divided by the average capital value of the firm over the period. Figures in parentheses are *t*-values.

debt ratios are negatively related to the variance of cash flow; in other words, firms with greater instability of cash flow do have lower debt-to-total-capitalization ratios.[74] The relationship was a bit stronger in the ten years from 1968 to 1977 than in the ten years from 1963 to 1972. It was also stronger when debt ratios were measured at book rather than at market values. While low correlations and small t-values (resulting in part from measurement error in our estimate of the variability of cash flow) indicate that the proxy for default risk used in the test explains only a small portion of the variation in debt ratios among firms, the results are at least consistent with the theory.

Efficiency Implications of the Existing Tax Structure

This section estimates the costs of the distortions of debt-capital, investment, dividend payout, and individual portfolio decisions resulting from the tax system.[75]

The Costs of Bankruptcy

Reliable studies of the costs of bankruptcy do not exist. The main problem is that data are not available. The Securities and Exchange Commission does not keep track of bankruptcy costs in any way that is generally accessible. Some private lenders have records that show some, but not all, of the costs of a limited number of bankruptcies with which they have been associated.[76] To obtain an order of magnitude, we estimate the costs of bankruptcy directly on the basis of a detailed examination of the costs of four recent bankruptcies and then estimate these costs indirectly using the capital asset pricing model.

74. The book value equations suggest a range of variation in D/V ratios of about 0.05 for deviations of σ^2/V plus or minus one standard deviation from its mean.

75. Measuring the cost of the distortions in saving decisions is beyond the scope of this chapter and is not examined here. For discussions of saving distortions, see Feldstein, "Welfare Cost of Capital Income Taxation"; Michael J. Boskin, "Taxation, Saving and the Rate of Interest," *Journal of Political Economy*, vol. 86 (April 1978), pt. 2, pp. S3–S28; and E. Philip Howrey and Saul H. Hymans, "The Measurement and Determination of Loanable-Funds Saving," *BPEA, 3:1978*, pp. 655–705.

76. Even if full data were available, however, it would be difficult to decide what costs ought to be included. For example, should the costs of a consultant who was called in to liquidate a number of stores in the bankruptcy of one supermarket chain be included as an administrative cost? This consultant may have increased the liquidation value of the stores enough to make his net value positive rather than negative.

DIRECT MEASUREMENT OF BANKRUPTCY COSTS. Cost data for four recent bankruptcies were obtained from files of two large institutional lenders that contained information on their own costs as well as on the costs of other lenders in cases where a consortium of institutions joined together to negotiate settlements. Certain general legal and administrative costs, such as trustees' fees of outside legal counsel, were obtained from the files of the private lenders and the Securities and Exchange Commission. However, the costs incurred by other private lenders were not available. It was assumed, therefore, that the ratio of identifiable costs incurred by these two lenders (both their own costs and their share of the estimated general legal and administrative costs) to their holdings of the firm's liabilities equaled the ratio of total legal and administrative costs to the firm's total liabilities. Table 4 shows these costs as a percentage of total liabilities for each of the four firms.

These cost estimates are probably biased downward for a number of reasons. First, all disbursements are not included; in some cases, continuing litigation is involved and substantial additional legal fees are anticipated. Moreover, the time and expenses of the private lenders' internal legal and financial staff, which may have exceeded the cost of outside expert counsel, are not included in the estimates. Finally, the prepetition liabilities significantly overstate the true value of the companies.

Table 4. Estimates of Identifiable Legal and Administrative Costs of Four Bankruptcies

Business	Date	Prepetition liabilities (dollars)	Costs as percent of liabilities
Manufacturer of steel products[a]	June 1977[b]	184,000,000	2.48
Manufacturer of ice cream and furniture[c]	June 1970– August 1978	43,000,000	8.90
Manufacturer of photo-typesetting equipment[a]	November 1974[b]	32,800,000	2.65
Operator of discount department stores[a]	November 1973– May 1975	90,800,000	6.25

Source: Authors' estimates based on files of two institutional lenders and the Securities and Exchange Commission.
a. Chapter XI bankruptcy.
b. Not yet complete.
c. Chapter X bankruptcy.

If the value of the settlements is only about one-third of the value of prepetition liabilities (a reasonable assumption in these cases), the estimated percentage costs would be three times those shown in table 4.

The case showing the highest cost percentage in the table illustrates that firms in bankruptcy often do not choose an early liquidation, even when it is in the best interest of the bondholders. In this case, the private lenders believed it was in their best interest to liquidate the firm immediately to maximize the recovery for the holders of the senior securities. The trustee refused to formulate a plan of reorganization until certain litigation against the company was resolved. This took three years and resulted in a $2 million liability. About two years later, the trustee filed a plan that was rejected by the creditors. At the end of almost eight years, an acceptable plan was finally approved. As a result, legal fees ate up a substantial share of the value of the assets that were available at the time the firm went into bankruptcy.[77]

The legal and administrative costs may have been only a small fraction of the total costs involved. In some cases the firm was unable to obtain trade credit and found its normal sources of supplies of inventories shut off. The companies themselves were often judged to be unreliable suppliers with an attendant unfavorable effect on sales. The onset of financial difficulty often led to a loss of key personnel, who preferred to work for a company with better long-term prospects. Finally, the management of these firms found it almost impossible to devote time and energy to business matters.

The case of the operator of discount department stores illustrates the typical pattern when discount chains go into bankruptcy. Charge account customers stop paying their bills, impairing the quality of the receivables. Employees walk off with merchandise from the shelves. The chain typically finds it impossible to obtain trade credit, which severely impairs its ability to finance its inventories. The very fact of bankruptcy can thus cause a dramatic change in the firm's stream of income and cash flow.

Court reorganizations, in contrast to liquidations, often involve a substantial transfer of claims from senior bondholders to subordinated bondholders and equity holders. One reason for this court bias is that the equity holders, the trade creditors, and the trustees are usually local people, but the senior debt holders are from outside the community. An-

---

77. One might speculate whether there was any significance in the fact that the trustee was a man in his sixties who was receiving $100,000 in trustee fees, the highest salary he had ever received.

other is that management typically owns substantial amounts of the equity and the courts often decide that management should have a continuing stake in the company after reorganization, which would provide an incentive to perform well. Still another reason is that the courts often feel the lender can afford to sustain some of the loss in order to permit the debtor to survive.

While the magnitude of this transfer cannot be estimated, there is conclusive evidence that such a transfer does in fact exist in court-ordered reorganizations. In a sample of recent bankruptcies (see table 5) the estimated value of the securities distributed to the senior debt holders was substantially less than their total claim, but subordinated debt holders received sizable settlements. Strict applications of me-first rules would imply that the senior debt holders should receive everything of value the corporation is able to distribute; nevertheless, the equity owners recovered something.

The last column of table 5 gives the percent of the total claims recovered by the senior bondholders on the assumptions that the securities received were of the highest quality and that the interest payments would be at the AA long-term corporate bond rate for newly issued securities. Since the securities received were in fact risky, it is clear that the senior bondholders received far less than the book amount of their claim.

The United Merchants case represents a clear departure from the me-first axiom. The senior debt holders received 35 percent of their claims in cash and 65 percent in notes. The subordinated debt holders received no immediate cash but were paid 100 percent of their claims in debt securities. The terms of the debt securities received by the subordinated debt holders were much more favorable than those delivered to the senior debt holders. The subordinated debt holders received their original interest rate and were entitled to full amortization by 1990, whereas the notes delivered to the senior lenders accrued no interest until July 1, 1985, and did not finally mature until 2025. In addition, the restructured subordinated debt was elevated to rank pari passu with the restructured privately held senior debt.

Senior debt holders agree to less than complete recoveries in such organizations for a number of reasons. First, the timing and nature of a future plan are uncertain. In the United Merchants case, a majority of the senior lenders felt that, unsatisfactory though the plan was, it was preferable to the unknown terms and timing of a settlement by independent trustee under chapter X of the Bankruptcy Act of 1898 as amended. The rule of thumb used by one major institutional lender is "Our institution is willing to give up 20 percent of what we should get on our bonds in order to keep the company out of the courts, in which case we might lose 30 percent or more." This 30 percent estimate is made up of 10 percent in administrative and legal fees and 20 percent via transfers from the bondholders to the equity holders.

Second, acceptance of a compromise reorganization plan avoids highly complex litigation that, if prosecuted, would take many years to resolve and would impair the business operations and growth prospects of the company. This was the situation in the Equity Funding case.

Third, the legal foundations for subordination have been perceived to be cloudy, and court practices thus influence informal reorganizations. In informal as well as formal reorganizations, there is typically a substantial "give-up" from the senior bondholders to subordinated bondholders and equity owners. Sometimes reorganizations can be arranged with little cost other than the give-up by the bondholders.

Even when a reorganization is easily effected without a bankruptcy proceeding, substantial legal costs may still be incurred later. A case in point concerns a manufacturer of men's clothing. This company's banks and major institutional lender entered into an intercreditors' agreement in 1977 that reorganized the various creditors' claims and provided for additional bank financing. Bankruptcy was not involved. The group is now being sued for allegedly controlling the company's board of directors and operating the firm in a manner deleterious to the interests of the company's shareholders. The damages claimed in the suit are almost three times as large as the total liabilities and capital of the company at the time the intercreditors' group was formed. Thus far, the legal expenses incurred and committed by the major institutional lender amount to almost 10 percent of the total loan of that lender.

In summary, reorganizations are typically less costly than bankruptcy and, if the parties agree, can be carried out with minimal transactions costs. However, the terms of the settlement usually require that the bondholders give up a significant percentage of the face value of their bonds to obtain the agreement of the management and the equity holders. Moreover, when disagreements arise, reorganization may be as costly as bankruptcy proceedings. Finally, with different classes of bondholders, it is often impossible to carry out an informal reorganization. Sometimes bondholders will prefer bankruptcy to reorganization because the financially distressed firm may be able to obtain new financing only by going

Table 5. Distribution of Securities in Recent Reorganizations

| Bankrupt firm and type of claim | Amount of claim (millions of dollars) | Percent of claim received in | | | Percent of equity in postplan company | Interest allowed | Interest rate (percent) | Year of completion of payment under plan | Value of securities paid to senior bondholder if riskless (percent) |
		Cash	Notes	Equity					
Colwell Mortgage Trust[a]									
Senior funded institutional debt	112.9	0	100	0	0	no	8	1984	95
Public subordinated debt	29.6	40	0	60	51[b]	no	n.a.	n.a.	…
American Export Industries, Inc.[a,c]									
Senior secured funded debt	10.7	80	0	0	0	yes	n.a.	1978	80
Public subordinated debt	62.9	27	0	0	0	yes	n.a.	1978	…
United Merchants and Manufacturers[a,d]									
Senior funded institutional debt	320.5	35	65	0	0	no	9[e]	2025	68
Public subordinated debt	18.5	0	100	0	0	yes	4[e]	1990	…

Daylin, Inc.[a,f]									
Senior funded institutional debt	68.8	11	76	13	15	yes	8	1999	n.a.
Public subordinated debt	32.4	0	21	79	53	yes	8	1999	...
Equity Funding Corp. of America[g,h]									
Senior funded institutional debt	44.4	0–4	0	76	39	yes	n.a.	n.a.	n.a.
Public subordinated debt	62.4	0	0	32	23	yes	n.a.	n.a.	...
Interstate Stores, Inc.[i,j]									
Senior funded institutional debt	90.9	52	40	0	0	yes	8	1985	97
Public subordinated debt	23.8	0	0	100	27.5[b]	yes	n.a.	n.a.	...

Source: Compiled by the authors.

n.a. Not available.

a. Filed under chapter XI of the Uniform Bankruptcy Act of 1978.

b. Voting stocks.

c. Claims filed July 12, 1977, and discharged August 29, 1978.

d. Claims filed July 12, 1977, and discharged June 30, 1978. Total claims amounted to $505.3 million.

e. As of September 1, 1985.

f. Claims filed February 26, 1975, and discharged August 29, 1976. Total claims amounted to $159.0 million.

g. Filed under chapter X of the Bankruptcy Act of 1898 as amended.

h. Claims filed August 4, 1973, and discharged March 31, 1976. Total claims amounted to $380.9 million.

i. Filed under chapters X and XI.

j. Claims filed May 22, 1974, transferred from chapter X to chapter XI, and substantially consummated but not yet officially discharged August 8, 1978.

through a formal bankruptcy proceeding. Such financing is often available because the new lenders can obtain a priority lien on the assets of the firm.

It appears, then, that by increasing the likelihood of financial distress, a highly levered capital structure may impose large and unpredictable costs on the firm, its security owners, and its lenders. These considerations help explain the current practice of bondholders to set fairly stringent debt limits. Even if the firm was willing to increase its leverage ratio, it might be unable to do so because of restrictions imposed by bondholders or because of the unwillingness of prospective bondholders to lend to the company.

INDIRECT MEASURE OF BANKRUPTCY COSTS. Not all efficiency costs of a high debt–equity ratio occur during formal bankruptcy. Firms in financial distress experience a variety of impediments that hinder their business activity and affect their operating earnings. These include difficulties in purchasing inventory, selling products, and retaining key employees. The firm may find its flexibility limited even before signs of financial distress occur. For example, a firm that had borrowed up to the limits imposed by its lenders could be forced to pass up a profitable investment opportunity because equity financing was the only alternative and the registration requirements of the Securities and Exchange Commission make this a time-consuming process. And when a firm's debt–equity ratio is high, the managers, acting in the interests of shareholders, face distorted investment incentives because of the opportunity to pass on possible losses to debt holders.[78] (To the extent that bondholders anticipate such behavior and charge an appropriate interest rate, shareholders themselves pay this efficiency cost.) Thus substantial costs may be incurred even if the firm never experiences a liquidity crisis.

Such costs cannot be measured directly. However, the total costs arising from extra debt, including the costs described in the paragraph above, can be approximated through the use of the first-order conditions for an optimal debt–capital ratio. As explained, when considering new financing, a firm will compare the tax advantages of having a dollar more debt instead of a dollar more equity with the implied increase in possible bankruptcy costs. In making this comparison, the costs of additional debt will

---

78. Covenants in the debt contract can to a degree prevent such behavior, but they are at best only partly effective.

Figure 1. Relationship between Marginal Efficiency Costs and Amount of Debt Financing

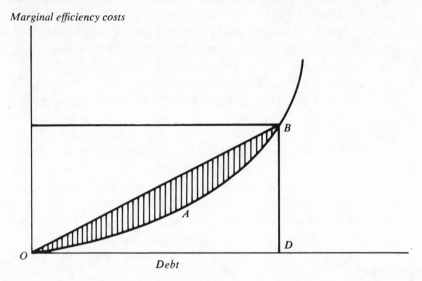

Marginal efficiency costs

Debt

include the costs just described as well as the more obvious costs of financial distress such as those measured in the preceding section.

Figure 1 illustrates how the total efficiency costs of bankruptcy can be measured. The efficiency costs of adding the first dollar of debt are very small, but the incremental costs of adding debt are higher as the amount of debt already outstanding is higher. If the curve *OAB* in figure 1 shows this rise in marginal costs, the area *OABD* measures the total efficiency costs created by a levered financial structure with debt *D*. To approximate the area of *OABD*, we use the area of the triangle *OBD*. Since firms with relatively unlevered capital structures run little risk of bankruptcy, the curve *OAB* will normally be convex. Thus the approximation of *OABD* by *OBD* will overstate the costs by the shaded area *OAB* in the figure.[79]

To get an idea of the quantitative importance of the efficiency costs, a value for *BD* is needed. Recall that, when the amount of debt is in equilibrium, the tax advantages, c^*, of additional debt and the incremen-

---

79. However, this estimate omits costs incurred by existing bondholders and other social costs of bankruptcy (disruption in trade or employment), thus offsetting the overstatement of costs in the approximation of *OABD* by *OBD*.

tal bankruptcy cost disadvantages will be equal. But the tax advantages of debt have already been approximated (see footnote 49). Inserting plausible parameter values for 1975 gives an estimate for *BD* of 0.0145,[80] or about a 1.4-cent tax incentive per year to replace a dollar of equity with a dollar of debt. (Compared with the *pretax* carrying costs of debt of 6.3 cents per year, this tax incentive is very large.) Then, given von Furstenberg's estimate for corporate debt of $440 billion in 1975,[81] the estimated efficiency cost (triangle *OBD* in figure 1) is $3.2 billion. This represents the annual efficiency costs arising from the existence of risky debt.

It should be reemphasized that this estimate of the annual efficiency costs is rough. As a result of the triangular approximation used, the estimate probably overstates the area *OABD* in figure 1. However, area *OABD* represents only the costs borne by the coalition of equity holders and the junior bondholders. True social costs of bankruptcy and the moral hazard costs associated with risky debt may well be much larger than *OABD*. Moreover, the estimate of the tax advantage of debt versus equity financing used in constructing the estimate of bankruptcy costs is imprecise.

Whatever the precision of the estimate, the direct legal and administrative costs of bankruptcy seem to be a small fraction of the total efficiency costs of risky debt. In 1975, for example, the total liabilities of bankrupt firms were $4.4 billion. For any plausible fraction of this total that is lost through bankruptcy costs (which was estimated to be no larger than 10 percent in the preceding section), the more obvious costs must be small relative to the total efficiency costs.

For purposes of comparison, our estimates of the total costs of bankruptcy are less than half of one percent of the gross national product in 1975, so they are small in an aggregate sense. However, corporation tax revenues in 1975 were $40.6 billion, so the excess burden costs could be about 10 percent of corporate revenues.

---

80. Equation 5 states that, in equilibrium,

$$c(D/K) = r[\tau - (1 - \alpha_b)] + (1 - \alpha)(1 - \tau)pr.$$

The right side provides a measure for *BD*, the tax advantage of debt, interpreted as an annual flow. Gordon and Bradford measure $\alpha = 1$ (see footnote 59). We then assume that $\tau = 0.48$ and $r = 0.063$ (the commercial paper rate in 1975). Finally, we argue in appendix B that α_b is about 0.75. Together these imply that *BD* in 1975 was about 0.0145.

81. Von Furstenberg, "Corporate Investment," p. 355, table 1.

Efficiency Costs of Inefficient Risk-Bearing

As already noted, the variation in individual tax rates implies an inefficiency in the allocation of risk across investors. In this section, the
order of magnitude of these costs is approximated.

Efficiency in the allocation of marketed lotteries implies that each person at the margin demands the same risk premium in return for absorbing
a given risk. With the current tax structure, in return for absorbing the
after-tax uncertainty in a dollar of equity in a given firm, each investor
would in equilibrium just be willing to accept the after-tax risk premium.
But because of the variation in individual marginal tax rates, the risk
premium per unit of risk will vary across investors.[82] This implies that
risk is allocated inefficiently—the allocation can be improved by trans-
ferring risk from those charging a large risk premium to those charging a
small one.

Figure 2 illustrates the relationship implied by the capital asset pricing
model between the risk premium received by an individual per unit of risk
and the individual's marginal tax rate.[83] Those with the lowest risk premium (those holding "too little" equity) are in the highest tax brackets;
to them, tax-free bonds are extremely attractive. Those in the zero tax
bracket also have little equity (and a low risk premium) because they
receive little advantage from the relatively high capital gains component
in equity. Those who are indifferent to whether they own taxable or tax-
free bonds have the largest risk premium.

The cost of this variation in the marginal risk premium among investors is difficult to estimate. For a marginal reallocation of a given risk
from an investor with a high risk premium to one with a low risk premium,
the efficiency gain is the difference in their risk premiums. In the example
in figure 2, the maximum such gain would be 34 percent of the riskless
market interest rate. The total gain from reallocation would be the sum
of all marginal gains accrued during the process of moving from the
initial equilibrium to a new equilibrium in which all individuals charge
the same risk premium for each risk.

---

82. The investor will be willing to absorb $1 - c$ percent of the uncertainty in a
dollar of equity in return for an after-tax risk premium $(1 - c)\bar{g} + (1 - m)\bar{d} -$
$\max[(1 - m)r_z, r_f]$. The risk premium per unit of risk is therefore $\bar{g} + [(1 - m)/$
$(1 - c)]\bar{d} - [1/(1 - c)] \max[(1 - m)r_z, r_f]$.

83. In graphing the expression derived in footnote 82, it is assumed that $c = 0.2m$,
$r_f = 0.75r_z$, $\bar{d} = 0.6r_z$, and $\bar{g} = r_z$.

Figure 2. Relationship between the Risk Premium and the Relative After-Tax Value of Dividends and Capital Gains

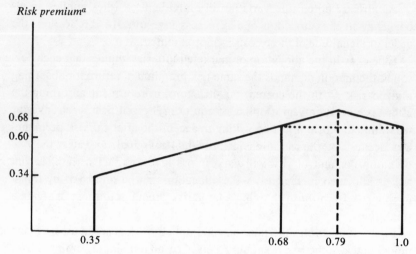

a. The risk premium is expressed as a fraction of $\dot{r}_z$.

The efficiency gains from this reallocation are estimated in appendix B under a set of simplifying assumptions.[84] If the riskless interest rate is 8 percent, the efficiency costs from the inefficient allocation of the risk in the $630 billion of corporate equity outstanding at the end of 1975 was $44 million.[85] Thus to the extent that the parameters chosen are reasonable, efficiency costs from inefficient risk-bearing appear to be small.

Efficiency Costs of the Dividend Payout Distortion

The effective personal income tax on dividends is much higher than that on capital gains for individual investors. As a result, individuals alter their portfolio composition toward assets with a higher capital gains component and corporations are induced to reduce their dividend payout rate. It is not even clear whether these changes in behavior have efficiency costs or efficiency benefits, let alone what the magnitude of the effect is.

84. According to assumptions in appendix B, the annual efficiency costs resulting from the inefficient distribution of corporate risks across investors can be approximated by $0.01\, r_z^2 V$, where V is the total amount of risky securities outstanding and r_z is the riskless interest rate.

85. The 1975 estimate of corporate equity outstanding is from von Furstenberg, "Corporate Investment," p. 355, table 1.

The problem is that the theory explaining the payment of dividends is still incomplete.

Three possible explanations were given earlier for why corporations pay dividends: (1) since some equity investors, particularly corporations, will prefer dividends to capital gains, it may be that the value of dividends in the market just equals that of capital gains; (2) despite the tax disadvantage, dividends have the advantage over capital gains of providing a means to fund consumption with lower transactions costs or with less risk of violating legal structures against the spending of "capital"; and (3) dividends are useful as a signal to investors of the firm's profitability. Each explanation has different implications for the efficiency effect of the tax distortion discouraging dividends.

Under the first explanation, individuals are indifferent, tax reasons aside, between dividends and capital gains. Therefore, the fact that their portfolios have securities with a higher capital gains component has no cost. Risk-spreading will be inefficient as a result of this shift, but this effect has already been measured.

Under the second explanation, any reduction in the cash component of the return on the portfolio of an individual who uses the proceeds for consumption will result in higher transactions costs for that individual (the brokerage costs involved in selling shares to replace lost dividends). To the extent that firms reduce their dividend payout rate, resulting in an increase in their internal funds, the transactions costs of firms will decline if they are able to avoid underwriting expenses for new issues of debt or equity. On the other hand, the transactions costs of firms will increase if in response they increase their purchases of debt or equity. Of course, firms of the former type will be much more inclined to reduce their dividends than the others. Without taxes, in equilibrium the various transactions costs would be traded off against each other. Introducing taxes results in a trade-off between extra taxes and extra transactions costs. Measuring the net increase in transactions costs induced by the tax distortion would be difficult.

When dividends play a signaling role, the firm trades off the improvement in investors' expectations resulting from higher dividends with the higher tax rate on dividends for investors and the increase in transactions costs for the firm resulting from a reduction in its retained earnings. Here, investors may well be indifferent between dividends and capital gains. The only efficiency costs involving the dividend payout rate are the costs to the firm of a reduced level of retained earnings. These costs would be smaller were the equilibrium dividend payout rate smaller. Therefore, any tax distortion that discouraged dividends would reduce the efficiency costs. Even if the total costs to the firm of using dividends as a signal rise as a result of this additional tax distortion, the real costs—in contrast to the tax costs—decline.

Thus, depending on the explanation for why dividends are paid, the tax distortion discouraging dividends may have no direct efficiency effect, or it may have an efficiency cost or an efficiency benefit. There is no a priori presumption which direction of effect is more important.

Efficiency Costs of the Tax Advantage of Noncorporate Investment[86]

In the capital asset pricing model, the equilibrium rate of return on capital in the corporate sector (after correcting for the risk premium and the bankruptcy premium) will exceed the equilibrium rate of return in the noncorporate sector.[87] With the use of plausible parameter values for 1975, this implies that in equilibrium the rate of return on capital in the corporate sector will be 27.4 percent higher than in the noncorporate sector.[88] In contrast, Shoven estimated that as a result of differential taxation on the returns to capital in the two sectors the equilibrium rate of return on capital in the corporate sector will be 53 percent higher than in the noncorporate sector.[89]

The excess burden costs implied by such a distortion should be approximately in proportion to the square of the size of the distortion. Our results then imply excess burden costs of only 26.7 percent—$(27.4/53.0)^2$—of the size of the distortion costs found by Shoven.[90] Shoven's estimate of the excess burden costs resulting from the misallocation of capital between corporate and noncorporate uses is $4.26 billion; our

86. Ignored here, as elsewhere, is the fact that a business may shift from a corporate to a noncorporate status as a result of the corporation tax.

87. The excess is $[\tau - (1 - \alpha_b)](r_z - \gamma r)/(1 - \tau)$, as derived in footnote 65, equation 11.

88. We assume that $\tau = 0.48$, $\alpha_b = 0.75$, $r_z = 0.063$, $r = 0.08$, and $\gamma = 0.3$.

89. See John B. Shoven, "The Incidence and Efficiency Effects of Taxes on Income from Capital," *Journal of Political Economy,* vol. 84 (December 1976), pp. 1261–83. In table 2, he shows that the tax rate on noncorporate capital is 31 percent, and that on corporate capital is 55 percent. If the after-tax rates of return are to be equal, the before-tax rates of return must differ by 53 percent.

90. This approximation is rough. Had we measured the rate of return in the noncorporate sector as a percentage of the return in the corporate sector throughout instead of the converse, the excess burden implied by our results would be 38.6 percent of that in Shoven; ibid.

estimate is therefore \$1.1 billion.[91] It may be noted that this distortion, which is the standard distortion considered in the public finance literature, seems to be only about a third as costly as the distortion in debt-equity decisions.

Evaluation of Tax Reform Proposals

As the preceding analysis has shown, the present procedures for taxing corporate earnings create sizable excess burden costs. Many changes in the tax laws have been suggested to alleviate these costs. In this section, we estimate the efficiency gains that might be realized by several different kinds of tax reform proposals.

Criteria for Evaluation

The method of evaluation is to compare the efficiency gains and revenue costs of small changes in tax rates resulting from the various proposals. In an optimal tax structure, the potential efficiency gains relative to the revenue costs resulting from small changes in tax rates should be the same for all taxes. When this ratio differs for different taxes, the excess burden can be reduced without reducing tax revenues. The tax change with the highest ratio of efficiency gain relative to revenue cost is a prime candidate for reduction. However, while such estimates suggest the most promising directions for tax reform, they cannot indicate how large a change would be appropriate.[92]

These estimates are concerned only with the distortions in corporate financial policy and in the allocation of capital between the corporate and the noncorporate sectors.[93] The distortion in savings behavior is omitted because we do not have a complete theory of how the market interest rate is determined. Distortions affecting the dividend payout rate are also ignored because so little is known about the reasons for dividend payments (even the direction of change in excess burdens is unknown). Also, only the partial equilibrium efficiency effects of tax changes are ex-

---

91. Since the excess burden costs are approximately proportional to the square of the size of the tax distortion, they are proportional to $[\tau - (1 - \alpha_b)]/(1 - \tau)^2$ $(r_z - \gamma r)^2$. This approximation will be used when considering the effects of tax changes in the next section.

92. See appendix D for an explanation of the derivation of the estimates.

93. Inefficiency in the allocation of risk across investors is too small to merit attention.

Table 6. Efficiency and Revenue Effects of Selected Tax Changes, 1975
Millions of dollars

Tax change	Efficiency gain	Revenue gain or loss
1. 1 percentage point reduction in the corporation tax rate	171	−123
2. 1 percentage point reduction in the capital gains tax rate	238	−193
3. Deductibility of 1 percent of dividends under the corporation tax	0	−70
4. Taxation of 1 percent of interest payments under the corporation tax	45	245

plored; secondary effects through shifts in demand among commodities are ignored.

In addition to comparing efficiency gains and revenue costs (see table 6), the windfall transfers among individuals resulting from the tax changes, as well as the degree to which the personal tax approximates either a comprehensive income tax or a consumption tax, are discussed. However, the relative importance of the efficiency and equity effects cannot be compared because the two criteria are not commensurate.

Reduction of the Corporation Tax

The efficiency gain resulting from a small cut in the corporation income tax rate is about 40 percent larger than the revenue loss (table 6, line 1). The last dollar of corporation income tax costs the private sector $2.40—$1.00 in lost income and $1.40 in increased inefficiency.[94] Either this tax is much more expensive to administer than other taxes, in which case it should be reduced, or it is more equitable than other taxes, which we find unconvincing. Alternatively, marginal government expenditures financed by this tax should be more than twice as "valuable" as marginal private expenditures, which we also find unconvincing.

Would changing the corporate rate have any important equity implications? It would not change the relation between personal income and personal tax obligations, so would not affect the degree to which the tax law approximates either a consumption or a comprehensive income tax. However, since debt–equity ratios will fall, more savings will be invested in equity, which will be treated more favorably under the present income

94. If the distortions in savings decisions had been included, the efficiency effect would be larger.

tax than it would be under a comprehensive income tax. (Consumption tax advocates might view this shift toward equity as an improvement, though.) Also, more businesses will incorporate, further converting ordinary income into capital gains.

One would expect a reduction in the corporation tax to cause capital gains on equity, but if the amount of equity outstanding is initially in equilibrium, this may not be the case. In the new equilibrium, equity holders will still value the returns (after the corporation tax) from a dollar of marginal real investment at a dollar. The price of equity may rise immediately, but firms will expand the supply of equity capital, cutting back the supply of bonds, until the price falls toward its original level. Anticipation of this eventual drop may restrain the initial rise. Even though in equilibrium the new marginal holder of equity values the return from a dollar of real investment at a dollar, the increased intramarginal holdings of equity will be valued at more than a dollar, so consumer surplus will have increased. Although price may not change significantly, there will be windfall gains in utility. Since those in higher tax brackets have relatively stronger preferences for equity than for bonds, this group would capture most of these windfall gains in utility. And existing bondholders, having a lower probability of bankruptcy, would also receive windfalls.

On balance, there appear to be large efficiency gains from a cut in the corporation tax rate, although there may also be some costs in tax equity. Larger changes in the corporation tax rate will not appear as favorable, however, since the excess burden declines as the square of the existing distortion.

Decrease in the Capital Gains Tax Rate

The implications of cutting the capital gains tax rate are similar to those of cutting the corporate rate. This change lessens the degree to which taxes discourage equity finance. Again, a dollar of government revenue effectively costs the private sector more than two dollars (table 6, line 2).

If the capital gains tax were maintained as a tax on realizations, there would be a further gain as a result of the weaker lock-in effect for securities holdings. The lock-in effect arises because an investor can postpone payment of tax on his accumulated capital gains without penalty by postponing the sale of the asset. With a lower tax at realization, the incentive to postpone realization is reduced.

An unexpected decrease in the capital gains tax will make equity more attractive. However, in equilibrium the returns from a dollar of real investment will continue to be worth a dollar on the stock market. Intramarginal holdings of equity will rise in value, implying a gain in utility for those with the strongest preference for equity. And existing bondholders will be better off because of the decreased possibility of default.

There thus appear to be large efficiency gains as well from cutting the capital gains tax rate. Advocates of a comprehensive income tax would oppose such a reduction in the capital gains tax rate on equity grounds, but advocates of a consumption tax might favor a reduction.

Partial Deductibility of Dividends

In spite of the concern about the double taxation of dividends, there seems to be no clear efficiency gain from allowing corporations to deduct part of their dividend payments, and yet there are clear revenue costs to the government (table 6, line 3). One way to understand this result is to recognize that corporations can avoid this tax by repurchasing shares instead of paying dividends. If they pay dividends, there must be a compensating advantage. It is unclear, however, whether the resulting changes in dividend payout rates produce efficiency gains or efficiency losses.[95] The resulting increase in dividend payouts would increase the percentage of corporate income that is taxable at the ordinary income tax rates, however. Thus a dividend deduction under the corporation income tax would make the individual income tax base more comprehensive and would improve the equity of the tax system.

These ambiguous results concerning the efficiency effects of the partial deductibility of dividends depend critically on the possibility of share repurchase as an alternative to paying dividends. To the extent that the repurchase of equity is costly, however, this partial deductibility should make debt–capital ratios fall and stimulate corporate investment, with implied efficiency gains.

Limited Deductibility of Interest Payments under the Corporation Tax

Eliminating the deductibility of 1 percent of interest payments under the corporation tax would produce both an efficiency gain and a revenue

95. If dividends are made partially deductible under the corporation tax, the amount of dividends and new issues of equity will increase until again $\alpha = 1$, so that dividends and retentions are valued equally, and $q = 1$. In this process α_b will not necessarily change at all. If it does not, the equilibrium debt–equity rate ratio will not change. Nor will the equilibrium allocation of capital between the corporate and noncorporate sectors change. The tax disincentives for dividends drop slightly because of the partial deductibility of dividends, but it is not clear whether this is an efficiency gain or a loss.

gain (table 6, line 4). Although this change might increase the distortion in saving decisions, the cost of this further distortion would have to be very large to offset the advantages of this tax change.

Since debt–equity ratios would drop if the deduction for interest were curtailed, more income would appear as capital gains, making the tax system less equitable from the point of view of those favoring a comprehensive income tax. Also, the higher corporation taxes might make the firm seem riskier to existing bondholders, resulting in a capital loss for them.

Partnership Treatment of Corporate Income

A more comprehensive proposal would be to eliminate the corporation tax entirely and attribute all profits proportionately to shareholders to be included in their taxable income, taxable at ordinary rates.[96] The efficiency gains under this proposal (see appendix D to this chapter) would consist of reductions of excess burdens resulting from distortions in financial policy ($3.2 billion) and in the allocation of capital between the corporate and noncorporate sector ($1.1 billion). These efficiency gains, totaling $4.3 billion, would be purchased at a cost of $23.4 billion in lost revenues.

Since all corporate earnings, whether from bonds or from equity, would be taxed at ordinary rates, the proposal would meet the conditions of a comprehensive income tax. If share prices rose by a different amount than the increase in retained earnings (and such differences are normally sizable), the difference would be treated as a capital gain, however. This would reduce the equity improvement from the partnership treatment. Nevertheless, a much smaller share of corporate earnings would take the form of capital gains, which would be an improvement on balance from the point of view of advocates of a comprehensive income tax.

The Expenditure Tax

An expenditure tax would eliminate all personal taxes on the return to savings, whether from interest receipts, dividends, or capital gains. Such a tax has been advocated on both efficiency and equity grounds by a number of economists.[97] Its most important advantage is the elimination of

96. See Charles E. McLure, *Must Corporate Income Be Taxed Twice?* (Brookings Institution, 1979).

97. For a discussion of the relative merits of an income tax and expenditure tax, see Joseph A. Pechman, ed., *What Should Be Taxed: Income or Expenditure?* (Brookings Institution, 1980).

the distortion in savings decisions created by the taxation of the returns on savings under the income tax.

If an expenditure tax were imposed and the corporation tax repealed, the distortion resulting from the risk of bankruptcy would disappear. However, if the corporation tax were left in place, the distortion would increase; we estimate excess burdens would rise by $3.5 billion. This suggests that proposals for an expenditure tax, if not accompanied by repeal of the corporation tax, should at least be accompanied by a reduction in the distortion favoring debt finance resulting from the corporation income tax.

Further analysis of an expenditure tax is beyond the scope of this paper. It is clear, however, that tax reformers should be concerned about the corporation tax when advocating a movement toward an expenditure tax.

Conclusions

In this paper, we have developed a model of corporate financial decisions when there is both uncertainty and the possibility of costly bankruptcy. This model was used to measure the distortions in behavior induced by the existing tax structure and their excess burden costs. The effects on efficiency costs and revenues of various possible modifications of existing taxes were also explored, and several major conclusions drawn.

First, as long as firms are competitive, explicit recognition of bankruptcy costs is essential if a model is to explain the observed corporate financial structure.

Second, debt–capital ratios increased steadily between 1946 and 1974, and have declined only slightly since then. This rise was accompanied by, and according to our theory was caused by, a simultaneous rise in nominal interest rates, and by increasing optimism (or reduced pessimism) about prospects for the economy, at least until the early 1970s.

Third, the efficiency costs arising from tax incentives to increase debt–capital ratios are substantial, on the order of $3 billion a year, or approximately 10 percent of corporation tax revenues.

Fourth, distortions in the allocation of capital for corporate and noncorporate uses do not appear to be as large as previously thought. Our estimate is one-quarter to one-third of the size of earlier estimates.

Finally, any of several directions of tax change aimed at lessening the distortion in debt–capital ratios merit serious consideration.

Appendix A: Glossary of Symbols

Symbol	*Definition*
c	Implicit tax rate on accrued capital gains
$c(D/K)$	Increase in annual bankruptcy costs caused by an increase in the firm's debt–capital ratio as a result of the replacement of a dollar of equity with a dollar of debt
C_D	Increase in annual bankruptcy costs resulting from a dollar of debt-financed real investment
C_E	Increase in annual bankruptcy costs resulting from a dollar of equity-financed real investment
d_i	Rate of return on the ith security through dividends taxable to the individual at ordinary rates
d_M	Rate of return on the market portfolio through dividends taxable to the individual at ordinary rates
g_i	Return on the ith security taxable at capital gains rates
g_M	Return on the market portfolio taxable at capital gains rates
m	Marginal tax rate on interest income for an individual
n	Marginal tax rate on dividends for an individual
p	Percent of a firm's after-tax profits paid out as dividends
q	Stock market valuation of the present value of returns from a dollar of marginal real investment
r	Market interest rate on corporate bonds
r_f	Market interest rate on tax-exempt bonds
r_z	Riskless market interest rate
s	Pretax marginal return on capital (after depreciation and expenses)
α	Ratio of after-tax value of a dollar of dividends to the after-tax value of a dollar of capital gains in the stock market
α_b	Ratio of after-tax value of a dollar of interest receipts to the after-tax value of a dollar of capital gains in the stock market
β_i	Riskiness of the ith security, measured as $\rho_{iM}\sigma_i\sigma_M/\sigma_M^2$
γ	Percent of debt finance used to finance new investments
δ	Before-tax risk premium on the uncertain returns from a dollar of real investment
ε	Stochastic element, with mean zero, in the return on a dollar of real investment
τ	Corporation income tax rate

Appendix B: Estimation of α_b through Comparison of Taxable and Tax-free Interest Rates

In this appendix, α_b, the value in the market of a dollar of interest payments relative to a dollar of capital gains, is estimated by comparing the equilibrium yields of the securities of the *same* corporate issuer: one taxable and one tax-exempt. If the two securities are identical in all respects except taxability of interest returns, so that they have identical risk, the risk premiums on the two securities, as valued in the market, must also be identical.[98] If $\alpha_b r_b$ represents the expected return on taxable bonds and $\alpha_f r_f$ represents the expected return on tax-free bonds with comparable risk (each as valued relative to the equivalent amount of capital gains), then $\alpha_b r_b$ must equal $\alpha_f r_f$. However, it is reasonable to suppose that α_f is about 1, since α_f represents the value in the market of tax-free interest relative to capital gains, and capital gains are at worst relatively lightly taxed. It therefore follows that α_b is about r_f/r_b.

We proceed by comparing the equilibrium yields of two securities issued (or guaranteed) by the same corporation: one taxable and one tax-exempt. The usual problem with such an exercise is the difficulty of finding taxable and tax-free issues with comparable risk. Fortunately, it is possible to find a sample of several corporate issuers who simultaneously sold tax-exempt and taxable bonds. In recent periods, corporations have often been able to finance part of the expenditure for a particular plant with tax-exempt industrial revenue bonds. These bonds are issued by the local municipality, but all debt-service requirements are the responsibility of the corporation. Since the bond interest is exempt from personal income taxes, these bonds yield less than equivalent taxable securities. Obviously, the firm would choose to do all of its borrowing with these types of securities, but at the time of our study the total amount of each issue was limited by the U.S. Treasury to $3,500,000. Thus firms will often finance a new plant with industrial revenue bonds up to the maximum limit and then finance the remainder with regular taxable securities. This provides an opportunity to see how corporate bonds are priced in the market when they differ only in the tax status of the interest paid.

During 1978 we could find five such joint issues, where the terms of

98. Were it not for the IRS ruling forbidding deduction of interest payments from debt undertaken to purchase tax-exempt bonds (26 U.S.C. sec. 265[2]), investors could go long in one security and short in the other and earn a riskless profit with no *net* investment.

Table 7. Yields of Taxable and Tax-exempt Simultaneous Bond Issues, 1978

Company	Date	Yields to maturity (percent)		Ratio of yields, nontaxable issue to taxable issue
		Taxable issue	*Nontaxable issue*	
Exel Ind	3/14/78	9.25	7.125	0.770
Carolina Fruit Carriers Corp.	4/25/78	9.875	7.50	0.759
Haverty Furniture	7/25/78	10.00	7.75	0.775
Luchenby Furniture	8/8/78	9.75	7.75	0.795
Perini Corp.	10/10/78	9.50	7.375	0.776
Mean				0.775

two issues were sufficiently similar to rule out any other influence on the yields of the bonds. The data, which are presented in table 7, indicate that $r_f = 0.775r$, implying that $\alpha_b \approx 0.775$.

A second method of estimating α_b is to compare the yields of taxable and tax-exempt issues of the same quality. Here we compared the yields of taxable and tax-exempt long-term issues of equivalent rating during calendar year 1978. Of course, this comparison controls less well for quality and other variations. For example, an AA bond rating may not imply the same quality for the two types of securities. Moreover, while an attempt was made to control for equivalence of call protection, it was simply not possible to ensure that the bonds compared were equivalent in all respects. Nevertheless, the estimates obtained were similar to those described above, although they suggest a somewhat lower value for α_b. During 1978 the ratio r_f/r generally ranged between 0.65 and 0.70.

Finally, it is interesting to note that McCulloch has in effect produced estimates for α_b by looking at how yields differ on long-term government bonds that sell at par and those that sell at discounts.[99] All the promised yield of the former is in fully taxable coupon payments; some of the yield of the latter is in favorably taxed capital gains (the difference between the market and redemption prices of the bonds). McCulloch's estimates imply a range for r_f/r of 0.70–0.78.

Taking all the evidence into account and giving special weight to the estimates based on the issues in table 7, where the best control was exer-

99. J. Huston McCulloch, "The Tax-Adjusted Yield Curve," *Journal of Finance*, vol. 30 (June 1975), pp. 811–30.

cised over the quality and terms of the two issues compared, we estimate that the tax-exempt interest rate (r_f) is approximately 75 percent of the taxable interest rate (r) for long-term securities.

It should be noted that these estimates apply only to long-term bonds. Comparing short-term prime housing notes (the highest quality government-guaranteed, tax-exempt security available) with U.S. Treasury bills of comparable maturity over year-end periods from 1961 to 1968 produced an average value for r_f/r of about 0.58. It appears that the value of α_b applicable to short-term issues is considerably lower than 0.75.

Appendix C: Approximation of the Excess Burden from Inefficient Risk-bearing

In footnote 82, we noted that the marginal risk premium on a security for a given investor would be $\bar{g} + [(1 - m)/(1 - c)]\bar{d} - [1/(1 - c)]$ max $[(1 - m)r_z, r_f]$. This will vary systematically across investors because of the variation in tax rates across investors. In this appendix, the efficiency gains from redistributing risk among investors until all investors have the same risk premium at the margin are approximated.

To do this, the following simplifying assumptions on relative magnitudes are made:

(1) $c = 0.2m$;   (2) $r_f = 0.75r_z$;   (3) $\bar{d} = 0.6r_z$;   and (4) $\bar{g} = r_z$.

With these assumptions, an investor's risk premium can be expressed as a function of his $\alpha = 1 - m/1 - c$. This relationship was shown in figure 2.

To estimate the total efficiency gains resulting from a reallocation of risk across investors, the following assumptions were made: (1) the distribution of investors (weighted by their equity portfolio) across values of α is uniform between 0.35 and 1.0,[100] and (2) each individual's risk premium is proportional to his holdings of risky securities.[101]

100. In the tax simulation file we used, the distribution of marginal tax rates of individuals is slightly heavier at the higher tax rates, but introducing tax-free investors ought to at least offset this.

101. This assumption essentially follows from the capital asset pricing model. To see this, let the individual's utility function be $f(\mu,\sigma^2)$ where μ, the mean return on the portfolio, equals $r'x$ and where σ^2, the variance of the return on his portfolio, equals $x'\Omega x$. Here r is the vector of expected after-tax returns on the available assets, x is a vector of the dollars invested in each security by the individual, and Ω is a matrix of covariances of after-tax returns among the securities. Manipulation of the first-order conditions then gives $x = -f_1[\Omega^{-1}(r - \alpha r_z)]/2f_2$, where $r - \alpha r_z$ represents the after-tax risk premium. As asserted, x is proportional to the after-tax risk premium. The qualification is that f itself depends on x.

Figure 3. Illustrative Distribution of Marginal Risk Premiums

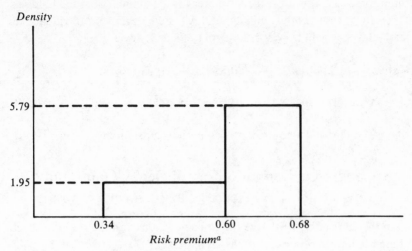

a. The risk premium is expressed as a fraction of r_z.

Assumption 1, along with our earlier assumptions, then implies that the distribution of the marginal risk premiums assigned to each share takes the simple form shown in figure 3. Taxpayers with a value of α greater than 0.68 have risk premiums between $0.60r_z$ and $0.68r_z$, and those with a value of α less than 0.68 have risk premiums between $0.34r_z$ and $0.60r_z$.

Assumption 2, applied to figure 3, implies that at the new equilibrium when all individuals have the same risk premium, this common risk premium will be $0.53r_z$.[102] By assumption 2, the efficiency gain when an individual trades from an initial risk premium x to the market equilibrium risk premium of ρ is just $\frac{1}{2}[(\rho - x)\Delta A]$, where ΔA measures the difference in the number of securities the individual owns between the two equilibriums—the marginal efficiency gain declines from $\rho - x$ to zero,

102. Let ρ represent the new equilibrium risk premium. Then it must be that the number of securities that individuals with an initial risk premium below ρ will buy will equal the number that those initially above ρ will want to sell. Assumption 2 implies that if the initial risk premium is x, the desired charge in holdings will be $(\rho/x - 1)A$, where A is the amount of initial holdings. Summing this expression over all individuals, we have

$$1.95 \int_{0.34r_z}^{0.60r_z} (\rho/x - 1)\, dx + 5.79 \int_{0.60r_z}^{0.68r_z} (\rho/x - 1)\, dx = 0,$$

where the amount of initial holdings is replaced by the density of initial holdings. Simple algebra implies that $\rho = 0.53r_z$.

giving an average of $\frac{1}{2}(\rho-x)$ per unit change in holdings. Also by assumption 2, $\Delta A = (\rho/x - 1)A$, where A is the amount of initial holdings. When these results are combined and when we sum over individuals, the total efficiency gain from spreading risk efficiently would be

$$V\{1.95 \int_{0.34r_z}^{0.60r_z} 1/2[(0.53r_z - x)(0.53r_z/x - 1)]\, dx$$

$$+ 5.79 \int_{0.60r_z}^{0.68r_z} 1/2[(0.53r_z - x)(0.53r_z/x - 1)]\, dx\} = 0.01r_z^2V,$$

where V is the total amount of risky securities outstanding.

Appendix D: Derivation of Efficiency Gains and Revenue Effects of Selected Tax Reform Proposals

In this appendix, we derive the efficiency gains and the revenue effects of the tax reform proposals discussed in the text.

Reduction in the Corporation Tax

The principal efficiency effect of reducing the corporation tax rate is to lower the distortion favoring debt over equity finance and the associated costs. The size of the initial excess burden is in proportion to $[\tau-(1-\alpha_b)]^2$. In appendix B, α_b was estimated to be 0.75, and it is assumed that this value will remain unaffected by the change in the corporation tax rate. A 1 percent reduction in τ would then lead to a 4.1 percent drop in the excess burden, or a gain of $132 million a year.

The size of the excess burden from the distortion of investment decisions is proportional to $\{[\tau-(1-\alpha_b)]/(1-\tau)\}^2 (r_z-\gamma r)^2$. If τ drops by one percentage point, D will drop by 2.1 percent according to the triangular approximation in figure 1. This change, together with the change in τ, implies that the excess burden on investment will fall by 3.4 percent, or $39 million a year. The total efficiency gain from a cut in the corporation tax rate is therefore $171 million a year.

In 1975, a cut of one percentage point in the corporate rate would have reduced revenues by $406 million, assuming corporate behavior did not change. The resulting $406 million reduction in corporate revenues would accrue to shareholders. If their average marginal tax rate was 0.157,[103] taxes on shareholders would increase by $64 million a year. But

---

103. This is the figure used by Martin Feldstein and Lawrence Summers in "Inflation, Tax Rules and the Long-Term Interest Rate," *BPEA, 1:1978*, pp. 61–99.

tax revenues would also increase as a result of the shift toward equity finance. According to the triangular approximation in figure 1, a 1 percent drop in τ will lead to a 2.1 percent drop in D. Given the availability of tax-free bonds with $r_f = 0.75r_z$, the marginal tax rate on bonds ought to be 25 percent. In contrast, the marginal tax rate on equity income would be $[1-(1-0.48)(1-0.157)] = 0.56$, a level 0.31 higher than that on debt. The shift in financial structure toward equity would then imply a revenue gain of $0.31r(0.021D) = \$180$ million, assuming $r = 0.063$ and $D = \$440$ billion.[104] Also, capital will shift slightly toward the corporate sector, where it is taxed more heavily. The change in the excess burden of \$39 million is approximately $t\Delta K$, where t is the tax distortion and ΔK is the amount of capital shifted to the corporate sector. Therefore, \$39 million also measures the increase in tax revenue resulting from this shift in capital. Thus the net revenue loss would be about \$123 million a year.

Decrease in the Capital Gains Tax Rate

As shown in footnote 91, the excess burden from the levered capital structure induced by the corporation tax is proportional to $[\tau-(1-\alpha_b)]^2$. Here, α_b is a weighted average of the values $(1-m)/(1-c)$ for each investor. A uniform 0.01 decrease in the effective tax rate c implies a change of approximately 1 percent in α_b, given that c is small. This change in α_b implies a 6.6 percent decrease in excess burden costs, on the assumption that $\alpha_b = 0.75$, or a gain of \$212 million a year (at 1975 income levels).[105]

This 1 percent change in α_b also implies, according to the triangular approximation in figure 1, that D will decrease by 3.3 percent. This decrease, together with the change in α_b, implies that the cost of the investment distortion will decrease by 2.4 percent, or \$27 million a year.

If the stock market grows normally at 8 percent a year on a base of \$630 billion in 1975,[106] the lost tax revenue, assuming no change in behavior, would be \$504 million. However, individuals will tend to shift toward equity. Based on the triangular approximation in figure 1, the amount of debt will decrease by 3.3 percent when $\alpha_b = 0.75$. If the combined tax rate on equity exceeds that on debt by 0.31 (as argued above) and assuming $r = 0.063$, the gain in revenue resulting from this shift toward equity would have been $0.31r(0.033D) = \$284$ million in 1975.

---

104. See von Furstenberg, "Corporate Investment," p. 355, table 1.

105. We assume that the dividend payout rate readjusts so as to maintain $\alpha = 1$ at the new equilibrium.

106. See von Furstenberg, "Corporate Investment," table 1.

Also, the fall in α_b will generate a flow of capital to the noncorporate sector. As noted, the revenue engendered by this movement will approximately equal the efficiency gain, which was measured as $27 million. The net revenue loss would therefore be $193 million. This is to be compared with the $238 million decrease in the excess burden.

Partial Deductibility of Dividends under the Corporation Tax

As noted above (footnote 95), if the tax rate on dividends is lowered by making 1 percent of dividends deductible under the corporation tax, the amount of dividends and new issues of equity will increase until again $\alpha = 1$, so that dividends and retentions are valued equally, and $q = 1$; α_b need not change at all in this process. If α_b does not change, the equilibrium debt–equity ratio does not change. Also, the equilibrium allocation of capital between the corporate and noncorporate sectors will not change. Because of the change, the tax disincentives for dividends drop slightly. However, it is not clear whether this is an efficiency gain or loss.

If there was no change in dividend payout rates, corporate revenues would drop by $0.01\tau Div$, or $154 million in 1975, when corporate dividends were $32.1 billion. However, shareholders will be taxed at an average marginal rate of 0.157 on this income,[107] implying an offsetting revenue gain of $24 million. The dividend payout rate will presumably increase in response to the tax change. According to Feldstein and Summers, the average personal marginal tax rate on dividends is higher than that on capital gains by 0.24, and with this change the corporate rate is lower by 0.005.[108] The only available estimate of the responsiveness of dividends to the relative tax rate is by Feldstein; on the basis of English data, he estimated that the elasticity of dividends to the opportunity cost in retained earnings was 0.9.[109] Under this proposal, the opportunity cost in retained earnings declines by 0.9 percent, implying a forecast increase in dividends of 0.8 percent. Tax revenues would then increase by (0.235) (0.008)(32.1), or $60 million in 1975. This gives a total revenue loss of $70 million.

107. Feldstein and Summers, "Inflation, Tax Rules, and the Long-Term Interest Rate."

108. Ibid. We ignore here for lack of information the decrease in corporation tax revenues resulting from different relative tax rates on dividends and capital gains for corporate holdings of equity.

109. M. S. Feldstein, "Corporate Taxation and Dividend Behavior," *Review of Economic Studies,* vol. 37 (January 1970), pp. 57–72.

Limited Deductibility of Interest Payments under the Corporation Tax

Let us assume that 1 percent of interest payments is no longer deductible. If we rederive the expression in footnote 91 for marginal excess burden costs from debt finance, we find that it now equals $r\{\tau-[1-\alpha_b(1-0.01\tau)]\}$. When $\alpha_b = 0.75$, the distortion drops by 1.6 percent and the excess burden by \$97 million. However, when the conditions for an equilibrium capital stock in the corporate sector are reexamined, $s-r_z$ increases by $0.01\gamma r\tau/(1-\tau)$ because of the heavier taxation of debt-financed capital. And with the use of the triangular approximation in figure 1, the amount of debt will drop by 1.6 percent, causing γ to drop. These changes cause a further shift of capital to the noncorporate sector, increasing the cost of this distortion by 4.6 percent, or \$52 million, which leaves a net efficiency gain of \$45 million.

If the market value of corporate debt is \$440 billion and the average long-term interest rate is about 0.09 (figures are for 1975), corporation tax revenues will increase by \$190 million if there is no change in behavior. Since corporate revenues drop by this amount, tax payments by shareholders drop by \$30 million, assuming their average marginal tax rate is 0.157. However, as a result of the drop in the distortion favoring debt, the amount of debt will drop. By the triangular approximation of figure 1, the debt decreases by 1.6 percent when $\alpha_b = 0.75$. If the tax rate on equity is 0.31 higher than that of debt, revenues increase by \$137 million. But, the shift of capital from the corporate to the noncorporate sector causes a revenue loss comparable to the efficiency loss, or about \$52 million. The total revenue gain is \$245 million.

Partnership Treatment of Corporate Earnings

Since the tax treatment of income from debt and equity is identical under this proposal, the tax distortion in financial policy would be eliminated, implying a drop of \$3.2 billion in excess burden costs. Also, there would no longer be a difference in the tax treatment of corporate and noncorporate capital, which implies that the \$1.1 billion distortion cost from the inefficient allocation of capital would be eliminated. Since $c = m$, and if the deviation between capital gains and retained earnings is ignored, private risk-bearing will also be efficient, gaining \$44 million a year.[110]

110. However, the risk borne by the government through its tax revenues will increase, implying inefficiency in investment decisions since the firm will ignore the costs to the government of bearing this risk.

Furthermore, the distortion in the dividend payout decision would be eliminated. However, when dividends are used as a signal, it is not clear whether this is an efficiency gain or loss.

To arrive at a crude revenue estimate, assume that the average marginal tax rate on equity is 0.31 above that on bonds. Then, the tax rate on equity will become just equal to that on bonds for those currently holding equity. Other individuals will shift from debt to equity to avoid bankruptcy costs, but this will have no tax consequence. Therefore, the revenue loss should be about 31 percent of the return on corporate equity, or $23.4 billion in 1975, assuming $630 billion in equity and a before-tax total rate of return of 12 percent.

The Expenditure Tax

Optimal corporate financial policy implies that $c(D/K) = r[\tau - (1-\alpha_b)]$. If an expenditure tax was imposed and the corporation tax repealed, this distortion would disappear. However, if the corporation tax was left in place and $\alpha_b < 1.0$ initially, the distortion would increase by $(1-\alpha_b)r$. If $\alpha_b = 0.75$ initially, the additional excess burden cost is $3.5 billion.

Comments by J. Gregory Ballentine

It has been argued for some time that the corporation income tax causes efficiency losses because it induces a misallocation of capital between the corporate and noncorporate sectors and because it acts as an extra tax on capital income, increasing the misallocation of consumption over time. Gordon and Malkiel conclude that the first of these misallocations is small, and they ignore the second. They do argue, however, that the tax causes a welfare loss principally through a distortion in corporate financial policy. This is an extremely important point. Previous analysis of the welfare loss associated with the misallocation of capital and the distortion in the timing of consumption suggests that the combined loss may be on the order of 1 percent of GNP. If this loss is in addition to the loss estimated by Gordon and Malkiel, the case for revising corporation tax policy appears very strong. If the only loss is the distortion in financial policy, the case is much weaker. After a brief summary of the paper, I will return to this matter, for in my opinion the Gordon-Malkiel analysis does not support the conclusion of little or no capital or consumption misallocation.

The paper briefly summarizes analysis of corporate financial policy in a world in which bankruptcy is costless. The conclusion of such analysis is by now fairly familiar; with the corporation income tax and realistic values of the appropriate personal income tax rates on dividends, interest, and retentions, firms will rely entirely on debt finance and no one will hold equity. That this result is counterfactual leads Gordon and Malkiel to conclude that potential bankruptcy costs must prevent firms from relying entirely on debt finance at the margin. That is, as firms react to the corporation income tax by increasing their use of debt finance, they find that the probability that they will go bankrupt, and thus incur bankruptcy costs, rises. Firms choose an intermediate financial policy at which the tax costs of extra equity finance are just balanced by the expected bankruptcy costs of additional debt finance.

Because it has been argued recently that bankruptcy costs are too small to offset the tax penalty on equity finance, Gordon and Malkiel provide an illuminating discussion of the many complexities surrounding the bankruptcy or reorganization of a firm. They stress the fact that difficult and prolonged negotiations are likely to be necessary to resolve the claims of bondholders and equity holders. Such negotiations are costly. Even if formal bankruptcy is avoided and an informal reorganization is agreed upon, much negotiation, with its attendant legal and administrative costs, is usually required. Gordon and Malkiel's emphasis on institutional details in this matter is an important contribution.

While they do present figures on the legal and administrative costs associated with four recent bankruptcies, the unavailability of data prohibits Gordon and Malkiel from making a direct computation of expected bankruptcy costs for U.S. firms. So they measure those costs indirectly by inferring their value from the values of the returns on debt and equity. That is, in their model the gap between the net-of-tax return on equity and the net-of-tax interest rate must be equal to the marginal expected bankruptcy costs of additional debt finance. Using reasonable values for the returns on debt and equity, they can then calculate marginal expected bankruptcy costs. By assuming such costs to be linearly related to the amount of debt finance, total bankruptcy costs can be approximated.

On the basis of this procedure, Gordon and Malkiel calculate the annual welfare loss from tax-distorted debt–equity ratios to be $3.2 billion in 1975. The linearity assumption implies that this is an overestimate, but other factors suggest it may be an underestimate.

Gordon and Malkiel also argue that the corporation income tax may induce inefficient risk taking and a distortion in dividend payout ratios.

Their rough estimates of the size of the loss arising from inefficient risk taking suggest that loss is quite small. No attempt is made to calculate a loss resulting from any possible distortion in dividend payout ratios. Such calculations must await a thorough and realistic model of the determination of these ratios.

The efficiency gains associated with a number of possible tax reforms are also evaluated by Gordon and Malkiel. Since the dominant source of any efficiency loss in their analysis arises from the tax-induced increase in debt–equity ratios, they find that tax reforms, such as lowering the corporation income tax or allowing dividends to be deducted from that tax base, are likely to provide significant welfare gains because they lower the extra tax on equity.

As I have mentioned, Gordon and Malkiel ignore the misallocation in the timing of consumption resulting from the corporation income tax and also argue that that tax causes only a small sectoral misallocation of capital. Both of these distortions are present if the tax drives a wedge between the marginal return to capital (cost of capital) in the corporate sector and the interest rate. (In this analysis the interest rate is taken to be equal to the return on noncorporate capital.) I believe that the wedge is there and that it is large; consequently I believe that the distortions in the timing of consumption and in the allocation of capital are potentially quite large.

The source of the wedge between corporate and noncorporate costs of capital can be seen by considering a firm's choice of financial policy. Repurchase of debt and new real investment are alternative uses of funds, so optimal financial policy implies that at the margin the same rate of return must be earned on those two alternatives. If there are no bankruptcy costs, the return on the repurchase of debt is simply the interest rate; thus the return on new real investment (the marginal return to capital) is equal to the interest rate independent of the level of the corporation income tax—which is to say, the tax does not cause a wedge.

Notice that this analysis assumes there are   bankruptcy costs. Therefore, it also implies that firms rely entirely on debt finance. Gordon and Malkiel show that, if there are bankruptcy costs, firms will not rely entirely on debt finance. As the corporation income tax causes them to shift to debt finance, they incur expected bankruptcy costs. The shift to debt stops when the expected bankruptcy costs from extra debt finance make debt no more attractive than equity. Of course, it is still true that at the optimum the return on new investment must be equal to the return on the repurchase of debt. But the crucial point, which Gordon and Malkiel do not stress, is that in this case the return on the repurchase of debt is the interest rate plus the decline in expected bankruptcy costs resulting from lowering the debt–equity ratio. Clearly there is a wedge between the marginal return to corporate capital and the interest rate, and that wedge is the expected bankruptcy costs of extra debt finance. Since firms only incur expected bankruptcy costs because of the tax penalty on equity finance (that is, in the absence of that tax penalty no risky debt will be issued), the wedge is caused by the extra tax on equity income.

When they turn to measuring the misallocation of capital, Gordon and Malkiel implicitly assume that the wedge is very small by explicitly assuming that expected bankruptcy costs are independent of the size of the firm. That is, according to their assumption a very large firm and a very small firm with identical debt–equity ratios must have identical total expected bankruptcy costs. Consequently bankruptcy costs do not enter the marginal cost of capital for a firm expanding at a fixed debt–equity ratio, and those costs then do not enter as a wedge between corporate and noncorporate costs of capital. In this case, the wedge exists only because of the tax on the fraction of capital financed by equity.

I find the assumption that total bankruptcy costs are fixed implausible and even inconsistent with Gordon and Malkiel's measurement of them. Gordon and Malkiel measure total bankruptcy costs by first inferring marginal bankruptcy costs (which I call c^*) from the gap between debt and equity returns; then they assume that marginal bankruptcy costs are *proportional to the level of corporate debt* (D in figure 1). Under this assumption total bankruptcy costs are equal to $\frac{1}{2}$ c^*D. This measurement of total bankruptcy costs directly contradicts the later assumption that bankruptcy costs depend only on the debt–equity ratio and are independent of the level of finance. Clearly Gordon and Malkiel's measure implies that if corporate debt and equity finance both increase in the same proportion total bankruptcy costs will also increase proportionately. That is, those costs are not fixed.

By omitting marginal bankruptcy costs from their calculation of corporations' marginal cost of capital, Gordon and Malkiel have underestimated the tax-induced wedge between corporate and noncorporate returns. Based on the Gordon-Malkiel description of the types of costs that are included in expected bankruptcy costs as well as their measure of expected bankruptcy costs, I conclude that those costs do enter firms' marginal cost of capital and that the corporation income tax does induce a large wedge between the return on new corporate capital and the interest rate. Consequently that tax leads to a misallocation of capital and it adds to the distortion in the timing of consumption. This in turn means that the Gordon-Malkiel calculations of the efficiency gains to be made from such tax changes as lowering the corporation income tax, allowing the deductibility of dividends from corporate profits, and integrating corporation and personal taxes are significant underestimates.

There are then at least three sources of significant efficiency loss resulting from current corporation tax policies. The contribution of the Gordon-Malkiel paper, and it is a major contribution, is that the heretofore ignored losses arising from a distortion in financial policies are measured. Some matters associated with their measure remain to be resolved, however. For example, Gordon and Malkiel describe several sources of bankruptcy costs that investors might bear. But in their discussion, they do not distinguish between social costs of bankruptcy and the private costs relevant to the firm's financial decision. Their calculations presume that the private costs that the firm takes into account are all social costs and that, except for the costs borne by senior bondholders, they are the only social costs. Some of the bankruptcy costs discussed, however, are not necessarily social costs. Potential liquidation losses that are matched by the gains of the purchasers of the firms' assets are an example. Given the large gap between the Gordon-Malkiel indirect measure of bankruptcy costs and their direct estimate of legal and administrative costs (which are social costs), this issue may be quantitatively important. Counterbalancing this is the possibility that some social costs, such as disruption in output during bankruptcy, may not be considered by the firm in evaluating its financial policy. Such costs are omitted from the estimate of social costs.

My final comment has to do with a matter that Gordon and Malkiel touch upon only briefly, but which is an important aspect of an overall evaluation of corporate taxation. Essentially they reject the conduit view of the corporation. Consequently they argue that the only income of stockholders that is relevant for equity comparisons is the dividends received and corporate retentions. As they state, this approach implies that the corporation tax is not an equity issue. I disagree. Indeed, but for a tax justified strictly by the benefit principle, I would say that any tax that transfers resources to the government is an equity issue. The corporation income tax is definitely an equity issue; and that tax's apparent effects on equity are no more attractive than its efficiency effects.

Comments by William C. Freund

I applaud the Gordon-Malkiel paper. It tackles a very difficult and controversial topic and, in the process, provides an excellent review of the literature.

Because of the nature of the model and the difficulties of measurement, the major conclusions of Gordon and Malkiel are necessarily rather weak. For example, they conclude that each firm will have its own optimal debt–equity ratio (firms with riskier investments will choose a lower ratio and firms with less risky investments will choose a higher ratio). Individuals will hold a diversified portfolio, with those in the lower tax brackets owning relatively less equity and those in the higher tax brackets specializing in equities and tax-exempt bonds. Such conclusions really do not add a great deal to what we know about the financial structure of corporations. But I do commend the Gordon-Malkiel paper for explicitly incorporating the role of inflation and the cost of bankruptcy in their model.

Professor Ballentine mentioned the weak conclusions and the guarded inferences that were drawn about dividends because so little is known about the reasons for the payment of dividends. The authors rightly acknowledge that, although a few attempts have been made to rationalize the payment of dividends, the size and stability of dividends remains a puzzle.

I wish that Gordon and Malkiel had considered some evidence in recent working papers of the National Bureau of Economic Research and had integrated the findings into their theoretical model and empirical analysis. For example, I wonder what they would have to say about a working paper by Feldstein and Slemrod.[111] At first glance this paper, which deals with the taxation of capital gains on individuals, may seem irrelevant. But there is a relationship between inflation and the supply of equity capital.

In the Feldstein-Slemrod study, which is based on IRS data for 1973, the authors found that individuals paid capital gains taxes on $4.5 billion of nominal capital gain, which turn out to be real capital losses of nearly $1 billion. Real capital gains tax rates have been soaring with inflation.

111. Martin S. Feldstein and Joel Slemrod, "Inflation and the Excess Taxation of Capital Gains on Corporate Stock," National Bureau of Economic Research Working Paper 234 (Cambridge, Mass.: NBER, February 1978).

These taxes affect not only the supply of equity savings by individuals and the total rate of savings, as suggested by Michael Boskin, but have an added effect on the institutionalization of savings. The Gordon-Malkiel paper seems to assume that there are only corporations on the demand side and individuals on the supply side and to ignore the institutionalization of saving.

Pension funds and insurance companies play a dominant role in the financial markets and affect the debt-equity preferences of corporations. The tax exemption of institutions affects the supply of institutional savings and therefore the flow of funds to the debt and equity markets.

Another article (originally a National Bureau paper) deals with the effects of taxation on the selling of corporate stock and the realization of capital gains.[112] For example, limiting the long-term capital gains tax rate to 25 percent would, according to the estimates by Feldstein, Slemrod, and Yitzhaki, nearly double corporate stock sales by individuals. It would almost triple the total value of net gains realized at 1973 levels. The analysis shows that reducing the tax on capital gains would reduce the lock-in effect on investment behavior. That would affect the financing preferences of corporations as well. Obviously, capital gains taxes favor retained earnings as a source of new equity and impede the efficient allocation of capital funds.

Finally, a most significant recent paper (originating at the National Bureau) tackles specifically the effects of tax and inflation rates on debt–equity ratios.[113] The authors demonstrate that, with current U.S. tax laws, even moderate rates of inflation can cause a substantial change in the equilibrium levels of debt–equity ratios and the net real yields on debt and equity investments. This occurs because current law taxes nominal income (nominal interest and nominal capital gains) but allows borrowers to deduct nominal interest payments.

The analysis and the empirical findings of these studies are suggestive. I think they are important to evaluating corporate financial policies. Perhaps they will not change the Gordon-Malkiel conclusions but, to the extent possible, they should be integrated into both their theoretical and empirical formulations.

112. Martin Feldstein, Joel Slemrod, and Shlomo Yitzhaki, "The Effects of Taxation on the Selling of Corporate Stock and the Realization of Capital Gains," *Quarterly Journal of Economics,* vol. 94 (June 1980), pp. 777–91.

113. Martin Feldstein, Jerry Green, and Eytan Sheshinski, "Inflation and Taxes in a Growing Economy with Debt and Equity Finance," *Journal of Political Economy,* vol. 86 (April 1978), pt. 2, pp. S53–S70.

ROGER E. BRINNER *and* STEPHEN H. BROOKS

Stock Prices

BUSINESSMEN, economists, and finance specialists have frequently
stated that the crises of the 1970s have "depressed" the stock market. The
regularly cited crises include the 1975 recession, increased regulatory burdens, the discovery that OPEC can hobble the industrial world, and accelerating inflation from a host of causes. Of these causes the link between
inflation and the stock market is the greatest subject of debate. At the end
of the 1960s stocks were widely assumed to be attractive investments
in an inflationary environment because they are based on real assets. The
assumptions were wrong. The past decade of rising inflation has been a
period of weak equity demand. Figure 1 displays the surprisingly strong
negative correlation between inflation and the growth in real equity
prices.[1] After adjustment for inflation, the stock market fell sharply in the
1970s even though real earnings were stable. An important issue is
whether investors as a group correctly assessed the impact of inflation on
corporate prospects or whether they reacted in a grossly exaggerated,
negative manner.

Certain observers have also argued that the tax reforms and generally
rising tax rates of the last decade were major contributors to the decline in

The authors particularly appreciate the comments and criticisms received from
Henry Aaron, Patric Hendershott, and the other conference participants.

1. The simple correlation between inflation and real growth of stock prices (defined as Standard and Poor's index of 425 industrial stocks divided by the consumer
price index) was -0.665. The simple correlation between inflation and real earnings
growth per share was -0.360. And the simple correlation between real growth of
stock prices and growth of real earnings per share was 0.462. All of these statistics
refer to the period 1955–78.

200   *Roger E. Brinner and Stephen H. Brooks*

Figure 1. Growth in Consumer Prices, Share Prices, and Corporate Earnings, 1955–78[a]

Percent

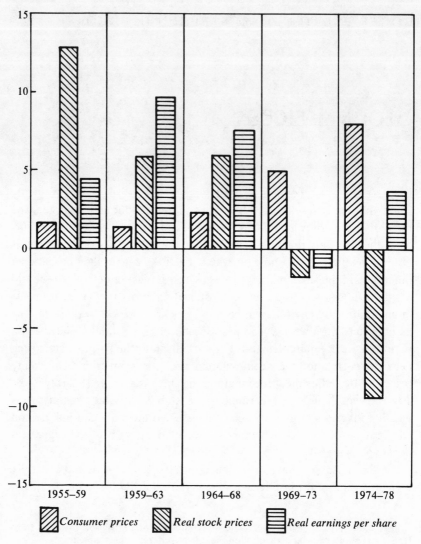

a. Average growth rate from beginning to end of designated periods, based on eight-quarter averages of the actual level values to minimize the influence of exceptional quarterly values.

the real value of common stock prices.[2] To the extent that taxes on capital gains and dividends rose faster than taxes on other sources of income, this argument is strong and deserves empirical evaluation. However, the general upward drift of marginal personal tax rates since 1965 has simultaneously reduced the returns on competing investments and has thus reduced the discount rate appropriate for evaluating future equity returns.[3] The net impact of tax changes is therefore more complex than has been recognized in many popular and professional discussions, and explicit, careful analysis is required.

No consensus now exists on the degree to which inflation and increased taxes are responsible for the decline in real stock prices, nor does one exist on whether stocks are currently underpriced in a fundamental sense. We address these diverse issues simultaneously with a rational model of stock prices, constructed with an explicit calculation of the present value of expected dividends and capital gains. The present value calculation reflects projected growth in dividends and retained earnings, and the tax rates applicable to corporate profits, dividends, and gains. The resultant posttax equity returns are discounted with a posttax bond yield to reflect the opportunity cost of equity investment. Deviations of this present value estimate from actual stock prices are evaluated for their correlation with other economic factors, such as inflation and monetary policy, and for the presence of irrational behavior.

Our results should encourage those who believe that there are strong, systematic ties between stock market prices and logically appealing economic variables. Share prices are sufficiently correlated to projected dividends and capital gains that, on the basis of *available* corporate earnings and net worth information, the resultant equity prices may be termed rational. However, the results strongly indicate that inflation has reduced the efficiency of equity markets by damaging the quality of traditional earnings information so that the market currently substantially undervalues corporate assets.

Our principal findings are as follows. First, if one makes fairly simple assumptions about the formation of expectations, stock prices are highly correlated with the expected present value of returns from equity invest-

2. Martin Feldstein, "Inflation and the Stock Market," *American Economic Review,* vol. 70 (December 1980), pp. 839–47.
3. Between 1965 and 1978 personal taxes (defined to include state and local taxes) have risen from 12.1 percent of personal income to 15.1 percent, according to national income and product accounts.

ment. Roughly 70 percent of the variation in actual share prices can be explained by the variation in a present value of future posttax dividends and capital gains. (The next section of the paper explains in considerable detail how we estimated the present value of these future returns.) However, substantial recent biases are evident.

Second, consumer confidence (as measured by the University of Michigan Survey Research Center Index of Consumer Sentiment) and credit market conditions explain about half of the remaining variation in share prices (about 15 percent of the total variation). Alternatively, the ratio of the reported book value of corporate assets (net of debt claims) to the true replacement cost of these assets—a ratio that reflects the potential for investor illusion, that is, undervaluation of the net worth of corporations in an inflationary environment—explains the same proportion of the unexplained variation. If these variables are employed together, they explain two-thirds of the variation not explained by the initial present value calculation.

Third, the statistical power of the confidence and credit condition variables is not particularly noteworthy, but the power of a variable measuring the ratio of book value to replacement cost reveals a potent illusion on the part of investors. The coefficient of this variable indicates that the investment community has failed to recognize at least 50 percent, and possibly 100 percent, of the pure nominal appreciation of real corporate net assets brought about by inflation. By 1978 this illusion had depressed the stock market by at least 20 percent.

Fourth, the presence of a substantial inflation illusion is further supported by lower correlations between share prices and alternative estimates of the present value of earnings and capital gains more closely linked to current inflation. The highest correlations between a present value composite and the stock market were found when expectation regimes that are relatively insensitive to prevailing inflation rates were used.[4]

Fifth, we measured the sensitivity of stock prices to tax rates in several ways. Most of the empirical literature on the behavior of share prices fails to consider the effect of taxes on the relative attractiveness of stocks (through dividends and capital gains) and competing investments. We find that the tax effects are important and are largely captured by a rational calculation of the posttax present value of dividends and capital gains.

4. In the appendix, we report the sensitivity of our results to alternative assumptions about future earnings, dividends, and capital goods price inflation.

The model also highlights the fact that taxes on competing returns must be considered in judging the full impact of proposed or actual tax reforms on the price of corporate shares. In particular, even though the average burden of taxes on dividends and gains has risen markedly since 1965, the simultaneous increase in the effective tax rate on interest income has minimized the depressive effect on the stock market. Other things being equal, the increase in taxes on bond interest would have raised the present value of any given stream of posttax dividends and gains by 17 percent. Subsequent sections of this study quantify the role of tax increases and decreases on the present value of dividends and capital gains.

Finally, the impact of changes in capital gains taxation can be easily exaggerated, in part because deferral of taxes until a gain is realized diminishes the absolute effect of a tax change, and in part because the impact of tax changes on the discount rate of accompanying tax law changes must be considered.

The paper is organized into three sections. The first describes our equity valuation model. The second explores the effect of forces other than the expected value of dividends and capital gains on share prices. These forces include uncertainty, taxes, and inflation. A brief concluding section winds up the paper.

The Equity Valuation Model

We begin by assuming that the price per share of common stock (P) is the risk-adjusted sum of the expected present value of after-tax dividends earned during the time the stock is held $[EPV(DIV)]$ plus after-tax proceeds from the sale of the stock at the end of the holding period $[EPV(PRO)]$:

(1)
$$EPV = EPV(DIV) + EPV(PRO)$$
and
(1a)
$$P = EPV \times \text{risk adjustment.}$$

The expected present value of the dividend stream over any specified holding period (H) is given by:

(2)
$$EPV(DIV) = \sum_{i=1}^{H} \frac{D_i^e(1 - t)}{[1 + r(1 - t)]^i},$$

where D^e is expected dividends per share, t is the marginal tax rate of dividend recipients, r is the yield on competing government securities of maturity similar to the stock holding period, and H is the holding period. The expected present value today of the sale proceeds at the end of the holding period is given by:

$$(3) \qquad EPV(PRO) = \frac{P_H^e - (P_H^e - P_0)t_{cg}}{[1 + r(1 - t)]^H},$$

where P_0 is the current-period purchase price of the stock, P_H^e is the expected selling price of the stock H periods after purchase, and t_{cg} is the capital gains tax rate.

A prime attraction of this model of equity valuation is that it explicitly evaluates the stock from the *posttax* standpoint of an investor whose holding period is *finite;* it therefore includes the value of both dividends and capital gains. In these regards the approach differs significantly from the conventional capital asset pricing model based on an infinite stream of pretax dividends alone.

To calculate the *EPV* for use in an equity pricing model, a host of problems must be solved. One must specify how expectations are formed. One must estimate effective marginal tax rates for dividends, capital gains, and returns to competing financial assets. One must choose a representative investment horizon because an infinite horizon would make the capital gains tax rate irrelevant. One must relate expected gross capital gains $(P_H^e - P_0)$ to the value of the expected accumulation of retained earnings over the holding period. Finally, one must specify the determinants of equity risks. Our strategy in this study was to test a variety of straightforward hypotheses for each expectation model, and then to apply these structures to carefully constructed data.

The stock price, earnings, and dividend data are based on Standard and Poor's averages for industrial stocks. The quarterly stock price observations are averages of daily quotations. The dividend series equals the cumulative payment over the most recent four quarters; hence the payments are at annual rates. The earnings are book earnings less corporation income tax, as reported by Standard and Poor's, for the current quarter and the previous three quarters. The earnings are adjusted from a traditional accounting definition to an "economic" definition by multiplying earnings by the ratio of inflation-corrected economic profits to reported profits for nonfinancial corporations. Corrected profits equal reported profits plus the inventory valuation adjustment, the difference between straight-line replacement-cost and book depreciation, and the reduction in the real value of net financial liabilities.[5]

Table 1 shows the calculations necessary to estimate the net gain from this reduction in real indebtedness (column 6). The final column shows the ratio of adjusted economic earnings to reported book earnings for the period 1956 through 1978.

The Expected Value of Dividends

Calculation of the expected present value of dividends, *EPV(DIV)*, requires specification of expectations concerning the dividends received during each year of the holding period. We assume that investors know current dividends per share and that they estimate the future *growth* in dividends according to the following process:

$$(4) \qquad D_i^e = D_0(1 + d^e)^i, \qquad i = 1, 2, \ldots, H,$$

where D_i^e is the expected level of dividends in the ith year of the holding period, D_0 is the level of dividends in the most recent year, and d^e is the expected annual growth rate in dividends determined in the current period. Thus substituting equation 4 into equation 2 gives

$$(2a) \qquad EPV(DIV) = \sum_{i=1}^{H} \frac{D_0(1 + d^e)^i(1 - t)}{[1 + r(1 - t)]^i}.$$

We tried alternative values of d^e, formed according to adaptive expectations, static expectations, and constant expectations. Under adaptive expectations, it is assumed that the expectations formed during the current period for the future value of a given variable will change from the

---

5. The unreported gain from the reduction in the real value of debt has been discussed at length by George M. von Furstenberg and Burton G. Malkiel, "Financial Analysis in an Inflationary Environment," *Journal of Finance*, vol. 32 (May 1977), pp. 575–92. Following their procedure, we focus on the reduction in real indebtedness associated with end-of-period net financial liabilities (net financial liabilities, drawn from flow-of-funds data for nonfinancial corporations, are the sum of long-term liabilities, short-term liabilities, net miscellaneous liabilities, profits tax liabilities, and net trade debt minus financial assets). The price deflator used to calculate the reduction in real value was the implicit price deflator for personal consumption expenditures plus gross private domestic investment. This deflator has the virtue of capturing the value of the real gain to the stockholder both as consumer and as entrepreneur.

Table 1. Adjusted Earnings Calculation, 1956–78
Billions of dollars unless otherwise specified

Year	Reported book profits (1)	Capital consumption adjustment (2)	Inventory valuation adjustment (3)	Net financial liabilities (4)	Growth in prices (percent) (5)	Net gain in real indebtedness (6)	Tax liabilities (7)	Adjusted after-tax earnings (8)	Ratio of adjusted earnings to reported earnings (9)
1956	43.0	−3.0	−2.7	51.0	2.6	1.6	20.0	18.9	0.8
1957	41.0	−3.3	−1.5	57.0	3.2	1.4	19.1	18.5	0.8
1958	34.7	−3.4	−0.3	57.9	1.5	0.8	16.1	15.7	0.8
1959	44.0	−2.9	−0.5	60.8	2.0	1.3	20.7	21.2	0.9
1960	40.5	−2.3	0.3	69.4	1.6	0.8	19.1	20.2	0.9
1961	40.4	−1.8	0.1	73.9	0.6	0.5	19.4	19.8	0.9
1962	45.1	1.0	0.1	80.1	1.4	1.3	20.6	27.0	1.1
1963	49.9	1.9	−0.2	87.2	1.2	0.9	22.7	29.8	1.1
1964	56.4	2.6	−0.5	95.5	1.3	1.1	23.9	35.7	1.1
1965	66.0	3.5	−1.9	109.5	1.8	2.2	27.1	42.8	1.1
1966	70.8	3.8	−2.1	129.1	3.0	4.3	29.4	47.4	1.1
1967	66.9	3.6	−1.7	147.5	2.6	3.6	27.6	44.7	1.1
1968	73.6	3.7	−3.4	167.9	4.1	7.2	33.5	47.5	1.2
1969	70.1	3.5	−5.5	191.8	4.7	9.3	33.2	44.1	1.2
1970	56.7	1.5	−5.1	217.4	4.6	9.0	27.2	34.9	1.2
1971	65.0	0.5	−5.0	236.2	4.6	9.8	29.8	40.5	1.1
1972	77.5	2.7	−6.6	256.1	3.7	8.8	33.4	49.0	1.1
1973	95.7	1.9	−18.6	296.9	5.7	21.1	39.4	60.6	1.1
1974	107.5	−3.0	−40.4	357.9	10.7	39.2	42.5	60.8	0.9
1975	103.7	−11.9	−12.4	384.6	9.0	25.8	40.3	64.8	1.0
1976	133.8	−14.4	−14.7	398.7	5.1	18.4	52.4	70.8	0.9
1977	148.5	−11.8	−15.1	446.4	6.3	27.3	59.4	89.3	1.0
1978	171.1	−12.6	−25.2	511.1	7.1	38.0	68.6	102.7	1.0

Sources: Calculations based on information from the Bureau of Economic Analysis and the Board of Governors of the Federal Reserve System.

expected value formed during the last period by some portion, α, of the difference between the actual observed value and the expected value for that last period, so that $d_t^e - d_{t-1}^e = \alpha(d_{t-1} - d_{t-1}^e)$.

Under "static" expectations, the rate of growth in per-share dividends in the most recent period is expected to be maintained for the holding period. This is equivalent to an adaptive model with α equaling 1. Under "constant" expectations, the average rate of growth in per-share dividends for the entire period is assumed to be the expected rate of growth in every period. Thus under constant expectations, current conditions have no effect on the expected future growth in dividends.

The Expected Value of the Proceeds from Sale

Computation of expected net proceeds from the sale of the stock at the end of the holding period requires the calculation of two numbers. The first is the expected value at the time of sale of the assets embodied in the original purchase. The nominal value of these assets will grow as the replacement cost of fixed capital assets increases over time. The second is the value of the new earnings retained in the firm during the holding period. We assume that the market evaluates retained earnings just as it evaluates the other assets of the firm. Like the assets embodied in the original purchase, the nominal value of these newly acquired assets will grow as the replacement cost of capital assets increases. Thus the capital gain attributed to the stock consists of the appreciation in the nominal value of the originally purchased assets, plus the gains in value resulting from the reinvestment of earnings over the holding period and the appreciation of these earnings.

The Market Valuation of Assets

Investors must, of course, form some judgment on how the market, at the end of the holding period, will value both the assets originally purchased and those arising from retained earnings during the holding period. The implicit stock market valuation of these assets relative to their replacement cost is conventionally referred as Tobin's q ratio.[6]

We assume that investors expect the market to adjust the replacement cost of assets by the average value of q over the estimation interval, 1955–

---

6. The q concept was first developed by James Tobin in "A General Equilibrium Approach to Monetary Theory," *Journal of Money, Credit, and Banking*, vol. 1 (February 1969), pp. 15–29.

78.[7] The average value of the stockholder q over this interval is 0.77. At first glance, a value of q less than one seems inconsistent with rational net investment because it seems to indicate that the new capital is being purchased at a price greater than the acquisition cost of old capital. But an average q less than one is indeed feasible in a rational world with non-homogeneous capital, information costs, transportation costs, and imperfect data.

Firms invest to maintain current capacity as well as to expand for future demands. Purchases of entire firms cannot meet maintenance needs or modestly increase basic capacity. Therefore, some new plant and equipment purchases will occur even if whole firms are available at lower average cost. Industries currently experiencing high rates of capacity utilization and anticipating substantial growth may consider mergers or acquisitions to expand capacity. The q values in such industries would therefore be expected to tend toward one. In fact, values of q greater than one are feasible if the short- and medium-term supply of new equipment is tight and the market for equipment is only partially cleared through price increases. The costs of acquiring information about the physical status of the existing firm's physical assets, plus the cost of dismantling and shipping those assets to another location, can also easily explain why the value of q may differ from one. The cost of ascertaining accurate earnings information is even more important. Inflation greatly complicates this process and simultaneously erodes confidence. We use the *average q* discount observed in the sample period from all of the causes rather than attempting to model the expected future q. In fact, the study itself can be viewed as a model of q, because it attempts to explain movements in share prices relative to expected economic returns.[8]

7. We have used the q ratio calculated by George von Furstenberg, with one important adjustment. See "Corporate Investment: Does Market Valuation Matter in the Aggregate?" *Brookings Papers on Economic Activity, 2:1977,* pp. 347–408. Von Furstenberg's q focuses on total assets and therefore accurately characterizes how the firm as a whole is valued relative to its replacement costs. However, the focus of this study is the equity interest in the firm. For our purposes, a stockholder-specific q is a more attractive concept. Therefore, we have subtracted the value of interest-bearing debt from both the replacement cost and the market values reported by von Furstenberg. In this way our q ratio encompasses only the assets claimed by the current holders of equity.

8. Modigliani and Cohn have recently developed a parallel theme, arguing that inflation and the associated high interest rates have led investors to miscalculate current and prospective earnings and to discount these earnings inappropriately. Franco Modigliani and Robert Cohn, "Inflation, Rational Valuation, and the Market," *Financial Analysts Journal,* vol. 35 (March–April 1979), pp. 24–44.

The Expected Sale Price

To pull together the preceding considerations, the expected sale price per share of common stock at the end of the holding period (P_H^e) is given by

$$(5) \qquad P_H^e = (q)(RC_0)(1 + PI^e)^H + q \sum_{i=1}^{H} RE_i^e (1 + PI^e)^{H-i},$$

where RC_0 is the replacement cost of the firm's assets at the time the share is purchased, q is the average value of the shareholder q for the period 1955–78 ($= 0.77$), PI^e is the expected average annual inflation rate in the implicit price deflator for business fixed investment, RE^e is expected retained earnings, and H is the expected holding period. We calculated and tested alternative patterns of expectations for the expected growth of the deflator for business fixed investment (see the appendix to this paper). The expected retained earnings series is the difference between expected per-share earnings and expected per-share dividends:

$$(6) \qquad RE_i^e = E_i^e - D_i^e,$$

where expected per-share earnings (E_i^e) are calculated in a manner analogous to that of expected dividends (D_i^e): [9]

$$(7) \qquad E_i^e = E_0(1 + g^e)^i,$$

where E_0 is the level of per-share adjusted earnings when the stock is purchased, and g^e is the constant expected average annual growth in adjusted earnings per share calculated across a number of alternative expectation regimes (see the appendix).

Thus, using equations 4, 6, and 7, we have

$$(6a) \qquad RE_i^e = E_0(1 + g^e)^i - D_0(1 + d^e)^i.$$

The Choice of Key Parameters

THE HOLDING PERIOD. We assumed a holding period of five years. Brinner has estimated that the average holding period on realized equity gains is 3.6 years;[10] but it is apparent that many gains are not realized for tax

9. See equation 4, above. In general, $g^e \neq d^e$. This is consistent with expected growth or decline in the dividend payout rate. Note that over the interval studied the dividend payout rate was far from stationary.

10. Roger E. Brinner, "Inflation and the Definition of Taxable Personal Income," in Henry J. Aaron, ed., *Inflation and the Income Tax* (Brookings Institution, 1976), pp. 121–45, especially p. 136.

purposes during the life of the investor. As Bailey noted, a very substantial share of all gains must not be realized until after a bequest to explain the low ratio of realized accrued gains.[11] On the other hand, daily market prices are likely to be dominated by traders who are realizing gains, and a reasonably short horizon is probably the best choice for a model of stock price behavior. We chose five years as a compromise figure, supported in retrospect by some correlation tests.

ESTIMATION OF TAX RATES. We gave the calculation of marginal tax rates considerable attention, because a primary goal of the study was to estimate the influence of tax variables on stock prices in a standard valuation model. Our key tax rate series is a weighted average of the marginal federal tax rates faced by people who reported dividends in adjusted gross income. The weights for each year are the shares of total dividends reported by members of a taxable income class in that year. The marginal tax rates are the marginal rates for the mean taxable income of the class.[12] This method produces relatively high estimates of tax rates, as the marginal rate is the applicable rate for the "last" dollar of dividend income and the weighting procedure represents only those who reported dividends in adjusted gross income. People who did not receive dividends or whose dividends were below the exclusion limits do not affect the calculation. However, dividend recipients without taxable income who face a zero marginal rate do enter the calculation.

The impact of state and local taxes was also included. In this case, the multitude of separate tax plans made detailed analysis impractical. The marginal state and local tax rate of dividend recipients was assumed to be 1.5 times the average effective state and local personal tax rate determined from national income and product accounts data.[13] This multiplicative factor represents the higher average effective rates on dividend recipients and the mild progressivity of many state and local personal tax systems. The combined effective marginal tax rate on dividend recipients, t, is then:

11. Bailey, "Capital Gains and Income Taxation."
12. The tax rate chosen was the rate applicable to joint returns for the given taxable income. Because a portion of the taxable income reported came from non-joint filers, our tax rates slightly understate the true tax rate on dividend income of all filers.
13. The state and local tax rate in the national income and product accounts is calculated as state and local personal tax and nontax payments divided by the sum of wage and salary accruals, dividends, personal interest, rental income including adjustments, and proprietor's income including adjustments. The denominator of this ratio comes as close to federal adjusted gross income as the national income and product accounts will allow.

$$t = t_{state/local}(1 - t_{federal}) + t_{federal}.$$

In this way, we also explicitly recognize the deductibility of state and local taxes from federal taxes.

We set the tax rate on capital gains at one-half the tax rate on dividend recipients. In the calculations of expected present value we assume that the investor anticipates that the tax rate will remain at its current value over the holding period.

This method of calculating tax rates implicitly ignores the purchases of stocks by nontaxable entities such as pension funds, by corporations, or by financial intermediaries such as mutual funds or insurance companies. Such purchasers of stock own approximately 25 percent of all stocks.[14] Our procedure is justifiable if, as we believe, the market must produce roughly an equilibrium return for the marginal individual common stock investor and his tax rate is most closely captured by the composite used here.

THE DISCOUNT RATE. We chose the three-to-five-year government bond rate for the before-tax discount rate, matching our presumed investment horizon. This rate fluctuates with the rate of return on competing assets of similar maturity. Except for the risk associated with unanticipated inflation, this interest rate reflects a riskless return, given the assumption of a fixed investment horizon. We assume that the differential risk of equity investment is captured through a proportional reduction of the present value calculated with discounting by the posttax bond rate. We elaborate this concept of risk adjustment below in the discussion of multiple regression results.

THE EPV PARAMETERS CHOSEN FOR FURTHER ANALYSIS. The appendix details the selection of the "best" pattern expectation for dividends, earnings, and the implicit price deflator for business fixed investment. On the basis of closest correlation with the actual stock market index, the best *EPV* was one that assumed adaptive expectations for adjusted per-share earnings growth with a speed-of-adjustment coefficient, α, of 0.025, implying a long mean lag of ten years; static expectations for per-share earnings, implying that the current rate of growth of dividends is expected to continue throughout the investment horizon; and constant expectations for growth in the implicit price deflator for business fixed investment, implying that the rate of growth for the deflator is expected always to equal

14. Marshall E. Blume, Dean Crockett, and Irwin Friend, "Stockownership in the United States: Characteristics and Trends," *Survey of Current Business* (November 1974), pp. 16–40, especially p. 18.

Figure 2. The Stock Market and the Expected Present Value, 1955–78

1941–43 = 10

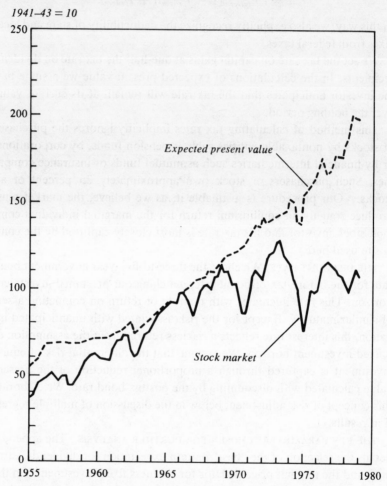

the average rate of growth for the entire sample period regardless of when the expectation is formed. The average rate of growth for the entire period for the deflator was 4.1 percent.

What interpretation can be given to this somewhat curious combination of expectation patterns embodied in the expected present value that most closely tracks fluctuations in the stock market? First, and most obvious, investors do not put great weight on current-year earnings growth, perhaps because expected earnings growth is based here on an "adjusted earnings" series that differs from reported book earnings. If the presence of earnings illusion described by Modigliani and Cohn is a real factor in valuation models,[15] then the lack of sensitivity to economic earnings is not surprising. Second, the higher sensitivity of dividend growth expectations to current conditions can be explained by the fact that the underlying series is itself sluggish. Slower adjustment speeds produce a smooth pattern of growth rates, which masks too much of the cyclical variation in dividends. Finally, the choice of a constant growth rate for the investment deflator is, among other things, evidence that the 1970s acceleration in prices was mostly (and wrongly) ignored in the valuation of existing assets.

The expected present value of dividends and final sales prices (*EPV*) and the stock market index are shown in figure 2. The correlation coefficient of the *EPV* with the stock market was 0.814. However, it is clear that the stock market failed to grow as rapidly as predicted by the *EPV* after 1968. By 1978 the share price index was only 54 percent of the *EPV*, much lower than the average share price–*EPV* ratio of 85 percent from 1955 through 1970. In the second half of this study we present a model of equity valuation that allows us to test alternative explanations for this rising undervaluation in the stock market.

The Impact of Taxes on the Present Value and on Share Prices

How much do changes in personal taxes alter the *EPV*? Changes in tax rates cut both ways. They obviously change the after-tax dividend stream and the sale proceeds. They also change the discount rate by altering the after-tax yield on competing assets. These two effects tend to offset one another. Whether a tax reduction would lower or raise the *EPV* is a priori ambiguous.[16]

15. Modigliani and Cohn, "Inflation, Rational Valuation, and the Market," p. 32.
16. Part of the ambiguity is attributable to the possibility that the expected dividend growth rate may logically exceed the discount rate for finite investment horizons. It can be shown that:

$$EPV(DIV) = \{D_0(1-t)(1+d^e)/[r(1-t)-d^e]\} \cdot (1 - \{(1+d^e)/[1+r(1-t)]\}^H)$$

or

$$EPV(DIV) = \{A\} \cdot \{B\} \qquad \text{and} \qquad \frac{\partial EPV(DIV)}{\partial t} = \frac{\partial A}{\partial t} B + \frac{\partial B}{\partial t} A.$$

The partial derivative of $\{A\}$ with respect to t is always positive. The partial derivative of $\{B\}$, on the other hand, is always negative. When average values for d^e and $r(1-t)$ are used, both A and B are negative, because the average posttax discount rate is less than the expected dividend growth rate. Therefore, the derivative of $EPV(DIV)$ with respect to t is the sum of a negative and a positive term. The magnitude of each of these is a function of H.

Figure 3. Effect of Cutting Taxes by Half on the Expected Present Value of Dividends Earned

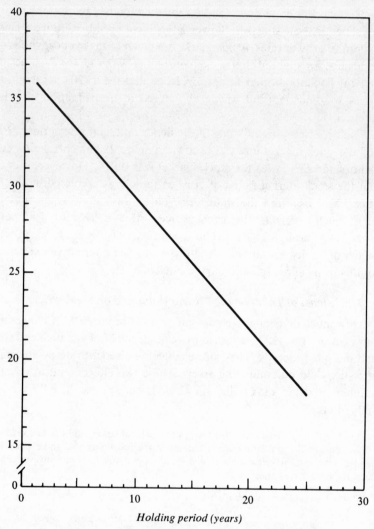

Percentage change in EPV (DIV)

Holding period (years)

Figure 4. Effect of Cutting Taxes by Half on the Expected Present Value of Proceeds from the Sale of Stock

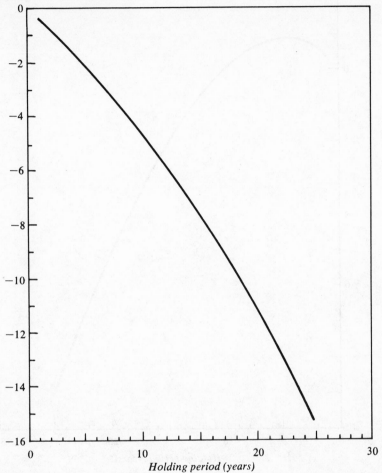

Percentage change in EPV (PRO)

Holding period (years)

In the illustrations that follow, the *EPV* is broken down into its two parts, *EPV(DIV)* and *EPV(PRO)*. Each part is then investigated to determine how it would change if all tax rates were halved. In calculating the new values for the expected present value of dividends, *EPV (DIV)*, and sales proceeds, *EPV(PRO)*, we set all other parameters at their average 1955–78 values. And we did not factor in the feedback effects of tax changes on any economic variable.

Figure 5. Effect of Cutting Taxes by Half on the Total Expected Present Value

Percentage change in EPV

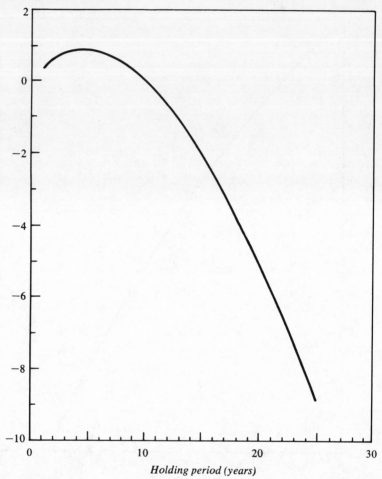

Holding period (years)

The sign of the partial derivative of the *EPV(DIV)* with respect to the tax rate based on this average assignment of key parameter values is still indeterminate until an investment horizon has been specified. With a five-year investment horizon, each one-point reduction in the tax rate, say, from 45 percent to 44 percent, increases the *EPV(DIV)* by 1.6 percent. However, longer investment horizons imply smaller proportional effects. Figure 3 shows the percentage-increase effect on *EPV(DIV)* for holding periods of twenty-five or fewer years of halving the tax rate applied to

Figure 6. Effect of the Capital Gains Tax on the Total Expected Present Value, 1955–78

Index: 1941–43 = 10

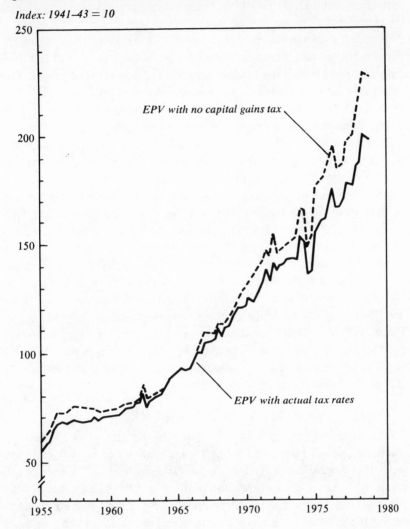

dividends and alternative investments. At the "standard" five-year horizon, the *EPV(DIV)* is increased 32 percent if tax rates are cut from 44
percent to 22 percent.

Cutting taxes unambiguously *lowers EPV(PRO)*, given these average
parameter values for all holding periods, because tax cuts increase the
relative yield of competing assets, $r(1-t)$, more than they increase the

proceeds from selling the stock. Figure 4 shows the proportional effect of cutting taxes in half on $EPV(PRO)$ for holding periods of twenty-five or fewer years.

Figure 5 shows the impact on the total EPV of the tax rate reduction. Halving the tax rate would raise the EPV for holding periods of less than ten years and lower it for holding periods of eleven years or longer. The increase in the EPV for holding periods under eleven years is small.

Because the impact of capital gains taxes on share prices has been so widely discussed, we calculated the effect of eliminating this tax without changing any other tax (see figure 6). Eliminating the capital gains tax would uniformly improve the market, but by a relatively small margin. Using expected growth rates for the average values for the period as a whole and eliminating the capital gains tax would have raised the EPV by an average of 6.4 percent. On the other hand, in the high-inflation environment of 1978, the EPV would have been 14.5 percent higher had there been no tax on capital gains. Expected sale proceeds naturally play a larger proportional role relative to dividends in a high-inflation situation.

These results highlight the important role that changes in the yield on alternative assets have in determining the after-tax yield on equity. They are, however, partial equilibrium results and are therefore only suggestive. Full equilibrium results would, among other changes, recognize that interest rates are themselves functions of tax rates on earnings as well as investment income and that corporate earnings reflected in the EPV would change if personal tax rates were lowered.[17]

Have Tax Changes Significantly Affected Stock Prices?

The expected present value of dividends and sale proceeds (EPV) shown in figure 2 above was the best such predictor of the stock market index that we estimated. To test the overall statistical significance of tax changes, the share price correlation of this best EPV was compared with the share price correlation of an analogous no-tax EPV. We constructed the no-tax EPV with the same pattern of expectations for the growth in

17. The important work in this area includes Martin Feldstein, Jerry Green, and Eytan Sheshinski, "Corporate Financial Policy and Taxation in a Growing Economy," discussion paper 556 (Harvard Institute of Economic Research, June 1977); Alan J. Auerbach, "Share Valuation and Corporate Equity Policy," National Bureau of Economic Research Working Paper 255 (Cambridge, Mass.: NBER, July 1978); and Patric H. Hendershott, "The Decline in Aggregate Share Values: Inflation and Taxation of the Returns from Equities and Owner-Occupied Housing," NBER Working Paper 370 (NBER, July 1979).

earnings, dividends, and the investment deflator, but with tax rates on capital gains, dividends, and competing assets set at zero.

We first regressed the logarithm of the stock market index on the logarithm of the with-tax *EPV* and then on the logarithm of the no-tax *EPV*. Our statistical test clearly rejected the null hypothesis that tax rates do not matter.[18]

The test results are a clear indictment of the failure of other research to include personal tax rates in a model of equity valuation. However, some have argued that, while the level of taxes is important, their year-to-year variability can be ignored. To test the validity of this hypothesis, we ran a second test in which we substituted an average-tax-rate *EPV* for the no-tax *EPV*. In this second alternative, *EPV* tax rates are set at their average levels over the estimation interval. Under this hypothesis, tax rates matter to the extent of their average level, but the variation in the tax rates around that average does not explain a significant portion of the variation in the stock market. Errors from the regression of the stock market on this average-tax *EPV* were again compared with the errors from the with-tax *EPV* regression. The test results suggest that the average tax rate does contribute to explaining stock prices but that variability in tax rates has significant additional explanatory power.[19]

Share Price Variation Not Explained by Expected Present Values

The objective of the expected present value variable is to provide a stable benchmark of comparison to actual share prices (P) so that any additional influences can be separately identified. These extra factors can be classified in three categories: discounting due to uncertainty and risk; correlation with the business cycle; and illusions or persistent irrationality. In symbols,

$$P = EPV \times f(\text{uncertainty, cycle, illusion}).$$

18. To test the statistical significance of recognizing nonzero tax rates, we used a test for nonnested hypotheses developed by H. White and L. Olson in "Determinants of Wage Change on the Job: A Symmetric Test of Non-Nested Hypotheses" (December 1977). The null hypothesis is that the difference between mean squared errors in the two regressions is insignificant. The White-Olson statistic is distributed normally with mean zero and variance one. The value of the test statistic was found to be 7.6, a value that clearly rejects the null hypothesis.

19. The White-Olson statistic was 4.8, considerably less than that derived from the test against the no-tax *EPV* but still rejecting the hypothesis of no significant difference between the constant average taxes and the actual level of taxes.

This section reports the results of regression analysis that measures the three systematic deviations of dividend and gain expectations from the simple formulas used to construct the present values.

The Effects of Uncertainty and the Business Cycle

The expected present values are nearly always greater than the observed market price, a result easily attributable to an additional risk discount. The present values use the five-year government bond yield as the alternative asset yield for discounting. Government bonds have no default risk and provide a certain stream of nominal payments. The only risk, if bonds are held to maturity, is the potential loss of real value through unanticipated inflation. Equity investment is associated with a less certain dividend stream and a risky final sale value.

We considered, and rejected, dealing with risk by adding an arbitrary constant to the bond rate in the calculation of the discounted present values. This procedure did not seem appropriate or sufficiently flexible. The near-term dividend receipts are virtually as certain as bond interest. Even the five-year forward dividend returns are highly predictable and arguably offer a smaller *real* risk in a volatile inflationary environment than bond interest payments. The expected capital gain is admittedly highly uncertain, but this uncertainty is not suitably represented by a constant increment to the discount rate. We therefore chose to model the present value as if the returns were certain and then to allow the risk to enter through the other arguments of the regression equation.

Manipulation of the formulas of the familiar "infinite-horizon" stock valuation model may clarify this point. As Malkiel notes,[20] the expected return on equities (r_E) and the current share price (P_0) are related in the infinite-horizon model by a simple function of current dividends (D_0) and the estimated long-run growth rate of earnings and dividends (g): $P_0 = D_0(1 + g)/(r_e - g)$. The analogous, infinite-horizon version of expected present value of dividends developed in this study using the bond rate (r_B) for discounting is $EPV = D_0(1 + g)/(r_B - g)$. If taxes are to be recognized, the D_0 is the posttax dividend, and r_B is the posttax bond yield. Comparing these two expressions implies that $p = EPV(r_E - g)/(r_B - g)$. If, as suggested, the implicit discount rate for equity investment (r_E) were to equal the bond rate (r_B) plus a risk premium (Δ), this expression simplifies further to $p = EPV[1 + \Delta/(r_B - g)]$, or, in logarithmic terms,

$\log(p) = \log EPV + \log[1 + \Delta/(r_B - g)]$, or approximately, $\log(p) = \log(EPV) + \Delta/(r_B - g)$.

In the regressions reported later, the constant term, the consumer sentiment index, and the financial variables can be interpreted as jointly representing the final term, $\Delta/(r_B - g)$, plus any other systematic deviations of "market" expected present values from our "formula" present values. Our regression specification thus allows for the testing of increasing or decreasing risk discounts while simultaneously evaluating other influences.

Regression analysis of the industrial share price versus the expected present value confirms a pattern of a high basic correlation between price and *EPV*, plus autocorrelated residual variation, which can be partially explained by cyclical indicators (see table 2).

The expected present value is sufficient by itself to explain 75 percent of the variation in share prices if a unit elasticity is not forced on the relationship (equation 2-1), or 69 percent of the same variation if a unit elasticity is forced (equation 2-2).[21] The errors are highly autocorrelated as should be expected, given the simplicity of this format and hence the likelihood of omitted variables. In equation 2-2 we constrain the coefficient of the logarithm of *EPV* to equal one to see how much explanatory power declines if we impose the assumption that a 1 percent change in *EPV* is matched by a 1 percent change in stock prices. As is apparent, explanatory power declines modestly.

The addition of the University of Michigan Index of Consumer Sentiment and the financial market variables raises the explained variation to 85 percent of the total variation (equation 2-3). Each increase of one percentage point in consumer sentiment is found to boost the stock market by seven-tenths of a percentage point, other things being equal. The two financial variables stand for a large set of elements that could affect investors' perceptions or expectations of market performance. Such concepts would include the existence or prospect of a credit squeeze, the degree of monetary stimulus, and the general riskiness of the market. The financial variables were chosen because they are widely used leading indicators and are accessible to the investing public. Each additional percentage point of real money growth is found to raise the stock market by 3.4 percentage points. Each percentage point reduction in the spread between

21. Strictly speaking, the explanatory power is with respect to variation in the logarithm of the share price index, not the index itself.

Roger E. Brinner and Stephen H. Brooks

Table 2. The Roles of Risk and Inflation Illusions in the Price–EPV Relation[a]

Equation number	Explanatory variable[b]	Coefficient	Summary statistics		
			$\bar{R}^2$	Durbin-Watson	Standard error
2-1	Constant	0.751 (0.219)	0.746	0.143	0.163
	Log (*EPV*)	0.786 (0.047)			
2-2	Constant	−0.243 (0.018)	0.693	0.126	0.180
	Log (*EPV*)	1.000 (0.136)			
2-3	Constant	−0.882	0.848	0.260	0.126
	Log (*EPV*)	1.000			
	Mich. sentiment index	0.722 (0.154)			
	Real money growth	3.441 (0.716)			
	Bond rate − prime rate	0.042 (0.015)			
2-4	Constant	0.248 (0.045)	0.868	0.295	0.118
	Log (*EPV*)	1.000			
	Log (*BOOK/REPL*)	−0.839 (0.074)			
2-5	Constant	−0.190 (0.168)	0.911	0.428	0.097
	Log (*EPV*)	1.000			
	Mich. sentiment index	−0.033 (0.150)			
	Real money growth	3.364 (0.548)			
	Bond rate − prime rate	0.008 (0.012)			
	Log (*BOOK/REPL*)	0.702 (0.086)			

Table 2 (*continued*)

Equation number	Explanatory variable[b]	Coefficient	Summary statistics		
			$\bar{R}^2$	Durbin-Watson	Standard error
2-6	Constant	−1.191 (0.319)	0.929	0.559	0.086
	Log (*EPV*)	1.273 (0.056)			
	Mich. sentiment index	0.360 (0.156)			
	Real money growth	1.778 (0.587)			
	Bond rate − prime rate	0.016 (0.011)			
	Log (*BOOK/REPL*)	1.092 (0.111)			

a. Dependent variable: logarithm of Standard and Poor's stock price index. Period of estimation: 1955–78, quarterly data. Standard errors of the coefficients are in parentheses.
b. The variables are defined in the text and at the end of the appendix.

the bond rate and the prime rate cuts the share price index by 4.2 percentage points.[22]

The Power of Inflation to Depress the Market

Equations 2-4, 2-5, and 2-6 report a test for an inflation illusion. They include the logarithm of the book-to-replacement-value ratio as an explanatory variable. This variable permits a relatively straightforward test of whether investors are willing or able to construct "economic" present values or whether they rely on faulty book-value information in assessing corporate net worth. As indicated in figure 7, from 1955 through 1969 the inflation-related distortion of corporate reports was insignificant. Thereafter it was dramatic: reported net worth rose only 58 percent but true "economic" net worth rose 130 percent from the beginning of 1970 to the end of 1978.

22. Traditional "risk" variables such as moving standard deviations of growth, inflation, or share prices did not provide significant evidence of increasing risk in the 1970s. This finding conforms to results from a recent study by William C. Brainard, John B. Shoven, and Laurence Weiss, "The Financial Valuation of the Return to Capital," *Brookings Papers on Economic Activity, 2:1980*, pp. 453–502. They argue that a generalized increase in risk premiums is difficult to support empirically as the cause of weak share prices. They come to this conclusion by testing several appealing, theoretically motivated measures of risk as determinants of equity prices.

Figure 7. Three Indexes of Corporate Value: Share Prices, Book Value, and Replacement Cost, 1955–78

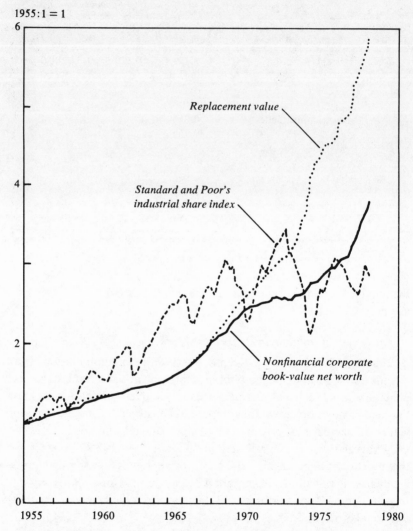

1955:1 = 1

The book value of nonfinancial corporate firms (*BOOK*) is defined as the historic cost of physical assets minus the market value of net financial liabilities. Except for differences between market and book values of liabilities, this series corresponds quite closely to the flow-of-funds concept of nonfinancial corporate net worth. The replacement-cost net worth

(*REPL*) series exceeds the book-value series because physical assets are recorded on a replacement-cost basis net of straight-line depreciation rather than on a historic cost basis net of accelerated depreciation.[23]

Book-value net worth is a misleading concept for it subtracts apples (current market values of liabilities) from oranges (historic cost of assets); replacement-value net worth, which subtracts the market value of liabilities from the market value of physical assets, is a better concept. If the market were able to see through the distortions that inflation creates in official accounting systems, it could be expected to track replacement net worth. This net worth should also be closely tied to the present value of dividends and future retained earnings since physical asset prices ought to parallel earning power. If inflation befuddles accountants and investors, then share prices might be expected to track the only available concept—book value—and essentially to ignore economic (replacement) net worth and its logical twin, the expected present value of this study.

An estimated coefficient of 1.0 on the logarithm of this ratio of book to replacement value would indicate that investors were wholly deluded by the distortions in accounts caused by inflation; a coefficient of 0.0 would indicate that investors had seen through the fog. Any intermediate coefficient would suggest that the market has ignored only part of the real value of corporate net worth.[24]

Equation 2-4 suggests that the market may in fact have ignored 84 percent of the difference between net book value and the higher current net replacement value. Moreover, inclusion of this variable increases the percentage of variation in stock prices explained from 69 percent in the otherwise similar equation 2-2 to 87 percent in equation 2-4.

Equation 2-5 adds the illusion variable to equation 2-3, thereby raising the percentage of variation explained from 85 percent to 91 percent. Only real money growth and the "illusion" variable remain statistically significant here as multicollinearity problems mount. If the true coefficient of log (*BOOK/REPL*) lies within a two-standard-error range of the esti-

23. The liability market value and the asset replacement-cost data were generously provided by George von Furstenberg.

24. An algebraic presentation may clarify this point. If the market reflects replacement net worth, then $p = EPV = REPL$/number of shares. If the market reflects only the book value, then $p = BOOK$/number of shares. A coefficient of 1 in a regression such as equation 4, log $(p/EPV) = A + $ log (*BOOK/REPL*), therefore means that the *EPV* and *REPL* have been effectively eliminated from the regression because the formula *EPV* should approximate the per share replacement value (*REPL*/number of shares) regardless of market evaluation.

mated value, the stock market has failed to recognize between 53 percent and 87 percent of the difference between replacement cost and book value.

Equation 2-6 is identical to equation 2-5 except that the coefficient of log (EPV), constrained to have a value of one in 2-5, is estimated freely in 2-6. The overall standard error of the regression falls from 0.097 to 0.086, the Michigan Index of Consumer Sentiment regains its statistical significance and quantitative importance, and the coefficient of real money growth declines. The estimated inflation illusion effect remains highly significant, statistically and quantitatively.

All of the equations reported in table 2 had seriously autocorrelated error terms (signified by the low Durbin-Watson statistics). We address this problem below.

Share Price Sensitivity to Taxes

Figure 8 presents the historical patterns of four tax rates that influence the net return on funds invested by the corporate sector. The dividend rate (t) was described in detail in an earlier section of this paper. The maximum capital gains rate (t_{cg}) is the maximum conceivable personal tax rate on capital gains, allowing for maximum "unearned" income tax rates, the minimum tax, and the potential for "earned income" taxation at rates above their normal ceiling.[25] The corporate rate (t_c) is the maximum marginal tax rate on corporate source income. Both it and the dividend rate have been purged of the surtax in 1968–70. The combined rate (t_{equity}) represents the cascaded effects of all of these taxes on a marginal dollar of pretax corporate income.[26]

Taxes play a prominent role in the calculations of expected present value and hence in the regression model. However, testing for any further separate effects is worthwhile because emotional responses to tax-rate increases may produce an exaggerated market impact. Table 3 presents simple correlations between alternative tax parameters and share prices; and table 4 presents multiple regression analyses, including a subset of the tax variables.

---

25. This series was provided by the Office of Tax Analysis, U.S. Treasury Department.

26. This may be written as $t_{equity} = t_c + (1 - t_c) [(dpo)t + (1 - dpo) teff_{cg}]$, where *dpo* is the dividend payout ratio, and $teff_{cg}$ (the *effective* tax rate on capital gains) equals $(0.8t/2 + 2t_{cg})/[1 + r(1 - t)]^5$. An arbitrarily weighted average of one-half the dividend rate and the maximum capital gains rate has been discounted to reflect the advantage of tax deferral.

Figure 8. Historical Patterns in the Taxation of Corporate Capital, 1955–78

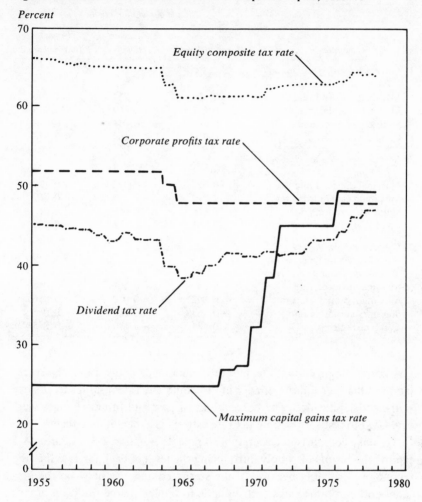

Percent

The strength of the simple correlations presented in sections 1 and 2 of table 3 is surprising unless one begins with an extremely naive view of the stock market and its relation to tax rates. On the other hand, the relatively strong correlations reported in section 3 of the table and the autocorrelated errors consistently noted in earlier specifications prompted us to perform a number of additional regressions. The residuals of the "preferred" equation identifying risk and illusion influences on share prices are significantly negatively correlated with the dividend tax rate, the statu-

Table 3. Correlations between Tax Parameters and Share Price

	Simple correlation coefficients		
Tax rate	Current level	4-quarter change	1-quarter future change
1. Correlation with Standard and Poor's share price index			
Marginal dividend rate	−0.384	0.254	0.166
Maximum capital gains rate	0.672	0.469	0.145
Statutory corporate rate	−0.897	0.051	0.010
Combined rate	−0.750	0.169	0.078
2. Correlation with the share price– EPV ratio			
Marginal dividend rate	−0.677	−0.372	−0.192
Maximum capital gains rate	−0.590	−0.010	−0.069
Statutory corporate rate	0.065	0.068	−0.019
Combined rate	−0.311	−0.415	−0.226
3. Correlation with the risk- and illusion-adjusted regression residuals (equation 2-5, above)			
Marginal dividend rate	−0.546	−0.101	−0.010
Maximum capital gains rate	0.092	0.050	−0.056
Statutory corporate rate	−0.355	0.062	−0.065
Combined rate	−0.487	−0.170	−0.045

tory corporate profit tax rate, and the "combined" equity rate. The correlation of the four-quarter change in this combined rate just fails to achieve statistical significance. The correlations of past and future changes were evaluated to test for possible tax rate as well as expectation effects.

To make comparison easier, table 4 repeats equation 2-5. Equation 4-1 reports the results of simply introducing the level of each tax rate into the regression. Probably because of the strong collinearity between the personal and corporate rates (attributable to the legislative tradition of cutting or raising them in tandem) the result is peculiar: each one-point increase in personal dividend taxes cuts share prices by about 5 percent, but a one-point increase in the corporate rate is projected to *raise* share prices by about 2.5 percent. Both of these effects are significant by normal statistical standards. The estimated coefficient of the maximum tax rate on capital gains is insignificant and has the wrong sign.

To deal with the problem of collinearity in tax rates, we employed the variable representing the composite tax rate, t_{equity}, in equations 4-2 and 4-2a. The *EPV* coefficient is freely estimated in equation 4-2a, and con-

Table 4. Testing for Additional Tax Influences in the Price–EPV Relation

Equation number	Explanatory variable[a]	Coefficient	$\bar{R}^2$	Durbin-Watson	Standard error
2-5	Constant	0.190 (0.168)	0.911	0.428	0.097
	Log (*EPV*)	1.000			
	Mich. sentiment index	−0.033 (0.150)			
	Real money growth	3.364 (0.548)			
	Bond rate − prime rate	0.008 (0.012)			
	Log (*BOOK/REPL*)	0.702 (0.086)			
4-1	Constant	0.359 (0.217)	0.954	0.836	0.070
	Log (*EPV*)	1.000			
	Mich. sentiment index	0.344 (0.130)			
	Real money growth	2.442 (0.497)			
	Bond rate − prime rate	−0.013 (0.009)			
	Log (*BOOK/REPL*)	0.358 (0.181)			
	Log $(1 - t_{div})$	2.878 (0.415)			
	Log $(1 - t_{cg})$	−0.231 (0.174)			
	Log $(1 - t_c)$	−1.192 (0.452)			
4-2 and 4-2a	Constant	1.062/1.051 (0.202/0.763)	0.936/ 0.936	0.546/ 0.546	0.080/ 0.082
	Log (*EPV*)	1.000/1.002 (.../0.100)			
	Mich. sentiment index	0.272/0.272 (0.136/0.151)			
	Real money growth	2.267/2.262 (0.497/0.579)			

Table 4 (*continued*)

Equation number	Explanatory variable[a]	Coefficient	$\bar{R}^2$	Durbin-Watson	Standard error
			Summary statistics		
	Bond rate − prime rate	0.009/0.009 (0.010/0.011)			
	Log (*BOOK/REPL*)	0.658/0.661 (0.073/0.171)			
	Log (1 − t_{equity})	1.151/1.146 (0.189/0.358)			
4-3	Constant	0.388 (0.516)	0.971[b]	1.9059	0.055
	Log (*EPV*)	1.000			
	Mich. sentiment index	0.486 (0.152)			
	Real money growth	1.449 (0.637)			
	Bond rate − prime rate	0.016 (0.012)			
	Log (*BOOK/REPL*)	0.520 (0.183)			
	Log (1 − t_{equity})	0.768 (0.459)			
	Lagged error	0.821 (0.066)			

a. The variables are defined in the text and at the end of the appendix. Standard errors of the coefficients are in parentheses.
b. The r^2 without error feedback = 0.925.

strained to 1 in equation 4-2. The estimated coefficients of *EPV* and of all other variables except the difference between the bond rate and the prime rate are unaffected by the constraint. Based on the coefficients in equation 4-2, share prices rise by approximately three percentage points beyond the tax impact embodied in the expected present value for each one-point decline in the composite tax rate. This result suggests that irrational responses to tax changes (in other words, responses not traceable to tax-caused changes in the *EPV*) may have caused the tax decreases of the late 1950s through 1965–66 to boost the market by approximately 20 percent, while the tax increases from 1966 through 1978 may have then cut share prices by about 10 percent.

To remove the autocorrelation of residuals still apparent in equation 4-2, we simultaneously estimated the first-order autoregressive error coefficient in equation 4-3. The tax variable is no longer found to be statistically significant as its estimated coefficient declines by almost one-half

Figure 9. Actual Standard and Poor's Index, Regression Estimate, and the "Economic" Expected Present Value, 1955–78

Index: 1941–43 = 10

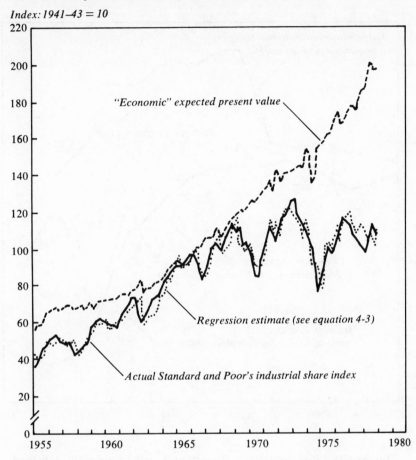

while the estimated standard error increases. The consumer confidence, real money growth, and illusion variables retain their significance.

In this final equation, the 1955–66 tax changes are seen to have raised share prices by 12 percent *beyond* the tax impact on the *EPV*. Subsequent tax increases cut share prices by an estimated 7 percent. (Recall, however, that these effects are not found to be statistically significant.) To refer back to the earlier discussion of tax rates and *EPV*s, the 1955–65 tax rate changes raised the *EPV* by 0.5 percent. The 1966–78 rate increases then cut the *EPV* by 0.4 percent. The total estimated impact of taxes on the price of shares was thus a gain of 12.5 percent during the first subperiod and a loss of 7.5 percent during the second subperiod.

Figure 10. Sources of Variations in Share Prices from the Expected Present Value, 1955–78

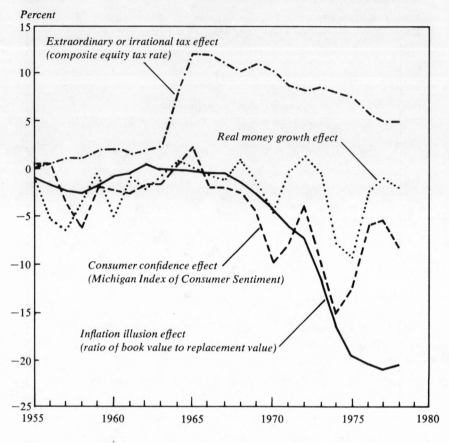

Percent

The tax effect is quantitatively important though of marginal statistical quality. It is obviously insufficient to explain the depressed level of the stock market in the 1970s. Figure 9—a graph of the share price index, the expected present value of dividends and sales proceeds without any risk adjustment, and the estimated share price from equation 4-3—clearly indicates that a much wider gap than this tax effect has developed during the past ten years. It is apparent that equation 4-3 tracks the stock market well after 1968 only because changing consumer confidence and illusion have been included in the analysis.

Figure 10 summarizes the major quantitative influences besides the *EPV* on share prices. The initial year of the regression analysis, 1955, has been arbitrarily chosen as numéraire. The figure shows that, for example, the extremely weak stock market of 1974 was generated by three strong depressants. In the aftermath of Watergate, economic policy turned extremely restrictive and consumer confidence collapsed. Slow real money growth cut share prices by 7 percent from their fundamental *EPV*. Two other factors cut prices by 16 percent each—a lack of confidence and the understatement of corporate net worth through traditional accounting measures. The composite tax rate on equity was in fact approximately four points below its 1955 numéraire value and thus contributed modest positive support relative to the 1955 position.

Conclusion

The final regression specification suggests significant roles for (1) current cyclic conditions, (2) economic fundamentals, and (3) illusion in the pricing of shares. Not surprisingly, consumer confidence and stimulative monetary policy support market prices. On the other hand, investors appear to weigh "true" economic prospects and "foggy" accounting measures of corporate net worth approximately equally, as witnessed by the 0.5 coefficient of the ratio of book to replacement value in the last regression. This ratio was virtually stable from 1955 through 1968, but by 1978 had fallen to 65 percent of its 1968 value, implying a depressive impact on the stock market of approximately 20 percent. The substantial role of illusion operating through the inflation distortion of corporate net worth, and perhaps through exaggerated responses to tax increases, is clearly shown in figure 10. The era of escalating inflation ushered in by the fiscal stimulus of the Vietnam War coincides with a sharp departure of share prices from their arguable equilibrium values.

The suggestion of a strong inflation illusion is certainly not unique to this study. As the weak stock market performance of the 1970s has become clear, quite a few authors have remarked on the negative impact of inflation.[27] Recently, Malkiel and Modigliani-Cohn[28] debated whether this correlation is due to increasing risk or to illusion.

27. See Phillip Cagan, "Common Stock Values and Inflation," National Bureau of Economic Research, Supplement 13 to the *54th Annual Report* (September 1974); John Lintner, "Inflation and Common Stock Prices in a Cyclical Context," National Bureau of Economic Research, *53rd Annual Report* (September 1974), pp. 23–36; Zvi Bodie, "Common Stocks as a Hedge Against Inflation," *Journal of Finance*, vol. 31 (May 1976), pp. 459–70; and Brainard, Shoven, and Weiss, "Financial Valuation of the Return to Capital."

28. See Malkiel, "Capital Formation Problem"; and Modigliani and Cohn, "Inflation, Rational Valuation, and the Market."

The illusion effect identified by this paper lends support to the Modigliani-Cohn thesis that illusion has a prominent influence. As economists, Modigliani and Cohn are apprehensive about their results because they feel that persistent irrational behavior is indicated. In this paper we argue that, while the market may in fact be undervalued in a fundamental sense based on "true" economic data, the market price may still be appropriately termed rational: share prices accurately reflect available, though faulty, information.

A bull market is possible for the 1980s. If widely used measures of corporate worth should be restated to capture assets on the same current value basis as liabilities, a 20 percent jump in share prices could be achieved. The accounting profession is contemplating changes in this direction with its efforts in the field of replacement cost analysis. Most discussions of this area have focused on the impact on annual profits,[29] but the effects on balance sheets will be proportionately greater. If a complete and correct accounting overhaul is achieved, there is good reason to believe the market will respond vigorously.

Appendix: Calculating the Expected Present Value

The *EPV* is:

$$EPV = \sum_{i=1}^{H} \frac{D_0(1-t)(1+d^e)^i}{[1+r(1-t)]^i} + \frac{P_0 t_{cg}}{[1+r(1-t)]^H}$$

$$+ \frac{(1-t_{cg})}{[1+r(1-t)]^H} qRC_0(1+PI^e)^H$$

$$+ q \sum_{i=1}^{H} [E_0(1+g^e)^i D_0(1+d^e)^i](1+PI^e)^{H-i},$$

where the variables are as defined in the text. Alternative expectation regimes were tested for each of the three expectation variables: d^e, the growth in per-share dividends; g^e, the growth in per-share adjusted after-tax economic earnings; and PI^e, the growth in the price deflator for business fixed investment. A total of five expectation regimes were tested.

---

29. As we argued earlier in the text, earnings adjustments of two types are necessary. First, depreciation should be calculated on a replacement cost basis, and second, the reduced real value of debt must be recognized. These two adjustments would produce an earning series consistent with balance sheets updated to reflect assets measured in replacement value terms, except that the earnings measure would correctly not include pure inflation gains in equity-financed nominal asset values.

Figure 11. Percentage Growth in Earnings per Share, 1955–78

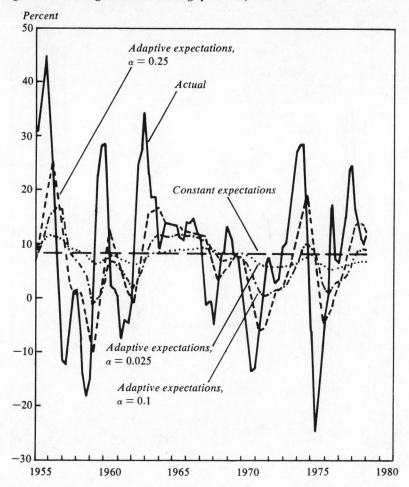

Percent

Adaptive expectations,
$\alpha = 0.25$

Actual

Constant expectations

Adaptive expectations,
$\alpha = 0.025$

Adaptive expectations,
$\alpha = 0.1$

Three were adaptive expectations with varying speeds of adjustment ($\alpha = 0.025$, 0.1, and 0.25). The fourth—static expectations—assumes that the most recent observed rate of growth of the indicated variable would persist thereafter. This is the most volatile regime. The fifth—constant expectations—assumes that the future rate growth would be equal to its average over the entire interval. It is, of course, invariant with respect to time and is the most sluggish expectation regime. Figures 11–13 show the actual growth rates for each series plotted against those determined

Figure 12. Percentage Growth in Dividends per Share, 1955–78

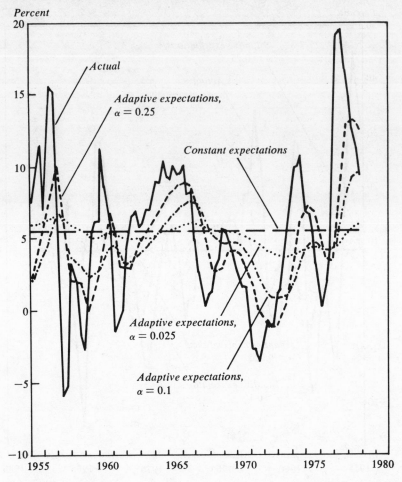

by the alternative expectation regimes. (Note that the static expectation series is not included in the three charts since it duplicates the actual growth rate of the series.)

A total of 125 *EPV*s were calculated for each possible combination of expectation regimes. The *EPV* with the highest correlation with the stock market was that which assumed earnings expectations formed by an adaptive process with a speed of adjustment of 0.025, static dividend expectations, and constant investment deflator growth.

Figure 13. Percentage Growth in the Deflator for Business Fixed Investment, 1955–78

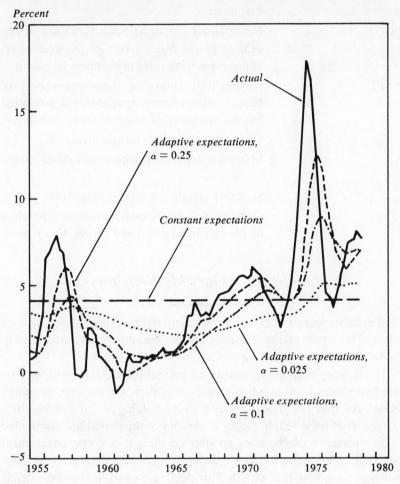

Percent

Definition of Terms

EPV	Expected present value of posttax dividends and capital gains (see text)
Mich. sentiment index	University of Michigan, Survey Research Center, Index of Consumer Sentiment
Real money growth	Four-quarter change in the logarithm of the $M1$-GNP deflator ratio
Bond rate	New-issue rate for high-grade corporate bonds

Prime rate	Short-term bank loan rate for prime commercial customers
BOOK	Nonfinancial corporate book value net worth, defined as the historic cost of physical assets minus the market value of net financial liabilities
REPL	Nonfinancial corporate replacement cost of physical assets net of straight-line depreciation less the market value of net financial liabilities
t	Marginal personal tax rate on dividends
t_{cg}	Maximum marginal personal tax rate on capital gains
t_c	Statutory marginal corporation tax rate
t_{equity}	Composite equity investment rate incorporating dividend, capital gains, and corporation rates

Comments by Gary M. Wenglowski

As a member and partner of an investment banking firm, I lived through much of the equity market environment that the authors have attempted to model. So my view is that of a practitioner.

The authors use a model based on a present value equation to test several hypotheses regarding the impact of inflation and taxation on equity values. An after-tax dividend stream over a holding period and the after-tax proceeds from selling stocks at the end of the period are discounted to their present value by using an after-tax three-to-five-year government bond rate. The present values most closely correlated with actual stock prices assume, first, that expected dividends are equal to actual dividends in each year; second, that the expected earnings growth of stocks is constant and equal to the average annual earnings growth between 1956 and 1976; and third, that the holding period is five years.

The correlation between the resulting present values and the actual Standard and Poor's 400 industrial stock index is shown in figure 9 of the paper. The correlation is surprisingly high, particularly in the period after 1972 when the stock market was volatile. How I wish we had had the benefit of this model to guide us through that period. However, I believe that the high correlation may be deceptive and that it masks important problems in the model's specification.

My main concern about the proposed stock valuation model is the specification of the discount rate in the present value formula. The authors have used a ten-year government bond rate on an after-tax basis to discount the returns from investment in common stocks. In theory, the discount rate for common stocks should exceed the government bond rate by a premium for the higher risk of investing in stocks. This incremental risk is usually conceived as including the pitfalls companies face as a result of the business cycle and the changing leverage on their balance sheets. Also, as a practitioner in the financial markets, I have sensed a new element of incremental risk in stock investing since the early 1970s—the continuing surprisingly poor performance of the stock market itself. That is the risk of irrational market valuation. It shows up in the willingness of investors to pay a higher price–earnings ratio for control of a company when a corporate takeover occurs than they are willing to pay for a company's shares. Presumably, this is because in the latter case they are depending on the market's valuation of those shares to eventually make their profit.

The incorrect specification of the discount rate in the present value formula shows up on figure 9 in the present values being consistently above Standard and Poor's index, which the authors duly note. They also note that the difference between the calculated present values and the index reflects the difference between the true discount rate for stocks and the ten-year government bond rate. However, the authors do not focus on the fact that their calculated present values exceed the stock index by the greatest margin in the 1963–66 period and that there is little difference between the calculated present values and Standard and Poor's index for 1974–76. The implication is that the true capitalization rate for stocks exceeded the bond rate by its greatest margin in the mid-1960s and that it was identical to the bond rate in the 1974–76 period. In other words, the results imply that the incremental risk in buying common stocks was at its largest in the mid-1960s and has been almost nonexistent in recent years. This is counterintuitive and raises serious questions about the model's validity and the conclusions based on it. I will not dwell on the factors that have made investment in common stocks riskier in the more recent period because I think they are almost beyond dispute. I simply list the 1975 recession, the most severe in the postwar period; the advent of peacetime wage and price controls, which affected 1973 and 1974 profit margins; and the significant numbers of business failures in the banking and real estate investment trust sectors during the period.

This surprising implication for the risk premium attached to investment in common stocks may reflect an error in specifying the earnings variable that the market has been discounting. Although investors question reported earnings during high inflation, it is not clear that the adjusted earnings used by the authors are good estimates of what investors discount. There is little quarrel with the view that inventory profits and reported profits that include a deficiency in depreciation allowances should not be considered true earnings. However, there are real questions concerning whether the Commerce Department's inventory valuation adjustments accurately measure inventory profits, given the crude assumptions on which they are calculated. There is also the question of whether the decline in the real value of debt should be added to earnings. A major proponent of that adjustment, Franco Modigliani, attended the conference.

So I believe the close correlation between the calculated present values and Standard and Poor's index is misleading, even though the authors point to it as a major support for their model. My suggestion would be that a valuation model be estimated with alternative measures of earnings and an equity capitalization rate that is allowed to vary with changing risk in order to capture the determinants of share prices during the past twenty years.

The major conclusion of the paper on the effect of tax changes on stock prices is weakened by the failure of the model to incorporate a changing risk premium in the equity capitalization rate. The authors concluded that tax changes do affect stock prices, but they use their calculations of present value to demonstrate that the effects are small. They assert that share prices respond to changes in tax laws through changes in *both* the post-tax flows *and* the discount rate. They point out that the net effects may be small, because a tax cut raises after-tax dividends and stock sales profits as well as the after-tax bond rate, which they use as a discount rate in their model. However, because their present value calculations do not allow for a changing risk factor in the equity capitalization rate and for the effect of tax law changes on that risk factor, it clearly omits a major channel through which changes in tax law affect stock prices. Equity investors view government tax changes as signals of change in the government's attitude toward investment, and therefore as indicators of changes in the risks attached to owning common stocks. Failure to allow for changing risk in stock ownership significantly weakens the authors' conclusions about the effect of taxes on stock prices.

JOSEPH J. MINARIK

Capital Gains

FEDERAL income tax treatment of capital gains is highly controversial. Long-standing equity and administrative issues continue to arouse heated debate: whether capital gains should be taxed at all; what preferential treatment, if any, gains should be given relative to ordinary income; to what extent net losses should be deducted from ordinary income; whether appreciated gifts and bequests should be taxed, or what basis they should carry to recipients; and many more. But perhaps because of the sluggish progress of the U.S. economy, the effect of capital gains taxation on economic growth and efficiency has claimed a great deal of attention. Economists and laymen argue about whether capital gains taxation reduces capital investment or distorts its allocation, thereby slowing the rate of growth of output and productivity. These questions were discussed during the congressional deliberations in 1978 that yielded significant reductions in the taxation of capital gains, and widely disseminated economic analyses of these issues may have had an important influence on the legislative outcome. The influence of capital gains taxation on the economy must be understood to evaluate the 1978 decision and to choose appropriate future policy; the purpose of this paper is to increase this understanding.

I am grateful to Gerald E. Auten, Barry Bosworth, Ralph B. Bristol, Jr., John A. Brittain, Harvey Galper, Robert W. Hartman, Jerry A. Hausman, Bruce K. MacLaury, Benjamin A. Okner, Arthur M. Okun, Joseph A. Pechman, George L. Perry, and Emil M. Sunley for their helpful suggestions; to Timothy A. Cohn, Katharine J. Newman, and Laurent R. Ross for research assistance; and to Arthur Morton and Nancy E. O'Hara, who supervised the computer programming. Support for this research was provided by the National Science Foundation; support for research using the IRS Seven-Year Panel of Taxpayers was provided by the U.S. Treasury Department.

Three Issues in Capital Gains Taxation

While numerous arguments have been raised for preferential treatment of long-term capital gains, this discussion will focus on three major issues: the bunching of long-term gains, the opportunities for timing the realization of gains and losses, and the lock-in effect of the tax on capital gains.

With progressive taxation of long-term gains upon realization, the included portion of a long-term gain is taxed at the taxpayer's highest marginal tax rate on ordinary income. If the gain is large relative to the taxpayer's typical ordinary income, it could fall into still higher marginal rate brackets and incur a tax liability significantly higher than if part of the gain were taxed each year during which the asset was held.[1] This bunching problem has been widely recognized in the general literature on capital gains taxation, though the data available have not permitted estimation of the frequency or the amount of overtaxation caused by bunching until quite recently.

Some experts have argued that bunching should be remedied through more exact methods than the present general exclusion of 60 percent of long-term gains. One possible solution would be to average capital gains and other income over the period the asset was held (or some maximum period longer than the five years available to any taxpayer under current law). Goode points out that income averaging would provide relief for a taxpayer whose taxable income (including the gain) was substantially larger than usual, but none if his income including capital gains was stable, however bunched an individual gain might be. Averaging would complicate the tax forms and require records from earlier years, but many transactions could be disqualified from averaging because they were too small relative to average total income for averaging to significantly affect the tax liability.[2]

An alternative to income averaging would be proration of capital gains over the number of years the asset was held or some maximum period. The portion representing appreciation in the current year would be taxed as

1. For example, taxation in full of a $100,000 gain (held for two years) in 1978 would result in a liability of $24,180 for a single person claiming the standard deduction and having no other income. If the gain were split evenly between the two years, the total liability would be only $19,280. The problem is more serious the longer the holding period; it is nonexistent if the gain does not push the taxpayer into a higher marginal rate bracket.

2. Richard Goode, *The Individual Income Tax*, rev. ed. (Brookings Institution, 1976), pp. 191–95.

usual; the remainder for previous years would be taxed at the same effective rate as that for the current year. The effect would be to moderate the rate progression applied to the gain; the share of the gain prorated to earlier years would not be allowed to reach into higher marginal rate brackets. David points out that proration, unlike averaging, would be based only on the current year's tax return and thus would require no record keeping beyond the asset's basis; also unlike averaging, proration would reduce the tax liability on a large gain held over several years even if taxable income, including gains, was stable. Goode argues that prorating more than a small number of gains would be unwieldy, and Wetzler contends that to adopt proration in addition to general income averaging would enormously complicate the tax code.[3]

The third way to solve the bunching problem is taxation of gains as they accrue rather than when they are realized. Accrual taxation would involve formidable problems, including the valuation of assets rarely sold, the inventorying of all assets with the filing of each return, and the payment of taxes on accrued gains that had not been realized in cash.[4]

Some experts contend that the bunching problem, while potentially serious under particular circumstances, is not worrisome in practice. They see bunching as the result of the taxpayer's privilege to defer the realization of the gain until a time of his choosing and thus defer taxation of the appreciation. Concessions such as averaging or proration would reduce the tax liability upon realization to approximately the sum of the liabilities that would have been due in each year if the gain had been taxed on accrual. This would give the taxpayer the advantage of the time value of money while the tax was deferred. Some experts argue that the deferral of taxes on capital appreciation is a significant benefit to recipients of capital gains and thus makes the need for other preferential treatment less urgent. Wetzler has proposed a deferral charge as compensation for the implicit interest-free loans from the federal government to holders of appreciating assets.[5]

3. Martin David, *Alternative Approaches to Capital Gains Taxation* (Brookings Institution, 1968), pp. 166–80; Goode, *Individual Income Tax,* p. 192; James W. Wetzler, "Capital Gains and Losses," in Joseph A. Pechman, ed., *Comprehensive Income Taxation* (Brookings Institution, 1977), pp. 130–32.

4. David, *Alternative Approaches to Capital Gains Taxation,* pp. 183–85.

5. Wetzler, "Capital Gains and Losses," pp. 115–53. See also Roger Brinner and Alicia Munnell, "Taxation of Capital Gains: Inflation and Other Problems," Federal Reserve Bank of Boston, *New England Economic Review* (September–October 1974), pp. 3–21.

A further issue is the taxpayer's opportunity to time the realization of gains and losses. Consider the owner of a diversified portfolio of securities who relies on their appreciation to meet his cash needs. If his assets on the average increase in value but some decline, he can sell a balanced group of appreciating and depreciating assets with a total net gain of zero and pay no tax. The rest of his appreciating assets can be left to grow in value and under current law can be contributed to charity or bequeathed with no capital gains tax. Further, the heirs will not be liable for capital gains tax on the appreciation that occurred before they inherited the property. Some experts argue that the potential for deferring the tax and timing the realization renders further preferences somewhat redundant, but others believe that taxpayers with small portfolios cannot diversify sufficiently to take advantage of this. Available data have not permitted detailed analysis of the offsetting of gains and losses.[6] It is known that in 1962, of 4.3 million returns reporting net capital gains, 0.7 million realized some losses; and of 1.5 million reporting net losses, 0.7 million realized some gains.[7]

Some experts argue that taxation of gains locks investors in to assets that do not offer the best available yield. The lock-in effect takes two forms. First, the requirement that assets be held for a minimum length of time before preferential treatment is granted inhibits the sale of assets held for less than that period. Seltzer found that the five graduated holding periods in the law from 1934 to 1937 significantly reduced the turnover of capital assets.[8] Fredland, Gray, and Sunley demonstrated that realizations in 1962 were significantly reduced just before, and significantly increased just after, securities were held for six months.[9]

A lock-in effect also occurs when the tax that would be due upon the sale of an appreciated asset absorbs the profit from selling that asset and purchasing another with a higher pretax yield.[10] Brannon examined time

6. David, *Alternative Approaches to Capital Gains Taxation,* pp. 73–81.

7. U.S. Treasury Department, Internal Revenue Service, *Statistics of Income— 1962, Supplemental Report, Sales of Capital Assets Reported on Individual Income Tax Returns* (Government Printing Office, 1966), p. 60, table 6, and p. 86, table 9.

8. Lawrence H. Seltzer, *The Nature and Tax Treatment of Capital Gains and Losses* (National Bureau of Economic Research, 1951), pp. 167–72.

9. J. Eric Fredland, John A. Gray, and Emil M. Sunley, Jr., "The Six Month Holding Period for Capital Gains: An Empirical Analysis of Its Effect on the Timing of Gains," *National Tax Journal,* vol. 21 (December 1968), pp. 467–78.

10. Suppose that an investor paid $500 for stock that is now worth $1,000, and that the stock yields 10 percent with no prospect of further capital gain. If the effective tax rate on the gain is 20 percent, the investor could not profitably switch to a

series data and found evidence of reduced realizations as the result of capital gains taxation, but precise estimates were impossible because of data limitations.[11] Auten used pooled annual aggregate data by income class and identified a lock-in effect.[12] Feldstein, Slemrod, and Yitzhaki contend that actual realizations are highly sensitive to reductions in taxes applicable to capital gains, and that tax cuts would thus encourage enough additional realizations to increase total tax revenue. Using 1973 tax returns, they estimated a very high elasticity of realizations to the applicable marginal tax rate and computed on that basis that reducing the maximum tax rate on long-term capital gains from 45.5 percent to 25 percent would increase revenue.[13] Auten and Clotfelter, using a panel of tax returns for the 1967–73 period, found a smaller response to taxpayers' average tax rates over time. They also found a response to fluctuations in the tax rates (caused by variations in deductions and other income) that was greater than the response to average tax rates in some specifications.[14] Some experts counter that the lock-in effect is not so much the result of an insufficient preference for capital gains realizations as of forgiving income tax on capital gains held until death or given to charity and postponing tax on appreciation of assets given to other individuals. They claim that eliminating those preferences would be the best way to reduce the lock-in effect.[15]

---

new security unless it yielded over 11.1 percent. The disincentive to reallocate funds from the security yielding 10 percent to any other yielding between 10 and 11.1 percent is the lock-in effect. Charles C. Holt and John P. Shelton, "The Lock-In Effect of the Capital Gains Tax," *National Tax Journal,* vol. 15 (December 1962), pp. 337–52; Beryl W. Sprinkel and B. Kenneth West, "Effects of Capital Gains Taxes on Investment Decisions," *Journal of Business,* vol. 35 (April 1962), pp. 122–34.

11. Gerard M. Brannon, "The Lock-In Problem for Capital Gains: An Analysis of the 1970–71 Experience," in *The Effect of Tax Deductibility on the Level of Charitable Contributions and Variations on the Theme* (Washington, D.C.: Fund for Policy Research, 1974).

12. Gerald E. Auten, "Empirical Evidence on Capital Gains Taxes and Realizations" (Treasury Department, Office of Tax Analysis, 1979).

13. Martin Feldstein, Joel Slemrod, and Shlomo Yitzhaki, "The Effects of Taxation on the Selling of Corporate Stock and the Realization of Capital Gains," *Quarterly Journal of Economics,* vol. 94 (June 1980), pp. 777–91.

14. Gerald E. Auten and Charles T. Clotfelter, "Permanent vs. Transitory Tax Effects and the Realization of Capital Gains" (Treasury Department, August 23, 1979).

15. Martin J. Bailey, "Capital Gains and Income Taxation," in Arnold C. Harberger and Martin J. Bailey, eds., *The Taxation of Income from Capital* (Brookings Institution, 1969), pp. 11–49; David, *Alternative Approaches to Capital Gains Taxation,* pp. 145–64; Goode, *Individual Income Tax,* pp. 200–03, 209–10.

Bunching of Long-Term Gains

As mentioned earlier, the bunching of long-term gains in a single year under a progressive income tax can increase tax liabilities. On the other hand, taxation is deferred over the years in which the gains accrued, in effect constituting an interest-free loan of the tax liability on the accrued gain from the government to the asset holder. And taxpayers can choose the year in which they realize their gains to minimize their tax liability.

It is impossible to disentangle the relative effects of bunching and deferral with existing data. It is possible, however, to look at the bunching question and the timing of realization with the Internal Revenue Service Seven-Year Panel of Taxpayers, a random sample of identical filers' tax returns over the period 1967–73.[16]

The panel file shows only the total net gain or loss for any one year, and so it is impossible to gauge precisely the holding period over which any individual gain or loss item accrued. However, the file can show whether a net gain in one year is an isolated event or whether gains are realized in every year. It can also show whether the net gain in a particular year is taxed at a higher or lower marginal rate than is typical for the taxpayer over the duration of the panel. Because of the particular limitations and capabilities of the panel file, this analysis cannot compare the taxation of gains as they accrue, as opposed to lump sums when they are realized (that is, the type of bunching that is cited by advocates of proration). Rather, it will provide some indication of the frequency of realized gains that are large relative to average income over several prior and subsequent years (that is, the additional tax that would be prevented by a general capital gains averaging provision that corrected for losses as well as gains).

The bunching problem arises when a taxpayer realizes a long-term gain that is large relative to his average income.[17] Such a taxpayer would bear a far higher liability on that gain upon realization than he would under accrual taxation or a proration or averaging provision. In contrast,

16. The file contains information on a uniform random sample of taxpayers; thus its coverage of upper income taxpayers with large amounts of capital gains is limited. The sample includes the returns of 21,382 taxpayers for at least one year each, but some of these did not file returns in all of the seven years. For this analysis the sample is limited to 3,430 taxpayers who filed returns in at least five of the seven years and realized capital gains or losses in at least one of the years in which they filed returns.

17. The archetypical case is the sale of a business or partnership interest upon retirement

another taxpayer who is an active trader in capital assets may time his realizations along with his receipts of ordinary income and his itemized deductions, so that his income including capital gains is stable.[18] For such a taxpayer, mandatory averaging of capital gains over several years would increase rather than decrease total tax liabilities.

The relative frequency of realizations of "once in a lifetime" gains and of carefully timed recurrent gains should have an important influence on public policy. If highly bunched gains are common, policy should lean in the direction of protection from such extremes; but if many taxpayers already average by timing their gains, other income, and deductions appropriately, policies to ameliorate bunching are less urgent. This is especially true in light of the complexity of special provisions for taxpayers and tax authorities and the potential for abuse.[19]

To measure the extent of bunching, table 1 shows tax liabilities, by income class, for taxpayers in the panel file who realized long-term capital gains or losses in at least one year. Column 2 shows the average tax liability over the period with the 1973 tax law applied in each year and no income averaging permitted.[20] Column 3 shows the tax that would have been due under a complete income and deduction averaging system.[21] The difference between these columns is the additional tax that is due because of all fluctuations of income and deductions, including but not restricted to capital gains. For the entire population, this difference is about 9 percent of the tax liability without averaging. Column 4 is the total tax liability if capital gains, but no other income or deduction item, were averaged over the period.[22] For the entire population, averaging

18. The same effect obtains if a taxpayer, to maintain his consumption, realizes gains when his other income is low.

19. For some tax experts, the deferral of tax liability would be a compelling argument against concessions to recipients of long-term capital gains regardless of the impact of bunching.

20. A single tax law is used because taxpayers who plan their realizations to minimize their tax liability are likely to attempt to stabilize their taxable income, and because changes in tax laws are difficult to anticipate. From that point of view, use of different tax laws over the period would mask the taxpayer's behavior. Income averaging is omitted for the same reason.

21. That is, the tax due on the average amount of ordinary income and the average amounts of net long-term and net short-term gain, less the average amounts of deductions and personal exemptions.

22. That is, the average tax that would be due if tax were calculated in each year on the actual amounts of ordinary income, deductions, and exemptions, and the average amounts of net long-term and net short-term gain or loss over the period. This tax system is applied as an analytical device rather than a policy proposal.

Table 1. Average Annual Tax over a Five-to-Seven-Year Period for Taxpayers Who Realized Capital Gains

Dollars unless otherwise specified

Adjusted gross income net of capital gains	Number of returns[a] (1)	Tax with actual income and deductions per return per year[b] (2)	Tax with averaged income and deductions per return per year (3)	Tax with averaged capital gains and actual other income and deductions per return per year (4)	Percentage of tax saving through complete averaging achieved by averaging of capital gains only (5)
Less than 0	16	133	45	1,302	−1,328.7
0–1,000	27	91	17	143	−70.6
1,000–2,000	85	80	28	67	25.1
2,000–3,000	128	155	95	135	34.1
3,000–4,000	158	250	182	225	36.6
4,000–5,000	163	377	277	344	32.3
5,000–10,000	949	805	699	758	44.1
10,000–15,000	921	1,570	1,426	1,481	61.9
15,000–20,000	459	2,656	2,428	2,496	70.0
20,000–25,000	220	3,701	3,403	3,538	54.7
25,000–50,000	227	7,487	6,917	7,248	41.9
50,000 and over	77	33,408	30,943	31,256	87.3
Total or average	3,430	2,521	2,298	2,390	58.6

Source: Internal Revenue Service Seven-Year Panel of Taxpayers.

a. Includes returns of taxpayers who submitted tax returns for at least five of the seven years and realized capital gains in at least one of those years.

b. Under provisions of the 1973 law.

capital gains over the seven years would reduce tax liabilities by about 5 percent. Thus capital gains bunching accounts for approximately 59 percent of the additional taxation caused by the absence of a complete averaging system. This fraction generally increases with income net of gains; in fact, averaging of only gains over the period would increase taxes for the two lowest income classes as a whole.

This result suggests that some taxpayers, even those at higher income levels, may time their gains to coincide with years in which their ordinary income is below average and their deductions are higher than normal. This question is explored further in tables 2, 3, and 4, which show the effect of averaging capital gains only over the entire sample period for taxpayers whose tax would be increased by such averaging—12.5 percent of the population. As mentioned earlier, this occurs when taxpayers with

Table 2. Tax Returns with Taxes Increased by the Averaging of Capital Gains, by Income Other Than Capital Gains

Income other than capital gains (dollars)	Total number of returns	Returns with taxes increased by capital gains averaging		Percentage increase in tax caused by capital gains averaging
		Number	Percent	
Less than 0	16	8	50.0	6,192.1
0–1,000	27	5	18.5	199.4
1,000–2,000	85	18	21.2	47.0
2,000–3,000	128	26	20.3	32.8
3,000–4,000	158	38	24.1	21.9
4,000–5,000	163	37	22.7	28.0
5,000–10,000	949	125	13.2	22.3
10,000–15,000	921	63	6.8	17.6
15,000–20,000	459	37	8.1	8.3
20,000–25,000	220	26	11.8	7.8
25,000–50,000	227	40	17.6	8.3
50,000 and over	77	7	9.1	6.0
Total or average	3,430	430	12.5	13.2

Source: Same as table 1.

Table 3. Tax Returns with Taxes Increased by the Averaging of Capital Gains, by Number of Years Gains Were Realized

Number of years gains were realized	Total number of returns	Returns with taxes increased by capital gains averaging		Percentage increase in tax caused by capital gains averaging
		Number	Percent	
1	1,283	108	8.4	14.0
2	569	68	12.0	10.3
3, 4, or 5[a]	808	98	12.1	6.5
4, 5, or 6[b]	306	67	21.9	11.8
5, 6, or 7[c]	464	89	19.2	21.2
Total or average	3,430	430	12.5	13.2

Source: Same as table 1.

a. Three years for taxpayers with five tax returns in the sample; three or four years for those with six returns; and three, four, or five years for those with seven returns.

b. Four years for taxpayers with five tax returns in the sample; five years for those with six returns; and six years for those with seven returns.

c. Five years for taxpayers with five tax returns in the sample; six years for those with six returns; and seven years for those with seven returns.

Table 4. Tax Returns with Taxes Increased by the Averaging of Capital Gains, by Amount of Capital Gains

Capital gains (dollars)	Total number of returns	Returns with taxes increased by capital gains averaging		Percentage increase in tax caused by capital gains averaging
		Number	Percent	
Less than 0	751	64	8.5	8.1
0–1,000	1,940	206	10.6	10.2
1,000–2,000	302	63	20.9	10.8
2,000–3,000	137	32	23.4	12.2
3,000–5,000	137	27	19.7	13.0
5,000–10,000	88	21	23.9	9.7
10,000–25,000	46	10	21.7	22.2
25,000 and over	29	7	24.1	32.8
Total or average	3,430	430	12.5	13.2

Source: Same as table 1.

fluctuating ordinary income realize capital gains in years of low ordinary income and thus stabilize their total income. Further, frequent traders are likely to time their realizations to coincide with years in which their tax rates are low—one in five taxpayers with gains in all years or all but one year would have their taxes increased by mandatory averaging of gains, as against one in eight for the population as a whole. The frequency of such tax increases is a U-shaped function of income other than gains, but an increasing function of total gains. Tax increases caused by the averaging of gains equal approximately 13 percent of liability based on actual gains.

The tendency to time realizations is evident in the data themselves. With the use of yearly percentage deviations ($\%DEV$) of adjusted gross income (net of all capital gains), itemized deductions (exclusive of state income and sales taxes), and net capital gains from the mean values for individual taxpayers for the duration of the panel, the following regression equation was obtained from the panel data (t-statistics are given in parentheses):

$$\%DEVGAIN = 1.3231 - 0.0601\ \%DEVAGI + 0.4254\ \%DEVDED.$$
$$\qquad\qquad\qquad (3.067) \qquad\qquad\qquad (13.189)$$

$$\bar{R}^2 = 0.0075;\ \text{standard error} = 200.321$$

The equation indicates that, if a taxpayer's adjusted gross income (AGI) in any one year is 1 percent higher than his mean adjusted gross income over the seven years of the panel, his net capital gains *(GAIN)* will be about 0.06 percent lower than his mean value. Further, if his itemized deductions *(DED)* are 1 percent higher than his mean deductions over the seven years, his net capital gains will be about 0.4 percent greater than his mean value. Both coefficients are consistent with the hypothesis that taxpayers tend to realize gains when their tax rates are temporarily reduced, although the deductions effect seems to be much more pronounced than the income effect.

These results suggest that many taxpayers do experience bunching of capital gains, as conventionally assumed, and incur higher tax liabilities as a result. The income averaging system now in the law reduces such excess liabilities. On the other hand, others time their gains and losses when their deductions are high and their other income is low in order to reduce their tax liabilities; those who realize the greatest gains and who realize them most frequently are the most likely to time their realizations. This benefit of the realization principle for capital gains recipients is often overlooked.

Timing of Capital Gains and Losses

Because the data used in the preceding analysis include only net short-term and net long-term capital gains or losses, it was not possible to measure the extent to which individual gain or loss transactions were used to offset each other. The 1973 Internal Revenue Service Sales of Capital Assets File provides detail on individual capital transactions and therefore can be used to analyze the timing of capital gains and losses during a single year.[23]

Table 5 summarizes the information on realized capital gains and losses in the 1973 file. Column 3 shows that 24 percent of all returns with net gain reported at least some losses, and that the frequency of realizing offsetting gains and losses increases sharply as income increases. The ratio

23. The Sales of Capital Assets File contains information on the approximately 50,000 tax returns from the IRS Individual Tax Model File (which contains a total of approximately 100,000 tax returns) that include capital transactions. Each transaction is detailed with the type of asset, the dates of acquisition and sale of the asset, and the cost basis and purchase price. The Sales of Capital Assets File shares the stratified sample design of the Individual Tax Model File, with 100 percent sampling of tax returns with adjusted gross income above $200,000. Thus the Capital Assets File includes a rich sample of tax returns with large and numerous capital asset transactions, but has also been stratified accurately to replicate the entire population.

Table 5. Capital Gains and Losses on Federal Income Tax Returns, 1973

Adjusted gross income net of capital gains (dollars)	Number of returns with net gain (1)	Number of net gain returns with some losses (2)	Percent of net gain returns with some losses (3)	Gross gain divided by net gain (4)	Number of returns with net loss (5)	Number of net loss returns with some gains (6)	Percent of net loss returns with some gains (7)	Gross loss divided by net loss (8)
None	121,979	21,404	17.6	1.3	25,449	5,932	23.3	1.9
0–2,500	308,969	58,866	19.1	1.5	101,570	53,021	52.2	1.4
2,500–5,000	299,363	56,719	19.0	1.6	119,672	19,120	16.0	1.4
5,000–7,500	284,160	34,464	12.1	1.5	124,637	23,742	19.1	1.5
7,500–10,000	311,023	74,756	24.0	1.4	125,035	39,535	31.6	3.5
10,000–15,000	536,069	95,290	17.8	1.6	283,754	85,199	30.0	1.5
15,000–20,000	423,784	100,355	23.7	1.6	343,242	113,548	33.1	1.8
20,000–25,000	269,874	78,082	28.9	1.5	254,347	83,984	33.0	1.4
25,000–30,000	194,498	59,809	30.8	1.5	159,861	80,267	50.2	1.6
30,000–50,000	312,968	122,800	39.2	1.7	265,850	104,771	39.4	1.9
50,000–100,000	142,776	66,690	46.7	1.7	116,732	60,895	52.2	2.0
100,000–200,000	33,481	17,714	52.9	1.5	23,655	14,904	63.0	2.1
200,000–500,000	6,898	4,059	58.8	1.4	4,063	2,836	69.8	1.9
500,000–1,000,000	721	436	60.5	1.3	382	301	78.8	2.2
1,000,000 and over	228	148	64.9	1.3	144	117	81.3	1.9
Total or average	3,246,791	791,592	24.4	1.5	1,948,393	688,172	35.3	1.8

Source: Internal Revenue Service Sales of Capital Assets File.

Table 6. Ratio of Stock Sales to Dividends for Returns with Net Stock Gains

Class of net stock gain (dollars)	Number of returns	Stock sales divided by dividends
0–2,500	718,576	2.5
2,500–5,000	163,942	4.9
5,000–7,500	76,615	4.7
7,500–10,000	32,224	7.9
10,000–15,000	57,787	4.1
15,000–20,000	19,327	4.5
20,000–25,000	19,779	8.3
25,000–30,000	11,063	6.0
30,000–50,000	21,123	7.1
50,000–100,000	15,721	7.8
100,000–200,000	8,387	17.3
200,000–500,000	3,658	13.4
500,000–1,000,000	1,066	12.9
1,000,000 and over	603	19.5
Total or average	1,149,871	6.6

Source: Same as table 5.

of gross gain to net gain decreases slightly with income. Columns 7 and 8 show similar results for net loss returns, but with the ratio of gross loss to net loss increasing with income.

A further aspect of the timing issue is the degree to which shareholders at various net gain or loss levels turn over their portfolios in any given year. Table 6 shows that the ratio of stock sales to dividends rises sharply as net stock gains increase. Moreover, returns with large net stock gains reported ratios of stock sales to dividends that are high relative to the ratio of the value of all stock outstanding to total dividend payments.[24] Thus for many investors with large portfolios, the potential for realization of larger amounts of capital gains in response to reduced tax rates on gains is limited.[25]

24. The ratio of stock sales to dividends for returns with net stock gains of $1,000,000 or more was 19.5. Based on the average 1973 dividend yield of 0.0306 (*Economic Report of the President, 1979*, p. 285, table B-88), the ratio of total portfolio value to dividends averages 32.7.

25. Simulations of the tax implications of unlocking accrued gains often rely on a proportional increase in realized gains based on changes in effective tax rates (such as Feldstein, Slemrod, and Yitzhaki, "Effects of Taxation"). On this basis, much of the simulated increase in realized gains (in absolute terms) comes from tax returns that already have large amounts of realized gains. Table 6 suggests that many of those returns may have limited additional gains to realize.

Table 7. Relationship of Stock and Nonstock Gains and Losses, Returns with Net Stock Gain, 1973

Adjusted gross income net of capital gains (dollars)	Number of returns	Returns with nonstock net gain		Returns with nonstock net loss	
		Percent of all returns	Nonstock gain divided by stock gain	Percent of all returns	Nonstock loss divided by stock gain
None	18,061	37.4	1.5	17.7	−0.2
0–2,500	89,444	3.3	0.8	21.4	−0.5
2,500–5,000	62,618	21.2	7.1	3.5	−0.8
5,000–7,500	77,616	9.9	1.8	17.8	−0.2
7,500–10,000	104,890	8.7	0.8	15.4	−0.4
10,000–15,000	167,090	9.1	0.7	6.6	−0.2
15,000–20,000	156,916	13.0	1.2	12.7	−0.5
20,000–25,000	121,529	20.1	0.8	11.1	−0.7
25,000–30,000	92,487	18.2	0.8	17.4	−0.7
30,000–50,000	160,678	20.4	0.7	16.1	−0.3
50,000–100,000	74,601	26.2	0.6	16.8	−0.4
100,000–200,000	19,232	32.4	0.6	19.7	−0.3
200,000–500,000	4,150	38.9	0.6	23.8	−0.4
500,000–1,000,000	432	43.8	0.4	26.1	−0.5
1,000,000 and over	127	49.6	1.1	32.4	−0.1
Total or average	1,149,871	15.4	1.0	13.8	−0.4

Source: Same as table 5.

A final consideration for any analysis focused on stock gains is the degree to which gains or losses on other types of assets might confuse the analysis. Tables 7 and 8 show that 30 percent of all tax returns with gains or losses on corporate stock also have gains or losses on other assets. The degree to which taxpayers use losses on stock, which is a relatively liquid asset, to offset gains on nonstock assets, which may be less liquid, is striking. Nonstock losses are particularly large relative to stock gains in the $1,000,000 and over ordinary-income class, where 59 percent of all returns with net losses on stock have net gains on other assets, and on average there is more than $1 of stock loss for every $2 of nonstock gain. The prevalence of such offsetting gains and losses suggests that the relationship between marginal tax rates and gains on corporate stock cannot be analyzed without regard to other factors.[26]

Two conclusions may be drawn from this analysis. First, estimates of

26. For example, an upper income taxpayer with large nonstock gains may show a high first-dollar tax rate on stock gains owing to his normal tax rate and the appli-

**Table 8. Relationship of Stock and Nonstock Gains and Losses, Returns with
Net Stock Loss, 1973**

Adjusted gross income net of capital gains (dollars)	Number of returns	Returns with nonstock net gain		Returns with nonstock net loss	
		Percent of all returns	Nonstock gain divided by stock loss	Percent of all returns	Nonstock loss divided by stock loss
None	12,934	49.3	−4.9	24.1	1.4
0–2,500	59,326	14.3	−7.3	0.9	0.3
2,500–5,000	64,287	17.1	−1.9	2.3	6.8
5,000–7,500	68,609	18.1	−3.0	16.1	2.3
7,500–10,000	65,447	7.7	−2.9	5.8	0.9
10,000–15,000	190,480	16.1	−1.8	7.9	1.7
15,000–20,000	254,904	16.1	−2.6	16.8	0.5
20,000–25,000	196,318	18.9	−2.2	8.5	0.4
25,000–30,000	136,442	26.1	−1.2	10.8	0.2
30,000–50,000	227,225	19.4	−2.0	11.9	1.3
50,000–100,000	102,470	28.6	−2.1	14.2	0.6
100,000–200,000	22,050	38.1	−2.4	13.9	0.6
200,000–500,000	3,858	47.6	−2.9	16.6	1.0
500,000–1,000,000	401	50.6	−4.9	21.9	0.6
1,000,000 and over	148	58.8	−1.9	25.0	0.2
Total or average	1,404,899	19.3	−2.4	11.0	0.7

Source: Same as table 5.

the relationship of tax rates and capital gains realizations must take account of offsetting gain and loss transactions, lest serious errors be made.
Second, the timing option often permits tax-free reallocations of investments in corporate stock and other capital assets. For those with holdings
large enough to permit diversification, the timing option is particularly
significant.

Locking In Caused by Marginal Tax Rates

A final question is the effect of the level of capital gains tax rates on
asset holders' decisions to realize. As mentioned earlier, taxes on capital

---

cation of the minimum tax and maximum tax offset. If that taxpayer realizes large
stock losses to offset those nonstock gains, a regression will show an overlarge negative coefficient on the basis of this nonmarginal strategy. In the opposite case, large
nonstock losses (or capital loss carry-overs) may produce a zero tax rate and large
positive stock gains in circumstances with little relevance for estimating the elasticity of responses to marginal changes of nonzero tax rates.

gains do make realization and reinvestment less profitable, but because the incentive effects of the tax law are based largely on expectations of the relative future performance of alternative investments, the magnitude of the tax effects in practice is uncertain. Empirical analysis has been limited by a lack of appropriate data, but the 1973 Sales of Capital Assets File permits such analysis.

This analysis is restricted to realizations of gains and losses on corporate stock because stock investments are highly liquid and are typically made for the purpose of capital gain. The analysis here follows the general methodology of Feldstein, Slemrod, and Yitzhaki, but with some refinements.[27]

Even though the capital assets file is by far the richest source of data available on realizations of capital gains, it cannot support analysis that uses a sophisticated structural model of taxpayer behavior.[28] In particular, the lack of information on investors' holdings and purchases of stock, in detail comparable to that on sales, prevents the application of a model based firmly in theory.

Instead, I begin with a reasonable reduced-form model:

Realized long-term corporate stock gains = F (dividends, other income, gains on other assets, carry-over and losses on other assets, itemized deductions, business losses, and the marginal tax rate).

Realization of gains is probably a function of the size of the taxpayer's portfolio. Tax returns provide no direct measure of portfolio size, but the

27. "Effects of Taxation."
28. The theoretical underpinning of the lock-in effect is the work of Holt and Shelton, "Lock-In Effect," and Sprinkel and West, "Effects of Capital Gains Taxes." The short- and long-run effects of the capital gains tax can be seen from the example presented earlier. An investor paid $500 for stock that has now stabilized in value at $1,000 and that yields 10 percent of current value. With an effective capital gains tax rate of 20 percent, the investor can only be made better off by switching to a stock that yields 11.1 percent or more. If the capital gains tax rate is reduced to 15 percent, stock yielding 10.8 percent or better will increase the investor's income stream. At the time of the tax cut, the investor who held his stock under the higher tax rate would immediately switch if he knew of any alternative asset yielding between 10.8 and 11.1 percent. That is the short-run effect.

In the longer run, a lower capital gains tax rate would reduce the yield differential necessary to induce any investor to switch to an asset of higher yield. If yields fluctuate over time, the lower the capital gains tax rate is, the greater the likelihood in any period that some alternative asset will reach a yield high enough to induce the investor to switch will be. That is the long-run effect.

The theory is complicated in application by investor uncertainty, as well as by the commingling of yield and capital gains objectives.

amount of dividends can be used as a proxy indicator.[29] Those with large holdings may be active traders and may realize large fractions of their accrued gains each year. On the other hand, those with small portfolios may realize all their gains in a single sale. Thus the qualitative effect of portfolio size on the amount of gains realized in a given year is uncertain. After finding that the tax rate does not have a statistically significant effect on capital gains realizations for the entire population, Feldstein, Slemrod, and Yitzhaki removed from their sample all cases with dividends of less than $3,000.[30]

The equations in this paper likewise show no apparent relationship between tax rates and realizations for the entire population, so tax returns with dividends below $3,000 were removed from the analysis. However, some effort was devoted to finding the degree to which locking in caused by tax rates does appear for various portfolio sizes. Dividends were entered into the equations in a quadratic form to allow for nonlinearities and also as an interaction term with the tax rate.

Income from sources other than stock sales might also influence realization behavior. A small income might induce stock sales to maintain current consumption. A high income would certainly obviate the need for stock sales to maintain consumption, but it might also be associated with financial sophistication and frequent trading. Adjusted gross income net of stock gains is entered into the equations in a quadratic form to allow for nonlinearities. An interaction term with the tax rate is also used. Inclusion of actual stock gains in the income variable would result in multicollinearity with any tax rate on gains. Inclusion of an average amount of stock gains in income would impart a negative bias to the coefficient (because such a variable would underestimate adjusted gross income for returns with high gains and overestimate income for those with low gains).

In general, older taxpayers would be expected to be more reluctant to realize gains, because appreciation on assets transferred at death would

---

29. Feldstein, Slemrod, and Yitzhaki, "Effects of Taxation," p. 781, note that upper income (and thus higher tax rate) shareholders may hold more low-yield growth stocks, citing Marshall E. Blume, Jean Crockett, and Irwin Friend, "Stock-ownership in the United States: Characteristics and Trends," *Survey of Current Business* (November 1974), p. 18. Such regressions therefore tend to understate the effect of tax rates on realizations.

30. At the 1973 average dividend payout rate of 3.06 percent (*Economic Report of the President, 1979,* table B-88), this represents a portfolio of almost $100,000. Feldstein, Slemrod, and Yitzhaki, "Effects of Taxation," p. 782, state that tax returns with at least $3,000 of dividends received 79 percent of all dividends reported.

never be subject to income tax. At the same time, older taxpayers, with their reduced labor income, are more likely to need the proceeds of asset sales to maintain accustomed levels of consumption. The incomes of the aged who do not realize gains may be so low that they need not file tax returns, thus making realizations more frequent among the filing population. Further, large stock gains relative to dividends may reflect realizations of capital gains on shares held for long periods of time, which the elderly are most likely to have in their portfolios. Tax returns permit the identification of taxpayers (single or either spouse filing a joint return) over sixty-five years old; a dummy variable is used in the equations to differentiate such returns.

A distinction must be drawn between the effects of temporary and permanent tax rate reduction. A taxpayer might find the capital gains tax rate extraordinarily low in any given year for several reasons. He might choose to borrow heavily in order to invest for gains, and thus have large deductions for investment interest and a taxable income (and thus marginal tax rate) lower than normal. He might choose to make substantial gifts to charity, which are deductible and reduce his taxable income. He may have extraordinary business losses that reduce his gross income below its normal level. Finally, he may have capital losses on assets other than stock (or accumulated loss carry-over) that would offset equal amounts of stock gain.[31] A stockholder with a portfolio of appreciated stock in any of these circumstances might choose to realize some or all of his gains in order to take advantage of his temporarily low marginal tax rate. If tax rates were reduced permanently by law, the same taxpayer might choose to realize those gains in the first year, thus reducing his stock of accrued gains for succeeding years; or he might not react immediately because he could realize those gains in later years at the same tax rates. In any event, the influence of transitory factors must not be confused with the continuous effects of statutory tax rates.

31. Alternatively, a taxpayer may realize large capital losses on stock to offset large capital gains on other assets. The IRS Sales of Capital Assets File contains a number of high-income returns with such offsetting gains and losses. Inclusion of these cases in the regression analysis without some control for the offsetting gains and losses overstates the effect of marginal tax rates on realizations. Because those returns show large positive gains before stock losses are considered, their marginal tax rate on gains appears high; the high tax rate is then associated, not with zero gains, but with negative gains, which overstates the absolute value of the negative coefficient. Controlling for the offsetting transactions through an independent variable (as described in the text) has a significant effect on estimated realizations.

To eliminate the transitory effects, several independent variables are added to the regression equations.[32] The sum of capital loss carry-over and gains or losses on assets other than stock (and short-term gains or losses on stock) is included. The value is entered as either a positive or a negative variable, according to its sign, to allow for different taxpayer responses to nonstock gains as opposed to nonstock losses and carry-over. The expected sign is negative, with carry-over and losses on assets other than stock expected to attract offsetting stock gains, and gains on other assets expected to attract stock losses. The amount of business losses is also included, with an expected negative sign. Finally, the amounts of deductions for cash and noncash charitable contributions and interest paid (other than on home mortgages) are included.[33]

The tax rate variable can be defined in several different ways. The effective tax rate on the last dollar of capital gains is the relevant cost for the investor's decision to realize additional gains, though not the cost of realizing the actual gains, and it is strongly collinear with the amount of gains realized. The first-dollar tax rate avoids this multicollinearity, but it is at best not representative of the tax that may be due on a more reasonable amount of gains, and at worst can be very misleading if there are small amounts of carry-over or other losses.[34] Any approximation based on a combination of these two shares their defects. The variable used here is the effective tax rate on a predicted amount of stock gain, which is based

32. Without these independent variables the equations estimate the short-run effect of the tax on realizations, as described in note 28, above. With the independent variables, the result is closer to the long-run effect.

33. These deductions represent only 24.9 percent of total itemized deductions for 1973, so there is no danger that the deductions variable will generate an approximate identity between adjusted gross income and taxable income. Internal Revenue Service, *Statistics of Income—1973, Individual Income Tax Returns* (GPO, 1976), pp. 48–49, table 2.2, p. 53, table 2.5, and pp. 56–57, table 2.7.

All of the variables used to control for transitory influences may in some sense be endogenous to the realization decision. For example, while an investor may be encouraged to realize a gain by a large charitable contribution he had made, he might also make such a contribution to reduce the tax on an earlier or subsequent realization. The exact nature of this simultaneous relationship is difficult to model, and because the effect of the independent variables on the estimated elasticities is relatively small, no attempt is made to generalize the model to encompass the simultaneity.

34. For example, the tax on the first $100 of stock gain for a return with $1,100 of short-term loss carry-over is zero; if the carry-over was only $1,000, however, the gain would be taxed at the ordinary rate, which could be as high as 70 percent. If the typical stock gain for such tax returns was substantially larger than $100, neither of those figures would be indicative of the real tax price of realization.

on the amounts of dividends and adjusted gross income net of stock gains.[35] This formulation has the virtues of avoiding both the simultaneity of capital gains realizations with the tax rate (because the predicted amount of gain on which the tax rate is calculated is not directly related to the taxpayer's actual gains) and the distortion of the tax rate caused by small amounts of losses or carry-over (because the predicted gain is large enough to swamp typical amounts of losses or carry-over).[36]

The equations are estimated with ordinary least squares. All the variables on both sides of the equation are divided by dividends, as a correc-

---

35. The predicted amount of stock gain is the average within fifty-six subpopulations cross-classified by dividends and adjusted gross income.

36. This approach differs from that of Feldstein, Slemrod, and Yitzhaki, "Effects of Taxation," pp. 780–81. They used an instrumental variable technique predicting the last-dollar tax rate on actual gains, using the last-dollar tax rate on predicted gains and the first-dollar tax rate as instruments. This formulation yields a weighted average of the two tax rates and is unsatisfactory (as was argued above) both because the variable predicted in the first stage is not appropriate for the second-stage equation and because the tax rates used as instruments are subject to distortion from carry-over and losses on other assets. To demonstrate the basic similarity of these two approaches but to isolate the difference, the Feldstein, Slemrod, and Yitzhaki equation was replicated but with the new tax rate formulation. Feldstein, Slemrod, and Yitzhaki report the following result from an unweighted regression (t-statistics are given in parentheses):

$$GAINS/DIVIDENDS = 35.0 + 0.18\ AGE65 - 1.23 \log (DIVIDENDS)$$
$$\quad\quad\quad\quad\quad\quad (0.50)\quad\quad\quad (10.34)$$
$$- 0.50 \log (AGI) - 0.50\ TAX,$$
$$(4.31)\quad\quad\quad (13.11)$$

where $GAINS$ is long-term gains on stock, $AGE65$ is a dummy variable taking the value 1 if a personal exemption for sixty-five or over is claimed, AGI is adjusted gross income net of stock gains plus predicted stock gains in AGI (based on net AGI and dividends), and TAX is the instrumental variable (no first-stage equation is reported). When the tax rate is changed to the formulation to be used in this paper, the result is:

$$GAINS/DIVIDENDS = 30.17 + 0.36\ AGE65 - 1.22 \log (DIVIDENDS)$$
$$\quad\quad\quad\quad\quad\quad (1.07)\quad\quad\quad (10.85)$$
$$- 0.80 \log (AGI) - 0.25\ TAX.$$
$$(10.74)\quad\quad\quad (17.02)$$

The Feldstein, Slemrod, and Yitzhaki result implies an elasticity of realizations with respect to the tax rate of −23.8; the result with the new tax rate is −11.8. Though numerically different, both estimated elasticities might fairly be described as astronomical. These results are presented only to compare the Feldstein, Slemrod, and Yitzhaki and the new tax rate formulations; it will be shown below that all the coefficients in both these equations are greatly biased.

tion for heteroscedasticity.[37] The results of the equation are shown in table 9. Equation 1, for returns with dividends of at least $3,000 and omitting the independent variables for the transitory effects, shows that long-term stock gains over the relevant range is a decreasing function of income from sources other than stock and an increasing function of dividends, all else being equal.[38] The dummy variable for elderly taxpayers shows a negative and statistically significant coefficient, indicating that the inhibiting effect of potential tax avoidance through step-up of basis overrides the greater financial need of some of the elderly and leads to lower stock sales in that group.

The tax rate and interaction coefficients in equation 1 yield an elasticity estimate of -0.44 at the means of all the variables, indicating that a capital gains tax rate reduction would result in a loss of tax revenue. However, such an inference must be considered tentative in light of the a priori arguments expressed earlier for either a rising or a falling elasticity with respect to portfolio size. Equation 1 allows an examination of this question because its interaction terms generalize the relationship between the elasticity and portfolio size. The next to last line in table 9 shows that the estimated elasticities are -0.21 in the $3,000–$10,000 dividend class, -0.31 in the $10,000–$20,000 class, -0.42 in the $20,000–$50,000 class, and -1.49 for recipients of dividends of $50,000 and over. Thus only for portfolios of over approximately $1,500,000 of corporate stock

37. The same equation without the normalization of all variables by dividends (for returns with at least $3,000 of dividends) provides approximately the same elasticity estimate at the mean dividend, income, and tax rate values as the normalized equation, but elasticity estimates at typical variable values for portfolio sizes larger than average rise until, for returns with more than $50,000 in dividends, they are counterintuitively positive.

38. Feldstein, Slemrod, and Yitzhaki ("Effects of Taxation") found a strongly significant negative relationship to dividends. The differences between their findings and mine apparently result because they used an unweighted regression and I computed with the sample weights. Weighting of the regressions is required because the sample is selected according to stratified sampling rates based on adjusted gross income, which includes all of short-term and one-half of long-term capital gains. Therefore, all else being equal, returns with larger capital gains are more likely to be in the sample than returns with smaller gains. Under these circumstances coefficients derived through ordinary least squares will be biased. Weighted least squares produces consistent estimates, though the accuracy of the estimates of the standard errors depends on the sample size, which in this case is extremely large. See Jerry A. Hausman and David A. Wise, "Stratification on Endogenous Variables and Estimation: The Gary Income Maintenance Experiment," in Charles Manski and Daniel McFadden, eds., *Econometric Analysis of Discrete Data* (MIT Press, forthcoming).

Table 9. Regression Results on Realizations of Long-Term Stock Gains, 1973

Independent variable[a] or summary statistic	Dividend class and equation number					
	$3,000 and over (1)	$3,000 and over (2)	$3,000–$10,000 (3)	$10,000–$20,000 (4)	$20,000–$50,000 (5)	$50,000 and over (6)
Constant	2,925 (4.259)	1,946 (2.876)	3,565 (1.219)	−27,390 (1.420)	−50,460 (3.435)	40,900 (3.965)
Age dummy	−1,231 (3.686)	−731.6 (2.217)	−649.4 (1.138)	−1,216 (0.937)	−4,397 (2.914)	−4,180 (1.280)
Dividends	0.5121 (4.157)	0.3807 (3.123)	−0.08057 (0.072)	4.276 (1.495)	3.405 (3.571)	0.2652 (1.941)
Dividends^2	0.3865 (10^{-6}) (0.550)	−0.4311 (10^{-7}) (0.063)	0.2733 (10^{-4}) (0.272)	−0.1213 (10^{-3}) (1.199)	−0.2955 (10^{-4}) (1.968)	−0.1348 (10^{-6}) (1.253)
Adjusted gross income	0.008712 (1.184)	0.002423 (0.306)	0.007469 (0.535)	−0.1208 (5.402)	−0.1355 (6.325)	−0.2439 (9.884)
Adjusted gross income^2	0.8561 (10^{-9}) (1.470)	−0.3746 (10^{-8}) (4.959)	−0.5716 (10^{-8}) (4.057)	0.1794 (10^{-9}) (0.057)	−0.2385 (10^{-8}) (0.351)	0.5046 (10^{-8}) (7.153)
Gains on other assets	...	−0.1093 (15.650)	−0.1260 (9.879)	−0.05393 (3.146)	−0.05382 (3.876)	−0.07818 (5.456)
Carry-over plus losses on other assets	...	−0.001871 (0.105)	0.03498 (1.076)	−0.1700 (4.138)	−0.3598 (12.356)	−0.0369 (2.183)
Interest deductions	...	0.2473 (5.750)	0.2224 (2.861)	0.4987 (4.703)	0.0986 (1.196)	0.2227 (3.201)
Cash charitable contributions deductions	...	1.010 (12.940)	0.9633 (6.658)	1.170 (7.497)	0.9415 (6.941)	0.9552 (7.926)

Noncash charitable contributions deductions	...	1.939 (21.698)	1.859 (11.106)	2.363 (12.970)	2.351 (15.394)	2.808 (31.472)
Business losses	...	−0.1257 (11.371)	−0.1526 (7.497)	−0.009194 (0.346)	−0.1936 (7.982)	−0.2222 (9.099)
Marginal tax rate	−524.8 (8.284)	−334.4 (5.281)	−445.4 (4.380)	...[b]	1,119 (3.312)	−1,109 (2.693)
Marginal tax rate^2	28.63 (12.664)	13.20 (5.521)	16.15 (3.757)	...[b]	...[b]	...[b]
Marginal tax rate times dividends	−0.01569 (2.352)	−0.01321 (2.007)	...[b]	−0.02378 (3.196)	−0.06334 (5.051)	−0.01187 (2.267)
Marginal tax rate times AGI	−0.004812 (14.452)	−0.001658 (3.943)	−0.002059 (2.729)	0.004174 (4.021)	0.003683 (4.013)	0.00492 (5.793)
Corrected $\bar{R}^2$	0.0170	0.0560	0.0586	0.0758	0.1313	0.1453
F	58.47	119.29	42.54	30.98	62.66	123.39
(Degrees of freedom)	(9; 29,879)	(15; 29,873)	(14; 9,323)	(13; 4,741)	(14; 5,698)	(14; 10,068)
Corrected standard error of estimate	5.065	4.963	5.624	3.384	2.040	2.109
Elasticity from own equation	−0.44	−0.79	−0.76	−0.79	−1.08	−1.27
Elasticity from equation 1	−0.44	−0.44	−0.21	−0.31	−0.42	−1.49
Elasticity from equation 2	−0.79	−0.79	−0.65	−0.86	−0.70	−1.22

Source: Internal Revenue Service Sales of Capital Assets File. Standard errors of the variables are in parentheses.

a. The dependent variable is long-term stock gains. All variables are divided by dividends.

b. Coefficient failed test of statistical significance; variable was therefore omitted from equation for computation of elasticity.

would capital gains tax cuts generate sufficient additional realizations to result in an increase in revenue.

Equation 2 uses the same general specification on the same population but adds the variables used to control for fluctuations in tax rates. The relationship of gains to adjusted gross income becomes significant and negative rather than insignificant and positive. The variable for gains on other assets shows a large and significant negative coefficient, as expected. This coefficient is consistent with the data in tables 7 and 8, which demonstrated that many taxpayers seek to match their realized gains on other assets with stock losses to minimize their tax liabilities. The variable for nonstock losses (including carry-over) has a smaller coefficient and is statistically insignificant. The business loss variable is also significant with the expected sign. The variables for itemized deduction items all show the expected sign and statistical significance. The elasticity estimate for the entire population is −0.79, which is higher than that for the equation without the additional independent variables. The puzzle of this discrepancy is somewhat reduced when the elasticities for various portfolio sizes are computed. As shown in the bottom line of table 9, equation 2 yields elasticities of −0.65, −0.86, −0.70, and −1.22 for the dividend classes in ascending order. It is reasonable that the independent variables for transitory influences reduce the measured tax effect most for taxpayers with large portfolios, who would tend to be more diversified and thus to have some shares that could profitably be switched with a temporary reduction in their effective tax rates. Taxpayers with smaller portfolios would be less likely to respond to fluctuations in tax rates because their portfolios would probably be less diversified, and measurement of the incremental effect of the fluctuations might therefore be more tentative.

To confirm the elasticities estimated from equation 2, the same equation was run on subsamples corresponding to the dividend classes specified above. The elasticity estimates were quite similar at −0.76, −0.79, −1.08, and −1.27. These results suggest again that taxpayers with stock portfolios larger than $1,500,000 would increase their realizations of gains by a greater percentage than a cut in the capital gains tax, and further indicate that those in the $600,000–$1,500,000 range would increase realizations very slightly more than tax rates were reduced. The range of elasticities for the regressions on the subsamples is thus slightly higher than would be expected from the overall elasticity estimated in equation 1.

Apart from the elasticity estimates, the subsamples confirm the expected signs on the control variables for deductions and gains and losses on other assets. The only unexpected sign arises in the smallest portfolio class for the coefficient on carry-over and losses on other assets, but that coefficient is not statistically significant.

Why does the top end of the wealth distribution respond so much more strongly to variations in tax rates? Two possibilities come to mind. First, the potential absolute variation in tax rates is much greater for those who are wealthiest. This is simply because their highest potential tax rate is much larger than the highest potential rate for those with smaller property incomes (while the lowest possible rate is zero for both groups). This larger range of tax rates suggests that tax minimization is more profitable for wealthier taxpayers because the same change in tax rates means more to the recipient of a larger amount of gains.

Second, it is entirely possible that the incomes and deductions of the well-to-do fluctuate more than those of the less well-off. The equations identify likely causes of lower than average taxable income, and the relevant variables generally have large coefficients of the expected sign. However, it is much more difficult to identify *above* average taxable income when items from all sources are extremely large. Thus taxpayers who have small realizations and high tax rates may be responding to upward fluctuations of income and would time their realizations in the same fashion even if statutory tax rates were lower.

It is possible, with the results of equations 3 through 6 in table 9, to estimate the revenue effect of the capital gains tax provisions of the Revenue Act of 1978 at 1973 income and capital gains levels.[39] Realized stock gains increase by 5.3 percent, with most of that growth at income levels in excess of $50,000. Table 10 shows the resulting change in tax liabilities. Tax revenues are reduced by $692 million, or 5.8 percent, and 65 percent of the tax reduction is received by taxpayers with incomes over $100,000.[40]

39. The features included are the reduction of the portion of long-term gains included in adjusted gross income from 50 to 40 percent, and the removal of the excluded portion of long-term gains from tax preferences in the minimum tax and the maximum tax. The change in the law is assumed to have no effect on taxpapers with less than $3,000 of dividends.

40. Use of the coefficients from either equation 1 or equation 2 would result in a greater revenue loss than that presented in table 10. This revenue loss estimate includes transactions in corporate stock only. It is highly likely that sales of other assets are far less tax sensitive, because stock is the most liquid asset generally purchased to achieve capital gains. For this reason, the actual revenue loss for transactions in all assets is probably significantly greater than the estimate for only corporate stock.

Table 10. Changes in Tax Liability Resulting from the Capital Gains Tax Reductions of the Revenue Act of 1978, 1973 Income Levels

Adjusted gross income (dollars)	Number of returns[a] (thousands)	1973 tax liability (millions of dollars)	Tax liability under 1978 act (millions of dollars)	Change in tax liability (millions of dollars)	Change in tax liability (percent)	Change in tax liability (dollars per return)
Less than 0	15.1	11.6	1.9	−9.7	−83.9	−645.4
0–2,500	83.3	0.3	0.0	−0.3	−98.0	−3.6
2,500–5,000	98.8	9.5	8.6	−0.9	−9.1	−8.8
5,000–7,500	106.3	33.6	30.8	−2.8	−8.4	−26.5
7,500–10,000	119.8	85.1	83.7	−1.4	−1.7	−12.0
10,000–15,000	244.7	324.0	317.4	−6.6	−2.0	−27.1
15,000–20,000	310.6	666.6	652.4	−14.3	−2.1	−46.0
20,000–25,000	245.0	726.4	708.2	−18.1	−2.5	−74.0
25,000–30,000	171.4	666.6	657.6	−9.0	−1.4	−52.6
30,000–50,000	329.3	2,316.9	2,241.8	−75.2	−3.2	−228.2
50,000–100,000	171.6	2,748.6	2,647.2	−101.5	−3.7	−591.5
100,000–200,000	48.0	1,964.6	1,843.8	−120.8	−6.1	−2,518.8
200,000–500,000	11.6	1,239.7	1,101.5	−138.2	−11.1	−11,880.3
500,000–1,000,000	1.7	495.1	413.6	−81.5	−16.5	−48,030.0
1,000,000 and over	0.6	546.2	434.6	−111.6	−20.4	−181,501.1
Total or average	1,957.6	11,834.9	11,143.0	−691.9	−5.8	−353.4

Sources: Internal Revenue Service 1973 Sales of Capital Assets File and Individual Tax Model File.
a. With dividends of at least $3,000.

Summary and Conclusions

This paper has presented research in two areas that have been largely unexplored in the past owing to a lack of appropriate data. The bunching of capital gains was found to increase tax liabilities for about 88 percent of those who realized gains. However, this leaves 12 percent who time their realizations of capital gains in years when they are subject to low tax rates because their incomes are lower or their deductions higher than usual. This smaller group disproportionately includes those with large capital gains. The five-year averaging provision in the law already provides some relief for those whose gains are taxed at higher than average rates because of bunching. The other side of the coin—the self-averaging permitted taxpayers through the timing of realizations—is a benefit of the current tax system that is often ignored.

The second new feature of this analysis is the identification of the use of realizations of offsetting capital gains and losses in a single year as a tax-minimization device. The data indicate that higher income taxpayers are likely to realize offsetting gains and losses; such taxpayers have diversified portfolios and may thus realize accrued gains without incurring any tax liability. This tendency is not restricted to relatively liquid assets like stock; rather, other assets were traded in offsetting transactions, and there was a striking tendency for stock losses to be used to offset nonstock gains. These results suggest that taxpayers with small net gains or losses may in many cases have reallocated substantial shares of their portfolios in offsetting transactions, sometimes among several types of assets.

Additional evidence regarding the lock-in effect of the capital gains tax has also been presented. Available estimates of the lock-in effect have been quite imprecise. The most recent estimate indicated an extremely large, continuing lock-in effect. Much of this large measured effect was caused by an incorrect statistical procedure; much of the remainder was the response of taxpayers to fluctuations in their own effective tax rates, as opposed to the level of statutory capital gains rates. This same timing of gains in low tax rate years (and losses in high tax rate years) can be expected whatever the statutory capital gains rates. Once this timing response was removed, the continuing additional realizations to be expected from reductions in capital gains tax rates was found to be much smaller than previous estimates. Further, taxpayers who responded sufficiently to capital gains tax cuts to produce increased federal tax revenue were shown to be a small segment of the population (those with stock portfolios larger than $600,000). As a result, the capital gains tax reduction in 1978 reduced tax revenues on balance.

Appendix A: History of the Capital Gains Tax Provisions

This appendix provides a brief history of the treatment of capital gains under the federal individual income tax. The discussion is limited to the required holding period for preferential treatment; the fraction of capital gains included in adjusted gross income; alternative or additional taxes on gains; the treatment of capital losses; the definition of assets eligible for capital gains treatment; and the deferral of tax on realized gains.[41]

A summary of the holding period, inclusion, alternative tax, and loss-offset provisions is presented in table 11. The capital gains preference has taken the form of an exclusion of part of the gain from adjusted gross income and a limited maximum rate of tax on the gain, provided the gain has been held for some minimum length of time. As is evident from the table, both the minimum holding period required to qualify for the exclusion and the rate of the exclusion itself have changed considerably over the history of the individual income tax. From the introduction of the income tax in 1913 until 1921 there was no preference. In 1922, a 12½ percent alternative tax rate for gains on assets held at least two years was introduced. From 1934 through 1937 long-term gains fell into four categories according to the length of holding period; the longer an asset was held, the smaller the portion of the gain included in taxable income. From 1938 through 1941 there were two categories of long-term gains, with the inclusion rate again lower for assets held longer. The simple long-term–short-term dichotomy was reinstated in 1942 and has endured. In addition to the exclusion, a maximum tax rate on gains was in effect from 1938 until 1968, varying from 15 to 26 percent. Under the 1969 act the maximum rate of 25 percent was restricted to the first $50,000 of long-term gain; it was repealed entirely for tax years beginning in 1979.

41. More complete, though dated, treatments of these questions are available in David, *Alternative Approaches to Capital Gains Taxation;* and *The Federal Tax System: Facts and Problems,* Committee Print, Joint Economic Committee, 88 Cong. 2 sess. (GPO, 1964).

Since 1969 there have been, under certain circumstances, additional taxes on capital gains. The first of these, the so-called minimum tax, was designed to increase the tax on large long-term capital gains. The excess of the excluded portion of long-term gains (plus certain other preferences) over certain exemptions and deductions was taxed at a flat rate (10 percent through 1975 and 15 percent thereafter).[42] Beginning in 1979 the excluded portion of capital gains was removed from the minimum tax base and added to the the base of a new alternative minimum tax, which also included all of adjusted gross income less personal exemptions and itemized deductions claimed for medical expenses and casualty losses. The alternative minimum tax base was subjected to a progressive tax rate schedule that ranged from 10 to 25 percent. The final tax liability is the ordinary tax or the alternative minimum tax, whichever is greater.[43] The premise of the alternative minimum tax is thus that the tax liability should not be less than some fraction of gross income, unless extraordinary medical expenses or casualty losses significantly reduce the ability to pay.

Because capital gains receive preferential treatment, some taxpayers expend considerable legal effort to convert ordinary income into capital gains. The Internal Revenue Service and the Congress have retaliated with legislation and regulations. The result is a legal battleground that encompasses over half of the internal revenue code and a large fraction of the workload of tax administrators.

Capital gains were first defined in the law in 1922, when the preferential treatment of long-term gains began. The principles behind the definition have remained the same ever since. The law first defines capital assets as property, and then excludes certain types of property from that definition. The two most important exclusions are the incomes received in the ordinary course of business (such as the sale of a manufacturer's product)

42. As of 1979, only tax preference items in excess of one-half of ordinary tax liability or $10,000, whichever was larger, were subject to the minimum tax. Tax preference items other than the excluded half of long-term capital gains included excess itemized deductions, accelerated depreciation on low-income rental housing or other real property, accelerated depreciation on personal property, amortization of pollution control or child care facilities, stock options, bad debt reserves of financial institutions, depletion, and intangible drilling costs.

43. Technically, the alternative minimum tax is equal to the excess of that tax, computed on the alternative minimum tax base and the 10–25 percent rate schedule, over the ordinary tax, computed in the usual way; the taxpayer then pays the ordinary tax plus the alternative minimum tax, if any.

Table 11. History of the Capital Gains Provisions under the Federal Individual Income Tax

Tax year or period	Holding period	Percent of gain taxed as ordinary income	Alternative tax (highest rate on long-term gains)	Treatment of losses
1913–15	All	100	None (highest rate: 7 percent)	Not deductible
1916–17	All	100	None (highest rate: 15 percent in 1916, 65 percent in 1917)	Deductible only from capital gains
1918–21	All	100	None (highest rate: 77 percent in 1918, 73 percent in 1919–21)	Deductible in full from income of any kind
1922–23	2 years or less	100	None	Deductible in full from ordinary income, but not from capital gains
	Over 2 years	100	12½ percent; but total income tax must be no less than 12½ percent of total net income	Deductible in full from income of any kind
1924–31	2 years or less	100	None	Deductible in full from income of any kind
	Over 2 years	100	12½ percent	Creditable at 12½ percent, provided total income tax is no less than if losses were deducted in full from ordinary income
1932–33	2 years or less	100	None	Losses from stocks and bonds deductible only from gains on stocks and bonds. Other losses deductible in full from income of any kind
	Over 2 years	100	12½ percent	Creditable at 12½ percent, provided total income tax is no less than if losses were deducted in full from ordinary income
1934–37	1 year or less	100	None	Net losses, reduced by the appropriate inclusion rate based on the holding period, deductible to the extent of included capital gains plus $2,000
	Over 1 year to 2 years	80	None (highest rate: 50.4 in 1934–35, 63.2 in 1936–37)	

Year	Holding period	Percent of gain taken into account	Tax rate	Treatment of losses
	Over 2 years to 5 years	60	None (highest rate: 37.8 in 1934–35, 47.4 in 1936–37)	Deductible only from gains on assets held 18 months or less; excess losses to the extent of net income may be carried forward to the next tax year
	Over 5 years to 10 years	40	None (highest rate: 25.2 in 1934–35, 31.6 in 1936–37)	
	Over 10 years	30	None (highest rate: 18.9 in 1934–35, 23.7 in 1936–37)	
1938–41	18 months or less	100	None	Net loss reduced by the appropriate inclusion rate deductible from other income or creditable at 30 percent, whichever gives the greater tax
	Over 18 months to 2 years	66⅔	30 percent of included gain (highest rate: 20 percent in 1938–39 and 1941, 22 percent in 1940)	
	Over 2 years	50	30 percent of included gain (highest rate: 15 percent in 1938–39 and 1941, 16.5 percent in 1940)	
1942–51	6 months or less	100 (of excess over 50 percent of long-term loss, if any)	None	Net loss (short-term loss plus 50 percent of long-term loss, or excess of short-term loss over 50 percent of long-term gain, or excess of 50 percent of long-term loss over short-term gain) deductible from included gain plus $1,000 of ordinary income; excess carried forward for 5 years as short-term loss
	Over 6 months	50 (less short-term loss, if any)	25 percent (26 percent effective September 1, 1951)	
1952–63	6 months or less	100 (of excess over long-term loss, if any)	None	Net loss (sum of long- and short-term loss, or excess of short-term loss over long-term gain, or excess of long-term loss over short-term gain) deductible from other income up to $1,000; excess carried forward for 5 years as a short-term loss
	Over 6 months	50 (of excess over short-term loss, if any)	26 percent (1952–53) 25 percent (1954–63)	

Table 11 (*continued*)

Tax year or period	Holding period	Percent of gain taxed as ordinary income	Alternative tax (highest rate on long-term gains)	Treatment of losses
1964–69	6 months or less	100 (of excess over long-term loss, if any)	None	Net loss (sum of long- and short-term loss, or excess of short-term loss over long-term gain, or excess of long-term loss over short-term gain) deductible from other income up to $1,000; excess short-term losses carried forward indefinitely as short-term loss; excess long-term losses carried forward indefinitely as long-term loss; short-term loss carry-overs used first
	Over 6 months	50 (of excess over short-term loss, if any)	25 percent	
1970–76	6 months or less	100 (of excess over long-term loss, if any)	None	Net loss (sum of short-term loss and 50 percent of long-term loss, or excess of short-term loss over long-term gain, or 50 percent of excess of long-term loss over short-term gain) deductible from other income up to $1,000; excess short-term losses carried forward indefinitely as short-term loss; excess long-term losses carried forward indefinitely as long-term loss; short-term loss carry-overs used first
	Over 6 months	50 (of excess over short-term loss, if any)	25 percent on first $50,000 of gain only. Additional tax of 10 percent (15 percent in 1976) on excluded half of gain under certain circumstances (highest rate: 0.3221375 in 1970; 0.3875 in 1971; 0.455 in 1972–75; 0.49125 in 1976)	
1977	9 months or less	100 (of excess over long-term loss, if any)	None	Net loss (sum of short-term loss and 50 percent of long-term loss, or excess of long-term loss, or excess of short-term loss over long-term gain, or 50 percent of excess of long-term loss over short-term gain) deductible from
	Over 9 months	50 (of excess over short-term loss, if any)	25 percent on first $50,000 of gain only. Additional tax of 15 percent	

Year	Holding period	Additional tax on gains	Percent of gain excluded / deduction of losses	Treatment of net losses
1978	1 year or less	None	100 (of excess over long-term loss, if any)	other income up to $2,000; excess short-term losses carried forward indefinitely as short-term loss; excess long-term losses carried forward indefinitely as long-term loss; short-term loss carry-overs used first
	Over 1 year	25 percent on first $50,000 of gain only. Additional tax of 15 percent on excluded half of gain under certain circumstances (highest rate: 0.49125 January 1–October 31; 0.349 November 1–December 31)	50 (40 after October 31 only) (of excess over short-term loss, if any)	Net loss (sum of short-term loss and 50 percent of long-term loss, or excess of short-term loss over long-term gain, or 50 percent of excess of long-term loss over short-term gain) deductible from other income up to $3,000; excess short-term losses carried forward indefinitely as short-term loss; excess long-term losses carried forward indefinitely as long-term loss; short-term loss carry-overs used first
1979	1 year or less	None	100 (of excess over long-term loss, if any)	
	Over 1 year	Graduated additional tax on full amount of gains under certain circumstances (highest rate: 28 percent)	40 (of excess over short-term loss, if any)	Net loss (sum of short-term loss and 50 percent of long-term loss, or excess of short-term loss over long-term gain, or 50 percent of excess of long-term loss over short-term gain) deductible from other income up to $3,000; excess short-term losses carried forward indefinitely as short-term loss; excess long-term losses carried forward indefinitely as long-term loss; short-term loss carry-overs used first

Sources: U.S. Department of the Treasury, *Federal Tax Rates, 1913 to 1940* (Government Printing Office, 1941), pp. 530–32, and *Federal Tax Rates, 1940 through 1950* (GPO, 1951), pp. 277–78; *Revenue Act of 1951*, H. Rept. 586, 82 Cong. 1 sess. (GPO, 1951); *Brief Summary of the Provisions of H.R. 8363, "The Revenue Act of 1964,"* Committee Print, Senate Committee on Finance, 88 Cong. 2 sess. (GPO, 1964); *Tax Reform Act of 1969*, H. Rept. 91-782, 91 Cong. 1 sess. (GPO, 1976), pp. 162–69; *Tax Reform Act of 1976*, H. Rept. 94-1515, 94 Cong. 2 sess. (GPO, 1976), pp. 232–35; and *General Explanation of the Revenue Act of 1978*, Committee Print, Joint Committee on Taxation, 96 Cong. 1 sess. (GPO, 1979), pp. 251–60.

and gains on property used in a trade or business. In both of these general categories, however, numerous exceptions have been made. For example, in 1943 gains from sales of timber were defined as capital gains even though the timber might be sold routinely in the ordinary course of business. Gains from sales of coal (1951) and iron ore (1964) royalty rights were defined as capital gains, even though the royalties themselves would have been taxed to the original owner as ordinary income.[44] Likewise, certain business assets can be sold for capital gains so long as recovery of depreciation already taken against ordinary income is taxed in full. Taxpayers continue to test the capital gains definition with their particular circumstances, and the resolution of each case adds to the already large body of legislation, regulations, rulings, and case law.

Just as capital gains are not added in full to taxable income, so capital losses are not subtracted in full. From 1913 through 1916 capital losses could not be offset against capital gains at all. Since that time, the law has been more generous—allowing losses to be offset against gains, allowing net losses to be carried forward to later tax years, or allowing the offset of some (in certain years, all) of capital losses against ordinary income.[45] Treatment of losses is an important economic issue because risk-taking is affected by the treatment of both successful and unsuccessful risks.

The tax law has always recognized capital gains when they are realized rather than as they accrue. This presents an important opportunity for tax reduction by holding rather than selling appreciating assets. By postponing sale, the owner of appreciating property implicitly allows all of his investment to earn its current market return instead of selling the asset and reinvesting only the after-tax proceeds at the market rate. Certain provisions of the tax code extend the opportunity of deferral to involuntary conversions, exchanges of property of like kind, certain exchanges of

44. *Revenue Act of 1951,* H. Rept. 586, 82 Cong. 1 sess. (GPO, 1951); and *Brief Summary of the Provisions of H.R. 8363, "The Revenue Act of 1964,"* Committee Print, Senate Committee on Finance, 88 Cong. 2 sess. (GPO, 1964), p. 6.

45. The offsetting of short-term losses against long-term gains is itself an issue, since all of short-term but only part of long-term gains are included in adjusted gross income. From 1942 through 1951 short-term losses were deducted from *the portion of long-term gains that was included* in adjusted gross income. This allowed taxpayers to realize long-term gains and half as much in short-term losses and pay no tax; it also meant that taxpayers realizing equal amounts of short-term gains and long-term losses were taxed on half their gains at ordinary rates. Since that time, short-term losses have been deducted from *total* long-term gains before the included portion is computed.

insurance policies, and certain exchanges of securities in corporate organizations, reorganizations, and mergers. Still another opportunity is probably the most common: the deferral of recognition of the fully reinvested gain on owner-occupied homes.

One of the most significant deferral opportunities is available through the transfer of assets either by gift or at death. Property transferred by gift is subject to federal gift taxation, but no income tax is assessed on the accrued gain. The donee receives the property subject to the donor's basis with an adjustment for gift taxes paid, and if the donee chooses to sell the property, capital gains taxes are collected on the entire appreciation from the date the donor acquired it. Property transferred by bequest is subject to the federal estate tax, but again the appreciation goes untaxed under the income tax. Further, the donee accepts as the basis the value of the property as of the time of bequest, meaning that any appreciation accrued during the donor's lifetime is never subject to capital gains tax. The deferral of taxation through gift or bequest is considered a major problem by some tax experts, because appreciating property can change hands between generations without capital gains tax, thus increasing the concentration of wealth. Further, property owners may keep assets that are economically inferior to available alternatives because the present value of the tax savings at death will exceed the yield differential between the assets, capitalized and discounted over the owner's expected lifetime.

Appendix B: Historical Data on Capital Gains

Realizations of capital gains are extremely volatile over time, as is shown in table 12. Several offsetting factors are at work. When assets appreciate and gains accrue more rapidly, some taxpayers choose to realize those gains rather than leave them at risk. Taxpayers with accrued losses have incentives to realize them in order to offset gains, and to move them into apparently more profitable assets. When asset prices are stable or falling, there is less appreciation to realize, but stagnant and falling incomes with no gains encourage realizations to maintain consumption levels. Losses are also likely to be realized to maintain consumption, but published statistics generally do not reveal the true extent of loss realizations because of the limitation on loss offsets against ordinary income.

Table 12 indicates that realizations are significantly correlated with the state of the economy and of the stock market. Net gains are significantly positively correlated with both the level of corporate profits and stock

Table 12. Realized Net Capital Gains and Net Capital Losses on Individual Income Tax Returns and Selected Economic Indicators, 1954–77

Year	Net gains (thousands of dollars)	Net losses (thousands of dollars)	Corporate profits (billions of dollars)	Standard and Poor's index	Percent change, gross domestic product deflator	Real rate of growth of GNP (percent)	Baa corporate bond rate (percent)
1954	3,731,862	379,446	37.8	29.69	1.4	−1.3	3.51
1955	5,126,350	375,213	46.7	40.49	2.2	6.7	3.53
1956	4,991,131	438,465	45.9	46.62	3.2	2.1	3.88
1957	4,128,228	642,695	45.4	44.38	3.4	1.8	4.71
1958	4,879,114	549,110	40.8	46.24	1.6	−0.2	4.73
1959	6,796,602	522,115	51.2	57.38	2.2	6.0	5.05
1960	6,003,859	704,284	48.9	55.85	1.7	2.3	5.19
1961	8,290,879	670,085	48.7	66.27	0.9	2.5	5.08
1962	6,821,421	1,050,393	53.7	62.38	1.8	5.8	5.02
1963	7,468,326	1,019,344	57.6	69.87	1.5	4.0	4.86
1964	8,909,143	969,991	64.2	81.37	1.6	5.3	4.83
1965	11,069,464	888,606	73.3	88.17	2.2	5.9	4.87
1966	10,960,261	1,018,979	78.6	85.26	3.3	5.9	5.67
1967	14,593,683	911,798	75.6	91.93	2.9	2.7	6.23
1968	18,853,870	864,221	82.1	98.70	4.5	4.4	6.94
1969	16,078,215	1,494,887	77.9	97.84	5.0	2.6	7.81
1970	10,655,553	1,648,870	66.4	83.22	5.4	−0.3	9.11
1971	14,558,580	1,403,581	76.9	98.29	5.1	3.0	8.56
1972	18,396,678	1,321,387	89.6	109.20	4.1	5.7	8.16
1973	18,200,682	1,529,396	97.2	107.43	5.8	5.5	8.24
1974	15,377,899	1,907,774	86.5	82.85	9.7	−1.4	9.50
1975	15,799,165	1,727,272	107.9	86.16	9.6	−1.3	10.61
1976	20,207,101	1,645,248	141.4	102.01	5.2	5.7	9.75
1977	23,363,333	2,586,729	159.1	98.20	5.9	4.9	8.97

Sources: Internal Revenue Service, *Statistics of Income: Individual Tax Returns*, various years; *Economic Report of the President, 1979*, tables B-2, B-3, B-19, B-65, and B-88.

market indexes, as are changes in net gains.[46] Profits and stock market indexes are also positively correlated with the absolute value of net losses, indicating that asset holders respond to rising prices by cashing in their losses for more profitable reinvestment or by offsetting their gains with losses. Upward movements in profits and the stock market are correlated with smaller loss realizations, however, because rising markets wipe out some accrued losses. Faster growth and acceleration of growth of the gross national product are associated with increased realization of net gains. High interest rates are associated with greater net gains and net losses; rising interest rates are associated with decreases in realizations of net gains and increases in realizations of net losses. Net gains and net losses tend to be larger when the inflation rate is higher; an acceleration of inflation is associated with an increase in net losses.

Comments by James W. Wetzler

Whenever it cuts the capital gains tax rate, Congress claims that the additional transactions induced by the tax cut will prevent any decline in revenues, and whenever it raises the tax rate, Congress claims credit for the assumed revenue gain with little reference to possible lock-in effects. The most recent cycle in congressional attitudes on lock-in lasted only two years. Clearly, empirical research to narrow the range of disagreement on this issue is a high priority, and both Joseph Minarik and Martin Feldstein, Joel Slemrod, and Shlomo Yitzhaki, on whose work Minarik builds, should be commended for undertaking the assignment.[47]

How much do economists really know about the extent to which changes in tax rates on capital gains affect investors' decisions to sell assets? I am afraid that, despite the best efforts of Minarik and Feldstein-Slemrod-Yitzhaki, the answer is, relatively little.

---

46. This reflects the important role of gains on corporate stock in total gains. In 1962 stock transactions accounted for $7.1 billion of $17.3 billion total gross gains and $4.1 billion of $6.3 billion total gross losses. Internal Revenue Service, *Statistics of Income—1962, Supplemental Report: Sales of Capital Assets Reported on Individual Income Tax Returns*, table 1, p. 21. The inferences discussed here are based on correlation coefficients rather than a general regression model because the various measures of economic conditions are highly collinear among themselves. Without a richer body of time series data, these results should be taken as tentative.

47. Feldstein, Slemrod, and Yitzhaki, "Effects of Taxation."

Let me start with the relevant theory, which logically should precede any empirical work but which is omitted by both Minarik and Feldstein-Slemrod-Yitzhaki. It is easy to show that a wealth-maximizing investor who owns an asset that has appreciated in value will not sell that asset and switch to an alternative asset unless the expected rate of return on the alternative investment is enough higher than that on the original asset to justify the capital gains tax on the appreciation and other costs of making the transaction. The extra rate of return on the alternative asset needed to induce the switch is proportional to the capital gains tax rate and to the ratio of the appreciation on the asset to its value. If there is a step-up in basis at death, the needed excess return also varies inversely with life expectancy.[48]

Investors' expectations about rates of return on different assets are unobservable, of course. Therefore, to derive any testable hypotheses, some assumptions must be made about how these expectations are formed and how they change over time. For example, it might be assumed that, having just bought an asset, an investor expects it to have a higher rate of return than any alternative assets but that, as time passes, his expectations about the rate of return on his own asset and on alternative assets follow random walks. Eventually, these fluctuations in expectations will cause some alternative asset to improve sufficiently in the investor's estimation to overcome his original preference, the transactions cost of making a switch, and any applicable tax consequences. At this point, the investor switches to the new asset.

The result of this exercise would be a theory of investors' holding periods. For any particular asset on which there was a given amount of unrealized appreciation and which was owned by an investor with a given tax rate, the holding period would be a random variable. A change in the capital gains tax rate would change the mean, and probably the other moments, of the probability distribution of holding periods.

A final step in building the theory should be to show how a given change in the probability distribution of holding periods would be translated into a change in realizations of capital gains. Presumably, a discrete shortening of the mean holding period, perhaps as a result of a cut in the capital gains tax rate, would lead to an initial surge of realizations followed by a decline to a level above the original starting point. In the long run the effect on

---

48. See Holt and Shelton, "The Lock-In Effect of the Capital Gains Tax," and Wetzler, "Capital Gains and Losses," pp. 135–37.

realizations of a given shortening of the holding period will depend on the rate at which assets appreciate.[49]

With this as background, I turn to Minarik's paper. In the appendix Minarik presents historical data on realizations of capital gains and losses, but he does not use these data to draw conclusions about the effects of tax changes on realizations. For what it is worth, a simple comparison of changes in tax rates and changes in aggregate realizations of gains gives little support to those who believe that tax rates strongly influence realizations. The explicitly temporary 7.5 percent increase in capital gains tax rates from the 1968 income tax surcharge, which took effect in midyear, did not prevent a large rise in realizations in that year. The 1977 data show that realizations of net gains rose 10 percent over 1976 despite the sizable capital gains tax increase enacted in 1976 and a weak stock market. The behavior of realizations after the Tax Reform Act of 1969 is hard to interpret because that act gave investors a crazy quilt of incentives by phasing in an increase in tax rates on large gains of high-bracket taxpayers, extending and phasing out the surcharge, and enacting a minimum tax effective in 1970. Thus it is hard to evaluate the meaning of the sharp drop in realizations in 1970 or the equally sharp increases in 1971 and 1972.[50]

One interesting empirical result presented by Minarik is that a sizable number of investors make use of their flexibility about when to realize a gain to even out their income over time. It is not clear whether these taxpayers are responding to the potential tax savings resulting from this self-averaging or whether they sell assets when taxable income is low just because that is when they need the cash. In either case, Minarik's results suggest that the bunching problem is less serious than has been assumed and that, among capital gains recipients, some of the variation in the mar-

49. These calculations are relatively simple under the assumption that the holding period changes from one value to another but are considerably more difficult when an entire probability distribution of holding periods is shifting and when adjustments are made for the effect of any change in holding periods on the amount of gain passing tax-free at death.

50. Since this paper was written, data on capital gains realized in 1979 have become available. They show a sufficient increase in realizations to make the actual revenue raised by the capital gains tax in 1979 approximately what might have been expected under the law in effect before the 1978 tax cut. This outcome is closer to the result predicted by Minarik's equation than to that predicted by Feldstein-Slemrod-Yitzhaki. The 1979 data indicate the short-run response to the tax cut, of course, not the steady-state response.

ginal tax rate applying to the first dollar of gain reflects transitory changes in income.

The major part of Minarik's paper is a reappraisal of Feldstein-Slemrod-Yitzhaki's highly publicized study claiming that a cut in the maximum capital gains tax rate from its 1973 level to 25 percent would lead to a threefold increase in realizations of gains. (Presumably, a cut to 25 percent from the higher 1977 tax rates would lead to a still larger increase in realizations.) The Feldstein-Slemrod-Yitzhaki study consisted of cross-section regressions relating an individual's sales of corporate stock and net gain realized on corporate stock to his marginal capital gains tax rate. The regressions were estimated from the Internal Revenue Service's 1973 study of individual transactions in capital assets.

Both Minarik and Feldstein-Slemrod-Yitzhaki should be faulted for proceeding with empirical tests without first having straightened out the relevant theory. I suspect that, once the theory of investors' holding periods and the precise link between holding periods and realizations is worked out, the system will have a reduced form in which an individual's realized gains is a dependent variable and his marginal tax rate is one of the independent variables. At that time, regressions such as those of Minarik and the earlier study may be useful in estimating some of the parameters of the system. In isolation from the relevant theory, however, their results are very hard to interpret.

For example, the short-run response of realizations to a change in the tax rate should be larger than the long-run response. Do Feldstein-Slemrod-Yitzhaki's and Minarik's coefficients measure the short-run effect, the long-run effect, or something in between? Also, a transitory decline in income affects realizations both by lowering the tax rate and by creating a need for cash. Thus if much of the variation in marginal tax rates reflects transitory changes in income, it may be impossible to get an unbiased estimate of even the short-run effect of a ceteris paribus change in tax rates.

Under these circumstances, the main contribution of Minarik's regressions is that they bring the estimated coefficient of the tax rate variable down from the stratospheric height it attained in the Feldstein-Slemrod-Yitzhaki study. The latter completely ignored the question of whether a short-run or a long-run response was being estimated. Minarik, in contrast, adds several independent variables designed to control for factors causing temporary changes in marginal capital gains tax rates in an attempt to purge the tax rate variable of transitory influences. These new variables raise the coefficient of the tax rate variable for people with medium-sized portfolios and lower it for people with large portfolios. Only for people with very large portfolios do Minarik's equations confirm Feldstein-Slemrod-Yitzhaki's conclusion that a cut in capital gains tax rates will increase realizations enough to raise revenue.

Some of Minarik's independent variables, however, probably represent something other than a measure of transitory changes in tax rates. For example, the correlation between charitable contributions and capital gains is more likely to result from the propensity of people with gains to make contributions than from the effect of contributions in temporarily lowering the marginal tax rate. It would be better to drop that variable. Business losses may affect the realization of gains not only by temporarily lowering the marginal tax rate but, more significantly, by creating a need for cash.

Problems arise in measuring the marginal capital gains tax rate. For taxpayers with capital losses or loss carry-forwards, the marginal tax rate for a capital gain is zero in the year the gain is realized; however, realization of the gain would reduce the loss carry-forward available for future years. Thus the true marginal rate for these taxpayers is the present value of the expected future tax benefit that would otherwise have been obtained from the forgone loss carry-forward. To the extent that there are errors in measuring the tax rate variable, the size of its coefficient will be biased downward.

Another issue is the quality of the underlying data. My understanding is that the 1973 capital asset tapes are of poor quality in the sense that, for many individual transactions, the reported gain does not equal the reported sale price minus the reported purchase price and that the reported total gain of many taxpayers does not equal the sum of the gains and losses from the individual transactions. I would be interested in knowing what efforts both Minarik and Feldstein-Slemrod-Yitzhaki made to deal with these problems.

I conclude from all this that we still know relatively little about the magnitude of changes in realizations, in both the short and the long run, that would result from a change in capital gains taxes. As the most promising direction for further research, I suggest more theoretical work on how holding periods are determined and how changes in holding periods are translated into changes in aggregate realizations, followed by statistical tests with the cross-sectional data to relate variation in holding periods to marginal capital gains tax rates. My guess is that a better approach to estimating the effect of tax changes on realizations will prove to be equations that use tax rates to explain variations in holding periods across individuals, rather than the variation in realizations per se.

FRANK DE LEEUW *and* LARRY OZANNE

Housing

A SERIES of past studies have established a strong case that the federal
income tax favors investment in housing over investment in many other
financial and real assets.[1] In the case of owner-occupied housing, the reason is that the housing services an owner provides for himself are not
counted as income, although certain of the expenses of providing these
services—namely, property tax payments and mortgage interest payments—are deductible in calculating taxable income. Capital gains on
owner-occupied housing, furthermore, largely escape taxation. In the case
of rental housing, the main factors are depreciation allowances for tax
purposes far in excess of economic depreciation, rapid write-off of con-

The authors are grateful for financial support from the Office of Tax Analysis
and for many helpful comments by readers too numerous to mention. A version of
this study appeared in the *Survey of Current Business,* vol. 59 (December 1979),
pp. 50–61.

1. Henry J. Aaron, *Shelter and Subsidies: Who Benefits from Federal Housing
Policies?* (Brookings Institution, 1972), pp. 53–73; George S. Tolley and Douglas B.
Diamond, "Homeownership, Rental Housing, and Tax Incentives," in *Federal Tax
Policy and Urban Development,* Hearings before the Subcommittee on the City of
the House Banking, Finance, and Urban Affairs Committee (Government Printing
Office, 1977), pp. 114–95; Richard Goode, *The Individual Income Tax* (Brookings
Institution, 1964), pp. 120–29; David Laidler, "Income Tax Incentives for Owner-
Occupied Housing," in Arnold C. Harberger and Martin J. Bailey, eds., *The Taxa-
tion of Income from Capital* (Brookings Institution, 1969); Harvey S. Rosen,
"Housing Decisions and the U.S. Income Tax: An Econometric Analysis," *Journal
of Public Economics,* vol. 11 (February 1979), pp. 1–23; Emil Sunley, "Tax Advan-
tages of Homeownership Versus Renting: A Cause of Suburban Migration?" in
National Tax Association–Tax Institute of America, *Proceedings of the Sixty-third
Annual Conference on Taxation* (Columbus, Ohio: NTA–TIA, 1971), pp. 377–92;
and Paul Taubman and Robert Rasche, "The Income Tax and Real Estate Investment," in *Tax Incentives* (Lexington Books, 1971), pp. 113–42.

struction-period interest and taxes, and a low tax rate on capital gains, which constitute the major part of the return to rental housing.

There are two reasons for reexamining the taxation of housing. One is that the standard view does not encompass the large effect of inflation on returns to housing investment in recent years. The other is that there have been substantial legislative changes during the last twelve years in the treatment of "excess" depreciation, of tax preference income, of construction-period interest and taxes, and of capital gains.

This paper looks at the tax treatment of housing in the light of high rates of inflation and recent legislation. But first, it introduces and illustrates its central tool of analysis, a procedure for calculating the present value to an investor of purchasing a durable physical asset subject to complex tax treatment. While present value calculations have often been used in analyzing rental housing investment, this mode of analysis is here pushed further than previously—for example, in making comparisons between rental housing, owner-occupied housing, and plant and equipment, and in differentiating between the short-run impact of a tax change on the price of an asset and the long-run impact on the rental price of its services. Using the latter, we present estimates of the long-run impact of tax changes on tenure choice and quantities of housing services. Many issues beyond the scope of this study could profitably be analyzed with the present-value procedures used here.

The central tool of analysis is then used to illustrate the standard view of housing taxation, to examine the effect of inflation, and to review the effect of recent legislation. The main conclusions drawn are:

—The standard view well describes the tax treatment of housing in the mid-1960s.

—Basically, high rates of inflation are favorable to investment in housing.

—For owner-occupied housing, therefore, the tax treatment under current economic conditions is even more favorable than it was in the mid-1960s.

—However, inflation is less favorable to investment in rental housing than to investment in owner-occupied housing.

—Inflation is still less favorable—in fact, it is typically not favorable at all—to investment in plant and equipment.

—Recent legislation has significantly reduced the profitability of rental housing. The tax advantages of rental housing, if they exist at all under current inflation rates and legislation, are small.

These conclusions rest on assumptions as well as facts. One key assumption is point-for-point responsiveness of mortgage rates to the general rate of inflation; one key fact is relatively high mortgage-to-value ratios for both owner-occupants and rental investors (ratios of 0.75 and 0.80 are used in the paper). Also, some of the conclusions rest on the definition of a "neutral" alternative set of tax provisions against which to compare current housing taxation. The alternative used in this paper is a tax on sales minus all expenses (including economic depreciation) and on some fraction of capital gains, with the bases for both depreciation and capital gains adjusted for inflation. The sensitivity of the conclusions to this definition of a comparison case and to key assumptions and facts is explored in the paper and in an appendix available from the authors.

The final section of the study discusses some issues in housing taxation policy. It concludes that there is a strong case for tightening the tax treatment of owner-occupied housing, although this is difficult to do without disappointing the expectations of many recent home buyers. The case for any further tightening of the tax treatment of rental housing is weak. For rental housing, a case can be made for offering some of the benefits of inflation adjustment in the calculation of depreciation and capital gains in exchange for a more realistic allowable rate of depreciation.

The Present Value of a Housing Investment

The central tool of analysis of this study, a procedure for calculating present value, tallies benefits and costs of an investment for every time period, including imputed benefits and complex tax impacts, and then applies a rate of discount to the year-by-year net financial benefits to arrive at present value. We begin with a simple example for a relatively familiar type of investment, a new owner-occupied home.

A Representative Mid-1960s New Owner-Occupied Home

The benefits and costs of investment in an owner-occupied home, as tables 1 and 2 illustrate, can be organized into three phases. In the initial phase there are a down payment and certain transactions costs; in the second, or operating, phase there are imputed rental benefits, actual outlays for operating expenses, property taxes, interest, and amortization, and tax savings; and in the final phase, when the house is sold, there are proceeds of the sale, transactions costs, a mortgage repayment, and possibly additional taxes.

The example in the tables is designed to be representative of new housing investment in the early 1960s, when the rate of inflation was negligible and house prices and mortgage rates were much lower than they are currently. The tables list all the assumptions that describe a represen-

Table 1. A Representative Mid-1960s Investment in New Owner-Occupied Housing

Item	Value
Assumptions	
Initial cost (dollars)	25,000
Land	4,845
Structure	20,155
Ratio of imputed rent to initial cost	0.090
Ratio of operating costs to initial cost	0.026
Depreciation rate (percent)	1.2
Holding period (years)	12
Expected annual rate of price increase (percent)	
Land	3.0
Structure	0
Imputed rent	0
Operating costs	0
Mortgage characteristics	
Interest rate (percent)	5.0
Term (years)	25
Ratio of mortgage to value	0.75
Tax characteristics	
Property tax rate (percent)	2.0
Marginal income tax rate (percent)	30.0
Taxable fraction of imputed rent	0
Taxable fraction of property tax	−1.0
Taxable fraction of mortgage interest	−1.0
Taxable fraction of capital gains	0
Costs and benefits (dollars)	
Initial year	
Down payment	−6,250
Closing costs (2.5 percent of initial cost)	−625
Cash flow	−6,875
Operating years (imputed rent less outlays after tax)[a]	
1	201
2	175
3	148
4	122
5	95
6	68
7	41
8	13
9	−15
10	−42
11	−71
12	−99
Terminal year	
Sale price	24,345
Selling cost (7.5 percent of sale price)	−1,826
Mortgage repayment	−12,497
Tax on capital gain	0
Tax on mortgage payment	0

Table 1 (*continued*)

Item	Value
Cash flow	10,022
Capital gain (sale price less selling cost less initial cost)	−2,481
Summary measures	
Demand price, discount rate of 4 percent (dollars)	25,000
Percent difference from initial cost	0
Long-run rent–cost ratio restoring a real after-tax rate of return of 4 percent	0.09000
Percent difference from actual	0

Source: Frank de Leeuw and Larry Ozanne, "The Impact of the Federal Income Tax on Investment in Housing," *Survey of Current Business*, vol. 59 (December 1979), p. 51. Figures are rounded.
a. For derivation of imputed rent less outlays after tax in each year, see table 2.

tative new housing investment in the 1960s, assumptions about land and structure costs, operating costs, expected rates of increase in various prices, rate of economic depreciation, mortgage terms and rate, property tax and income tax provisions, expected number of years of occupancy, and the value of the services provided—that is, the rent the house could earn, or its imputed rent.[2]

The principal conclusions of this paper are by no means sensitive to all of these assumptions. Most of the major assumptions to which results are sensitive—expected inflation rates, tax provisions, and mortgage rates— are examined and varied in the paper. Sensitivity to other assumptions is explored in the appendix available from the authors.

In the initial year, as table 1 shows, outlays consist of a down payment of 25 percent of the assumed $25,000 price and closing costs equal to 2.5 percent of the price, for a total outlay of $6,875. In general, the contribution of the initial transactions to present value is

(1) $$-(1 - m + c)V_0,$$

where m is the ratio of mortgage to value, c is the ratio of closing costs to value, and V_0 is the initial value of the property.

In the operating years (table 2) imputed rent is a benefit that begins at 9 percent of the initial cost and is reduced in subsequent years by depreciation of the structure. On the outlay side are operating costs, property taxes, mortgage interest, and amortization of the debt, but two of these items, property taxes and mortgage interest, are in part offset by tax

2. The assumptions are based on housing data from the Census Bureau, the Federal Housing Administration, the National Association of Realtors, and numerous other sources, and on studies by housing experts. An appendix listing principal sources of information for the assumptions is available from the authors of this paper.

Table 2. Costs and Benefits in Operating Years for New Owner-Occupied Housing, Mid-1960s
Dollars

Operating years	Imputed rent	Outlays					Tax saving on		Imputed rent less outlays after tax
		Operating costs	Property taxes	Mortgage interest	Amortization	Imputed rent less outlays	Property tax	Mortgage interest	
1	2,250	650	500	938	393	−230	150	281	201
2	2,228	650	497	918	413	−250	149	275	175
3	2,207	650	496	897	433	−270	149	269	148
4	2,185	650	495	876	455	−290	148	263	122
5	2,164	650	493	853	478	−309	148	256	95
6	2,144	650	492	829	501	−328	148	249	68
7	2,123	650	491	804	526	−348	147	241	41
8	2,103	650	490	778	553	−367	147	233	13
9	2,083	650	489	750	580	−386	147	225	−15
10	2,063	650	488	721	609	−405	146	216	−42
11	2,044	650	487	690	640	−424	146	207	−71
12	2,024	650	487	658	672	−443	146	198	−99

Source: Same as table 1. Figures are rounded.

savings. The tax savings turn the pretax net cost of the investment into an after-tax net gain during the first eight operating years, but a small after-tax net operating loss remains in later years. In general, the contribution of operating-year transactions (actual and imputed) to present value is

$$(2) \qquad \sum_{i=1}^{n} \left[\frac{R_i - O_i - (1 - t)PT_i - (1 - t)MI_i - MA_i}{(1 + d)^i} \right],$$

where R is imputed rent, O is operating costs, PT is property taxes, MI is mortgage interest, MA is mortgage amortization, d is a discount rate, and t is a marginal income tax rate. The subscript i denotes the year and runs from 1 to n, the holding period for the investment.

At the end of the twelfth year, sale of the house at a price of \$24,345 reflects the net effect of the assumed inflation in land prices (see table 1) and the structure depreciation rate. Selling costs of 7.5 percent of the sale price and repayment of the remaining mortgage debt are deducted from the sale price for a terminal-year cash flow of \$10,022. The contribution of terminal transactions to present value is given by

$$(3) \qquad \frac{(1 - s)V_n - \left(mV_0 - \sum_{i=1}^{n} MA_i\right)}{(1 + d)^n},$$

where s is the ratio of selling costs to sale price, V_n is the final sale price, mV_0 is the initial mortgage, ΣMA_i is the sum of operating-year amortization payments, and $(1 + d)^n$ is the discount factor applicable to the terminal year n.

These year-by-year costs and benefits can be combined in various ways to summarize the outcome of the investment. In this study two summary measures are emphasized; a short-run summary, which will be labeled the "demand price" of the investment, and a long-run summary, which will be labeled the "equilibrium rent–value ratio." The demand price is simply the present value of all of the costs and benefits at an assumed real discount rate of 4 percent,[3] added to the initial cost of the investment. It is

3. Four percent is a broad average of the after-tax real rate of return (including capital gains) on fixed investment in the U.S. economy during the post–World War II era. See Laurits R. Christensen and Dale W. Jorgenson, "U.S. Income, Saving and Wealth, 1929–69," *Review of Income and Wealth,* series 19 (December 1973), pp. 329–62. When the expected rate of inflation is varied, as in some of the results reported later in this article, the nominal rate of discount is varied by the same amount; for instance, when expected inflation is assumed to be 6 percent a year, a discount rate of 10 percent rather than 4 percent is used.

the maximum amount that a home buyer would be willing to pay if he wished to realize a real after-tax rate of return of at least 4 percent. At a real discount rate of 4 percent, as table 1 shows, the present value of the investment is precisely zero, so that the demand price is equal to the $25,000 cost of the dwelling in this case.

If the demand price of an investment is different from the cost, then the market is not in long-run equilibrium. Initially, if the demand price is above cost, the result will be either a large return to the home buyer or a large profit for the builder or developer. In either case, market forces are set in motion that lead to growth of the stock of housing in the form of either more new housing or better maintenance of the existing stock. As the stock expands, the imputed rent per unit of housing services will fall (or rise at a rate below trend) and the return on housing will also fall. These forces may be expected to persist until they restore some normal relationship between the after-tax rates of return on new housing and rates of return on other investments.

While the present-value calculations employed in this study say nothing about the timing or form of changes in the stock of housing, they can be used to calculate what change in rent it would take to restore a given rate of return. In the example presented in tables 1 and 2, it takes no change in rent to achieve an after-tax return of 4 percent, since demand price already equals cost at a real discount rate of 4 percent. To illustrate this use of present-value calculations, the "base case" of tables 1 and 2 can be compared with a case identical to it in all respects except for a major tax provision.

This comparison appears in table 3, in which the first column is simply a summary of the results shown in table 1. The second column of the table (case 2) shows the results of an investment identical to that of tables 1 and 2, except it is assumed that mortgage interest is not deductible in calculating taxable income.

The summary measures (results) are shown in the bottom section of the table. When interest is not deductible, the demand price is only $22,688. Under this alternative tax treatment the tax saving resulting from interest payments (see table 2) is zero, and the value of the house to the investor falls below the $25,000 cost by more than $2,000. If tax law were actually changed in this way, the change would cause a sharp drop in the incentive to invest in new owner-occupied housing.

Eventually, less investment would lead to a smaller stock (or smaller growth in the stock than would otherwise take place) and a higher im-

Table 3. Effects of the Mid-1960s Tax Law and of Changes in the Law on Owner-Occupied Housing

Item	Case 1: mid-1960s tax law[a]	Case 2: mortgage interest deductibility disallowed	Case 3: taxation of imputed rent less all expenses
Assumptions			
Initial cost (dollars)	25,000	25,000	25,000
Ratio of imputed rent to initial cost	0.09000	0.09000	0.09000
Expected annual rate of price increase (percent)	0	0	0
Mortgage interest rate (percent)	5.0	5.0	5.0
Results			
Demand price, discount rate of 4 percent (dollars)	25,000	22,688	21,436
Percent difference from initial cost	0	−9.2	−14.3
Long-run imputed rent–cost ratio restoring a real after-tax rate of return of 4 percent	0.09000	0.10034	0.11137
Percent difference from 0.09000	0	11.5	23.7
Effect of long-run change in rent on			
Owner-occupied fraction of all households (percentage points)	0	−3.0	−6.5
Housing services per owner-occupant household (percent)	0	−7.8	−16.0

Source: De Leeuw and Ozanne, "Impact of the Federal Income Tax on Investment in Housing," p. 53.
a. From table 1.

puted rent. Some households would choose to be renters rather than owner-occupants. Among owner-occupants some would choose smaller flows of housing services. These reductions in quantity would raise the value per unit of service. Table 3 shows that the ratio of imputed rent to value that would restore the real after-tax rate of return of 4 percent is 0.10034, 11.5 percent above the 0.09 of the base case.

Given this 11.5 percent change in rent, it is possible to carry the analysis one step further by using the results from studies of the demand for housing. Elasticities of tenure choice and of quantity demanded with respect to price represent estimates of what a change in price does to the quantities of owner-occupied and rental housing demanded in the long run. The estimates underlying table 3 imply that an 11.5 percent increase in rent would be accompanied by a 3.0 percent decrease in the percentage of households that are owner-occupants (and a corresponding increase in the percentage that are renters) and a 7.8 percent decrease in the amount of housing per homeowner.

The estimates rely heavily on a cross-section study by Rosen.[4] In applying his results, we have taken into account the highly nonlinear relationship he estimated between tenure choice and its determinants by working through a few policy changes for ten cases representing the distribution of incomes and tax rates rather than for just one typical case. The ratios of results for a weighted sum of the ten disaggregated cases (weights reflect the proportion of households represented by each case) to results for the one typical case have been used to adjust single-case results throughout this paper.

These estimates apply to an extremely long run. They rest on the assumption that the supply of housing is perfectly elastic, an assumption certainly inappropriate for a period as short as a year or two; in fact, in our view, it is not even appropriate for a period as long as ten or fifteen years when the size and shape and location of the existing stock at the start of the period can still have an appreciable influence on housing conditions at the end of the period. For any period shorter than the very long run, the estimates at the bottom of table 3 overstate tenure and quantity effects.

These long-run price and quantity estimates can themselves be used to estimate the welfare loss associated with a tax treatment and the long-run revenue consequences of a tax change, which can differ substantially from short-run revenue impacts. We have not developed such estimates for this study.

A Representative Mid-1960s Rental Development

The example in tables 4 and 5 represents investment in new unsubsidized rental housing in the mid-1960s, when the rate of inflation was negligible. The division into initial, operating, and termination phases is much the same for rental housing as for owner-occupied housing. The tax laws governing rental housing, however, are much more complicated, and these complications are reflected in the assumptions and the actual outcome of the investment.

The rental housing investor is assumed to invest through a real estate partnership and to be in the 50 percent marginal tax bracket. Two of the tax complications currently faced by this class of investors, the "recap-

4. "Housing Decisions."

Table 4. A Representative Mid-1960s Investment in New Rental Housing

Item	Value
Assumptions	
Initial cost (dollars)	300,000
Land	36,000
Structure	250,189
Interest and taxes	13,811
Ratio of rent to initial cost	0.11700
Economic depreciation rate (percent)	1.4
Holding period (years)	13
Mortgage characteristics	
Interest rate (percent)	5.0
Term (years)	25
Ratio of mortgage to value	0.80
Expected annual rate of price increase (percent)	
Land	3.0
Structure	0
Rent	0
Operating costs	0
Tax rates (percent)	
Property tax	2.0
Marginal income tax	50.0
Minimum tax	0
Depreciation[a]	
Useful life (years)	35
Construction-period interest and taxes (percent)	
Expensed	100
Amortized over 10 years	0
Capital gains (historical-cost basis; percent)	
Subject to recapture as ordinary income	0
Subject to income tax	50
Operating-year losses as offset to other income (percent)	95
Costs and benefits (dollars)	
Initial year	
Down payment	−60,000
Closing costs (2.5 percent of initial cost)	−7,500
Tax saving from expensing of construction-period	
interest and taxes	6,906
Cash flow	−60,594
Operating years (rent less outlays after tax)[b]	
1	4,597
2	3,890
3	3,202
4	2,530
5	1,874
6	1,231
7	601
8	−18

Table 4 (*continued*)

Item	Value
9	−628
10	−1,229
11	−1,823
12	−2,412
13	−2,996
Terminal year	
Sale price	272,655
Selling cost (5.5 percent of sale price)	−14,996
Mortgage repayment	−150,929
Recapture tax	0
Capital gains tax	−22,855
Minimum tax	0
Cash flow	83,876
Capital gain (sale price less selling cost less initial cost plus depreciation)	91,418
Summary measures	
Demand price, discount rate of 4 percent (dollars)	300,000
Percent difference from initial cost	0
Long-run rent–cost ratio restoring a real after-tax rate of return of 4 percent	0.11700
Percent difference from actual	0

Source: De Leeuw and Ozanne, "Impact of the Federal Income Tax on Investment in Housing," p. 54. Figures are rounded.

a. Historical-cost basis, double-declining balance formula.

b. For derivation of rent less outlays after tax in each year, see table 5.

ture" (upon sale) of a proportion of depreciation in excess of straight-line and the minimum tax rate on tax preference income, were not part of the tax code in the mid-1960s and so can be ignored for the moment. The capital gains fraction subject to tax was 50 percent at that time, and capital gains were (and are) calculated on the basis of historical cost.

The 1954 Tax Reform Act permitted depreciation for tax purposes on residential rental property as much as twice the straight-line rate, using a declining-balance formula. Under the typical assumption of a useful life of thirty-five years, this translates into a first-year depreciation rate of 2/35, or 5.7 percent, compared to an estimated economic rate of only 1.4 percent. Tax depreciation is based on historical cost, so that its contribution to present value falls as the rate of inflation rises. In the zero-inflation case of tables 3 and 4, it is the most powerful tax advantage of rental housing.

Construction-period interest and taxes in the mid-1960s could be deducted as a current business expense. Losses during operating years could (and can) be used to offset other taxable income, and it is assumed that 95 percent of operating-year losses are used in this way.

The outcome in the initial year depends on the down payment, closing costs (assumed to be 2.5 percent of the $300,000 value of the property), and the tax benefit from expensing construction-period interest and taxes. In the example the net outlay is $60,594.

During the operating years (see table 5), cash flow before taxes consists of rent less four items: operating costs, property taxes, interest, and amortization. The net outcome ranges from a small positive amount in the first year to a loss of nearly $4,000 in the last operating year. Tax benefits also contribute more in the early years than later, because of the declining-balance depreciation formula. Consequently, net financial benefits after taxes begin at more than $4,500 in the first year, fall below zero in the eighth year, and drop to a loss of nearly $3,000 in the last year.

It is anticipated that the property will be held for thirteen years, a period that maximizes the present value of the investment. The sale price of $272,655 represents the net outcome of rising land prices and a slowly depreciating structure, as in the owner-occupied case. Selling costs are assumed to be 5.5 percent of the sale price, somewhat lower than the corresponding assumption for owner-occupied property. Mortgage repayment and a capital gains tax are also due at time of sale, leaving a net cash flow of $83,876.

Once again, the example was designed to represent an equilibrium in which the short-run demand price is exactly equal to the $300,000 cost and the long-run rent–value ratio is equal to the assumed actual ratio of 0.117.

Shortcomings of Present-Value Analysis

Present-value analysis, like any other analytical tool, has shortcomings that it is important to keep in mind. One of them is that some of the economic assumptions are held fixed even when there are changes in tax provisions or other economic conditions that might lead them to change. This is *not* true of the mortgage rate and the nominal discount rate, which are assumed to change with the underlying rate of inflation. But it is true, for example, of the ratio of land cost to structure cost; if a change in the tax treatment of new rental housing alters the optimal combination of land and structure, that alteration is not reflected in the present-value calculations presented here.

Table 5. Costs and Benefits in Operating Years for New Rental Housing, Mid-1960s
Dollars

Operating years	Outlays						Tax calculation			Rent less outlays after tax
	Rent	Operating costs	Property taxes	Mortgage interest	Amortization	Rent less outlays	Depreciation allowance	Profits[a]	Profits tax[b]	
1	35,100	11,700	6,000	12,000	5,029	371	14,297	−8,897	−4,226	4,597
2	34,668	11,700	5,948	11,749	5,280	−9	13,480	−8,208	−3,899	3,890
3	34,241	11,700	5,897	11,485	5,544	−384	12,709	−7,550	−3,586	3,202
4	33,821	11,700	5,848	11,207	5,821	−756	11,983	−6,918	−3,286	2,530
5	33,406	11,700	5,801	10,916	6,112	−1,123	11,298	−6,309	−2,997	1,874
6	32,998	11,700	5,755	10,611	6,418	−1,486	10,653	−5,721	−2,718	1,231
7	32,595	11,700	5,711	10,290	6,739	−1,845	10,044	−5,151	−2,447	601
8	32,197	11,700	5,669	9,953	7,076	−2,201	9,470	−4,595	−2,183	−18
9	31,805	11,700	5,629	9,599	7,430	−2,552	8,929	−4,051	−1,924	−628
10	31,419	11,700	5,590	9,228	7,801	−2,900	8,419	−3,517	−1,671	−1,229
11	31,038	11,700	5,553	8,838	8,191	−3,244	7,938	−2,990	−1,420	−1,823
12	30,663	11,700	5,518	8,428	8,601	−3,584	7,484	−2,468	−1,172	−2,412
13	30,292	11,700	5,485	7,998	9,031	−3,921	7,056	−1,947	−925	−2,996

Source: Same as table 4. Figures are rounded.
a. Rent less outlays, except amortization, less depreciation allowances.
b. Profits times tax rate times loss-offset fraction (95 percent).

Second, it is debatable whether rates of return will eventually move all the way back to some assumed economywide after-tax real rate of return. To the extent that housing is an imperfect substitute for other assets (or is a substitute for consumption), the rate of return for housing investment after a change in tax laws or economic conditions would tend to move back only part of the way toward the prechange equilibrium. To the extent that housing is an important component of national wealth, furthermore, the economywide real rate of return itself will be affected by developments in the housing market.

Third, the analysis of present value is also limited in that it does not take account of the liquidity or borrowing difficulties of some households. While for most homeowners the higher housing prices of recent years have been more than offset by capital gains and tax benefits, for some would-be homeowners high prices have made it almost impossible to acquire a down payment and enter the homeownership market. It would be difficult to adapt the procedures used in this study to represent the situation faced by these households.

Restriction of the analysis to new housing is another limitation. For many purposes, to be sure, close substitutability of new and existing housing means that it is probably sufficient to analyze the present value of new housing alone and assume that the price of existing housing adjusts so that it earns the same rate of return. For rental housing, however, tax laws applicable to new structures are generally more generous than those applicable to existing structures. The differences should affect investors' expectations about the eventual sale price of a new structure. It would be possible, though difficult, to use present-value analysis to help estimate the appropriate price impact and to modify new investors' price expectations accordingly. We have not attempted to do so here.

A final point about the present-value and related calculations of this study is that they bear a close relation to the concept of user cost. The rent at which the present value of an investment equals zero is one definition of user cost. The long-run rent–value ratio used here, when multiplied by cost, also solves for the rent at which present value equals zero. Under simplifying assumptions—no transactions costs or capital gains taxes, mortgage rate equal to nominal discount rate, and a number of others— the procedure used can be reduced to a formula that closely resembles familiar user-cost expressions. The procedure used in this study has advantages over a user-cost formula in handling complexities such as transactions costs or recapture of excess depreciation and in drawing a distinction between short-run asset price effects and long-run rent effects. But the same economic reasoning underlies both analytical tools.

The Impact of Tax Changes and Inflation

With the use of present-value calculations, this section first restates the standard view that housing receives favorable income tax treatment under the assumptions of zero expected inflation and mid-1960s tax law. "Favorably treated" implies a comparison with some other treatment. The case used for comparison in this study is an unincorporated commercial enterprise that pays an income tax on sales minus all expenses (including economic depreciation) and on some fraction (50 percent in the 1960s) of realized capital gains. With respect to inflation, the comparison case is one in which the bases for both depreciation and capital gains are adjusted by the price of rental services.[5]

The comparison case follows current tax law for unincorporated business enterprises except for provisions that most economists believe clearly distort the allocation of resources. Instead of these distortionary provisions—specifically, instead of depreciation allowances in excess of economic depreciation and historical-cost bases for depreciation and capital gains—the comparison case is based on provisions that are more neutral with respect to allocation. Comparisons of the actual tax treatment of housing with this neutral case fully bear out the standard view that investment in housing received favorable tax treatment under mid-1960s conditions.

Following these comparisons is an investigation of the effect of inflation on the profitability of owner-occupied housing, rental housing, and plant and equipment. The conclusions are that inflation confers substantial benefit on investment in owner-occupied housing, less benefit on rental housing investment, and no benefit at all in the plant and equipment case analyzed.

The section then examines the impact on rental housing of legislative changes since the mid-1960s—changes dealing with construction-period interest and taxes, recapture of excess depreciation, the minimum tax on tax preference income, and capital gains. On balance, these changes have reduced the returns to investment in rental housing.

5. Advocates of inflation adjustment of tax bases generally favor using a general price index for making the adjustments. The rental price used in this study is a proxy for a general price index for goods and services.

Finally, the section reviews the standard view of housing taxation in the light of high rates of inflation and recent legislation. It concludes that owner-occupied housing is currently treated even more favorably than it was in the mid-1960s but that rental housing, if it has any tax advantage currently, has only a very small one.

The Standard View

The favorable tax treatment of homeownership arises from the deductibility of some of the expenses of homeownership—property tax payments and mortgage interest payments—and the failure to tax the imputed income from owner-occupancy. Conceptually, though not practically, the simplest way to eliminate this favorable treatment is to tax imputed rent minus costs, with costs including not only interest and property taxes but also operating costs and economic depreciation. The effect of this alternative treatment—taxation of imputed rent less all expenses—is shown in case 3 of table 3. It leads in the short run to a demand price 14.3 percent lower, and in the long run to a rent–cost ratio 23.7 percent higher, than actual mid-1960s tax treatment. Under demand and tenure-choice elasticities estimated by Rosen, the long-run effect of moving from current taxation practice to taxing imputed rent and allowing deduction of all costs would be a 6.5-percentage-point reduction in the fraction of households that are owner-occupied[6] and a 16.0 percent reduction in the average housing services per owner-occupant.

For rental housing, the illustration of the standard case follows the same basic logic. Case 1 of table 6 summarizes the typical mid-1960s case presented in tables 4 and 5. Case 2 summarizes an alternative treatment in which depreciation for tax purposes is equal to the estimated economic depreciation rate of 1.4 percent a year rather than the commonly used double-declining-balance formula based on a useful life of thirty-five years. The result is to lower the demand price in the short run by 7.2 percent and to raise the long-run rent by 13.2 percent.[7] This long-run change in rent would reduce the fraction of households that rent by an estimated

6. The estimate is somewhat larger than Rosen's estimate of 4.4 percent ("Housing Decisions," p. 21). The difference appears to be due to differences between the Michigan panel sample of households he used and the sample of IRS returns we used for our disaggregated computations.

7. The principal reason for the larger percentage impact on rent than on demand price is that it is not the full change in rent but only the change in rent after tax that contributes to the investor's return.

Table 6. Effects of Mid-1960s Tax Law and of Changes in the Law on Rental Housing

Item	Case 1: mid-1960s tax law	Case 2: change to economic depreciation	Case 3: capitalization of construction-period interest and taxes	Case 4: cases 2 and 3 combined
Assumptions				
Initial cost (dollars)	300,000	300,000	300,000	300,000
Ratio of rent to initial cost	0.11700	0.11700	0.11700	0.11700
Expected annual rate of price increase (percent)	0	0	0	0
Results				
Demand price, discount rate of 4 percent (dollars)	300,000	278,380	294,767	272,023
Percent difference from initial cost	0	−7.2	−1.7	−9.3
Long-run rent–cost ratio restoring a real after-tax rate of return of 4 percent	0.11700	0.13242	0.12056	0.13696
Percent difference from 0.11700	0	13.2	3.0	17.1
Effect of long-run change in rent on Renter fraction of all households (percentage points)	0	−8.5	−2.0	−10.8
Housing per renter household (percent)	0	−7.2	−1.6	−9.4

Source: De Leeuw and Ozanne, "Impact of the Federal Income Tax on Investment in Housing," p. 56.

8.5 percentage points and reduce the quantity of housing services per rental household by 7.2 percentage points.

A change in the treatment of construction-period interest and taxes is not as important a matter as shifting to economic depreciation. Case 3 shows the results of fully capitalizing these expenses rather than following the mid-1960s practice of expensing them (tax law changes since the mid-1960s have moved treatment of these expenses to a position between the two extremes).

The estimated effects of the two changes together appear in the final column of the table. Depreciation allowances based on economic depreciation and capitalization of construction-period interest and taxes would eventually raise the level of rents by 17.1 percent (case 4). This magnitude is smaller than the 23.7 percent increase for owner-occupants shown in table 3, suggesting that the income tax treatment of a representative owner-occupant investment as of the mid-1960s was more favorable than the treatment of a representative rental investment.

To sum up, present-value calculations based on mid-1960s conditions fully support the standard propositions that the taxation of housing is favorable compared with an investment in which full income is taxed, depreciation allowances approximate true economic depreciation, and all construction costs are capitalized.

The Impact of Inflation

Under the present tax system inflation is basically favorable to investment in housing, provided mortgage rates rise by no more than the increase in the rate of inflation. The effect of inflation is to shift returns from the operating years to the termination year of an investment, and thereby to shift the tax base from ordinary income to capital gains. During operating years returns are lower because interest outlays tend to rise in proportion to the level of interest rates (for example, to double if interest rates are 10 percent rather than 5 percent), or much more than in proportion to the general price level. In the terminal year real returns are higher because debt repayment is fixed in dollar value and hence does not rise with the price level at all.

A highly simplified example of a durable investment will clarify the influences at work. The example ignores transactions costs and depreciation, although the latter is discussed separately in connection with rental housing. It assumes a single nominal rate of interest equal to $(1 + r)(1 + \dot{p}) - 1$, or approximately $r + \dot{p}$, where r is a real interest rate and $\dot{p}$ is a rate of price increase. The implied assumption that nominal interest rates respond approximately point for point to changes in the rate of inflation will be discussed and modified later.

The example describes an investment project worth V dollars, in which the investor initially makes a down payment of $V(1 - b)$, where b is the loan-to-value ratio. The loan is a fixed-dollar bond, with repayment due in entirety at the end of its term, rather than a level-payment mortgage.

In operating years the investor receives a net rent (rent less operating costs and property taxes) that is assumed to rise with the inflation rate, pays interest on his borrowing, and pays an income tax on net rent less interest. The contributions of these operating entries to present value is calculated by dividing them by $[(1 + r)(1 + \dot{p})]^i$, where i is the year in which they occur. The operating-years component of present value is

$$(4) \quad \sum_{i=1}^{n} \left[\frac{1}{(1 + r)(1 + \dot{p})} \right]^i \{ R(1 + \dot{p})^i - [(1 + r)(1 + \dot{p}) - 1]bV \}(1 - t),$$

where n is the investor's holding period, R is initial rent, and t is the income tax rate (assumed constant for the moment).

When the investment is sold, the investor receives a price that equals the initial value inflated by the subsequent price increase, repays the loan, and pays a capital gains tax. The discounted value of these items is

$$(5) \qquad \frac{V(1 + \dot{p})^n - bV - tg[(1 + \dot{p})^n V - V]}{[(1 + r)(1 + \dot{p})]^n},$$

where g is the portion of capital gains subject to tax.

The components of present value vary in their sensitivity to the inflation rate, $\dot{p}$. The present value of net rent is not sensitive to inflation, because the current-dollar stream of rent and the discount factor are affected by $\dot{p}$ in exactly the same way. Interest outlays, however, are highly sensitive, because interest payments respond much more to inflation than does the discount factor. For example, if the zero-inflation interest rate, r, equals 4 percent, a rise in the inflation rate from zero to 8 percent will approximately triple the flow of interest payments in every year—from 4 percent of bV to 12.3 percent (equal to 1.04 times 1.08, less 1.0) of bV. The discount factor, in contrast, will go up by only 8 percent in the first year and by gradually increasing amounts thereafter. The discount factor does not triple its zero-inflation value until the fifteenth year.

The derivative of the entire expression for present value with respect to $\dot{p}$ is given by

$$(6) \qquad \frac{\partial(PV)}{\partial \dot{p}} = t(b - g)\left[\frac{nV}{(1 + r)^n(1 + \dot{p})^{n+1}}\right].$$

If g is zero, as is typical for owner-occupied housing, present value clearly rises with inflation. If g is 40 percent, as is typical for many other assets, present value rises with inflation (in this simplified case) as long as b, the loan–value ratio, exceeds 0.4. This relationship holds strictly only if all the simplifying assumptions of this example hold;[8] but it is true generally that if capital gains are taxed at a rate sufficiently lower than operating income inflation raises the present value of an investment.

---

8. One of the simplifying assumptions in this analysis is the assumption of a constant marginal tax rate. Under a progressive income tax, inflation pushes taxpayers into higher brackets unless it is offset by periodic tax cuts or by systematic indexation of tax brackets. The working assumption in this study is that this inflationary effect on tax brackets *is* offset; inflation is not equated with an automatic growth in the share of income taken by taxes. Periodic tax cuts during recent years suggest that this is a realistic assumption. In the appendix, however, the effect of the alternative assumption that tax schedules are not revised in the presence of inflation is considered.

The result in the simplified example closely resembles present-value results for owner-occupied housing. As the solid line in the left panel of figure 1 shows, the demand price for the mid-1960s $25,000 house would rise to nearly $27,000 under an expected 6 percent inflation rate and an 11 percent mortgage rate (6 percent above the base-case mortgage rate of 5 percent). Under these circumstances, the equilibrium rent–value ratio in the long run would fall by nearly 10 percent. Expected inflation at an annual rate of 12 percent, with a corresponding increase in the mortgage rate to 17 percent, would raise the short-run demand price to nearly $28,000 and eventually lower the rent–value ratio (not shown in the figure) by more than 15 percent.

The inflation effects just described, the base cases in figure 1, allow the mortgage rate to rise point for point with the increase in the rate of inflation. Historical experience for many countries suggests that this is a reasonably accurate long-run generalization. It implies that real before-tax interest rates do not vary systematically with the rate of inflation, an implication that is in turn consistent with (though not equivalent to) the assumption that inflation does not systematically affect the marginal productivity of capital.

Figure 1 also shows the results of other assumptions about mortgage rates. One such assumption is that the real after-tax mortgage rate, rather than the real before-tax mortgage rate, is unchanged in the face of inflation. Mortgage rates must rise faster than point for point with inflation to be consistent with this assumption; if borrowers face a 30 percent marginal tax rate, the required increase is $1 \div (1-0.3)$, or 1.43 percentage points for each one-point increase in the inflation rate. If interest rates do change this rapidly—from 5 percent to more than 22 percent as the rate of inflation goes from zero to 12 percent—then the real after-tax cost of mortgage finance stays constant, and, as shown in figure 1 by alternative A, the demand price for owner-occupants stays approximately constant as the inflation rate changes. At the same time, interest rate increases of this magnitude imply that, unless the productivity of capital rises sharply with inflation, bondholders receive a rapidly increasing share and equity holders a falling share of the returns to capital (before taxes) as inflation rates increase.

A more realistic assumption in the short run, though probably not in the long run, is that mortgage rates rise less than point for point with inflation. As shown in the figure, the assumption that mortgage rates rise only half as rapidly as inflation (alternative B) causes an increase in demand

Figure 1. Inflation, Mortgage Rates, and the Demand Price for Housing[a]

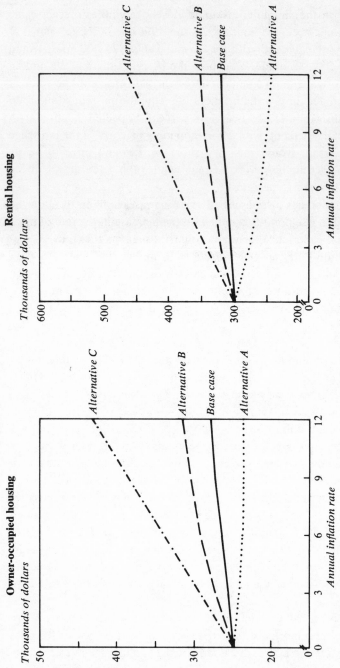

a. The lines labeled "Base case" are based on a point-for-point response of the mortgage rate to the inflation rate; for example, the mortgage rate rises from 5 to 8 percent when the expected inflation rate (as measured by the expected increase in rental prices) rises from 0 to 3 percent.

The alternative cases, labeled A, B, and C, are based on the following assumptions:

Alternative A lets the mortgage rate rise by $1/(1 - t)$ percentage point for each additional point in the expected inflation rate, where t is the marginal income tax rate of a representative dollar invested in new housing (0.3 for owner-occupied housing, 0.5 for rental housing).

Alternative B lets the mortgage rate rise by 0.5 percentage point for each additional point in the expected inflation rate.

Alternative C, like B, lets the mortgage rate rise by 0.5 percentage point for each additional point in the expected inflation rate, and in addition lets expected price increases for land and structures rise by 1.5 percentage points for each point in the expected inflation rate (as measured by the expected increase in rental prices).

price as the rate of inflation rises. A steeper increase follows from the assumption that not only do mortgage rates rise less rapidly than inflation but that expected increases in structure and land prices rise by 1.5 times the rate of inflation. As alternative C in the left panel of figure 1 shows, these assumptions lead to a demand price of more than $43,000, 73 percent above cost, under 12 percent inflation.

While a full analysis of the dynamics of recent housing market developments is well beyond the scope of this study, these results are nevertheless suggestive. They suggest that the recent boom in house prices may be heavily influenced by the rise in expected inflation together with a relatively small—far less than point for point—rise in mortgage rates. If that is the case, the boom may end as the normal relation between interest rates and inflation rates is restored.[9]

Inflation is not so favorable to investment returns for rental housing as for owner-occupied housing. One reason, not covered in the simple example analyzed above, is that depreciation allowances are based on historical cost and hence do not rise over time with the price level. Depreciation formulas that appear very generous under zero rates of inflation are much less so when inflation reaches double-digit rates. The other reason, which is covered in the example above, is that the taxation of capital gains, including purely nominal gains, is much more common for rental housing than for owner-occupied housing.

The right panel of figure 1 quantifies the impact of inflation on rental housing. The solid line, based on the assumption of a point-for-point reflection of inflation increases in mortgage rate increases, shows that the base-case demand price of $300,000 under zero percent inflation would increase by 4.2 percent under 6 percent inflation and by 6.2 percent under

9. A number of recent unpublished studies have argued persuasively that the user cost of owner-occupied housing has fallen in recent years when account is taken of the effects of inflation on capital gains and tax benefits. Douglas Diamond, "Taxes, Inflation, Speculation, and the Cost of Homeownership" (North Carolina State University, October 1979); Patric H. Hendershott and Sheng-Cheng Hu, "Inflation and the Benefits from Owner-Occupied Housing," National Bureau of Economic Research Working Paper 383 (Cambridge, Mass.: NBER, August 1979); and Kevin Villani, "The Tax Subsidy to Housing in an Inflationary Environment: Implications for After-Tax Housing Costs" (U.S. Department of Housing and Urban Development, March 1979). As Diamond points out, these results all rest in part on the incompleteness of the economy's adjustment to recent inflation rates and can therefore be read as suggesting that the user cost of owner-occupied housing will rise when interest rates and expected capital gains return to normal alignment with general inflation rates.

12 percent inflation. The corresponding increases for owner-occupied housing are larger—7.2 percent under 6 percent inflation and 11.2 percent under 12 percent inflation—because of the effects of historical-cost depreciation and taxation of nominal capital gains on rental, but not on owner-occupied, housing investment. Working in the other direction is the tax rate for the typical investor in rental property, which is higher than for the typical homeowner, since a high tax rate limits the increase in after-tax mortgage costs. The difference due to tax rates, however, is not enough to offset the difference due to historical-cost bases for depreciation and capital gains.

For rental housing, the assumption that mortgage rates rise enough to keep after-tax mortgage costs constant leads to a decline in demand price as inflation increases. In the rental case, the required mortgage rate increase per point of inflation is $1 \div (1-0.5)$, or 2 percentage points; as inflation rises from zero to 12 percent, the required mortgage rate therefore goes from 5 percent to 29 percent. Clearly, this is a case of theoretical rather than practical significance.

A short-run case of practical interest, once again, is the case of partial adjustment to inflation, as depicted by the curves for alternatives B and C. The top curve is based on the assumptions that mortgage rates rise only half as rapidly as inflation and that expected structure and land prices rise more rapidly than inflation. Demand price rises rapidly with inflation under these assumptions, but not as rapidly for rental as for owner-occupied housing. Again, these figures are suggestive of forces at work in recent years—in this case, forces leading to a shift from rental to ownership tenure, including conversion to condominium ownership of a growing number of rental structures. However, the recent shift away from rental housing has also been influenced by other forces, including legislative changes of the last decade, which will be analyzed below.

An important question in appraising recent and prospective investment trends is how the impact of inflation on housing investment compares with its impact on business plant and equipment. Figure 2 attempts to answer the question with an example of the present value of a typical investment in a nonfinancial corporation.

The plant and equipment example looks at the investment from the point of view of a stockholder who purchases equity for $9,200 in the initial year and sells it after seven years. The firm in which he invests benefits from an investment tax credit and borrows to convert the $9,200 equity investment into $20,000 of new plant and equipment. With the use

Figure 2. Inflation and Demand Prices for Owner-Occupied Housing, Rental Housing, and Plant and Equipment[a]

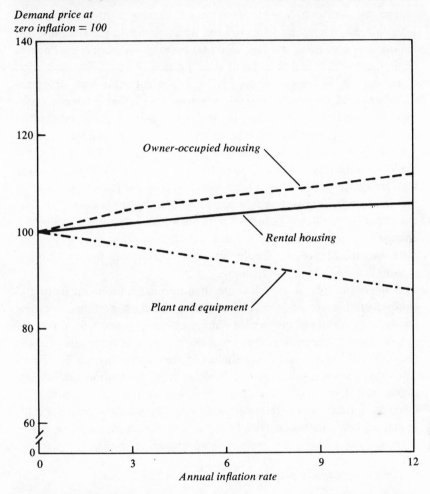

*Demand price at
zero inflation = 100*

a. In all three cases, the borrowing rate is assumed to rise by one percentage point for each additional point in the inflation rate.

of this capital stock, it produces output from inputs of capital stock, materials, and labor; calculates profits based on historical-cost depreciation and a portion of inventory profits; pays taxes and dividends; and divides its after-tax cash flow between further investment in capital stock and investment in other assets. During the years the stock is held, the investor's realized benefit from these activities is confined to the dividends he receives minus the income tax he pays on them. When the stock is sold, however, the investor benefits from an after-tax capital gain.

The calculations indicate that the present value of plant and equipment —in contrast to housing—does not rise with inflation at all. The same two factors that operate in the case of rental housing—historical-cost depreciation allowances and taxation of some portion of nominal capital gains —are part of the reason for the decline in present value with high rates of inflation. There are also two other factors. One is that many firms continue to keep accounts on a first-in, first-out basis, with the result that the taxation of some portion of capital gains from inventory holdings (inventory profits) reduces present value as inflation increases. The other is that the loan–value ratio for plant and equipment investment is typically lower than for housing; and a lower loan–value ratio means fewer benefits from the shift from operating-year earnings to terminal-year cash flow that accompanies inflation.[10] A further possible influence on present value is a change in perceived riskiness caused by inflation. The plant and equipment example, however, like the housing cases in both figures 1 and 2, ignores possible changes in riskiness.

Some of the special complications that arise in analyzing the plant and equipment case are dealt with by assuming certain fixed ratios—for example, a fixed ratio of dividends to after-tax earnings and a fixed ratio of indebtedness to the book value of real assets. These assumptions limit the generality of the analysis. Nevertheless, it seems clear that the basic factors that cause present value to fall rather than rise with inflation—historical-cost depreciation, taxation of nominal capital gains, taxation of inventory profits, and a relatively low loan–value ratio—are important in making inflation less beneficial to plant and equipment investment than to investment in housing, especially owner-occupied housing.[11]

Recent Legislation and the Value of Rental Investment

Returns to rental housing were substantially affected by tax legislation in 1969, 1976, and 1978. This legislation (1) ended the expensing of construction-period interest and taxes and shifted to amortization of these outlays over a number of years; (2) provided for recapture (that is, taxation as ordinary income rather than capital gains) of the excess over

10. Equation 6 included the loan–value ratio as one of the key determinants of the response of the present value of an investment to inflation.

11. A more detailed description of the plant and equipment example is available from the authors.

Table 7. The Impact of Recent Legislative Changes on Rental Housing

Item	Case 1: pre-1969 tax law	Case 2: 1969 and 1976 changes	Case 3: reduced tax on capital gains, 1978	Case 4: cases 2 and 3 combined
Assumptions				
Initial cost (dollars)	600,000	600,000	600,000	600,000
Ratio of rent to initial cost	0.1000	0.1000	0.1000	0.1000
Expected annual rate of price increase (percent)	6.0	6.0	6.0	6.0
Mortgage interest rate (percent)	9.0	9.0	9.0	9.0
Results				
Demand price, discount rate of 10 percent (dollars)	622,889	597,265	633,933	607,945
Percent difference from case 1	0	−4.1	1.8	−2.4
Long-run rent–cost ratio restoring a real after-tax rate of return of 4 percent	0.0919	0.1010	0.0880	0.0972
Percent difference from case 1	0	9.9	−4.2	5.8
Effect of long-run change in rent on Renter fraction of all households (percentage points)	...	−6.5	2.9	−3.9
Housing per renter household (percent)	...	−5.4	2.3	−3.2

Source: De Leeuw and Ozanne, "Impact of the Federal Income Tax on Investment in Housing," p. 59.

straight-line depreciation upon sale of a property; (3) introduced a minimum tax on tax preference income (that is, income from certain sources that would otherwise be exempt from income taxation); and (4) lowered from 50 to 40 percent the proportion of capital gains subject to income taxation.

The first three of these changes reduced the present value of investment in rental housing, but the fourth change had the opposite effect. In addition to the legislative changes, there have been Internal Revenue Service and judicial rulings that have generally had the effect of reducing the value of investment in rental housing.

To measure the impact of these four changes, the mid-1960s economic assumptions used earlier are inappropriate. Instead, the results shown in table 7 are based on a set of assumptions—including a $600,000 cost,[12] 6

12. The total initial cost serves simply as a scale factor (for both rental and owner-occupied housing), so that doubling the initial cost simply doubles all the dollar costs and benefits.

percent expected inflation, and a 9 percent mortgage rate—more appropriate to the mid-1970s. Under these assumptions, pre-1969 investment law (case 1) yields a demand price of $622,889, or 3.8 percent above cost, and a long-run rent–cost ratio of 0.0910, 8.1 percent below the assumed actual ratio of 0.1000.

Taken together, the first two tax changes reduce the demand price to $597,265 (case 2), or 4.1 percent lower than the pre-1969 case. The long-run rent–cost ratio is raised to 0.1010, or 9.9 percent higher than in case 1. These changes are the result of tightening the tax treatment of rental housing in 1969 and 1976.[13] Most of the change is due to the ten-year write-off rather than the expensing of construction-period interest and taxes.[14]

The reduction in 1978 of the fraction of capital gains subject to taxation offset some of the effect of the 1969 and 1976 tightening, as case 3 shows. The capital gains change, however, applied not only to rental housing but to a broad class of other investments, whereas the 1969 and 1976 reforms were specifically directed at rental housing and certain other tax shelters. For this reason and because of the IRS and judicial rulings since 1969 not measured in case 2, the worsening position of rental housing relative to other investment is understated by case 4, which measures the effect of the capital gains change together with those of the 1969 and 1976 reforms.

The Standard View Reconsidered

The analysis at the beginning of this section restated the standard view that, according to pre-1969 tax law and apart from the effects of inflation, both owner-occupied and rental housing are strongly favored by the income tax. It is now possible to reconsider this view in the light of high

---

13. One element in this tightening, the minimum tax, was imposed in 1969, tightened in 1976, and then loosened somewhat in 1978. The 1978 change consisted of removing the untaxed portion of capital gains from the list of preference items covered by the minimum tax and subjecting that portion to a complex alternative tax that only a handful of taxpayers are likely to have to pay. Excess depreciation remains on the list of preference items. The results in table 7 refer to the 1978 version of the minimum tax, not the 1976 version.

14. The estimates of long-run rent impact in this section tend to be larger than the user-cost impacts of the same legislative changes estimated by Tolley and Diamond in "Homeownership." The principal reason is that Tolley and Diamond measured the effect on the annual flow of dollars caused by each change, and we calculated the change in rent that, *after tax,* would offset that effect.

inflation rates and recent legislation. The analysis below suggests that under current law and taking account of high rates of inflation, owner-occupied housing is even more strongly favored than in the mid-1960s but that it is questionable whether favored treatment of rental housing investment persists.

OWNER-OCCUPIED HOUSING. It was shown earlier that for owner-occupied housing taxing imputed rent less all expenses (including economic depreciation) would reduce the demand price by about 14 percent and increase the long-run rent–value ratio by about 24 percent (table 3). These results referred to zero inflation. Results for positive inflation rates are broadly similar, provided that depreciation allowances are based on the inflation-adjusted value of the capital stock, not on its historical cost (if depreciation allowances are based on historical cost, then the gap in demand price or rent between the base case and the alternative widens as inflation rates increase).

Comparing current housing taxation law with taxation under a neutral alternative requires not only changing the treatment of imputed rent and depreciation but also taxing some portion of capital gains. For capital gains, as for depreciation, the method of dealing with inflation critically affects the results. This study reports on results in which the basis for capital gains, like the basis for depreciation, is adjusted for inflation and in which the capital gains tax applies not only to the dwelling itself but also to capital gains on the outstanding mortgage.[15]

While the capital gains tax employed here as an alternative to current housing practice does adjust for inflation, it adheres to current practice in two other respects. First, only 40 percent rather than all of the capital gains are subject to tax. Second, the tax is levied on realized capital gains, not on accrued capital gains. In the case of mortgage debt, a small realized capital gain occurs at each amortization payment. Because the mortgage is far from fully amortized when the property is sold, the bulk of the

15. The view of income taxation underlying this alternative to the current treatment of housing is that the goal is to tax both net income from current operations and any change in net worth. The current value of capital used up in production should be subtracted from income and added to the change in net worth. If the change-in-net-worth component is defined after adjustment for inflation, then the inflation adjustment should apply to balance-sheet items fixed in nominal dollars as well as to those whose values depend on market prices. Rises in the dollar value of real assets are reduced before taxation by this adjustment, and the value of a debt that is fixed in dollar terms but rises in real value should be turned into a capital gain by the same process.

realized gain occurs when the outstanding debt is repaid at the termination of the investment.[16]

The estimated results of taxing imputed rent after deducting inflation-adjusted depreciation and 40 percent of real capital gains are shown in figure 3. The base case (represented by a solid line in each panel) is not the mid-1960s case of table 1 but rather a mid-1970s case in all respects except the inflation and mortgage rates, which take on three alternative values. Compared to this base case, the alternative tax treatment represented by the dashed lines would reduce the demand price for owner-occupied housing by 12.1 percent at zero inflation, by 13.3 percent at a 6 percent inflation rate, and by 13.7 percent at a 12 percent inflation rate. Most of this reduction is due to the taxation of imputed rent less expenses; the contribution of taxing real capital gains, as just defined, is minor. The long-run consequences for rents and hence for tenure choice and services per owner-occupant, shown in the footnote to the figure, are quite large. The standard view of the tax treatment of owner-occupied housing, in short, carries over fully to the current inflationary environment.

The dotted lines in the two panels of the figure are of interest because they represent a tax alternative that would leave the returns to owner-occupied housing largely unaffected by inflation. The tax provisions that lead to these results are a combination of taxing rent after all expenses (including inflation-adjusted depreciation), *plus* taxation of 100 percent rather than 40 percent of inflation-adjusted capital gains. Even though capital gains continue to be taxed on realization rather than on accrual, the demand price and the long-run rent–value ratio are largely immune to the underlying rate of inflation. Demand price, for example, rises from $53,654 at zero inflation to only $54,826 at 12 percent inflation. At high rates of inflation, this treatment would leave demand prices well below those of the case in which only 40 percent of capital gains are taxed.

RENTAL HOUSING. For rental housing, it was shown earlier that under tax law before 1969 and at zero inflation, the shift from double-declining-balance depreciation to estimated economic depreciation and to full capitalization of construction-period interest and taxes would, for a representative new rental property, lower the demand price by about 9.3 percent.

---

16. The results make no allowance for the possibility that taxing capital gains on mortgage debt would reduce the mortgage rate. If allowance had been made, the capital gains adjustment would be smaller.

Figure 3. Effects of Mid-1970s Tax Law and Alternatives on Owner-Occupied Housing

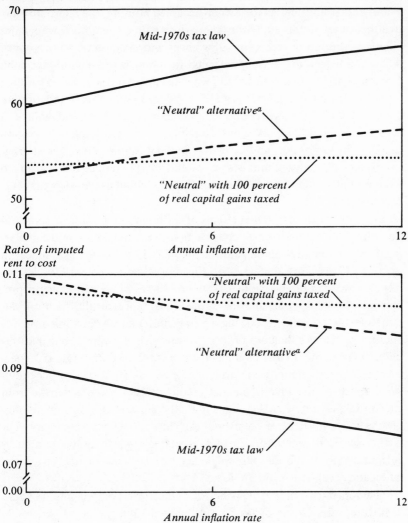

Demand price (thousands of dollars)

Ratio of imputed rent to cost

Annual inflation rate

a. The long-run effects of a change from the mid-1970s tax law to a "neutral" alternative are as follows:

Annual inflation rate	Owner-occupant fraction of all households (percentage points)	Housing services per owner-occupant (percent)
0	−5.5	−13.6
6	−6.5	−16.0
12	−7.3	−17.7

Under current tax law, the corresponding reduction would be only about half as large, principally because of ten-year amortization of construction-period outlays and recapture provisions introduced in 1969.

For rental housing, as for owner-occupied housing, the alternative tax treatment used in this study for comparison with current tax law includes inflation-adjusted depreciation allowances and taxation of 40 percent of inflation-adjusted realized capital gains, including gains on mortgage debt. For rental housing, in contrast to owner-occupied housing, this treatment leads to a tax advantage that is steadily reduced as the rate of inflation increases. Current tax law continues to confer a sizable tax advantage at zero inflation but limits the gains from inflation by requiring depreciation based on historical cost and by taxing nominal capital gains. The alternative treatment analyzed in this study would sharply reduce returns at zero inflation but would not limit the gains from inflation in the ways that current law does.

Estimates of the combined effects of shifting to an economic depreciation rate, fully capitalizing all construction-period expenses, and calculating depreciation and capital gains on an inflation-adjusted basis appear in figure 4. (The cases are based on the representative mid-1970s investment analyzed in table 7, above.) The solid lines in the two panels represent mid-1970s tax law, and the dashed lines represent the "neutral" alternative tax treatment. The figure indicates that at zero inflation the alternative reduces demand price by a little over 5 percent, but that this difference narrows to less than 2 percent when the inflation rate is 12 percent. Since many nonhousing investments benefit from special tax provisions (such as the investment tax credit), this 2 percent benefit from current tax law represents no benefit at all compared to a sizable number of alternative investment opportunities. Thus, in contrast to owner-occupied housing, the standard view that rental housing is favorably treated by current tax law is substantially weakened by consideration of recent legislation and of high rates of inflation.

The dotted lines in the two panels, like the corresponding lines in figure 3, illustrate the effects of taxing 100 percent rather than 40 percent of inflation-adjusted capital gains (in addition to the other changes already discussed). Again, the figure suggests that this combination of tax provisions would make returns to investment largely independent of the rate of inflation, but would also reduce returns at high rates of inflation substantially below those of cases in which only 40 percent of capital gains are taxed.

Figure 4. Effects of Mid-1970s Tax Law and Alternatives on Rental Housing

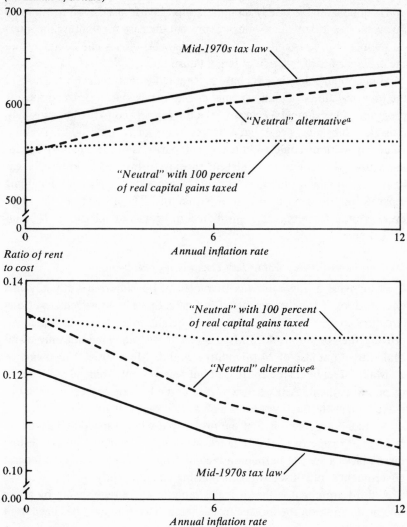

Demand price
(thousands of dollars)

Mid-1970s tax law

"Neutral" alternativeᵃ

"Neutral" with 100 percent
of real capital gains taxed

Annual inflation rate

Ratio of rent
to cost

"Neutral" with 100 percent
of real capital gains taxed

"Neutral" alternativeᵃ

Mid-1970s tax law

Annual inflation rate

a. The long-run effects of a change from the mid-1970s tax law to a "neutral" alternative are as follows:

Annual inflation rate	Renter fraction of all households (percentage points)	Housing services per renter household (percent)
0	−5.9	−4.9
6	−4.1	−3.4
12	−3.0	−2.5

Housing Taxation Issues

To conclude, we briefly summarize frequently used arguments for a favorable tax treatment of housing, present the case for limiting the interest deduction for owner-occupied housing, and offer some comments on the present state of taxation of rental housing.

Many other policy issues could profitably be analyzed with the help of the present-value calculations emphasized in this study. Housing subsidy programs, for example, generally take the form of construction subsidies, mortgage subsidies, accelerated depreciation, or rent subsidies. Present-value calculations could yield useful comparisons of the effects of spending a fixed dollar total on different subsidy forms. It would also be enlightening to analyze the present value of property tax changes, including separate tax rates on land and on structures. These policy issues, however, are too far removed from the central focus of this study to be included here.

Arguments for Favorable Tax Treatment of Housing

Proponents of favorable tax treatment of housing frequently advance one or more of four arguments. The first is that the improvement of one structure confers an external benefit on neighboring structures—that improving the condition of 26 Main Street raises the value not only of 26 Main Street but also of 24 Main Street and 28 Main Street. The owner of 26 Main Street bears the entire cost but receives only some of the benefits of his investment. A tax subsidy, it is argued, is an appropriate way to make benefits to the investor as high as the total benefits to society.

A second argument is that the property tax falls especially heavily on residential properties. The reliance of local governments on real estate taxes places a special burden on income from housing, which the federal government could offset by taxing housing income lightly.

A third argument is that it is desirable to encourage saving by a low rate of taxation on the income from saving. The argument has been used to oppose the double taxation of corporate income more often than to support the exemption of owner-occupant imputed income. However, if it is saving in general rather than saving in some particular form that is desirable, the argument can be applied to housing as well.

Finally, there is the argument that homeownership should be encouraged because it makes better neighborhoods and better citizens. In economic terms, owner-occupants have a strong financial interest in maintaining a desirable neighborhood. The argument, however, is generally cast in broader terms than individual financial interest.

Probably none of these arguments can be either conclusively refuted or firmly established. Our own view is that they have some validity, as do many arguments for the special treatment of other categories of investment. Since none of the four arguments seem to justify tax benefits that rise with the income tax bracket of the beneficiary, that particular feature of the present tax benefits to owner-occupants is especially hard to defend. But the arguments do mean that substantial room for disagreement about the ideal housing taxation policy will remain.

Limiting the Interest Deduction for Owner-Occupied Housing

Even if some tax benefits for housing can be defended, the case for limiting the current very high benefits enjoyed by owner-occupants is a strong one. These benefits have been growing substantially with the increases in inflation and mortgage rates. It is hard to argue that there has been any corresponding growth in the desirability of subsidizing owner-occupied housing. A large fraction of the benefits, furthermore, go to high-income households, not to households that are close to the margin in choosing between becoming homeowners and remaining renters.

Two technical—as opposed to political—problems of limiting the tax benefits for owner-occupied housing are avoiding the highly complex procedures that would be necessary to tax imputed rent directly and avoiding, as far as possible, disappointing the expectations of many recent buyers of homes by sharply reducing their tax benefits. A good solution to both problems would be placing a ceiling on the size of the interest deduction for computing taxable income.[17] The ceiling could be set high enough so that it would affect few taxpayers at the time it was enacted but would have an increasing effect as inflation drove up house prices and hence the average size of mortgages. As table 8 suggests, completely eliminating the interest deduction would not only reduce the tax benefits of owner-occupants but would also make the value of a housing investment insensitive to the expected general rate of inflation. A ceiling on the interest deduction would be a relatively painless way of gradually making these changes.

17. Earlier discussions are contained in the testimony of George Peterson in *Federal Tax Policy and Urban Development*, Hearings, pp. 3–34; and Edward Cohan, "Carter Would Limit Relief for Interest Paid on Mortgages," *New York Times*, September 13, 1977.

Table 8. Disallowing the Deductibility of Interest for Owner-Occupied Housing

Item	Zero inflation	6 percent inflation	12 percent inflation
Assumptions			
Initial cost (dollars)	60,000	60,000	60,000
Ratio of imputed rent to initial cost	0.0900	0.0900	0.0900
Mortgage interest rate (percent)	5.0	11.0	17.0
Case 1: mid-1970s tax law			
Demand price (dollars)	59,692	64,114	66,456
Percent difference from initial cost	−0.5	6.9	10.8
Long-run imputed rent–cost ratio restoring a real after-tax rate of return of 4 percent	0.09057	0.08201	0.07690
Percent difference from 0.0900	0.6	−8.9	−14.6
Case 2: interest deduction disallowed			
Demand price (dollars)	54,145	54,545	54,790
Percent difference from initial cost	−9.8	−9.1	−8.7
Long-run imputed rent–cost ratio restoring a real after-tax rate of return of 4 percent	0.10087	0.10060	0.10057
Percent difference from 0.0900	12.1	11.8	11.7
Effect of long-run change in rent on			
Owner-occupant fraction of all households (percentage points)	−3.2	−3.1	−3.0
Housing services per owner-occupant (percent)	−8.2	−8.8	−7.9

Not surprisingly, there are difficulties in treating mortgage interest for owner-occupied housing differently from interest generally. While homeowners borrowing in the residential mortgage market would, for outlays above the ceiling, pay full interest costs, other homeowners could effectively be paying only an after-tax interest rate. That would be the case, for example, for a homeowner who could pay for his house by selling taxable bonds or by borrowing against business assets rather than by borrowing in the mortgage market. Probably only a small fraction of households would fall in these categories, however.

Even a limited interest deduction would be worth more to a taxpayer in a high bracket than to one in a low bracket. To eliminate the differential subsidy to those in high tax brackets, conversion of the interest deduction to a tax credit is the remedy usually suggested. A tax credit, however, is more complex than a ceiling on deductions. Furthermore, while a ceiling does not eliminate the differential subsidy per dollar of deduction, it does sharply limit the subsidy per taxpayer, since it is high-bracket homeowners who would be most affected by the ceiling. A tax credit without a ceiling could easily be more advantageous to high-bracket homeowners than a deduction with a ceiling.

Future Directions for Rental Housing Taxation

The case for tightening the tax treatment of housing is much weaker for rental housing than it is for owner-occupied housing. Rental housing has benefited less from inflation and has been affected more by recent tax reforms. For these and other reasons, investment in new rental housing has not fared nearly as well as investment in owner-occupied housing in recent years.

If strong interest in moving toward indexation of the tax base develops over the next few years, there may be an opportunity for rationalizing the tax treatment of rental housing. A move toward realistic depreciation allowances could be combined with indexation in the treatment of depreciation and capital gains and phasing out of recapture. The cost to investors of lower depreciation would offset some of the benefits of indexation, so that the combination of changes would prevent indexation from reestablishing a significant tax shelter for rental real estate.

Comments by George Peterson

I shall begin by summarizing what the de Leeuw-Ozanne paper attempts to do, point out what it does not attempt to do, and then raise several specific points about the approach used. I will conclude with some reflections on the policy issues surrounding housing taxation.

The basic proposition of the paper is that a high rate of inflation has made the tax treatment of housing relatively more favorable than the treatment of other investments because of the deductibility of mortgage interest payments and because owner-occupants of housing enjoy virtual exemption from capital gains taxation. The after-tax user cost of capital for owner-occupied housing falls as the rate of inflation increases, at least when the mortgage rate increases no faster than the general inflation rate. For rental housing, the same factors operate but are offset by the fact that the depreciation treatment of housing becomes less generous as inflation rises because of the use of historical costs as a depreciation basis. In fact, de Leeuw and Ozanne argue that the lesser gain from inflation realized by rental housing has been largely offset by the recent legislative changes that have tightened the taxation of rental housing. Investment in plant and equipment benefits less from inflation than all types of housing, in large part because of the lower loan–value ratios that are used to finance it.

Inflation operating through the tax system is expected to divert an increasing share of total investment to the residential sector and particularly to owner-occupied housing. The authors suggest that this finding requires a substantial modification of the standard view of housing taxation. I would prefer to call it reinforcement of the new orthodoxy, for several papers in the last few years have argued that the user cost of owner-occupied housing capital falls with inflation.

De Leeuw and Ozanne did not write a second half of their paper providing an empirical examination of the effects they discuss. The paper does not look empirically at how expectations about housing inflation are formed. Such expectations are crucial to the magnitude of the after-tax gap between housing and other investments.

The only estimates of the investment impact of the tax treatment are drawn from Harvey Rosen's studies.[18] And as the authors point out, Rosen's results refer to a very long-run equilibrium, two decades or more, in which housing supply is totally elastic. For the very short run, de Leeuw and Ozanne do calculate an equilibrium demand price for fixed housing capital under various alternatives, but they do not investigate the adjustment process by which that particular price differential between the market demand price and producer cost is removed. So there is no guidance to the sectoral investment effects of the tax treatments they are discussing.

I am sympathetic with the authors' avoidance of that deeper exploration into difficult empirical work. I think it is worth noting that now that we have had almost a decade's experience with drastically different metropolitan rates of increase in housing price, we may be in a position to estimate the lag structure determining anticipations of future housing price changes and to link these, as well as the equilibrium tenure and investment choices, to metropolitan housing investment decisions.

Several specific approaches in the paper deserve comment. First, the authors rely throughout on present-value calculations rather than on the estimates of the user cost of capital used in other papers in this book. The

18. Especially "Housing Decisions."

methods are essentially equivalent, of course. The after-tax return in equity in a house is simply the discount rate, which equates the present value of after-tax revenues to the equity investment. The use of present value has some practical advantages in handling single events like transactions costs or tax liability from realized capital depreciation; those terms can convert user-cost expressions into extremely cumbersome operational terms.

But the present-value construction keeps the nonlinearities inside the computer program and limits the value of the approach for the illustration of specific cases. It is difficult to grasp how the results shown for the typical cases analyzed in the text would change under alternative assumptions even though they devote a portion of an appendix (not included in this book) to trying to clarify that for us.

The problem is compounded because many of the economic assumptions built into the present-value calculation are held fixed, when preferably they should be treated endogenously as to outcome of the different tax treatments. The authors, however, assume a fixed-structure loan ratio, although it presumably would shift with the tax treatment structures. For example, the depreciation rate, which is assumed to be fixed, would shift with maintenance outlays, which in turn would be affected by shifts in the demand price. This apparently is true even of the tax situation of individuals in some of the simulations. If I understand their simulations correctly, the investor in the 22 percent marginal tax bracket is assumed to remain in that bracket and to bear a 22 percent marginal tax rate even when the mortgage interest deductions are removed. The truth probably is that most people in that situation would stop itemizing and claim the standard deduction, and many would face a new marginal rate. So I am not certain that the present-value approach is an innovation that will prove helpful in analyzing investment responses empirically.

The second point I would like to mention is that most of the focus in the de Leeuw-Ozanne paper is on a higher equilibrium rate of inflation that is fully anticipated. I think most of the recent disruption in the housing market has stemmed from unanticipated inflation.

An actual inflation rate in excess of the rate anticipated when the mortgages were taken out gives rise to ex post excess real returns on housing or extremely low actual cost of capital in the housing sector. For a number of metropolitan markets, people, using actual depreciation rates, have calculated that the cost of capital is negative for recent time periods. Hendershott and Hu recently estimated expected rates of return on the basis of a geometric weighting procedure, using the inflation rates of the last six years, and came up with ex post real rates of return on housing of some 5 to 8.5 percent a year in excess of expected rates. Using that same weighting procedure, they estimated that the anticipated cost of capital was around 5 percent for the housing sector versus more than 15 percent of return on plant and equipment capital investment.[19]

It is extremely important, I think, to understand the adjustment process in the transition from this period of out-of-equilibrium housing markets to one of equilibrium markets. This transition has several specific implications for the adjustment process. In the last few years mortgage rates have risen less rapidly than expected inflation, promoting a boom in housing prices and housing investment. This situation cannot persist indefinitely. If it reverses, if mortgage rates stay up and expected inflation subsides, the price of housing will probably rise less rapidly than the prices of other goods or may actually decline.

Similarly, I think it is crucial to understand how expectations about the future performance of housing prices are formed. Hendershott and Hu simply assume a geometric weighting procedure.[20] Experience with differential rates of housing price increase in different metropolitan markets may now make it possible to determine the lag structure under which housing price expectations are formed.

Let me, then, briefly consider the inefficiencies that might arise from the current inflation-induced "undertaxation" of housing. The most frequently mentioned is the overconsumption of housing. It has paid to invest in rooms, even ones that were not used, because the ex post user cost has been negative. This is one of the major inefficiencies attributable to inflation.

Second, the accumulation of equity in owner-occupied housing may have depressed saving. Some of the tax proposals simulated in the paper would extinguish large amounts of home equity, and such reductions in personal wealth would tend to increase the saving rate. This question, not addressed in the de Leeuw-Ozanne paper, may relate to several of the other papers in this book.

Third, the changes in income tax treatment described in this paper would affect various parts of metropolitan areas quite differently. The tax laws principally increase the value of high-priced housing, stimulate in-

19. Hendershott and Hu, "Inflation and the Benefits of Owner-Occupied Housing," pp. 10, 28.
20. Ibid.

vestment, and stimulate housing price appreciation primarily at the fringe of the outer areas of the metropolitan region. These effects introduce inefficiencies of a different kind. Many planners say that the stimulation of low-density housing is undesirable and causes economic problems. And the loss of value for housing in the central area that is already low cost certainly has some tax base implications for jurisdictions located there.

Finally, I direct your attention to a social experiment that Canada hoped to carry out. Canada does not allow tax deductions for either mortgage interest or property taxes; as a result, the proportion of high-income Canadian households that own their homes is not much higher than the fraction of low-income households that own in the United States. The Conservative Progressive party pledged to allow tax credits for mortgage interest and for property taxes, and in September 1979 announced a plan that would allow a 25 percent tax credit for up to $5,000 of mortgage interest for each household and a flat credit for property tax payments. It was not enacted because the party was voted out of office, in part as a result of this proposal. This legislative change would have eventually produced evidence on how tax laws affect housing consumption and tenure choice. To my knowledge virtually no one attempted to justify the introduction of credits on the grounds that Canada should increase investment in the residential sector. And few supported the government's position that there should be higher rates of owner-occupancy. The proposal was discussed almost entirely as a wealth, or income, redistribution, a form of tax relief aimed specifically at lower- and middle-income households. The second issue was the allegedly desirable creation of windfall gains for current owners. And third, the possible effect of the tax change on unemployment in the construction industry was emphasized.

The lesson of this debate, I suppose, is that most of the tax alternatives being discussed in the housing sector are not going to be evaluated by the public on the basis of how they affect allocative efficiency; instead, issues of income and wealth redistribution will predominate.

Comments by Harvey S. Rosen

It is now well understood that in the United States inflation and taxation interact in a way that changes the relative values of certain assets. The paper by de Leeuw and Ozanne focuses on how the interaction affects the values of owner-occupied housing, rental housing, and business plant and equipment. The heart of the paper consists of a series of numerical examples in which they compute the present values of investments in each of the assets under alternative assumptions on the tax structure and inflation rates.

As the authors note, their procedure is closely related to computations of the "user cost of capital" that appear in the neoclassical investment literature.[21] The main contribution of this paper is its very careful incorporation into the analysis of the relevant tax laws for housing investment. A nice feature of the paper is its concise, clear statement of the relevant tax provisions.

Although the calculations for the various housing modes incorporate more realism than their predecessors, several troublesome assumptions remain. Some, such as the assumption of a fixed ratio of land cost to rental cost, are noted by the authors. A few others come to mind: the authors postulate that the holding period is independent of the economic environment and that the rate of real economic depreciation closely approximates depreciation for tax purposes. Nevertheless, I think the basic conclusion—that during the 1970s the combination of taxation and inflation made rental housing less attractive to investors than owner-occupied housing—is correct.

I am less sanguine about the calculations for plant and equipment. Recent research on the relationship between the financial structure of a firm and the effective cost of investment raises questions that are not dealt with in the calculations by de Leeuw and Ozanne.[22] It would be nice to see a series of computations on how the effective price of an asset varies with taxes, inflation, *and* the underlying theory of firm behavior. But de Leeuw and Ozanne's main focus is on owner-occupied versus rental housing, and as mentioned above, refinement of these calculations probably would not change their substantive conclusions much.

Enlightening though their computations are, however, they do not provide a complete picture of the impact of taxes on recent experience in the housing market. I will devote a little time to exploring some other issues.

21. Dale W. Jorgenson, "Econometric Studies of Investment Behavior: A Survey," *Journal of Economic Literature,* vol. 9 (December 1971), pp. 1111–47.

22. See, for example, Joseph E. Stiglitz, "Taxation, Corporate Financial Policy, and the Cost of Capital," *Journal of Public Economics,* vol. 2 (February 1973), pp. 1–34; and R. W. Boadway and N. Bruce, "Depreciation and Interest Deductions and the Effect of the Corporation Income Tax on Investments," *Journal of Public Economics,* vol. 11 (February 1979), pp. 93–105.

Table 9. Some Data on Housing in the Mid-1970s

Year	Median value of owner-occupied housing units (dollars) (1)	New home mortgage yields (percent) (2)	Owner occupancy rate (3)
1973	24,100	7.95	0.645
1974	27,200	8.92	0.646
1975	29,500	9.01	0.646
1976	32,300	8.99	0.647 ·
1977	36,900	9.01	0.648

Sources: Column 1, U.S. Department of Commerce, *Annual Housing Survey: Current Housing Reports*, Series H-150 (Government Printing Office, 1975–79). Column 2, *Economic Report of the President, 1979*, p. 258. Column 3, Dwight M. Jaffee and Kenneth T. Rosen, "Mortgage Credit Availability and Residential Construction Activity," paper presented at Brookings Conference on Taxation, October 1979, p. 19.

To lend some concreteness to the discussion, consider the figures in table 9. The first column shows the path of owner-occupied housing values from 1973 to 1977. The nominal increases are enormous, presumably reflecting at least in part the kinds of effects discussed in the third section of de Leeuw and Ozanne's paper. Moreover, the capital gains rates tend to exceed the mortgage rates in column 2. As a very rough approximation, one could say that owner-occupiers were consuming "free housing" over this period. Yet column 3 indicates that there was hardly a rush into owner-occupied housing; the proportion of households that were owner-occupiers stayed just under 0.65.

It is not hard to come up with explanations for this phenomenon. I begin by considering a few possibilities not directly related to taxes and inflation. An obvious candidate for explaining column 3 is transactions costs. Renters may want to become owner-occupants but find it too costly to do so immediately. This consideration suggests it might be useful to incorporate into the present-value calculations a less narrow view of transactions costs that takes into account the various psychological and pecuniary costs of moving.

Another possible explanation of the table is that it reflects a slow short-run response on the supply side of the market. De Leeuw and Ozanne, of course, take great care to distinguish between short- and long-run effects, but one wonders whether inflation was generating shifts in supply as well as demand.

Given the investment framework chosen by de Leeuw and Ozanne, the main problem is failure to consider the effects of taxes and inflation on the perceived risks of housing investment. Ex ante, individuals do not know how much prices will rise.[23] The theory of optimal portfolio selection indicates that investment choices depend on both expected returns *and* risk. Loosely, we can think of de Leeuw and Ozanne as having told us about the former but not much about the latter. In terms of table 9, it may be that the reason households did not move to take advantage of "free" housing was that they failed to predict the price increases or viewed them as uncertain. It would be interesting to see both theoretical and empirical work on how inflation and taxes affect the riskiness of the return to home-ownership.

It should be clear that most of these comments concern not the quality of the de Leeuw-Ozanne computations but how they are used to assess the behavioral impacts of taxes and inflation. Essentially, the present-value results are substituted into behavioral equations that are driven mainly by the relative prices of renting and owning. While such equations are useful and informative, I think that the next stage of research should be the development of more sophisticated equations.

Finally, to deal with the normative issues raised in the paper's last section, it may be useful to restate some of the discussion, taking advantage of the conceptual framework provided by the literature on optimal taxation. The efficient tax treatment of housing is not necessarily a "neutral" one; to minimize excess burden one must take into account other distortions in the economy, including externalities and taxes on other commodities and assets. My inclination is to agree with Aaron that the "neighborhood" and "good citizenship" effects are not very persuasive reasons for subsidizing owner-occupied housing.[24] Nevertheless, a subsidy may still be efficient if certain conditions on the elasticities of other taxed goods are satisfied.[25] In this connection, note that it is possible to rationalize on efficiency grounds a subsidy that depends on the household's marginal tax rate. If the elasticity of demand for housing varies systematically with income, there may be a case for differential taxation.

---

23. Feldstein and Summers have suggested that over time there has been an increased sensitivity of individuals' optimal inflation forecasts to recent inflationary experience. It would be interesting to see if the same was true of housing prices. Martin S. Feldstein and Lawrence Summers, "Inflation, Tax Rules, and the Long-Term Interest Rate," National Bureau of Economic Research Working Paper 232 (NBER, February 1978).

24. Aaron, *Shelter and Subsidies*.

25. W. J. Corlett and D. C. Hague, "Complementarity and the Excess Burden of Taxation," *Review of Economic Studies*, vol. 21 (January 1953), pp. 21–30.

GEORGE M. VON FURSTENBERG

Saving

IN THIS STUDY I attempt to explain how government, personal, and corporate saving rates—the three saving rates that combine to yield the national saving rate—are determined in the United States.[1] The novel features of the analysis are the introduction of a "fiscal surprise" variable in the explanation of the personal saving rate and the identification of the degrees of interdependence between the three sectoral saving rates.

Past research on saving has often emphasized that saving out of different components of income may vary. This happens not just because these components are not necessarily of equal permanence but also because they go to income and age classes whose saving rates differ from those of other groups. While preserving some of the distinction between transitory and permanent components of income through the use of cyclical variables, I do not focus on saving from different components of disposable income. Instead I recognize that even components of the net national product that are not part of disposable income—that is, retained earnings and taxes—may have a pronounced effect on personal saving. Because retained earnings constitute corporate saving and because taxes minus government expenditures define government saving,

The author thanks Clifford R. Wymer for his econometric advice and the use of his maximum-likelihood estimation programs, and Fernando A. Santos and Kellett W. Hannah for valuable research assistance. Comments by the editors, Robert W. Kilpatrick, Willem Buiter, and the official discussants also helped improve portions of this paper, although not all suggestions were followed. The author bears sole responsibility for the views expressed.

1. As defined in the national income and product accounts, investment by government is not part of government saving; nor is investment in consumer durables part of personal saving, although it strongly influences such saving.

all the components of national saving are interdependent. This implies that the ultimate effect on national saving of raising one of its components may differ significantly from the direct effect. In this chapter I will explore the extent to which the government can raise national saving either by increasing its own saving or by influencing corporate retentions taking the offsets involved into account.

After presenting the major findings and basic specifications, I discuss the characteristics and stability of the fiscal policy rule implicit in the behavior of the government saving rate. I then develop and implement the estimation plan for private saving rates. This is followed by a section enumerating the explanatory variables that failed in the analysis. The paper concludes with some comments on the fiscal policy implications of the study.[2]

Before proceeding with the analysis, it is useful to summarize the major conclusions of the study.

1. Empirical analysis of aggregate U.S. time series has not, and in my opinion cannot, provide conclusive evidence regarding the effect of saving incentives on the personal saving rate. The reason is that the relevant explanatory variable, the expected after-tax real rate of return on household net worth, cannot be measured precisely. Whether one finds a positive or negative effect depends on the choice of measure. As a result, the sum total of the time series evidence is no more conclusive in this area than the theory.

2. The direction of the effect of an equal rise in taxes and transfer payments on the personal saving rate is clear in theory. Increased public provision for old age, ill health, unemployment, and other contingencies should reduce households' necessity to provide similar protection through private saving. Those who are taxed might therefore consume no less and current transfer recipients might consume more than they would without these government programs. However, the personal saving rate has shown no tendency to decline from cycle to cycle. If theory is correct, there must be some hitherto unidentified factors that would have caused the personal saving rate to rise had it not been for the simultaneous increase in taxes and transfers.

---

2. The first appendix contains the notations and definitions of all variables used in the regressions. The second outlines the methods used to estimate the amount of, and real after-tax rates of return on, household net worth and the amount of social insurance net worth, which are among the variables that failed to perform as expected.

3. Simultaneous increases in tax and transfer rates have become so much a part of the fiscal pattern that any temporary acceleration of one relative to the other has little effect on the national saving rate. If there is an unusually large increase in transfer payments, household saving increases in the expectation that taxes will soon catch up. Households will also save most of a tax cut that is out of line with the government's normal policies. Such discretionary policy changes have little effect on aggregate demand. In other words, fiscal surprises generated through taxes or transfers do not seem to work.

4. A change in the rate of government purchases of goods and services alone has a powerful effect on national saving. Without including any cyclical repercussions, the national saving rate moves by about 90 percent of such a change. The effect of a surprise tax change would be only one-tenth. When the multiplier effects are included, the ultimate change in aggregate demand may be about twice as large in each instance. Thus if there is no slack in the economy, increased government purchases reduce national saving; if there is slack, increased purchases raise output. However, since it is difficult to vary government purchases countercyclically, this policy instrument usually cannot be mobilized in a timely fashion.

5. Since government purchases cannot be varied quickly enough and variations in tax and transfer rates do not have much effect on aggregate demand, it may be possible to alter the national saving rate by substituting one tax for another without changing the ratio of taxes to net national product. Unfortunately, the effect of such substitutions on the supply of saving is uncertain. Reduced taxation of the incomes from capital in the corporate sector, balanced by increased taxation of labor incomes, may, however, stimulate business fixed investment, as the chapter by Hendershott and Hu in this book suggests. Because the response of all components of national saving—government, corporate, and personal—to cyclical changes is large, increased investment demand will not be limited by an "inadequate" supply of saving in periods of recovery. Furthermore, business fixed investment represents only one of several competing uses of national saving; residential investment and net foreign investment are among the others.

6. An increase in inflation-induced inventory profits reduces the corporate saving rate because it is usually associated with higher taxes and dividends. However, some of this damage is undone because households save more when corporations save less. This offset means that a change in

330 *George M. von Furstenberg*

the tax accounting rules or in the tax treatment of dividends changes the net private saving rate only about one-third as much as the corporate saving rate. Again, however, total national output, and hence national saving and domestic investment, are likely to grow if investment incentives are increased during periods of slack. In this as in other cases, concern about the adequacy of private saving should not impede changes in the tax structure for efficiency reasons, provided the reforms are appropriately timed during the business cycle.

Basic Features of the Estimation System

Since national saving and investment are related to one another, it is hazardous to take the supply side of the economy as given. The size and composition of government spending, taxes, subsidies, and regulations, as well as decisions about the rate of growth of the money supply, have income, substitution, wealth, and expectation effects. All these may modify both actual and potential output and hence the ability and willingness of individuals and businesses to save. Any shift in saving rates, in turn, can influence actual output in the short run and potential output in the long run. It is thus risky to estimate saving rates without embedding the behavioral variables in a model of total output and income determination. While I do not have such a model, I allow for the possibility that the three components of the national saving rate may be correlated negatively except for the common influence of the business cycle.

There is considerable risk of simultaneity bias in equations that are estimated for the individual components of national saving. The bias is greatest when output changes are induced by changes in personal or government outlays and least when they arise from disturbances in domestic or foreign investment. In the former case, saving rates are part of the cyclical disturbance; in the latter, they respond to cyclical forces originating elsewhere. Deviations in saving rates that correlate positively with deviations in investment rates may also prevent cyclical biases in saving equations.[3] An autonomous decline in the purchases of consumers accompanied by a rise in net exports or an increase in the rate of inventory change may be one example of such an offset in the short run. An unexplained fall in government saving that crowds out domestic fixed invest-

---

3. Negative, or cyclically reinforcing, correlations of the error terms are equally possible. A sudden decline in confidence throughout the economy may raise the personal saving rate and lower the domestic fixed investment rate more or less simultaneously.

ment would be another. The severity of the simultaneity bias thus depends on one's view of the appropriate model of the economy: the bias is greatest in Keynesian and least in classical formulations.

Bias is reduced in this paper by expressing the key variables as fractions of the net national product. While tax and nontax receipts show a strong cyclical pattern superimposed on a rising trend, the corresponding tax rate shows no significant cyclical variation. However, the transfer payments rate displays marked countercyclical variations and the rate of spending on consumer durable goods shows marked procyclical variations. An unexpected rise in transfers or cut in taxes has little effect on the potential output gap, because the reduction in government saving is offset by an increase in personal saving. As a consequence, the coefficients estimated on the transfer rate and the tax rate may be greater than the coefficients that would be produced by the cyclical factors and the passage of time that govern the expected level of these rates. Similarly, a reduction in spending on consumer durables, such as a sudden slump in car sales, raises both the personal saving rate and the potential output gap in the same quarter.[4] The coefficient estimated on the spending rate for consumer durables may thus account for more than the normal degree of substitution of personal saving for investment in consumer durables that occurs during a representative business cycle.[5]

Dealing in rates rather than levels by dividing the key variables by the net national product also serves a noneconometric purpose. It is natural that the government saving rate should be calculated as a ratio to the net national product because taxes are levied on almost all the income and

4. The correlation between the rate of spending on consumer durable goods and the potential output gap is -0.55, and it is -0.60 between the rate of consumer durable goods spending and the change in the gap from two quarters earlier. The exact definitions of the variables involved, $CDUR$ and GAP, are given in appendix A.

5. It is conceivable that the coefficients on the potential output gap, transfer rate, tax rate, and consumer durable spending rate will be biased away from 0 and toward ± 1 through failure to provide for endogenous determination. However, endogenizing these variables in a complete system suggests that this bias does not raise the estimated coefficients as consistently as expected. See George M. von Furstenberg, "Domestic Determinants of U.S. Net Foreign Investment," International Monetary Fund, *Staff Papers,* vol. 27 (December 1980). When a similar specification for the personal saving rate (augmented by money supply and demographic factors) was used, the absolute value of the coefficients on the potential output gap, the transfer rate, and the tax rate declined, while that on the rate of consumer durable spending rose. The implication that a rise in taxes net of transfers lowers the personal saving rate remained but was far less dramatic than in this paper. However, the result that a fiscal surprise tax cut raises personal saving by about 90 percent of the amount involved was confirmed.

product flows contained in it. However, it is less obvious that corporate or personal saving should also be related to such a broad aggregate rather than to sector incomes, such as corporate profits or disposable personal income. Since pay-out ratios from reported after-tax corporate profits change little from cycle to cycle and dividends are sticky, variations in the corporate saving rate reflect inflation adjustments to reported profits and cyclical changes in the adjusted corporate profit share in the net national product. Cyclical improvements in profits are due to the declining average total costs of many firms as they move up to the preferred level of capacity utilization. Like the inflation-accounting factors, recent changes in the tax rate on unadjusted corporate profits influence the adjusted after-tax profits and hence adjusted retentions. Most fiscal surprises originate outside the corporate sector, and it is hard to see how any such surprise can affect after-tax profits, which result from past investment decisions and recent tax changes, through channels other than the corporation tax rate and possibly the potential output gap. Because the feed-through of the various factors to adjusted retentions seems sufficiently apparent, it is unnecessary to model the corporate profit share and the pay-out decision explicitly. Instead, reliance will be placed on estimating a partially reduced form.

The reasons for estimating personal saving as a fraction of net national product are more fundamental. All components of net national product, rather than only the components and transfer payments that appear in disposable personal income, may influence personal saving decisions. It is, of course, the expected permanent level of resource availability, not just the current level, that enters personal saving decisions. Still, even after cyclical influences have been accounted for by use of the potential output gap, personal saving may not be a stable function of disposable income; it may depend also on corporate saving and on all types of taxes used to finance government outlays. In particular, a rise in the aggregate tax rate that is matched by a decline in the ratio of adjusted retained earnings to net national product may affect the personal saving rate even if disposable income does not change. According to Martin Feldstein and others, retained earnings are perceived as an addition to household net worth. Lowering them thus produces an equivalent increase in personal saving.[6] Paul David

6. See Martin S. Feldstein, "Corporate Taxation and Dividend Behavior," *Review of Economic Studies,* vol. 37 (January 1970), pp. 57–72; and Martin S. Feldstein and George Fane, "Taxes, Corporate Dividend Policy and Personal Savings: The British Postwar Experience," *Review of Economics and Statistics,* vol. 55 (November 1973), pp. 399–411.

and John Scadding have argued that increased taxes may be associated with increased government consumption, which is regarded by taxpayers as being equivalent to personal consumption; this would suggest that the government saving rate and the private saving rate are independent.[7] If these presumptions about consumer behavior are correct, changing either the tax rate or the corporate saving rate would have no effect on the private saving rate at a given level of disposable income. Also worth investigating is whether a simultaneous rise in taxes and transfers leaves the personal saving rate unchanged when it is assumed that disposable income is not the income concept on which saving decisions are based.

The specification of fiscal variables requires further refinement, since consumers may be assumed to react differently to unsystematic and systematic changes in taxes and transfers. The rate of government saving and dissaving is found to vary so regularly over the business cycle that fiscal behavior is largely predictable.[8]

Deviations of the government saving rate from the rate implied by past practice are treated as unsystematic variations or fiscal surprises. Households anticipate that such deviations will prove temporary and take the expected shifts in fiscal policy into account in their saving decisions.[9]

7. Paul A. David and John L. Scadding, "Private Savings: Ultrarationality, Aggregation, and 'Denison's Law,'" *Journal of Political Economy,* vol. 82 (March–April 1974), pp. 225–49.

8. Some comments on how anticipated fiscal policy responses can affect private sector planning are contained in Martin Neil Baily, "Stabilization Policy and Private Economic Behavior," *Brookings Papers on Economic Activity,* 1:1978, pp. 11–59, especially pp. 39–41. (Hereafter *BPEA.*) Since Baily is concerned with the systematic response of fiscal policy to aggregate demand shocks, unanticipated fiscal policy could be defined by the failure of fiscal variables to respond as expected to economic events.

9. Defining unanticipated changes in fiscal policy without taking account of the government's stabilization activities would not be in keeping with the premises of this paper. For an example of such disregard, see Steven M. Sheffrin, "Unanticipated Money Growth and Output Fluctuations," *Economic Inquiry,* vol. 17 (January 1979), pp. 1–13, especially p. 5. Barro uses percentage deviations of federal government expenditures from trend to construct temporary movements that he attempts to link to estimated money growth. See Robert J. Barro, "Unanticipated Money Growth and Unemployment in the United States," *American Economic Review,* vol. 67 (March 1977), pp. 103–05; and Barro, "Unanticipated Money, Output, and the Price Level in the United States," *Journal of Political Economy,* vol. 86 (August 1978), p. 551. In both articles Barro must implicitly be assuming the absence of any surprise in government expenditure determination. Otherwise he could not have used the current percentage deviation of such expenditures from trend to estimate the expected current rate of growth of the money supply, which he equates with the regression prediction of that rate.

Fiscal surprise is thus entered as one of the explanatory variables in the equation for the personal saving rate.[10]

Major Findings

As shown in table 1, net personal saving was, on the average, twice as large as net corporate saving in the period 1955–78. The standard deviation of the latter is larger than that of the former, but not as large as the standard deviation of government saving. Ex post, government dissaving absorbed an average of 8.5 percent of net private saving and raised the standard deviation of net national saving above that of net private saving.[11]

On the basis of the size of the $\bar{R}^2$, the percentage of the variations that can be explained is highest for corporate saving and lowest for government saving. The unexplained variation in net national saving is thus twice the unexplained variation in net private saving, or 11.2 percent versus 5.6 percent. With a 1979 net national product of $2.1 trillion, the root-mean-square error in the net national saving rate of 0.0059 suggests that errors in net national saving of plus or minus $12 billion or more could occur in one out of three cases, while errors of this size would be expected in only one out of twenty cases in net private saving.

10. Personal saving is taken to include the statistical discrepancy. Raymond Goldsmith has advised the author that, since flow-of-funds saving of households and unincorporated businesses exceeds personal saving and incomes earned in illegal activities are not counted, both disposable personal income and personal saving are frequently underestimated in the national income and product accounts. Thus the addition of the statistical discrepancy to personal saving seems warranted, even though that discrepancy has not always been positive.

11. An attempt to estimate the entire system of personal, corporate, and government saving rates and the overidentifying restrictions implied by the structural model and by the (in this case, trivial or noninteractive) identity requirement that the components of saving sum to the national saving rate yielded a strong indication of inconsistency in the full-information maximum-likelihood estimation. The chi-square value of the log-likelihood ratio was so high, 1266 with 58 degrees of freedom (yielding a normal deviate of 39.6), that the hypothesis that the overidentifying restrictions are consistent with the sample had to be rejected. For comparison, the chi-square value of 44.5 with 24 degrees of freedom for the system composed of the personal and corporate saving rates alone exceeded the critical value of 36.4 at the 5 percent level in the upper tail by far less. Although the hypothesis of consistency should, strictly speaking, still be rejected at the 5 percent (though not at the 0.5 percent) level, this chi-square test is known to be passed very rarely in practical applications and is regarded as too severe in cases involving fewer than several hundred observations.

Table 1. Summary Statistics of Net National Saving and Its Components, 1955:2-1978:4

Saving	Mean	Standard deviation	Root-mean-square error	$\bar{R}^2$
Net private saving	0.07401	0.01243	0.00294	0.944
Personal saving[a]	0.04986	0.00926	0.00248	0.928
Corporate saving[b]	0.02415	0.01076	0.00178	0.972
Government saving	−0.00627	0.01481	0.00505	0.884
Net national saving	0.06774	0.01767	0.00592	0.888

Source: Column 1 of table 5 and columns 6 and 7 of table 7.
a. Includes the statistical discrepancy.
b. Includes corporate retained earnings from the rest of the world.

The effects of changes in economic conditions on private and national saving are summarized in table 2. Over 50 percent of any increase in the gap between potential and actual output is absorbed by a fall in national saving either simultaneously or with a short lag. Since net national saving is only 6.8 percent of net national product on the average, the marginal cyclical national propensity to save greatly exceeds the average propensity. A decline in net national saving must be matched by an equal ex post decline in the sum of net domestic investment and net foreign investment by the United States. However, these two items will not decline as much as saving *on account of* the recession, since an autonomous reduction of investment may precipitate the cyclical decline in the first place. Furthermore, foreign and domestic investment may move in opposite directions.

In the longer run, the growth in the rate of spending on consumer durables would return to its trend value of close to zero (0.0033 in footnote d of table 2), and this would reduce personal saving as the positive effect of a temporary decline in consumer durable spending from past averages was eliminated. More pertinent, however, is that a permanent increase in the potential output gap would lead both to a reappraisal of the norm that underlies countercyclical fiscal policy and to a gradual revision of permanent income and employment expectations in the private sector. In the very long run, after all stock and expectation adjustments had been completed, net national saving should be unaffected, provided that only the level of the net national product, but not its long-run growth rate or the capital intensity of production, was lowered permanently. The results in table 2 should therefore be interpreted strictly in the short-run, cyclical context.

Another partial experiment is to hold the gap (and all other determi-

Table 2. Effect of an Increase of One Percentage Point in the Potential Output Gap on the Net National Saving Rate

Percent of the net national product

Source of effect	Personal saving[a]	Corporate saving[b]	Government saving	Net national saving
Direct effect	−0.466	−0.274	−0.367	−1.107
Cross-effect from decline in corporate saving	0.185	...	...	0.185
Cross-effect from decline in government saving[c]	0.294	...	...	0.294
Indirect effect from decline in consumer durable spending rate[d]	0.105	...	...	0.105
Simultaneous effect	0.118	−0.274	−0.367	−0.523
Lagged effect from induced rise in unemployment[e]	...	...	−0.141	−0.141
Cross-effect of induced rise in unemployment	0.113	...	...	0.113
Total effect after one year	0.231	−0.274	−0.508	−0.551

Source: Calculations based on column 1 of table 5 and columns 6 and 7 of table 7.

a. Includes the statistical discrepancy.

b. Includes corporate retained earnings from the rest of the world.

c. Since the coefficients on taxes (−0.783) and transfers (0.807) are almost identical, it makes little difference whether the decline in government saving takes the form of lower taxes, increased transfer payments, or a combination of both. Since estimated side relations showed that the cyclical response of transfers is two to three times as pronounced as that of taxes (the response of the latter is insignificant), I used a coefficient of 0.8 on the former.

d. Since the coefficient of the consumer durable spending rate ($CDUR$) in column 6 of table 7 is −1.000, the effect was obtained from the side relation:

$$CDUR = 0.0033 - 0.1047\ GAP + 0.7674u_{-1},$$
$$(2.67)\quad (-4.07)\qquad\quad (11.60)$$
$$R^2 = 0.692;\ \text{Durbin-Watson} = 2.12$$

where GAP is the potential output and u_{-1} is the lagged error term.

e. The rise in the unemployment rate is assumed to be one-third of the preceding increase in the percentage output gap.

nants of government saving) constant and increase corporate profits tax liabilities (table 3). The effects of such a fiscal surprise are initially very weak, as the increase in government saving and the reduction in corporate saving are largely offset in the personal sector. As the effect of the tax rise on corporate retentions wears off, an increase in saving amounting to 10 percent of the tax increase emerges after two years. The same result would be obtained from a surprise increase in any other tax.[12]

12. The errors that are explained by ρ (the coefficient of u_{-1}) in the first equation of table 5 constitute part of the fiscal surprise as measured. Since ρ is 0.81 in that table, fiscal surprises, once generated, are expected to diminish only gradually in succeeding quarters. Not all transitory elements of fiscal posture included in "fiscal surprise" are therefore altogether surprising.

Table 3. Effect of an Increase of Ten Percentage Points in the Corporate Profits Tax Rate on the Net National Saving Rate[a]

Percent of the net national product

Source of effect	Personal saving[a]	Corporate saving[b]	Government saving	Net national saving
Direct effect	...	−0.830	1.000	0.170
Cross-effect from decline in corporate saving	0.560	...	...	0.560
Cross-effect from tax increase	−0.783	...	...	−0.783
Cross-effect from fiscal surprise[c]	−0.113	...	...	−0.113
First-year effect	−0.336	−0.830	1.000	−0.166
Effect on corporate saving in second year	...	0.466	...	0.466
Cross-effect of change in corporate saving	−0.314	...	...	−0.314
Cumulative second-year effect	−0.650	−0.364	1.000	−0.014
Elimination of remaining effect on corporate saving	...	0.364	...	0.364
Cross-effect of change in corporate saving	−0.246	...	...	−0.246
Total effect after two years	−0.896	0.000	1.000	0.104

Source: Calculations based on column 1 of table 5 and columns 6 and 7 of table 7.
a. Includes the statistical discrepancy.
b. Includes corporate retained earnings from the rest of the world.
c. A fiscal surprise amounting to an increase of 0.01 in the ratio of total taxes to net national product produced by the rise in the corporate profits tax rate.

These results imply that a tax cut of unusually large proportions during a cyclical decline would have less inflationary implications but also smaller effects on real economic activity than is commonly claimed. The high degree of offset between personal saving and government saving expected under such conditions indicates that Edward Denison's advice that "policymakers should be cautious in appraising their ability to influence private saving behavior" and the David-Scadding suggestion that taxes may not affect private saving should both be viewed with skepticism.[13] Under certain conditions, the national saving rate will prove sticky because the private saving rate is flexible.

Nor do these results support the view that the private sector reduces its

13. Edward F. Denison, "The Contribution of Capital to the Postwar Growth of Industrial Countries," in *U.S. Economic Growth from 1976 to 1986: Prospects, Problems, and Patterns*, vol. 3: *Capital*, Committee Print, Joint Economic Committee, 94 Cong. 2 sess. (Government Printing Office, 1976), p. 59; and David and Scadding, "Private Savings."

planned outlays when government purchases rise without regard to how the increased purchases are financed.[14] An increase in the deficit at a given level of the potential output gap generated by a surprise increase in government purchases raises personal saving by 11 percent of the amount involved, while a balanced-budget expansion involving no surprises lowers personal saving by 78 percent of that amount. Hence private outlays are cut by 11 percent of the increase in government purchases in the first case and by 22 percent in the second. Government debt and taxes do not have the same effects on aggregate demand, though the difference in effects per dollar of change in government purchases (0.89 when debt financed versus 0.78 when tax financed) is small.[15]

Historically, fiscal changes have had little effect on the private saving rate because the ratios of both transfer payments and taxes to the net national product did not rise in the sample period. However, a number of fiscal changes could have a significant effect. For instance, a reduction in transfer payments and an equal increase in government purchases would lower private saving by about 80 percent of the amounts reallocated. And as already noted, an equal increase in taxes and government purchases would have almost the same effect in reducing saving. Since neither of these policies would change government saving, national saving would fall by as much as private saving in these two instances. These policy measures reduce saving and are thus highly effective in stimulating aggregate demand.

I was not able to quantify the effects on personal saving of either the after-tax real rate of return on net worth or the ratio of private net worth to disposable income, even though at least the last of these variables

14. That view may be attributed to Robert Barro, among others. See especially Robert J. Barro, "Are Government Bonds Net Wealth?" *Journal of Political Economy*, vol. 82 (November–December 1974), pp. 1095–1117, and "Reply to Feldstein and Buchanan," ibid., vol. 84 (April 1976), pp. 343–49, for a discussion of the conditions under which the adjustment of private transfers would fully offset the governmentally imposed transfers implied by social security or public debt issue. For a detailed reconsideration of the issue, see J. Ernest Tanner, "Fiscal Policy and Consumer Behavior," *Review of Economics and Statistics*, vol. 61 (May 1979), pp. 317–21.

15. For a comprehensive examination and critique of the recent literature on the "Ricardian" equivalence of government debt and taxes, see Willem H. Buiter and James Tobin, "Debt Neutrality: A Brief Review of Doctrine and Evidence," in George M. von Furstenberg, ed., *Social Security Versus Private Saving* (Ballinger, 1979), pp. 7–67; and James Tobin and Willem H. Buiter, "Fiscal and Monetary Policies, Capital Formation, and Economic Activity," in George M. von Furstenberg, ed., *The Government and Capital Formation* (Ballinger, 1980), pp. 73–151.

Table 4. Effect of an Unexpected Increase of One Percentage Point in the Inflation Rate on the Net National Saving Rate

Percent of the net national product

Source of effect	Personal saving[a]	Corporate saving[b]	Government saving	Net national saving
Direct effect	...	...	0.087	0.087
Indirect effect of inventory profits on corporate saving[c]	...	−0.129	...	−0.129
Cross-effect of increase in government saving	−0.070	...	...	−0.070
Cross-effect of decline in corporate saving[d]	0.087	...	...	0.087
Total effect	0.017	−0.129	0.087	−0.025

Source: Calculations based on column 1 of table 5 and columns 6 and 7 of table 7.

a. Includes the statistical discrepancy.

b. Includes corporate retained earnings from the rest of the world.

c. The side relation below yielded a 0.19 decline in the ratio of the inventory valuation adjustment to net national product ($IVAC$) per 0.01 rate of increase in the quarterly GNP deflator (DI) over the same period:

$$IVAC = -0.0042 - 0.1903\ DI + 0.8345 u_{-1}.$$
$$(-1.86)\quad (-1.98)\qquad (14.07)$$

$$\bar{R}^2 = 0.755;\ \text{Durbin-Watson} = 1.71$$

Multiplying −0.19 by 0.677, the coefficient on $IVAC$ in the last column of table 7, yielded this indirect effect.

d. The direct effect was again multiplied by −0.8 to obtain the indirect effect of a cut in transfers or a rise in taxes, as explained in footnote c, table 2.

should affect saving.[16] Furthermore, there were indications that inflation has a small transitory positive effect on personal saving, which I discounted.

However, inflation entered the regression estimates through two other channels. Unexpected increases in the rate of inflation lead to a small but predictable increase in government saving. On the other hand, an increase in the inflation rate produces a rise in inventory profits, which reduces corporate saving. Again, however, both of these changes tend to be offset to a large degree in the personal sector, so that there is little net effect on the national saving rate (table 4).

16. The variables are constructed painstakingly in appendix B. Regarding the former, Feldstein has established "the theoretical indeterminacy of the effect on private saving of switching to a consumption tax or reducing the tax on capital income by any other compensated tax changes." Bradford considers major tax alternatives and their contribution to efficiency also within a tax substitution framework and offers specific recommendations for change. See Martin Feldstein, "The Rate of Return, Taxation, and Personal Savings," *Economic Journal*, vol. 88 (September 1978), pp. 482–87, especially p. 486; and David F. Bradford, "The Economics of Tax Policy Toward Savings," in von Furstenberg, ed., *The Government and Capital Formation*, pp. 11–71.

Government Saving

In the United States fiscal policy has been used in a repetitive manner
during each of the business cycles since the end of the Korean War. As a
result, the size of the deficit (relative to the net national product) under
different economic conditions can be predicted by consumers and businessmen with a fair degree of certainty. To the extent that discretionary
actions correspond to expectations, they become essentially endogenous.
Conversely, unusual actions are regarded as aberrations that will be maintained for only a few quarters before they are undone.

The fiscal policy rule was derived by calculating the normal state of
fiscal affairs that has prevailed since the beginning of 1955. Fiscal policy
is represented by the ratio of the government surplus or deficit (as defined
in the national income and product accounts) for all levels of government
combined to the net national product. The basic variables that are assumed to determine the government saving rate are the relative potential
output gap and the change in the unemployment rate lagged by half a
year. The coefficient on the gap is intended to capture not just the effects
of the automatic stabilizers but also the normal discretionary responses to
cyclical developments, whether they are officially billed as temporary or
permanent. The lagged change in the unemployment rate is a transitional
element that was added because experience has shown that it takes time
for major discretionary fiscal actions to be implemented. Since the unemployment rate lags behind the gap, the implication is that the government
saving rate is higher in the first year or more after the start of a cyclical
downswing than the level that would correspond to a given gap ratio and
then subsequently declines below that level.

Two additional variables that are not associated with normal cyclical
changes in the government saving rate were included in the analysis. The
first is the difference between the actual and the officially expected inflation rate. If the actual inflation rate exceeds the expected rate, a higher
surplus is achieved promptly because of the operation of the automatic
stabilizers. However, since the politically acceptable inflation rate
changes, there is no reason to suppose that the normal government saving
rate is raised permanently by higher rates of inflation.[17]

17. The inflation rate is the annualized rate of change in the GNP deflator from
the preceding quarter. The expected inflation rate can be inferred from the annual
data reported in the *Economic Report of the President* only since 1963. It is held at
its starting level of a little less than 1 percent (0.007) in all earlier quarters and dis-

The second additional variable is a fiscal abnormality, that is, an unusual expenditure increase or tax cut. Two such events occurred during the sample period. The first was the underbudgeting of expenditure increases during the Vietnam War; the second was the extraordinary response to the 1974–75 recession that took the form of a large one-time income tax rebate in the second quarter of 1975.[18] These extraordinary measures are treated as nonrandom events that suspend the fiscal policy rule and not as random errors that occur in the observance of the rule.

After distributing the results quarterly to form a continuous pattern,[19] the annualized estimates of abnormal expenditures or tax cuts were divided by the net national product to conform to the dimension of the dependent variable. The resulting variable was given the sign of the effect of the fiscal abnormality on the surplus, so that abnormal expenditure increases and tax rebates were both entered as negative numbers. The coefficient on the fiscal abnormality variable is expected to be unity, on the assumption that these nonrandom disturbances are not compensated for in other parts of the budget. This expectation was subsequently confirmed.

---

tributed quarterly in later years to smooth the series. Rounded to the nearest one-quarter of a percent, the annual expected inflation rates inferred for the years 1963 through 1978 were 0.75, 1.5, 2.25, 1.75, 2.5, 3.0, 3.25, 4.5, 3.0, 3.25, 3.0, 7.0, 10.0 (without energy programs), 6.0, 5.5, and 6.0 percent. The idea of using the forecasts in the *Economic Report* comes from William Fellner, *Toward a Reconstruction of Macroeconomics* (American Enterprise Institute for Public Policy Research, 1976), pp. 118–24.

18. The size of the rebates in the second quarter of 1975 is easily quantified. It is the sum of the one-time rebate of 1974 taxes ($8 billion) and of the one-time payment of $50 to each recipient of social security benefits ($1.7 billion), which together amounted to almost $39 billion at an annual rate. The war-induced military expenditure overruns were obtained by taking the difference between the first budget estimates and actual expenditures for fiscal years 1966–68. On the advice of Robert W. Kilpatrick and Thomas Cuny of the Office of Management and Budget, I used budgetary subfunction 051, excluding the deductions for offsetting receipts, for the actual Department of Defense military budget outlays in "Federal Government Finances" (Office of Management and Budget, January 1978). The matching first budget estimates were obtained from *The Budget of the United States Government* for fiscal years 1966, 1967, and 1968 (Defense Department military agency classification, administrative budget). On this basis, military outlays appear to have been underbudgeted by $6.4 billion in fiscal 1966, $10.4 billion in 1967, and $5.2 billion in 1968.

19. The estimates for the numerator of the fiscal abnormality variable from 1965:3 through 1968:2 were 3.0, 5.5, 7.5, 9.6, 10.4, 10.4, 10.4, 10.4, 8.2, 6.2, 4.2, and 2.2 (billions of dollars at annual rates; minus signs omitted).

Table 5. Determinants of the Government Saving Rate, 1955:1–1978:4

Independent variable or regression statistic	All levels of government				Federal (entire period) (5)	State and local (entire period) (6)
	Entire period (1)	1955:1 to 1960:4 (2)	1961:1 to 1969:4 (3)	1970:1 to 1978:4 (4)		
Constant	0.00281 (0.92)	0.01191 (1.54)	0.00205 (0.50)	0.00016 (0.05)	−0.00106 (−0.24)	0.00454 (1.12)
GAP	−0.36738 (−6.35)	−0.45674 (−4.24)	−0.16986 (−1.56)	−0.37406 (−5.46)	−0.35138 (−5.43)	−0.03855 (−1.53)
$U_{-2} - U_{-4}$	−0.42262 (−3.06)	−0.53216 (−2.20)	−0.33895 (−0.75)	−0.39985 (−2.32)	−0.31838 (−2.12)	−0.07468 (−1.31)
$PI - EPI$	0.08658 (2.40)	0.07305 (0.89)	0.01885 (0.25)	0.14700 (3.01)	0.09295 (2.40)	−0.00616 (−0.44)
AN	1.01272 (7.23)	...	1.24071 (2.33)	0.89188 (5.77)	0.97211 (6.43)	...
u_{-1}	0.81006 (12.82)	0.85779 (6.76)	0.71075 (4.98)	0.57525 (3.66)	0.86722 (16.68)	0.95154 (29.84)
$\bar{R}^2$	0.877	0.880	0.663	0.920	0.879	0.880
Standard error	0.00519	0.00557	0.00549	0.00467	0.00572	0.00225
Durbin-Watson	1.499	1.550	1.393	1.635	1.831	2.496

Source: Calculations of the author based on data in the national income and product accounts of the U.S. Department of Commerce. Figures in parentheses are *t*-statistics. For notation and definition of the variables, see appendix A.

With adjustment for first-order serial correlation[20] and standard notation for the error terms, the regression equation for the fiscal policy rule (using the notation in appendix A) for the ninety-six quarters from 1955 through 1978 is:

$$GS = a_0 + a_1 GAP + a_2(U_{-2} - U_{-4}) + a_3(PI - EPI) + a_4 AN + \rho u_{-1} + \epsilon.$$

The regression was fitted to the entire sample period and to the subperiods 1955:1–1960:4, 1961:1–1969:4, and 1970:1–1978:4.

The fiscal policy rule calculated from this equation is shown in table 5, column 1. The estimates for 1955:1–1960:4 (table 5, column 2) are close to those for the entire period, suggesting that the fiscal policy rule was already well established in the early years of the Eisenhower administration. A formal test of the separate estimates for the three subperiods provided no support for the hypothesis that the fiscal policy rule was not stable for the entire period.[21]

It is clear from the results in the last two columns of table 5 that the rule for all levels of government combined is influenced by the actions and responses of the federal government much more than by the fiscal behavior of state and local governments. Nevertheless, it is reasonable to assume that the federal government takes state and local fiscal behavior into account in determining its own actions, so that the equation for total

20. The procedure used by Data Resources, Incorporated, for estimating the parameters of a linear regression model with first-order autocorrelation incorporates the first observation as described in Charles M. Beach and James G. MacKinnon, "A Maximum Likelihood Procedure for Regression with Autocorrelated Errors," *Econometrica*, vol. 46 (January 1978), pp. 51–58.

21. The test was as follows: the squared sum of errors (*SSE*) was obtained for the combined run (*SSE_c*) and for each of the three subperiod regressions (*SSE_1*, *SSE_2*, and *SSE_3*) with $h = 24$, $m = 36$, and $n = 36$ quarterly observations, respectively. Given an equal number of $K = 6$ regressors in each equation, these results were then used to calculate the *F*-statistic.

$$\frac{(SSE_c - SSE_1 - SSE_2 - SSE_3)/2K}{(SSE_1 + SSE_2 + SSE_3)/(h + m + n - 3K)} \sim F_{2K, h+m+n-3K}.$$

The resulting *F* value was 0.84, indicating that the estimates for three subperiods are not significantly different from the estimates for the entire period. The formula is an extension of the two-period test statistic shown in Jan Kmenta, *Elements of Econometrics* (Macmillan, 1971), p. 373. The generalization comes from R. L. Brown, J. Durbin, and J. M. Evans, "Techniques for Testing the Constancy of Regression Relationships Over Time," *Journal of the Royal Statistical Society*, vol. 37 (1975), B series, pt. 2, pp. 149–92, especially p. 156.

government saving (table 5, column 1) is used to infer the fiscal policy rule.[22]

What do the numerical results in the first column of table 5 then have to tell us? The small and statistically insignificant intercept suggests that, under steady growth conditions when the potential output gap is zero, the consolidated budget for all levels of government would be about balanced or yield a small surplus.[23] If under such conditions inflation were one percentage point higher than expected, the surplus would be increased 0.09 percent of net national product, or $1.9 billion at 1979 levels (given a 1979 net national product of around $2,100 billion). Now assume the gap rises by one percentage point. Then the surplus would fall by about 0.37 percent of net national product, or $7.8 billion, in the same quarter. As a result, the unemployment rate would grow by about 0.33 percentage point over the two succeeding quarters, and this would cause $U_{-2} - U_{-4}$ to be positive for a few quarters thereafter. If the coefficient on $U_{-2} - U_{-4}$ is about -0.4, the surplus rate would fall temporarily by another 0.13, giving a total decline of 0.5 percent of net national product, or $10.5 billion. About three-quarters of this would persist after the unemployment rate stabilized.

If this is what typically happens, is it reasonable to assume that private decisionmakers expect it to happen? Furthermore, are their expectations so firm that they regard any budgetary outcome that differs from that predicted by the fiscal policy rule as a temporary aberration? Statistically, there is a tendency for budget outcomes to return to the norm because ρ is significantly less than unity in the first equation in table 5 (even at the 1 percent level). This suggests that a stable reaction function could rationally have been attributed to the government by the private sector, although there is no assurance that this assumption was made.

While matters may have been slightly different during the 1950s in this regard, most people are convinced that significant government surpluses will not persist, not even at full employment. In a cyclical downturn, the political attractions of budget balancing are overcome by the desire to reverse the economic decline. The rule of thumb—that the gov-

22. The *Economic Report of the President* has contained estimates of the full-employment or high-employment budget and budget surplus for all levels of government combined since the early 1970s. Detailed discussions of the expected fiscal behavior of state and local governments that must be taken into account in federal budget planning have appeared in almost every issue since the mid-1950s.

23. In 1947 a proposal along these lines was made by the Committee for Economic Development for the federal government's budget policy. See *Taxes and the Budget: A Program for Prosperity in a Free Economy* (New York: CED, 1947).

ernment deficit is higher by about one-third of any increase in the potential output gap, and vice versa—may long have been internalized by private parties. They may also be aware that the size of the politically acceptable deficit is influenced by a higher than expected inflation rate and by recent changes in the unemployment rate.

One need claim no more than this broad understanding of fiscal policy-making to hypothesize that expectations are conditioned by the fiscal policy rule. Moreover, the rule does not imply unsustainable debt accumulation or any other obvious disaster that would force its abandonment;[24] there is no economic reason why it should not be adhered to for a long time.

The systematic element of the fiscal policy rule may be obtained by calculating the normal level of government saving from the first equation of table 5. Setting the fiscal abnormality and systematic error terms equal to zero yields a measure of the government saving rate that is unaffected by fiscal surprises and past errors. The difference between the actual and normal government saving rate so constructed then consists of (1) non-random errors caused by fiscal abnormalities, (2) the random error of the actual regression estimate with adjustment for first-order serial correlation of the error terms, and (3) the inherited but diminishing error explained by ρu_{-1}. These errors will not persist for long so they may be treated as temporary fiscal shocks. For simplicity, their sum will be referred to as the fiscal surprise variable, FS. Thus, if $FS > 0$, the surplus is higher than one would expect and households may ignore some of the extra fiscal stringency by spending more. Conversely, if $FS < 0$, they may save more than they would if the same fiscal posture was in line with the policy rule. In other words, households will expect a relaxation of fiscal policy in the future if $FS > 0$ and a tightening if $FS < 0$.

Private Saving

Having derived the fiscal surprise variable, I can now attempt to explain the private saving rates. This is done below in table 6 for the corporate sector and in table 7 for the personal sector. To avoid the technical

24. The rule implies that a temporary change in the deficit will not affect the future government saving rate, so that government saving is independent of past accumulations of government debt. For a discussion of expectations based on sustainable rules of fiscal policy and how they bear on the issue of the government debt burden, see George M. von Furstenberg and Burton G. Malkiel, "The Government and Capital Formation," *Journal of Economic Literature,* vol. 15 (September 1977), pp. 835–78, especially p. 859.

problems of manipulating sectoral net saving rates, which can be negative at times,[25] the derivation of the regression specification starts out with nonsaving rates, which are simply 1 minus the saving rate. These nonsaving rates are multiplicative functions of various conditioning variables, the net national product, and the potential output gap.[26] Converting to logarithms and changing signs then yields the sectoral saving rates as dependent variables.

Interdependence of Private Saving Components

There are good reasons to suppose that various components of private saving are interdependent. Take, for instance, retained earnings of financial and nonfinancial corporations. Since loan demand is highly cyclical, the retained earnings of some classes of financial intermediaries will cor-

25. Negative sectoral saving rates cannot be transformed into logarithms. Furthermore, the logarithms of positive sectoral saving rates cannot be combined to estimate saving rates at the higher level of aggregation that may be called for.

26. Specifically, with S the amount of saving in any sector,

$$(1) \qquad (NNP - S) = (1 - a_0) \prod_{i=1}^{m} e^{a_i x_i} \prod_{j=m+1}^{m+n} y_i^{a_i}.$$

The m variables of type x in the exponent of the natural logarithm are the conditioning variables and the n variables of type y are base variables. The distinction is that percentage changes in y variables are associated with percentage changes in $(NNP - S)$ but absolute changes in x variables are unassociated with percentage changes in $(NNP - S)$. In practice, x-type variables tend to be rates or relative prices and y-type variables represent bases, such as (permanent) NNP, from which nonsaving is assumed to be made subject to the conditioning variables, x.

To derive a saving rate from equation 1, assume the product of the base variables is $NNP^{a_{m+1}} (GNPK72/GNP72)^{a_{m+2}}$, where $GNPK72/GNP72$ is the ratio of potential to actual GNP. Then dividing through by NNP and taking logarithms yields:

$$(2) \qquad \ln (1 - S/NNP) = \ln (1 - a_0) + \sum_{i=1}^{m} a_i x_i + (a_{m+1} - 1) \ln NNP$$

$$+ a_{m+2} \ln (GNPK72/GNP72),$$

or approximately,

$$(3) \qquad S/NNP = a_0 - \sum_{i=1}^{m} a_i x_i - (a_{m+1} - 1) \ln NNP - a_{m+2}[1 - (GNP72/GNPK72)].$$

The last two variables in equation 3, which are denoted $LNNP72$ and GAP, respectively, are included in all the regressions, while the conditioning variables differ by sector. (All national income accounts variables are conceptually entered in real terms, but the ratio of any two nominal variables is equal to the ratio of the corresponding real variables assuming the same deflators apply.)

relate positively with the business cycle. On the other hand, the earnings of other intermediaries, such as saving and loan associations, may be depressed by rising short-term interest rates. Rising interest rates and bank earnings imply higher costs for nonfinancial corporations that are net debtors. Thus the retained earnings of financial and nonfinancial corporations are linked either directly or indirectly. The error terms may conceivably be related across equations if the saving rates are estimated independently. The technique of full-information maximum-likelihood estimation of equations will therefore be used to check whether information contained in the covariance of the residuals of the two corporate savings rates can improve the estimates.

There may be even stronger interdependence at a higher level of aggregation. It has been argued that retained earnings of the corporate sector as a whole influence personal saving. If households "pierce the corporate veil" and allow for corporate retentions in making their saving decisions, there is a direct relationship between these major components of private saving, with personal saving responding to predicted rather than actual irregular values of corporate saving.[27] Also, a net worth variable should capture the indirect influence of corporate retentions on personal saving to the extent that they raise the value of corporate equities. However, as indicated later, the coefficients of the net worth variable in personal saving equations are statistically insignificant. This supports the hypothesis that corporate retentions affect personal saving directly through their influence on household saving decisions rather than indirectly through any immediate effect on corporate equity values.

As another example of possible interdependence, government consumption, or taxes minus transfer payments, may be regarded by households as a partial substitute for private consumption. In such circumstances, a rise in the ratio of taxes to net national product may raise the ratio of personal saving to disposable income but leave the ratio of private saving to the net national product unaffected. Paul David and John Scadding have supported the equivalent proposition, that the gross private

27. The regression results in table 7 confirm that the coefficient on corporate saving (*C&RW*) is weakened in the equations for personal saving (*PERS&SD*) if errors in *C&RW* are not eliminated. Thus this coefficient turns out to be only −0.455 in the ordinary least squares estimate and −0.675 in the full-information maximum-likelihood estimate of personal saving. The coefficient on corporate saving was strengthened further, to −0.681, in the full-information maximum-likelihood estimation of the complete system described in note 5, above.

saving rate is invariant to the tax rate, on the conjecture that consumers regard tax-financed government expenditures as consumption.[28]

While the trade-off may not be dollar for dollar, consumers may nevertheless reduce their consumption by some percentage of a tax-financed increase in government purchases. For example, an increase in defense purchases resulting from an expansion of the armed forces is certain to reduce the personal consumption expenditures of inductees and to raise government consumption, although tax financing is not required to produce this effect. Robert Barro has therefore shifted the fiscal substitution proposition from taxes net of transfer payments to government purchases, arguing that the latter reduce private purchases, no matter how financed.[29] Since government purchases are equal to taxes net of transfers minus the expected budget surplus and the fiscal surprise as here defined, the latter would appear as an element of Barro's formulation, though not separately identified.

To test whether ordinary least squares or the full-information maximum-likelihood estimation technique is more appropriate in view of the possible interdependencies among saving components, the separate components were estimated first. If there was no interdependence, the regression equation for the aggregate would be the sum of the component equations. To test for interdependence, the adjusted coefficient of determination, $\bar{R}^2$, for the aggregate was compared with the Carter-Nagar $\bar{R}^2$ for the full-information maximum-likelihood system of component equations. If the latter exceeded the former, disaggregated systems estimation would be preferred to the ordinary least squares estimation at the higher level of aggregation.

Interdependence appears to be weak between segments of the corpo-

28. "Private Savings," p. 241. For a detailed discussion of these views and their relevance to the effects of fiscal policy on steady growth, see George M. von Furstenberg, "The Effect of the Changing Size and Composition of Government Purchases on Potential Output," *Review of Economics and Statistics,* vol. 62 (February 1980), pp. 74–80; and von Furstenberg, "Public Versus Private Spending: The Long-Term Consequences of Direct Crowding Out," in von Furstenberg, ed., *The Government and Capital Formation,* pp. 243–63.

29. See Barro, "Are Government Bonds Net Wealth?" pp. 1095–1117; Barro, "Reply to Feldstein and Buchanan," pp. 343–49; and Barro, *The Impact of Social Security on Private Saving, Evidence from U.S. Time Series, with a Reply by Martin Feldstein* (American Enterprise Institute for Public Policy Research, 1978). On pp. 42–45 of the last publication, Feldstein gives a number of reasons why government saving should not be an argument in personal consumption (or saving) functions.

rate sector. Presumably because of offsetting factors, retained earnings of nonfinancial corporations exhibited no interrelation with the retained earnings of financial corporations from domestic sources. However, the interdependence between corporate and personal saving was sufficiently pronounced to warrant the use of the full-information maximum-likelihood estimation technique.[30]

Regression Estimates

This section reports on the preferred regressions for various private saving rates. Estimates of the determinants of net corporate saving for the nonfinancial and financial sectors separately, and for the corporate sector as a whole, are given in table 6. Estimates for the personal sector, the corporate sector, and the entire private sector are given in table 7. Results using the ordinary least squares and full-information maximum-likelihood techniques are given in both tables.

CORPORATE SAVING. The same explanatory variables are used in the regressions for nonfinancial and financial corporations. These include the logarithm of the net national product in 1972 dollars, the potential output gap, the respective inventory valuation and capital consumption allowance adjustments, and changes in the effective corporation tax rate on reported profits in the last year and the two preceding years. The effects of tax rate changes for both financial and nonfinancial corporations decline as the change ages and they remain significant through the second year for nonfinancial corporations and the third year for financial corporations. Net saving of nonfinancial corporations declines by over two-thirds of any rise in inventory profits because such profits increase both taxes and dividends.[31] There is no inventory valuation adjustment for financial corporations and their capital consumption adjustment is very small.

The third ordinary least squares run reported in table 6 is a regression for the net saving of nonfinancial and financial corporations combined. When independence of the component regressions is assumed, the coefficients for the entire corporate sector should replicate the coefficients for variables that appear in only one of the component equations and should be the sum of the coefficients of variables that appear in both equations.

---

30. Net retained earnings originating in the rest of the world are included in retentions of the entire corporate sector at this stage.

31. Since organized labor focuses on unadjusted profits of corporations, there is also the possibility that wage demands will be stimulated by inventory profits in a negotiation setting, but this effect is unlikely to be large.

Table 6. Estimates of the Corporate Saving Rate, 1955:2–1978:4

Independent variable or regression statistic	Ordinary least squares estimates					Full-information maximum-likelihood estimates	
	Nonfinancial corporations (1)	Financial corporations (2)	All corporations[a] (3)	All corporations[a] (4)	All corporations[b] (5)	Nonfinancial corporations (6)	Financial corporations (7)
Constant	0.02538 (10.20)	0.00560 (16.81)	0.03075 (13.73)	0.03142 (13.74)	0.03380 (13.50)	0.02530 (29.54)	0.00559 (52.20)
LNNP72	−0.00354 (−0.47)	−0.00286 (−2.65)	−0.00674 (−0.99)	...	...	−0.00204 (−0.17)	−0.00316 (−2.59)
GAP	−0.25645 (−9.88)	−0.00416 (−1.04)	−0.25394 (−9.85)	−0.27154 (−12.75)	−0.27226 (−12.70)	−0.25411 (−8.79)	−0.00393 (−0.99)
TC04	...	...	...	−0.08752 (−4.28)	−0.08712 (−4.26)	...	...
TC48	...	...	...	−0.04396 (−2.15)	−0.05447 (−2.70)	...	...
TNFC04	−0.04450 (−2.15)	...	−0.03950 (−1.98)	...	...	−0.03744 (−1.99)	...
TNFC48	−0.04001 (−1.79)	...	−0.02648 (−1.23)	...	...	−0.02496 (−1.23)	...
TNFC812	−0.01760 (−0.92)	...	−0.01799 (−0.94)	...	...	−0.00274 (−0.16)	...

$TFC04$	...	-0.01073 (-7.93)	-0.02508 (-3.18)	...	...	-0.01149 (-9.28)
$TFC48$	...	-0.00673 (-4.78)	-0.00607 (-0.75)	...	...	-0.00676 (-5.28)
$TFC812$	...	-0.00311 (-2.45)	-0.00066 (-0.09)	...	...	-0.00311 (-2.67)
$CCANFC$	0.23605 (1.10)	...	0.23488 (1.15)	...	0.28992 (1.39)	...
$CCAFC$	...	0.79661 (2.25)	1.35555 (0.67)	...	...	0.80825 (2.50)
$IVAC$	0.71518 (11.65)	...	0.69136 (11.64)	0.71600 (12.54)	0.69205 (12.00)	0.69384 (12.68)
u_{-1}	0.91707 (22.61)	0.89718 (19.86)	0.91077 (20.67)	0.92479 (24.03)	0.93147 (25.64)	0.92898 (24.83)
$\bar{R}^2$	0.965	0.936	0.972	0.973	0.971	0.967[c]
Standard error	0.00192	0.00032	0.00182	0.00180	0.00183	...[d]
Durbin-Watson	1.893	1.713	1.965	2.042	2.012	...[d]

Source: Calculations of the author based on data in the national income and product accounts. Figures in parentheses are t-statistics. For notation and definition of the variables, see appendix A.
a. Excludes corporate retained earnings from the rest of the world.
b. Includes corporate retained earnings from the rest of the world.
c. Carter-Nagar $\bar{R}^2$.
d. Not computed.

Table 7. Estimates of the Personal, Corporate, and Net Private Saving Rates, 1955:2–1978:4

Independent variable or regression statistic	Ordinary least squares estimates					Full-information maximum-likelihood estimates	
	Personal saving[a] (1)	Corporate saving[b] (2)	Net private saving (3)	Net private saving (4)	Net private saving (5)	Personal saving[a] (6)	Corporate saving[b] (7)
Constant	0.23006 (9.77)	0.03380 (13.50)	0.26573 (10.29)	0.27797 (11.66)	0.28939 (22.49)	0.25444 (10.86)	0.03255 (19.36)
GAP	−0.41075 (−8.98)	−0.27226 (−12.70)	−0.55250 (−12.68)	−0.54913 (−13.55)	−0.55939 (−15.26)	−0.46604 (−9.68)	−0.27415 (−13.09)
TC04	...	−0.08712 (−4.26)	−0.02740 (−0.75)	...	...	...	−0.08301 (−4.47)
TC48	...	−0.05447 (−2.70)	−0.06475 (−1.85)	...	...	...	−0.03640 (−1.98)
IVAC	...	0.69205 (12.00)	0.25053 (2.38)	0.24293 (2.37)	0.24481 (2.40)	...	0.67722 (12.43)
C&RW	−0.45473 (−4.60)	...	...	...	...	−0.67463 (−5.47)	...

	(1)	(2)	(3)	(4)	(5)	(6)
TAX	-0.73768 (8.19)	...	-0.80851 (-7.86)	...	...	-0.78282 (-9.28)
$TRANS$	0.83573 (7.38)	...	0.88466 (6.95)	...	...	0.80749 (7.82)
$TXTR$	...	...	...	-0.83136 (-8.19)	-0.88004 (-16.08)	...
FS	-0.09286 (-1.10)	...	-0.05237 (-0.55)	-0.05423 (-0.57)	...	-0.11343 (-1.47)
$CDUR$	-1.02383 (-9.38)	...	-1.03705 (-8.25)	-0.98712 (-8.02)	-0.99441 (-8.19)	-1.00025 (-9.71)
u_{-1}	0.87516 (15.64)	0.93147 (25.64)	0.88140 (15.71)	0.89145 (17.96)	0.89548 (18.59)	0.85551 (17.04) 0.95899[d] (27.37)
$\bar{R}^2$	0.916	0.971	0.941	0.941	0.941	0.960[c]
Standard error	0.00269	0.00183	0.00302	0.00304	0.00302	0.00259[d] 0.00184[d]
Durbin-Watson	2.135	2.012	2.106	2.098	2.125	...

Source: Calculations of the author based on data in the national income and product accounts. Figures in parentheses are t-statistics. For notation and definition of the variables, see appendix A.

a. Includes the statistical discrepancy.
b. Includes corporate retained earnings from the rest of the world.
c. Carter-Nagar $\bar{R}^2$.
d. Calculated as $[N/(N - K)]^{0.5}$ times the root-mean-square error of the estimated residuals, where $N = 95$ (quarters) and $K = 8$ in system regression 6 and $K = 6$ in regression 7.

This expectation is roughly met for all variables included in the run for nonfinancial corporations, but not for those appearing only in the regression for financial corporations (which carry far less weight in the total). Nevertheless, systems estimation for nonfinancial and financial corporations, shown in the last two columns of table 6, yields a lower Carter-Nagar $\bar{R}^2$ than the ordinary least squares run for all corporations. On this basis, it was concluded that it is preferable to estimate net corporate saving as a whole rather than to use full-information maximum-likelihood estimation for the components.

The regression for all corporations can be simplified further by eliminating all explanatory variables that were found to be statistically significant in the third run (table 6, column 4). When the taxes of nonfinancial and financial corporations are combined, changes in the effective corporate tax rate in the last year and the year before last are significant. However, the capital consumption adjustment variable is not significant and is thus not included in this run.

The last step is to add net retained earnings originating in the rest of the world to net saving in the domestic corporate sector (table 6, column 5). Basically, retained earnings from abroad are stationary after dividing by the net national product, and there is strong serial correlation of the deviations from the mean that could not readily be explained by a variety of economic variables.[32] Thus the specification selected is identical to that of the preceding run. The intercept and ρ are raised by the addition of retained earnings from abroad, while the remaining coefficients are

32. The first explanatory variable was derived from the updated series for actual and potential output in manufacturing in major industrial countries (originally reported in Jacques R. Artus, "Measures of Potential Output in Manufacturing for Eight Industrial Countries, 1955–78," International Monetary Fund, *Staff Papers,* vol. 24 [March 1977], pp. 1–35) by weighting the gap for Canada by 0.5 and the gaps for Japan, France, Germany, Italy, and the United Kingdom by 0.1 each. The resulting composite variable for the foreign output gap in manufacturing was expected to correlate negatively with net retentions originating in the rest of the world, but the statistical relation was slight. Adding the potential output gap in the United States on the theory that the earnings of foreign affiliates are derived, in part, from exports to the United States did not help matters. Changes in relative wholesale prices, such as in the ratio of the producer price for crude nonfood materials except fuel to the producer price index, were positive and significant only when run in combination with the foreign and domestic gap variables, both of which were insignificant. Furthermore, most of the explanatory power of the last regression stemmed from the adjustment for first-order serial correlation of the residuals.

largely unaffected. This specification is also used in the full-information maximum-likelihood estimation of total net private saving.

PERSONAL SAVING. It is not clear that the nonsaving of the household sector is a stable fraction of the net national product or of disposable personal income. Hence the derivation of the explanatory variables tried in the regression for net personal saving (table 7, column 1) requires some discussion. If personal saving responds differently to different components of the net national product, whether or not these components are received by persons or credited to corporations or governments on their behalf, it is the composition of net national product that matters. David and Scadding would not expect personal saving to be depressed by an increase in the ratio of taxes or of taxes minus transfers to the net national product even though disposable personal income would fall at a given level of net national product.[33] On the other hand, Feldstein would expect a rise in corporate saving to reduce personal saving almost equally.[34] He would therefore expect personal saving to fall proportionately much more than disposable income when corporate saving rose. To identify these behavioral responses, taxes, transfers, and corporate saving were added to the list of explanatory variables in the personal saving equations in table 7.[35]

David and Scadding would assume that an equal rise in taxes and

---

33. "Private Savings."

34. "Rate of Return, Taxation, and Personal Savings."

35. To allow for the variability of the saving factor on *NNP*-linked base variables, which is identified as the intercept a_0 in equation 3, this factor is multiplied by Y^*/NNP, where Y^* is an income concept defined as:

$$(4) \qquad Y^* = NNP(1 - b_1 TAX + b_2 TRANS - b_3 C\&RW).$$

If b_1, b_2, and b_3 were all unity, Y^* would be equal to YD plus the statistical discrepancy, SD, minus interest paid by consumers to business. Transfers as defined in this paper include net interest paid by governments (except interest paid to foreigners) and the deficit or surplus of government enterprises as well as transfer payments (except government transfer payments to foreigners). Adding the statistical discrepancy to disposable income is consistent with adding it to personal saving. Subtracting interest paid by consumers to business amounts to excluding such interest payments from personal outlays as well, because these interest payments are already netted against interest received by persons to obtain the adjusted concept of disposable income. However, I do not work with this concept directly but let the regression determine Y^*, to which a fixed saving coefficient, a_0, can be attached. Redefining the intercept as $a_0 (1 - b_1 TAX + b_2 TRANS - b_3 C\&RW)$ accounts for the addition of *TAX, TRANS,* and *C&RW* to the list of explanatory variables in the personal saving equations of table 7.

transfers that left taxes less transfers unchanged had no effect on personal saving. This is confirmed by the results in column 1 of table 7, since the regression coefficients on taxes and transfers (a_0b_1 and a_0b_2) are both about 0.8. These authors would also assume, however, that an isolated rise in taxes or decline in transfers that produced an equal increase in taxes less transfers would have no effect. This hypothesis is decisively refuted by the results; in fact, taxes and transfers affect personal saving more than consumption.

Feldstein's hypothesis that there is a high degree of substitution between corporate and personal saving tests out rather better.[36] Although significantly less than -1, the coefficients shown on corporate saving range from -0.45 to -0.67 in the personal saving equation in table 7. If the latter figure is accepted as being more reliable, this implies that an increase in corporate saving cuts personal saving thirteen times as much as a decline in the growth of the net national product. While this is still well short of the value of 20 that would be required for complete dollar-for-dollar offset between personal and corporate saving when the long-run marginal propensity to save is 0.05, Feldstein is clearly more right than wrong.

Since the income-equivalence coefficients on taxes, transfers, and corporate saving (b_1, b_2, and b_3) that can be deduced from the personal saving equation are all far from unity, the results imply that personal saving is not a stable function of (permanent) disposable income, as is frequently supposed. Rather, any rise in taxes net of transfers or in retained earnings reduces personal saving disproportionately more than disposable income.

Two additional variables are shown in column 1 of table 7. One is the fiscal surprise variable derived earlier, which is intended to allow for the possibility that, say, a deficit that is unusually large ($FS<0$) will lead

36. A complete statement of Martin Feldstein's position appears in his contribution, "Corporate Tax Integration," in *An Evaluation of New Proposals to Reduce the Corporate Income Tax Burden: Encouraging Capital Formation Through the Tax Code*, Committee Print, Joint Seminars of the Task Force on Tax Policy and Tax Expenditures and the Task Force on Capital Needs and Monetary Policy of the Senate Committee on the Budget, 94 Cong. 1 sess. (GPO, 1975), pp. 165–97. Howrey and Hymans find that business cash saving reduces personal cash saving by about 70 cents on the dollar for the period 1955–74. This result is close to my full-information maximum-likelihood estimate. See E. Philip Howrey and Saul H. Hymans, "The Measurement and Determination of Loanable-Funds Saving," *BPEA*, *3: 1978*, pp. 655–85, especially p. 681.

consumers to doubt that this budgetary situation will last. They may then prepare for a future tax hike or a cut in government spending by saving more. The coefficient on the fiscal surprise variable should thus be negative. The second additional variable is spending on consumer durable goods.[37] A negative coefficient should attach to unusually high expenditures of this kind, and this is the case in table 7.

The same explanatory variables plus those used in the regression for corporate saving are used in the ordinary least squares regression for the total net private saving rate (table 7, column 3). Because corporate saving appears with a coefficient of -0.45 in the regression for personal saving, the coefficients in the equation for corporate saving should contribute only 55 percent of their strength to the combined run. The coefficient on the potential output gap in column 3 comes close to the weighted sum of the corresponding coefficients in the earlier columns, and the coefficient on consumer durable spending changes little. However, several of the other coefficients deviate markedly from the levels that would be expected if the two runs were independent.

This finding suggests that the full-information maximum-likelihood system estimation may be more appropriate than independent ordinary least squares estimation in this instance. Furthermore, the appearance of corporate saving among the explanatory variables in the equation for personal saving increases interdependence. Correspondingly, the Carter-Nagar $\bar{R}^2$ for the system of the two equations is higher than the $\bar{R}^2$ for the ordinary least squares estimate of net private saving in column 3 or the simplified alternatives presented in columns 4 and 5. Full-information maximum-likelihood system estimation is therefore preferred in this instance.

Even so, it is interesting to compare the two simplified ordinary least squares equations for net private saving with other equations in table 7. Both exclude the corporation tax rate change variables that were insignificant in equation 3 even though they are significant in equations 2 and 7. A coefficient of -0.08 or -0.09 on the variable for the tax change in the last year implies that a 0.01 increase in the tax rate expressed as a

---

37. The variable $CDUR$ was constructed as the ratio of expenditures on consumer durables, CD, to NNP minus the average of that ratio over sixteen preceding quarters so that

$$CDUR = CD/NNP - \left[\sum_{i=1}^{16} (CD/NNP)_{-i} \right] \Big/ 16.$$

fraction of corporate profits reduces corporate retentions by an amount almost equal to the tax increase in the first year, on the assumption that the ratio of before-tax profits to net national product is between 10 and 11 percent. However, this effect diminishes rapidly as time passes. Another modification used in the table's equations 4 and 5 was to combine the tax and transfer variables into a single variable, taxes less transfers, because the absolute values of the coefficients on the tax and transfer rates were found to be so close. This closeness persists in the full-information maximum-likelihood estimate in column 6. It may be concluded that a simultaneous rise in taxes and transfers has practically no effect on the ratio of personal saving to net national product.[38]

A rise in taxes accompanied by a rise in government purchases that leaves the fiscal surprise variable unchanged reduces personal saving in relation to net national product by almost 80 percent of that increase. It reduces personal saving even more if the tax rise lifts the government budget surplus unexpectedly because it is not accompanied by an increase in government spending. In that case the reduction amounts to almost 90 percent because the fiscal surprise rises by as much as taxes.[39] In either event higher taxes less transfers should be associated more closely with an equal reduction in the ratio of personal saving to the net national product than with an equal cut in personal consumption expenditures. This is the opposite of what David and Scadding have suggested. However, it is not certain that the results of the time series regressions can be used to infer the effects of unusual combinations of policy changes.

Taxes less transfers changed comparatively little over the sample period because the growth in the ratio of taxes to net national product was accompanied by roughly equal growth in the ratio of transfers to net na-

38. A disproportionate influence of taxes and transfers on personal saving has been found by others. See Lawrence J. Kotlikoff, "Testing the Theory of Social Security and Life Cycle Accumulation," *American Economic Review*, vol. 69 (June 1979), p. 408; Lester D. Taylor, "Saving out of Different Types of Income," *BPEA, 2:1971*, pp. 383–407; F. Thomas Juster and Paul Wachtel, "A Note on Inflation and the Saving Rate," *BPEA, 3:1972*, pp. 765–78; and Juster, "Uncertainty, Price Expectations and the Personal Saving Rate: Some Preliminary Results and Questions for the Future," in Burkhard Strumpel and others, eds., *Survey of Consumers, 1972–73* (University of Michigan, Institute for Social Research, 1975), pp. 5–30.

39. At given values of taxes and transfers, a fiscal surprise produced, for instance, by a cut in government purchases reduces personal saving by 11 percent of the rise in fiscal surprise, according to the full-information maximum-likelihood estimate. However, as explained in footnote 5, caution should be exercised since the sum of the coefficients on the fiscal surprise and tax variable proved more robust in alternative specifications than the division between them.

tional product.[40] But while the net effect of the expansion of the public sector on personal saving has been small so far, the potential effects could be large. Contrary to the interpretation of David and Scadding, the historical stability of cycle averages of the private saving rate does not require that consumers ignore taxes in formulating their saving plans. All it requires is that they take account of taxes and transfers equally, since both grew by almost equal amounts in relation to net national product over the sample period, and since corporate saving changed little between cycles.

Since corporate and personal saving rates are both free of simple trends, as evidenced by the insignificance of the coefficient on the net national product, the net private saving rate is also trendless in this respect. The gross private saving rate can therefore show such trends only to the extent the ratio of the adjusted capital consumption allowance to GNP has shown a trend, for instance, because the composition of the capital stock has changed from structures toward more equipment.[41] Again, however, no such trend is evident.

The offset between deviations of the consumer durable spending rate from its past average level (*CDUR*) and personal saving is about one to one. The coefficient on the potential output gap is -0.47 in the full-information maximum-likelihood estimate of personal saving and -0.27 in that of corporate saving. Since the mean of the personal saving ratio is 0.05 and that of corporate saving is 0.024, a 0.01 increase in the potential output gap produced by a one percentage point decline in the ratio of actual to potential GNP lowers personal saving by 9.4 percent and retained earnings by 11.2 percent. Cyclical changes thus have a stronger effect on corporate saving than on personal saving, as one would expect.

Explanatory Variables That Failed

A number of explanatory variables that were tried in the corporate and personal saving equations were rejected because their influence either

40. From 1955:1 to 1978:4, taxes rose from 27.5 to 36.4 percent of the net national product and transfers from 5.7 to 12.4 percent, but taxes less transfers grew from 21.8 to only 23.9 percent over this twenty-four-year period. The correlation between taxes and transfers was 0.89, but the correlation between taxes and taxes less transfers was only half as large; transfers and taxes less transfers were uncorrelated when ratios to the net national product were used throughout.

41. The resulting rise in the depreciation rate on the aggregate stock of capital need not raise the ratio of capital consumption allowances (adjusted) to the net national product if the capital–output ratio has declined.

was not statistically significant or was in the wrong direction. These variables were not discussed in the preceding section to avoid interrupting the discussion of the significant variables.

Variables for Corporate Saving

Since the inflation premium that compensates the lender for the expected reduction in the real value of his nominal-dollar claim is included in the interest payments deducted by corporations, the official retained-earnings figures understate real retained earnings.[42] What is, in fact, a repayment of debt in real terms is regarded as a current factor cost to the debtor and as income to the creditor. If investment responds to profits net of real, not nominal, interest paid, economic forces that lower the measured ratio of retained earnings to the net national product may be at work during an inflationary period.

This was tested by adding the ratio of net interest paid divided by the net national product to the basic regression for saving of nonfinancial corporations (column 1, table 6) and, alternatively, the reduction in real indebtedness estimated by Burton Malkiel and the author.[43] Neither variable yielded significant results, perhaps because uncertainty and the risk premiums required for investment have grown along with the expected rate of inflation.[44]

In the saving equation for financial corporations (column 2, table 6), two interest-spread variables were tried. The first was the difference between the average prime rate charged by banks and the Federal Reserve Bank of New York discount rate,[45] which was taken to indicate changing regulatory or rate-setting pressure on bank profits. The second was the difference between the average market yield on U.S. government three-month bills and the yield on U.S. Treasury securities at a constant matu-

42. See Henry J. Aaron, ed., *Inflation and the Income Tax* (Brookings Institution, 1976); and John B. Shoven and Jeremy I. Bulow, "Inflation Accounting and Nonfinancial Corporate Profits: Financial Assets and Liabilities," *BPEA, 1:1976,* pp. 15–57.

43. See George M. von Furstenberg and Burton G. Malkiel, "Financial Analysis in an Inflationary Environment," *Journal of Finance,* vol. 32 (May 1977), p. 578, table 1, col. 3. Because the (generally negative) capital consumption and (positive) real indebtedness adjustments may work in opposite directions (but with the same absolute effect per unit of change) on adjusted retained earnings, the sum of these adjustments was also tried. However, this combination also failed to yield statistically significant results.

44. On this, see Burton G. Malkiel, "The Capital Formation Problem in the United States," *Journal of Finance,* vol. 34 (May 1979), pp. 291–306.

45. These data were obtained from selected issues of the *Federal Reserve Bulletin.*

rity of twenty years.[46] This variable was intended to capture changing disintermediation pressure on the profits of financial institutions. No significant effects of these variables were found, perhaps because these spreads may affect the earnings and retentions of commercial banks and savings institutions in opposite directions.

Thus changing interest payments or rate spreads did not help account for variations in retained earnings in either the nonfinancial or the financial corporate sectors. This may explain the lack of interdependence between the savings equations of nonfinancial and financial corporations found in the preceding section.

Variables for Personal Saving

It has often been argued that farmers save more than nonfarm households. However, adding the difference between the income of farm proprietors and the average level of that same variable over the twelve preceding quarters to the explanatory variables in the personal saving equation was unproductive. Since there is a high degree of correlation between farmers' income and changes in the relative price of food,[47] opposing factors may be at work. An (unexpected) rise in farm income raises the saving of farmers and of the personal sector as a whole, but the associated increase in the relative price of food lowers the saving rate of nonfarm households as increased outlays for essentials eat into saving.

Along similar lines, it was hypothesized that a rise in the ratio of the deflator for domestic absorption (personal consumption, net investment, and government purchases) to the net national product deflator might reduce the personal saving rate, which it can do if the demand for increasingly expensive imports, such as crude oil or energy products, is highly inelastic so that less is spent on other goods including future consumption (saving). However, these effects were small and statistically insignificant.

Table 8 reports on the results of a number of attempts to capture the influence of inflation, uncertainty, and net worth on saving. The variables for inflation ranged from the actual and officially expected inflation rates, and the difference between them, to a distributed lag on past quarterly changes in the actual inflation rate as measured by the consumer price index. A second-degree Almon lag polynomial on the latter variable estimated without end constraints over sixteen quarters produced unusual

46. These data were obtained from the U.S. central data bank of Data Resources, Incorporated.

47. The relative price variable was constructed as $CPIFOOD/CPIFOOD_{-4} - CPI/CPI_{-4}$. Its correlation with net farm proprietors' income was 0.81.

Table 8. Alternative Regressions for the Personal Saving Rate, 1955:2–1978:4[a]

Independent variable or regression statistic	Regression number							
	1	2	3	4	5	6	7	8
Constant	0.26558 (11.37)	0.24170 (10.75)	0.25775 (8.73)	0.22583 (8.32)	0.26221 (8.70)	0.23652 (8.58)	0.26089 (10.31)	0.23317 (11.10)
GAP	−0.41738 (−9.48)	−0.42299 (−9.29)	−0.42526 (−8.96)	−0.43399 (−9.13)	−0.42077 (−8.63)	−0.42420 (−8.68)	−0.42207 (−9.43)	−0.42749 (−9.44)
C&RW	−0.42782 (−4.48)	−0.42431 (−4.15)	−0.44154 (−4.34)	−0.43965 (−4.20)	−0.44667 (−4.38)	−0.44278 (−4.24)	−0.44714 (−4.25)	−0.44447 (−4.35)
TAX	−0.81551 (−9.75)	−0.75689 (−8.78)	−0.82182 (−9.61)	−0.76772 (−8.91)	−0.85004 (−8.22)	−0.83571 (−7.96)	−0.84678 (−8.89)	−0.82720 (−8.57)
TRANS	0.77906 (7.81)	0.81156 (7.36)	0.80262 (7.21)	0.83632 (7.41)	0.77880 (6.40)	0.77038 (6.08)	0.78406 (7.82)	0.78481 (7.45)
FS	−0.02318 (−0.30)	−0.07442 (−0.91)	−0.02202 (−0.28)	−0.07036 (−0.87)	−0.00599 (−0.07)	−0.03186 (−0.37)	−0.00810 (−0.10)	−0.03704 (−0.45)
CDUR	−0.98219 (−8.09)	−1.00202 (−8.45)	−0.97702 (−8.01)	−0.99052 (−8.26)	−0.96928 (−7.83)	−0.96865 (−7.83)	−0.96994 (−7.90)	−0.97018 (−7.94)
DICPIQ[b]	3.35564 (2.24)	3.54241 (2.12)	3.39837 (2.24)	3.71558 (2.24)	3.30517 (2.17)	3.56820 (2.21)	3.32103 (2.21)	3.61437 (2.25)

	(1)	(2)	(3)	(4)	(5)	(6)	(7)	(8)
RRAT	−0.20370 (−2.76)	...	...	...	−0.18426 (−2.19)	...	−0.18365 (−2.20)	...
RRFS	...	−0.11788 (−1.43)	−0.19037 (−2.40)	−0.12866 (−1.57)	...	−0.14072 (−1.74)	...	−0.13965 (−1.74)
NW/YD	...	...	0.00227 (0.46)	0.00525 (0.95)	0.00257 (0.52)	0.00624 (1.27)	...	...
NSW/YD	...	...	...	...	0.00314 (0.45)	0.00786 (1.13)	...	...
SUMNW	...	...	...	...	...	...	0.00273 (0.63)	0.00668 (1.63)
u_{-1}	0.73313 (7.74)	0.83608 (12.21)	0.74147 (7.61)	0.81707 (10.92)	0.72570 (7.10)	0.76890 (8.30)	0.72896 (7.63)	0.77508 (9.28)
$\bar{R}^2$	0.920	0.918	0.919	0.918	0.919	0.918	0.920	0.919
Standard error	0.00262	0.00265	0.00263	0.00265	0.00264	0.00265	0.00263	0.00264
Durbin-Watson	2.189	2.209	2.187	2.177	2.183	2.164	2.184	2.162

Sources: Calculated by the author based on data in the national income and product accounts, and appendix B, table 10, columns 7 and 8, and table 11, columns 10 and 11. Figures in parentheses are t-statistics. For notation and definition of the variables, see appendix A.

a. Includes statistical discrepancy.

b. The statistics shown are the sum of the regression coefficients on quarterly percentage changes in the CPI over sixteen quarters, starting with the latest quarter, which were estimated with an unconstrained second-degree Almon lag polynomial. The time pattern of the coefficients forms an inverted U without sign change. The positive effect of changes in the rate of inflation on the personal saving ratio reaches a maximum around the middle of the sixteen-quarter interval that is over twice as large as the beginning and ending coefficient values.

results. A rise in the inflation rate was found to raise the saving rate to an increasing extent for the first eight quarters and to a decreasing extent for the next eight quarters, suggesting that the effect of a rise in the inflation rate on the personal saving rate is positive but transitory.[48] Because the sum of the lag coefficients on the inflation rate was just significant at the 5 percent level, this variable was retained in all regressions reported in table 8.[49]

The dispersion of inflation rates is known to be a positive function of the level of those rates,[50] so that it is difficult to distinguish the effects of inflation and uncertainty on saving. Thus real wage uncertainty was estimated directly in an attempt to discriminate between these effects. This uncertainty index was constructed as a moving sum of the absolute deviations of adjusted hourly earnings in 1967 dollars from trend[51] for five years, ending with the current year, and distributing the results quarterly. According to the index, uncertainty was lowest in 1968–69 and highest

48. On the basis of simple regressions that include real balances of net liquid assets and inflation and unemployment rates, a saving-increasing effect of both unexpected and expected inflation has been found for the United States in David H. Howard, "Personal Saving Behavior and the Rate of Inflation," *Review of Economics and Statistics*, vol. 60 (November 1978), pp. 547–54. He notes that the effect of expected inflation on personal saving is indeterminate. However, if expectations of a higher rate of inflation lower real income expectations, expenditures on nondurables should fall and saving may rise. See William L. Springer, "Consumer Spending and the Rate of Inflation," *Review of Economics and Statistics*, vol. 59 (August 1977), pp. 299–306. On the other hand, "classical theory suggests that fully anticipated inflation which is expected to continue for some time should lead to higher expenditures for durables or other goods suitable for hoarding if the effective rate of interest paid to households does not adjust fully to anticipated inflation." Susan W. Burch and Diane Werneke, "The Stock of Consumer Durables, Inflation, and Personal Saving Decisions," *Review of Economics and Statistics*, vol. 57 (May 1975), p. 145.

49. However, the estimates may not prove robust in the future as additional observations are added from the current wave of inflation.

50. See Angus Deaton, "Involuntary Saving Through Unanticipated Inflation," *American Economic Review*, vol. 67 (December 1977), pp. 899–910; and Paul Wachtel, "Inflation and the Saving Behavior of Households: A Survey," in von Furstenberg, ed., *The Government and Capital Formation*, pp. 153–74. The question of whether the variance of the general price change causes the variance of the relative price change is explored in Alex Cukierman, "The Relations between Relative Prices and the General Price Level: A Suggested Interpretation," *American Economic Review*, vol. 69 (June 1979), pp. 444–47.

51. The index refers to the total private nonagricultural economy and is adjusted for overtime (in manufacturing only) and for interindustry employment shifts. It is reported, for instance, in the *Economic Report of the President, 1979*, p. 224. The annual trend rate of growth in real adjusted hourly earnings was estimated to be 2.74 percent for 1949–55, 1.94 percent for 1955–68, 1.49 for 1968–73, and 0 percent thereafter.

at the beginning and end of the sample period. However, the expectation that real wage uncertainty would be related positively to the personal saving rate was not borne out; in fact, the estimated coefficient was negative and highly significant. A variable whose movement is U-shaped over the estimation period with a negative coefficient or a variable that forms an inverted U over the sample period with a positive coefficient[52] can thus contribute to goodness of fit in conjunction with the other variables in table 8. However, its economic identification with uncertainty failed.

Spurious correlations also seem to bedevil the interest rate and net worth variables shown in table 8. The coefficient on the smoothed after-tax real rates of return on net worth is always negative, regardless of whether the Feldstein-Summers[53] or my own deflation procedure is used. Even more disturbing, in the latter case the coefficient is significant statistically.[54]

These findings suggest that saving incentives are not likely to increase personal saving, even though the experience of some European countries has been more favorable.[55] Furthermore, the national income accounting system, which treats the inflation premium in interest paid as a factor cost and return, understates the saving of government and nonfinancial corporations and overstates the income and saving of persons during a period of inflation.[56] If personal income and personal saving were cor-

52. Tobin's q for nonfinancial corporations would follow this pattern. See George M. von Furstenberg, "Corporate Investment: Does Market Valuation Matter in the Aggregate?" *BPEA, 2:1977*, pp. 347–97, especially pp. 351–55. However, a positive coefficient on q would be unexpected in saving equations if q varies inversely with perceived rate-of-return risks unless one shares Marshall's apparent conjecture that capital risk affects saving adversely. On this, see David L. Hanson and Carmen F. Menezes, "The Effect of Capital Risk on Optimal Saving Decisions," *Quarterly Journal of Economics*, vol. 92 (November 1978), pp. 653–70. A variable that has a U-shaped pattern over the period 1955–78 is the proportion of people twenty-five to thirty-four years of age in the total civilian population.

53. Martin Feldstein and Lawrence Summers, "Inflation, Tax Rules, and the Long-Term Interest Rate," *BPEA, 1:1978*, pp. 61–99.

54. For further discussion of these variables, see appendix B.

55. See, for instance, Martin Pfaff, Peter Hurler, and Rudolf Dennerlein, "Old-Age Security and Saving in the Federal Republic of Germany," in von Furstenberg, ed., *Social Security Versus Private Saving*, pp. 277–312.

56. A detailed exploration of this issue is provided in Jeremy J. Siegel, "Inflation-Induced Distortions in Government and Private Saving Statistics," *Review of Economics and Statistics*, vol. 61 (February 1979), pp. 83–90. For further explanation of this issue, see von Furstenberg, "The Rhetoric of Tax 'Reform,'" in *Federal Budget Policy, Employment, and Inflation: Proceedings of Tax Foundation's 28th National Conference* (New York: Tax Foundation, 1977), pp. 27–35; and Clarence L. Barber, "Inflation Distortion and the Balanced Budget," *Challenge*, vol. 22 (September–October 1979), pp. 44–47.

rected to exclude these premiums, saving would be lowered as inflation progressed. Since the rate of return on household net worth declined steadily over the sample period, the rate-of-return variable could be positive and significant outside the national income framework. Even then the coefficients estimated on arrays of variables with strong time trends could easily offset or reinforce each other in various ways, so that it would be impossible to isolate the economic effects of saving incentives.

The same skepticism can be applied to the results on the cyclically adjusted private net worth and net social insurance wealth variables (columns 3, 4, 5, and 6 of table 8). Both have nearly identical, though statistically insignificant, positive coefficients where negative coefficients would be expected on the basis of life cycle theory.[57] In that theory, saving is determined by deviations of actual from desired net worth at successive ages. It would be anomalous for changes in desired net worth to be as large as or larger than changes in actual net worth produced by market revaluations or legislative actions.

If one takes the Kaldorian view that capitalists save more than workers,[58] one might be able to rationalize a positive coefficient on private net worth. Clearly, however, this line of reasoning cannot be extended to the social insurance wealth variable without obliterating the class distinctions involved. Furthermore, to the extent that real after-tax rates of return can

57. The positive coefficient on the ratio of private net worth to disposable personal income is particularly disappointing in view of Bhatia's finding that undistributed corporate profits have no independent effect on household consumption and influence consumption, if at all, only via expected capital gains, which are treated as a component of wealth by households in making spending decisions. See Kul B. Bhatia, "Corporate Taxation, Retained Earnings, and Capital Formation," *Journal of Public Economics,* vol. 11 (February 1979), p. 123. Mishkin also found a positive relation between changes in household net worth (particularly via the stock market) and consumption in a recent recession. See Frederic S. Mishkin, "What Depressed the Consumer? The Household Balance Sheet and the 1973–75 Recession," *BPEA, 1:1977,* pp. 123–64.

58. See B. J. Moore, "Equities, Capital Gains, and the Role of Finance in Accumulation," *American Economic Review,* vol. 65 (December 1975), pp. 872–86; and Hans Brems, "Alternative Theories of Pricing, Distribution, Saving and Investment," *American Economic Review,* vol. 69 (March 1979), pp. 161–65. However, for the United States, income distribution effects on consumption have generally been found to be weak. See Alan S. Blinder, "Distribution Effects and the Aggregate Consumption Function," *Journal of Political Economy,* vol. 83 (June 1975), pp. 447–75; and Philip A. Della Valle and Noriyoshi Oguchi, "Distribution, the Aggregate Consumption Function, and the Level of Economic Development: Some Cross-Country Results," *Journal of Political Economy,* vol. 84 (December 1976), pp. 1325–34.

be regarded as proxies for the real income of capitalists obtained from a given net worth, the coefficients on the rate-of-return variable should be positive, not negative. There is no obvious escape from the conclusion that the rate of return and wealth effects suggested by the results in table 8 are spurious when considered jointly.

Although the pairwise correlations between the net worth and the two rate-of-return variables (*RRFS* and *RRAT* in table 8) are −0.57 and −0.89, coefficient-splitting does not seem to account for the unexpected regression results that remain even if these variables are entered separately. Still, the failure of these variables to work as expected may be due to changes in the economic environment that prevent them from revealing their effects. The progressive decline in the trend rate of growth of adjusted hourly real earnings that accelerated toward the end of the last decade coincides with an accelerating rate of decline in both rate-of-return variables. If the reduced growth in real earnings was to some extent unforeseen at the time of entry into gainful employment, workers might find in midcareer that they could not maintain the consumption program originally planned and still meet their saving goals.[59] Despite the reduced rewards for saving, they might therefore have to start saving sooner in their life cycle and at lower incomes than originally intended. The transitional effect of disappointed expectations about earnings growth may well be a rise in the aggregate rate of saving. The prospects of earlier retirement and greater longevity may also have raised the target net worth ratio over the sample period.

Similarly, a rise in social insurance wealth that is accompanied by growing concern about the crisis in social security financing and rising fears about recontracting by younger generations may not increase reliance on government-created, as opposed to privately controlled, net worth.[60] Even privately controlled net claims on the government, such as

59. For documentation, see footnote 51. The decline in the rate of technical change after 1966, which would have led to negative growth rates of output after the 1973 energy shock if the levels of inputs had not grown, is detailed in Barbara M. Fraumeni and Dale W. Jorgenson, "The Role of Capital in U.S. Economic Growth, 1948–1976," in George M. von Furstenberg, ed., *Capital, Efficiency, and Growth* (Ballinger, 1980), pp. 9–250. Unexpected declines in the rate of technical change are likely to reduce income growth for both workers and capitalists below expectations.

60. See Bulent Gultekin and Dennis E. Logue, "Social Security and Personal Saving: Survey and New Evidence," in von Furstenberg, ed., *Social Security Versus Private Saving*, pp. 65–132.

those evidenced by private ownership of public debt, may not be perceived as being on a par with other components of net worth by the private sector as a whole if higher future taxes, increased macroeconomic instability, or reduced real economic growth are expected.[61] Even so, one may suspect that only weak effects can readily be swamped by changes in other potentially relevant factors that were omitted from the regressions.

Concluding Comments

This study shows that government saving habitually moves with cyclical and other factors in a well-defined pattern. Therefore, only deviations from a rule that implies government dissaving on the average but with large swings over the business cycle are treated as fiscal surprises.

In this expectational milieu the crucial distinctions are not between an automatic and a discretionary fiscal change or between a temporary and a permanent change. This allows one to dispense with labels for particular fiscal actions.[62] What matters is not the labels attached to isolated policy steps but whether the resulting overall fiscal stance is consistent with the rule or off the trajectory to which it is expected to return. So long as there are no political or economic grounds for suspecting that the fiscal policy rule will change, a rational assumption is that the rule will continue to be observed and that government debt will grow indefinitely.[63] Further development of the concept of the fiscal rule and its measurement may yield clearer insights than have been obtained in this study.

Additional work on other input variables may also prove rewarding. A great deal of care was lavished on the construction of the real after-tax rate-of-return variables, including accrued capital gains. Because I was dissatisfied with the common practice of picking the rate of return on a single asset, such as corporate bonds, to represent the saving incentives of households when actual household portfolios are, and must be, much

61. For the earliest development of these points, see Franco Modigliani, "Long-Run Implications of Alternative Fiscal Policies and the Burden of the National Debt," *Economic Journal,* vol. 71 (December 1961), pp. 730–55.

62. The finest recent example of the conventional piecemeal approach is Alan S. Blinder, "Temporary Taxes and Consumer Spending," National Bureau of Economic Research Working Paper 283 (Cambridge, Mass.: NBER, October 1978).

63. A necessary condition for the existence of a steady-growth solution is, of course, that the real government debt outstanding (including the debt implicit in net social security claims on the government) grow at the same rate as other real stocks and flows.

more diversified to hedge against inflation and other factors, I calculated rates of return on a more representative portfolio. The difference this broadening makes is striking. The nominal rate-of-return series derived in appendix B, before taxes and deflation are applied, has *zero* correlation with the nominal series used by others. This suggests that one should be suspicious of simple proxies, such as corporate bond yields, in studies of saving behavior under inflationary conditions. There are assets, such as real estate, in household portfolios that provide superhedges against inflation; other assets, such as demand deposits, provide no inflation protection at all.[64] Households diversify their portfolios to hedge against inflation surprises. It would be a mere coincidence if the yield on a single asset were to track the changing investment opportunities of households when inflation rates changed rapidly. Even a broad measure of real after-tax portfolio returns is, however, so bedeviled with time trends and measurement problems that one should share the fears about spurious correlation expressed by Howrey and Hymans,[65] even if the "expected" coefficient on after-tax rates of return should happen to turn up in a particular multiple regression. This is all the more advisable if the appropriateness of a coefficient depends on personal judgment and not on any conclusive economic theory.

A robust result of this study is that government saving, corporate saving, and personal saving are highly interdependent and cannot usefully be studied in isolation. In particular, permanent disposable income is not the income concept relevant for explaining personal saving.[66] Rather, two-thirds of corporate saving and an even larger percentage of taxes net of transfers appear to be substituted for personal saving at the margin. A rise in corporate saving and net taxes lowers the ratio of disposable income to the net national product, but personal saving is reduced proportionately much more than disposable income. Thus personal consumption expenditures cannot easily be reduced by redistributing income away from the household sector. If this finding is correct, theories of household

64. However, by economizing such deposits and increasing turnover, their implicit service yield may be raised in response to higher rates of inflation. See Benjamin Klein, "Competitive Interest Payments on Bank Deposits and the Long-Run Demand for Money," *American Economic Review*, vol. 64 (December 1974), pp. 931–49; and Anthony M. Santomero, "The Role of Transaction Costs and Rates of Return on the Demand Deposit Decision," *Journal of Monetary Economics*, vol. 5 (July 1979), pp. 343–64.

65. Howrey and Hymans, "Measurement and Determination," p. 682.

66. This is also implied in ibid., pp. 669–70, 681–84.

behavior need to be refined beyond the assertion that households lift corporate and government veils or that corporate and government saving contribute to households' perception of life-cycle resource availability. Until they are so refined, the possibility remains that the statistical offset between corporate saving and taxes on the one hand and personal saving on the other is not behavioral but fronting for something else.

If the government's ability to stimulate personal consumption through tax-transfer measures is as limited as the foregoing evidence suggests, its power to contribute to recovery through conventional fiscal means, such as across-the-board tax changes, should not be exaggerated.[67] While higher government purchases would stimulate aggregate demand, the difficulties of varying government expenditures in a timely fashion for countercyclical purposes are well known. Furthermore, the tax net of transfer rates has changed appreciably only within but not between cycles. The policy drama that has surrounded successive tax debates since at least 1964 should not be allowed to obscure the stability of the fiscal policy rule that has been followed implicitly since the end of the Korean War.

Adherence to the rule appears to have contributed to the net private saving rate changing fairly little across cycles to date. This outcome could change if a different fiscal policy were followed persistently in the future. Whether or not a particular component of the national saving rate, or any grouping of the components, remains approximately constant depends heavily on whether expectations regarding traditional fiscal policies can be broken. There is no economic law that says they should not be.

Appendix A: Data Definitions and Notation

National Income and Product Account Variables

CCA   Capital consumption adjustment divided by net national product (*NNP*)
GS   Government saving (surplus or deficit) divided by *NNP*
IVA   Inventory valuation adjustment divided by *NNP*

67. Even though agreeing with Tanner, "Fiscal Policy," p. 319, in this respect, one should realize that tax reductions can stimulate aggregate demand even if they have little or no initial effect on national saving. A rise in the rate of the investment tax credit or any other tax change that affects spending incentives via substitution effects at the margin may increase aggregate demand. The point here is only that income effects alone are unlikely to have much impact and that substitution effects must be aimed at in devising an effective tax reduction (or tax increase) program. In view of the political attraction of voting only for balanced or across-the-board tax cuts, the chances of activating substitution effects are slim unless the conventional pattern can be broken by instituting differential tax changes.

NNS	Net national saving divided by *NNP*
NPS	Net private saving divided by *NNP*
PERS	Personal saving divided by *NNP*
REA	Undistributed profits of corporations with *IVAC* and *CCAC,* divided by *NNP*
RW	Net retained earnings originating in the rest of the world, divided by *NNP*
SD	Statistical discrepancy divided by *NNP*
T	Corporate profits tax liability divided by corporate profits before tax
TAX	Total government receipts, excluding federal grants-in-aid to state and local governments, divided by *NNP*
TRANS	Total government expenditures net of federal grants-in-aid to state and local governments minus government purchases of goods and services and minus federal government transfer and interest payments to foreigners, all divided by *NNP*
TXTR	The difference between *TAX* and *TRANS*, *TAX* − *TRANS*
YD	Disposable personal income

National Income and Product Account Suffixes

C	Corporations
FC	Financial corporations
NFC	Nonfinancial corporations
72	Variables expressed in 1972 dollars
mn	Numbers indicating that variables are entered as the difference of their level lagged *m* and *n* quarters

Constructed Variables

AN	Fiscal anomalies associated with underbudgeted defense expenditures during the buildup phase of the Vietnam War and with the rebates of 1974 taxes paid in 1975:2, both divided by *NNP,* as explained in the section on government saving
CDUR	Expenditures on consumer durables, *CD,* divided by *NNP,* minus the average level of this expenditure rate over 16 preceding quarters,

$$\sum_{i=1}^{16} (CD/NNP)_{-i}/16$$

DI	The rate of change in successive quarterly values of the GNP deflator, entered as a fraction

DICPIA   The change in the annual rate of inflation measured by the consumer price index

DICPIQ   The quarterly rate of change in the consumer price index, $(CPI - CPI_{-1})/CPI_{-1}$, minus that same rate of change one quarter earlier, $(CPI_{-1} - CPI_{-2})/CPI_{-2}$, yields the change in the quarterly rate of inflation

GAP   Equals 1 minus the ratio of actual GNP in 1972 dollars to the estimate by Data Resources, Incorporated, of potential output, $GNPK72$, or $1 - GNP72/GNPK72$.

ICPIA   The annual percentage rate of inflation measured by the consumer price index

LNNP72   The logarithm of NNP in 1972 dollars

PI−EPI   The difference between the actual and the officially forecast annualized quarterly rates of change in the GNP deflator, as explained in the section on government saving. Inflation rates are expressed as fractions of the GNP deflator rather than in percent

T   Time dummy, which equals 1 in 1953 and grows by increments of 1 each year thereafter (appendix B)

$U_{-2} - U_{-4}$ The difference between the total unemployment rate from the household survey lagged 2 and 4 quarters. Unemployment rates are expressed as fractions of the labor force rather than in percent and are quarterly averages of monthly rates

Estimated Variables

CR   Rate of nominal capital gains on corporate equities, derived in appendix B

FS   Fiscal surprise variable estimated in the section on government saving as the difference between the actual government surplus and the normal regression-predicted surplus, divided by NNP. The estimates of 100 times the fiscal surprise variable are given in table 9 (in percent of *NNP*)

NW/YD   The cyclically adjusted ratio of net worth to disposable personal income, from column 7 of table 10 (see appendix B)

NSW/YD   The cyclically adjusted ratio of net social insurance wealth to disposable income, from column 8 of table 10 (see appendix B)

RRAT	The smoothed after-tax real rate of return on net worth (*NW*), from column 10 of table 11 (see appendix B), entered as a fraction
RRFS	The smoothed after-tax real rate of return on net worth (*NW*) constructed with the Feldstein-Summers estimates of the expected inflation rate, from column 11 of table 11 (see appendix B), entered as a fraction
SUMNW	The sum of *NW/YD* and *NSW/YD*
u_{-1}	The lagged systematic error term used in the first-order serial correlation adjustment when $u = \rho u_{-1} + \epsilon$ and ϵ is the random error term

Table 9. Estimates of the Fiscal Surprise Variable, Quarterly[a]

	Quarter			
Year	1	2	3	4
1955	−0.166	0.299	−0.110	0.440
1956	0.910	0.957	1.024	1.269
1957	0.808	0.694	0.509	0.413
1958	−0.310	−1.095	−1.478	−0.965
1959	0.024	0.073	0.470	0.602
1960	2.156	2.223	1.793	1.688
1961	1.267	0.955	1.170	0.805
1962	−0.373	−0.198	−0.043	0.099
1963	0.674	1.500	1.036	0.630
1964	−0.027	−0.774	0.056	0.531
1965	0.738	0.521	−1.044	−1.473
1966	−1.316	−1.170	−1.566	−2.122
1967	−2.743	−2.755	−2.786	−2.532
1968	−2.241	−2.635	−1.441	−1.202
1969	0.275	0.477	0.159	0.714
1970	0.618	−0.323	−0.367	−0.543
1971	−0.851	−1.061	−0.760	−0.702
1972	−0.193	0.038	0.009	−0.790
1973	−0.552	−0.372	−0.507	−0.579
1974	0.345	0.388	0.994	0.467
1975	−0.233	−3.284	−0.691	−0.869
1976	−0.952	−0.489	−0.559	−0.306
1977	0.846	0.285	−0.651	−1.039
1978	−0.429	0.335	0.392	0.404

a. Entries are 100 times the fiscal surprise ratio, *FS*.

Appendix B: Derivation of Estimates

This appendix presents the sources and methods used to derive the time series that were developed especially for this study.

Household Net Worth and Social Insurance Wealth

The concept of household net worth used in this study is broader than many but narrower than some.[68] It includes the market value of land other than farmland and the replacement cost of nonfarm structures, as well as the market value of corporate equities. All other financial assets are entered at face value from the flow-of-funds tabulations, so that the resulting estimate of net worth does not depend directly on interest rates. The concept excludes the replacement cost of the net stock of consumer durables (now available from the Bureau of Economic Analysis) and consumer and installment credit attributed to such assets (around 27 percent of the total financial liabilities of the household sector and 30 percent of the monetary interest paid by it). This was done to maintain consistency with the national income and product accounts and to avoid having to impute a net rate of return on these leveraged consumer assets. To eliminate the cyclical element, the ratio of net worth to disposable income was multiplied by a cyclical adjustment factor derived from a regression of the log of the net worth ratio on the log of the ratio of actual to potential GNP in 1972 dollars.[69] The adjusted ratios are shown in table 10, column 7.

Net social insurance wealth includes not only the net assets of the old

68. For example, only a stock price index is used to represent wealth in Robert E. Hall, "Stochastic Implications of the Life Cycle–Permanent Income Hypothesis: Theory and Evidence," *Journal of Political Economy,* vol. 86 (December 1978), p. 984. Only net stocks of fixed, nonresidential business capital (valued at the national income accounts estimate of replacement cost and not at market) and nongovernmental residential housing are added to form the wealth measure used in Tanner, "Fiscal Policy." On the other hand, consumer durables and owners' equity in unincorporated farms and businesses are included in the household net worth concept used in the MIT-Penn-SSRC model. For a detailed discussion, see David F. Seiders, *Household Sector Economic Accounts,* Staff Paper 83 (Board of Governors of the Federal Reserve System, 1974). Since changes in owners' equity in unincorporated enterprises affect only a small group of households with a high propensity to save accrued capital gains, this component was omitted from the estimate of net worth that is supposed to affect personal consumption expenditures and saving.

69. Cyclical adjustment is called for because household saving is unlikely to be affected by variations in the net worth ratio that are expected to be transitory. The

age and survivors insurance (OASI) trust fund,[70] but also the unfunded liabilities of civil service, military, and state and local government pension and retirement funds and of the pension plans of private corporations.[71] Although the effect of the business cycle on social security wealth is weak, the ratio of net social insurance wealth to disposable income was also adjusted by a cyclical factor.[72] The adjusted ratios are shown in table 10, column 8.

---

regression for 1955:1 through 1979:1 is:

$$\Delta \ln (NW/YD) = 0.003 + 1.130 \, \Delta \ln (GNP72/GNPK72).$$
$$(0.34) \quad (3.84)$$

$\bar{R}^2 = 0.36$; standard error $= 0.043$; Durbin-Watson $= 1.43$

Since the constant term is very small and statistically insignificant, time trends may be presumed to be absent and the adjustment factor applied to NW/YD was taken to be $(GNP72/GNPK72)^{-1.13}$. The Δ indicates quarterly change.

70. Data through 1974 were obtained by converting to current dollars the estimates of Alicia H. Munnell, "The Future of the U.S. Pension System," in Colin D. Campbell, ed., *Financing Social Security* (American Enterprise Institute for Public Policy Research, 1979), pp. 244–47. Munnell's social security wealth series was extrapolated in constant 1972 dollars for the four years beyond 1974 at a decelerating rate to reflect the Social Security Act Amendments of 1977 and 1978. The values assumed were $1.6 billion, $1.65 billion, $1.7 billion, and $1.7 billion (1972 dollars). After reflating by the GNP deflator, the yearly estimates were blown up as explained in the next footnote.

71. For 1975 the unfunded liabilities of civil service, military, and state-local plans are estimated to amount to $630 billion; Alicia H. Munnell, "Pensions for Public Employees," paper prepared for the Joint Committee on Public Pensions (National Planning Association, August 1978), p. 135. For the same year, the unfunded liabilities of private uninsured pension plans were estimated as $75 billion; Raymond W. Goldsmith, "The National Balance Sheet of the United States, 1953–75," draft, March 1978, p. 148. The sum of $705 billion is 34.66 percent of the $2,034 billion of net OASI wealth estimated for the year 1975 in current dollars. Similarly, Goldsmith (p. 150) estimates that the sum of the items other than OASI was $40 billion in 1953. This is 20 percent of the OASI wealth of $200 billion estimated for 1953. I therefore blew up the (extrapolated) OASI wealth estimate in current dollars by multiplying the OASI figures by 1.2 in 1953, 1.26 in 1965 (with increments to 1965 of 0.005 per year), 1.33 in 1972 (increments of 0.01 per year), 1.335 in 1973, 1.34 in 1974, 1.3466 in 1975, and 1.35 thereafter. The estimate of net social insurance wealth at the end of 1978 was taken to be 1.05 of the estimate of $3,491 billion for the year 1978 derived in this fashion. For all earlier years, the year-end estimates in column 6 of table 10 are averages of the annual estimates for adjoining years.

72. The adjustment factor $(GNP72/GNPK72)^{0.236}$ applied to NSW/YD was derived from the following regression for the period 1958:1 through 1979:1:

$$\Delta \ln (NSW/YD) = 0.036 - 0.236 \, \Delta \ln (GNP72/GNPK72).$$
$$(6.71) \; (-1.30)$$

$\bar{R}^2 = 0.03$; standard error $= 0.027$; Durbin-Watson $= 0.42$

Table 10. Assets, Liabilities, and Net Worth of Households, 1954–78
Billions of dollars unless otherwise specified

End of year	Nonfarm Land (1)	Nonfarm Structures (2)	Total financial assets (3)	Financial liabilities (4)	Net worth (NW) (5)	Net social insurance wealth (NSW) (6)	Cyclically adjusted ratios NW/YD (7)	Cyclically adjusted ratios NSW/YD (8)
1953	64.9	187.3	535.1	78.5	708.8	241	...	...
1954	72.6	202.0	628.5	89.7	813.4	267	3.087	1.009
1955	84.9	222.2	708.5	103.9	911.7	305	3.213	1.072
1956	97.4	238.9	754.6	116.9	974.0	339	3.268	1.119
1957	108.9	255.1	742.2	126.9	979.3	368	3.417	1.166
1958	121.9	275.4	878.8	139.8	1,136.3	399	3.590	1.200
1959	140.0	296.9	946.7	155.7	1,227.9	433	3.803	1.244
1960	148.6	311.7	973.9	169.7	1,264.5	465	3.854	1.292
1961	161.8	323.6	1,118.0	186.0	1,417.4	524	3.904	1.377
1962	172.8	336.2	1,093.5	202.4	1,400.1	590	3.705	1.482
1963	184.7	351.9	1,223.7	223.4	1,536.9	659	3.716	1.553
1964	197.9	367.8	1,335.1	244.8	1,656.0	748	3.680	1.640

Year	Column 1	Column 2	Column 3	Column 4	Column 5	Column 6	Column 7	Column 8
1965	212.7	382.2	266.4	1,470.6	1,799.1	848	3.515	1.710
1966	224.4	395.9	283.5	1,462.3	1,799.1	958	3.338	1.806
1967	237.7	429.5	304.5	1,688.6	2,051.3	1,078	3.533	1.890
1968	250.8	489.8	330.9	1,914.2	2,323.9	1,211	3.736	1.999
1969	274.7	536.2	352.3	1,862.8	2,321.4	1,361	3.569	2.045
1970	280.1	562.5	370.5	1,926.9	2,399.0	1,531	3.435	2.099
1971	306.9	599.3	406.7	2,153.9	2,653.4	1,726	3.524	2.214
1972	342.6	669.2	459.6	2,389.0	2,941.2	1,999	3.339	2.315
1973	395.7	772.9	512.7	2,300.9	2,956.8	2,293	3.172	2.406
1974	446.2	871.2	551.3	2,198.2	2,964.3	2,580	3.217	2.461
1975	494.1	956.4	593.1	2,547.4	3,404.8	2,859	3.144	2.449
1976	556.6	1,077.4	666.8	2,928.9	3,896.1	3,114	3.283	2.469
1977	647.5	1,253.4	776.9	3,097.6	4,221.6	3,370	3.168	2.400
1978	748.3	1,448.6	869.8	3,374.3	4,701.4	3,666	3.087	2.332

Sources: Column 1, Raymond W. Goldsmith, "The National Balance Sheet of the United States, 1953–75," draft (March 1978). Nonfarm land values are estimated after 1975 by assuming that the ratio of land value to the value of structures remains constant at 51.66 percent. Column 2, the net stock of nonfarm residential capital, current cost valuation, was supplied by the Bureau of Economic Analysis. Columns 3 and 4, Federal Reserve Board of Governors, flow-of-funds accounts for households, personal trusts, and nonprofit organizations; for column 4, total liabilities of the household sector minus installment consumer credit and other consumer credit outstanding. Column 5, sum of columns 1, 2, and 3 minus column 4. Column 6, see the text. Columns 7 and 8, columns 5 and 6 divided by disposable personal income in the first quarter of the succeeding year, adjusted as explained in the text.

Rates of Return

Rates of return were calculated only for household net worth because, with nearly universal coverage, the individual has little opportunity to vary the size of his social security wealth. The calculation of the real after-tax rates of return involved two steps. First, nominal returns were obtained for the various components of net worth and these returns were taxed if they were subject to present or future taxes. Second, the resulting after-tax nominal rates of return were converted to real rates by the use of alternative estimates of expected inflation rates and then smoothed.

The returns on the assets enumerated in table 10 include all monetary and imputed interest and rental income, dividends, and accrued capital gains received by households and are net of depreciation with capital consumption adjustment. Monetary interest paid by households, except for the 30 percent assumed to be paid on consumer and installment credit, was subtracted. The before-tax figures were converted to after-tax amounts by estimating marginal tax rates on each of four components of income from capital: (1) imputed incomes, (2) net monetary incomes, (3) accrued capital gains on corporate equities, and (4) accrued capital gains on land and structures. The method was as follows:[73]

1. The marginal federal tax rate on all imputed incomes was assumed to be zero.

2. Marginal federal tax rates on monetary household incomes from capital were estimated by assigning the statutory marginal tax rate applicable to the taxable income by which the bottom 85 percent of total federal income taxes had been generated. These rates can be obtained for the years 1961 through 1975 from the Internal Revenue Service, *Statistics of Income, Individual Income Tax Returns*.[74] They range from a low of 30.5 percent in 1964 to a high of 39 percent in 1974 during that time.[75] These

73. The derivation and intended meaning of the marginal tax rate used to obtain after-tax rates of return are not always explained in the literature. Boskin, for instance, merely states that he used the average marginal tax rate on interest income from *Statistics of Income*. See Michael J. Boskin, "Taxation, Saving, and the Rate of Interest," *Journal of Political Economy*, vol. 86 (April 1978), p. S11.

74. To identify the sources, see appendix table B-6 of the successive editions of Joseph A. Pechman, *Federal Tax Policy* (Brookings Institution, 1966; rev. edition, 1971; and 3d edition, 1977).

75. Under 1976 law the average marginal federal income tax rates on the dividend and interest receipts of individuals have been estimated as 39 percent and 35 percent, respectively, in Martin Feldstein and Lawrence Summers, "Inflation and the

rates are meant to represent the average marginal federal income tax rate, assuming that an additional dollar of monetary income from capital is not associated with an increase in deductions. Taken literally, this means not only that borrowing is not increased or that debt–equity ratios decline, but also that the entire additional dollar is saved since the deduction for state sales taxes may otherwise rise.[76]

To take account of income taxes levied by lower jurisdictions, the federal rates were blown up by the factor $1 + (1 - f)s$, where f is the federal income tax rate and s is the ratio of state and local taxes to federal taxes. This procedure added one percentage point to the federal rates each year from 1955 through 1961, two points in 1962–68, three points in 1969–71, and four points thereafter. The resulting estimates are in column 3 of table 11.

3. The undiscounted marginal income tax rate on capital gains was taken to be one-half of the marginal rates in column 3 of table 11 plus one-tenth of the maximum tax rate on capital gains, with the tax on tax preference items ignored. The expected maximum rate at the time of realization was assumed to have increased from 25 percent to 35 percent in 1969, although the actual maximum was raised in three steps from 1968 to 1971. Furthermore, the expected maximum was assumed to have dropped to 30 percent in 1978, although a lower maximum (equal to 28 percent) was applied to the last two months of that year when the legislation finally emerged. Changes in loss offset provisions and in the minimum holding period required to qualify for long-term capital gains treatment were also ignored.

Since accrued capital gains are taxed only when realized, the capital gains rates were adjusted to allow for the tax deferral. This was done by

---

Taxation of Capital Income in the Corporate Sector," National Bureau of Economic Research Working Paper 312 (NBER, January 1979), pp. 14 and 21. My assumed federal income tax rate of 36 percent for all monetary incomes from capital combined is consistent with their estimate for 1976. Bradford has estimated total federal taxes on the returns to saving of 36 percent for the year 1977:4–1978:3. See Bradford, "Economics of Tax Policy Toward Saving."

76. Marginal tax rates on taxable income rather than on adjusted gross income or a broader income concept are also implicit in the estimates by Feldstein and Summers, "Inflation and the Taxation of Capital Income," and by Colin Wright, "Saving and the Rate of Interest," in Arnold C. Harberger and Martin J. Bailey, eds., *The Taxation of Income from Capital* (Brookings Institution, 1969), p. 300. An updated version of the latter series was used by Howrey and Hymans, "Measurement and Determination," p. 673.

Table 11. Derivation of After-Tax Rates of Return on Net Worth, 1955–78
Billions of dollars unless otherwise specified

	Income from capital		Marginal income tax rate (percent)	After-tax			Expected inflation rate (percent)	After-tax rates of return (percent)			
Year	Imputed (1)	Net monetary (2)	(3)	Net monetary (4)	Capital gains (5)	Total return (6)	(7)	Nominal (8)	Real (9)	Real smoothed (10)	Alternative to col. 10 (11)
1955	15.3	18.0	35.0	11.7	37.9	64.9	0.40	7.98	7.55	6.08	3.80
1956	16.7	18.9	35.0	12.3	31.8	60.8	0.44	6.67	6.20	6.82	4.72
1957	18.3	20.3	35.0	13.2	−10.3	21.2	0.60	2.18	1.57	5.77	3.91
1958	19.8	20.9	35.0	13.6	85.6	119.0	0.82	12.15	11.24	4.68	3.10
1959	21.9	22.0	37.0	13.9	3.0	38.8	1.09	3.41	2.29	4.95	3.77
1960	24.3	22.9	37.0	14.4	4.7	43.4	1.39	3.53	2.11	4.12	3.41
1961	25.9	23.6	37.0	14.9	77.5	118.3	1.70	9.36	7.53	2.96	2.69
1962	28.0	25.7	36.0	16.4	−52.4	−8.0	2.04	−0.56	−2.55	3.16	3.34
1963	30.2	27.7	36.0	17.7	63.3	111.2	2.38	7.94	5.43	3.65	4.29
1964	32.1	30.5	32.5	20.6	41.2	93.9	2.73	6.11	3.29	1.97	2.93
1965	35.0	34.1	34.0	22.5	71.3	128.8	3.09	7.78	4.55	4.02	5.32
1966	38.5	36.1	34.0	23.8	−16.8	45.5	3.45	2.53	−0.89	4.62	6.18
1967	41.3	38.1	37.0	24.0	147.0	212.3	3.81	11.80	7.70	3.50	5.12
1968	43.4	41.4	38.0	25.7	197.3	266.4	4.18	12.99	8.46	2.47	4.14
1969	47.2	43.7	39.0	26.7	−24.8	49.1	4.55	2.11	−2.33	2.91	4.62

Year	(1)	(2)	(3)	(4)	(5)	(6)	(7)	(8)	(9)	(10)	(11)
1970	51.1	49.0	38.0	30.4	100.4	18.9	4.32	4.92	-0.57	1.54	3.33
1971	55.7	51.0	35.0	33.2	159.0	70.1	6.63	5.29	1.27	-0.68	1.04
1972	61.4	53.3	39.0	32.5	174.1	80.2	6.56	5.66	0.85	-0.55	0.60
1973	66.2	60.6	40.0	36.4	96.1	-6.5	3.27	6.03	-2.60	0.21	1.36
1974	76.3	72.5	43.0	41.3	135.2	17.6	4.57	6.40	-1.72	0.32	1.52
1975	86.7	77.0	42.0	44.7	304.0	172.6	10.26	6.77	3.27	0.05	1.05
1976	93.1	86.7	40.0	52.0	309.3	164.2	9.08	7.14	1.81	0.71	1.55
1977	105.0	96.0	42.0	55.7	272.0	111.3	6.98	7.51	-0.49	1.20	2.50
1978	117.5	105.9	43.0	60.4	364.6	186.7	8.64	7.88	0.70	0.68	1.84

Sources: Column 1, sum of the imputed interest and rental incomes reported in the national income accounts, table 8.3, lines 67, 68, and 71, and table 8.2, line 43, in *Survey of Current Business*. Column 2, sum of monetary interest, rental income, and dividends, table 8.2, line 26, table 8.3, line 33, and table 2.1 *minus* 70 percent of monetary interest paid, table 8.3, line 57. (The net interest implicit in the line items entering into columns 1 and 2 is equal to personal interest income in table 2.1 minus imputed net interest paid by farms to persons; table 8.3, line 78.) Column 3, see the text. Column 4, $(1 - t)$ times the entries in column 2, where t is the tax rate in column 3. Column 5, sum of the entries in columns 5 and 9 of table 12 below. Column 6, sum of the entries in columns 1, 4, and 5. Column 7, see the text. Column 8, ratio of the entries in column 6 to the estimates of net worth in column 5 of table 10 above at the end of the preceding year. Column 9, derived from column 8 using column 7. Column 10, values obtained from column 9 with a five-year moving average process centered at the year shown. To construct such averages for the beginning and ending years of the series, the after-tax real rate of return was assumed to be 7.55 percent in 1953 and 1954 (the same as in 1955) and 0.70 in 1979 and 1980 (the same as in 1978). Column 11, derived from column 8 using other estimates (by Martin Feldstein and Lawrence Summers, "Inflation, Tax Rules, and the Long-Term Interest Rate," *BPEA, 1:1978*, p. 87) of the predicted inflation rate (augmented by assuming 6 percent for 1977 and 7 percent for 1978) and taking five-year centered moving averages of the resulting real rate-of-return estimates (augmented by 5.14 percent in 1953 and 1954, the same annual rate as in 1955, and by 1.53 percent in 1979 and 1980, the same as in 1978).

assuming a holding period of five years for corporate equities.[77] Tax benefits from deferral were estimated by assuming that nominal capital gains, once generated, appreciate at the nominal interest and discount rate, and that all gains remaining after tax are reinvested and the principal that originally produced the capital gain is withdrawn.[78]

4. The effective capital gains tax rate on land and structures is obtained in exactly the same way, by using a holding period of twenty years and the average annual yield on Treasury securities at a constant twenty-year maturity for the discount rate. The lengthening of the holding period is to take account of rollover provisions for capital gains on the principal owner-occupied residence. The (recently broadened) one-time dollar exclusions allowed on the realization of capital gains by the elderly are ignored in this calculation. Even so, the rates shown in column 8 of table 12 are quite low and show no tendency to rise over time.

One may object to adding the different types of returns if they entail

---

77. Longer holding periods are suggested in Martin J. Bailey, "Capital Gains and Income Taxation," in Harberger and Bailey, eds., *Taxation of Income from Capital,* pp. 11–49. However, the actual average holding period need not be equal to the expected average holding period anticipated at time of purchase. Furthermore, the rate of turnover may be a function of the rate and dispersion of capital gains and losses because of tax loss and loss offset considerations as well as of the statutory tax rates and estate plans that apply. It has been estimated that limiting the tax rate on realized gains to 25 percent would cause an almost threefold increase in realization in the first year. See Martin Feldstein, Joel Slemrod, and Shlomo Yitzhaki, "The Effects of Taxation on the Selling of Corporate Stock and the Realization of Capital Gains," *Quarterly Journal of Economics,* vol. 94 (June 1980), pp. 777–91. However, no reliable way of endogenizing the average holding period has yet been invented, although the work by Joseph Minarik in this volume moves us closer in this direction.

78. The problem is to determine the benefit of having the total gains of $CG(1 + r)^n$, realized after n years, taxed only at the end of the holding period at the rate t. Tax proceeds are then $tCG(1 + r)^n$. This amount can be compared to the future value of the capital gains taxes paid over n years if accrued capital gains, consisting of the base amount CG and appreciation at the annual rate, r, of the after-tax amount remaining, were taxed each year. The sum of the alternative tax payments, brought forward to year n for comparability, is:

$$tCG(1 + r)^n + tr(1 - t)CG\{(1 + r)^{n-1} + [1 + (1 - t)r](1 + r)^{n-2} + [1 + (1 - t)r]^2(1 + r)^{n-3} \dots\}.$$

When the latter amount is divided by the former and the resulting factor is applied to t, the benefits from the tax deferral reduce the statutory capital gains tax rate, t, to the rate t_e, where $t_e = t^2/[t + (1 -t)A]$, and $A = 1 - \{[1 + (1 - t)r]/(1 + r)\}^n$. Setting n equal to 5 and using the average annual market yield on three- to five-year government securities for r gives the effective capital gains tax rates on corporate equities shown in column 4 of table 12.

different degrees of fundamental risk and leverage risk. However, in the housing sector, leverage risks on net returns do not appear to have risen (the ratio of home and other mortgage obligations of the household sector to the replacement cost of the net stock of residential capital and land has remained between 30 and 35 percent). The degree of leverage of net worth other than real estate appears to have risen over time, but this is due largely to the poor performance of corporate equities in recent years. Hence comparability of the nominal rates of return on total net worth does not seem to have suffered because of changes in leverage.

However, the relative importance of dividends in net monetary returns has fallen and that of net monetary interest received has risen. The contribution of nominal capital gains has been unstable, with capital gains on land and structures overtaking capital gains on corporate equities as time progressed. Because corporate stocks are riskier than bonds and land and structures are probably less risky than corporate stocks, the net change in the aggregate portfolio risk exposure may be small.[79]

Since the rates of return are conceptually comparable over time, an average or smoothing process over adjoining years can be used to estimate expected rates of return. However, before doing this, an adjustment was made to take account of the unusual behavior of the stock market under rising inflation. This adjustment is called for if investment characteristics that they did not actually possess were attributed to common equities. No one expects bonds to be a hedge against unanticipated increases in the rate of inflation and, for reasons explained in the chapter by Frank de Leeuw and Larry Ozanne in this book, real estate may be expected to be a superhedge. Thus households, aware of inflation hazards, can arrange their portfolios to diversify risks. However, if they attribute hedge characteristics to an asset and it does not have such characteristics, they will be making a systematic error that may cause the actual rate of return to differ from the expected rate for an extended period.

---

79. Still, it is possible that rising inflation rates have made most types of nominal returns on capital more risky over time and have increased the riskiness of all investments, thereby raising the real internal rates of return applied to future earnings. See Malkiel, "Capital Formation Problem"; Franco Modigliani and Richard A. Cohn, "Inflation, Rational Valuation and the Market," *Financial Analysts Journal*, vol. 35 (March–April 1979), pp. 24–44; William Fellner, "American Household Wealth in an Inflationary Period," in Fellner, ed., *Contemporary Economic Problems, 1979* (American Enterprise Institute for Public Policy Research, 1979), pp. 153–89; and the chapters by Roger Gordon and Burton Malkiel and Roger Brinner and Stephen Brooks in this volume.

Table 12. Derivation of After-Tax Capital Gains on Corporate Equities and Nonfarm Real Estate, 1954–78
Billions of dollars unless otherwise specified

| | Corporate equities | | | | | Nonfarm real estate | | | |
| | Before-tax gains (unadjusted) (1) | Windfall gains (−) or losses (2) | Marginal statutory tax rate (percent) (3) | Effective tax rate (percent) (4) | After-tax adjusted gains (5) | Before-tax gains | | Effective tax rate (percent) (8) | Total after-tax gains (9) |
Year						Land (6)	Structures (7)		
1954	71.9	...	...	...	...	0.9	−0.1	...	...
1955	50.1	−6.8	20.0	18.2	35.4	1.0	1.9	14.0	2.5
1956	16.9	20.2	20.0	17.9	30.4	1.2	0.4	13.7	1.4
1957	−39.3	23.5	20.0	17.6	−13.0	1.4	1.7	13.2	2.7
1958	104.5	−7.6	20.0	18.0	79.4	1.6	5.5	13.3	6.2
1959	28.0	−28.4	21.0	18.1	−0.3	1.7	2.1	13.3	3.3
1960	−6.1	12.2	21.0	18.3	5.0	2.0	−2.3	13.4	−0.3
1961	105.7	−7.8	21.0	18.5	79.8	2.1	−4.8	13.5	−2.3
1962	−61.3	1.6	20.5	18.1	−48.9	2.3	−6.3	13.1	−3.5
1963	79.4	1.4	20.5	18.0	66.3	2.5	−6.0	13.0	−3.0
1964	51.0	1.6	18.8	16.2	44.1	2.6	−5.9	11.7	−2.9

	1	2	3	4	5	6	7	8	9
1965	73.1	7.7	19.5	16.8	67.2	11.7	−7.0	12.1	4.1
1966	−59.0	30.8	19.5	16.3	−23.6	12.6	−4.9	11.6	6.8
1967	149.7	−1.8	21.0	17.7	121.7	13.3	15.6	12.5	25.3
1968	146.4	38.7	21.5	17.9	152.0	14.0	37.7	12.4	45.3
1969	−108.3	38.3	23.0	18.5	−57.1	14.8	22.2	12.7	32.3
1970	−14.9	16.2	22.5	17.9	1.1	16.2	4.0	12.0	17.8
1971	110.1	−45.9	21.0	17.3	53.1	16.6	2.6	11.6	17.0
1972	85.9	−32.4	23.0	19.0	43.3	18.1	24.3	13.0	36.9
1973	−194.8	103.9	23.5	19.0	−73.6	20.2	56.5	12.5	67.1
1974	−205.6	131.1	25.0	19.8	−59.7	23.4	65.4	12.9	77.3
1975	158.5	−35.8	24.5	19.5	98.8	26.4	57.9	12.5	73.8
1976	170.7	−86.2	23.5	18.9	68.5	29.2	79.6	12.0	95.7
1977	−44.2	21.9	24.5	19.8	−17.9	32.9	115.3	12.8	129.2
1978	18.5	36.1	24.5	19.2	44.1	38.3	124.3	12.3	142.6

Sources: Column 1, year-end to year-end increase in the value of corporate equities outstanding held by households, personal trusts, and nonprofit organizations, minus net purchase of such equities by the same sector during the year; Federal Reserve Board of Governors, Flow-of-Funds Accounts. Column 2, one-half of rates in column 3 of table 11 above plus 0.1 of maximum rate expected on capital gains (35 percent after 1968, 30 percent after 1977). Column 4, see the text. Column 5, $(1 - t)$ percent of sum of entries in columns 1 and 2, where t is the rate in column 4. Column 6, 1.43 percent of land value for households at end of preceding year until 1965 and 5.91 percent from 1965 on; derived from Goldsmith, "National Balance Sheet, 1953–75," tables 31, 33, and 35. Column 7, change in net stock of residential capital, nonfarm, current cost valuation (supplied by the Bureau of Economic Analysis) minus net investment in the same type of capital. Column 8, see the text. Column 9, $(1 - t)$ percent of the sum of entries in columns 6 and 7, where t is the rate in column 8.

Adjustment for Windfall Losses on Corporate Equities

As Phillip Cagan and Robert Lipsey have explained, the standard theory of inflation, at least up to the mid-1960s, held that stocks are a hedge against inflation.[80] In fact, they may even be a superhedge during the transitional adjustment to higher rates of inflation as demand shifts away from monetary assets. This view has clearly not been corroborated by the behavior of stock prices since the mid-1960s.[81]

Although some attempts have been made to explain this phenomenon with the benefit of hindsight,[82] it seemed absurd to assume that the performance of the stock market since the late 1960s has lived up to expectations. Unless the large windfall losses during this period were added to the actual returns, the estimates of expected rates of return would be biased downward to an increasing extent in recent years.

To measure the bias, the annual rate of nominal capital gains on corporate equities from 1955 through 1978[83] was regressed on the prospective change in the potential output gap from the current year[84] and on the change in the annual rate of inflation, measured by the consumer price index, from the preceding to the current year. The regression was:

$$CR = 0.0882 - 4.0201 \, \Delta(1 - GNP72/GNPK72) - 3.8824 \, DICPIA.$$
$$(3.90) \quad (-2.58) \quad\quad\quad\quad\quad\quad\quad (-1.98)$$
$$\bar{R}^2 = 0.62; \text{ standard error} = 0.1088; \text{ Durbin-Watson} = 1.85$$

This equation was solved first for the predicted values of the dependent variable and then with the change in the inflation rate set to zero. An ex-

---

80. Phillip Cagan and Robert E. Lipsey, *The Financial Effects of Inflation,* National Bureau of Economic Research General Series, 103 (Ballinger, 1978), pp. 4–5.

81. In a recent paper, Hendershott attributes part of the decline in share values to the favorable tax treatment of income from owner-occupied housing. Patric H. Hendershott, "The Decline in Aggregate Share Values: Inflation and Taxation of the Returns from Equities and Owner-Occupied Housing," National Bureau of Economic Research Working Paper 370 (NBER, July 1979). See also James W. Wetzler, "Capital Gains and Losses," in Joseph A. Pechman, ed., *Comprehensive Income Taxation* (Brookings Institution, 1977), pp. 115–62; and Harvey S. Rosen, "Housing Decisions and the U.S. Income Tax," *Journal of Public Economics,* vol. 11 (February 1979), pp. 1–24.

82. See, for instance, Martin Feldstein, "Inflation and the Stock Market," National Bureau of Economic Research Working Paper 276 (NBER, August 1978).

83. To obtain the annual rate, the nominal capital gains in column 1 of table 12 were divided by the value of corporate equities at the end of the preceding year.

84. The stock market was allowed to anticipate cyclical events for up to one year, so that the change in the gap from the current to the succeeding year was used to construct this variable. An increase of one percentage point (0.01) in the gap was assumed from 1978 to 1979.

cess of the latter solution over the former indicates capital losses caused by a rise in the rate of inflation; a shortfall signifies gains caused by a decline in inflation. Converting the estimated windfall gain or loss rates back into dollar amounts yields the results shown in column 2 of table 12. The series indicates that only half of the large windfall losses generated by rising rates of inflation in 1973 and 1974 were offset by windfall gains in the following two years before a new string of windfall losses began.

Combining these windfall elements with accrued capital gains and taxing them as shown in table 12 yields the after-tax adjusted capital gains in column 5 of that table. The total return, shown in column 6 of table 11, was obtained by adding imputed and after-tax net monetary income from capital. Dividing by net worth at the end of the preceding year (from table 10) yields the after-tax nominal rate of return in column 8, table 11.

Real Net Rates of Return

To estimate the after-tax real rates of return, the expected inflation rate must be subtracted from the nominal rates of return.[85] I use the rate predicted with a regression on time to approximate the expected rate of inflation. Prediction errors then balance out for the period 1953–78.

The specification used to estimate the expected inflation rate was intended to achieve a number of objectives. Because inflation was high in 1950 and 1951, the expected inflation rate should fall toward the mid-1950s and then rise, first at an increasing and then at a decreasing rate.[86] It is difficult to believe that the expected inflation rate continued to rise at an increasing rate through 1978, since this implies that the inflation rate was not expected to be contained. Furthermore, the double-digit inflation rate of 1974 should come as a rude surprise because it was far above almost all 1973 forecasts.[87]

85. More precisely, if the nominal rate is r and the expected inflation rate is i, the real rate, R, is obtained from the equation: $R = (1 + r)/(1 + i) - 1 = (r - i)/(1 + i)$. Deriving the after-tax real rate of return in this fashion should not be taken to imply any theory of nominal rate determination such as that embodied in the Fisher equation. On this, see Maurice D. Levy and John H. Makin, "Anticipated Inflation and Interest Rates: Further Interpretation of Findings on the Fisher Equation," *American Economic Review*, vol. 68 (December 1978), pp. 801–12.

86. To capture this, the regression was started in 1953, although in table 11 the predicted values are used only from 1955 on.

87. An estimate of about 7 percent for the year-to-year change in the GNP deflator (reported in the *Economic Report of the President, February 1974*, p. 28) is representative of the forecasts made up to the beginning of 1974. However, the mean expected price change over the next twelve months obtained by the University of Michigan Survey Research Center exceeded 10 percent during parts of 1974.

With the use of the year-to-year percentage change in the consumer price index as the dependent variable, a specification along these lines is:

$$ICPIA = a_0 + a_1 T^\delta + a_2 \ln T,$$

where T equals 1 in 1953 and grows by increments of 1 each year thereafter. With preassigned values of δ ranging from 0.2 to 1 and the elimination of a small, statistically insignificant intercept, the preferred equation is:

$$ICPIA = 1.407\ T^{0.75} - 2.553 \ln T.$$
$$(4.89) \qquad (-2.97)$$

$\bar{R}^2 = 0.70$; standard error $= 1.58$; Durbin-Watson $= 1.13$

By taking the first and second derivatives with respect to T, it can be seen that the predicted inflation rate declines until 1955 ($T = 3$), rises at an increasing rate until 1974 ($T = 22$) to a level of 6.4 percent (when the actual rate was 11.0 percent), and subsequently continues to rise at a decreasing rate, reaching 7.9 percent in 1978 (table 11, column 7).

Martin Feldstein and Lawrence Summers's expected inflation rate is a weighted (discounted) average of ten years of quarterly Box-Jenkins inflation forecasts.[88] This rate jumps from 4.3 percent in 1973 to 8.0 percent in 1974 and then back to 5.2 percent in 1975. Although this procedure is undoubtedly correct for deriving expected real rates on long-term bonds, it is not obviously correct for estimating real capital gains on other assets such as real estate. In the case of inflation hedges, it seems reasonable to assume that this year's (smoothed) real rate of return will repeat itself regardless of what the inflation rate may turn out to be next year. Hence the regression estimate of the expected inflation rate was regarded as a suitable measure for converting nominal to real rates of return when capital gains are included in the return.[89] The result is shown in column 9 of table 11.

To eliminate cyclical and other transitory effects, the annual real after-tax rates of return were averaged over five years, centered on the current

88. Feldstein and Summers, "Inflation, Tax Rules, and the Long-Term Interest Rate," p. 87.

89. Howrey and Hymans, "Measurement and Determination," p. 673, use the mean expected price change variable derived from the Survey Research Center (see footnote 87, above) also without extrapolation and discounting as a separate variable to allow for both the effect of a real rate of return on saving and a separate inflation effect.

year. Column 10 of table 11 gives the real after-tax returns using the regression estimate of the expected inflation rates, and column 11 gives the estimates based on the Feldstein-Summers expected inflation rate. Because the proper adjustment for inflation is uncertain, both estimates of the after-tax real rate of return were tried in the regressions of the personal saving rate.[90]

Other Estimates

Although researchers are likely to differ in the choice of deflation procedures and tax rates, the most important differences in alternative series of after-tax real rates of return are likely to arise from disagreement over the selection or construction of the appropriate nominal rate of return. Some researchers have used the rate of return on a single class of assets, such as Moody's Aaa or Baa bond yield, to represent the rate-of-return incentives of households.[91] Since according to most estimates these nominal yields do not appear to rise by more than the expected rate of inflation, the after-tax real rates of return almost invariably decline when inflation rises. As corporate bonds are not a hedge even against expected increases in the rate of inflation on an after-tax basis and other assets are a hedge, bond rates are not a suitable gauge of the changing returns available on diversified household portfolios over time.

If a broader series is used, one should remember that not all series available in the literature are equally suitable for representing the saving incentives of households. The capital gains relevant for households are established in financial and real estate markets; they are not equal to the hypothetical revaluation gains arising from inflation-produced increases in the replacement cost of the stock of capital goods.[92] In fact, one such

90. The correlation between my own and the Feldstein-Summers expected inflation rate is 0.796, after the annual data have been distributed quarterly using an integral curve approximation routine to a quadratic fitted successively to three adjoining annual data points.

91. Recent examples are Boskin, "Taxation," and Howrey and Hymans, "Measurement and Determination."

92. This comment applies equally to wealth estimates used in household behavior functions. Thus Tanner, "Fiscal Policy," uses the official (Bureau of Economic Analysis) estimates of the replacement cost of the net stock of nonresidential business capital and of nongovernmental residential structures to construct his private sector wealth variable as if the ratio of the market value of the financial claims to these assets to their replacement cost (Tobin's q ratio) were necessarily unity.

broad nominal series that has been used in a study of saving[93] has a correlation of almost precisely zero with the nominal rate-of-return series in table 11, though it correlates quite closely with the Aaa and Baa bond series. The last two series are also uncorrelated with the series derived here because nominal rates of return on net worth are not found to rise systematically with inflation over time. Rather, the slow growth of dividends and the growing stagnation of the stock market offset the rise in nominal interest income and in accrued capital gains on land and residences in my broad-based measure. The absence of any correlation between alternative input variables purporting to capture the same rate-of-return effects on saving suggests that care in constructing these variables may be worthwhile.

Comments by Ann F. Friedlaender

Twenty some years ago Denison noted that the private saving ratio has shown a remarkable constancy since 1929. From this Denison's law was formulated, which states that private saving is an invariant fraction of national income. Since private saving is the sum of corporate and personal saving, this constancy of the private saving ratio implies that changes in corporate saving must be precisely offset by changes in personal saving. To explain this, Feldstein has argued that individuals are able to pierce the "corporate veil" and subsume corporate retention in their personal saving decisions. Similarly, the constancy of the private saving ratio also implies that individuals are insensitive to government saving. In explanation, David and Scadding have argued that consumers regard tax-financed government expenditures as belonging to the category of consumption and hence that government consumption is a substitute for private consumption.

Von Furstenberg's paper builds on these arguments and attempts to quantify the full range of interrelationships that may exist between government saving, personal saving, and corporate saving. To this end, he

93. Boskin, "Taxation," includes the nominal rate of return for the private national economy estimated annually by Laurits Christensen and Dale Jorgenson through 1969 among several measures tried. This series appeared in Christensen and Jorgenson, "U.S. Income, Saving, and Wealth, 1929–1969," *Review of Income and Wealth,* series 19 (December 1973), p. 344 (last column). It includes revaluation gains on physical assets rather than nominal capital gains on financial claims to those assets.

estimates functions for the government saving ratio, the corporate saving ratio, and the personal saving ratio. Government saving is postulated to depend on macroeconomic variables such as the GNP gap, changes in the unemployment rate, and inflation, but to be independent of private saving behavior. The corporate saving ratio is postulated to depend on economic activity as expressed through the net national product (*NNP*) and the GNP gap, corporation tax variables, depreciation, and inventory profits. And the personal saving ratio is postulated to depend on the GNP gap, government taxes and transfers, corporate retentions, consumer durables purchases, and unexpected government saving (or dissaving).

Hence von Furstenberg postulates a block recursive system in which the government directly affects corporate saving through taxes and directly affects personal saving through taxes and unexpected taxes or expenditures. The government also indirectly affects personal saving through corporate retentions.

Von Furstenberg's empirical results largely support Feldstein's contention that individuals pierce the corporate veil, but contradict David and Scadding's contention that personal saving decisions are invariant to government saving. Indeed, von Furstenberg finds that increases in taxes have a twofold direct negative effect on personal saving. First, increases in taxes and government saving are viewed as substitutes for personal saving; and second, insofar as increases in taxes lead to an unexpected increase in government saving, consumers respond by consuming more. Countering this, however, is the indirect effect of government saving via corporate retentions. If the increase in government saving results from an increase in corporation taxes, corporate retention will be reduced, leading to an increase in personal saving. Thus the net impact of changes in the government saving rate depends on the direct response of both personal saving and corporate saving to changes in government saving and the indirect response of personal saving to corporate saving.

For example, von Furstenberg's empirical results indicate that a 10 percentage point rise in the corporate profits tax that yielded a 1 percentage point rise in the government tax ratio (taxes/*NNP*) and the government saving ratio will have a direct effect on the corporate saving ratio, reducing it by 0.83 percentage point. Similarly, this change will have a direct effect on the personal saving ratio; the increase in the ratio of taxes to *NNP* leads to a reduction in the personal saving rate of 0.78 percentage point, and the unexpected increase in government saving reduces this rate another 0.11 percentage point. Counteracting this, however, is the indirect effect of the full corporate retentions on personal savings, which gives rise to an increase in the personal saving rate of 0.56 percentage point. The net effect of all of these changes is an actual reduction in the total saving rate of 0.17 percentage point. While von Furstenberg estimates that this is partially offset in subsequent years by increases in corporate saving, the total change in national saving is substantially less than that implied by the initial increase in government saving.

Thus von Furstenberg's results indicate that, although the total national saving rate is relatively constant, its components are not: the corporate saving rate responds to change in government saving, but the personal saving rate responds to changes in the corporate and government saving rates. Consequently, von Furstenberg's paper raises serious questions about the validity of Denison's law.

While I am hardly a believer in Denison's law, I have to admit that I did not find von Furstenberg's analysis entirely convincing. Basically, I wish that he had lavished as much care and thought on the specification of his savings relationships and their underlying behavioral structure as he did on the construction of specific variables. Since I believe that a considerable number of questions can be raised concerning the appropriateness of his specifications, I also believe that his results should be viewed with skepticism.

I now turn to some particulars, taking them in more or less the order in which they were presented in the paper.

1. Von Furstenberg postulates that the government saving rate can be described by a stable reaction function. From this, he infers that consumers view government saving as following an expected behavioral pattern. If, however, the government deviates from its expected behavior in any one period, consumers will react and adjust their saving accordingly. Hence the fiscal surprise variable becomes a determinant of personal saving as well as other variables that I will discuss below.

Since von Furstenberg stresses the importance of the stability of the government's reaction function, it seems useful to raise a few questions about its specification.

1a. A reaction function is obtained from the behavioral response of the government, which is assumed to maximize a specified utility function with respect to its control variables, subject to the reduced form coefficients that relate the relevant endogenous variables in the economy to the exogenous variables. Thus a reaction function is only meaningful if the dependent variable is a government instrument. However, while specific taxes or expenditures may be government instruments, I wonder if it is reasonable to treat the government surplus or deficit as an instrument and then to estimate a reaction function for the government saving rate.

1b. Furthermore, even granting that von Furstenberg's specification of a government reaction function for the saving rate may be appropriate, I find it surprising that this reaction function is stable over the postwar period. Since the reaction function is itself a reduced-form expression that depends on the underlying welfare weights and the reduced-form coefficients of the economy, a constant reaction function implies that the changes in the welfare weights are exactly balanced by changes in the underlying reduced-form coefficients of the economy. While von Furstenberg makes some allowance for this by introducing a variable representing abnormal expenditures into the reaction function, it is not obvious that this is the appropriate way to take changes in the underlying utility function or structures of the economy into account.

1c. Also, there is little reason to believe that the federal government and state and local governments have the same reaction functions. Indeed, von Furstenberg estimates that these two levels of government have substantially different saving functions. If this is correct, however, it seems inappropriate to combine them and treat the combined governments as having a single reaction function. Since the underlying behavior of the two levels of government is probably quite different, it would have been more appropriate to estimate different saving relationships with different arguments for each level of government.

2. In von Furstenberg's treatment of personal and corporate saving, I am troubled by his estimation plan, which postulates that the personal saving rate and the corporate saving rate can each be derived from a basic relationship that ties sectoral consumption to a number of conditioning variables and base variables in a multiplicative fashion. Through appropriate manipulation, von Furstenberg then derives an expression for a sectoral saving rate that is a function of *NNP*, the GNP gap, and a number of variables that are appropriate to each sector. While such a general specification may make it easy to pursue a parallel treatment of corporate and personal saving and to obtain additive saving rates, I do not think that such parallelism is justified. Corporations and individuals save for very different reasons and have very different behavioral responses. It is thus unlikely that the general reduced form postulated by von Furstenberg adequately describes the true saving behavior of either corporations or individuals. Indeed, the significance of the disturbance

term, which von Furstenberg includes to adjust for first-order serial correlation, implies that there may be a large number of missing variables and that the saving functions are misspecified. Instead of von Furstenberg's ad hoc specification of the sectoral savings rates, I would have preferred to see considerably more analysis of the underlying behavioral determinants of corporate and personal saving.

2a. Specifically, with respect to the saving rate of individual corporations, the amount of corporate retentions depends on a complex set of relations dealing with the profitability of the firm, the firm's investment decisions as well as its decision concerning its balance of internal debt, and equity finance. These, in turn, depend on macroeconomic conditions; the return to capital; the tax structure covering personal income, corporate income, and capital gains; tax incentives provided by accelerated depreciation and investment credits; and the capital and debt structure of the firm.

While it is unlikely that any simple reduced-form equation such as that postulated by von Furstenberg could adequately describe this behavioral process, it seems clear that any reduced form that attempted to do so would have to include many more variables than those used by von Furstenberg. Not only does von Furstenberg's speculation suffer from an inappropriate use of a reduced form, but it also suffers from a failure to include variables that influence corporate retention such as tax differentials on dividends and capital gains.

2b. Similarly, although I am no specialist on the behavior of financial corporations, it seems to me that their retention rate cannot be fully explained by a specification that excludes variables reflecting conditions in the money and housing markets. Again, I argue that von Furstenberg's specification fails to take into account the underlying behavioral relationships that explain the saving behavior of financial corporations.

2c. The personal saving rate presents similar problems of specification and modeling. Von Furstenberg assumes that the substitution effects among personal saving, government saving, fiscal surprise, and corporate saving can be captured by a specification that effectively treats them as shift parameters on the basic saving rate. In doing this, he neglects any analysis of the process by which consumers treat government or corporate saving as a substitute for personal saving. But if government saving or corporate saving affects personal saving, how does it do so? What is the behavioral response that lets individuals pierce the corporate or the government veil? In the absence of such an analysis, it is difficult to take von

Furstenberg's results at face value, since it is entirely possible that they are the product of spurious correlation in which personal saving, corporate saving, and government saving are all related to some omitted variables.

Indeed, the savings-investment equilibrium condition almost guarantees that von Furstenberg's regression reflects spurious correlation. In equilibrium, $S + T = I + G$, where S represents private saving, T represents net taxes, I represents investment, and G represents expenditures. By splitting savings into personal saving (Sp) and corporate saving (Sc), solving for personal saving, and dividing everything by NNP, the following relationship is obtained:

$$Sp/NNP = G/NNP + I/NNP - Sc/NNP - T/NNP.$$

The last two expressions enter directly into von Furstenberg's regression, but the first two do not. If, however, the GNP gap, NNP, and consumer durable purchases are thought of as proxies for these variables, von Furstenberg's personal saving equation can be interpreted as an equilibrium condition. In this case, the coefficients of the corporate saving variable and the tax-minus-transfer variable are effectively constrained to be minus one, which is remarkably close to those given by von Furstenberg's results. Of course, von Furstenberg's equation is not precisely equal to the equilibrium condition, but it appears to be sufficiently close to raise the issue of whether he is actually estimating the equilibrium relationship instead of a behavioral relationship.

If true, this might explain why the real rate-of-return variables and the net worth variables could have yielded unsatisfactory results since their correlation with investment or real government expenditure is unclear. To the extent that von Furstenberg's personal saving equation is closer to the savings-investment equilibrium condition than a true behavioral relationship, his results are not surprising. Unfortunately, however, in this case they are not very useful either.

In conclusion then, I must admit that I remain skeptical about Denison's law and the substitution hypothesis concerning the relationship among government saving, corporate saving, and personal saving. Although it is entirely possible that personal saving is a stable function of national income or that individuals treat corporate saving or government saving as a substitute for their own saving, without a coherent theory that would explain such behavior I remain unconvinced by the empirical results. While this is an admittedly difficult subject, I think the time has come to do some analysis and estimation of the underlying structural relationships instead of relying on simplistic reduced-form specifications that tend to obfuscate rather than clarify these relationships.

Comments by Warren E. Weber

This interesting paper has three main purposes: to determine the rule that governs the behavior of the government saving rate; to examine the interrelationships among the rate of government saving, the rate of personal saving, and the rate of corporate saving; and to examine the effects of various fiscal measures on total saving once such interrelationships have been taken into account. I will address each of these major purposes in turn.

The Theory of Economic Policymaking

The first purpose of this paper is to determine a "stable reaction function" for the rate of government saving. The idea of a reaction function implies that discretionary fiscal policy decisionmaking is involved. The starting point for any determination of the rule governing the behavior of government saving should be a theory of the way in which government policy is made. Although von Furstenberg does not give an explicit statement of such a theory, there is an implicit one contained in his contention:

In the United States fiscal policy has been used in a repetitive manner during each of the business cycles since the end of the Korean War. As a result, the size of the deficit (relative to the net national product) under different economic conditions can be predicted by consumers and businessmen with a fair degree of certainty. To the extent that discretionary actions correspond to expectations, they become essentially endogenous. Conversely, unusual actions are regarded as aberrations that will be maintained for only a few quarters before they are undone.

In my opinion, this implicit theory of von Furstenberg's may be cast in the following explicit form. My purpose in making such an explicit formulation is to point up some possible difficulties with his empirical specification of the government saving function. Let x_t denote the vector of target variables for the economy in period t, x_t^* the vector of politically desired values for these target variables in period t, and gs_t the value of the government's control variable (the government saving rate) in period t. Then an optimal (and stable, in the sense of unchanging parameters) reaction function for gs_t similar to von Furstenberg's will result from the following minimization problem.

Suppose that the political consensus on the (expected) "loss" associated with a given configuration of x_t is a function of the difference between x_t and x_t^* and can be represented by[94]

$$(5) \qquad L = L(x_t - x_t^*).$$

The effects of changes in gs_t on the target variables are given by the system of structural equations determining the behavior of the economy. These constraints can be written as

$$(6) \qquad x_t = f(gs_t, x_{t-1}).$$

Further, suppose that there are certain automatic stabilizers for fiscal policy built into the economy, so that there is an automatic component to the government saving rate (gs_t^a), which can be represented as

$$(7) \qquad gs_t^a = g(x_t).$$

The reaction function for the discretionary component of the government saving rate (gs_t^d) results from minimizing equation 5 subject to equations 6 and 7 and will be of the form

$$(8) \qquad gs_t^d = h(x_t^*, x_{t-1}).$$

This reaction function contains only lagged target variables and desired values of target variables. Current values of target variables will not appear.

Adding equations 7 and 8 gives the function determining the government saving rate as

$$(9) \qquad gs_t = g(x_t) + h(x_t^*, x_{t-1}).$$

The function explaining the government saving rate used by von Furstenberg is

$$(10) \qquad gs_t = g(GAP_t, U_{t-2} - U_{t-4}, PI_t - EPI_t),$$

where GAP_t is one minus the ratio of actual to potential GNP in period t,

---

94. The variable $L(.)$ is often specified to be a quadratic function of $x_t - x_t^*$ in the optimal economic policy literature. Such a specification is convenient since in the case of linear constraints, minimization of $L(.)$ yields linear reaction functions. However, there is no need to specify a functional form for $L(.)$ in this discussion.

U_t is the unemployment rate in period t, PI_t is the inflation rate in period t, and EPI_t is the officially expected inflation rate in period t. Since equations 9 and 10 are similar, it appears that von Furstenberg's reaction function for government saving can be justified as being the result if policymakers were attempting to optimally control the economy.

However, some of the similarities between equations 9 and 10 disappear on further examination. In particular, by including the GAP_t and $PI_t - EPI_t$ variables, von Furstenberg imposes what may be unjustifiably strong restrictions on the functional form of his reaction function. Consider, for example, the case of the GAP_t variable. The inclusion of a target variable such as current GNP in the government saving function can be justified by the effects of current GNP on the automatic component of government saving. The inclusion of potential GNP, however, must be justified by its being a component or a proxy for a component of x_t^*. Thus potential GNP should affect discretionary government saving. Viewed from this perspective, there seems to be no reason for including actual and potential GNP in the very restrictive manner implied by the GAP_t variable. The same holds for $PI_t - EPI_t$. On the other hand, the variables GAP_t and PI_t would seem reasonable if one were specifying the loss function (equation 5) rather than the reaction function (equation 9).[95]

The above discussion also points out that a simultaneous equations estimation bias will exist if either 9 or 10 is estimated. As equation 6 clearly points out, the x_t are affected by the values of the gs_t, so that they are not independent of any stochastic components in either 9 or 10.

One of the major purposes of von Furstenberg's estimation of the reaction function for the government saving rate is to obtain a measure of its unanticipated component (which he calls fiscal surprise) to be used in his regressions explaining the personal saving rate. The fiscal surprise variable is defined to be the difference between the actual government saving rate and the anticipated government saving rate, which is the product of the independent variables times their regression coefficients. The difficulty with this procedure is that von Furstenberg's anticipated government saving rate is not the optimal predictor of the government saving rate since the government's reaction function was assumed to have autocorrelated errors. Last period's error multiplied by the autocorrelation coefficient is

95. In fact, von Furstenberg may exhibit some confusion about the two functions since he justifies the inclusion of $PI_t - EPI_t$ in equation 10 by arguing, "If the actual inflation rate exceeds the expected rate, a higher surplus is achieved promptly because of the operation of the automatic stabilizers."

information that is available and useful to private decisionmakers in forecasting government actions. Assuming that households do not use this information not only seems inconsistent with the spirit of the paper but also leads to measures of fiscal surprise that are inefficient and serially correlated.

Estimation of Saving Rates

In estimating corporate and personal saving rates, von Furstenberg takes account of the possibility that these rates may be interdependent. He allows for such interdependencies first by allowing the stochastic disturbance terms that affect the various equations to be contemporaneously correlated and then by allowing the unanticipated components of the government saving rate and the corporate saving rate to be independent variables in his personal saving rate regression equations.

I am sympathetic toward von Furstenberg's approach of taking into account the fact that households may pierce both the corporate and the government veils in making their consumption and savings decisions. However, I question whether he has been totally consistent in his application of this approach to the regression equations he estimates.

First, if households are capable of piercing both the corporate and the government veils, then for the sake of consistency corporations should be assumed to be able to pierce the government veil. Logically, therefore, the fiscal surprise variable should appear in the regressions attempting to explain the corporate saving rate. However, it is not included.

Second, in the discussion of why the fiscal surprise variable rather than the total government surplus variable is the correct one to include in the regression equations, von Furstenberg makes the point that the systematic component of fiscal policy can be anticipated by private sector decisionmakers and will therefore be incorporated into the parameters of their saving rate equations. On the other hand, for corporate saving, he implicitly takes the opposite point of view when he includes the actual corporate saving rate rather than the unanticipated component of the corporate saving rate in the personal saving equation. It would be more consistent with his overall argument to use unanticipated saving rates for both the corporate and government components. If households pierce the corporate veil, then, according to von Furstenberg's own argument, the systematic components of the corporate saving rate will already be accounted for in the parameters of the personal saving rate function.

I conclude my discussion of this section by attempting to explain the disturbing results that von Furstenberg obtains on his wealth and interest rate variables in the section "Explanatory Variables That Failed." The wealth variable, though insignificant, enters his personal saving rate regressions with the wrong sign (positive instead of negative). However, the wealth variable, which is actually net wealth divided by disposable income, has been multiplied by 1.13 times $(1 - GAP_t)$ in each time period. Thus the effects of changes in GAP_t may overwhelm the effects of wealth, and since GAP_t is also included in the regressions, the wealth variable may be insignificant because it is redundant. It is interesting to note that the wealth variable and GAP_t have regression coefficients of opposite signs in table 8, as would be implied by this explanation.

Von Furstenberg rejects the results with the real interest rate variable because it enters the regressions with negative and, in the case of the $RRAT$ variable, statistically significant coefficients. He argues that a positive coefficient is to be expected. However, this is only true when the dependent variable in the regression is the *level* of saving. When the dependent variable is the saving *rate,* a negative coefficient can occur. The reason is that real rate of return and the level of income should be positively related. Thus an increase in the rate of return will increase both the numerator and denominator of the dependent variable, and if the effects of changes in the real rate of return on income are relatively greater than the effects on savings, the negative coefficient obtained by von Furstenberg would result.

Before leaving this section, however, let me turn once again to the question of consistency of von Furstenberg's treatment of the variables used in his regressions. In constructing his nominal rate-of-return series, which formed the basis for the $RRAT$ and $RRFS$ variables, actual nominal returns earned in a particular time period were used for all categories of assets except corporate equities, which adjusted for windfall gains and losses. The adjustment was made because "unless the large windfall losses [on corporate equities] during this period were added to the actual returns, the estimates of expected rates of return would be biased downward to an increasing extent in recent years." Thus the rate-of-return series is to be interpreted as an expected one rather than an actual one. My question of consistency, then, is why no attempt was made to adjust the returns on other categories of assets such as residential structures and corporate bond holdings for windfall gains and losses as well. In other words, von Furstenberg's nominal rate-of-return series embodies the implicit assumption that returns on all categories of assets except corporate equities can be perfectly anticipated. Such an assumption seems too strong.

After total nominal returns on assets were calculated, they were divided by total wealth to obtain the before-tax nominal rate-of-return series. This series was then carefully adjusted by using marginal tax rates to obtain the nominal after-tax rate of return.[96] However, if one considers portfolio composition to be a variable of household choice, then actual returns are endogenous to the model, and their inclusion causes a simultaneous equations bias that also affects the estimated regression coefficients.

Policy Implications

The two major policy implications of von Furstenberg's paper are that a surprise increase in the tax rate will have little or no effect on the national saving rate and that a balanced budget increase in both government expenditures and taxes that generates no fiscal surprise will lead to a substantial lowering of the national saving rate. Thus the paper finds that surprise tax cuts do not much stimulate aggregate demand whereas balanced budget increases in government expenditures do.

The important and interesting innovation in von Furstenberg's evaluation of fiscal policy is the distinction he draws between systematic or predictable policy on one hand and surprise or unanticipatable policy on the other. As stated earlier, I am in sympathy with the approach of dividing fiscal policies into these two categories and allowing each to have a different effect.

However, this approach is not without a major potential pitfall, especially when the only characterization of predictable fiscal policy is in terms of the surplus or government saving rate. The pitfall is that, since the effects of a policy depend on the degree to which it was anticipated, the evaluation of a particular contemplated policy action requires a prior determination of the extent to which it is already included in the reaction function for the government saving rate. For example, suppose one wants to determine the effects of a tax cut in the current economic circumstances. Should such a cut be considered a fiscal surprise or is it the predictable response of government saving to a fall in the ratio of actual to potential output?

---

96. The adjustment using marginal tax rates for variables in the household decision problem raises the question of why average rather than marginal tax rates are independent variables in the regression equations for corporate saving.

Conclusion

The major strength of the paper is its approach to the evaluation of fiscal policies on saving, and for this reason my comments have centered almost exclusively on the parts where this approach has not been consistently applied. In particular, there are two aspects of the approach to investigating the determinants of the national saving rate that lead me to advocate that future work build upon the framework suggested here. The first is that the estimated saving rate functions attempt to account for the interrelationships between the saving decisions of the household, corporate, and government sectors. The second is that the estimated saving functions allow for the different impacts of anticipated and unanticipated fiscal changes.

However, any future empirical evaluations of the effects of fiscal policy on saving using the approach of this paper would be considerably strengthened if two modifications were made. First, I advocate switching the focus from the reaction function for the government saving rate to separate reaction functions for government expenditures and taxes, perhaps with some type of constraint on the surplus imposed through the loss function. Such a modification of the approach would overcome what I identified as a potential pitfall, since now tax and spending changes could be more accurately decomposed into their anticipated and unanticipated components.

Second, I advocate more explicit modeling of the behavior of the household and corporate sectors to take account of the effects of the anticipated as well as the unanticipated components of government actions. In particular, the role of anticipated fiscal policy actions in the formation of expectations concerning future income and interest rates should be made more explicit. Further, government expenditures could be included in the households' utility function with current taxes (and future tax liabilities to the extent that they are discounted) included in the budget constraint. Or household ownership of firms could be explicitly included in the household budget constraint so that the personal and the corporate saving decisions were simultaneously determined. In addition to decreasing the ad hoc nature of the current specification, more explicit modeling might also allow the evaluation of the major institutional changes in the application of fiscal policy that result from decisions to modify the form of the government's reaction functions. The current specifications do not have this capability.

CHARLES T. CLOTFELTER *and* C. EUGENE STEUERLE

Charitable Contributions

In 1978 an estimated $32.8 billion was contributed by living individuals to the nation's charitable organizations.[1] Representing 2.25 percent of disposable personal income, these donations accounted for 83 percent of giving from all sources: living individuals, bequests, corporations, and other institutions. Donations of time and talent were also of great importance; one estimate indicates that annually over 6 billion hours of time are given to charitable and religious organizations.[2] Many of these contributions support educational, scientific, religious, and cultural activities, promote the public good, and enhance the opportunities of individuals unrelated to the donors. It is therefore not surprising that charitable giving is often seen as a close substitute for many government programs and that public policy toward such giving has received a great deal of attention.

The most important federal policy affecting charitable giving is the deduction for contributions allowed in the individual income tax. Enacted in 1917, the deduction appears to have been designed originally to ensure that the income tax did not discourage charitable giving. Since then the incentive effect of the deduction (or disincentive effect of the

We are grateful to Roy Wyscarver for programming assistance and to Gerald Auten, Gerard Brannon, John Brittain, Harvey Galper, William Reece, Gabriel Rudney, and Dudley Wallace for helpful comments and discussions.

1. "Giving USA—1979 Annual Report" (New York: American Association of Fund Raising Council, 1979).

2. James N. Morgan, Richard F. Dye, and Judith H. Hybels, "Results from Two National Surveys on Philanthropic Activity," in Commission on Private Philanthropy and Public Needs, *Research Papers Sponsored by the Commission on Private Philanthropy and Public Needs,* vol. 1 (Government Printing Office, 1977), pp. 157–323.

tax) has remained the primary justification for the deduction.[3] A second justification occasionally advanced is that a deduction is a necessary adjustment to maintain horizontal equity across taxpayers. For example, Andrews argues that charitable contributions are properly subtracted in defining an income tax base.[4] As Goode points out, however, this justification has never been widely accepted in the United States.[5] Thus policy debate on the charitable deduction has tended to highlight the size and the propriety of the deduction's incentive effect.[6]

Basic to an evaluation of this incentive effect is a determination of its magnitude. If contributions are like other consumer goods, the gross amount of contributions made will be inversely related to the "price" of giving. For an itemizer with a marginal tax rate t, the net cost of making a $1 contribution or of consuming $(1 - t) \times \$1$ is the same; thus his relative price of giving is $1 - t$. If taxpayers' contributions are sensitive to this price of giving, then different tax treatments of contributions and different schedules of tax rates may have significant effects on the amount of charitable giving.

In this paper we examine the empirical question of what effect tax incentives have on charitable giving. In particular, we are interested in the sensitivity of price elasticity estimates to the specification of the relationship between giving and price. Using tax data for 1975, we estimate price elasticities for the population to be about $- 1.25$ if we assume specifications and functional forms similar to those used in earlier studies of contributions. We find, however, that estimates of the price elasticity tend to vary by income class and are sensitive to the specification of the regression model. The estimates from the most reasonable cross-sectional specifications range from $- 0.4$ to $- 0.9$ for low-income taxpayers to $- 1.7$ to $- 1.8$ for high-income taxpayers. Evidence on changes in contributions over time also indicates that the price elasticity for the population is significantly less than zero, with our most reasonable estimates ranging from

3. Richard Goode, *The Individual Income Tax* (Brookings Institution, 1976).

4. William D. Andrews, "Personal Deductions in an Ideal Income Tax," *Harvard Law Review*, vol. 86 (December 1972), pp. 309–85.

5. *Individual Income Tax*, p. 161.

6. Some authors have also discussed the efficiency of the deduction in promoting activities with favorable externalities. For instance, Hochman and Rodgers have argued that a tax credit would probably be preferable to a deduction on the efficiency grounds that all charitable activities should be subsidized at an equal rate rather than at rates varying with income. Harold M. Hochman and James D. Rodgers, "The Optimal Tax Treatment of Charitable Contributions," *National Tax Journal*, vol. 30 (March 1977), pp. 1–18.

− 0.6 to − 1.1 in value, depending on specification and data. Because these ranges are wide, we hesitate to assign a precise numerical value to the average price elasticity for the population.

At a price elasticity of 0, giving is unresponsive to price incentives or tax reductions for contributions. The more negative the price elasticity, the greater is the increase in contributions relative to the cost to the government of providing a price incentive. At a price elasticity of − 1, the loss in government revenues resulting from a marginal change in price is exactly equal to the increase in contributions generated by the change.[7] We believe that special emphasis should not be placed on − 1 as the dividing point for deciding whether to support or oppose public policies affecting charitable contributions. Consideration needs to be given not only to the "efficiency" of a price incentive, but also to its equity and to practical problems of administration. Any policy on charitable contributions, for instance, needs to take into account the ability of taxpayers to keep records, the "equal" treatment of taxpayers, and the extent to which the tax system rewards those who are most "tax conscious." On the efficiency question, charitable contributions are only partial substitutes for some government expenditures, not complete substitutes for all government expenditures. Even as substitutes, contributions may be spent more or less efficiently than government expenditures. For instance, if the efficiency of expenditures for the public welfare is increased by decentralized decisionmaking, then the argument for price incentives is strengthened, as is the argument for equalizing the price incentive for taxpayers. In any case, the policy choice depends on much more than whether a given parameter is more or less than − 1 in value.

The U-Shaped Curve of Giving

A useful starting point for the analysis of individual giving is an examination of the average propensity to make contributions at various income levels. Figure 1 shows rates of giving by income class. The horizontal axis is marked by income percentiles so as to give equal weight to each tax return or household in the population. Each income class is thus weighted by the percentage of returns or households that fall in that in-

---

7. Let R = revenues, G = contributions, P = price, t = marginal tax rate, and Z = a constant. If $(dG/G)/(dP/P) = -1$, and $R = Z - tG$, then

$$dR = -dP \cdot G + (P - 1)\, dG = -[(P \cdot dG)/G] \cdot G + (P \cdot dG) - dG = -dG.$$

Figure 1. Rates of Giving by Income Class

Contributions as percent of income

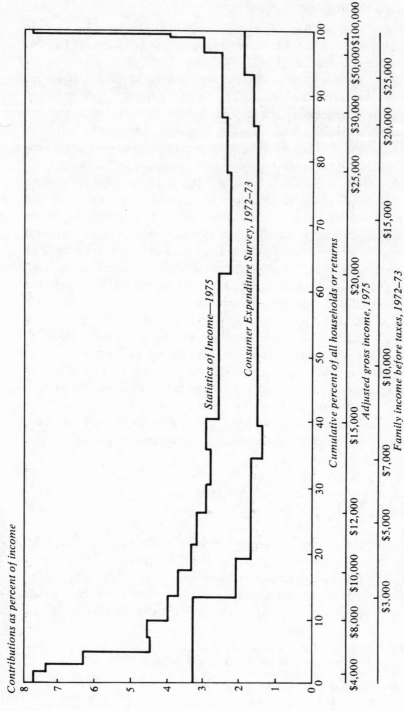

Sources: U.S. Internal Revenue Service, *Statistics of Income—1975: Individual Income Tax Returns*, covering itemizers only; and Bureau of Labor Statistics, *Consumer Expenditure Survey, 1972–73*, covering all households, regardless of whether itemized or not.

come class. Below the percentile distribution are corresponding absolute income levels. Despite the difference in coverage and methodology of the sources,[8] the data indicate that giving as a percent of income takes on a U-shaped curve. The rate of contributions is relatively high at lower income levels, then declines steadily as income begins to increase. The rate remains fairly constant for taxpayers and families that fall into the ranges of income surrounding the median income level. Only for the wealthiest quartile does the rate of giving begin to increase, and high rates are reached again only at the income levels of a minute portion of the population.[9]

Previous Research on Tax Incentives and Charitable Contributions

Charitable contributions have received greater attention in empirical analysis than any other itemized deduction. Besides the easy availability of data for itemized contributions, a primary reason may be that households have considerable discretion over charitable expenditures. Unlike most other deductions, contributions are not a necessary expenditure brought on either by hardship such as illness or by a past commitment such as a long-term debt. Instead, in each year taxpayers may choose to contribute amounts ranging from nothing to very large proportions of their incomes; this discretion has encouraged a comparison between charitable giving and conventional consumer demand. The empirical work itself has revealed a remarkable degree of consensus in methodology and, to a lesser extent, findings over a wide variety of data sets.

Until the 1960s there was no systematic econometric analysis of the effect of taxes on the level of charitable contributions. In 1960 Kahn provided a careful consideration of trends in itemized charitable deductions and concluded that, for low- and middle-income taxpayers, there

8. The differences in figure 1 reflect a variety of factors, including inaccurate reporting on surveys, the special characteristics of low-income itemizers, and the higher average giving of itemizers than of the population as a whole. Some further details on the limitations of survey data and tax return data are discussed on pages 422–24, below.

9. No simple constant elasticity of giving with respect to income can explain a U-shaped giving pattern of individuals. That is, with a constant elasticity, the rate of giving would be constant, steadily declining or steadily increasing as income increased. If $G = aY^b$, and both a and b are constants, then $d(G/Y)/dY = (b-1)aY^{b-2}$. A U-shaped curve therefore implies that the income elasticity must vary with income or that other variables affect giving patterns, or both.

was no evidence that taxes actually have a measurable effect on giving. According to Kahn, the evidence seemed to hold out the possibility of an incentive effect only for taxpayers with higher incomes.[10]

Taussig

In the first econometric study of charitable giving known to us, Michael Taussig analyzed individual tax returns of itemizers in 1962 using the 1962 Treasury tax file.[11] Taussig's sample of 47,678 itemizers represented a rich data base, although about a third of the itemizers in the complete sample were omitted from his sample. His model of charitable giving is based on consumer demand theory; as such, it has provided the basis for subsequent econometric models of giving. Taussig takes contributions to be a function of disposable income (adjusted gross income minus taxes paid) and the marginal tax rate. According to him, the latter is used in place of an explicit "price" (one minus the marginal tax rate) because the marginal tax rate, not the price, is the direct policy instrument. Taussig also adopts the constant elasticity specification that has characterized the subsequent econometric models of giving. In addition to income and marginal tax rate, he includes variables reflecting marital status, family size, age, medical expenses, and capital gains. In general, the estimated equations indicate that marginal tax rates have little or no effect on the level of individual giving but that income is quite important.

Taussig estimated equations for six income classes, as shown in table 1. Income elasticities in each equation are significantly greater than one, but marginal tax rate elasticities (translated into price elasticities in table 1) are not significantly different from zero for income classes below $100,000. For income classes above $100,000, price elasticities are significant but quite small, ranging from −0.04 to −0.10 when calculated at mean marginal tax rates for each class. Taussig presents corroborating evidence to suggest that the incentive effect of taxes increases with income. For example, he compares the marginal tax rates of big givers and small givers (as measured by percentage of income contributed) within

10. As Kahn points out, however, such an incentive effect is of little importance in evaluating the charitable deduction if the deduction is intended merely as a necessary refinement in obtaining taxable income. Only if the deduction is intended to be a subsidy for giving is this incentive effect important. C. Harvey Kahn, *Personal Deductions in the Federal Income Tax* (Princeton University Press, 1960), p. 72.

11. Michael K. Taussig, "Economic Aspects of the Personal Income Tax Treatment of Charitable Contributions," *National Tax Journal,* vol. 20 (March 1967), pp. 1–19.

income classes and shows that only in the highest income classes did big givers have significantly higher marginal rates than small givers (although, by the same token, only in the highest income classes is it possible to have large differences in marginal tax rates). He also shows that actual giving rises faster than "predicted" giving—based on the net cost of other deductions—arguing that such a pattern is consistent with an incentive effect at higher income levels.

Whatever the importance of these informal tests, Taussig's econometric analysis supports the notion that tax incentives stimulate charitable giving very little. Other researchers have suggested possible explanations for these results, remarkable because they contrast with results of subsequent econometric work on the subject. Schwartz has suggested that Taussig's inclusion of capital gains might have biased the marginal tax rate variable toward zero.[12] Feldstein faults Taussig's methodology on three points: the incompleteness of the sample, the use of a price variable that was itself dependent on the amount of giving, and the estimation of five separate equations, which reduced the variance of the income and marginal tax rate variables.[13]

Schwartz

A second econometric study of charitable giving, by Robert Schwartz, employs a somewhat different model and data quite different from those used in Taussig's study.[14] Emphasizing the important role of utility interdependence in the theory of altruistic behavior, Schwartz shows that such a theory implies that a person's giving will depend in part on his income position relative to potential recipients. Schwartz therefore includes "other" income in addition to "own" income in some specifications of his contributions equations. The data used by Schwartz come from *Statistics of Income* information on aggregate income, deductions, and taxes by income class. Schwartz compiled time series data on average disposable income, price of giving (one minus the average marginal tax rate), and average contributions for three broad adjusted gross income classes: 0–$10,000, $10,000–$100,000, and $100,000 and over. Annual data were available for thirty-one of the years between 1929 and 1966.

12. Robert A. Schwartz, "Personal Philanthropic Contributions," *Journal of Political Economy*, vol. 78 (November–December 1970), pp. 1264–91.

13. Martin Feldstein, "The Income Tax and Charitable Contributions: Part I—Aggregate and Distributional Effects," *National Tax Journal*, vol. 28 (March 1975), pp. 81–100.

14. Schwartz, "Personal Philanthropic Contributions."

Table 1. Findings of Econometric Studies of Aggregate Contributions

Study	Data source	Income group (thousands of dollars)	Sample size	Estimated elasticities Price	Estimated elasticities Income
Taussig	Tax file, 1962	0–25	15,400	...	1.31 (0.04)
		25–100	16,285	...	1.99 (0.05)
		100–200	10,450	-0.10[a]	3.10 (0.06)
		200–500	4,508	-0.06[a]	2.54 (0.09)
		500+	1,035	-0.04[a]	1.75 (0.12)
Schwartz	Statistics of Income, time series, 1929–66	0–10	31	-0.68 (0.49)	0.28 (0.16)
		10–100	31	-0.76 (0.20)	0.92 (0.16)
		100+	31	-0.41 (0.10)	0.45 (0.09)
Feldstein	Statistics of Income, pooled, 1948–68	4–100	117	-1.24 (0.10)	0.82 (0.03)

Feldstein-Clotfelter	FRB survey (1963)	1.721+	1,406	−1.15 (0.20)	0.87 (0.14)
Feldstein-Taylor	Tax file, 1962	4+	13,770	−1.09 (0.03)	0.76 (0.02)
	Tax file, 1970	4+	15,291	−1.28 (0.06)	0.70 (0.02)
Boskin-Feldstein	SRC survey, 1974	1–30	1,621	−2.54 (0.28)	0.69 (0.06)
Dye	SRC survey, 1974	1–50	1,780	−2.25 (0.27)	0.53 (0.06)
Abrams-Schmitz	Statistics of Income, pooled, 1948–72	4–100	136	−1.10 (0.08)	0.81 (0.02)
Reece	BLS, Consumer Expenditure Survey, 1972–73	...	...	−1.19[b]	0.88[b]

Sources: Michael K. Taussig, "Economic Aspects of the Personal Income Tax Treatment of Charitable Contributions," *National Tax Journal*, vol. 20 (March 1967), p. 6, table 1; Robert A. Schwartz, "Personal Philanthropic Contributions," *Journal of Political Economy*, vol. 78 (November–December 1970), p. 1276, table 2; Martin Feldstein, "The Income Tax and Charitable Contributions: Part I—Aggregate and Distributional Effects," *National Tax Journal*, vol. 28 (March 1975), p. 87, equation 2; Martin Feldstein and Charles Clotfelter, "Tax Incentives and Charitable Contributions in the United States: A Microeconomic Analysis," *Journal of Public Economics*, vol. 5 (January–February 1976), p. 11, equation 6; Martin Feldstein and Amy Taylor, "The Income Tax and Charitable Contributions," *Econometrica*, vol. 44 (November 1976), p. 1206, equations 2.5 and 2.4; Michael J. Boskin and Martin Feldstein, "Effects of the Charitable Deduction on Contributions by Low-Income and Middle-Income Households: Evidence from a National Survey of Philanthropy," *Review of Economics and Statistics*, vol. 59 (August 1977), p. 352, equation 1; Richard F. Dye, "Personal Charitable Contributions: Tax Effects and Other Motives," in National Tax Association–Tax Institute of America, *Proceedings of the Seventieth Annual Conference, 1977* (Columbus, Ohio: NTA–TIA, 1978), p. 313, equation 3; Burton A. Abrams and Mark D. Schmitz, "The 'Crowding-Out' Effects of Governmental Transfers on Private Charitable Contributions," *Public Choice*, vol. 33, no. 1 (1978), model III; and William S. Reece, "Charitable Contributions: New Evidence on Household Behavior," *American Economic Review*, vol. 69 (March 1979), p. 147, equation 3. Figures in parentheses are standard errors.

a. Schwartz, "Personal Philanthropic Contributions," p. 1280.
b. Elasticities calculated at means; standard errors not available.

Following Taussig, Schwartz adopted a constant elasticity model, merely substituting tax price for marginal tax rate as the price variable. Other explanatory variables included the above-mentioned "other" income, a time trend, a dummy variable for World War II (1941–45), and a dummy variable for years before the introduction of the standard deduction (1929–41). The resulting price and income elasticities—for equations covering all years and excluding the other income—are shown in table 1. The point estimates of the price elasticities are all larger than those given by Taussig, and the income elasticities are all smaller. The estimated price elasticities are significantly different from zero for incomes over $10,000 (which is above the median income in 1966), and the income elasticities are significantly different from one in the lowest and highest income groups.

Two aspects of this study merit special attention. First, the time series constructed by Schwartz produces correlations between the price and income variables that are dramatically different from any observed in other published studies. Whereas the typical correlation between price and income in cross-section studies is negative and usually quite high, the correlations presented by Schwartz are generally positive, reaching $+0.95$ in the regression for incomes below $10,000. This unusual correlation, apparently the result of the gradual reduction over time in marginal tax rates on nominal incomes, distinguishes this data set from those based on cross sections. The second point relates to the interpretation of the income elasticity in Schwartz's regressions. Where Y is own income and Y_0 is "other" income, giving (G) can be expressed as a function of own income, price (P), and relative income (Y/Y_0):

$$(1) \qquad G = AY^aP^b(Y/Y_0)^c,$$

which is equivalent to one of the models estimated by Schwartz:

$$(2) \qquad G = AY^{a+c}P^bY_0^{-c}.$$

Schwartz argues that, if equation 1 is correct, cross-section equations that omit the relative income measure will produce an overestimate of the "true" income elasticity, a, because absolute income is positively correlated with the omitted variable, relative income. In this way he explains Taussig's much higher estimated income elasticities. Schwartz goes further to interpret his elasticity estimates of equation 2 as implying that relative income is a more important determinant than absolute income. Despite the theoretical attractiveness of including relative income, however, it is important to emphasize the hazard in attempting to allocate the income effect between absolute and relative income. In fact, Schwartz avoids estimating equation 1 simply because of the high multicollinearity between the two income measures.

Feldstein

In the first of several studies of the effects of tax incentives on charitable giving, Feldstein analyzed the same *Statistics of Income* data that provided the basis for Schwartz's time series estimates.[15] Feldstein, however, used finer income brackets and also pooled observations for different years to create a time series of cross sections covering the even years between 1948 and 1968. With seventeen adjusted gross income classes available each year for eleven years, this procedure yielded a maximum of 187 observations. In practice, only brackets with mean net incomes between $4,000 and $100,000 were used in estimation. For each income class he calculated the disposable income, average price, and average giving of itemizers in constant dollars. This pooling procedure provides more variation in income and price than Schwartz's more aggregate observations while preserving some of the independence between price and income measures caused by changes in the tax law over time. A major disadvantage of aggregate data remains the rough measure of tax price: rather than taking the average of prices in an income group, the data require calculating the price for a given average taxable income.[16]

The model estimated by Feldstein uses the same constant elasticity specification as was used by Schwartz, although relative income is excluded from most equations. Feldstein redefined the price and income variables, however, to remove possible simultaneity bias. Instead of using actual marginal tax rates and actual taxes, Feldstein set these variables to the values they would take in the absence of contributions. Although this change appears to make little difference with aggregate data, it is quite important in micro data.[17] Income is defined as adjusted gross income minus taxes if there were no contributions, although an alternative of taxable income plus contributions minus taxes if there were no contributions is also tried and found to yield similar results.

15. Feldstein, "Income Tax and Charitable Contributions: Part I."
16. Martin Feldstein and Amy Taylor, "The Income Tax and Charitable Contributions," *Econometrica*, vol. 44 (November 1976), pp. 1202–04, note that this difference is small, however.
17. Since taxable income decreases with increased giving, price increases. Using actual prices would result in a positive bias in estimated price elasticities.

The basic estimates suggest a much higher price elasticity than Taussig or Schwartz obtained, with point estimates clustering around −1.2. The income elasticity was estimated to be about 0.8 and generally was significantly less than one. The addition of a trend variable shows a secular decline in giving of slightly over 1 percent a year, though Feldstein notes that this result could be due to the drop in the relative income of included income classes.[18] When relative income itself was added to the equation,[19] the absolute income elasticity fell and the elasticity of relative income was larger, as Schwartz had found. Feldstein examines the possible variation in price elasticity by income class in two ways. First, he presents separate regressions for four income classes implying that the price elasticity declines, from −1.8 in the under $10,000 class to −0.3 in the over $100,000 class. However, the use of an interaction term between income and price (page 90, note) yields the opposite conclusion, that the price elasticity *rises* with income.[20]

Besides his treatment of gifts of appreciated assets, which is discussed below, one final contribution of Feldstein's study is the simulation of changes in contributions based on changes in tax policy. Using his basic log-linear model of giving, Feldstein calculated the value of contributions generated under various tax regimes that would change price or price and income. As an illustration, Feldstein calculated that eliminating the deduction in 1968 would have resulted in a decrease in contributions made by itemizers from $11.1 billion to $7.3 billion.

Feldstein-Clotfelter

Feldstein and Clotfelter employ much the same methodology in analyzing survey data on individuals collected for the Federal Reserve Board.[21] This data set was the first analyzed to include nonitemizers in the sample and to provide measures of wealth, permanent income, age, and other demographic variables. Although the income and wealth measures are clearly preferable to adjusted gross income as a measure of income, the

18. Furthermore, this result disappears when the entire sample is used. Feldstein, "Income Tax and Charitable Contributions: Part I," p. 88n.

19. Ibid., p. 93.

20. Feldstein rejects the latter specification because it yields a positive price elasticity for incomes below $8,300. Ibid., pp. 90–91n.

21. Martin Feldstein and Charles Clotfelter, "Tax Incentives and Charitable Contributions in the United States: A Microeconomic Analysis," *Journal of Public Economics,* vol. 5 (January–February 1976), pp. 1–26.

lack of tax return data is a disadvantage in calculating the price of giving. Taxes and marginal tax rates had to be calculated on the basis of approximations of taxable income.[22] The final sample used in the study consisted of 1,406 households with incomes over the twentieth percentile in 1963. High-income households were overrepresented. Income measures based on both current and permanent income were employed.

As in several other studies, gifts of appreciated assets were accounted for in the measure of price in order to reflect the ability of taxpayers to deduct the full value of gifts of appreciated assets without paying capital gains tax on the gains. As noted by Schwartz and developed by Feldstein and Feldstein-Taylor, the price of contributing an appreciated asset is:

$$(3) \qquad P_a = 1 - m - mc\,(1 - B/V),$$

where m is the marginal tax rate on ordinary income, mc is the marginal tax rate on capital gains income, and $(1 - B/V)$ is the (discounted) gain-to-value ratio of the asset.[23] Because this price and the price on cash gifts $(P = 1 - m)$ are highly collinear, a weighted average of the two was used, the weights being based on the taxpayer's income class. Search techniques were employed to determine the optimal value of $(1 - B/V)$ since this ratio is unknown. The authors determined this ratio to be 50 percent.

The estimated price and income elasticities using this price measure and the two-year average of disposable income are quite close to those previously obtained by Feldstein. The basic elasticity estimates in an equation using these variables and including three age dummies and the log of wealth are -1.15 for price and 0.87 for income, as shown in table 1. These results show little sensitivity to variations such as the exclusion of nonitemizers, the exclusion of young and middle-aged households, and the addition of a large number of demographic variables. Among the demographic variables used, only a dummy variable for communities of 250,000 to 1 million is significant (it has a positive effect); education, sex, and race are all insignificant. The authors find some variation in the price elasticity of giving, with higher elasticities in lower income and wealth brackets, but the standard errors of such estimates are quite large.

22. Estimated itemized deductions, excluding contributions, were based on the value of owned residences and income. Ibid., p. 8n.

23. Since the tax on capital gains can be postponed or even avoided, mc typically overstates the expected tax rate on capital gain income. See Feldstein, "Income Tax and Charitable Contributions: Part I," and Feldstein and Taylor, "Income Tax and Charitable Contributions," pp. 1202–04.

Feldstein-Taylor

In a further analysis of individual tax return data, Feldstein and Taylor examined the tax files for 1962 and 1970.[24] These files offered the opportunity to obtain accurate tax data, to examine the variability of the price elasticity by income, and to directly compare Taussig's results using the same 1962 tax file. Unusual care was used in calculating marginal tax rates: state income taxes and federal tax provisions such as income averaging and the alternative tax on capital gains were accounted for in the marginal rate calculations. In addition, the basic price measure embodies the assumption of a 50 percent discounted gain-to-value ratio for gifts of appreciated assets. As shown in table 1, the estimated price and income elasticities based on both files—in equations including one dummy each for age and marital status—are quite close to those obtained in the previous two studies. Both price elasticities are significantly different from -1.0.

These findings clearly do not agree with those obtained by Taussig using the same 1962 data. The authors suggest two possible explanations. First, Taussig used actual marginal tax rates and actual taxes; Feldstein and Taylor made both tax computations assuming no contributions had been made, that is, using the price on the first dollar of contributions. Any spurious positive correlation between price and giving would thus be eliminated by using such hypothetical values. Second, Feldstein-Taylor included in their estimates the portion of the sample inadvertently omitted by Taussig.

Because of the large number of observations available for high-income taxpayers, the Feldstein-Taylor study offers the best previously published information on the variation by income class in the price elasticity of contributions. Three different specifications were used to measure this variation. First, Feldstein and Taylor report that a simple interaction term between price and income implies that the price elasticity increases with income; however, they reject this specification because it implies a positive price elasticity over some low-income ranges. Second, they estimated separate equations for each of four income classes for 1962 and 1970. Except for a very large elasticity for the lowest income group in 1962, these results also suggest that the price elasticity rises with income. For 1970, the estimates ranged from an exceptionally low -0.35 (standard

24. "Income Tax and Charitable Contributions."

error, 0.52) for the lowest income group to −1.74 (standard error, 0.08) for incomes over $100,000. Finally, the authors estimated a single equation allowing for variations only in the price elasticity. In contrast to the previous two tests, these elasticities fall (from −2.3 to −1.3) as income rises, leaving unresolved the matter of variations in price sensitivity.[25]

Boskin-Feldstein and Dye

Two studies, one by Boskin and Feldstein and one by Dye, examine a national survey of philanthropy taken in 1974 by the University of Michigan's Survey Research Center.[26] Like the Federal Reserve Board survey used by Feldstein and Clotfelter, the sample includes nonitemizers as well as itemizers and information on a number of demographic variables, but contains little explicit tax information. Unlike the FRB survey, the SRC data contain relatively few high-income households. For this reason Boskin and Feldstein used only households with incomes below $30,000, and Dye only households below $50,000. Another weakness is that data on household income are available only for broad income classes.[27] Taxable income was calculated from the mean income or midpoint of each bracket, data on deductible expenses, and reported itemization status. Since itemization may in fact be a function of the size of contributions, the method employed in these studies of calculating price may be partly responsible for the unusually large estimated price elasticities.

The estimated price elasticities in both studies are quite high: −2.54 by Boskin and Feldstein and −2.25 by Dye. The income elasticities are correspondingly lower: Boskin and Feldstein obtained an estimate of 0.69

25. Sunley reestimated Feldstein and Taylor's basic equation using 1973 tax data and obtained similar estimates for the price and income elasticities. When he included an interaction term between price and income, the estimated price elasticity varied from near zero for taxpayers with income of $10,000 to −1.3 for taxpayers with income of $200,000. See Emil M. Sunley, "Federal and State Tax Policies," in David W. Breneman and Chester E. Finn, Jr., eds., *Public Policy and Private Higher Education* (Brookings Institution, 1978), pp. 304–05.

26. Michael J. Boskin and Martin Feldstein, "Effects of the Charitable Deduction on Contributions by Low-Income and Middle-Income Households: Evidence from a National Survey of Philanthropy," *Review of Economics and Statistics,* vol. 59 (August 1977), pp. 351–54; and Richard F. Dye, "Personal Charitable Contributions: Tax Effects and Other Motives," in National Tax Association–Tax Institute of America, *Proceedings of the Seventieth Annual Conference, 1977* (Columbus, Ohio: NTA-TIA, 1978), pp. 311–17.

27. Income classes up to $30,000 are (in thousands) 1–2, 2–4, 4–8, 8–10, 10–15, 15–20, and 20–30.

and Dye—in an equation including a wealth measure—one of 0.53. Both studies indicate that age is an important determinant of contributions, with giving increasing with age. A central question posed by both studies is whether the price effect is actually just an "itemization effect," and whether price differences other than those resulting from itemization status are inconsequential in their effect on giving. In support of this notion, Dye reports that the estimated price elasticity for itemizers alone is not significantly different from zero and also that an equation substituting an itemization dummy for price explains the variation in giving for the entire sample as well as the basic equation. Boskin and Feldstein counter this with a constrained estimate of the price elasticity for itemizers. Imposing an income elasticity estimated for nonitemizers on itemizers, they obtained a high and significant price elasticity (-2.32; standard error, 0.60).[28] Because the income elasticity must be constrained to obtain a significant price elasticity, the issue of an itemization effect for this sample remains clouded. It is useful to note, however, that an unconstrained regression for itemizers alone by Feldstein and Clotfelter as well as all the estimates by Feldstein and Taylor (whose sample was restricted to itemizers) indicate a significant price effect apart from any "itemization effect."

Abrams-Schmitz

Abrams and Schmitz augmented and then reestimated Feldstein's pooled *Statistics of Income* data, extending the series to 1972.[29] Their basic estimates involve simply a replacement of the time trend variable by several alternative measures of the growth of government expenditures for social programs, including social security. Since the trend in such expenditures has been upward over the century and since the authors did not also include the trend variable, it is not surprising that such expenditures have a negative effect (the same sign as Feldstein's trend variable in the $4,000–$100,000 sample) and that the price elasticity changes little. Despite the inconclusiveness of this econometric test, it is certainly conceivable that public expenditures are seen as a substitute for private

28. They also estimated the basic equation with essentially an itemization dummy and obtained a significant, though smaller, price elasticity and an insignificant "itemization effect."

29. Burton A. Abrams and Mark D. Schmitz, "The 'Crowding-Out' Effect of Governmental Transfers on Private Charitable Contributions," *Public Choice*, vol. 33, no. 1 (1978), pp. 29–39.

philanthropy. In particular, Schwartz notes that the interdependent utility model implies a reduction in giving as a response to increased government aid to potential recipients.

Reece

Reece analyzed data on charitable contributions from the 1972–73 Bureau of Labor Statistics *Consumer Expenditure Survey*.[30] Because of the disaggregation among types of contributions that is available from the survey, Reece appropriately adopted a Tobit estimating procedure to account for the large number of zero entries. An equation explaining one aggregate measure of contributions[31] with price, income, age, and other characteristics of potential recipients yields point estimates of -1.19 for the price elasticity and 0.88 for the income elasticity. All other explanatory variables are insignificant.

Studies of Contributions by Type of Donee

Although most empirical studies have treated giving as a single "good" that can be purchased with income, it is reasonable to view giving, like consumption, as being made up of several goods. A taxpayer's contributions to his church, for example, are likely to be quite a different "good" from his contributions to the United Way or his alma mater. Such gifts may differ in the amount of recognition the taxpayer receives for his gift, the amount and kind of pressure to contribute applied to him, and the kind of "services," if any, he may receive from the donee. It would not be surprising, therefore, if the "demands" for these various goods were quite different, each exhibiting its own price and income elasticities. If so, the aggregation of contributions embodied in the above studies will obscure important differences in responses to tax incentives, and estimates based on such aggregate data would offer little assistance in assessing the distributional impact of changes in tax policy. Fortunately, some data by type of donee are available and have been analyzed in three studies that used estimation techniques similar to those reported above (see table 2).

In the second part of a two-part study, Feldstein examined the impact of the income tax on religious organizations, educational institutions,

---

30. William S. Reece, "Charitable Contributions: New Evidence on Household Behavior," *American Economic Review*, vol. 69 (March 1979), pp. 142–51.

31. This measure includes all giving minus support payments to nonfamily members (including alimony), gifts, and the "other" category.

Table 2. Findings of Econometric Studies on Contributions, by Type of Charity

Description	Type of donee	Estimated elasticities	
		Price	Income
Feldstein	Religious organizations	−0.49[a]	0.63[a]
Data: *Statistics of Income*,		(0.08)	(0.03)
1962		n.e.[b]	0.38[b]
Sample size: 17			(0.03)
		−0.78[c]	0.52[c]
		(0.02)	(0.01)
	Educational institutions	−2.23[a]	1.22[a]
		(0.54)	(0.19)
		n.e.[b]	1.54[b]
			(0.08)
		−1.97[c]	1.31[c]
		(0.08)	(0.05)
	Hospitals	−2.44[a]	1.08[a]
		(0.62)	(0.22)
		n.e.[b]	1.87[b]
			(0.12)
		−1.90[c]	1.26[c]
		(0.09)	(0.06)
	Health and welfare organi-		
	zations	−1.19[a]	0.85[a]
		(0.12)	(0.04)
		n.e.[b]	0.83[b]
			(0.02)
		−1.25[c]	0.83[c]
		(0.02)	(0.01)
	All others	−2.63[a]	0.65[a]
		(0.23)	(0.08)
		n.e.[b]	1.10[b]
			(0.06)
		−1.55[c]	1.03[c]
		(0.05)	(0.03)
Fisher	Institutions of higher education	−2.31	2.31
		(0.91)	(0.24)
Data: Aggregate contribu-			
tions by income class,			
Michigan, 1974–75			
Sample size: 18			

Table 2 (*continued*)

Description	Type of donee	Estimated elasticities	
		Price	Income
Reece[d]	Charities not deducted from		
Data: BLS, *Consumer Ex-*	paycheck and those		
penditure Survey,	deducted (1)	−0.98	1.43
1972–73	Religious organizations (7)	−1.60	0.40
	Educational institutions (8)	−0.08	1.64
	Other (11)	−3.07	0.00

Sources: Martin S. Feldstein, "The Income Tax and Charitable Contributions: Part II—The Impact of Religious, Education, and Other Organizations," *National Tax Journal,* vol. 28 (June 1975), p. 217, table 3; Ronald C. Fisher, "The Combined State and Federal Income Tax Treatment of Charitable Contributions," in NTA-TIA, *Proceedings, 1977,* p. 402, table 3, equation 6; Reece, "Charitable Contributions," p. 148, table 2. Numbers in parentheses are standard errors.
  n.e. Not estimated.
  a. Unconstrained estimates.
  b. Price elasticity constrained to equal −1.24 before regressions were run.
  c. Ratio of price and income elasticities equal.
  d. Numbers in parentheses in column 1 refer to equation number.

hospitals, health and welfare organizations, and all others.[32] Using 1962 tax return data in which giving by type of organization was detailed, he estimated income elasticity by three different specifications and price elasticity by two different specifications.[33] In the first specification, a constant elasticity was assumed for each type of giving, even though Feldstein notes that this specification is inconsistent with a constant price elasticity for all giving. A second specification imposed a price elasticity from "extraneous information" (meaning: from an earlier study). The third specification required a constant ratio of price to income elasticity for all types of giving. Despite the limits of these econometric specifications, the models clearly reflect a large difference in patterns of giving by type of charity. For educational institutions and hospitals, giving comes primarily from income classes above $50,000; both price and income elasticities are greater than 1.1 in absolute value. For religious organizations, giving comes primarily from low- and moderate-income classes, and elasticities (when estimated) are low and average much less than 0.8 in absolute value. Health and welfare organizations have price and income elasticities similar to those obtained by Feldstein in the first part of his two-part study

32. Martin S. Feldstein, "The Income Tax and Charitable Contributions: Part II—The Impact on Religious, Education, and Other Organizations," *National Tax Journal,* vol. 28 (June 1975), pp. 209–26.
33. A third specification fixes the price elasticity according to "extraneous information."

for aggregate contributions; contributions to "others" have high price elasticities, and income elasticities range between 0.65 and 1.10.

In a second study focusing on particular types of contributions, Fisher estimated the combined impact of federal deductibility and a 50 percent state credit for contributions to Michigan colleges and universities.[34] He found income elasticities of around +2.3 and price elasticities of around −2.3. He was constrained, as many others had been in previous studies, to use certain averages per income class. Also, he did not have data on actual giving, but rather, data on the amount of grant received.

Reece estimated price and income elasticities for giving to charities, to religious organizations, and to educational institutions through charitable deductions from pay, and for certain support, gifts, and political transfers (generally noncharitable).[35] His data source was the 1972–73 Bureau of Labor Statistics *Consumer Expenditure Survey.* Using a maximum-likelihood Tobit technique and defining the dependent variable as approximately equaling contributions for which a tax deduction is allowed, he estimated price and income elasticities similar to the constant elasticities reported in previous studies using tax return data (for example, Feldstein and Taylor). However, when he confined the dependent variable to charities (excluding religious and educational) not deducted from paychecks and contributions to charities deducted from pay, he found a price elasticity of about −0.98 and income elasticity of 1.43. According to Reece, this is consistent with models of utility interdependence which imply that the utility of others is a luxury. In other regressions, Reece obtained a high price elasticity (−1.60) for religious organizations and a low elasticity (−0.08) for educational institutions, although his goodness-of-fit measure is weak in the latter case. While these results differ from those reported by Feldstein and Fisher, data limitations make comparisons difficult.

New Estimates of Taxpayer Responses to Tax Incentives for Charitable Giving

The Data

The data used in this study come from two sources. The principal one is the 1975 Treasury tax file, a stratified, random sample of individual in-

34. Ronald C. Fisher, "The Combined State and Federal Income Tax Treatment of Charitable Contributions," in NTA-TIA, *Proceedings, 1977,* pp. 397–403.
35. "Charitable Contributions."

come tax returns filed for tax year 1975. The file contains information on contributions, income, taxes paid, age, and other characteristics of taxpayers. With the 1975 Treasury individual income tax calculator, it was possible to determine the marginal tax rates of taxpayers while taking into account the interaction of numerous tax provisions dealing with tax preferences and the special treatment of certain types of income, as well as rate schedules, filing status, and deductions.[36] Because tax returns contain information on the contributions of itemizers only, it was necessary to restrict the sample to avoid sample selection bias. This involved omitting itemizers who would not have itemized if they had made no contributions. Since these taxpayers have first dollar prices of one and are included only by virtue of their (often large) contributions, the contributions of taxpayers with prices of one tend to be overstated. Most of these taxpayers are nonitemizers and are thus excluded. Of the 50,000 taxpayers in the 1975 tax file, 26,397 were itemizers who satisfied the condition that they would have itemized regardless of the level of their contributions.

A secondary data set is the Treasury's Seven-Year Panel of Taxpayers. This represents a 1-in-5,000 sample of all individual tax returns for the years 1967–73. Unlike the 1975 tax file, the sample is not stratified but is random across the population of filers. Thus while the file provides information on the giving of individual taxpayers over time, the size of the sample is small at upper income levels. Of 7,063 itemizers in 1970, only 88 had average incomes of over $50,000. For this reason, taxpayers with average incomes above $50,000 were excluded in the analysis of the panel.

Because tax files contain information on the contributions of itemizers only, a low-income observation in either of these files (restricted to itemizers) represents a special type of low-income household—one with sub-

---

36. For a description of this calculator, see Roy A. Wyscarver, "The Treasury Personal Individual Income Tax Simulation Model," Office of Tax Analysis Paper 32 (U.S. Treasury Department, 1978). Because this tax calculator does not normally take into account income averaging, the marginal tax rates of taxpayers identified as averagers in 1975 were estimated from information on normal tax liability, marginal rate without income averaging, and tax savings resulting from income averaging. The estimating equation was fitted for a sample of averagers in 1973 for whom marginal tax rates had been obtained through a simulation of the income averaging provisions of the tax code. This simulation procedure, described in Charles T. Clotfelter, "Tax Incentives and Charitable Giving: Evidence from a Panel of Taxpayers," *Journal of Public Economics*, vol. 13 (June 1980), pp. 319–40, was developed largely by Gerald Auten. In general, the inclusion of income averagers in the 1975 sample made little difference in parameter estimates; however, they are included in all samples analyzed below.

stantial tax deductions despite its low income. Although survey data may provide a better sample of low-income households, tax information has the following advantages: (1) while some income sources are not reported, income reported on tax returns does not suffer from the more severe misreporting problem of most surveys; (2) the availability of detailed information from income tax returns (and in this case, a detailed tax calculator) allows exact measurement of marginal tax rates; (3) tax files are generally much larger and contain much more relevant tax-related information; and (4) charitable contributions are believed to be reported more accurately on tax returns,[37] primarily because the taxpayer is required to keep some records for tax purposes.[38]

Estimates of the Basic Specifications

Following the practice of previous studies, we adopt a log-linear equation as the basic specification of individual giving behavior. The dependent variable in the basic equation is the logarithm of contributions plus $10, denoted $\ln(G + 10)$. The price measure is the logarithm of a weighted average of prices reflecting gifts of assets as well as cash (ln $P50$), defined in equation 3, above, and assuming for assets a discounted gain-to-value ratio of 50 percent.[39] The basic income measure (Y) is adjusted gross income minus the tax liability that would have been due if no contributions had been made. Dummy variables for marital status (MRD), for the presence of dependents (DEP), and for five age groups are added to reflect important demographic differences among taxpayers. Equation 3-1 in table 3 shows the estimates based on this specification. The point estimate of the price elasticity is −1.268, with a standard error of 0.052. The estimated income elasticity is 0.776, with a standard error of 0.018. These results are quite close to estimates for the 1961 and 1970

37. For instance, the contributions reported by itemizers in the 1974 Survey of Philanthropy conducted by the University of Michigan's Survey Research Center differ greatly from those reported on tax returns in the same year. In this case, especially for higher incomes, the average amounts reported in the survey were substantially larger than those on tax returns. Whether this is a misreporting problem or a sample problem cannot be determined.

38. Contributions may, of course, be overstated by taxpayers. Furthermore, the incentive to overstate contributions is proportional to the marginal tax rate, making it virtually impossible to separate the true incentive effect on contributions from any systematic overstatement effect.

39. For taxpayers with dividend or capital gains income, $P50 = C \cdot P1 + (1 − C)$ $[P1 − (0.5 \cdot mc]$, where mc is the marginal tax rate on capital gains, $P1$ is the price of making cash contributions, and C is the proportion of gifts given in cash by the taxpayer's adjusted gross income group.

Table 3. Equations Explaining Charitable Contributions in 1975[a]

Dependent variable: ln $(G + 10)$

	Equation number and sample		
Variable	3-1; full 1975 tax file	3-2; full 1975 tax file	3-3; 1975 tax file; joint filers, aged 35–55
ln $P50$	−1.268 (0.052)	...	−1.243 (0.076)
ln $P1$	...	−1.358 (0.068)	...
ln Y	0.776 (0.018)	0.830 (0.018)	0.708 (0.026)
MRD	0.260 (0.029)	0.235 (0.030)	...
DEP	0.196 (0.022)	0.191 (0.022)	0.392 (0.033)
Age group			
30–34	0.379 (0.036)	0.373 (0.036)	...
40–49	0.563 (0.035)	0.561 (0.035)	0.108 (0.029)
50–59	0.691 (0.035)	0.700 (0.036)	0.218 (0.032)
60–64	0.903 (0.045)	0.928 (0.045)	...
65 and over	1.197 (0.044)	1.250 (0.044)	...
Intercept	−3.271 (0.159)	−3.875 (0.239)	−2.102 (0.240)
$\bar{R}^2$	0.472	0.468	0.366
Sample size	26,397	26,397	13,485
Mean contribution (dollars)	10,676	10,676	4,624
Mean income (dollars)	70,231	70,231	59,405

a. For explanation of the symbols, see the text. Numbers in parentheses are standard errors.

tax files obtained by Feldstein and Taylor and are similar as well to price elasticities obtained by Feldstein, Feldstein and Clotfelter, and Reece.[40]

40. For comparison, the identical Feldstein and Taylor specification (equation 2.4), which uses income, first-dollar price, and dummies for marital status and age of over sixty-five to explain ln $(G + 1)$, was estimated using the current data, and that yielded a price elasticity of −1.452 (standard error, 0.062) and income elasticity of 0.826 (standard error, 0.022), compared to −1.285 and 0.702, respectively, in Feldstein and Taylor's 1970 equation (see table 1).

The standard error on the price elasticity estimate implies a 95 percent confidence interval of -1.37 to -1.17. When other factors are held constant, contributions from married couples are 30 percent larger than for single taxpayers, other heads of household, and married taxpayers filing separate returns. The presence of dependents also raises contributions by 22 percent. Age is found to exert a large positive effect on giving: the dummy variables for successive age classes increase monotonically. Taxpayers in the forty to forty-nine age bracket give a full 75 percent more than otherwise similar taxpayers under thirty, and giving by taxpayers over sixty-five exceeds that of taxpayers in their forties by more than 40 percent. These differences may reflect differences in wealth holdings, as well as other attributes commonly associated with age. In any case, a strong age effect is common to all the results presented in this paper and is consistent with the findings of previous studies.

Equation 3-2 substitutes the first dollar price of cash gifts ($\ln P1$) for the weighted average price reflecting gifts of appreciated assets. As in previous studies, this substitution makes little qualitative difference, with the point estimate of the price elasticity rising slightly, to -1.358. In equations estimated for the 1975 tax file in the remainder of the paper, therefore, $\ln P50$ is used as the price variable; the price relevant to cash gifts is used in the panel file.

As an additional check of the stability of the estimates, the model was reestimated for a homogeneous subsample from the 1975 tax file of married taxpayers between the ages of thirty-five and fifty-five. As shown in equation 3-3, this restricted sample produces estimates of the price and income elasticities that are generally close to those obtained from using the entire sample; the only major difference is the approximate doubling of the effect of dependents.

Variations in Price and Income Elasticities

The assumption of constant price and income elasticities is clearly a simplification. Because of the importance of these parameters for tax policy, it is useful to investigate how each may vary over the income distribution. For instance, since the current deduction is allowed generally only to higher income taxpayers, it is important to know whether tax revenues would decrease more than contributions increased if the deduction were extended to lower income taxpayers or if a flat rate credit were substituted for the deduction. As noted above, previous studies have examined the variation in price and income elasticities by income, but the results have been mixed. To test the constancy of price and income elasticities, we estimated several equations that allow for variation according to the income and price of the taxpayer. Our purpose was not merely to test whether such variation exists, but also to determine the sensitivity of the measurement of the elasticities to the specifications of the models.

Table 4 shows the implied price and income elasticities at various income levels for several specifications. Where elasticities are not constant, they are calculated at the mean price and income for the income class. The first specification employed is one that adds an interaction term ($\ln Y \cdot \ln P$) to the basic specification of equation 3-1. This allows price and income elasticities to vary by income and price; however, the specification is restricted insofar as the change in the price and income elasticities are forced to move together. That is, income increases and price decreases as individuals move into higher income and tax brackets. The specification restricts the absolute values of the income and price elasticities to rise or fall together. When an interaction term is added, the absolute value of the price elasticity rises substantially with income (as does income elasticity with increases in the absolute value of price). The implied price elasticity is -0.382 for the lowest income class of the sample and rises in absolute value to -1.668 at income levels above \$100,000. At $Y = \$4,000$, the lowest income for any observation included in the regression, the equation in note b, table 4, implies a price elasticity of -0.105. As shown in figure 1, over 62 percent of all returns with itemized deductions had adjusted gross incomes of \$20,000 or less, and 96 percent had adjusted gross incomes of less than \$50,000. Thus for the great majority of taxpayers the implied price elasticity is less in absolute value than 1. This result is somewhat similar to that obtained by Feldstein and Taylor. Because they find positive price elasticities at income levels below \$7,455, they reject the specification, though not on the basis of any statistical test.

The second specification in table 4 is an adaptation of the translog model,

$$\ln G = a + b_1 \ln P + b_2 \ln Y + b_3 \ln Y \times \ln P + b_4 (\ln P)^2 + b_5 (\ln Y)^2,$$

with additional independent variables for age, dependents, and marital status.[41] The income elasticity equals $b_2 + b_3 \ln P + 2 b_5 \ln Y$, and the price elasticity equals $b_1 + b_3 \ln Y + 2 b_4 \ln P$. The advantage of this model is that it allows both price and income elasticities to vary and does

41. L. R. Christensen, D. W. Jorgenson, and L. J. Lau, "Transcendental Logarithmic Production Frontiers," *Review of Economics and Statistics,* vol. 55 (February 1973), pp. 28–45.

Table 4. Price and Income Elasticities by Income Class

Model description	Actual or implied elasticity of giving with respect to	Income level (dollars)				
		4,000–10,000	10,000–20,000	20,000–50,000	50,000–100,000	100,000 and over
General model expansion						
Basic log model with interaction term (ln Y · ln P)[a,b]	Price	−0.382 (0.071)	−0.657 (0.062)	−0.905 (0.056)	−1.273 (0.052)	−1.668 (0.056)
	Income	0.553 (0.021)	0.589 (0.020)	0.654 (0.019)	0.815 (0.018)	0.899 (0.019)
Translog model[a,c]	Price	−0.423 (0.134)	−0.732 (0.116)	−0.972 (0.094)	−1.253 (0.060)	−1.506 (0.057)
	Income	0.552 (0.048)	0.578 (0.037)	0.646 (0.028)	0.827 (0.050)	0.908 (0.020)
Interclass variation only						
Constant income elasticity[d]	Price	−2.172 (0.274)	−1.387 (0.119)	−1.260 (0.065)	−1.114 (0.055)	−1.506 (0.057)
	Income	...	...	0.777 (0.022)	...	...
Basic log model by income class[e]	Price	−0.945 (0.664)	−1.346 (0.315)	−1.657 (0.108)	−1.360 (0.140)	−1.779 (0.120)
	Income	0.393 (0.209)	0.621 (0.094)	0.364 (0.066)	0.668 (0.138)	1.089 (0.054)

a. Elasticities are calculated at the mean income and mean price of each income class. Estimated standard errors of price and income elasticities, also calculated at the mean for each class, are shown in parentheses.

b. Based on the equation:

$$\ln G = 3.387 \ln P + 0.478 \ln Y - 0.421 \ln Y \cdot \ln P + \ldots$$
$$(0.257) \qquad (0.024) \qquad (0.023)$$
$$R^2 = 0.479$$

c. Based on the equation:

$$\ln G = 4.306 \ln P - 0.247 (\ln P)^2 + 0.706 \ln Y - 0.014 (\ln Y)^2 - 0.538 \ln Y \ln P + \ldots$$
$$(0.629) \qquad (0.124) \qquad (0.266) \qquad (0.013) \qquad (0.067)$$
$$R^2 = 0.479$$

d. $R^2 = 0.475$.

e. From lowest to highest income class, $R^2 = 0.074, 0.091, 0.141, 0.075, 0.224$.

not constrain them to vary together as does the previous specification. Nonetheless, the results are consistent with the first method: the price elasticity is -0.423 in the lowest income class and gradually rises in absolute value as income and price rise. At $Y = \$4,000$ and $P = 0.86$, the implied elasticity is -0.082. As in the interaction model, the price elasticity is close to -1 in the \$20,000–\$50,000 income range and rises above 1.5 in absolute value in the highest income class.

One may suspect that the uniformity of these results is because both specifications add an interaction term, $\ln Y \cdot \ln P$. However, similar results were produced by a third specification in which no interaction term was introduced, and the price elasticity was allowed to vary only according to the price and not the income of the taxpayer.[42] What is common to these specifications is that, when the price elasticity is allowed to vary according to income, price, or both, the regressions consistently imply that price elasticity is small at lower income (or higher price) levels, becomes more negative as income increases, and is less than -1 only for a small portion of the population at higher income levels.

The third method used is to hold income and price elasticities constant within income groups but to allow them to vary across such groups. Two separate approaches were used to allow interclass variation. In the first, the income elasticity is held constant in a single regression across the sample population while the price elasticity is allowed to vary by income class. The second approach is to estimate separate regressions for each income class, thus allowing all parameters, including those for income, price, age, and so on to vary from income class to income class. Both approaches were used and the results are reported in table 4 under the heading "Interclass variation only." When the income elasticity is held constant across the population, price elasticities do vary by income class, although the differences are not great except for the lowest income class, where the price elasticity is greater than 2 in absolute value. Given the particular characteristics of low-income itemizers, and their high rate of giving (see figure 1), their coefficient of price must be interpreted with caution. Elasticities for the remaining classes are similar to the constant elasticity of equation 3-1.

42. In this specification, Y, $\ln Y$, P, $\ln P$, and other demographic variables were used as dependent variables. Unlike methods 1 and 2, the price elasticity is a function of price alone. The estimated price elasticity was similar to those shown for methods 1 and 2, although the estimated income elasticity was more constant across income classes.

In separate regressions for each income class, estimated price elasticities vary between -1.346 and -1.779 for all income classes except the $4,000–$10,000 class, for which the price elasticity is -0.945 and insignificant. These results are much more constant than those reported by Feldstein and Taylor for either 1962 or 1970, and the price elasticities tend to be somewhat higher. Indeed, Feldstein and Taylor's 1970 results appear closer to our results using methods 1 and 2.[43]

In summary, the pattern of variation in price elasticities depends on the way in which variation is allowed. Models that add independent variables in which price is a component tend to show price elasticities that increase in absolute value as income increases. The price elasticity is small at low incomes and exceeds one in absolute value only for a small part of the population. Models allowing interclass, but not intraclass, variation, however, tend to imply higher and more constant price elasticities across all income groups except perhaps the lowest. Still, parameter estimates have not been consistent across tax files when separate regressions have been run for each income class.

For the population of itemizers represented here, a summary means of comparing a general model expansion with a basic constant elasticity model is to simulate under each model the effects of eliminating the present tax deductibility of contributions. For each individual in our restricted sample, therefore, we calculated the change in giving that would be predicted by two estimated equations if the current price of giving were replaced by a price of one. When a constant price elasticity of -1.268 is assumed for everyone (equation 3-1), hypothetical giving declines by 43.4 percent for the population represented by the sample.[44] However, when the equation for the basic log model with interaction term is used (allowing the price elasticity to be different for each individual), the de-

43. Three other specifications were also tried. The first, which used giving as a percent of income as the dependent variable, gave unrealistic results. The implied price elasticity was about -2 at the lowest levels, less than -3.5 at income levels around $20,000, and about -1 at incomes of $20,000 and above. The second and third specifications applied the basic log model with interaction term and the translog model to separate income classes. In these specifications, most coefficients of variables of price and income, including the interaction term, were insignificant in practically all income classes. In view of the restricted range of variation for price and income within these income classes, this result is not surprising.

44. For the basic equation, simulated giving was found by solving the equation

$$G_1/G_0 = (A Y^\alpha P_1^\beta e^{\Gamma X + \mu})/(A Y^\alpha P_0^\beta e^{\Gamma X + \mu}),$$

where G, Y, P, X, and μ represent, respectively, giving, income, price, a vector of other variables, and an error term. Current price is denoted by P_0, and P_1 represents the simulated price. Where $P_1 = 1$, the equation reduces to $G_1 = G_0 P_0^{-\beta}$.

cline in giving is only 35.4 percent. Since ending deductibility would have caused a 34.4 percent increase in the weighted average of the price for the sample, this decline implies an "average" elasticity of only −1.031. Within a 95 percent confidence interval, the possible decline ranges from 32.5 to 38.1 percent, implying average elasticities of −0.948 to −1.110. It is worth emphasizing that these simulation results are based on the population of itemizers in 1975 who would have remained itemizers even if none of their contributions had been deductible. Since this population is a subset of the entire population of itemizers, care should be used in applying these findings.

Analyzing Giving Behavior over Time

To arrive at estimates of the price and income elasticities of giving based on the analysis of giving behavior over time, we examined both aggregate data for income classes and individual panel data. There are two reasons for examining charitable giving over time as well as in cross sections. First, there may be lags or dynamic interactions in giving behavior over time that would not be observed in the pattern of giving in any one year. Second, observing changes over time may enhance the prospect of distinguishing the separate effects of price and income on giving.

Feldstein and Taylor devote considerable attention to the problem of identifying separate income and price elasticities when the two variables are so closely related. They point out that, despite the relatively small standard errors of estimated coefficients, identification still may be a serious problem if the functional form relating price and income is nonlinear.

In any one year price is an exact nonlinear function of taxable income and marital status. Although net income is not perfectly correlated to taxable income and marital status does vary in cross-section samples, correlation between price and income tends to be quite high. It would thus be desirable to observe independent changes in price, such as those due to changes in the tax law over time. To obtain an estimate of the price elasticity that is not dependent on cross-section variation in prices and income, Feldstein and Taylor analyzed changes in giving for sixteen income groups between 1962 and 1970. Holding real income classes constant for the two years, they compared changes in giving with changes in prices for these income classes. They calculated arc elasticities, A, for each class by the formula

$$A = \frac{\ln (G70/G62)}{\ln (P70/P62)},$$

Table 5. Relative Giving, Average Price, and Implied Arc Elasticities, 1962, 1970, and 1975

Income (thousands of dollars)			Ratio of contributions to income			Price of gifts including assets			Arc elasticities		
1962 range[a]	1970 midpoint[a]	1975 midpoint[b]	1962[a]	1970[a]	1975	1962[a]	1970[a]	1975	1962–75	1962–70	1970–75
10–12	13.6	19.6	0.035	0.031	0.025	0.749	0.761	0.761	−21.17	−7.64	...[c]
12–15	16.6	22.2	0.037	0.032	0.026	0.717	0.733	0.686	7.98	−6.58	3.13
15–20	21.6	31.3	0.040	0.033	0.031	0.653	0.692	0.619	4.77	−3.32	0.56
20–30	30.8	44.5	0.048	0.041	0.040	0.530	0.600	0.511	4.99	−1.27	0.15
30–40	43.2	62.3	0.060	0.046	0.055	0.432	0.506	0.455	−2.93	−1.68	−1.39
40–50	55.5	80.1	0.092	0.064	0.054	0.367	0.440	0.420	−3.95	−2.00	3.65
50–60	67.8	97.8	0.115	0.067	0.066	0.287	0.392	0.397	−1.71	−1.73	−1.19
60–70	80.1	115.6	0.152	0.075	0.093	0.279	0.380	0.360	−1.93	−2.29	−3.98
70–80	95.6	133.4	0.179	0.097	0.099	0.218	0.348	0.364	−1.16	−1.31	0.45
80–100	114.1	160.1	0.189	0.118	0.102	0.280	0.370	0.358	−2.51	−1.69	4.42
100–150	154.1	222.4	0.224	0.143	0.190	0.290	0.323	0.354	−0.83	−4.16	3.10
150–200	215.8	311.3	0.229	0.162	0.165	0.314	0.323	0.341	−3.97	−12.25	0.34
200–350	339.1	489.2	0.256	0.202	0.204	0.325	0.338	0.348	−3.32	−6.04	0.34
350–500	524.0	756.1	0.230	0.195	0.214	0.321	0.349	0.355	−0.72	−1.97	5.45
500–750	770.6	1,111.9	0.257	0.213	0.300	0.366	0.366	0.365	−56.55	...[c]	−125.18
750–1,000	1,078.9	2,001.4	0.284	0.300	0.234	0.384	0.335	0.326	1.18	−0.40	9.12

a. Feldstein and Taylor, "Income Tax and Charitable Contributions," p. 1211, table 2.
b. With use of the consumer price index, same real midpoint as 1962 class.
c. Undefined; zero denominator.

where G and P represent average contributions and price for the income class. To account for a time trend in giving and to produce an average elasticity, Feldstein and Taylor then estimated a variant of the basic constant elasticity equation using the sixteen constant dollar income groups as observations:

(4) $$G70/G62 = C(P70/P62)^b e^u,$$

where C is a constant, b is the price elasticity, and u is an independent random variable. This equation uses the changes in tax law over the period—particularly the reduction in rates in 1964—to yield an independent shift in prices. The estimated price elasticity of -1.39, using the price accounting for gifts of appreciated assets, agrees quite closely with other estimates in the study. It is interesting to note that the estimated constant term implies that there was an exogenous decline in contributions over the period 1962–70 of about 1 percent a year.

Because our study makes use of a sample of itemizers in 1975, we decided to test the stability of the Feldstein-Taylor results by repeating their analysis for the periods 1962–75 and 1970–75. Both their results and ours are presented in tables 5 and 6. Unlike the period 1962–70, arc elasticities for 1970–75 (table 5, last column) are often positive. When regressions are estimated for 1970–75 using prices and weights similar to those used for 1962–70, three of the four price elasticities also turn out to be positive, although the standard errors are so large that the estimates are not significantly different from zero (table 6). The one significant price elasticity for 1970–75 is negative (-1.092) and results from using a weighted rather than an unweighted regression.

For the longer period, 1962–75, the arc elasticities are primarily negative in higher income classes but positive in the lower classes containing most itemizers. Regression results for this period using different prices and weights are fairly consistent: price elasticities are significant, less than one in absolute value (though not significantly less), and significantly different from the 1962–70 results. The intercept terms for 1962–75 generally imply the same exogenous annual rate of decline (1.4 percent to 1.9 percent, except for the weighted regression, where it equals 2.9 percent) that is implied by the 1962–70 results (1.1 percent and 1.9 percent, where reported), although there is no reason why that rate might not be expected to change over the periods involved. Since the years 1962–75 encompass the period 1962–70, this dissimilarity in price elasticities between the two periods is quite pronounced, although it might have been

Table 6. Price Elasticities Based on Changes in Contributions and Price for Real Income Groups, Selected Periods, 1962–75[a]

Description	1962–75	1962–70[b]	1970–75
Unweighted equations using P50			
Price elasticity	−0.813	−1.393	0.559
	(0.062)	(0.189)	(0.684)
Intercept	−0.217	−0.143	0.018
	(0.051)	(0.033)	(0.049)
$\bar{R}^2$	0.37	0.78	−0.02
Unweighted equations using P1			
Price elasticity	−0.840	−1.540	0.479
	(0.261)	(0.214)	(0.743)
Intercept	−0.162	−0.083	−0.001
	(0.061)	(0.040)	(0.047)
$\bar{R}^2$	0.38	0.77	−0.04
Weighted equations using P50			
Price elasticity	−0.629	−1.575	−1.092
	(0.379)		(0.285)
Intercept	−0.315	...[c]	−0.209
	(0.015)		(0.017)
$\bar{R}^2$	0.96	...[c]	0.91
Unweighted equations using P50 and *dropping bottom 3 classes*			
Price elasticity	−0.972	−1.344	0.433
	(0.294)		(0.737)
Intercept	−0.168	...[c]	0.050
	(0.063)		(0.052)
$\bar{R}^2$	0.45	...[c]	−0.06

a. Numbers in parentheses are standard errors.
b. Data from Feldstein and Taylor, "Income Tax and Charitable Contributions," p. 1212.
c. Not reported in ibid.

anticipated by noting the difference in results from the two independent periods, 1962–70 and 1970–75. In short, this replication does not provide support for the hypothesis that the price elasticity is greater than one in absolute value. The high degree of aggregation involved in the procedure, however, makes the specific estimates suspect.

In a second analysis of giving behavior over time, we analyzed data from the Internal Revenue Service Seven-Year Panel of Taxpayers, described above. In particular, we examined the giving behavior of taxpayers who itemized in both 1968 and 1973. Although this group would probably

Table 7. Price and Income Elasticities Based on Changes in Personal Giving, 1968–73[a]

Equation	Income measure	Price elasticity	Income elasticity	Other variables included
7-1	Current net income	−0.623 (0.306)	0.426 (0.065)	None
7-2	Current net income	−0.884 (0.316)	0.325 (0.068)	Dummy variables for marital status, dependents, and five age categories
7-3	Permanent income	−0.658 (0.336)	0.417 (0.071)	Dummy variables for marital status, dependents, and five age categories, and transitory income component

a. Current net income is current adjusted gross income minus taxes paid if no contributions were made. Permanent income is predicted adjusted gross income in individual regressions of adjusted gross income on a time trend. Equations were of the form:

$$\ln (G73 + 10) - \ln (G68 + 10) = a + b_1(\ln P73 - \ln P68) + b_2(\ln Y73 - \ln Y68) + \dots$$

Numbers in parentheses are standard errors.

not be representative of all itemizers, let alone all taxpayers, this selection procedure still yields a unique sample of data on giving behavior over time for individuals. Because the panel contains few high-income individuals, we selected taxpayers with average adjusted gross income over the period, in 1970 dollars, of between $2,886 (the equivalent of $4,000 in 1975) and $50,000. This produced a sample of 2,533 taxpaying units. Giving and net income were defined as above, and the price of cash gifts was used because gifts of appreciated assets are an inconsequential portion of all gifts for taxpayers at these income levels. In addition to net current income, we also employed a measure of permanent income, the fitted value in individual regressions of ln AGI on a time trend.[45]

Table 7 presents estimates of price and income elasticities based on the analysis of changes in individual giving. Equation 7-1 explains changes in giving by changes in current net income and price, all in logarithms. The estimated price elasticity of −0.623 is considerably smaller than the basic estimates using the 1975 tax file, but its standard error is relatively large, giving the estimate a 95 percent confidence interval of −1.2 to −0.02. The estimated income elasticity (0.426) is also smaller than that

45. For each taxpayer a regression was estimated of the form: $\ln AGI_t = d_1 + d_2$ $(t - 1966) + u_t$, $t = 1967$–73. The change in fitted values thus reflects the seven-year trend in adjusted gross income (AGI).

based on the 1975 data. When dummy variables for marital status, dependents, and age are included, the price elasticity rises to −0.884, and the income elasticity falls. In equation 7-3 permanent income and a transitory income component are substituted for current net income. Again, the estimated price elasticity is less than one in absolute value, though it is not significantly less. These estimated price elasticities are somewhat larger than those estimated from similar equations over shorter time periods, reported in Clotfelter,[46] probably reflecting lags in adjustment of individual giving behavior.

Both analyses of changes in giving over time thus yield price elasticities that generally fall between zero and −1. However, both sets of estimates are relatively imprecise, as indicated by their large standard errors.

Conclusion

We have addressed the empirical question of what effect tax incentives have on charitable giving. As in previous studies on this question, only one type of tax incentive was actually observed—the personal deduction in the income tax—but the existence of significant elasticities seems to imply that contributions would respond to other incentives as well, such as a tax credit or an "above-the-line" adjustment to income, at least in the long run. A major reservation to such a conclusion would be the view held by Morgan, Dye, and Hybels[47] that the typical taxpayer is unaware of marginal tax rates and of the effect of tax incentives on giving. However, it seems just as likely that many taxpayers, particularly itemizers, use approximations and rules of thumb that render their behavior very similar, on average, to a perfectly informed optimizer.

As for the magnitude of the price elasticity itself, our review of previous empirical work and our own analysis point to a consensus of sorts. With few exceptions, almost all the estimates are significantly different from zero, and they are greater than 1 in absolute value for higher income classes. In that sense, the findings of this paper are consistent with the bulk of previous findings. However, we are considerably more uncertain about the actual value of the price elasticity than the standard errors associated with cross-section, constant-elasticity equations would indicate. Because of the close nonlinear relationship between income and price in the cross-section studies, the standard errors associated with estimates are likely to

46. "Tax Incentives and Charitable Giving."
47. "Results from Two National Surveys on Philanthropic Activity."

overstate the estimate's precision. Also, elasticities seem to vary by income, and a constant elasticity function yields only some average for the sample used. Our estimates based on the analysis of changes in giving behavior appear to bear out the uncertainty about the elasticity. While those results are generally consistent with a significantly negative elasticity, they do not provide the basis for confident identification of a precise elasticity. At the same time, the estimates based on changes in giving may well reflect lags in adjustment, with the long-run elasticity exceeding one in absolute value. Our study, in short, finds no pervasive flaws in the empirical work on this question. Still, the sensitivity of the price elasticity to changes in specification means that caution should be used in making policy prescriptions on the basis of such findings.

Comments by Gerard M. Brannon

Clotfelter and Steuerle summarize the extensive literature on the effect of tax deductibility on charitable contributions and then make their own contributions. Briefly, this recent literature suggests a price elasticity of a little over one (absolute) for the taxpaying population as a whole, but heretofore erratic results have been obtained when price elasticity was estimated separately for income classes or for types of charity.

The price elasticity of contributions for all taxpayers appears crucial to the judgment "Is it efficient to have a contributions deduction in the tax law to stimulate contributions?" (In keeping with the spirit of this book, I forgo the question "Is it fair?") The efficiency question should depend on whether $e\,U(C/G) > 1$, where e is the absolute value of the price elasticity of contributions, and $U(C/G)$ is the ratio of social utility from a dollar spent by charity to that of a dollar spent by government. The extensive Filer Commission report and its compendia laid a groundwork by assembling a mass of data on what charities do and providing a variety of qualitative assessments of charitable performance in specific areas (not all favorable to charities).[48] How even to define the relevant marginal social utility here has been barely explored beyond the vaguest arguments about pluralism. The econometric literature seems to assume that $U(C/G)$ is close to one over a wide range of contributions, which makes it critical

48. *Research Papers Sponsored by the Commission on Private Philanthropy and Public Needs.*

Table 8. Income, Contributions, and Marginal Tax Rates, Selected Income Classes, Itemized Returns for 1975

Adjusted gross income (thousands of dollars)	Contribution		Marginal tax rate	Adjustment for appreciated property	Price of contributing $1 (dollars)
	Dollars	Percent of income			
4,000	308	7.7	14	...	0.86
8,000	340	4.2	19	...	0.81
11,000	360	3.3	20	...	0.80
13,000	377	2.9	21	...	0.79
15,000	435	2.9	22	...	0.78
17,000	460	2.7	24	...	0.76
19,000	513	2.7	26	...	0.74
22,000	506	2.3	28	...	0.72
26,000	624	2.4	30	...	0.70
35,000	875	2.5	36	1	0.63
100,000	4,000	4.0	58	7	0.35

Source: U.S. Internal Revenue Service, *Statistics of Income—1975: Individual Income Tax Returns.*

to the efficiency question to know if the absolute value of the price elasticity is more or less than one.

Despite the apparent agreement that the price elasticity is greater than one, the situation is uncomfortable. One problem can be seen by visual inspection of the data. At one end, people have low incomes, low tax rates, and small contributions. At the other end, people have high incomes, high tax rates, and large contributions. The large contribution behavior could be attributed to either income or tax rates.

The recent econometric literature, which Clotfelter and Steuerle broadly support, attributes the large contributions at upper income levels to the high tax rates, not to the high income. Literally, this literature says that the income elasticity of contributions is less than one! Without tax deductions, rich people are stingier relative to income than poor people. Why this statistical result emerges can be seen in figure 1, where, through most of the income distribution, the ratio of contributions to income falls as income and tax rates rise.

To provide some feel for what is going on, I present in table 8 a numerical version of figure 1—I selected a sample of taxpayers spread along the income axis and estimated their contributions from the average curve. Then I inserted the marginal tax rate of the median taxpayer at the various income levels (when arrayed by size of marginal tax rate) and adjusted the effective marginal rate in the top brackets for the effect of gifts of appreciated property.

What is conspicuous in table 8 is that in the income brackets up to $22,000, where the ratio of contributions to income is falling, the level of income is five times greater than it is in the bottom bracket, but the price of contributions has fallen modestly. Above $22,000, where the ratio of contributions rises, income increases about the same way, but now the price of contributions falls much more (by 50 percent compared to the fall for the lower brackets of about 14 percent). When one fits a single equation to this set, it is understandable that the price of contributions will seem to have a stronger effect in explaining the large contributions at the high income levels.[49]

One kind of qualitative consideration raised by thinking about table 8 is that the contributions of rich and poor may be quite different in price-income sensitivity. Low-income contributions tend to go heavily to religious organizations, which plausibly have a low income elasticity since they involve, to some extent, buying a service. The contributions of the rich are plausibly more price and income sensitive.

Turning to the specific work of Clotfelter and Steuerle, I note first that they have done another cross-section analysis on later data but with the same result: price elasticity greater than absolute 1 and income elasticity lower. More interesting is that they investigate several related topics that give some new perspectives on the earlier research.

1. Time series. Feldstein and Taylor, examining data for the 1960s, were able to compare contributions at the same real income level with the lower tax rates after 1964. The result was a decline in real contributions, a result consistent with a price elasticity greater than absolute 1. Clotfelter and Steuerle find this almost completely reversed for the period 1970–75, and consequently, over a period long enough to cover both studies, they find only a moderate, less than one, price elasticity.

2. Income level. Heretofore it has been a bit of an embarrassment to the apparent agreement on high price elasticity that erratic results were obtained when efforts were made to measure elasticity separately for low and high incomes. Clotfelter and Steuerle deal with this problem satisfactorily by introducing terms for interaction between the income and price variables to obtain quite consistent results, with price elasticity rising from

---

49. The various authors of this econometric literature used a richer data base than I did (see table 8); they had intraclass variation also. The table still suggests how difficult it is to interpret their results.

Table 9. Revenue Loss from Contributions Deduction and Contributions Induced (Clotfelter-Steuerle Estimates)

Adjusted gross income (thousands of dollars)	Contributions (millions of dollars)	Tax rate	Revenue loss (millions of dollars)	Contributions induced (millions of dollars)
Under 5	193	5	9	4
5–10	1,280	15	192	81
10–15	2,323	21	488	357
15–20	2,570	24	617	452
20–25	2,119	28	593	576
25–50	3,730	26	1,343	1,305
50–100	1,448	54	796	997
100 and over	1,728	65	1,123	1,691
Total	15,391	...	5,161	5,463

0.4 at the bottom to 1.7 at the top and income elasticity rising from 0.6 to 0.9.

This result is interesting in several ways. It helps deal with the sort of problem with the older studies that I was concerned about in table 8. Moreover, this difference in elasticities by income level suggests that a single statistical measure of "overall elasticity," even if statistically valid, is not adequate to predict the balance of revenues lost to contributions induced, which involves a different weighting of high- and low-elasticity cases. (This point was suggested to me by Joseph Pechman.) Given different elasticities at high and low income levels, the overall relation of revenue lost to contributions induced must be investigated, as in table 9 (based on *Statistics of Income* for 1975).

It still turns out, with "tax weighting," that contributions induced exceed the revenue lost, but the margin is less than the 20 percent suggested by a statistical elasticity of 1.2.

3. Finally, Clotfelter and Steuerle make a unique contribution to the literature by examining data from a panel of taxpayers who itemized in both 1968 and 1973. The price elasticity obtained in this panel comes out below an absolute one, but the panel is limited to taxpayers with incomes from $4,000 to $50,000, and, as I read the figures, the panel results are about what one would have expected, given the income-level-differentiated estimates of elasticity in table 4.

On the whole, the picture of price elasticity greater than absolute one for contributions stands up. Clotfelter and Steuerle's work deals with some problems in this literature and contributes some new insight into income level differences. It is still a tricky problem.

Comments by John A. Brittain

This paper provides an excellent wrap-up of recent empirical analysis of the effects of income tax policy on the charitable contributions of living persons. The authors also present valuable new analysis based on the 1975 Treasury tax file and other sources. The clarity of the paper is remarkable for presentations of this kind, and its unpretentious tone is refreshing, if perhaps too modest.

Objectives of This and Earlier Studies

One important element missing from the paper is the rationale for the particular choice of elasticity to be estimated—namely, the elasticity of aggregate contributions with respect to the price of giving (the complement of the marginal tax rate). A zero value for this elasticity would be easy to interpret. A lack of response of giving to price changes would indicate that tax rates could be cut without reducing contributions; more specifically, deductibility of contributions could be curtailed without depressing giving. Not surprisingly, virtually all estimates have shown the expected negative price elasticity of giving. One problem, however, is that the much-stressed minus-one value for this elasticity as an important crossover point is never clarified. Earlier interpretations of this benchmark suggested that it marks the point at which the loss in revenue resulting from deductibility is equal to the associated increase in contributions. In other words, this degree of sensitivity of contributions to the price of giving is just sufficient to offset the cost of deductibility at the margin. Moreover, an elasticity more negative than unity would point to a "free lunch," where the stimulation of contributions more than made up for the revenue cost of certain policy changes.

Although the revenue-contribution relationship may have been clarified in earlier work, it would have been useful to have the underlying assumptions and derivations reviewed here as an aid to interpretation of the findings. More important, the practical meaning of the revenue-contribution offset itself could have been usefully explored. For example, what would be the effects of specified percentage curtailments of the current 100 percent deductibility? What are the welfare implications of a rise in contributions associated with an equal decline in revenues? How adequately do these increments to contributions substitute for public expenditures of the same amount? Obviously the answers to these questions entail value judgments, but the appropriate tax policy toward contributions depends on them, in addition to the empirical relationships. In short, the reader would derive more from the econometric work presented if the complex question of the policy implications of the findings had been addressed.

To turn from these policy matters, what were the methodological objectives of this study and its predecessors? In general, they have attempted to identify what might be called a supply function for individual contributions (G) as determined by the price of giving (P), individual income (Y), and other explanatory variables (OV). As indicated, the statistical focus has been on the elasticity of G with respect to P, and this has led to various models of the general relationship between $\log G$, $\log P$, and $\log Y$:

$$(6) \qquad \log G = f(\log P, \log Y, OV).$$

The basic log-linear constant elasticity specification of this relationship has generally yielded price elasticities negative by more than unity. However, always present has been the nagging reality that a strong relationship between two of the explanatory variables lurked in the background:

$$(7) \qquad \log P = g(\log Y).$$

Since the price of giving (P) faced by an individual is the complement of his marginal tax rate, the observed relationship between P and Y is inevitably strong and negative. The work by Clotfelter and Steuerle can best be reviewed by stressing their attempts to deal with this statistical problem by specifications that allow the price elasticity to vary with income.

The Models with Variable Elasticities

In table 3 Clotfelter and Steuerle report results of the simple log-linear specification:

$$(8) \qquad \log G = a + b \log P + c \log Y + d\,OV + u.$$

With their price variables based on cash gifts only and one variable allowing for asset gifts, their constant price elasticity estimates came to -1.36 and -1.27, respectively—significantly into the free-lunch range below minus one. These results are consistent with those of earlier studies. But, as before, there is no way of knowing to what extent these negative co-

Table 10. Variations in Elasticities and Other Statistics, by Income Class, Based on Clotfelter and Steuerle's Table 4, Basic Log-linear Model with Interaction Term

Statistic	Income class (thousands of dollars)				
	4–10	10–20	20–50	50–100	100 and over
Price elasticity	−0.382	−0.657	−0.905	−1.273	−1.668
Income elasticity	0.553	0.589	0.654	0.815	0.899
Mean price[a]	0.837	0.768	0.658	0.449	0.368
Mean income[a] (thousands of dollars)	7.73	14.85	26.76	64.14	163.92
Mean marginal tax rate[b]	0.163	0.232	0.342	0.551	0.632
Tax rate elasticity[c]	0.074	0.199	0.470	1.562	2.865
"Contribution" of P and Y to G/Y (percent)[d]	0.99	0.78	0.71	0.85	1.00

a. Estimated from tabulated elasticities and portion of regression equation, table 4, note b.
b. Complement of mean price.
c. Estimated as |price elasticity| · (mean tax rate)/(mean price).
d. Ratio of net price and income components of regression equation (table 4, note b) to mean income.

efficients should be attributed to the known negative association between P and Y. Certainly it would be rash to interpret the estimated constant elasticity as indicating the effect of exogenous changes in P alone when it is clear that P is inversely related to Y.

The authors follow previous studies by adding to equation 8 the interaction variable $\log P \cdot \log Y$, allowing for the interaction of price and income (see table 4, note b). Since the price elasticity is the policy variable of interest, it is convenient to restate their fitted equation (in natural logarithms) as:

$$(9) \quad \ln G = 0.478 \ln Y + (3.387 - 0.421 \ln Y) \ln P + \ldots$$
$$(0.024) \qquad (0.257) \quad (0.023)$$

This form offers an intuitive rationale for the interaction term. The "contribution" of price to the explanation of giving is a log-linear function of P with both parameters varying with Y. These varying functions of price seem entirely appropriate, given the strong relationship between P and Y. The price elasticities are given by the variable coefficient of $\ln P$ in equation 9.

Some of the results and implications of equation 9 are summarized in table 10. The price elasticities are shown to vary strongly by income, varying from −0.382 at an income of $7,730 to −1.668 at an income of $163,920. The implied elasticities with respect to the marginal tax rate are also derived there and vary even more strongly, from 0.07 at the low class mean to 2.87 at the high class mean. The low tax effect on giving at low income levels seems plausible, given the small effect on the price of giving of a relative change in a low tax rate.[50]

What are the statistical merits of the results from equation 9 as summarized in table 10? It is worth noting that the sampling error in the variable elasticity function in equation 9 appears to be dominated by the 0.257 standard error for ln P, suggesting that the price elasticity in the low income range may not differ significantly from zero. Five points can be made in support of the interaction model. First, with respect to goodness of fit, the t-ratio for the interaction term itself (about 18) suggests strongly that providing for the association of P and Y greatly improves the explanation of giving.[51]

A second question to be considered in appraising Clotfelter and Steuerle's elasticity results in table 10 is the giving *ratio* implied by their model. The authors report that their attempt to explain the giving–income ratio itself produced unrealistic results. However, if they had explained ln G/Y with the same variables as in equation 9 above, the price elasticity would have been unchanged and only the coefficient of ln Y would have changed (from 0.478 to −0.522). A remarkable implication of that revised equation is shown in the last line of table 10. The total "contribution" of the price and income variables in equation 9 to the giving–income *ratio* varies hardly at all with income. Variables P and Y together (including their effects via the interaction term) are shown to influence G in opposite directions and contribute on balance a fairly constant 1 percent to the estimates of G as a percent of Y. There is even a slight U-shaped pattern in the effect of P and Y on the G/Y ratio—a result consistent with the U-shaped observed ratio reported in figure 1.[52] The indicated minimal net effect of P and Y on variations in the giving ratio thus gives some additional plausibility to equation 9.

A third criterion that can be considered in appraising equation 9 is the behavior of the price elasticities at extreme income values. Clotfelter and Steuerle note that Feldstein and Taylor obtained variable elasticities similar to those in table 10 but rejected them because their equation yielded positive elasticities at income levels below $7,455. However, no statistical test was invoked. In any case, the same test can be applied to Clotfelter

50. These elasticities are relevant to appraising the effect on contributions of overall tax rate changes, rather than policy changes aimed at contributions only.

51. Note should be taken here, however, of warnings by Feldstein and Taylor of potentially misleading standard errors in the presence of nonlinearities.

52. There is no way to compare the predicted values of G/Y from equation 9 to the giving–AGI ratios of 2 to 8 percent in figure 1. The constant term and coefficients for other valuables were not reported by Clotfelter and Steuerle in equation 9.

and Steuerle's result in equation 9. It shows that the estimated price elasticity is positive only for incomes below \$3,120 and negative by more than unity only for incomes above \$33,500. It seems unlikely that any statistical test would reject equation 9 because of these implausible results for very low incomes. For example, the elasticities would be *significantly* positive for even lower incomes.

Fourth, it should be noted that Clotfelter and Steuerle's results for varying price elasticities with the interaction model are supported by their more general "translog" formulation, which does not force price and income elasticities to vary together. The price elasticities for the five income class means vary from -0.423 to -1.506, or almost the same breadth and range as in the interaction model. Moreover, the results for the translog model may be somewhat more acceptable in that the implausible zero elasticity point appears to be reached only at an even lower income level, if at all.[53]

Fifth, in case the interaction term remains a cause of skepticism, the authors note that a specification allowing price elasticity to vary only with price produced similar results. In sum, a tentative vote is cast here in favor of the sharp variations in elasticity indicated by the interaction and translog models over the constant elasticity models with price elasticities around -1.3 throughout.

Competing Elasticity Models

The authors refer to other tests with specifications allowing for variations in price elasticity. The first holds income elasticity artificially constant across incomes. Not surprisingly, the results are similar to those with the constant elasticity model. Somewhat more persuasive at first glance are the constant price elasticity models run for separate income *classes*. Again the answers are similar to those for the aggregate constant elasticity models. However, this too was to be expected, since income varies greatly within these classes, and the price coefficient may again be picking up the effect of these income variations. To isolate the price elasticity in each income class, equation 8 was fitted to each class separately (allowing intraclass variation in price elasticity). Here the coefficients for price and income were generally insignificant. Clotfelter and Steuerle attribute this result to limited variation of P and Y. However, without the interaction term, these variables were strongly significant and relatively constant. Their unreported results that include the interaction term thus cast doubt

53. It is not possible to estimate this point from the data presented by Clotfelter and Steuerle since the translog elasticity depends on both price and income.

on the latter result. The erratic results with the interaction term do not indicate that the model without it was correctly specified.

The time series analysis by Clotfelter and Steuerle, and Feldstein and Taylor before them, seeks to get around the price-income link by using independent changes in price arising from statutory changes in the tax laws. The approach appears promising, but the standard errors at this stage are awkwardly large. In any case, the estimated price elasticities were generally so low as to give no support to the high constant price elasticities emerging from the cross-section analysis.

Conclusion

The new cross-section work by the authors has been ably carried out, and it has probably pushed this line of inquiry to the limits of its productivity. Their attempts to isolate price and tax effects with the aid of statutory tax rate changes deserve to be followed up. At least two measurement questions should be considered in any further research. The 8 percent contribution–income ratio shown for low incomes suggests that adjusted gross income may be a misleading measure of permanent income and donor capacity at that end of the scale. For example, the income variable might well be revised to exclude capital losses or unusually high deductions in that range.[54] Also, the contributions variable itself is suspect according to Treasury estimates indicating substantial *over*statement of donations by upper income households.

Finally, the authors' cautious conclusions seem warranted in view of the work to date. They note a "consensus of sorts" showing price elasticities to be significantly negative, but only greater than one in absolute value for higher income classes. They deserve credit for laying this out so well. They also recommend caution in making policy prescriptions on the basis of the findings. Although this warning is certainly in order, an effort to spell out the policy implications of their tentative findings would be very useful. In this context they might put the Treasury file and these models to work simulating revenue effects of various tax policies toward contributions. In this way the estimated effects of tax rate changes, deductibility reductions, and tax credits or above-the-line adjustments to income could advance understanding beyond that achieved by a priori interpretation of elasticities.

54. This is related to the points made by Joseph Minarik in his paper in this book; he notes a tendency for capital loss bunching and for high deductions to offset ordinary income in the lower income brackets.

Conference Participants

with their affiliations at the time of the conference

Henry J. Aaron *Brookings Institution*

Martin J. Bailey *University of Maryland*

Martin Neil Baily *Brookings Institution*

J. Gregory Ballentine *University of Florida*

Alan S. Blinder *Princeton University*

Michael J. Boskin *Stanford University*

Barry Bosworth *Brookings Institution*

David F. Bradford *Princeton University*

Gerard M. Brannon *American Council of Life Insurance*

Harvey E. Brazer *University of Michigan*

Roger E. Brinner *Data Resources, Inc.*

John A. Brittain *Brookings Institution*

Stephen H. Brooks *Data Resources, Incorporated**

E. Cary Brown *Massachusetts Institute of Technology*

Gary T. Burtless *U.S. Department of Health, Education, and Welfare*

Lawrence Chimerine *Chase Econometrics*

Charles T. Clotfelter *Duke University*

Frank de Leeuw *U.S. Department of Commerce*

Martin S. Feldstein *National Bureau of Economic Research*

William C. Freund *New York Stock Exchange*

* On leave at the Council of Economic Advisers.

Ann F. Friedlaender *Massachusetts Institute of Technology*

Harvey Galper *U.S. Treasury Department*

Richard Goode *International Monetary Fund*

Roger H. Gordon *Princeton University*

C. Lowell Harriss *Columbia University*

Jerry A. Hausman *Massachusetts Institute of Technology*

Patric H. Hendershott *Purdue University*

Sheng-Cheng Hu *Social Security Administration*

Charles E. McLure *National Bureau of Economic Research*

Burton G. Malkiel *Princeton University*

Joseph J. Minarik *Brookings Institution*

Franco Modigliani *Massachusetts Institute of Technology*

Richard A. Musgrave *Harvard University*

Larry J. Ozanne *Urban Institute*

Joseph A. Pechman *Brookings Institution*

Rudolph G. Penner *American Enterprise Institute*

Nicholas S. Perna *General Electric Company*

George E. Peterson *Urban Institute*

Harvey S. Rosen *Princeton University*

John B. Shoven *Stanford University*

C. Eugene Steuerle *U.S. Treasury Department*

Emil M. Sunley *U.S. Treasury Department*

Stanley S. Surrey *Harvard University*

George M. von Furstenberg *International Monetary Fund*

Warren E. Weber *Virginia Polytechnic Institute*

Gary M. Wenglowski *Goldman, Sachs and Company*

James W. Wetzler *Joint Committee on Internal Revenue Taxation*

Index

Aaron, Henry J., 209n, 283n, 326, 360n
Abrams, Burton A., 418–19
Accelerator, interaction with cost of capital, 102–03, 105, 109, 111, 115, 128
Accrual taxation of capital gains, 243, 267
AFDC. *See* Aid to families with dependent children
Aged, capital gains realization by, 257–58
Aid to families with dependent children (AFDC), 34; effect on labor supply, 46–47, 60–61
Ando, Albert K., 88n, 90, 100n
Andrews, William D., 404
Artus, Jacques R., 354n
Ashenfelter, Orley, 49n
Assets: factors affecting sale of, 278; market valuation, 207–08; replacement cost, 5, 207, 224–25
Auerbach, Alan J., 92n, 140, 218n
Auten, Gerald, 14, 245, 423n

Bailey, Martin J., 210, 245n, 283n
Balassa, Bela, 91n
Ballentine, J. Gregory, 192
Bankruptcy Act of *1898,* 166
Bankruptcy costs, 7; data availability on, 163, 193; and debt–capital ratio, 162; examples of, 165; marginal, 171, 195; measurement of, 164–72, 195; under no-tax structure, 134–38; reorganization costs versus, 136, 166, 167, 193; risk and, 146–51; upper limit on, 145

Barber, Clarence L., 365n
Barro, Robert J., 333n, 338n, 348
Baumol, William J., 137n
Beach, Charles M., 343n
Berndt, Ernest R., 102n, 117n
Bhatia, Kul B., 366n
Bhattacharya, Sudipto, 154n
Bischoff, Charles W., 90, 102n
Black, Fischer, 153
Blinder, Alan S., 366n, 368n
Blume, Marshall E., 211n, 257n
Boadway, R. W., 324n
Bodie, Zvi, 233n
Bonds, 6; in bankruptcy liquidation, 136–37; discount rate, 211, 239; personal income taxation of, 141; risk in investment in, 143–44
Book value, replacement cost versus, 224–26
Boskin, Michael J., 72, 163n, 198, 390n, 417–18
Bradford, David F., 139n, 140, 147n, 148, 152n, 153, 172n, 339n
Brainard, William C., 91n, 223n, 233n
Brannon, Gerard M., 244, 245n, 437
Brems, Hans, 366n
Breneman, David W., 417n
Brennan, M. J., 147n
Brinner, Roger E., 10–12, 209, 243n
Brittain, John A., 21, 441
Brooks, Stephen H., 10–12
Brown, R. L., 343n
Bruce, N., 324n
Brunner, Karl, 112n
Buiter, Willem H., 338n

449

VOTES, MONEY, AND THE CLINTON IMPEACHMENT

BOOKS IN THIS SERIES

VOTES, MONEY, AND THE CLINTON IMPEACHMENT

Irwin L. Morris

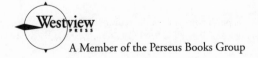
Westview
PRESS

A Member of the Perseus Books Group

Copyright © 2002 by Westview Press, A Member of the Perseus Books Group

Westview Press books are available at special discounts for bulk purchases in the United States by corporations, institutions, and other organizations. For more information, please contact the Special Markets Department at The Perseus Books Group, 11 Cambridge Center, Cambridge MA 02142, or call (617) 252-5298.

Published in 2001 in the United States of America by Westview Press, 5500 Central Avenue, Boulder, Colorado 80301–2877, and in the United Kingdom by Westview Press, 12 Hid's Copse Road, Cumnor Hill, Oxford OX2 9JJ

Find us on the World Wide Web at www.westviewpress.com

Library of Congress Cataloging-in-PublicationData.
Morris, Irwin L. (Irwin Lester), 1967-
  Votes, money, and the Clinton impeachment / by Irwin Morris.
    p. cm.
  Includes bibliographical references and index.
  ISBN 0-8133-9808-8 (pbk); 0-8133-3960-X
    1. Clinton, Bill, 1946—Impeachment. 2. Clinton, Bill 1946—Public opinion. 3. United States—Politics and government—1993–2001. 4. United States. Congress. Senate—Voting History—20th century. 5. United States. Congress. House—Voting—History—20th century. 6. Campaign funds—United States—History—20th century. 7. Political culture—United States—History—20th century. 8. Public opinion—United States—History—20th century. I. Title.
E886.2 .M68 2001
973.929'092—dc21   2001046725

10   9   8   7   6   5   4   3   2   1

For Chris, Maddie, and Cameron

CONTENTS

List of Tables and Figures

Tables

Figures

PREFACE

We are all living through history. Generations from now, historians will study the events of our time, just as there are now historians who study every previous era. Living through history is nothing special. But occasionally we get the opportunity to experience "history," those rare events that will someday hold the attention of generations yet to be born, and that is exceptional. Sometimes we are even aware of the significance of the events that become part of our daily lives and so we live *self-consciously* through "history"—something truly rare.

Living through the Clinton impeachment was one of those extraordinary opportunities that come along only a few times a century. During the scandal and its aftermath, one could watch history unfold, all the time realizing the significance of the events themselves. For those of my generation—those between the baby boomers and generation x-ers—this is one of the first, if not *the* first, truly historic phenomena in domestic U.S. politics. You just don't see presidents impeached every day. Maybe every century, but not every day.

Living through history, actually paying attention when something happens that people will talk about for centuries (decades, at least) is an exhilarating experience. It can also be a depressing experience. The Clinton-Lewinsky scandal and the subsequent public political spectacle rarely showcased the best in human beings. Quite often they seemed to highlight the worst. Living through history can also be a disturbing experience, particularly if you learn something you'd rather not know. Of course, history has a tendency to do that: to teach us what we need to know, ought to know, have to know just at the time we would prefer to continue on in the dark.

The Clinton-Lewinsky scandal, the president's impeachment and Senate trial, and the public reaction to all of these can be the type of history that teaches. I won't detail my argument at this point; that's why I wrote the book. But if I'm right—if money plays a different and far more significant role in the U.S. system than we had previously realized—we must face some difficult problems and make a serious effort to solve them. And we need to do so quickly because the stakes are high.

This book is intended for a broad audience. My argument is straightforward and uncomplicated and should be readily accessible to those with a rudimentary knowledge of U.S. politics. Although a thorough understanding of the quantitative analyses presented in several chapters requires a basic background in statistics, I have tried to present the results in such a way that the argument is still clear and comprehensible for those without statistical training. Overall, I believe I have succeeded.

A number of friends and family members talked with me about portions of this book more times than most of them care to remember. I was able to make a clearer argument and focus more consistently on what was important because of having talked with them, and I'm thankful for their help and support. Somewhat more extensive conversations with various colleagues were also quite helpful, and I am especially grateful to those—Paul Herrnson, Jim Gimpel, Karen Kaufmann, and Ric Uslaner—who took the time to read and provide comment on various drafts of the book proposal and/or sections of the manuscript. Their contributions have improved the manuscript immeasurably, but I alone am responsible for all of its shortcomings.

Finally, I appreciate the continued support of my wife, Chris, and my children, Maddie and Cameron. Frequently, brutally early mornings at the computer kept Daddy from being a fun playmate during the afternoon, but there were few complaints. I owe all three of you, and I promise not to write any more books for awhile. Not a long while, but awhile.

I

INTRODUCTION

Here, in the last weeks of a dizzying year, was the dizziest day of them all. It was a day of memorable speeches and vacuous ones, of gestures grand and petty, of shock, confusion, the momentous and the banal, of sudden shifts in mood and shattered logic, of wrong notes and portentous chords, a day of heroes and opportunists in such a frenzy of maneuvering that they could be one and the same person from one hour to the next.

So this is what history feels like before the historians get hold of it.

—David Von Drehle, Washington Post,
December 20, 1998: sec. A, p. 37

Impeachment Revisited

On July 27, 1974, the House Judiciary Committee of the 92nd Congress passed the first of three articles of impeachment against President Richard Nixon. Six Republicans joined 21 Democrats in supporting this first article of impeachment. At this point in the Watergate investigations, the public's opinion of Nixon's performance was at a historically low level; his job approval rating was an abysmal 26 percent. Nixon resigned shortly thereafter to avoid impeachment and subsequent removal from office.

Almost 25 years later, on December 12, 1998, the House Judiciary Committee of the 105th Congress passed four articles of impeachment against President William Jefferson Clinton on a party-line vote. One week later, two of the four articles passed the House of Representatives. A day after President Clinton's impeachment, his job approval rating was 68 percent, one of the highest job approval ratings since the Johnson administration (*Washington Post*/ABC News Poll 1998). At the culmination of the Senate trial on the impeachment articles, the Senate refused to accept either article of impeachment, but the votes on both articles were far closer[1] than public opinion would have led us to expect.

Although comparisons between the Watergate and Lewinsky scandals are controversial, they are also unavoidable. Impeachment proceedings of any type are relatively uncommon. Impeachment proceedings against presidents are extraordinarily rare. In an effort to grasp what happened—to the president, the Congress, and to us—we understandably attempt to draw parallels and identify distinctions between similar events with which we have had previous experience. This is all to say that the Watergate scandal is an integral part of the context in which we view the Clinton impeachment.

Reasonable people disagree about the relative reprehensibility of the charges levied against Presidents Nixon and Clinton, and they disagree about the seriousness of the crimes each man may have committed. In at least one respect, however, the contrast between Nixon and Clinton is clear. As the House moved to impeach Nixon, he was a singularly unpopular president who had lost the support of the U.S. public. No reasonable observer at the time suggested that Americans supported Nixon in his efforts to remain president. This was clearly not the case with Clinton. During the House impeachment of Clinton, the president had very high approval ratings, and opinion polls showed that a large majority of Americans opposed his impeachment.

Writing more than 200 years ago, Alexander Hamilton concluded: "[T]he republican principle demands that the deliberate sense of the community should govern the conduct of those to whom they intrust the management of their affairs" (*Federalist Pa-*

pers 1982, v. 71). For Hamilton, as well as many of the other founders of the nation, a functioning representative system required correspondence between community interests and the actions of the government, at least on the central issues of the day. The founders were not advocates of government by plebiscite. Many of them distrusted extensive public participation in the affairs of government, and even if they had not, the technological infrastructure of the time (both in terms of communication and transportation) would have made widespread public involvement in national politics practically impossible.

The founders did, however, have a profound respect for the significance of the term "representation." One could not expect representatives to constantly concern themselves with the details of their constituents' opinions on all of the issues that came before Congress, but on the central issues of the day, citizens had a right to expect their public servants to act in a manner consistent with their (the constituents') reasoning and preferences. At the very least, if a representative decided to replace constituents' preferences with his or her own, that person must not be allowed to corrupt the voting process when those constituents wished to replace him or her.

Obviously, the Clinton impeachment was a "central issue" of our day. During the impeachment proceedings in the House and the trial in the Senate, members of Congress consistently cited the votes on the articles of impeachment as the most important of their careers. Why, then, on the most important political issue of the late twentieth century, did the House (and even the Senate, to some extent) behave in a manner so inconsistent with public opinion? And what does this striking discrepancy between representatives' actions and the public will indicate about representation in our political system? This book is an attempt to answer these two questions.

Background

As David Von Drehle so aptly writes, it was a "dizzying" year for politics, strange and unusual in almost every respect (Von Drehle 1998). The plain facts of the case—even those on which both sides agreed—were nothing less than striking. Independent prosecutor Kenneth Starr[2] spent more than four years and $40 million investigating President and Mrs. Clinton's involvement in a series of complex real estate transactions in rural Arkansas that came to be known as "Whitewater." This investigation never led to a single official charge against the president, and neither the president's nor Mrs. Clinton's role in the financial transactions associated with the Whitewater land development deals ever played any significant role in the impeachment proceedings.

A completely unrelated legal proceeding, a sexual harassment suit brought by Arkansan Paula Jones—a suit subsequently thrown out by the presiding federal judge—paved the way to the president's impeachment.[3] Clandestine recordings by a career bureaucrat, Linda Tripp, of her conversations with a young former White House intern, Monica Lewinsky—witness in the Paula Jones sexual harassment lawsuit—provided the foundation for charges that nearly cost Clinton his presidency. The colorful characters involved in this scandal (Clinton, Lewinsky, Starr, Tripp, and others) acted out a unique drama—a political morality play as much as a sexual morality play—on the stage of modern U.S. history.

As the 1998 mid-term elections neared, pundits and political analysts predicted dour days for the president's party. Even under the best of conditions, the incumbent president's party regularly loses seats in the House and Senate during mid-term elections, especially mid-term elections in which the president is a lame duck. Given the special circumstances surrounding the 1998 elections, nearly everyone expected Republicans to make significant gains in either the House or the Senate (or, more likely, both) as the public stiffly rebuked the president and the Democrats who had supported him during the scandal.

Surprisingly, just as the scandal had little or no impact on Clinton's own personal popularity, it also had little effect on members of his party. The Republicans failed to gain an advantage in either the House or the Senate during the November elections. In addition, in an unprecedented turn of events during a scandal-scarred election year,[4] the Democrats held their own in the Senate and gained five seats in the House. For only the second time in this century (and the first time since 1934), a president's party increased its membership in one house without losing seats in the other in a mid-term election.

The shock of this mid-term electoral setback throttled the Republican Party leadership. House Speaker Newt Gingrich, the architect of the Republicans' Contract with America and the man most responsible for the Republican majorities in both houses of Congress, quickly came under fire from prominent conservatives like Richard Armey (R.–Tex.) and Tom Delay (R.–Tex.) for failing to stay the course begun at the Republican revival during the elections of 1994. Gingrich, already weakened by a failed conservative coup to gain control of the Republican Party, was quickly overwhelmed, and he became the first casualty of the party's stark November failure. It was an utterly unexpected turn of events. During a year of presidential scandal, the president's party posted the best mid-term election results since the 1930s, and the majority party in the House of Representatives exiled its leader. Bill Clinton, the "Comeback Kid," had apparently done it again.

But the public repudiation of Republican efforts to impeach the president had surprisingly little impact on the impeachment process. Republicans, especially the more conservative members of the party, responded swiftly and simply to the mid-term election results. Little more than six weeks after the election, the House Judiciary Committee and the House of Representatives impeached the president. In the moralistic aftermath of the impeachment votes, the Republicans again lost one of their own, as Speaker-designate Robert Livingston (R.–La.) resigned after admitting his own marital infidelity. In less than six weeks, the House had lost two Speakers, another first in U.S. history. That the Senate failed to convict the president on either article of impeachment does little to mitigate the surrealistic spectacle of the Clinton-Lewinsky scandal and the legislative impeachment process. It was a dizzying year indeed.

Briefly, the Facts

Looking back, it all started innocently enough.[5] In July 1995, Monica Lewinsky began her White House internship. Less than six months later, she was promoted to a full-time, paid position in the

Office of Legislative Affairs at the White House. According to the independent counsel's report, Lewinsky first met the president during her internship. A few days before the end of her internship and the beginning of her paid staff position, she and the president shared their initial intimate encounter. Over the course of the next few months, Clinton and Lewinsky had several encounters of a sexual nature. By the spring of 1996, staff concerns about the relationship between Lewinsky and the president had resulted in Lewinsky being transferred to a public relations position at the Pentagon. In the Public Affairs Office at the Pentagon, Lewinsky met Linda Tripp, a former secretary in the Bush and Clinton administrations and fellow White House exile.

During the summer of 1997, Lewinsky confided in Tripp during a series of lunches and midnight telephone calls, describing her relationship with the president. Clinton questioned Lewinsky about the extent to which she had discussed their relationship with friends, but she denied any disclosure. In early fall, Tripp began covertly recording her conversations with Lewinsky. At the same time, multiple anonymous telephone calls to the Rutherford Institute, the funding agency for the Paula Jones lawsuit against the president, suggested the existence of a sexual relationship between Lewinsky and the president. Jones was charging Clinton with on-the-job sexual harassment during his tenure as Arkansas governor, and the Jones' legal team made a connection between their client's suit and Lewinsky's relationship with the president. Shortly before Thanksgiving, Tripp was subpoenaed as a witness in the *Jones* case. In early December, the Jones' lawyers listed Lewinsky as a material witness. Before the end of the year, the Jones' attorneys had served Clinton with papers requesting information about notes and communications between himself and Lewinsky.

In January 1998, Tripp contacted independent counsel Kenneth Starr and agreed to make another secret tape of a conversation with Lewinsky with the aid of agents from the Federal Bureau of Investigation. On January 15, after obtaining this final secret tape, Starr requested official permission from the Justice Department to extend the scope of his Whitewater inquiry. Two days later, in his deposition in the Paula Jones suit, Clinton denied having any "sexual relations" with Lewinsky. On January 21, Starr's investigation into Clinton's relationship with Lewinsky was made public, and Clinton issued a public denial of any "inappropriate relationship" with Lewinsky.

In April 1998 Federal Circuit Court Judge Susan Webber Wright dismissed the *Jones* lawsuit, but Starr's investigation continued. During the summer, Starr provided a broad grant of immunity to Lewinsky and subsequently subpoenaed Clinton. Approximately three weeks after the videotaping (and subsequent public broadcast of the tape) of Clinton's testimony, Starr delivered his report to Congress, citing 11 potentially impeachable offenses. Two days later, Congress made the report public.

To evaluate the allegations contained in *The Starr Report,* Henry Hyde (R.–Ill.), chairman of the House Judiciary Committee, initiated hearings. The 1998 elections overshadowed the work of the House Judiciary Committee during the weeks preceding the election. In fact, at one point it appeared that the committee would not act on any of the offenses cited in the independent counsel's report. On election day, Democrats prevented Republican gains in the Senate and made small gains themselves in the House, producing the best electoral results for the party of a sitting president in 64 years. A few days later, in response to growing unrest among rank and file House Republicans, Newt Gingrich resigned from both the Speakership and the House of Representatives.[6]

Given the public's surprising support for Democrats during the 1998 elections, the continuation of House Republican efforts to impeach the president took many Washington insiders by surprise. What surprised no one, however, was the overtly partisan nature of the battle waged during the impeachment hearings held by the House Judiciary Committee. The debate during committee hearings plainly manifested a partisan conflict. Although Democrats criticized the president's behavior and personal judgment, they also pushed for a legislative punishment short of impeachment (such as censure). Republicans on the Judiciary Committee unanimously opposed these attempts to build support for an executive censure. Little more than a month after the elections, the House Judiciary Committee reported out four articles of impeachment, each passing on a strict party-line vote. After deliberations on the floor of the House, two of the articles of impeachment were approved by the House membership and two articles of impeachment were rejected. Because the Christmas holiday break was imminent, the Senate deferred consideration of the articles of impeachment until the following year.

In the interim, between the passage of the articles of impeachment by the House and the end of the calendar year, a sexual scandal ended the leadership hopes of Speaker-designate Robert Livingston (R.–La.). Public disclosure of a past marital infidelity forced him to withdraw his name from consideration for the Speakership. Ironically, in the wake of Clinton's scandalous relationship, the Republicans lost two of their most prominent congressional leaders.

After the start of the first session of the new, 106th Congress, the Senate initiated its own hearings and deliberations on the articles of impeachment. Although various alternatives to votes on the articles of impeachment were suggested, both articles stood a floor vote on February 12, 1999. Both failed, ending a brief but extraordinary period in U.S. history.

Legislative Politics in Unusual Times

Presidential impeachments are rare events. Before Clinton, only one president, Andrew Johnson, had ever endured impeachment. House Speakers seldom resign, and marital infidelity rarely prevents an anointed Speaker-to-be from assuming the top legislative position in the federal government. That a beleaguered and scandalized president would see his party post gains during a mid-term election runs counter to conventional wisdom. In clear contradiction to the preferences of a large majority of Americans, Republicans on the House Judiciary Committee pursued the impeachment process, rolled the Democrats on the House Judiciary Committee, and voted to impeach the president all by themselves. And then the House, or more accurately, the House Republicans—in clear contradiction to the preferences of a large majority of Americans—impeached the president.[7]

Politically speaking, what happened? I begin to answer this question by considering representatives' own explanations of their behavior. In newspaper articles, on television talk shows, in the House Judiciary Committee hearings, and on the floor of the House, the stories were similar.[8] Members on both sides of the aisle characterized their own actions—and those of fellow partisans—in terms of ethics and character, of the rule of law and the Constitution. The president's opponents claimed to be voting their consciences, repulsed by Clinton's deceit. They portrayed the impeachment and their efforts to remove the president from office as the only reasonable response to his behavior. Tom Delay (R.–Tex.) described the ethical conflict manifested in the impeachment debate in the following terms: "It was about honor and decency and integrity and truth . . . about relativism versus absolute truth" (McLoughlin 1999: 206).

Supporters of the president also claimed the moral high ground during the impeachment proceedings. Arguing that Clinton's actions did not rise to the level of "high crimes and misdemeanors," they portrayed their opposition to the president's impeachment as an effort to protect the Constitution and preserve our system of government. Christopher Shays, a moderate Republican from Connecticut, generously attributed the conflict—mainly between Republicans and Democrats—to honest differences in conscience:

> I believe that the impeachable offenses have not been proven and that the proven offenses are not impeachable. But they are close. And that's why I understand why members who happen to be primarily Democrats concluded that the president should not be impeached, and members on my side of the aisle, primarily Republicans believed he should be impeached. *With no exception, I truly believe that every member of Congress of this institution is voting his or her conscience.* (emphasis added; *House Debates,* December 19, 1998: H11972)

Unlike Shays—one of the few House Republicans who opposed impeachment—most legislators viewed their opponents' motives as little more than base partisanship. Democrats were especially interested in attributing Republican impeachment efforts to a mean and

vindictive partisan plot dedicated to the embarrassment and removal of a popular Democratic president. During debate, Democrats frequently mentioned the partisan nature of the impeachment
proceedings. For many of the president's supporters (nearly all
Democrats), the drive to impeachment was fueled by a deep personal animosity toward the president held by a large number of
members on the Republican side of the aisle, and they repeatedly attributed the impeachment "machine" to nothing less than a partisan
conspiracy. Often the attribution was in the starkest of terms. Representative Maxine Waters (D.–Calif.), for example, during the
House Judiciary Committee hearings, described the impeachment
process as

> . . . a Republican coup d'etat. . . . [T]he Republicans will couch
> this extremist radical anarchy in pious language which distorts
> the Constitution and the rule of law. Bill and Hillary Clinton are
> the real targets, and the Republicans are the vehicles being used
> by the right-wing Christian Coalition extremists to direct and
> control our culture. (McLoughlin 1999: 179)

This is language consistent with Hillary Clinton's charge of a "vast
right-wing conspiracy" against her husband.

The basic facts support a partisan explanation for the conflict engendered by the efforts to impeach the president. During the Starr investigation, the impeachment trials in the House and the Senate, and
in the aftermath of the full spectacle, nearly all analyses of the Clinton impeachment identify partisanship as the most important factor
in determining legislative behavior. Gary Jacobson writes that the
politics of impeachment "epitomizes the sharp partisan divisions that
split both the Congress and the public" (2001: 254; see also Rozell
and Wilcox 2000). From all outward appearances, partisan attachments played a dominant roll in molding and influencing legislative
behavior during the impeachment proceedings. First, the House Judiciary Committee votes on each of the articles of impeachment were
split perfectly along party lines: all Republicans in favor, all Democrats opposed. Second, on the floor of the House, party cohesion was

quite high on the roll call votes on the four articles of impeachment, particularly so for the two articles that were successful. Even though party cohesion waned somewhat on the failed articles, a majority of Republicans still voted for both articles, and a majority of Democrats opposed both articles. Although party cohesion was somewhat weaker in the Senate, there was still considerable evidence that partisan ties were dominating the impeachment process. Only five of the 55 Republicans voted against the article of impeachment charging obstruction of justice, and only 10 of the 55 Republicans voted against the article of impeachment charging that the president committed perjury. In both cases, all of the Democrats voted against the articles. However, neither the Republican nor the Democratic leadership would admit to any significant or organized efforts to ensure party loyalty. In fact, several leaders explicitly stated that no organized efforts were made to sway votes among fellow partisans.[9]

Media reports of the impeachment process mirrored the congressional rhetoric: accounts of the impeachment process attributed legislative behavior to both differences of conscience and partisan conflict. Syndicated columnist David Broder wrote:

> The [impeachment] case is one on which men and women of good will can conscientiously differ. The Senate has an abundance of such people, Republicans and Democrats who will look beyond partisanship and public opinion polls and weigh the needs of the nation and the dictates of the Constitution (*Star Tribune,* December 23, 1998, p. 21A).

According to a *Miami Herald* article published immediately after the December impeachment votes, "Partisanship and precipice met in the U.S. House of Representatives yesterday, and the Republican majority leapt into the abyss by impeaching President Clinton on two articles" (December 20, 1998: sec. A, p. 15). As the process dragged on into 1999, the media increasingly emphasized the role of partisanship in the members' actions and their rhetoric.

If media accounts and legislators' own descriptions of the politics of impeachment are accurate, this was an exceptional time, a brief

period in U.S. history during which the engine of conventional politics—constituents and their interests—was forgotten. According to
numerous opinion polls taken immediately before the impeachment
votes in the House, approximately 60 to 65 percent of Americans
opposed impeachment, and opponents of impeachment outnumbered its supporters 2 to 1. The majority votes for two of the four
articles of impeachment suggest that more than a few representatives left plenty of constituents high and dry. Likewise, the Senate
votes on the impeachment articles—although neither received a majority—evidenced far more opposition to the president (and support
for removal) than existed in the general electorate. Evidently, a significant number of legislators ignored their constituents' preferences
throughout the impeachment proceedings. This is decidedly not
something the founders would have understood, and it is not conventional politics.

What About "the Public?"

Such disparity between public opinion and legislators' behavior is
rare on issues of this magnitude. Scholarship on legislative behavior
indicates that the engine of legislative politics on major issues about
which the public has clear and identifiable opinions is constituency
preferences. When conflicts between partisan allegiances and constituency pressures occur, constituents' opinions regularly trump fellow partisans' preferences, for the simple reason that members' careers are in the hands of the voters.

When national party leaders' objectives are inconsistent with local
constituents' interests, party leaders usually lose. This view of the
relative power of party leaders and constituents is not without its
critics. Prominent works argue that political parties are more important (and powerful) than the bulk of research admits (see, in particular, Aldrich 1995; Cox and McCubbins 1993). In addition, modern party leaders still retain certain traditional prerogatives that
may be useful in gaining legislators' acquiescence to leadership objectives. Likewise, the increasing importance of party financing in
congressional campaigns and the growth of member PACs has ap-

parently mitigated the limited significance of partisan attachments in legislative politics (Jacobson 1997; Herrnson 2000). Nevertheless, the claim that partisanship dominated the legislative politics of the impeachment process is inconsistent with the overwhelming preponderance of research on the modern Congress.[10]

It is also difficult to believe that legislators based their decisions about impeachment votes on their own personal moral sense, regardless of their constituents' preferences. It is equally hard to accept that legislators privileged their own interpretation of the Constitution—in particular, the impeachment clause—instead of the interpretations of their constituents. Certainly, members regularly evaluate policy issues and make strategic decisions based on their own individual conclusions about the optimal policy.[11] However, this desire to make good policy is nearly always subservient to the more primary goal of winning re-election.[12] Efforts to achieve personal policy objectives are most often made on issues that are either relatively unimportant to a member's constituency or immensely complex, where the connection between specific legislative activities and policy outcomes is difficult to make (Arnold 1990). Clearly, presidential impeachment fits in neither of these categories.

Although partisanship and personal conscience are the basis for most popular explanations of the impeachment process, the desire for re-election—and thus a constant concern for constituents' interests—is the foundation of the reigning scholarly paradigm of legislative behavior. Richard Fenno identifies re-election as one of the goals of members of Congress, and David Mayhew claims that it is the primary goal of legislators. Given the extent of public support for the president, it appears that many legislators, mostly Republicans, disregarded constituency preferences to support the party line or assuage their own consciences. Whether one thinks partisanship or conscience dominated impeachment politics, neither appears to be an electorally-optimal strategy.

Obviously, there is a stark inconsistency between popular explanations of impeachment politics and our understanding of conventional legislative behavior. According to our understanding of legislative decision making on prominent and important issues (like impeachment)—issues on which constituents have strong and stable positions—constituency preferences should dominate legislative behavior. If, however, the dynamics of the impeachment process were based on partisanship and personal ethics, then it would seem that the literature requires some revision. Was impeachment that rare and exceptional issue that turned conventional politics on its head? Or have we misunderstood—and improperly explained—the politics of impeachment? Can scholarship help us understand the Clinton impeachment, or was this impeachment, as important as it was, the anomalous case? And how powerful is our theory if it only leads to a misunderstanding of the single most important domestic political event in modern times?[13]

This book is an attempt to answer these questions. Where others see the play of partisanship and the conviction of personal ethics, I find legislators following the lead of their constituents. In this respect, the politics of impeachment were in no way exceptional. First, I show that in both the House and the Senate, constituency preferences dominated the decision-making calculus for many members. Nearly all Democrats and a significant number of Republicans treated the impeachment issue in a manner that was consistent with the preferences of their constituents. Explaining the behavior of the majority of members of Congress, both House and Senate, does not require the assumption of unusual partisan dynamics or an acceptance of the self-sacrificing (and electorally disadvantageous) obligation of personal ethics. Most, although far from all, members behaved in a manner that was completely consistent with their constituents' preferences. Those who ignored their constituencies appear to have been fully cognizant of the potential electoral fallout from their votes, and they responded accordingly (at least in the House) by raising historically large campaign war chests to scare off their challengers or to defeat them if they had the courage to enter the fray. Exactly why these representatives voted against their constituencies is an open question (and I will discuss and evaluate some of the more compelling answers), but their response was obvious: raise money, and a lot of it.

The legislators who defied their individual constituencies did so with the knowledge that campaign contributions from PACs, individuals, and political parties (mainly the Republican party) would aid their efforts to recapture their discontented constituencies and build a foundation for an extended legislative career.[14] In the end, these extra resources, which I refer to as "impeachment" funds, made a substantial difference at the polls in 2000. In one sense, financial resources paved the way for the impeachment of the president, and they were crucial to the Republican efforts to maintain control of the House and the Senate.

Why Study the Clinton Impeachment?

The legislative dynamics of the Clinton impeachment are theoretically provocative and, for that reason alone, are worth studying. As an extreme example of the dynamics of representative politics, we watched a legislative body frustrate the expressed preferences of a large majority (nearly two-thirds of the U.S. adult population) in the most widely publicized floor votes in U.S. history. The popular explanation for this unusual behavior is three-fold: legislators followed their hearts, their party leaders, or both. Although this explanation has some superficial plausibility, it is inconsistent with scholarly theories of legislative behavior. Political parties in the United States are relatively weak replicas of political parties in most other industrialized democracies, and members focusing on their own personal ethical perspectives—when they clearly contradict the expressed wishes of a large majority of the adult population— would seem to be taking an extreme political risk. This behavior is also inconsistent with current characterizations of individual legislative behavior. As John Wright clearly states:

> ... [W]hen the expected electoral consequences of their actions are considerable and when the position of their party conflicts with the preferences of their constituency, legislators are likely to ignore the appeals of party leaders and side with their constituents (1996: 72).

The Clinton impeachment has all of the hallmarks of a legislative scenario in which financial concerns—directed campaign contributions, coordinated expenditures, and soft money considerations—would play no role: Voters had strong opinions about a widely publicized issue that generated more controversy than any other issue in living memory. In general, it has been difficult to demonstrate that PAC contributions—or campaign contributions more broadly conceived—have a significant impact on legislative behavior, particularly roll call voting. This is especially true for highly visible and highly controversial issues; the research that does show some impact of contributions on behavior suggests that the effects will only be present or only "have large effects on roll call votes that have low public visibility" (Wright 1996: 144). Clearly, the impeachment roll calls were anything but low visibility. However, I will argue that certain members of Congress—impeachment supporters with constituencies opposed to Clinton's impeachment—raised unusually large campaign contributions and related financial support from individual contributors and PACs. I find that campaign contributions mattered—providing the margin of victory, perhaps—on the most visible and controversial issue of the day, very much *not* what current theory tells us to expect. This inconsistency between our understanding of these events and our understanding of legislative behavior more generally indicates that we have something important to learn.

The Clinton impeachment also provides a unique opportunity to analyze and reflect on the nature of representative government in the United States at the turn of the millennium. Although most members' votes reflected the preferences of their constituencies, a nontrivial number did not. These few formed the margin of victory in the House and cut the margin of loss in the Senate. The U.S. public came ever so close to losing a popularly elected president to a minority faction.

James Madison, one of America's first and greatest political scientists, was quite concerned about the danger that factions posed to the political system. For him, one of the great benefits of a majoritarian system was the way in which it prevented the empowerment of minority factions. Clearly, if a minority rose up against the public interest and the common good, the people could use the vote to disempower that political faction. But Madison's own description and analysis of the institutional and political aspects of our system of checks and balances suggests that he was unsure that the majoritarian principal would provide sufficient protection for the voters and the public interest. In our time, when financial resources play such an important role in political campaigns, it would seem that Madison's misgivings were well founded. I discuss these and related representational issues in the light of my analysis of the politics of impeachment and the electoral aftermath of the 2000 elections.

What This Book Is Not

Clearly, the Clinton impeachment was a major event, a truly "big deal." As such, it has spawned a host of books designed to tell various parts of the story from a wide array of perspectives. That said, I would like to point out what this book, my book, is not. First, this book is not a comprehensive examination of the scandal. It provides no new evidence about what Clinton, Lewinsky, or various other actors did or did not do. I have no unique personal or professional knowledge that bears on these issues. There will be other books— probably many—to do that.

Second, I am not especially concerned with the issues of constitutional interpretation raised during this institutional conflict. Whether Clinton's behavior rose to the level of an "impeachable offense" simply is not a relevant issue for my argument. Similarly, I do not discuss the constitutionality of lame duck impeachments (see Ackerman 1999). Clearly, these issues are fundamentally important. They are, however, topics for other books.

Finally, this book takes no position on the ethics of the behavior of those involved in the scandal or the impeachment process, except when substantial evidence indicates the repudiation of constituency interests. Although the behavior of many representatives clearly contradicted national public opinion, representatives are not elected by a national constituency; they are elected by district-level constituencies (and senators by state-level constituencies) and are responsible to them, not to a national-level constituency. Not surprisingly, blatant disregard for local constituencies was relativity rare. Of course, those rare cases turned out to be important. This book is a study of the legislative politics of the Clinton impeachment and an examination and discussion of the implications of this study for our understanding of the nature of legislative behavior and democratic politics: nothing more; nothing less.

Chapter Outline

In Chapter 2 I describe the Clinton impeachment. This description includes a narrative of the events leading up to and including the Starr investigation, the House Judiciary Committee hearings, the impeachment votes in the House, and the votes on removal in the Senate. I also present a cast of important characters—Clinton, Lewinsky, Starr, Tripp, and various members of the House and the Senate—and a rudimentary introduction to the constitutional issues involved in a presidential impeachment. This "history" of the process is not intended to provide a detailed description of the subtle but distinctive interpretations of events by the various individuals involved. It is simply a basic chronology of the events themselves. In that chapter I also describe the political rhetoric surrounding the impeachment process. The chapter simply provides the basic background of the Clinton impeachment that I assume in subsequent chapters of the book.

I doubt that any political event in history has been the subject of more opinion polling in a shorter amount of time than the impeachment of President Clinton. Numerous media organizations and polling firms conducted whole series of opinion polls tapping national attitudes on the various issues and topics surrounding the impeachment of the president. In Chapter 3, I present a small but representative sample of the polling results from a number of the most prominent media outlets (e.g., CNN/ABC News, *The Washington Post, USA Today*, and the Gallup Poll). Aside from highlighting the consistency of the results—a consistency borne out over time as each of the polls captured the subtle ebb and flow of support for the president—I show that the overwhelming majority of Americans (somewhere between 60 and 65 percent of the general population) opposed the impeachment of the president and his subsequent conviction, and I discuss the reasons for this opposition.

After establishing the high level of general public opposition to the impeachment and subsequent conviction of the president, I discuss current (popular) explanations for the divergence between public opinion and legislative behavior. According to most characterizations of roll call voting behavior in the House of Representatives on the articles of impeachment, partisanship and personal conscience explain the variance in members' votes. On the one hand, votes for impeachment are rationalized as a response to party allegiance for Republicans or a personal ethical repugnance to the president's actions. Conversely, opposition to the articles of impeachment is viewed as support for the Democratic Party and its president; a conscientious aversion to the treatment of the president; or an individually based, limited interpretation of the constitutional nature of impeachment. At this point, I begin a discussion—continued in subsequent chapters—of the representational issues involved in the repudiation of public opinion on impeachment.

Certainly, party ties and issues of conscience were not completely irrelevant during the impeachment proceedings. Nevertheless, in Chapter 4 I argue that their significance was strategically overemphasized. Alternatively, I find that in a majority of cases, House members voted in accordance with the preferences of their constituencies. I present some evidence suggesting that after accounting for constituency preferences and legislator ideology (which is, itself, related to constituency preferences), partisanship had little impact on roll call votes on the articles of impeachment. Chapter 5 includes an analysis of Senate roll call voting on removal that mirrors the House-based analysis in Chapter 4. As one would expect, I argue that constituency pressures played a somewhat more limited roll in Senate decision making.

In Chapter 6 I analyze the relationship between constituency opinion, partisanship, and campaign fundraising among House incumbents and their challengers. I focus on the fundraising patterns of Republicans who voted against their constituents' preferences on

impeachment and the fundraising patterns of the House impeachment managers, and I estimate the portion of incumbent war chests
attributable to the unpopularity of the impeachment proceedings:
"impeachment funds." Chapter 7 is an examination of the electoral
impact of campaign contributions. I focus specifically on the difference that the impeachment funds made in individual elections and
the cumulative impact of these funds on the partisan balance in the
House of Representatives.

In Chapter 8 I examine fundraising patterns in the Senate and attempt to estimate the impact of unpopular roll call votes on subsequent fundraising by Republican incumbents and their challengers. I
also look at the impact of the impeachment proceedings on individual Senate elections and the partisan balance in the Senate more
generally.

I find that even under the truly exceptional circumstances of impeachment, it was basically politics as usual. Because of the exceptional financial resources at their disposal, few legislators lost seats
because of their support for impeachment regardless of their constituents' preferences. In sum, partisanship and conscience were less
important and conventional constituency politics and political
money were more important than popular treatments of the Clinton
scandal and the impeachment process admit. Frankly, the financial
dimension of impeachment politics was rather more important than
I initially expected. That the size of one's bank account (politically
speaking) could make such a difference on an issue of constitutional
import that is unlikely to be rivaled in our time is nothing short of
deeply disturbing. I conclude with a discussion of the implications
of my findings for our understanding of the role of money and the
power of minority factions in modern U.S. politics. In the face of
some sobering conclusions, I describe the type of campaign finance
reform that might actually make a difference. I admit that significant reform is difficult under the best of circumstances, but as citizens (and constituents) we deserve better. If there is even the hint of
a possibility that impeachments (or control of the chambers of Congress) can be bought or sold, we are very much at the end of our
rope.

2

THE SCANDAL

History is full of chance encounters that make a difference.[1] The Clinton-Lewinsky scandal began with one such encounter. On May 8, 1991, Governor Bill Clinton attended a conference sponsored by the Arkansas Industrial Development Commission in the Excelsior Hotel in Little Rock, Arkansas. At this conference, he met a young clerk working at the registration desk. Her name was Paula Corbin, and after her marriage to Steve Jones, she would be known as Paula Jones. According to Jones, Danny Ferguson, an Arkansas state trooper assigned to the governor's detail, approached her and indicated that the governor would like to meet her in a hotel room. She agreed to meet the governor. To this day it is unclear what her expectations regarding the substance or outcome of the meeting were. Jones alleged that during the meeting Governor Clinton made several unwanted sexual advances toward her. She claims to have rebuffed each advance and to have stormed out of the room.

In the aftermath of this meeting, Jones told no more than a few intimates about this encounter with Clinton. Yet more than two and one-half years later, an article by David Brock in *The American Spectator* described a set of circumstances similar to hers and Clinton's, and the woman's name was simply "Paula." The title of this article was "His Cheatin' Heart." Just over a month after the publication of this article, Attorney General Janet Reno named Robert

Fiske to head the investigation into the Whitewater affair. On August 5, 1994, the Special Division of the U.S. Courts of Appeal would replace Fiske with Kenneth Starr.

Shortly after the publication of the article, Jones and her husband discussed her options with a lawyer named Daniel M. Traylor. Given the nature of the current legal system, Traylor quickly realized that a suit against *The American Spectator* was unlikely to be financially beneficial. Given the conventional First Amendment protections and the fact that Brock's article did not specifically identify Jones, it would be difficult, if not impossible, to prove libel. A suit against President Clinton, on the other hand, might prove to be a financial windfall.[2] In February 1994, Paula Jones denounced Clinton publicly for sexual harassment. On May 4, the *Washington Post* published an article detailing Jones's allegations against Clinton, and on May 6, Jones filed suit against Clinton.

Although Clinton would fight the very constitutionality of Jones's lawsuit—arguing that sitting presidents are not subject to civil suit while in office—the Supreme Court, in *Jones v. Clinton,* disagreed with Clinton and his lawyers, refused his request for immunity, and ordered the state court to proceed with the handling of the suit. During this suit, in what can only be described as an amazingly convoluted and bizarre chain of events, the Jones' legal team learned of an alleged relationship between a 21-year-old White House intern and President Clinton. If true, this information could be used in arguments designed to establish a pattern of sexual harassment. The Jones' lawyers included this young intern on the witness list for the Jones' civil suit. The rest, as they say, is history.

Looking back, Lewinsky's relationship with the president started innocently enough. In July 1995, Monica Lewinsky began an internship at the White House. Although Lewinsky obtained an internship at least in part because of family contacts with a prominent financial supporter of the Democratic Party (Walter Kaye), her ticket to the executive mansion was obtained through completely conventional channels. Internships are regularly distributed to those with important political contacts. In fact, White House internships are not especially difficult to get, and many individuals without political contacts regularly work as White House interns.

Less than six months after the start of her internship, Lewinsky was promoted to a full-time, paid position in the Office of Legislative Affairs at the White House. According to the independent counsel's report, Lewinsky first met the president during her internship. On November 15, 1995, just a few days before the end of her internship and the beginning of her paid staff position, she and the president had their initial intimate encounter. Over the course of the next five months, Clinton and Lewinsky had several encounters of a sexual nature.

While this relationship was ongoing, Clinton and Lewinsky had frequent personal contacts and regularly spoke with each other by telephone. They also exchanged personal gifts. By the spring of 1996, staff concerns about the relationship between Lewinsky and the president—in particular, the inordinate amount of time the president spent with the junior staffer—prompted Lewinsky's transfer to a public relations position at the Pentagon. In late March 1997, Clinton and Lewinsky had their final intimate contact. On May 24, Clinton informed Lewinsky that their relationship would have to cease. Lewinsky would thereafter refer to this day as "D-Day" or "Dump Day" (Toobin 1999). In the Public Affairs Office at the Pentagon, Lewinsky met Linda Tripp, a former secretary in the Bush and Clinton administrations and fellow White House exile.

Just over a year after Lewinsky's transfer to the Pentagon (during the summer of 1997), she confided in Tripp during a series of lunches and midnight telephone calls, detailing her relationship with the president. Although Clinton quizzed Lewinsky about the extent to which she had discussed their relationship with friends, she denied any disclosure.

Tripp, a White House secretary during the early stage of the Clinton administration, had attempted to publish a book describing a series of illicit affairs that Clinton pursued during the early years of his presidency. She contacted a small-time agent named Lucianne Goldberg about this book project. Although the original project did not pan out, Tripp contacted Goldberg again when Lewinsky began to confide in her. Lewinsky's story was, apparently, more bankable (from a literary standpoint) (Toobin 1999).

In early fall, Tripp began covert recordings of her conversations with Lewinsky. At the same time, multiple anonymous telephone calls to the Rutherford Institute, the funding agency for the Paula Jones lawsuit against the president, suggested the existence of a sexual relationship between Lewinsky and the president (Toobin 1999). Because Jones was charging Clinton with on-the-job sexual harassment during his tenure as Arkansas governor, the Jones' legal team quickly made the connection between their client's suit and Lewinsky's relationship with the president, although Lewinsky had not (and still has not) ever charged that the president in any way harassed her. A few days before Thanksgiving, Tripp was subpoenaed as a witness in the *Jones* case. In early December, the Jones' lawyers listed Lewinsky as a material witness. Before the end of the year, the Jones' attorneys had served Clinton with papers requesting information about notes and communications between himself and Lewinsky.

During the latter part of December 1997, Lewinsky talked with Vernon Jordan, a close friend of Clinton's whom she had only recently met, about various job possibilities. Some suggest that Jordan actually helped Lewinsky find a job. On December 17, Clinton contacted Lewinsky by phone and informed her that she was on the witness list in the Paula Jones civil suit. They briefly discussed a "sanitized" account of their personal relationship (Toobin 1999). Just after Christmas, Betty Currie was sent to Lewinsky's apartment to obtain the gifts given to her by the president. Strangely enough, she apparently returned home with these gifts and hid them under her bed.

In early January 1998, Lewinsky's first formal involvement in the *Jones* case was the submission of a signed affidavit denying the existence of a sexual relationship between herself and Clinton. Shortly thereafter, Tripp contacted independent counsel Kenneth Starr and agreed to make another secret tape of a conversation with Lewinsky with the aid of agents from the Federal Bureau of Investigation. On January 15, after obtaining this final secret tape, Starr requested official permission from the Justice Department to extend the scope of his Whitewater inquiry. It is important to note that no material relationship existed between the Whitewater land transactions and

Monica Lewinsky's relationship with Clinton. There is no evidence that Lewinsky played any role in the Whitewater transactions.

Starr's involvement in the Lewinsky matter was even more unlikely than the remoteness of the unrelated *Whitewater* case suggests, because he was not the original independent counsel on the *Whitewater* case. Robert Fiske, a prestigious defense attorney with the New York law firm of Davis, Polk, and Wardwell, was Attorney General Janet Reno's first choice after President Clinton announced that he supported the appointment of a special counsel to investigate Whitewater. Fiske had been appointed as U.S. Attorney for the Southern District of New York by Gerald Ford, and he had also served the Carter administration in that post. Once appointed, he took a leave of absence from his firm and immediately initiated an investigation into Whitewater and—on his own initiative—the unusual circumstances surrounding Vincent Foster's death.

Shortly after Fiske released a report indicating that Foster's death was suicide, President Clinton signed the statute reauthorizing the independent counsel. At that point, Attorney General Reno requested that the panel of three judges in the Special Division—the unit given responsibility for approving special counsels—ratify her decision to choose Fiske, a man several months into his job. The Special Division panel—composed of two Republicans and one Democrat—refused.[3] Fiske was subsequently replaced by Kenneth Starr.

Fiske was a professional counsel with years of experience as a practicing criminal attorney and prosecutor. He had relevant experience both inside and outside the government. When Kenneth Starr was appointed independent counsel, he had yet to participate—as defense counsel or prosecutor—in a single criminal case (Toobin 1999: 73). Whereas Fiske had been known as a moderate, Starr had very solid conservative credentials. In contrast to Fiske, who had taken a leave of absence from his law firm, Starr continued to work for his Washington firm as he investigated the Whitewater (and related) allegations (O'Connor and Hermann 2000).

Starr's interest in circumstances clearly beyond the original outlines of the Whitewater land deals became obvious almost immediately. In fact, the purview of Starr's investigation would eventually include the firing of several members of the White House Travel Office (or "travelgate"), Vince Foster's suicide, and the accumulation of Federal Bureau of Investigation files on prominent Republicans by several White House aides (or "filegate"). Starr never offered any indictments dealing with the original Whitewater land deals or any of the unrelated issues (aside from the president's relationship with Lewinsky) that he investigated during his tenure as special counsel. But of course the Lewinsky allegations were more than problem enough for the president.

Two days after Starr requested the Justice Department's permission to investigate Clinton's relationship with Lewinsky, Clinton—in his deposition in the Paula Jones suit—denied having any "sexual relations" with Lewinsky. On January 21, Starr's investigation into Clinton's relationship with Lewinsky was made public, and Clinton issued a now-famous public denial of any "inappropriate relationship" with Lewinsky. This denial would soon haunt the president.

Although Federal Circuit Court Judge Susan Webber Wright dismissed the *Jones* lawsuit in April 1998, Starr's investigation continued.[4] After extended negotiations during the following summer, Starr provided a broad grant of immunity to Lewinsky and subsequently subpoenaed Clinton. Clinton's extensive legal efforts to avoid testifying himself and to prevent his aides and associates from testifying were summarily rejected by the U.S. Supreme Court (O'-Connor and Hermann 2000). Approximately three weeks after the videotaping (and subsequent public broadcast of the tape) of Clinton's testimony, Starr delivered his report to Congress, citing 11 potentially impeachable offenses. Among the most serious of the allegations listed in the report of the independent counsel were perjury, subornation of perjury, abuse of power, and obstruction of justice. It is worth noting again that no aspect of the original Whitewater investigation was material to any of the allegations of impeachable offenses leveled against Clinton by the independent counsel. As Karen O'Connor and John Hermann have noted:

> Had Clinton settled the *Jones* case, he never would have had to give the Jones deposition. Had he not been deposed in *Jones,* the

independent counsel never could have investigated his relationship with Lewinsky. True, the relationship might have been made
public, but because both parties initially denied it, it would have
likely been assigned to the long list of rumors concerning Clinton
and a host of other women. (2000: 55)

Two days later, Congress, by a vote of 363 to 63, made the report
public.

House Response to the Report of the Independent Counsel

Although there was strong bipartisan support for some type of inquiry into the allegations against Clinton, there were disagreements—disagreements that basically broke along party lines—
about how extensive the investigation should be, what latitude
the House Judiciary Committee should be given to subpoena witnesses and gather evidence, and the timetable of the inquiry.

Rick Boucher (D.–Va.) proposed an inquiry into the allegations
Starr was investigating that would have a final deadline before the
end of the calendar year. This was a longer timeframe than the
one included in a previous Boucher proposal that failed in the
House Judiciary Committee (Baker 2000). Although this satisfied
most Democrats, it did not satisfy Republicans. By a partisan vote
of 258 to 176,[5] the House approved House Resolution 581, the
inquiry proposal sponsored by Henry Hyde (R–Ill.), chair of the
House Judiciary Committee. House Resolution 581 provided
broad subpoena and evidence-gathering powers, set no deadline
for the end of the inquiry, and did not restrict its subject matter.
Efforts to preempt the inquiry with some type of censure resolution were strongly opposed by nearly all Republicans and some
Democrats and were unsuccessful. The inquiry vote was the last
formal House vote dealing with impeachment prior to the 1998
congressional elections.

To evaluate the allegations contained in *The Starr Report,* the
House Judiciary Committee initiated hearings. The hearings included a report by the independent counsel and a host of witnesses.

These witnesses addressed a variety of issues not directly related to an examination or verification of the facts of the case. To attack the claim of some Clinton supporters that the president had not committed a serious offense even if he did commit perjury during a civil proceeding, Republican witnesses included individuals who had received jail sentences for committing perjury in civil cases. Democratic witnesses included experts on constitutional law brought in to give their opinions of the proper interpretation of "high crimes and misdemeanors."[6]

The committee included 21 Republicans and 16 Democrats.[7] Numerous votes taken by the committee split precisely along party lines. Almost immediately, it became obvious that the committee's proceedings would be characterized by stridently partisan rhetoric. Because they were in the minority, the Democrats were particularly fond of highlighting the partisan character of the proceedings. Two quotes from the December 10–12, 1998, committee debate on the articles of impeachment provide a clear sense of the character of the proceedings. First, the ranking Democrat on the committee, John Conyers (Mich.) concluded:

> The majority have simply rubber-stamped the unexamined, untested, double hearsay and conclusions of the independent counsel without conducting any factual investigation of its own. . . . My friends across the aisle, please let me remind you that it is you who are trying to overturn the results of two national elections, you who are attempting a legislative takeover of the executive branch, and you, not the president, who have the burden of coming forward with evidence. (McLoughlin 1999: 137–38)

On the other side, Bill Coble (Va.) argued:

> I represent a district far removed from the Beltway. . . . Here we are surrounded by Beltway advisers who demand fees in excess of $500 per hour. And many of these adept advisers, lawyers, and counselors are spinmeisters. They attach their spin, and often-times confusion results. But when I return to my district . . . my

> mind begins to clear, as I am at a point removed from the Beltway
> spin. All of a sudden I am aware of the definition of sex. All of a
> sudden I know the meaning of "alone." I know what "is" is, as
> do the majority of my constituents. (McLoughlin 1999: 140)

The committee debates following the report of the independent
counsel and the testimony of various witnesses were partisan specta-
cles composed of speeches filled with language like that used above.

One of the primary obstacles to inter-party agreement was the
wording of the Constitution itself, in particular the phrase "high
crimes and misdemeanors." As with much of the Constitution, the
section on impeachment is open to broad interpretation. The
founders borrowed the practice of impeachment from the English
political system. However, in the English system there were no limitations placed on the types of offenses that could serve as a basis for
impeachment, so the founders' use of the phrase "high crimes and
misdemeanors" was specifically designed to prevent the widespread
use of the impeachment power as a political tool (Gerhardt 2000). It
is also clear that the founders were unwilling to provide more explicit guidelines for determining what behaviors constituted impeachable offenses.

Congressional debates over the definition of "impeachable offenses" tend to be structured by advocacy. Support or opposition
for any particular definition of "high crimes and misdemeanors" depends on whether one supports or opposes the individual being
charged. As Gerhardt writes:

> Debates over the proper definition of impeachable offenses in
> Congress have thus featured tug-of-wars. Those seeking impeach-
> ment defend relatively broad, amorphous standards that they can
> show have been easily met in a given case, and those opposing
> impeachment support very narrow standards that they claim have
> not been met (2000: 155).

In effect, the founders ensured that decisions regarding impeachment and the definition of impeachable offenses be made de novo as

circumstances arose. As concerned as many representatives and senators were with what the founders meant when they wrote "high
crimes and misdemeanors," it is highly unlikely that they agreed on
a single interpretation of the phrase. If they did, we have no record
of this agreement or its specifics.

Not surprisingly, the imminent mid-term elections overshadowed
the work of the House Judiciary Committee. In fact, at one point it
appeared that the committee would not act on any of the offenses
cited in the independent counsel's report. In the months leading up
to the November elections, Republican spirits soared as Clinton
plunged deeper into the morass of the Lewinsky scandal. Shortly before election day, expectations were still high. Not only was history
on their side—the president's party tends to lose seats in mid-term
elections—but Clinton had helped immensely with a tailor-made
scandal. On the morning of the election, one journalist described
House Speaker Newt Gingrich—the very center of the Republican
universe in Congress—as follows:

> [He] woke up on election day confident that by the time his head
> hit the pillow, the Republicans would pick up seats, strengthen
> their hold on the House, and embolden the drive to impeach the
> president. . . . Within a few hours, he was on the telephone in a
> conference call with Republican congressmen around the country,
> boldly predicting a splendid day and a gain of some twenty seats
> (Baker 2000: 140).

It was not to be.

On election day, Democrats shocked Republicans by preventing
gains in the Senate and by making small gains in the House, producing the best electoral results for the party of a lame duck president
in 64 years. This result would have been a big surprise in a normal
mid-term election year. During a mid-term election in which the sitting president faced imminent impeachment, it was nothing less
than unbelievable. In a *New York Times* article published just after
the election, R. W. Apple concluded that, "[b]oth conservatives and
moderates in the party said the Republicans had to get back to ba-

sics. Even Speaker Newt Gingrich conceded that the results "should sober every Republican," and called for "new strategic thinking" (1998: 1). According to Pennsylvania Governor Tom Ridge, "If you make it a referendum on a President with a 67 percent approval rating, as they tried to do, you shouldn't be surprised if the election goes against you" (Apple 1998: 1). Likewise, Senator John McCain (R.–Ariz.) concluded, "I just hope this debacle is a wake-up call for our people. You've got to be for something—smaller government, better education, something. We're seen as the party that's against everything" (Apple 1998: 1).

Ironically, it appears that the very issue that Republicans had expected to provide such a boost for their campaigns and their party's electoral fortunes actually favored the Democrats. In the weeks leading up to the election, as Republicans struggled to find the best way to present the impeachment issue to win votes, Democratic pollsters and political advisors were pushing their candidates to "engage" the impeachment issue and to push it along the campaign trails (Baker 2000). Recent research on the 1998 election confirms Democratic analysis regarding the usefulness of the impeachment issue. Much of the Republicans' failure in 1998 is attributable to their handling of the Lewinsky scandal. According to Alan Abramowitz:

> . . . [T]he failure of the Republican party to make expected gains in the House and Senate in the 1998 midterm election was due largely to voter dissatisfaction with Kenneth Starr and congressional Republicans over their handling of the White House scandal and the impeachment inquiry. (1999: 8)

The drive to satisfy the conservatives who make up such a large part of many Republicans' primary constituencies resulted in the alienation of more moderate Republicans, those who either voted for moderate Democrats or who decided not to vote at all (Abramowitz 1999).

The mid-term election results were an unprecedented and unexpected failure for congressional Republicans, particularly those in the House. A few days later, in response to growing unrest among rank and file House Republicans, Gingrich resigned from both the Speakership and the House of Representatives.[8] Conservative Republican leaders had grown increasingly dissatisfied with Gingrich's leadership during the prelude to formal impeachment proceedings. Party leaders never developed a successful strategy for capitalizing on the president's misfortune, and eleventh-hour efforts to push impeachment as an important campaign issue appeared to do more harm than good. While Democratic advisors pushed impeachment as an issue, Republicans began to shy away from the potential negative fallout (Baker 2000). Gingrich's last-minute media buy ($10 million worth), designed to pillory Clinton and fellow Democrats, had failed; even worse, it had mobilized Democrats outraged at the treatment of their president (Baker 2000; Toobin 1999).

Unable to effectively leverage impeachment, the conservative leadership sought a new Speaker. Considerable support quickly built for a senior Southern Republican, Appropriations Committee chairman Robert Livingston (La.). As chairman of the Appropriations Committee, Livingston's relationship with Gingrich had not been friendly. After considering his circumstances and those of Gingrich immediately after the election, Livingston faxed an ultimatum to Gingrich indicating that he, Livingston, would not run for the Speakership if Gingrich agreed to a long and detailed list of "rules" for the relationship between the Speaker and the chairman of the House Appropriations Committee. Gingrich failed to respond within the timeframe Livingston set, and Livingston began his run for Gingrich's job (Baker 2000). Shortly thereafter, Gingrich chose to resign.

Given the public's surprising support for Democrats during the 1998 elections, the continuation of House Republican efforts to impeach the president took many Washington insiders by surprise. Explanations for the Republicans' tenacity in the face of defeat vary. What surprised no one, however, was the overtly partisan nature of the battle waged during the impeachment hearings of the House Judiciary Committee. As one of the most ideologically-oriented committees in the House, most of the members of the Judiciary Committee were relatively well insulated from an electoral standpoint, and efforts to build bridges across partisan and ideological divides were rare. The debate during committee hearings plainly manifested this partisan conflict. Although Democrats criticized the president's behavior and personal judgment, they also pushed for a legislative punishment short of impeachment (such as censure). Republicans on the Judiciary Committee unanimously opposed these attempts to build support for an executive censure, and refused to seriously consider censure as a legislative option.

Little more than a month after the elections, the House Judiciary Committee reported out four articles of impeachment, each passing on a strict party-line vote. Each of the articles of impeachment dealt specifically with the Lewinsky scandal, Clinton's testimony in the Jones hearings, and his alleged efforts to influence the testimony of other witnesses in the Jones hearings. Article 1 charged the president with committing perjury before independent counsel Starr's grand jury. The second article charged the president with committing perjury during his deposition in the *Jones* civil case. The third article charged him with obstruction of justice, specifically citing him for behavior designed to "delay, impede, cover up, and conceal the existence of evidence." The fourth and final article of impeachment charged the president with misuse and abuse of office by committing perjury in his responses to the 81 questions submitted by the House Judiciary Committee.

After deliberations on the floor of the House, two of the articles of impeachment were approved by the House membership—articles 1 and 3—and two articles of impeachment were rejected. Due to the upcoming Christmas holiday break, the Senate deferred consideration of the articles of impeachment until the following year.

In the interim, between the passage of the articles of impeachment by the House and the end of the calendar year, a sexual scandal ended the leadership hopes of Speaker-designate Robert Livingston (R.–La.). Public disclosure of a past marital infidelity forced him to withdraw his name from consideration for the Speakership. Ironically, in the wake of Clinton's scandalous relationship, the Republicans lost two of their most prominent congressional leaders.

After the start of the first session of the new, 106th Congress, the Senate initiated its own hearings and deliberations on the articles of impeachment. The Senate proceedings did not begin without controversy. One potential obstacle to the Senate impeachment trial was the issue of institutional continuity. Although some scholars (see Ackerman 1999) argued that a House impeachment and the Senate trial on the impeachment charges must take place during the same Congress, this contention failed to win widespread support and was quickly forgotten.

Although the presentations of the House managers' and the president's counsel were open to the public, the deliberations of the body on the articles of impeachment were closed—but not without a fight. In the end, a sufficient number of Republicans supported closed deliberations to win the day. In these closed sessions,[9] two issues dominated the deliberations: whether the House managers had proved beyond a reasonable doubt that the president had committed the alleged offenses and whether the offenses, if actually committed by the president, were impeachable. Some senators argued that the president had committed one or more of the alleged acts and that the acts were impeachable. Senator Bond (R.–Mo.) found that:

> If we are to have a government of laws and not of men and not of public opinion polls, then we must judge the President on the evidence presented to us. I believe that the acts that he committed constitute high-crimes and misdemeanors warranting his conviction. (*Congressional Record*, February 12, 1999: S1509)

Likewise, Senator Grams (R.–Minn.) concluded:

> I disagree in one aspect, but agree in another. I personally feel there is no room to disagree on whether the President is guilty of the charges in both Article One and Article Two; he committed perjury and he clearly obstructed justice. But I agree we will differ on whether these charges rise to the level of high crimes which dictate conviction. Again, I believe they do and have voted yes, on

both articles. (*Congressional Record,* February 12, 1999: S1499–S1500)

Other senators found the House managers' case less than compelling and argued that they had failed to prove it beyond a reasonable doubt, that the offenses did not warrant impeachment, or both. Senator Collins (R.–Maine) found insufficient evidence for conviction on the perjury charge but was convinced by the House managers on the charge of obstruction of justice. Nevertheless, she was not convinced that the specific character of Clinton's obstruction warranted impeachment. Accordingly, she concluded:

> [F]or impeachment purposes, obstruction of justice has more ominous implications when the conduct concealed, or the method used to conceal it, poses a threat to our governmental institutions. Neither occurred in this case. Therefore, I will cast my vote not for the current President, but for the presidency. I believe that in order to convict, we must conclude from the evidence presented to us with no room for doubt that our Constitution will be injured and our democracy suffer should the President remain in office one moment more. (*Congressional Record,* February 12, 1999: S1573)

Senator Biden clearly stated the position of those who were unconvinced by the House managers and House Republicans more generally: "In my judgment, trying to assume a perspective of principled political neutrality, the case before us falls far, far short on the facts and on the law" (*Congressional Record,* February 12, 1999: S1478).

Interestingly, during the Senate deliberations, members tended to admit to the reasonableness of the perspectives of those with whom they disagreed. This is in stark contrast to the sentiments expressed during the House debates. Although various alternatives to votes on the articles of impeachment were suggested (e.g., censure), both articles stood a floor vote on February 12, 1999. Both failed, ending a brief but extraordinary period in U.S. history.

Appendix 2-1

House Judiciary Committee Membership

Republicans	Democrats
Henry J. Hyde (Ill.), Chairman	John Conyers (Mich.), Ranking
F. James Sensenbrenner (Wis.)	Barney Frank (Mass.)
Bill McCollum (Fla.)	Charles E. Schumer (N.Y.)
George W. Gekas (Pa.)	Howard L. Berman (Calif.)
Howard Coble (N.C.)	Rick Boucher (Va.)
Lamar S. Smith (Tex.)	Jerrold Nadler (N.Y.)
Elton Gallegly (Calif.)	Robert C. Scott (Va.)
Charles T. Canady (Fla.)	Melvin L. Watt (N.C.)
Bob Inglis (S.C.)	Zoe Lofgren (Calif.)
Robert W. Goodlatte (Va.)	Sheila Jackson Lee (Tex.)
Stephen E. Buyer (Ind.)	Maxine Waters (Calif.)
Ed Bryant (Tenn.)	Martin T. Meehan (Mass.)
Steve Chabot (Ohio)	William D. Delahunt (Mass.)
Bob R. Barr (Ga.)	Robert Wexler (Fla.)
William L. Jenkins (Tenn.)	Steven R. Rothman (N.J.)
Asa Hutchinson (Arkansas)	Thomas R. Barrett (Wis.)
Edward Pease (Ind.)	
Christopher B. Cannon (Utah)	
James E. Rogan (Calif.)	
Lindsey O. Graham (S.C.)	
Mary Bono (Calif.)	

House Managers of the Senate Trial

Henry J. Hyde (Ill.), Chairman
F. James Sensenbrenner (Wis.)
George W. Gekas (Pa.)
Charles T. Canada (Fla.)
Stephen E. Buyer (Ind.)
Ed Bryant (Tenn.)
Steve Chabot (Ohio)
Bob R. Barr (Ga.)
Asa Hutchinson (Arkansas)
Christopher B. Cannon (Utah)
James E. Rogan (Calif.)
Lindsey O. Graham (S.C.)

3

PUBLIC OPINION AND THE CLINTON IMPEACHMENT

With Jina Hwang

On January 18, 1998, *The Drudge Report* published an item alleging that President Clinton had had a sexual liaison with a White House intern. Three days later, both *The Washington Post* and ABC News reported that independent counsel Kenneth Starr was investigating an alleged affair between a White House intern, Monica Lewinsky, and President Clinton. During the afternoon, Clinton denied that any sexual encounters ever occurred between himself and Lewinsky. Five days later, he repeated the original denial. The following day Hillary Clinton, on NBC's *Today* show, decried the "vast right-wing conspiracy" intent on engineering her husband's downfall.

In a few short days, Monica Lewinsky had gone from complete unknown to epicenter of the world's most media-conscious public. On January 15, only friends, family, coworkers, and the small group of lawyers intimately involved in the Jones case knew Lewinsky. Before the first of February, her name was a household word. Now that the public knew her name—and was starting to learn details about who she was (or might be)—the media scrambled desperately to figure out what the public thought of her alleged relationship with Clinton and how it was reacting to Clinton and his denials.

Immediately after the Lewinsky story broke, print and television media outlets were tapping public opinion about it. Every significant media outlet rushed to field overnight or two-day polls to assess the public's reaction to the allegations of a relationship between the president and Lewinsky (Andolina and Wilcox 2000). The public's evaluations of Clinton, his role in the scandal, and the proper course of action if the allegations against him were true were more negative at this point in time than they would be at any other point during the scandal. In the days leading up to the disclosure of his relationship with Lewinsky, Clinton's job approval rating hovered at 60 percent (Gallup Poll, January 16–18, 1998). In the days immediately following the disclosure, his job approval rating faltered, although only marginally. Gallup Poll figures show his approval dipping to 58 percent (January 23–25, 1998), and *Washington Post*/ABC News (January 22–25, 1998) poll figures indicate an even smaller drop to 59 percent.

Clinton's early response to the disclosure of the scandal—except for his initial denial—was, somewhat strangely for him, reticence. To the extent possible, he avoided discussions of the scandal, and he made every effort not to mention Lewinsky's name if and when questions about the scandal and his relationship with Lewinsky were asked. However, the story of the scandal had taken on a life of its own, and the president could—or did—do little to control it. As Jeffrey Toobin describes those first few days after the disclosure, "[T]he Lewinsky story had been careening down a hill, picking up momentum each day. Each new disclosure made the president look worse" (1999: 252). Clinton's unwillingness to enter the media fray during those first few days was costly in terms of public opinion. A growing majority of Americans believed the allegations that he had had a sexual relationship with Lewinsky while she was a White House intern, and most Americans thought Clinton had asked Lewinsky to provide false testimony during her Jones' hearing deposition (see Andolina and Wilcox 2000). The public also considered these serious offenses. According to a *Washington Post*/ABC News poll (January 22–25, 1998), more than 60 percent of the public believed the president should resign if he had lied under oath during the *Jones* trial, and 55 percent thought he should be impeached for the same behavior. By the end of January, Clinton's favorability rating was down from 62 percent in late October to 53 percent (Gallup Poll, January 25–26, 1998).

During his entire political career, Clinton's habitual response to personal or professional allegations of a scandalous nature was a direct frontal assault. This was the case during the Jennifer Flowers scandal early in his 1992 run for the Democratic presidential nomination. It was his modus operandi for dealing with the Whitewater allegations, Vincent Foster's unusual death, the firing of members of the White House Travel Office staff, and the various fundraising scandals. In this case, however, Clinton was not on the attack, at least not immediately. Exactly why is unclear. Quite possibly it was because it was difficult for him to decide whom to attack. The ultimate source of the scandal was Lewinsky (and her conversations with Tripp), but she was publicly untouchable (although Clinton associates made several attempts to discredit her), and Starr had yet to become fully involved in the investigation of the scandal. So the attack model was difficult to implement. As the opinion poll results indicate, the president's failure to respond was a public relations nightmare. The Lewinsky scandal dominated the news, so its importance was magnified. If the president persisted in his refusal to address the matter, his job approval and favorability numbers would continue to deteriorate.

Just before the end of January 1998, Clinton began to address the Lewinsky scandal more aggressively. In a now infamous denial, Clinton told a television audience, "I did not have sexual relations with that woman, Miss Lewinsky [mentioning her name in public for the first time]. I never told anybody to lie, not a single time." This was followed, strategically, by Hillary Clinton's *Today* show interview in which she decried the "vast, right-wing conspiracy" against her husband. The response of the Clinton team worked wonders for his public image. By January 28, Clinton's job approval rating had soared to 67 percent, his highest rating to that point

(Gallup Poll). His favorability ratings were also extraordinarily high. Nearly two-thirds of the American public (64 percent) had a favorable impression of Clinton in late January and early February 1998, a higher favorability rating than the president had had in more than a year (Gallup Poll, January 30-February 1, 1998). Along with the firming up of Clinton's job approval and favorability numbers came increased public support on those issues directly related to the scandal. More Americans believed the president's denial, and fewer Americans believed the president had been involved in suborning perjury by asking Lewinsky to lie during her Jones deposition. Likewise, fewer Americans thought the president should resign, and even fewer thought the president should be impeached (Andolina and Wilcox 2000).

Although the president's aggressive response to the Lewinsky allegations swayed public opinion in his direction, there was no avoiding the fact that the scandal would be a prominent public issue for some time to come. As long as the Lewinsky scandal remained a significant story, media outlets would tap public opinion on the scandal. Although public opinion polls on presidential popularity and presidential performance are common, during the active phase of the Lewinsky scandal—from original disclosure in January 1998 to the final Senate votes on the impeachment articles in February 1999—public opinion polls dealing with the president and the presidency were ubiquitous. Immediately following the disclosure of Lewinsky's relationship with Clinton, polling the public's opinion of the president, the presidency, and Congress became a growth industry. According to Kathleen A. Frankovic, survey director of CBS, CBS and the *New York Times* joined to conduct 48 separate surveys in 1998, 75 percent more than they had in any previous year, and many of these surveys focused on the Lewinsky scandal. These polls contained three times more questions about the Lewinsky scandal than early 1970s' polls had included about the Watergate scandal, the last time a U.S. president faced impeachment (Kotok 1999).

Survey questions plumbed a variety of different aspects of the Lewinsky scandal. There were the obvious questions about whether the president had lied (or committed perjury), whether he had had a sexual relationship with Lewinsky, and whether he had asked others (including Lewinsky) to lie to protect him. Respondents were asked whether the president should resign, and if he refused to resign, should he be impeached. Pollsters also asked about the handling of the Lewinsky matter by the independent counsel, particularly about the extent to which Starr had treated Clinton (and Lewinsky) fairly. Survey respondents were asked about the response of Congress to *The Starr Report,* the fairness and appropriateness of the impeachment hearings, and whether the president should be removed from office. Hardly any aspect of public opinion concerning the scandal or the individuals involved in the scandal went unexamined.

Because we have so much opinion poll data dealing with the scandal from the time period of the Starr investigation, the House Judiciary Committee hearings, the floor hearings in the House, and the Senate trial, we can estimate with some precision the public's evaluation of Clinton, its view of his impeachment, and whether Americans wanted him removed from office. In short, available public opinion data support the following conclusions:

1. Except for the first few days after the initial disclosure of the relationship between Clinton and Lewinsky, public evaluations of Clinton's job performance and Clinton's favorability numbers were consistently high. In many cases, these numbers were higher during 1998 than at any previous time in his presidency.
2. Again, following the initial reaction to the disclosure of Clinton's relationship with Lewinsky, the public did not support efforts to impeach the president. Not only did a majority of Americans oppose impeachment, but in nearly all cases—including polls taken closest to the actual impeachment votes—an overwhelming majority opposed impeachment.
3. Even larger majorities opposed removal from office than impeachment (where responses could be clearly distinguished).

There is simply no question that the American public opposed efforts to impeach the president and subsequently remove him from office.

One cannot fully appreciate the strikingly positive character of these opinion poll data without an accurate understanding of the sense of calamity and foreboding that immediately followed the initial disclosure of the Clinton-Lewinsky relationship. On January 25, the Sunday immediately following the original *Drudge Report* article, two prominent journalists openly questioned Clinton's ability to hold on to the White House more than a few short days. On NBC, Tim Russert put Clinton's survival chances at no better than even money, and on ABC, Sam Donaldson questioned whether Clinton's presidency would survive the week (Toobin 1999). Without a doubt, the situation looked untenable, and yet Clinton persevered, and the public followed. The public's evaluation of Clinton was, in general, significantly higher during and after the Lewinsky scandal than it had been before the scandal. In the next section, we discuss these data (and the related evaluations) in more detail.

Evaluations of the President and Opinions on Impeachment

Probably the most commonly asked public opinion question dealing with the president and his or her performance is the following "job approval" question: "Do you approve or disapprove of the way [the president's name] is handling his [her] job as president." This question is usually asked several times each month and has been for a number of years, so we can compare job approval ratings for many of the post-World War II presidents. Aggregate responses tend to be relatively stable; large percentage shifts are rare and are nearly always preceded by exceptional behavior or circumstances (e.g., Watergate).

During the first year of the Clinton administration, the president's job approval rating ranged from a low of 37 percent in early June to a high of 59 percent just a month after his inauguration. His average job approval rating for the first year of his administration—a

TABLE 3.1   Clinton Job Approval Ratings*

Year	Average Approval (percent)
1993	48.3
1994	44.8
1995	47.6
1996	54.5
1997	55.2
1998	61.9
1999	61.6
2000	59.9
2001**	66

*The figures are taken from various *Gallup Polls.*

**This is the average for the first two surveys, both in January, fielded in 2001.

time traditionally known as the honeymoon period—was 48.3 percent. In 1994, the president's average job approval rating dropped to 44.8 percent. Although Clinton's job approval rating would increase slightly in 1995, to 47.6 percent, he was still short of earning the support of half the U.S. public. Although there was a small increase to the mid-50s over the next two years, Clinton's approval ratings remained unexceptional. (See Table 3.1.)

After the disclosure of the Lewinsky scandal in January 1998, however, there was a significant and protracted increase in the president's approval figures. His 1998 figures alone were nearly 7 percentage points higher than those in his next highest year. Although there was a slight drop in 1999 and again in 2000, Clinton's approval ratings during these three years are significantly better than in any other year of his presidency (except 2001). As indicated previously, there was far more polling activity during the active phase of the Lewinsky scandal than at other times, so the 1998 and 1999 figures are actually based on significantly more data than those for other years.[1] This gives us an added measure of confidence in the average scores for these years. Clearly, there is no evidence that public evaluations of the president's job performance were negatively affected by the Lewinsky scandal.

Data on the president's favorability numbers paint a similar picture. When asked the following question—"What is your overall opinion of Bill Clinton: Is it favorable or unfavorable (or have you never heard of him)?"—more than 54 percent had a favorable impression of the president. Although "unfavorable" responses were also quite common (43 percent), the president's "favorable" percentage never dropped below 51 percent during the active phase of the Lewinsky scandal and the impeachment proceedings.

Congress did not fare as well as the president in these same opinion polls. There is a Congress job approval question—"Do you approve of the way Congress is handling its job?"—that is commonly asked in national surveys of political opinion. In 1998, the average job approval rating for Congress was 52 percent, almost 10 full points less than the president's job approval rating. And if we look at a graph of presidential job approval and congressional job approval over the course of the Lewinsky scandal, we see that the president outperformed Congress—sometimes by a significant amount—in every time period. (See Figure 3.1.)

Note also that the largest gap between presidential job approval and congressional job approval came right at the time when Congress was deciding to impeach the president. In fact, on a poll conducted on December 19 and 20, 1998—when the House approved two articles of impeachment against President Clinton—his approval rating reached an all time high of 73 percent ("Poll Readings" 1999). In the same poll, a stunning 81 percent called Clinton's presidency a success, quite an impressive achievement for a president who faced a trial on articles of impeachment alleging perjury, abuse of power, and obstruction of justice. Again, although the favorability figures for the president are slightly lower—and there is no direct analogue for Congress—the character of the relationship is the same: The president outperforms Congress from the standpoint of public opinion. (See Figure 3.2.)

We know that the public approved of the way in which Clinton was handling his job as president, but public opinion on job ap-

Figure 3.1 *

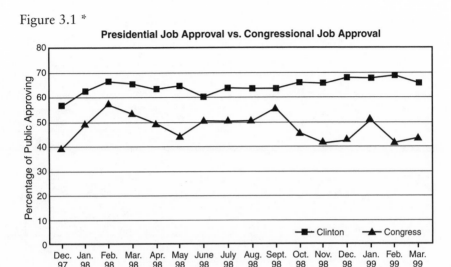

*Based on figures taken from various *Gallup Polls.*

proval and public opinion on presidential impeachment are distinct. It is certainly likely that Clinton's high job approval boosted public opposition to impeachment, but that has not yet been clearly demonstrated. More specifically, we are interested in the public's position on impeachment near the end of 1998 and on removal during the beginning of 1999. Basically, what was the public telling Congress that it wanted—with regard to impeachment and removal—at the time that Congress was directly addressing those issues?

During the latter part of 1998 and on into early 1999, the U.S. public, in large numbers, consistently opposed the congressional effort to impeach the president and subsequently remove him from office. In a poll fielded immediately after the House of Representatives impeached the president on December 19, 1998, only 35 percent of survey respondents indicated support for impeachment. Although Republicans in this sample overwhelmingly supported impeachment (73 percent), Independents (40 percent) and Democrats (12 percent) were strongly opposed (Gallup Poll, December 19–20, 1998). On the issue of removal from office, opinion poll data indicate strong support for the Senate's decision to acquit on both impeachment

Figure 3.2*

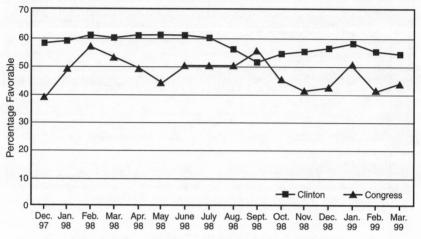

Presidential Favorability vs. Congressional Favorability

*Based on figures taken from various *Gallup Polls.*

charges. Results from February and March 1999 indicate that between 61 and 64 percent of the public supported the Senate's final
decision (Gallup Polls, February 12–13, 1999, and March 12–14,
1999). An ABC News poll taken on the day of the acquittal found
that three out of every five Americans supported Senate acquittal
(Langer 1999).

Aside from its opposition to impeachment and removal, the general public questioned the fairness of Congress's handling of the
Clinton impeachment. According to an October Gallup Poll, 50 percent of the U.S. public believed that Congress "did not conduct its
review of the charges against Bill Clinton in a fair and impartial
manner" (October 6–7, 1998). More than a year later, more than 50
percent of Americans (52 percent) considered the congressional handling of the charges against Clinton unfair (Gallup Poll, December
9–12, 1999). On the issue of filing criminal charges against Clinton
following his presidency, the public was strongly opposed—less
than 40 percent supported charging Clinton with a crime—immediately following his acquittal in the Senate (Gallup Poll, February

12–13, 1999). Finally, most Americans considered Clinton's impeachment harmful to the country as a whole. Nearly one-third of the public considered the process "very harmful," and another 42 percent considered the process "somewhat harmful" (Gallup Poll, February 12–13, 1999).

These opinion poll numbers present a clear picture of the average American's position on the Clinton impeachment at the time that the House was deciding whether to impeach and, subsequently, at the point that the Senate was evaluating the case for removal from office. When members of Congress were making their decisions about the case against Clinton, the public was clearly and vocally opposed to impeachment and removal. That simple fact cannot be denied. It is also important to realize that the crystallization of public opinion on the issue of impeachment did not occur late in the process. Public opposition to Clinton's impeachment solidified months before the final House vote was taken in late December 1998. Opinion polls in the months leading up to the 1998 election and the formal impeachment proceedings show strong and consistent opposition to impeachment and removal. This consistency is due largely to the fact that many Americans had made up their minds about whether Clinton should resign or be removed from office at the beginning of the scandal. According to Frank Newport of the Gallup Poll, the release of *The Starr Report* marked a turning point in public opinion, because many Americans made their final judgments about Clinton at that time (Ayres 1999). From the release of *The Starr Report* until the end of the trial, public opinion—whether for or against Clinton—remained stable, with 59 percent of Americans stating that nothing could happen to change their position on the removal of the president, and only 11 percent saying that they could be swayed by the evidence (Benedetto 1999).

Explaining Opposition to Impeachment

Given the media coverage of the Lewinsky scandal and the substance of the charges made against the president, the level of public support for Clinton—and the breadth and depth of public opposition to impeachment—were nothing less than striking. A comparison of the public's reaction to Clinton during the Lewinsky scandal and to Nixon during the Watergate scandal highlights the unusual level of support afforded Clinton.

Unlike Clinton, whose approval ratings remained in the 60 to 70 percent range even during the darkest days of the scandal, Nixon's average job approval rating (over two terms) was only 49 percent (Burnes 1998). In the summer of 1974, just before Nixon resigned, his approval rating was an incredibly low 24 percent (*The Gallup Poll Monthly,* July 1974). At this point, both Republicans and Democrats pushed for his removal or his resignation. By contrast, even after details of his scandal had been made public, Clinton still topped the Gallup Poll's list as the "most admired man" in the United States. With a few exceptions, presidents usually top this list. One of those exceptions was Nixon, who was beaten out by Henry Kissinger and Billy Graham during the final two years of his presidency.

There are several explanations for the difference between the public's support for Clinton and its opposition to Nixon. The first important distinction is that the specific scandals in which these two presidents were involved were quite different. Among other things, the Watergate scandal involved a pattern of behavior on the part of President Nixon to obscure the administration's role in the break-in at the Democratic Party's national headquarters at the Watergate hotel. There is compelling evidence—including secretly taped telephone conversations—that Nixon, on numerous occasions, obstructed justice and abused the powers of the office of the president to prevent the prosecution of members of the administration, his personal staff, and ultimately himself.

The Lewinsky scandal, on the other hand, was fundamentally about an improper sexual relationship between the president and a White House intern and the president's unwillingness to admit to this relationship in a civil legal proceeding. Although Clinton was also charged with abuse of power and obstruction of justice, there was significantly less evidentiary support for these charges in Clinton's case than in Nixon's. Most Americans believed that the Watergate scandal was fundamentally different from the Lewinsky scandal because the former addressed much more serious issues. Opinion poll data on the distinctiveness of the Watergate and Lewinsky scandals bear out this conclusion. Only 10 percent of those polled perceived the Lewinsky scandal to be more serious than the Watergate scandal, whereas 64 percent of the respondents thought Watergate was more serious than the Lewinsky scandal (Moore 1998).

According to former Nixon aide John Dean, most Americans "could not identify with wire tapping, break-ins, use of the FBI, IRS and CIA" (Lester 1998). Clinton's offenses, on the other hand, seemed a bit more human. Whereas Nixon's behavior was perceived as a threat to the integrity of our government, Clinton's actions were not viewed as a serious constitutional threat. James Hamilton (former associate counsel on the Senate Watergate Committee) argues that Nixon's actions were "great and dangerous offenses against the state," whereas former Representative Elizabeth Holtzman (a 1974 Judiciary Committee member) argues that Clinton's marital infidelity and his unwillingness to admit to it were not (Schmickle 1998: 19A). Therefore, the collection of Clinton's misdeeds "doesn't rise to what we saw in Watergate" and "does not involve the powers of the presidency" (Holtzman, quoted in Schmeckle 1998: 19A). Nixon lost the support of the public because his offenses were viewed as a threat to the constitutional order. Clinton's offenses, on the other hand, did not result in the loss of public support because they were perceived as character flaws rather than impediments to effective leadership or threats to popular government or the institution of the presidency.

In addition to the grave public perceptions of Watergate, another explanation for the difference in public opinions of Nixon and Clinton is the state of the nation, particularly the state of the national economy. It is widely accepted that the public's approval of a president is reflective of the state of the economy (see, among others, Kernell 1997). Presidents who enjoy strong economies are often rewarded with public support and votes (during election years), and presidents who face weak economies are usually punished (see Campbell 2000; Erikson 1989). Regardless of the president's actual responsibility for national economic circumstances, presidents and members of their party depend on good economic circumstances for the continued support of voters.

There were sharp differences in the state of the economy during the Nixon and Clinton administrations. In 1974, unemployment rates reached double digits and retail prices rose by 11 percent (Schmickle 1998). Many lost manufacturing jobs, and lower-paying service work was on the rise. Oil was scarce, and the oil and gasoline that were available were extraordinarily expensive.

During 1998, the U.S. national economy was enjoying the fruits of the longest sustained period of economic growth in modern U.S. history. Both inflation and unemployment were at levels that had not been seen in a generation, and interest rates—given the strong economy—were also at unusually low levels. Poverty was down, and people were leaving welfare rolls in record numbers. The national government was actually operating at a surplus, a situation that had seemed unlikely to the point of impossibility less than a decade before. The year that the Lewinsky scandal broke on the national media scene was one of the most prosperous years in U.S. history.

Clinton's advantage of presiding over good times was a major factor in his high approval ratings. Not only did he get high approval ratings for his handling of foreign policy (64 percent), race relations (76 percent), and education (69 percent), but at 81 percent, his approval rating for the handling of the economy hit record-setting marks (Page and Benedetto 1999). With 81 percent of Americans happy with Clinton's handling of the economy, it's not surprising that Clinton's job approval ratings were so high. With a strong economy and historically low unemployment, Clinton was viewed as an effective executive at the same time that he was seen as morally suspect. The drastic difference between Nixon's economy and Clinton's economy provides at least a partial explanation for the difference in public support for the two presidents.

It is important to remember that the public's astonishing and unfaltering support for the president was not a reflection of Americans' refusal to accept the president's guilt or less-than-moral character. Most Americans believed Clinton had had an inappropriate relationship with Lewinsky and that he had lied about this relationship during the course of his *Jones* deposition. An overwhelming majority, 79 percent, believed Clinton to be guilty of perjury, and 53 percent believed him to be guilty of obstruction of justice in the Paula Jones lawsuit (*USA Today*, January 12, 1999). Not surprisingly, the majority of Americans considered Clinton dishonest and untrustworthy. Only 24 percent of the public considered him honest and trustworthy, and an even smaller percentage of poll respondents (20 percent) thought that Clinton had demonstrated good moral leadership (Ornstein 1999). Although Americans harbored no illusions regarding Clinton's character, they clearly opposed his removal from office.

These contradictory views of the president—extraordinary support for his presidency accompanied by high levels of public disdain for his moral character and honesty are attributable to the fact that Americans balanced Clinton's performance as president and his character as a person and assessed them separately (Ornstein 1999). For many Americans, Clinton's behavior—in contrast to Nixon's—was a private, rather than a public, failing. This perspective extended to Clinton's handling of questions about his relationship with Lewinsky. If the affair itself were a private matter, the president could not be criticized too harshly for refusing to truthfully answer questions that should not have been asked in the first place. According to Molly Andolina and Clyde Wilcox, "For many Americans, Clinton's affair with Lewinsky was a private matter . . . [and many] believe that Clinton should never have been questioned about the matter" (2000: 189).

Clinton's own personal popularity also served him well during the Lewinsky scandal. Although his job approval numbers were higher during and after the scandal than they were prior to it, they were nevertheless quite solid in the three years immediately preceding the scandal. Clinton's favorability figures were similarly high prior to the scandal. Clinton was, quite simply, a very popular president, and this personal popularity insulated him somewhat from the fallout precipitated by the disclosure of his relationship with Lewinsky. Clinton had a capacity to relate to the public in an unusually effective way. In modern times, only Ronald Reagan was his equal as a communicator. As an empathizer, he was without peer. Nixon, of course, did not have Clinton's skills as a communicator. He had difficulty relating to the public and difficulty convincing Americans that he could relate to them. Not surprisingly, he did not enjoy the same level of personal popularity, and the public's response to Watergate was in no way softened or mitigated by their attachment to Nixon the person.

Public support for Clinton must also be viewed as public opposition to his political enemies, those who wanted to delve deeply into his relationship with Lewinsky, to impeach him, and remove him from office. As Andolina and Wilcox note, "Clinton benefited in this crisis from widespread public dislike of his enemies and skepticism of their motives" (2000: 187). At some level it is difficult to distinguish between dislike in an absolute sense and dislike in a relative sense. Because of Clinton's considerable popularity, his opponents—independent counsel Kenneth Starr, Speaker Gingrich, House Judiciary Committee Chair Henry Hyde, and the other House impeachment managers—faced a difficult task. Building public support for the impeachment of a popular president is an arduous task because the proponents are likely to be unpopular for no other reason than that they are opposing a popular president. That type of public opposition is nearly impossible to avoid.

Clinton's opponents not only faced the obstacle of challenging a popular president, their handling of the public relations of the Lewinsky investigation and the handling of the impeachment hearings were largely failures. The president's behavior should have cleared the way for his opponents to take and hold the high moral ground and the public support that would have come with that victory. But Clinton's opponents never effectively gained the advantage.

Admittedly, certain circumstances made it difficult to win the public relations battle with the president. First, the public perceived that the scandal was fundamentally about sex—and thus, fundamentally private. Failing to sway public opinion on this issue doomed efforts to build significant public support for Clinton's impeachment. Second, the public viewed the behavior of several of Clinton's most prominent opponents as illegal, unethical, or grossly unfair. Secretly taping intimate conversations with one's close friends (à la Linda Tripp) was not viewed as an appropriate investigative tool, and the use of these tapes by the independent counsel was quite unpopular. Similarly, the independent counsel's handling of Lewinsky—including issuing a grand jury subpoena to her mother—was viewed as excessive and unfair. Finally, the public was suspicious of the motives of Clinton's opponents. Although their language was suffused with ethics and moral rectitude, the president's enemies could never completely shake the impression that they were implementing a personal vendetta against a politically superior opponent. Fair or not, these factors undoubtedly influenced the public's perception of Clinton, his behavior, and the appropriate response to that behavior.

Finally, demographic and ideological differences between the supporters and opponents of impeachment also help us understand the underpinnings of responses to Clinton and the Lewinsky scandal. The majority of Americans were able to give Clinton favorable job ratings by separating his performance from his character. Clinton's opponents pushed Americans to do the exact opposite and tie the man and the president together. According to several Gallup Polls, a minority of Americans (38 percent of those polled) were of the same mind as Clinton's opponents and made up what the Gallup Organization labeled "the repulsed." Of this deeply critical group (97 percent felt negatively about Clinton as a person), 57 percent were conservative and 53 percent were Republican (Morello and Holguin 1999). Not surprisingly, Republicans and conservatives were most in favor of Clinton's impeachment, with 88 percent of "the repulsed" supporting Clinton's removal from office.

Clinton's supporters, on the other hand, were more ideologically diverse. After conducting a series of polls throughout the scandal, the Gallup Organization identified three separate groups of supporters with often conflicting feelings toward Clinton. The "admirers" made up 26 percent of those polled. Admirers supported Clinton not only as a president but also as a man. Only 1 percent of this group had negative feelings toward Clinton as a person. Somewhat surprisingly, only 29 percent of the "admirers" self-identified as liberals. More than half were women and more than half were Democrats. Half of all African Americans polled fit in the admirers group. Admirers, as would be expected, overwhelmingly (99 percent) opposed impeachment. A second group of supporters, the "pragmatists," made up 18 percent of those polled and, like the admirers, also included a relatively high proportion of women (53 percent). Although 73 percent felt negatively toward Clinton as a person, 94 percent favored the acquittal. Finally, the "forgivers," who also made up 18 percent of those polled, favored the acquittal of the president (91 percent) even though 40 percent felt negatively about the president as a person. Again, more than half were women (Morello and Holguin 1999).

The polls revealed a tendency for women and minorities (African Americans in particular) to support Clinton at significantly higher rates than white men. The relatively high opposition to impeachment among women and minorities may be a function of their evaluation of Clinton as an individual. It is more likely that it is at least partly a function of the general political dispositions of these groups and their aversion to the Republican party and many of its policies. Lowell Weicker, a former Connecticut senator, explained it this way: "If you are [a woman], if you are a minority, why would you want to kick out a man that you perceive as your friend and put yourself in the hands of a political party governed by the religious right?" (Nagourney 1998). While Clinton enjoyed his record-high ratings, the GOP received the lowest approval rating in the 14 years that the *New York Times* and CBS had asked the same question (Nagourney 1998). Most Americans preferred that Clinton, rather than congressional Republicans, have more influence on the direction the country was taking. This was a sharp turn from 1995, when Republicans took control of Congress for the first time in 40 years (*USA Today,* January 12, 1999). Throughout the scandal, the public was generally dissatisfied with the Republican Party. In January 1999, when Clinton's approval rating was at 67 percent, the GOP was at 40 percent and the Democrats at 57 percent

(USA/CNN/Gallup Poll, January 1999). Clinton's high approval ratings, therefore, may have partly reflected the public's overall dissatisfaction with the GOP.

The eventual acquittal of the president reflected the public's desire to keep Clinton in office: Support for impeachment was much greater in the Senate than among the general public. If an estimated 60 to 70 percent of voters favored the president, and if two-thirds opposed impeachment, why didn't the Senate's vote reflect national opinion? The discrepancy between the public opinion and Senate vote calls into question the relevance of public opinion polls. Perhaps frustrated by Clinton's good ratings, some Republicans like Republican National Chairman Jim Nicholson responded by stating that the polls did not matter: "We are really not governed by polls; we're governed by principles" (Page and Benedetto 1999). During the Clinton-Lewinsky scandal, polls added to the drama that unfolded before the nation. The polls in themselves seemed unbelievable at times, and they added "yet another surreal element [to] this surreal melodrama" (Ornstein 1999).

Although many House members said that their votes regarding the impeachment were matters of conscience, it's unlikely that they completely ignored Clinton's ability to sustain high levels of popularity with their constituents regardless of the troubles surrounding him. A more plausible explanation for the discrepancy between public opinion and House and Senate votes lies in the difference between national opinion and state/district opinion. Public opinion at the national level provides little information about the specific preferences of any particular state or district constituency. Because senators and representatives are not elected by national constituencies, we might reasonably expect a gap between the aggregate behavior of members of Congress and the aggregate preferences of their constituents. Perhaps the disjuncture between House and (to a lesser extent) Senate voting and public opinion is a function of misunderstanding the appropriate focal constituency. If we focus on the preferences of the proper constituencies (district and state populations), maybe public opinion did guide roll call voting on impeachment and conviction. The next two chapters examine the impact of district and state-level opinion on roll call votes on impeachment (in the House) and conviction (in the Senate).

Postscript: Public Opinion in the Aftermath

Recent opinion polls suggest that opposition to the Clinton impeachment has dissipated since the historic acquittal votes in the Senate. According to a recent ABC News poll, 45 percent of the U.S. public now approves of the House's decision to impeach Clinton (ABC News Poll, July 16, 2000). This is an increase from 40 percent immediately following the impeachment (ABC News Poll, December 20, 1998). Data from comparable Gallup polls suggest an even more striking change of heart. In a poll conducted December 9–12–1999 by the Gallup Organization, a full 50 percent of the U.S. public supported the House decision to impeach the president. This is a 15-point increase from the original post-impeachment poll in which 35 percent of the public supported impeachment (Gallup Poll, December 19–20, 1998). Likewise, support for Clinton's acquittal in the Senate waned in the months following the end of the scandal. Again, according to an ABC News poll, only 50 percent of the U.S. public now supports the Senate's decision to acquit Clinton (July 16, 2000). Immediately following the Senate votes in 1999, 60 percent of the American public supported acquittal (ABC News Poll, February 12, 1999). This result is not, however, corroborated by comparable opinion data. Results from a Gallup Poll fielded in December 1999 indicate that 57 percent of the U.S. public still supported the Senate's acquittal of the president (December 9–12, 1999).

One explanation for this change in public opinion is that a significant portion of the public has changed its mind about the seriousness of Clinton's offenses and, on further consideration, has decided that the case presented by the House managers (and conservative Republicans more generally) was more compelling than originally realized. This perspective suggests that if the House managers had been allowed to mount a full-scale prosecution during the Senate trial—with the ability to call a substantial number of witnesses—the public might have been convinced earlier, and removing Clinton from office might have become a serious possibility. Unfortunately, this explanation is not consistent with related public opinion data. For example, opinion poll results indicate that the proportion of the population that considers the congressional handling of Clinton's impeachment unfair has risen since the end of the impeachment proceedings (Gallup Poll, December 9–12, 1999). Similarly, fewer Americans think Clinton should be charged with a crime after leaving office, and nearly two-thirds of the public still considers the Clinton impeachment process either very harmful or somewhat harmful to the country (Gallup Poll, December 9–12, 1999). Overall the data do not support the contention that a sea change in public opinion has occurred on the Clinton impeachment.

A more reasonable explanation for the change in public opinion on the specific question of impeachment is that the public came to view impeachment—after the threat of removal had ended—as comparable to what it wanted all along: censure. Once it became clear that Clinton would not be forced out of office, impeachment could be interpreted as a form of extreme censure, and this is an interpretation that has been promulgated by at least a few public officials involved in the impeachment process. During the process, however, the public was correct to view impeachment as a far more serious threat to the president than censure. It is clear, regardless of the post-impeachment window dressing, that the president's opponents, particularly the House managers, aggressively sought the removal of the president during the Senate trial.[2] It is disingenuous to suggest, as some have, that impeachment was always a form of super-censure and that the president's administration was never seriously threatened. That was not the case during the impeachment proceedings, and the public was right to realize that it was not.

4

REPRESENTATION AND IMPEACHMENT

Sometimes legislators must make decisions that involve significant political trade-offs. Often they choose to seek the support (or avoid the disapproval) of one constituency while at the same time they are incurring the wrath of a second constituency. Although legislators must make political trade-offs on a regular basis, few situations have the high profile of the Clinton impeachment. The overwhelming national opposition to impeachment makes it very unlikely that the opponents of impeachment were concentrated solely in Democratic districts. In the case of the Clinton impeachment, it is more than likely that a large number of Republican legislators voted against the preferences of their geographic constituencies. In some cases, as we will find out, constituency preferences were clear and overwhelmingly opposed to impeachment in districts served by legislators who supported one or more of the articles of impeachment. By supporting impeachment, these Republicans risked alienating a majority of their constituents. In this chapter, I examine the factors that influenced representatives' votes on the four articles of impeachment brought against Clinton, focusing specifically on the impact of constituency opposition to impeachment, legislator ideology, and partisanship.

Background and Theory of Roll Call Voting

Disparity between public opinion and legislators' behavior—
whether for reasons of partisanship or personal ethics—is rare on issues of the magnitude of impeachment. Scholarship on legislative
behavior, particularly roll call voting, indicates that the engine of
legislative politics on prominent and contentious issues for which
the public has clear and identifiable opinions is constituency preferences. In one of the most theoretically significant and empirically
compelling examinations of roll call voting, John Kingdon concludes:

> ... [C]onstituency opinions have quite a marked effect on voting
> decisions. ... Legislators take account of constituency reaction
> long before and much more frequently than they worry explicitly
> about gain or loss of votes in the next election. ... [Simply put]
> the congressman considers constituency interest first (1989:
> 246–48).

R. Douglas Arnold makes a similar assertion: "Legislators ... have
strong incentives to consider citizens' potential preferences when
they are deciding how to vote" (1990: 272).[1] Although establishing
a clear and direct link between constituency preferences and legislative voting patterns is not easy, the general sense in the literature is
that a significant link exists (see Erikson 1978; Hill and Hurley
1999; Kuklinski and Elling 1977; Miller and Stokes 1963; Wood
and Anderson 1998).

The reasons for the congruence between legislative behavior and
constituency preferences are obvious. First, legislators depend on
the support of their constituents to remain in office. Failure to maintain sufficient constituency support increases the likelihood that an
incumbent will face an experienced and well-financed challenger,
[and experienced and well-financed challengers are far more likely
to unseat incumbents than challengers who are both inexperienced
and poorly funded (see Herrnson 2000)]. If David Mayhew's (1974)
contention that the primary objective of a member of Congress is to

win re-election is true, then paying attention to constituents' policy preferences makes good political sense.

We should also expect to see a correlation between constituency preferences and representative behavior because representatives and constituents often share a common background and social context. Representatives are required by law to serve constituencies in which they live. In most cases, representatives have spent years living in their districts, and in many cases they have spent a lifetime in their districts. The social and demographic forces that molded their constituents' ideological and policy preferences are the same social and demographic forces that have molded their own. We would normally expect two products of identical social forces—representative preferences and constituency preferences—to be quite similar and should not be surprised when that is actually the case.

We know that representatives have some latitude in their choices about how they will behave in Congress and how they will present themselves to their districts (see Fenno 1978). Although some will base their electoral appeal on their issue positions, others will soft pedal the issues and focus more on a personal appeal to their constituency. Ironically, we should expect to see issue position congruence between representatives and their constituents in both cases. In the first, it makes little sense to base one's electoral fortunes on issue positions that are unpopular in one's constituency. If staking a claim to certain issues and issue positions is the bread and butter of a representative's electoral appeal, he or she will make certain that his or her positions are shared by a majority of the constituency.

For the representative who depends on personal relationships to build a successful political career, taking particular stances on particular issues would appear to be less important. But we know (see Fenno 1978) that representatives who build their political careers on personal relationships tend to be from homogeneous districts and that most have spent their entire lives (or nearly so) in the district that they serve. Given the homogeneity of their districts and their intimate and long-standing connection to the political and social milieus of their districts, representatives who focus on personal relationships are likely to share their constituents' policy preferences because their own preferences were molded by exactly the same social and political forces that molded the preferences of their constituents (Fenno 1978, 2000). So, regardless of the specific character of a representative's relationship to his or her district, there is good reason to believe that a high level of congruence exists between legislators' and constituents' policy preferences.

When representatives behave in a manner inconsistent with constituency preferences, it is important that they provide a compelling rationale for the inconsistencies. Because legislators are usually so sensitive to constituency pressures, it is no surprise that much of the immediate post-impeachment activity focused on what Fenno refers to as "explanation" (1978: 149). One way to minimize the electoral fallout from unpopular position-taking on the Clinton impeachment was to characterize the consideration of the articles of impeachment as "questions of conscience," issues beyond the traditional constraints of constituency pressures.

As I noted in Chapter 1, members on both sides of the aisle characterized their own actions—and those of fellow partisans—in terms of ethics and character. Legislators, Republicans and Democrats alike, never tired of referring to the rule of law and the sanctity of the Constitution. The president's opponents, ostensibly repulsed by what they considered arrogant and deceitful behavior on Clinton's part, claimed to be voting their consciences. They portrayed impeachment as the only reasonable response to his behavior. Opponents of impeachment also claimed the moral high ground. Arguing that Clinton's actions did not rise to the level of "high crimes and misdemeanors," they portrayed their opposition to the president's impeachment as an effort to protect the Constitution. Although media treatment of the impeachment process did focus to some extent on questions of conscience, partisan characterizations of the political conflict over impeachment became increasingly prominent as the process continued.

When conflicts between partisan allegiances and constituency pressures occur, constituents' opinions usually trump fellow partisans' preferences, for the simple reason that members' careers are in the hands of the voters. Walter Oleszek puts it clearly and succinctly: "[I]t is still the constituents, not the president or the party or the congressional leadership, who grant and can take away a member's job" (1996: 43). Occasionally, the efforts of party leaders may overcome legislators' ties to their constituencies. More often than not, however, leaders actually urge members to pay attention to and abide by their constituents' preferences. According to Mayhew, "Leaders in both houses have a habit of counseling members to 'vote their constituencies'" (1974: 101).

Generally, when national party leaders' objectives are inconsistent with local constituents' interests, party leaders lose. This characterization of the relative power of party leaders and constituents is not without its critics. Some prominent work argues that political parties are far more important (and powerful) than the bulk of research admits (see, in particular, Cox and McCubbins 1993). And modern party leaders still retain certain traditional prerogatives that may be useful in gaining legislators' acquiescence to leadership objectives (such as the distribution of committee assignments, considerable influence over the choice of committee chairs, and, for the majority party in the House, the rule-granting power). Likewise, the increasing importance of party financing in congressional campaigns and the growth of member PACs (particularly leadership PACs) has tended to enhance the position of the party leadership in the members' decision-making calculus (Jacobson 1997; Herrnson 1998). Nevertheless, the claim that partisan politics dominated the impeachment process is wildly inconsistent with the overwhelming preponderance of research on the modern Congress. If party, rather than constituency, interests drove the impeachment proceedings and the floor votes of members in the House and the Senate, then exceptional times produced exceptional politics.[2]

Obviously, constituency preferences do not dominate members' behavior on all issues. All issues are not created equal. In some policy areas and on particular issues, constituents' opinions are very important, although the specific policy areas and issues vary by district. On many other issues, constituency preferences do not play an especially important role in determining representative behavior. Efforts to achieve personal or partisan policy objectives—when they are inconsistent with the preferences of constituents—are most often made on issues that are either relatively unimportant to a member's constituency or so complex that the connection between specific legislative activities and policy outcomes is difficult to make (Arnold 1990). But impeachment was not a trivial issue, and it was not a complex issue, at least not from the perspective of the voters. There is no evidence that voters struggled over their assessment of impeachment because the issue itself was too complicated. Just as the roll call votes on the articles of impeachment were not trivial or insignificant, the issue of impeachment was not perceived as especially complex.[3] Very few people, as the opinion polls indicate, were undecided about impeachment, and the result of a Clinton conviction on any of the articles of impeachment could hardly have been clearer, even to the perennially uninformed: The president is removed from office. The character of the impeachment issue suggests that constituents' preferences should matter.

Although constituency preferences should matter, it is not clear that they did. We know from Chapter 3 that a large majority of the U.S. public supported the president. Poll figures consistently showed that 60 to 65 percent of the public opposed impeachment and the subsequent conviction of the president on impeachment charges. Obviously, many legislators, nearly all Republicans, disregarded public preferences when they cast their votes on the articles of impeachment (at least the two that passed the House). Exactly why these representatives ignored public opinion is still unclear.

One reason may be that legislators who cast impeachment votes that were unpopular with their constituents believed—and maybe rightly so—that the impeachment proceedings would not be a significant issue in the 2000 elections. Given voters' political myopia, this may have been a reasonable belief. In modern U.S. politics, it is relatively easy to see why members of Congress might worry little about the electoral fallout from a handful of votes taken nearly two years prior to the current election, and the timing of the impeachment votes—just after the 1998 election—was perfect for those representatives who were hoping that their constituents would forget about the impeachment and their own role in the impeachment proceedings. But there is evidence that the impeachment issue influenced voters' opinions in 1998 (see Jacobson 1999), and that was before the House impeached the president. Likewise, there is some limited evidence that members considered constituency preferences when they cast their impeachment votes (Emmert and Lanoue 1999). So it seems unlikely that House members completely discounted the electoral impact of their impeachment votes in 2000.

Assuming that legislators did not trivialize the political significance of the impeachment proceedings and their own votes, how might we explain what appears to be strategically questionable behavior? Suppose incumbents seek to maintain a desirable relationship with their constituents, what might be referred to as a positive "equilibrium" (see Fenno 2000 for an analogous use of the term *equilibrium*). Significant events and behaviors may disrupt this equilibrium, and to return to the desired equilibrium a countervailing event must occur or a countervailing behavior must be initiated. Unfortunately, at least for the members, they may have objectives that are at cross purposes or that are inconsistent. This was almost certainly true for a significant number of House Republicans on the impeachment issue.

It is unlikely, given what we know of legislative behavior, that House members would willingly incite the disapproval of a sizable majority of their constituents unless they were attempting to avoid an even more significant electoral disaster in the near future and they expected to effectively compensate for disturbing this profitable electoral relationship with their constituents. In the impeachment context, it is not difficult to see how a large number of Republicans would both wish to avoid angering the party leadership and implement plans to compensate for the potential fallout associated with the unpopular impeachment votes.

Even on "questions of conscience," there are political rationales for ignoring one's constituents. Representatives might reasonably have viewed a vote against their party (but for their constituents, as many Republicans were cross-pressured) as a future obstacle to advancement within the party (to coveted committee slots, leadership positions, and/or higher office). It would hardly be expedient for legislators to say as much—one could not admit to stiffing one's constituents in the hopes of future party perquisites and privileges—but given the political dynamics of career development within the party and the significance of career development goals for many legislators, supporting the party in its primary political objectives makes at least some sense. It is easy to see how a contrary vote on such a significant issue on which the two parties' leaders were clearly split might prove detrimental to career advancement within the institution and the party. Whether future advancement would be adversely affected by a contrary vote, however, is difficult to determine.

As the political parties become increasingly important sources of campaign funds (not to mention soft money expenditures), particularly among Republicans, they are purported to have a greater role in influencing legislators' behavior than in the past. It is conceivable—although very unlikely, as I will explain below—that members feared some type of organizational retribution, such as national party funding of a primary challenger and/or denial of a desired committee assignment, if they failed to adhere to the party line on the impeachment issue. A legislator, fearing this type of punishment, might reasonably cross his or her constituency to avoid a primary fight if he or she might have an opportunity, in the near future, to compensate the large, aggrieved local constituency.

A legislator's hope for future career advancement should not be confused with a fear of political retribution for casting a vote against the party leadership. Whatever the legislators' reasoning, anti-constituent votes were not a function of a credible threat of partisan retribution. Although op-ed pages were filled with critiques of imagined threats by the Republican and Democratic leadership to punish recalcitrant members by funding primary challengers, individuals actually involved in the process, the legislators, consistently denied that they were pressured by party leaders to support the party's position on impeachment. By itself, this would not be reason enough to dismiss at least the possibility of some form of arm-twisting on the part of party leaders, but there are other reasons to think that party leaders had few incentives to push members of their party to vote against their constituents. Although many find the absence of excessive lobbying efforts a surprise, it should not be. The political circumstances of the time—particularly the partisan balance in the House—diminished the credibility of leadership threats and the impact of bully tactics.

At a time when the seats in the House were (and are) so evenly divided between the parties, a full-scale attack on even a small number of incumbents in one's own party is a dangerous strategy. First, serious short-term punishment would necessarily involve a well-funded, politically experienced primary challenger. To produce this well-funded challenger, the party—and individuals and PACs that traditionally support that party's candidates—would have to funnel resources that would otherwise have gone to one or more other partisans to the challenger. Under fire, the incumbent would likely respond by increasing his or her own efforts to raise campaign funds—again, funds that would have gone to fellow partisans. The primary election thus becomes very expensive for some set of partisans (due to lost contributions) who are not even directly involved in the election. If keeping (or winning) control of the House is important to party leaders (as it certainly is), this punishment strategy is very costly.

If the challenger is fortunate enough (or wealthy enough) to defeat the incumbent in the primary election, even more money must be raised to have a realistic chance of winning the general election. Open seat House races consistently boast the most expensive campaigns (see Herrnson 2000), and 2000 was no exception. The average House incumbent raised $875,910 during the 1999–2000 election cycle; candidates for open seats raised, on average, $1,147,744. So the difference between the average expenditure of incumbents and candidates for open seats is more than $270,000. In an electoral environment in which every dollar counts (as it did in 2000), punishing partisans for contrary votes on impeachment would have been an extremely costly strategy, from both a financial and a political perspective. Party leaders seriously concerned about retaining (or winning) the House would have found any significant punishment strategy for recalcitrant members seriously counterproductive. Members, knowing this, would never have considered punishment threats credible, and so leaders would not have embarrassed themselves by making them. Members interested in developing careers within the party had good reason to be concerned about how their votes on the impeachment articles would be perceived by party leaders. They did not, however, have reason to fear that leadership reactions to their votes would cost them their seats in the House.

The fact that the election following Clinton's impeachment was the first one of the twenty-first century and that it occurred during a year in which a decennial census was taken may also provide a partial explanation for some members' willingness to ignore their constituents' preferences. In a number of the states in which the Republican party is becoming increasingly prominent—Sunbelt states, particularly the South—and in which Republicans are gaining control of an increasingly large number of state legislatures, Republican incumbents may well have been looking toward their future constituencies (in most cases, more conservative because of favorable redistricting plans) when they cast their votes on impeachment. If these future-thinking incumbents could weather one potentially problematic election (2000) during which their support for impeachment would be a disadvantage, they might reap greater electoral and political rewards with their new constituency (in 2002).

Some members might also have been driven by a desire to build a political career beyond their own districts. Senate seats are always a potential objective for upwardly oriented representatives. It is certainly possible that a handful of representatives looking for a stepping stone to higher office used the impeachment issue to boost their chances of advancement. In some cases, this may have involved behaving in a manner that was relatively unpopular with one's current constituency (the district) and relatively more popular with one's hoped-for future constituency (the state).

Ideological disposition also may have influenced representatives' voting patterns on the articles of impeachment. In Chapter 3, we found that conservatives in the general public were significantly more likely to have negative feelings toward the president, and to support Clinton's impeachment and his removal from office than were liberals. The same may be true for representatives. It is certainly true that the debate over whether to impeach the president and the details of the articles of impeachment had strong ideological overtones, both in the House Judiciary Committee and on the House floor (see Chapter 2). Legislator conservatism may be positively associated with support for the articles of impeachment, and this increased support may not be fully captured by other factors that are related to ideology (such as partisanship).

Note that there is an important distinction between casting votes based on one's own ideological predilections and casting votes based on one's unbiased evaluation of the evidence of a case and interpretation of the law deemed relevant to the case. This distinction is a fundamental component of the literature on judicial decision making, and it is relevant here. There are two main perspectives toward judicial decision making. One school of thought posits that judges and justices base their rulings on the evidentiary specifics of a case and the particulars of the law related to that case. This school of thought is known as the "legal" model. A second school of thought posits that judges and justices base their rulings on their own ideological leanings and policy preferences. This is known as the "attitudinal" model.[4] These two models are not necessarily mutually exclusive, as some of the most recent research suggests, but neither are they indistinguishable. If, as a number of representatives claimed, they were guided by their own individual evaluations of the evidence against the president and their own idiosyncratic interpretations of the relevant law (in this case the Constitution), then we should *not* find an ideological dimension to roll call voting on the articles of impeachment.

In this chapter, I examine the voting behavior of legislators on the articles of impeachment against President Clinton. I begin by estimating district-level opinion and demonstrating that a majority of legislators—nearly all Democrats and a significant number of Republicans—actually voted their constituents' preferences. I then go on to show that even if one controls for seat safety, seniority, and ideology, district preferences still matter.

Estimating District-Level Opinion

During the impeachment process in the House of Representatives (and continuing on through the final consideration of the impeachment articles in the Senate), hundreds of national opinion polls estimated the level of public support for the president and for his impeachment. These opinion polls consistently showed that an overwhelming majority of the U.S. public (usually between 60 and 65 percent) opposed the impeachment and removal of President Clinton. We obviously have a very clear picture of national-level public opinion on the impeachment.

Unfortunately, comparable data for each individual congressional district do not exist. National surveys are rarely conducted with samples larger than 2,000 respondents; in fact, in many cases, national opinion surveys have significantly fewer respondents (1,000–1,200 respondents is not uncommon). Although 1,000–1,500-respondent samples are nearly ideal (from a cost/benefit standpoint) for estimating national opinion, samples of this size are far too small for generating direct estimates of district-level public opinion. In all likelihood, many of the 435 congressional districts are not represented in a 2,000-person national sample. Even if a national sample included, by chance (and this is very unlikely given the fact that many national survey samples fail to include individuals from each state), individuals from each congressional district, the district-level samples would be far too small for reliable inference.[5]

One way to avoid this problem would be to conduct district-level opinion surveys for each congressional district. Even if we were willing to limit ourselves to 50 respondents per district (and this figure is too low for reliable inference), we would still need a total sample of nearly 22,000 respondents. Obviously, the costs associated with this type of survey are prohibitive. In any case, we would need the opinion estimates from the time period of the consideration of the Clinton impeachment in Congress. Since that time is clearly past, we cannot conduct a survey like the one indicated above even if we had—and were willing to spend—the money to do it. So we must look for an alternative to opinion surveys of all the congressional districts, and we must be able to implement this alternative with the existing data.

One viable alternative to 435 district-level surveys is simulation of district-level opinion from national surveys (Erikson 1978). To implement the simulation procedure, one first identifies the individual-level demographic factors that influence opinion on the relevant issue. Then, using this information in conjunction with data on district-level constituency characteristics, one can generate an indicator of aggregate district opinion on the issue or topic of concern.[6] For example, if differences in personal income influence individual opinions about welfare—aversion to welfare programs increasing directly with wealth—then one could use this information, and information about aggregate income levels in the congressional districts, to estimate district-level support for welfare programs.

To estimate individual-level opinion on the Clinton impeachment, I use data gathered for the ABC News/*Washington Post* Impeachment Hearings Poll fielded on December 12–13, 1998, just before the full House vote on the articles of impeachment. The usable sample for this telephone poll is 1,004 and includes one or more respondents from each of the 48 contiguous states. The question used to tap individual opinion on impeachment was the following:

> The full House will vote on impeachment next week, and if the House impeaches Clinton the Senate will decide whether he should be removed from office. Based on what you know, do you think Congress should or should not impeach Clinton and remove him from office?

I coded responses in the following manner to create the scale for the dependent variable for this segment of the analysis:

- Should be impeached, Strongly (3)
- Should be impeached, Somewhat (2)
- Should not be impeached, Somewhat (1)
- Should not be impeached, Strongly (0) [7]

Modeling Roll Call Voting on Impeachment

Using demographic and preferential variables available in the survey, it is possible to estimate an individual-level model of choice. Ordinary least squares (OLS) regression is often used in these circumstances, although it is not the appropriate methodology for dealing with ordinal dependent variables. Because the coding of the dependent variable in this specific case is clearly at the ordinal level, I estimated a maximum likelihood ordered logit model. I then used coefficients from the individual-level model to estimate aggregate district-level opinions on the question of Clinton's impeachment.[8]

The district-level estimates of public support for the Clinton impeachment are striking. Although approximately 40 percent of the U.S. public supported Clinton's impeachment—a proportion reflected in the sample data—impeachment supporters were a majority in fewer than 15 percent of all congressional districts with incumbents running for re-election in 2000. (See Table 4.1.)

Note that all but one of the individuals serving a district in which a majority of voters supported Clinton's impeachment were Republicans, and all of these individuals—including Ralph Hall (D.–Tex.)—voted for at least one of the articles of impeachment. As one would expect, most of these representatives serve mountain states or Southern states, with a few Midwesterners sprinkled in. There is not a single member from a Northeastern state in this group. Significantly, if one extends the constituency preference boundary to 53 percent—obviously quite close to 50 percent and probably too close to make a substantial difference at election time—nearly all of the Republican House leaders—Armey (R.–Tex.), Delay (R.–Tex.), and Hastert (R.–Ill.)—and over half of the impeachment managers still in the House—Cannon (R.–Utah), Sensenbrenner (R.–Wis.), Buyer (R.–Ind.), Gekas (R.–Pa.), and Hyde (R.–Ill.)—are included.

On the other side of this issue, Democrats served all the districts in which at least 75 percent of the voting population opposed Clinton's impeachment. (See Table 4.2.) Regionally, this is a very different group from the members listed in Table 4.1. Many are from the Northeast, or large urban areas, or majority-minority districts in the

TABLE 4.1   Members Serving Districts Where Impeachment Was Most Popular

Year	District	Name	Percent Opposed to Impeachment	Party
TX	19	COMBEST	41.34	REP
IN	6	BURTON	42.15	REP
KS	1	MORAN	42.29	REP
TX	8	BRADY	42.57	REP
UT	1	HANSEN	42.77	REP
UT	3	CANNON	42.9	REP
TX	21	SMITH	43.75	REP
TX	26	ARMEY	44.56	REP
AL	6	BACHUS	44.89	REP
OK	5	ISTOOK	45.97	REP
NC	10	BALLENGER	46	REP
TX	3	JOHNSON	46.24	REP
TX	6	BARTON	46.52	REP
OH	2	PORTMAN	46.67	REP
AK	1	YOUNG	46.9	REP
CO	5	HEFLEY	47.09	REP
CA	21	THOMAS	47.49	REP
PA	9	SHUSTER	47.67	REP
NC	6	COBLE	47.77	REP
GA	9	DEAL	47.84	REP
CA	2	HERGER	47.92	REP
CA	47	COX	48.1	REP
WY	1	CUBIN	48.16	REP
WI	9	SENSENBRENNER	48.3	REP
MO	7	BLUNT	48.34	REP
FL	1	SCARBOROUGH	48.35	REP
IN	5	BUYER	48.6	REP
KS	3	TIAHRT	48.78	REP
OH	8	BOEHNER	48.81	REP
TN	1	JENKINS	48.91	REP
CA	45	ROHRABACHER	49.08	REP
NE	1	BEREUTER	49.18	REP
CA	4	DOOLITTLE	49.22	REP
IN	4	SOUDER	49.51	REP
TX	4	HALL	49.57	DEM
CA	51	CUNNINGHAM	49.72	REP
OH	4	OXLEY	49.96	REP

74

TABLE 4.2   Members Serving Districts Where Impeachment Was Most Unpopular

Year	District	Name	Percent Opposed to Impeachment	Party
CA	8	PELOSI	75.72	DEM
WI	5	BARRETT	76.25	DEM
CA	33	ROYBAL	76.6	DEM
NY	8	NADLER	76.76	DEM
GA	4	MCKINNEY	76.86	DEM
IL	4	GUTIERRES	77.06	DEM
FL	3	BROWN	44.76	DEM
CA	9	LEE	81.02	DEM
NY	12	VELAZQUEZ	81.02	DEM
NC	1	CLAYTON	81068	DEM
MS	2	THOMPSON	82.11	DEM
TX	30	JOHNSON	82.56	DEM
SC	6	CLYBURN	83.66	DEM
NC	12	WATT	83.97	DEM
CA	37	MILLENDER	83.99	DEM
TX	18	JACKSON-LEE	83.99	DEM
FL	23	HASTINGS	84.71	DEM
MO	1	CLAY	84.78	DEM
TN	9	FORD	85.08	DEM
CA	32	DIXON	85.18	DEM
VA	3	SCOTT	86.2	DEM
GA	5	LEWIS	86.37	DEM
CA	35	WATERS	86.46	DEM
NY	17	ENGEL	86.78	DEM
AL	7	HILLIARD	87.19	DEM
LA	2	JEFFERSON	87.61	DEM
PA	1	BRADY	87.69	DEM
MD	4	WYNN	87.82	DEM
NJ	10	PAYNE	88.6	DEM
FL	17	MEEK	88.74	DEM
NY	15	RANGEL	88.82	DEM
NY	6	MEEKS	88.9	DEM
NY	16	SERRANO	89.28	DEM
IL	7	DAVIS	89.53	DEM
MD	7	CUMMINGS	89.81	DEM
PA	2	FATTAH	89.98	DEM
IL	2	JACKSON	90.56	DEM
IL	1	RUSH	90.78	DEM
NY	10	TOWNS	90.84	DEM
MI	14	CONYERS	90.85	DEM
MI	15	KILPATRICK	90.85	DEM
NY	11	OWENS	92.38	DEM

South. Not one of these representatives voted for any of the articles of impeachment.

If we look at the roll call votes on the impeachment articles, we can see that every Democrat or Republican serving a constituency that supported impeachment voted for at least one article of impeachment, and a majority of members serving districts in which impeachment was opposed voted against all four articles of impeachment. Simply put, most legislators voted their districts. Now, it is obvious that Democrats were much more likely to vote in accordance with their constituents' preferences than Republicans. Only five Democrats voted against the preferences of the majority of their constituents, and each of these individuals supported one or more of the articles of impeachment. Conversely, a majority of Republicans voted against the preferences of a majority of their constituents. Only 56 House Republicans voted with their constituents, and 27 House Republicans voted against large majorities (>60 percent opposed to Clinton's impeachment) in their districts.

Even though many members' votes were not consistent with their constituents' preferences, one cannot avoid the fact that for well over half of the incumbents running for re-election in 2000, their votes on impeachment were the votes their constituents would most likely have cast. In the case of the impeachment votes in the House of Representatives, most legislators voted their electoral constituencies. For the majority of House incumbents in 2000, their public decisions about the Clinton impeachment were not electoral liabilities. Their votes were consistent with the preferences of a majority of their voting constituents. And yet, a sizable number of representatives clearly voted against the wishes of their constituents. Why?

First, legislators might have viewed their votes as an actual judgment on the facts of the case and the extent to which Clinton's behavior met the standard for impeachability. Legislators' public explanations of their own votes nearly all flowed from this vein. Both the journalistic and the more sensational "tell-all" treatments of the impeachment proceedings written by participants (see Baker 2000; Schippers and Henry 2000; Toobin 1999) attribute many House members' votes to ethical and legal evaluations. In fairness, the pro-impeachment books tend to view only impeachment supporters in these terms, as anti-impeachment books tend to view only impeachment opponents this way, but there are at least a few admissions of reasoned, ethical opposition (see Schippers and Henry's characterization of Representative Shays, R.–Conn.). Of course, it is nearly impossible to adequately evaluate this proposition in a more objective manner, mainly because we have no independent indicator of legislators' independent evaluations of the case against Clinton.

A number of alternative explanations for voting against one's constituency were examined by Emmert and Lanoue (1999) in the very first rigorous treatment of House roll call votes on the Clinton impeachment. They found ideology to be the primary determinant of vote choice for both Democrats and Republicans. Although Emmert and Lanoue's analysis is thought-provoking, it has several nontrivial shortcomings, at least for my purposes. First, although they incorporate a "Lame Duck" variable in an effort to control for members who were not returning to the House in 1999 (and thus were free of constituency pressures), their analysis almost certainly includes a large number of legislators who planned to retire at the end of the 106th Congress (and some of these had indicated as much before the impeachment votes). It is very unlikely that the structural determinants of these retirees are identical to those who intended to continue in office. To examine the possibility that Emmert and Lanoue understate constituency impact on the impeachment votes, I examine the impact of constituency pressure on members who actually decided to seek re-election in 2000.

Second, although Clinton's vote share is a reasonable surrogate for constituency preferences on the impeachment issues, it almost certainly underestimates the opposition to impeachment in districts with large African American populations (and overstates the opposition to impeachment in districts with relatively small African American populations). I use the indicator introduced previously (IMPOPP) to tap district-level opposition to impeachment.[9] The other explanatory variables included in my models are the same as those used by Emmert and Lanoue (1999): VOTE 98 (member's vote share in 1998 election), SENIOR (seniority), and ADA98 (ADA vote score in 1998).

Finally, Emmert and Lanoue's examination of each of the individual impeachment articles in separate models for the Republicans fails to adequately capture the integrated character of the roll call votes.[10] Technically, each vote was cast independently, and so Emmert and Lanoue have analyzed the Republican votes independently. But the members knew that voters would view these votes collectively. Voters might care about the difference between one "yea" vote and four "yea" votes, but it is very unlikely—and there is no evidence—that the voters actually made independent evaluations of the votes on the individual articles. To avoid this problem, I estimate an explanatory model that uses the sum of "yea" votes for each individual member as the dependent variable (or TOTAL).[11]

From a quick glance at Tables 4.3 and 4.4 it is easy to see that for Republicans, both ideology and district-level constituency opinion significantly affected the probability of casting one or more affirmative votes on the impeachment articles. (Table 4.3 includes state-level opinion on impeachment. Table 4.4 does not.) Seniority, vote margin, and state-level constituency opinion appear to have had no impact on the probability of casting affirmative votes on the impeachment articles. Because ideology is at least partly influenced, over time, by a legislator's perception of constituency opinion, the case made previously for a significant relationship between constituency opinion and vote choice on the impeachment articles—at least for Republicans—is doubly strengthened by these results. Whereas Emmert and Lanoue failed to find any evidence of a constituency effect among Republicans for three of the four articles of impeachment, a model specifically designed to capture the collective nature of the impeachment votes demonstrates that constituency effects mattered in a more general sense than previously realized.

For Democrats, only ideology appears to have had an impact on roll call votes on the articles of impeachment. (See Table 4.5.) These results mirror those of Emmert and Lanoue.[12] Because so few Democrats deserted the party on impeachment, identifying other factors of influence is quite difficult. The extreme skew of the dependent variable (many more votes against impeachment than votes for it)and the high correlation between ideology and constituency op-

TABLE 4.3   Explaining Republican Votes on the Articles of Impeachment

	Total	Frequency		
	4	110		
	3	42		
	2	18		
	1	3		
	0	6		

Parameter	Estimate	Standard Error	Chi-Square	Pr>ChiSq
Intercept	3.6598	2.312	2.5059	0.1134
Intercept 2	5.4559	2.3395	5.4384	0.0197
Intercept 3	7.3494	2.3898	9.4571	0.0021
Intercept 4	8.0678	2.4233	11.093	0.0009
ADA98	-0.0993	0.0155	41.1897	<.0001
IMPOPP	-0.0796	0.0363	4.8093	0.0283
VOTE98	-0.0162	0.012	1.8323	0.1759
SENIOR	0.0403	0.0275	2.1538	0.1422
SIMPOPP	0.0477	0.0388	1.516	0.2182

Percentage predicted correctly = 77.7
Proportionate reduction in error = 40.5 percent
Pseudo R^2 = 0.348
AIC = 318.225, SC = 346.912, -2 Log L = 300.225

position to impeachment lead me to question the robustness of the Democratic party results. Since we know that nearly every Democrat voted in a manner consistent with his or her constituents' preferences, these results alone should not lead us to ignore the substantive significance of constituency preferences for Democratic roll call voting on the articles of impeachment.

The above analysis assumes, as is commonplace in discussions of the Clinton impeachment, that party played a dominant role in determining roll call votes, even when controlling for constituency opinion, ideology, seniority, and seat marginality. If this were not true, then analyzing the roll call votes of Democrats and Republicans separately, as Emmert and Lanoue (1999) direct, would make little sense. Although partisan differences certainly appear important—at least at first glance—analytically evaluating partisan distinctiveness is worthwhile.

TABLE 4.4 Explaining Republican Votes on the Articles of Impeachment, Part II

	Total	Frequency
	4	110
	3	42
	2	18
	1	3
	0	6

Parameter	Estimate	Standard Error	Chi-Square	Pr>ChiSq
Intercept	4.9939	2.0605	5.8741	0.0154
Intercept 2	6.7852	2.0947	10.4922	0.0012
Intercept 3	8.6712	2.1536	1.6212	<.0001
Intercept 4	9.3819	2.1897	18.3576	<.0001
ADA98	-0.0946	0.0148	40.8831	<.0001
IMPOPP	-0.0585	0.0321	3.3175	0.0685
VOTE98	-0.0112	0.0112	1.0037	0.3164
SENIOR	0.0394	0.0274	2.0713	0.1501

Percentage predicted correctly = 77.7
Proportionate reduction in error = 40.5 percent
Pseudo R^2 = 0.348
AIC = 317.739, SC = 343.239, -2 Log L = 301.739

In fact, if we include Democrats and Republicans in the same model (see Table 4.6) and separate the effects of the relevant substantive variables with a party dummy variable (PARTY)[13] and appropriate interactive terms, we find that the PARTY coefficient is far from any conventional level of statistical significance. Admittedly, high multicollinearity—common in models with interactive terms—makes these results suspect, and I am unwilling to conclude that party failed to affect vote choice on the impeachment articles. Nevertheless, the significance of the constituency variable for Republicans (at the .10 level), even in the face of extreme multicollinearity, is further evidence that the impact of constituency opinion on roll call votes on the articles of impeachment has been incorrectly ignored or trivialized. Clearly, constituency opinion—at least for Republicans—mattered quite a lot.

But if constituency opinion mattered, we must still account for the large number of Republican legislators who thwarted their con-

TABLE 4.5   Explaining Democratic Votes on the Articles of Impeachment

Total	Frequency
3	3
2	3
0	173

Parameter	Estimate	Standard Error	Chi-Square	Pr>ChiSq
Intercept	29.6969	25.7991	1.325	0.2497
Intercept 2	35.2059	27.7221	1.6128	0.2041
ADA98	-0.2135	0.1052	4.1171	0.0425
IMPOPP	-0.4056	0.4	1.028	0.3106
VOTE98	-0.00003	0.00611	0	0.9956
SENIOR	-0.2662	0.2869	0.8611	0.3534

Percentage predicted correctly = 99.9
Proportionate reduction in error = 95.5 percent
Pseudo R^2 = 0.253
AIC = 20.757, SC = 39.88, -2 Log L = 8.757

stituencies by supporting one or more of the articles of impeachment. Clearly ideology played some role, and it is possible that partisan advancement (although it is not possible to analyze this contention explicitly) influenced some legislators.

The impeachment of a president is one of the most solemn and serious tasks the House of Representatives undertakes. It is the type of constitutional responsibility that draws a unique level of public attention, and it is something that, in the case of Clinton, clearly divided the U.S. public. Few voters were ambivalent about the Clinton impeachment. Realizing that constituency opinion did matter—it was not a completely trivial political force—it is still surprising that it did not matter more, particularly to Republicans. Among Republicans, in fact, nearly three dozen members voted against the clear preferences of overwhelming majorities of their constituencies (>60%) when they supported one or more of the articles of impeachment. If any set of votes should have cost these representatives their seats, it should have been the votes on impeachment. And yet very few of these incumbents actually lost their seats in 2000. The question is, why? One possible answer is that these endangered in-

TABLE 4.6 Explaining Democratic and Republican Votes on the Articles of Impeachment

	Total		Frequency	
	4		113	
	3		45	
	2		18	
	1		3	
	0		179	

Parameter	Estimate	Standard Error	Chi-Square	Pr>ChiSq
Intercept	4.5424	1.6975	7.1603	0.0075
Intercept 2	6.3879	1.7374	13.5183	0.0002
Intercept 3	8.1383	1.7974	20.5017	<.0001
Intercept 4	8.7323	1.8247	22.902	<.0001
ADA98*PARTY	-0.0878	0.014	39.5118	<.0001
ADA98	-0.1085	0.0586	3.4299	0.064
IMPOPP	-0.059	0.0312	3.593	0.0585
IMPOPP*PARTY	-0.1049	0.1563	0.4502	0.5023
PARTY	9.2031	8.8174	1.0894	0.2966

Percentage predicted correctly = 94.4
Proportionate reduction in error = 88.8 percent
Pseudo R^2 = 0.761
AIC = 337.993, SC = 372.918, -2 Log L = 319.993

cumbents raised a great deal of money for their campaigns to prevent losing. I examine that hypothesis in Chapter 6.

But before I look at how Republican incumbents who cast unpopular impeachment votes attempted to re-establish the positive "equilibrium" between themselves and their constituents, the pre-impeachment "equilibrium," I turn first to the Senate roll call votes on the articles of impeachment that passed the House. Ideology and, to a lesser extent, constituency preferences, carried the day in the House. Was the same true for the Senate?

5

REPRESENTATION AND CONVICTION

D etermining the president's guilt or innocence on the two successful articles of impeachment was no easier for the Senate
than it was for the House to consider and pass the articles in the
first place. The majority party, the Republicans, faced the daunting
task of public hearings on the articles and of dealing with an issue
that was both overwhelmingly supported by their fellow partisans
in the House and wildly unpopular with the U.S. public.

It is important to remember that the object of the Senate trial was
to evaluate the evidence to remove the president of the United
States. Once the two articles of impeachment had passed by a majority vote in the House of Representatives, a serious trial in the
Senate could not reasonably be oriented toward anything less, and
arguments to the contrary are specious and disingenuous. Supporters of a full-blown Senate trial undoubtedly sought Clinton's ouster.
A brief excerpt from Baker's *The Breach* emphasizes this fact and
the House managers' dedication to it:

> From the start, the senators made clear that the House team had no chance of
> winning. They would never get the two-thirds they needed for conviction. . . .

The assessment was bipartisan. Stevens (R-AK) . . . delivered it the most bluntly. "The president isn't going to be removed," Stevens said firmly. "I can produce thirty-four affidavits of senators tomorrow that would show that they won't vote for conviction."

Hyde was upset. "Well, if that's the situation, *there's no point in our being here*" (2000: 276; emphasis added).

Because the Senate trial was undoubtedly about removal, those who were supportive of the Republicans' efforts to remove the president from office describe the Senate's handling of the Clinton trial as a sham, a tragic farce. According to the chief investigative counsel for the House Judiciary Committee, David P. Schippers, the expectation among the Republicans most intent on Clinton's removal was that, "[I]f the Senate gave us a fair trial and if the Senators voted their consciences, President Clinton would be removed from office" (Schippers and Henry 2000: 258). Unfortunately for the managers and their conservative Republican supporters, the impeachment itself was the high water mark of the case against the president. Schippers concluded:

> . . . [I]t was all downhill from there. It was made blatantly clear to us [the House managers and their staff] that the Republican senatorial leadership did not want a real impeachment trial. That went double for the Democrats.(Schippers and Henry 2000: 260)

In general, popular treatments of the Clinton impeachment highlight the distinctiveness of the handling of impeachment by the House of Representatives and the trial by the Senate. The specific characterization of the differences depend upon the particular point of view of the author on impeachment and removal. Those positively disposed toward the president's case tend to be more complimentary of the Senate's handling of the impeachment case than they are of the House's handling of it (see, for example Baker 2000; Toobin 1999). Conversely, Clinton's opponents are demonstrably more critical of the Senate's handling of the trial than of the House's handling of the initial impeachment proceedings. The title of Schippers and Henry's book, *Sellout,* refers to the refusal of Senate Republicans to support the House managers (and House Republicans more generally) in their efforts to remove the president from office. Analyses of the Clinton impeachment that treat the House and Senate stages of the process in similar lights are consistently negative (see Posner 1999) and are relatively rare.

Why, then, did the Senate handle the issue of Clinton's impeachment in a manner so different from that of the House? Why did individual senators treat the issue differently than their colleagues in the House? This question must be addressed at two levels: the institutional and the individual. In the next section I discuss institutional differences, and in the subsequent section I discuss individual differences.

Institutional Distinctiveness of the House and Senate, and Why It Mattered for Impeachment

The House and the Senate are distinctive chambers. First, they differ in size. The 100-member Senate is significantly smaller than the 435-member House, and the interpersonal dynamics between the members are altered in predictable ways by the difference in size. The term lengths of their members are different, with Senators enjoying terms that are three times longer than those of House members. The House and Senate have, at least in some respects, different legislative responsibilities. The House is solely responsible for the initiation of spending bills, and the Senate has sole responsibility for ratifying treaties negotiated by the president and confirming the president's executive and judicial branch appointments. The House has a far more detailed and extensive organizational structure than does the Senate, and senators are responsible for far more diverse policy portfolios than are their House counterparts. Senators serve on more committees and are far more likely to hold substantive leadership roles (e.g., be chair or ranking member of a committee and/or subcommittee) than are representatives. Finally, the histories of the chambers and their pathways of institutional development are

distinct. Each of these differences played an important role in forming the distinctiveness of the House and Senate treatment of the
Clinton impeachment. It should come as no surprise that the House
and the Senate chose to handle the Clinton impeachment in ways
that were quite different.

The size factor and term length differences affect the interpersonal
dynamics within the chambers. Because the Senate is so much
smaller and because senators tend to serve with each other for
longer periods of time, the web of personal relationships that develops in the Senate tends to be more extensive than the web of personal relationships that develops in the House. Although the norm
of courtesy has lost some of its traditional standing in recent years,
it is still a substantially more important component of the personal
and political environment of the Senate than of the House. According to Norman Ornstein, Robert Peabody, and David Rohde, "[T]he
courtesy norm also continues to serve the interests of members.
. . . As one Republican senator said, 'It's the catalyst that maintains
a semblance of order'" (1987: 10). The interpersonal relations fostered by the courtesy norm provided the Senate with a means of
avoiding the type of rancorous debate that characterized the House
impeachment proceedings, and they made it possible for the Senate
to at least present the appearance of being a more serious tribunal
than the House.

Distinct constitutional responsibilities (and prerogatives) played
an important role in the difference between the impeachment proceedings in the House and those in the Senate. Impeachment is a
very serious threat to a sitting president, but it is not the same as removal. Although impeachments are rare, they are not without
precedent (e.g., Andrew Johnson's impeachment and Nixon's near-
impeachment). And although incredibly embarrassing, being impeached, in and of itself, has no necessary impact on the authority
of the sitting president. Conviction on impeachment charges, on
the other hand, results in the removal from office of a popular
president and may engender a serious constitutional crisis. Quite
simply, the constitutional and historical stakes associated with the

decision to remove a president from office are far greater than the stakes associated with the decision to impeach.

Conviction by the Senate also required a much larger majority of the voting membership than impeachment by the House. The difference between the majority voting rule for impeachment and the supermajority voting rule for conviction resulted from the founders' deep distrust of factional manipulation of the impeachment power for partisan objectives. As Hamilton argued, "[T]here will always be the greatest danger, that the decision [to remove from office] will be regulated more by the comparative strength of parties than by the real demonstrations of innocence or guilt" (*Federalist Papers* 1982, v. 65). The founders considered the Senate the most appropriate body for determining whether to remove the president from office because senators could most easily separate themselves from the temporary passions that might lead to an ill-considered attack on the president (*Federalist Papers* 1982, v. 65). But they also realized that even in the "dignified" Senate, partisan politics could carry the day, so they required a two-thirds vote to remove a sitting president from office. In the particular circumstances of the Clinton impeachment, the balance of power between supporters and opponents was such that the decision rule in the House provided for impeachment, but the decision rule in the Senate effectively prohibited conviction. Because the obstacles to conviction were far greater than the obstacles to impeachment, the Senate trial was a stark contrast to the House proceedings.

The House and Senate have different formal and informal leadership structures. The Senate is a much "flatter" organization than the House, and the chambers' distinctiveness in this regard has increased over time as the Senate norms of specialization and apprenticeship have faded (Ornstein, Peabody, and Rohde 1987). Senate leaders are less authoritative, and senators tend to be somewhat more independent than their House colleagues. Add this increased independence to the significantly higher decision rule for conviction (as opposed to removal), and it becomes even more difficult to see how conviction was a practical possibility. It is likely that if the chance of success in the Senate had been comparable to that in the House, the character of the proceedings would have been more comparable. There were significant differences, and the proceedings themselves reflected those differences.

Finally, the histories of the chambers differ in a way that is particularly important for the case of the Clinton impeachment. Even though it happened almost 140 years ago, the House did at one time impeach a president (Andrew Johnson). The Senate, even if by only a single vote, refused to convict Johnson and remove him from office. Subsequent scholarly evaluations of Johnson's impeachment suggest that it was highly suspect from a constitutional standpoint.[1] In early 1999, the Senate stood on the threshold of U.S. history in a way that the House had not, and in the end it was not willing to step off into the abyss.

Institutional differences between the House and the Senate do not tell the full story of each chamber's handling of the Clinton impeachment. Just as there were important differences of opinion among the representatives voting on impeachment, there were important differences of opinion among the senators voting on conviction. I turn now to an examination of senators' votes on conviction, focusing specifically on the difference between determinants of roll call votes on conviction and on impeachment.

Roll Call Voting in the Senate

A considerable portion of the research on roll call voting has focused on the House of Representatives. There are several reasons for the academic emphasis on the behavior of representatives. First, there are more representatives than senators. On any particular vote, there can obviously never be more than 100 senators voting. In the House, the limit on votes goes all the way up to 435. Plenty of roll call studies have been based on one or a few votes. With a sample of 100 (or more likely less, given the frequent no-shows and abstentions) it is often difficult to determine the distinct impact of independent variables that are highly correlated with each other (such as partisanship and ideology). Subtle effects are easier to disentangle in a sample of 435 representatives than in a sample of only 100 senators.

Another obstacle to rigorous analysis of roll call votes in the Senate—as compared to comparable analyses of House roll call votes—is the difference in the electoral timeframe between members of the two chambers. Every member of the House of Representatives runs for re-election every two years. In any single election year, only one-third of the senators run for re-election. Because representatives must run for re-election so frequently, they must pay greater attention to the potential reaction of their constituents to their roll call votes than must senators. There is a significant difference—from the standpoint of constituency attention—between a vote cast a year before a re-election run and a vote cast five years prior to a re-election run. Senators also serve a considerably longer period of time between their final re-election and their retirement (generally six years) than do representatives (obviously, no more than two years), so senators have more opportunities to cast roll call votes without worrying about constituency reactions than do representatives.

Research on roll call voting in the House and Senate indicates that the difference in electoral timeframe has important implications for institutional decision making. There is evidence that position in the electoral cycle influences roll call voting behavior among senators. Senators nearer to their own re-election campaigns tend to be somewhat more sensitive to constituency preferences than senators who have just won re-election or whose re-election campaigns are two or four years off (Fenno 1982; Thomas 1985).[2] This representational pattern is particularly pronounced on prominent issues of an exceptional nature such as the confirmation of a controversial presidential appointee. In their study of senators' votes on the Clarence Thomas confirmation, L. Marvin Overby, Beth Henshcen, Michael Walsh, and Julie Strauss (1992) found a much stronger relationship between constituency characteristics (e.g., relative size of the African American population in a state) and support for Thomas—for both Democrats and Republicans—among members facing imminent re-election campaigns than among members whose re-election years were more distant. In the specific case of the Clinton impeachment, various media accounts suggested that senators facing re-election in 2000 would be more likely to vote with their constituents (i.e., Republicans voting for acquittal) than colleagues who would not have to run again until 2002 or 2004.

Also, as in the House, retirements can influence roll call voting behavior. Members planning to retire rather than run for re-election, even those who are years away from actual retirement, may tend to base their votes on their own ideological leanings more than they would if they were planning to return to the Senate. Some members may not decide to retire until just before they must begin running for re-election, but others certainly have retirement in mind well before their re-election bid would have to start, and some probably have retirement in mind just after an election (especially if it is particularly brutal or it comes late in a career). Financial data suggest that retirees decide well before they inform the public. The important thing to remember is that chamber differences in the electoral timeframes and the distinctiveness of retirement patterns complicate Senate roll call studies to a far greater extent than they do House roll call studies.

Representatives cast more votes than senators, and it is easier to study roll call voting in the House than in the Senate because House members cast more recorded votes. Because debate is far more limited in the House than in the Senate, House votes are significantly more frequent. The House also takes somewhat more detailed recorded votes. Although the Senate might cast one or two votes on a particular issue, the House may cast a half dozen votes on the same issue. The increase in the number of votes—often on specific amendments—gives those analysts studying roll call voting behavior the means to distinguish between sets of often subtle forces that determine voting choices. Another reason the House takes more votes than the Senate is that the House enjoys a wider policymaking purview than the Senate. Revenue and taxation bills must be initiated in the House of Representatives, so a variety of issues that the representatives consider and record their votes on never reach the Senate.

The broader, more diverse electoral constituencies of the Senate also pose an obstacle to the rigorous analysis of roll call voting.[3] It is not always easy to identify the ways in which district constituencies influence voting on the floor of the House. Richard Fenno (1978), for example, argues that House members face a set of related but distinct constituency pressures. If identifying the preferences of House constituencies is difficult, it is significantly easier than identifying the preferences of Senate constituencies. States—except in those half dozen cases in which they are their own single districts—are larger and more demographically, economically, and politically diverse than any of the congressional districts contained within them. Obviously, this makes it more difficult to draw a clear connection between senators' voting behavior and the preferences of their constituents. The relative frequency of split Senate delegations—one senator from each political party—highlights the difficulties inherent in drawing connections between state-level constituencies and senators' policy-oriented behavior.[4]

For some time, researchers have had a great deal of difficulty clearly identifying specific constituency effects in roll call votes in the Senate. An interesting work by Wendy Schiller (2000) argues that constituency effects exist but that they can only be found when one understands—and accounts for—the representative dynamics inherent in the fact that each state constituency is served by a pair of senators. According to Schiller, once we understand the political dynamics of two individuals serving identical geographic constituencies we can begin to see how senators actually represent their constituencies in a host of different ways.

Although roll call voting in the House and Senate are in part driven by different dynamics, legislator ideology and partisanship shape voting patterns in both chambers. Recent efforts to distinguish between the role of partisanship in roll call voting in the House and in the Senate have found little difference between the chambers (Snyder and Groseclose 2000). Likewise, just as legislator ideology affects roll call voting patterns in the House—in general and on the issue of impeachment more specifically—recent research prevents us from ignoring its potential impact on senators' votes on the articles of impeachment (Levitt 1996).

Voting on Conviction in the Senate

Party lines in the Senate were not obviously more porous than those in the House. Only a slightly larger percentage of Senate Republicans voted against one or both of the articles of impeachment than did House Republicans on the same articles, and not a single Democrat voted for the articles. But senators were far less inclined to cite partisanship as the reason why their colleagues across the aisle disagreed with them. Senators tended to attribute their votes on conviction to the character of the evidence and the significance of the president's actions and whether they reached the standard for removal, and they publicly characterized their opponents' motives in much the same way. Senators studiously avoided direct attacks on the political motives of their colleagues. It was not that the senators agreed about whether the House managers had proved that Clinton committed certain untoward acts or whether Clinton's behavior warranted impeachment. They did not agree (except to the extent that they all found the president's actions revolting and deeply disappointing). But they were willing to disagree in a manner that minimized damage to the public's perception of the institution. Baker perfectly captures the esprit d'corps that flowed through the body at the history-making moment when the members cast their votes on the articles of impeachment:

> . . . [A] parade of senators sauntered casually to the front desk to record their votes. Others milled around, bantering and laughing aloud. Almost no one remained in his or her seat. Feinstein and staunch conservative John Ashcroft shook hands and talked in the center aisle. John Kerry, Chris Dodd, and Gordon Smith laughed cheerily together on the Democratic side. Lott joked with John Edwards. Pat Moynihan combed his hair in the back of the chamber, while Bill Frist wandered up to the gallery to sit with his wife and kids. The decorum of the trial was now gone. It was back to business as usual. (2000: 411–12)

We now face something of a quandary. The institutional differences between the House and Senate suggest that ideology should have played a more important role in the formation of Senate preferences on the articles of impeachment than in the House (where constituency preferences were quite important). But research on roll call voting in the Senate implies that partisanship and constituency preferences also play important roles in forming member preferences. On first glance, the distribution of support and opposition among the parties suggests that partisanship dominated Senate decision making. It is often difficult, however, to separate the independent effects of partisanship, ideology, and constituency preferences on roll call votes (particularly in the Senate). Finally, we know that the senators themselves focused on none of these factors when they explained their own votes—or, more problematically, the votes of those who disagreed with them.

In this chapter, I attempt to clarify our understanding of Senate decision making by examining the voting behavior of Senators on the articles of impeachment against the president. I begin by estimating state-level opinion and demonstrating that a majority of legislators—nearly all Democrats and a handful of Republicans—actually voted their constituents' preferences. I then evaluate the relative impact of partisanship, ideology, and constituency preferences on senators' votes on impeachment.

Estimating State-Level Opinion

During the full impeachment process in the House of Representatives (and continuing on through the final consideration of the impeachment articles in the Senate), hundreds of national opinion polls estimated the level of public support for the president and for his impeachment. As indicated in Chapter 3, these opinion polls consistently showed that an overwhelming majority of the U.S. public (usually between 60 and 70 percent) opposed the impeachment and removal of President Clinton. We obviously have a very clear picture of national-level public opinion on the impeachment.

Unfortunately, comparable data for each individual state—like congressional districts—do not exist. National surveys are usually far too small to include a sufficiently large sample of voters from each state, and it is not at all uncommon for voters in some states—obviously those with relatively small populations—to be excluded from the sample altogether. Even if a national sample included, by chance, individuals from each state, the state-level samples would be far too small for reliable inference. With the possible exceptions of California, Texas, New York, and Florida, few if any states would have a sufficient number of voters included in any reasonably sized national opinion poll sample to make accurate, valid estimates of state-level opinion.

This problem could have been avoided by conducting full-scale opinion surveys on impeachment in each of the states. Although that option would have been almost prohibitively expensive, it would have been the most accurate method for gauging state-level opinion. Unfortunately, no such set of surveys was ever administered. Since that time is clearly past, we cannot conduct a survey like the one indicated above even if we had—and were willing to spend—the money to do it. So we must look for an alternative to opinion surveys of all the states, and we must be able to implement this alternative with the existing data.

One viable alternative to 50 state-level surveys is simulation of state-level opinion from national surveys (Erikson 1978). Using the same procedure and the same opinion survey—the *Washington Post*/ABC News Impeachment Hearings Poll fielded on December 12–13, 1998—described in Chapter 4, I constructed estimates of public opposition to impeachment for each of the 50 states.

The state-level estimates of public opposition to the Clinton impeachment are just as striking as the district-level estimates generated for the House of Representatives. Although approximately 40 percent of the U.S. public supported Clinton's impeachment—a proportion reflected in the sample data—impeachment supporters were a majority in fewer than 10 percent of the states. A majority of voters in only four states—Utah, Alaska, Nebraska, and Kansas—supported the removal of the president from office. Of the senators up for re-election in 2000, only one, Orrin Hatch (R.–Utah) served a state in which a majority of the voters favored conviction of the president on the articles of impeachment. For a list of the percentage of voters opposed to removal, by state, see Table 5.1.

Not surprisingly, Democrats tended to serve states that were more strongly opposed to the president's conviction than do Republicans. The mean percentage of state population opposed to impeachment (57.7 versus 61.1 percent) and the median percentage of state population opposed to impeachment (58.7 versus 62.1 percent) are higher for Democrats than for Republicans. Of the four states most opposed to impeachment, none was served by a Republican senator. Of the four states most supportive of impeachment, only Nebraska had a Democratic senator (John Kerrey). He has since retired and has been replaced by a Republican.

Of the 55 Republican senators in the 106th Congress, only seven served states in which Clinton's impeachment was favored by a majority of the population. (See Table 5–2.) Bennett and Hatch from Utah, Murkowski and Stevens from Alaska, Hagel from Nebraska, and Brownback and Roberts from Kansas were the only Republican senators serving states in which a majority of voters supported Clinton's impeachment.

The remaining 48 Republicans served states where the opponents of impeachment outnumbered its supporters. This group includes a number of southern Republicans who served states where impeachment was especially unpopular. At first glance, several southern states appeared to have a surprisingly high percentage of impeachment opponents. In a region of the country that is traditionally conservative and in which the Republican Party has made such significant strides in recent years, how can one explain the level of opposition to impeachment? First, one must remember that our measure of impeachment is based on the level of Clinton support during the 1996 election and the relative size of the African American population. On both of these dimensions, many of the southern states score very highly. In addition, in those states that have relatively low scores on one or the other of these dimensions, the other score is quite high. For example, Clinton did poorly in South Carolina in 1996, but South Carolina has one of the largest African American populations in the country. Conversely, Arkansas and

TABLE 5.1   Percent of Voting Population Opposed to Removal, by State

State	Percent Opposed to Impeachment
UTAH	45.55
ALASKA	46.90
NEBRASKA	47.88
KANSAS	49.43
NORTH DAKOTA	50.14
MONTANA	50.89
SOUTH DAKOTA	52.25
OKLAHOMA	53.14
INDIANA	54.02
COLORADO	55.37
OREGON	55.91
NEVADA	56.28
KENTUCKY	56.55
NEW HAMPSHIRE	56.72
WYOMING	57.06
ARIZONA	57.06
IOWA	57.87
WISCONSIN	58.17
MAINE	58.21
WASHINGTON	58.36
TEXAS	58.73
MINNESOTA	58.79
IDAHO	59.03
WEST VIRGINIA	59.06
OHIO	59.19
MISSOURI	59.23
VERMONT	59.41
NEW MEXICO	59.67
PENNSLYVANIA	59.85
NORTH CAROLINA	60.61
VIRGINIA	60.77
ALABAMA	61.29
TENNESSEE	61.35
FLORIDA	61.71
CALIFORNIA	62.11
CONNECTICUT	62.53
HAWAII	63.10
MICHIGAN	63.14
SOUTH CAROLINA	63.17
GEORGIA	64.04
DELAWARE	64.97
ARKANSAS	65.04

(continues)

TABLE 5.1   (continued)

State	Percent Opposed to Impeachment
NEW JERSEY	65.13
MISSISSIPPI	65.42
RHODE ISLAND	65.53
ILLINOIS	65.62
MASSACHUSETTS	67.08
LOUISIANA	69.13
MARYLAND	69.19
NEW YORK	69.83

Tennessee have relatively small African American populations, but both were Clinton strongholds in 1996. That there was strong opposition to the Clinton impeachment should not be doubted. whether Southern Republican senators paid attention to that opposition is another question.[5]

Democrats, on the other hand, uniformly opposed the articles of impeachment. (See Table 5.3.) With one exception—Kerrey of Nebraska—all of the Democrats voted in a manner consistent with their constituents' preferences. For nearly half of the Democratic constituencies, impeachment opponents outnumbered impeachment supporters by a 3 to 2 margin (or greater).

If we look across parties for a constituency effect, it is very difficult to find. Calculating the simple opposition averages separately for senators who opposed both articles of impeachment, senators who opposed one article and supported the other, and senators who supported both articles, we find a small difference in the expected direction. Senators who opposed both articles serve states with slightly higher opposition rates than states served by senators who supported at least one of the impeachment articles. This difference is not, however, significant, and opposition to impeachment was actually slightly higher in states served by senators who opposed both articles than in states served by senators who supported only one article of impeachment. (See Table 5.4.)

98

TABLE 5.2   Republican Senators, Constituency
Opposition to Impeachment, and Votes on Conviction*

Name	State	Percent Opposed to Impeachment	Article 1	Article 2
BENNETT	UTAH	45.55	Yes	Yes
HATCH	UTAH	45.55	Yes	Yes
MURKOWSKI	ALASKA	46.62	No	Yes
STEVENS	ALASKA	46.62	Yes	Yes
HAGEL	NEBRASKA	47.88	Yes	Yes
BROWNBACK	KANSAS	49.43	Yes	Yes
ROBERTS	KANSAS	49.43	Yes	Yes
BURNS	MONTANA	50.89	Yes	Yes
INHOFE	OKLAHOMA	53.14	Yes	Yes
NICKLES	OKLAHOMA	53.14	Yes	Yes
LUGAR	INDIANA	54.02	Yes	Yes
ALLARD	COLORADO	55.37	Yes	Yes
CAMPBELL	COLORADO	55.37	Yes	Yes
SMITH	OREGON	55.91	Yes	Yes
Bunning	KENTUCKY	56.55	Yes	Yes
MCCONNELL	KENTUCKY	56.55	Yes	Yes
GREGG	NEW HAMPSHIRE	56.72	Yes	Yes
SMITH	NEW HAMPSHIRE	56.72	Yes	Yes
ENZI	WYOMING	57.06	Yes	Yes
THOMAS	WYOMING	57.06	Yes	Yes
KYL	ARIZONA	57.06	Yes	Yes
MCCAIN	ARIZONA	57.06	Yes	Yes
GRASSLEY	IOWA	57.87	Yes	Yes
COLLINS	MAINE	58.21	No	No
SNOWE	MAINE	58.21	No	No
GORTON	WASHINGTON	58.36	No	Yes
GRAMM	TEXAS	58.78	Yes	Yes
HUTCHISON	TEXAS	58.73	Yes	Yes
GRAMS	MINNESOTA	58.79	Yes	Yes
CRAIG	IDAHO	59.03	Yes	Yes
Crapo	IDAHO	59.03	Yes	Yes
DEWINE	OHIO	59.19	Yes	Yes
Voinovich	OHIO	59.19	Yes	Yes
ASHCROFT	MISSOURI	59.23	Yes	Yes
BOND	MISSOURI	59.23	Yes	Yes
JEFFORDS	VERMONT	59.41	No	No
DOMENICI	NEW MEXICO	59.67	Yes	Yes
SANTORUM	PENNSYLVANIA	59.85	No	No
SPECTOR	PENNSYLVANIA	59.85	Yes	Yes

*First-year senators are listed in lowercase letters.

(continues)

TABLE 5.2   (continued)

Name	State	Percent Opposed to Impeachment	Article 1	Article 2
HELMS	NORTH CAROLINA	60.61	Yes	Yes
WARNER	VIRGINIA	60.77	No	Yes
SESSIONS	ALABAMA	61.29	No	Yes
SHELBY	ALABAMA	61.29	Yes	Yes
FRIST	TENNESSEE	61.35	No	Yes
THOMPSON	TENNESSEE	61.35	Yes	Yes
MACK	FLORIDA	61.71	Yes	Yes
ABRAHAM	MICHIGAN	63.14	Yes	Yes
THURMOND	SOUTH CAROLINA	63.17	Yes	Yes
COVERDELL	GEORGIA	63.14	Yes	Yes
ROTH	DELAWARE	64.97	Yes	Yes
HUTCHINSON	ARKANSAS	65.04	Yes	Yes
COCHRAN	MISSISSIPPI	65.42	Yes	Yes
LOTT	MISSISSIPPI	65.42	Yes	Yes
CHAFEE	RHODE ISLAND	65.53	No	No
Fitzgerald	ILLINOIS	65.62	Yes	Yes

If I control for position in the electoral cycle by eliminating all senators whose terms were not up in 2000, the averages are slightly different, but the general pattern remains the same. (See Table 5.5.) Opposition to impeachment is slightly higher in states served by senators who opposed both impeachment articles than in states served by senators who voted for one or both articles of impeachment. Again, the difference is negligible and statistically insignificant.

At least for Senators, constituency pressures appear to have played a relatively small role in determining Senate roll call votes on Clinton's conviction. Is the same true for senator ideology? The answer is clearly "no." There is a huge ideological gap between those who voted for conviction and those who voted for acquittal on the impeachment charges. Using, as in Chapter 4, the roll call vote scores from the Americans for Democratic Action (ADA)[6] as an indicator of ideology,[7] I find that the average ideological score for impeachment opponents was almost 90, whereas supporters of one or more of the articles of impeachment had ideological scores in the single digits.[8] (See Table 5.6.) Position in the electoral cycle has no

TABLE 5.3 Democratic Senators, Constituency
Opposition to Impeachment, and Votes on Conviction[*]

Name	State	Percent Opposed to Impeachment	Article 1	Article 2
KERREY	NEBRASKA	47.88	Yes	Yes
CONRAD	NORTH DAKOTA	50.14	Yes	Yes
DORGAN	NORTH DAKOTA	50.14	Yes	Yes
BAUCUS	MONTANA	50.89	Yes	Yes
DASCHLE	SOUTH DAKOTA	52.25	Yes	Yes
JOHNSON	SOUTH DAKOTA	52.25	Yes	Yes
Bayh	INDIANA	54.02	Yes	Yes
WYDEN	OREGON	55.91	Yes	Yes
BRYAN	NEVADA	56.28	Yes	Yes
REID	NEVADA	56.28	Yes	Yes
HARKIN	IOWA	57.87	Yes	Yes
FEINGOLD	WISCONSIN	58.17	Yes	Yes
KOHL	WISCONSIN	58.17	Yes	Yes
MURRAY	WASHINGTON	58.36	Yes	Yes
WELLSTONE	MINNESOTA	58.79	Yes	Yes
BYRD	WEST VIRGINIA	59.06	Yes	Yes
ROCKEFELLER	WEST VIRGINIA	59.06	Yes	Yes
LEAHY	VERMONT	59.41	Yes	Yes
BINGAMAN	NEW MEXICO	59.67	Yes	Yes
Edwards	NORTH CAROLINA	60.61	Yes	Yes
ROBB	VIRGINIA	60.77	Yes	Yes
GRAHAM	FLORIDA	61.71	Yes	Yes
BOXER	CALIFORNIA	62.11	Yes	Yes
FEINSTEIN	CALIFORNIA	62.11	Yes	Yes
DODD	CONNECTICUT	62.53	Yes	Yes
LIEBERMAN	CONNECTICUT	62.53	Yes	Yes
AKAKA	HAWAII	63.10	Yes	Yes
INOUYE	HAWAII	63.10	Yes	Yes
LEVIN	MICHIGAN	63.14	Yes	Yes
HOLLINGS	SOUTH CAROLINA	63.17	Yes	Yes
CLELAND	GEORGIA	64.04	Yes	Yes
BIDEN	DELAWARE	64.97	Yes	Yes
Lincoln	ARKANSAS	65.04	Yes	Yes
LAUTENBERG	NEW JERSEY	65.13	Yes	Yes
TORRICELI	NEW JERSEY	65.13	Yes	Yes
REED	RHODE ISLAND	65.53	Yes	Yes
DURBIN	ILLINOIS	65.62	Yes	Yes
KENNEDY	MASSACHUSETTS	67.08	Yes	Yes
KERRY	MASSACHUSETTS	67.08	Yes	Yes

[*]First-year senators are listed in lowercase letters.

(continues)

TABLE 5.3 (continued)

Name	State	Percent Opposed to Impeachment	Article 1	Article 2
BREAUX	LOUISIANA	69.13	Yes	Yes
LANDRIEU	LOUISIANA	69.13	Yes	Yes
MIKULSKI	MARYLAND	69.19	Yes	Yes
SARBANES	MARYLAND	69.19	Yes	Yes
MOYNIHAN	NEW YORK	69.83	Yes	Yes
SCHUMER	NEW YORK	69.83	Yes	Yes

TABLE 5.4 Average Opposition to Impeachment by Conviction Votes (All Senators)

Votes for Conviction	Average Constituency Opposition to Impeachment (percent)
0	60.9
1	57.7
2	57.5

TABLE 5.5 Average Opposition to Impeachment by Conviction Votes (Senators Facing Re-election in 2000)

Votes for Conviction	Average Constituency Opposition to Impeachment (percent)
0	60.5
1	58.4
2	58.1

TABLE 5.6   ADA Scores by Conviction Votes (All Senators)

Votes for Conviction	Average ADA Score
0	89
1	6
2	4

TABLE 5.7   ADA Scores by Conviction Votes (Senators Facing Re-election in 2000)

Votes for Conviction	Average ADA Score
0	90
1	5
2	4.6

TABLE 5.8   Explaining Senate Votes on the Articles of Impeachment

Total	Frequency
0	49
1	5
2	45

Parameter	Estimate	Standard Error	Chi-Square	Pr>ChiSq
Intercept	11.024	7.5796	2.1154	0.1458
Intercept 2	9.7376	7.5336	1.6707	0.1962
ADA99	-0.1215	0.0378	10.3391	0.0013
IMPOPP	-0.0514	0.088	0.342	0.5587
PARTY	-6.5079	162.8	0.0016	0.9681
PELECT	-0.0708	0.0616	1.3211	0.2504

Percentage predicted correctly = 97.0
Proportionate reduction in error = 94.1 percent
Pseudo R^2 =
AIC = 60.019, SC = 75.589, -2 Log L = 48.019

significant effect on the ideological gap between those who voted for conviction and those who voted for acquittal on the impeachment charges. (See Table 5.7.) If anything, the ideological gap between the supporters and opponents of impeachment is slightly greater among those senators facing imminent re-election campaigns than among those senators whose re-election campaigns are more distant. These results suggest that when pressed, senators' personal ideological concerns win out over constituency preferences.

On closer inspection, personal ideology remains the primary explanation for the Senate voting pattern on the articles of impeachment. If we examine the impact of partisan, ideological, and constituency pressures simultaneously, we see that ideology easily dominates the explanatory model. (See Table 5.8.) I have estimated a logistic regression model similar to those presented in Chapter 4, and I find that ADA99 (senators' ADA scores from 1999) is significantly and negatively related to likelihood of supporting one or more of the articles of impeachment. As ADA scores increase, that is, as senators become more liberal, they are more likely to vote for acquittal. The PARTY variable is insignificant (and signed incorrectly). The constituency opposition variable (IMPOPP) is insignificant and signed incorrectly, and the electoral cycle variable (PELECT, a dummy variable coded "1" for senators facing re-election in 2000 and "0" otherwise) is also insignificant.[9]

Conclusion

Just as it did in the House, ideology played an important role in individual decision-making on the issue of impeachment. Liberal senators were far more likely to vote for acquittal than their more conservative colleagues. The distinct role of partisanship is, again, more limited than previously realized. This is certainly true if we take popular descriptions of impeachment politics seriously.

The interesting, but not completely unexpected, difference between the House and Senate is the absence of a strong constituency effect in the Senate. Although a majority of senators did actually take positions on removal that resonated with their constituents,

this position taking appears to be an artifact of the congruence between the members' underlying ideology and the preferences of the
senators' constituents. There is no evidence that an independent
constituency effect—one predicated solely on constituency preferences on the issues of impeachment and removal—existed. This is
just as true for senators facing re-election in the near term (2000) as
it is for senators whose next electoral challenges are some way off
(2002 and 2004). This finding raises two important questions:

1. Did those senators who crossed their constituencies on the
    Clinton impeachment attempt to make up for this deviation
    (possibly by raising extra campaign funds)?
2. Did those senators who crossed their constituencies on the
    Clinton impeachment suffer politically (at the ballot box)
    for their independence?

I examine both of these questions in Chapter 8.

6

MAKING UP: IMPEACHMENT, FUNDRAISING, AND ROLL CALLS IN THE HOUSE

There are only two important things in politics.
The first is money and I can't remember the second.

—*Mark Hanna (quoted in Donnelly, Fine, and Miller 1999: 3)*

The analysis presented in Chapter 4 indicates that both representative ideology and constituency preferences (at least for the Republicans) influenced roll call voting decisions on the articles of impeachment brought against President Clinton. But the statistical significance of the constituency preferences variable must not obscure the fact that a large number of representatives did not cast votes on the articles of impeachment that were unpopular with their constituents. Although nearly every Democrat voted his or her constituents' preferences, in dozens of Republican districts, what the constituents wanted failed to carry the day. And this is not a "small" politics issue. This is not about special privileges or exemptions for a concentrated political interest that will go largely unnoticed by the general public. This is the impeachment of a president.

On a public issue of such import—an issue on which public preferences were crystal clear—the practical irrelevance of so many constituents' preferences is remarkable.

In the wake of Clinton's impeachment, the district-level estimates of public support for the impeachment are striking. Although approximately 40 percent of the U.S. public supported Clinton's impeachment (Jacobson 1999)—a proportion reflected in the sample data—impeachment supporters were a majority in fewer than 15 percent of all congressional districts, and nearly all of those districts were held by Republicans. Given these results, it is no surprise that Democrats were much more likely to vote in accordance with their constituents' preferences than were Republicans. Only five Democrats voted against the preferences of the majority of their constituents, and each of these individuals supported one or more of the articles of impeachment. Conversely, a majority of Republicans voted against the preferences of a majority of their constituents. Only 56 House Republicans voted with their constituents, and 27 House Republicans voted against large majorities (>60 percent opposed to Clinton's impeachment) in their districts.

Admittedly, it is impossible to have a legislative career of any length without at one time or another frustrating nontrivial portions of one's local constituency. Even if we ignore those individuals in a representative's geographic constituency who are unlikely to vote for the representative in a primary or general election, there will be times when core constituencies—members of a representative's personal, primary, and or electoral constituencies (see Fenno 1978)—are seemingly ignored or actively opposed. That is the nature of representative politics in a diverse society. People will, from time to time, disagree.

In the regular course of representing a constituency, these instances of disjuncture between constituents and representatives tend to be temporary and are rarely of such significance that they have a meaningful negative impact on the course of a member's legislative career. There are two reasons for this. First, representatives make a concerted effort to smooth over policy rifts with important con-

mpeachment votes and the 2000 election miti-
n extreme shift in voting behavior.

also compensate constituents through increased
eral funds into their districts. This is tantamount
constituency, but it is not an uncommon prac-
rs 1994, 1995). Because compensation is mainly
cans, their majority party status is an important
age. Unfortunately, the tradition of Republican
mitigates against significant increases in pork
onstraint that implies that the distribution of
g is a zero-sum game. It may be impossible to
nts with individually optimal levels of con-

ans of overcoming the electoral fallout from an
nent vote, and the one on which I focus here, is
orts to raise campaign funds. In general, cam-
eans to an end. Money provides the means to
nhance electoral advertising (see Erikson and
, Gross, and Shields 1999). As Mayhew notes,
rces one of the most vital is money" (1974:
s one of the "resources that can be *translated*
9; emphasis added). For nearly all incumbents
ers the "campaign for resources" is an essential
vity (Herrnson 2000).

trategies, changes in roll call voting behavior
l generating federal revenue or resources for
dit claiming purposes) are distinct from cam-
a politically significant way. Ideological shifts
and pork barrel projects are specifically di-
nt's geographic constituency. Campaign funds
sources, and often these sources are not lo-
's district. This is especially true for PAC con-
on 2000). To raise additional campaign funds
alls resulting from unpopular impeachment
t reach out to individuals and organizations
n geographic constituencies. In exchange for

stituents. Representatives spend a great deal of time "explaining" themselves (their behavior in Washington, their votes, their policy positions and objectives, etc.) to their constituents (see Fenno 1978).[1] They attempt to predict, in advance, which of their public positions or roll call votes will be most problematic for them in their districts, and they prepare, sometimes compulsively, for the questions and criticisms they know they will face (Fenno 1978). Although politically successful representatives become adept at explaining themselves because they have to, dealing with angry critics is never an enjoyable prospect. It is especially unpleasant when these critics are (or were) one's supporters.

The easiest way to avoid having to provide difficult explanations about why you did not pay attention to what your constituents wanted on a particularly important issue is to pay attention to what your constituents want and give it to them. It is easy to explain why you followed your supporters' lead on an issue about which they are concerned, far easier than explaining why they are wrong or misguided (and you, by implication, are not).

There are times, of course, when representatives must make difficult decisions involving unavoidable political trade-offs. In the case of the Clinton impeachment, most Republicans faced some severe cross-pressures. For a majority of Republicans, their constituencies opposed inpeachment. Balanced against their constituents' interests were a variety of factors: the institutional benefits associated with supporting the party (e.g., a better committee assignment or a future shot at a leadership position); cultivation of a new, somewhat more conservative constituency (for those thinking ahead to the post-2000 redistricting); personal ideological orientation; and the dictates of one's conscience. The results presented in Chapter 4 suggest that ideological orientation played an especially important role in the final decisions many representatives made on the issue of impeachment. But regardless of the specific set of pressures or circumstances that led many Republicans to vote against their constituents, the plain fact is that they did. Assuming those representatives intended to keep their seats in Congress, how should we have expected them to respond?

Representatives who cast unpopular impeachment votes may have expected that impeachment would be a non-issue during the 2000 election. With nearly two full years between the floor votes on the articles of impeachment and the November elections in 2000, representatives might have expected the political landscape to have changed to such an extent that the voters would no longer care about representatives' individual roles in the impeachment process. With a presidential election taking center stage, maybe the voters could be expected to forget. Given voters' political myopia, this is a reasonable belief. In our political system, it is not too difficult to see why members of Congress might worry little about the electoral fallout from a handful of votes taken nearly two years prior to the current election. But the impeachment issue did influence voters' opinions in 1998 (see Jacobson 1999), and that was before the House impeached the president. It is highly unlikely that those members most likely to suffer from the prominence of the impeachment issue would also be the only members to think that the impeachment issue would be unimportant to voters. If that were true, it would turn the stereotype of the safe representative "running scared" on its head. There must be some other explanation.

Assuming legislators did not trivialize the electoral consequences of the impeachment proceedings and their roles in those proceedings, how might we explain what appears to be strategically sub-optimal behavior? Suppose incumbents sought to maintain a desirable relationship with their constituents, what I previously referred to as a positive "equilibrium". Unfortunately, at least for the members, they may have objectives that are at cross purposes or that are inconsistent (e.g., satisfying party leaders versus satisfying the constituency), and these cross pressures make disruptions difficult to avoid. This is almost certainly true for a significant number of House Republicans on the impeachment issue.

Members of Congress rarely risk the ire of their constituents unless they face primary and electoral constituencies that have conflicting preferences or have some means of compensating their constituents for the offending behavior (e.g., unpopular votes). On the issue of impeachment, one can easily see that a sizable number of

Republicans wishe
and attempted to
with the unpopula
political argument
impeachment coul
ing within the pa
those efforts. Like
a vote for impeach
the support of a
have intended to r
impeachment vot
the president. The
impeach Presiden
nored their consti
but few would ha
make up for their

David Mayhew
three basic elect
ing, and credit cl
turn to the elect
career in the Ho
or all of these be
havior in an eff
anti-impeachme
voted against in
number and va
tricts. Finally, t
paign funds tha
and frequency

A change in v
stituency. Beca
small set of r
stretch to assur
same constitue
proceedings su
of important i

time between the
gated the need for a

Legislators might
efforts to funnel fed
to "buying off" the
tice (Stein and Bicke
an issue for Republi
institutional advant
fiscal conservatism
barrel spending, a
pork barrel spendin
supply all incumbe
stituency benefits.

An alternative me
unpopular impeachm
to increase one's eff
paign funds are a m
both increase and e
Palfrey 1998; Goidel
"Of campaign resou
40–41), and money
into votes" (1974: 3
and credible challeng
and unavoidable acti

As compensatory s
(position taking) and
one's district (for cre
paign fundraising in
(even if temporary)
rected at an incumbe
are raised from man
cated in an incumben
tributions (see Herrns
to offset vote shortf
votes, candidates mus
well beyond their ow

these campaign funds from extra-district sources, members may provide some set of benefits to these contributors.[2] Given that campaign resources flow from beyond the borders of a candidate's electoral constituency, the extent to which contributor benefits are problematic, from a representational standpoint, is an open and important question.

If financial resources were evenly distributed across politically significant societal groups, then funding differences—and the location of funding sources—might be relatively unimportant. But these resources are not distributed evenly. Traditionally, the Republicans have held a significant advantage in the capacity to generate campaign funds (see Herrnson 2000).[3] If one political party tends to have a monetary advantage—as the Republicans have had in recent times—then the organizational and financial means to circumvent conventional representative politics are available. The potential for the use of campaign funds to compensate for legislators' unpopular policy positions is unsettling from the standpoint of normative democratic theory. That campaign funds might have been used for this purpose on an issue such as impeachment is deeply disturbing.

Even if representatives did not enter into quid pro quo relationships with their contributors—and there were so many contributors that it is hard to see how they could have—the use of campaign funds to obscure or mitigate the impact of unrepresentative activities is problematic. Let us suppose that not a single Republican contributor received any type of special treatment from the members that accepted his or her contribution. This is obviously an unrealistic assumption, but even if it were not, the use of campaign funds to preempt the expression of a constituency's true preferences is pathological.

Of course, some will say voters can always vote for whomever they wish; the money doesn't matter. That is true as long as the financial imbalance between the candidates is not so great as to tangibly affect the character and quality of the campaigns they run. Unfortunately, the financial imbalance between incumbents and challengers is that great, and the idea that gross disparities in campaign resources do not tip the scales heavily toward incumbents is naive. Even if we assume there is no quid pro quo relationship (which is unrealistic), we do not escape the representational thicket. Some crucial questions are unavoidable. Is it possible that financial resources paved the way for Clinton's impeachment, or at the very least enabled the conservative Republicans who pushed it through the House? Specifically, is there evidence of a trade-off between constituency opposition to impeachment and campaign funding levels? And now, some answers.

Impeachment Votes and Campaign Funding

Traditionally, Republican candidates have had a significant fundraising advantage over Democratic candidates (see Herrnson 2000). In one way, this fundraising advantage evaporated during the 1999–2000 election cycle. The campaign finance figures for the that election cycle show Democrats and Republicans in nearly a dead heat—$235,308,296 for House Democrats and $234,529,537 for House Republicans—but the Republicans have a significant advantage, nearly $7 million, once candidate contributions and candidate loans to their own campaigns are subtracted. More specifically, Republican incumbents outspent their Democratic counterparts by more than $120,000 per member, and Republican incumbents outspent Democratic challengers by more than $440,000 per member. Even these disparities understate the real gaps realized during the campaign period. During the first 15 months of the 2000 election cycle, House Republicans raised more money than their Democratic counterparts, and the gap between Republican incumbents and Democratic incumbents was even larger.[4]

Because campaign funds can enhance and increase advertising opportunities, some House Republicans might reasonably have gambled that they could raise sufficient campaign funds to overcome the negative electoral repercussions of an unpopular impeachment vote. On the other hand, few Democrats could afford to cross their constituents *and* their party leadership to support one or more of the articles of impeachment against the president. If Republicans perceived some trade-off between angered constituents and financial resources, then we should be able to find a clear and direct relationship between constituency opposition to impeachment and campaign receipts. This relationship should be especially strong for individuals, such as the House managers, who were prominent supporters of Clinton's impeachment.

To examine the impact of unpopular impeachment votes on campaign fundraising, I estimate regression models for both PAC contributions and individual contributions made to House incumbents from each of the major parties.[5] Because previous research indicates that a number of factors unrelated to the current issues of interest affect differences in campaign receipts—for example, leadership positions, previous vote margins, and ideology (see Herrnson 2000 and Jacobson 2001 for a review of this voluminous literature)—I include several control variables.[6]

In Table 6.1,[7] the model estimates for PAC contributions for Republicans clearly show that district-level opposition to the Clinton impeachment is directly related to funding levels. Even when con-

TABLE 6.1   Explaining PAC Contributions to House Republicans[*]

Variable	Parameter Estimate	Standard Error	t Value	Pr>|t|
Intercept	-149318	139230	-1.07	0.2851
PAC98	0.73956	0.06879	10.75	<.0001
VOTE98	67.06324	842.7976	0.08	0.9367
SENIOR	1292.009	1863.964	0.69	0.4892
LEAD	234592	93195	2.52	0.0128
IMPOPP	4450.318	2147.009	2.07	0.0398
MANAGER	-2039.22	54898	-0.04	0.9704
ROGAN	383956	163077	2.35	0.0197
ANTIPARTY	-56456	77798	-0.73	0.4691

$R^2 = 0.5513$
Adj $R^2 = 0.5293$

[*]Note that the campaign finance data for the 2000 election cycle used to produce the results presented in this table—and subsequent tables in this chapter—only include contributions through October 18, 2000. Complete data were unavailable at the time of the analysis.

trolling for leadership status, PAC contributions in the 1997–1998 electoral cycle, and vote share in the 1998 election, PAC funding was positively and significantly related to constituency opposition to impeachment. Every percentage point increase in district-level opposition to impeachment results in an increase of over $4,450 in PAC contributions. A 10-percentage-point difference between one representative's constituency and another representative's constituency would result in a $44,500 gap in campaign funding (all else being equal), with the representative from the constituency where the opposition to impeachment was greater raising the larger sum of money. On average, if opposition to impeachment (IM-POPP) were 55 percent in a representative's district, then just under a quarter of a million dollars ($244,750) of the representative's war chest would be attributable to efforts to raise PAC money to compensate for the unpopularity of impeachment.

This affect is not limited, somewhat surprisingly, to those individuals serving districts where opposition to Clinton's impeachment was especially strong. Although I do not present these results, even after incorporating (1) a dummy variable for districts in which opposition to impeachment was greater than 60 percent of the voting population and (2) an interactive term tapping the relationship between opposition and contributions for this group of incumbents, the overall opposition variable (IMPOPP) is still highly significant.[8] For Republican incumbents there is a general relationship between constituency opposition to the Clinton impeachment and increased PAC contributions.

This is a surprising finding, and it raises an important question. Why isn't the "impeachment" money limited to congressional districts in which impeachment was actually opposed by a large majority of the constituency? One explanation of why impeachment monies were not limited to these particular districts is that the impeachment issue produced a widespread devaluation of the Republican Party label. To return to that desirable electoral equilibrium that Fenno (2000) describes, Republicans everywhere were forced to raise extra campaign money. How much extra money had to be raised depended on the specific level of opposition to impeachment in one's district. Although Republicans in general raised money to combat the impeachment albatross, those who served districts in which impeachment was especially unpopular raised significantly more money.

The sign of the ANTIPARTY variable suggests that votes against impeachment, among Republicans, are associated with lower levels of PAC contributions, but the variable is statistically insignificant. The small number of impeachment opponents on the Republican side (five) makes it difficult, however, to draw statistically significant inferences, so a substantively important relationship may exist where statistical significance cannot be demonstrated. Somewhat surprisingly, there is no evidence that the House managers for the Senate impeachment trial differ—in terms of PAC campaign contributions—from their Republican colleagues. That House leaders receive inordinately large levels of PAC money is no surprise.

The political and institutional determinants of the total value of *individual* contributions present a somewhat different picture of the role of impeachment politics in campaign financing. First, just as in the case of PAC fundraising, we find a strong positive relationship between constituency opposition to impeachment and fundraising levels. According to the results presented in Table 6.2, every percentage point increase in constituency opposition to impeachment resulted in an increase of more than $8,200 in campaign funds raised from individual contributors. Unlike the case for PAC contributions, the House manager dummy variable is large, highly significant, and positively signed, indicating that the managers received significantly more in the way of individual contributions than did other Republican incumbents.[9] Even without the enormous Rogan war chest included in the House manager category (because there is a separate variable for Rogan), the impeachment boost in House manager funding is enormous (more than $400,000). Bob Barr (R.–Ga.) raised almost $3 million from individual contributions, and Henry Hyde (R.–Ill.) raised well over $2 million. Among House candidates (incumbents and challengers), House managers were first, third, and sixth on the individual contributions money list, and they were first, second, and fourth among Republicans on that list.[10]

TABLE 6.2   Explaining Individual Contributions to House Republicans

Variable	Parameter Estimate	Standard Error	t Value	Pr>|t|
Intercept	-248119	234415	-1.06	0.2914
IND98	0.84328	0.08049	10.48	<.0001
VOTE98	-1555.71	1421.008	-1.09	0.2752
SENIOR	1342.416	3121.062	0.43	0.6677
LEAD	-7174.74	153978	-0.05	0.9629
IMPOPP	8250.289	3600.004	2.29	0.0232
MANAGER	431408	92043	4.69	<.0001
ROGAN	4035867	271168	14.88	<.0001
ANTIPARTY	-71118	130137	-0.55	0.5855

$R^2 = 0.7632$
Adj $R^2 = 0.7516$

TABLE 6.3   Explaining PAC Contributions to House Democrats

Variable	Parameter Estimate	Standard Error	t Value	Pr>|t|
Intercept	86618	73835	1.17	0.2424
PAC98	0.72565	0.0534	13.59	<.0001
VOTE98	5.08422	20.84393	0.24	0.8076
SENIOR	4055.859	1162.987	3049	0.0006
LEAD	-39496	89661	-0.44	0.6601
IMPOPP	-573.174	920.3687	-0.62	0.5343
ANTIPARTY	-36849	60453	-0.61	0.543

$R^2 = 0.6376$
Adj $R^2 = 0.6246$

Comparable models for Democratic incumbents[11] present a strikingly different picture of the political dynamics of both individual contribution patterns and PAC contribution patterns. (See Tables 6.3 and 6.4.) In neither case is there a significant relationship between constituency opposition to impeachment and contribution levels. For Democrats, votes on the Clinton impeachment played no role—or no significant role—in subsequent funding dynamics. Al-

TABLE 6.4   Explaining Individual Contributions to House Democrats

Variable	Parameter Estimate	Standard Error	t Value	Pr>|t|
Intercept	228330	112420	2.03	0.0438
IND98	0.50127	0.04947	10.13	<.0001
VOTE98	-8.33635	35.19104	-0.24	0.813
SENIOR	-317.883	1985.273	-0.16	0.873
LEAD	84751	154890	0.55	0.585
IMPOPP	-920.035	1468.023	-0.63	0.5317
ANTIPARTY	-104021	101883	-1.02	0.3087

$R^2 = 0.4646$
Adj $R^2 = 0.4454$

though district-level opposition to impeachment is clearly related to campaign fundraising on the Republican side of the aisle, there is no relationship between these two variables among Democrats.

Perhaps most interesting, constituency opposition to impeachment was positively and significantly related to overall campaign fundraising among Democratic challengers. In fact, the overall funding boost per percentage point change in constituency opposition to impeachment was greater for Democratic challengers (just over $18,300) than for Republican incumbents ($12,700).[12] I also find a huge funding boost (over $500,000) for those Democrats who challenged House managers. (See Table 6.5)

There is some evidence, then, that Democrats were targeting (at least with respect to their fundraising) the Republican incumbents most likely to be vulnerable because of their stand on impeachment or their role in the impeachment process. It is important to note that the underlying structural fundraising disadvantage faced by challengers is far too great to be overcome by the relative difference in "impeachment" funds. Although Democratic challengers were able to boost their own campaign fundraising because of the unpopularity of the Clinton impeachment, the funding increase was far too small to overcome the general fundraising advantage enjoyed by Republican incumbants.

TABLE 6.5   Explaining Overall Contributions to the Challengers of
House Republicans

Variable	Parameter Estimate	Standard Error	t Value	Pr>|t|
Intercept	-268053	404819	-0.66	0.5088
TOT98	0.07741	0.08931	0.87	0.3874
VOTE98	-7588.48	2474.95	-3.07	0.0025
SENIOR	-3437.63	5362.951	-0.64	0.5224
LEAD	-42660	259699	-0.16	0.8697
IMPOPP	18351	6488.025	2.83	0.0053
MANAGER	504809	160277	3.15	0.0019
ROGAN	2854232	473206	6.03	<.0001
ANTIPARTY	185734	226546	0.82	0.4135

$R^2 = 0.4021$
Adj $R^2 = 0.3727$

Conclusion

Where others see the play of partisanship and the conviction of personal ethics, I find many legislators following the lead of their constituents. In this respect, the politics of impeachment were in no way exceptional. After estimating district-level opinion on the issue of impeachment, I show that nearly all Democrats and a nontrivial number of Republicans voted in a manner consistent with their constituents' preferences. Explaining the behavior of a large number of representatives does not require the assumption of unusual partisan dynamics or an acceptance of the self-sacrificing (and electorally-disadvantageous) obligation of personal ethics.

Constituency pressures do not, however, provide a complete explanation for the legislative politics of impeachment. A significant number of Republican representatives clearly behaved in a manner that was inconsistent with the wishes of those they represent. It is these Republicans who made the greatest effort during this electoral cycle to raise campaign funds. The data indicate that constituency-level opposition to Clinton's impeachment is directly associated with increased campaign receipts among Republicans. The impact of constituency-level opposition to impeachment on campaign receipts among the House managers is even greater.

Campaign fundraising, by itself, is not especially problematic from the standpoint of democratic theory. But if fundraising (and campaign spending) affect electoral outcomes, then we must begin to question the effectiveness of our system of representation, and the proper role of campaign funds in democratic elections must be revisited. In the next chapter, I examine the impact of impeachment funds on the 2000 House elections.

Appendix

Variable List

LEADER—*a dummy variable coded 1 for the Speaker of the House, majority leader, minority leader, and both party whips and 0 otherwise*

SENIOR—*number of years served in the House of Representatives by the incumbent as of 2000*

VOTE98—*percentage of the two-party vote received by the incumbent in the 1998 election*

IMPOPP—*a measure of the percentage of constituents opposed to Clinton's impeachment*

ANTIPARTY—*a dummy variable coded 1 for Republicans opposing all impeachment articles and Democrats supporting one or more impeachment articles and 0 otherwise*

MANAGER—*a dummy variable coded 1 for representatives who served as House managers for the Senate impeachment trial and 0 otherwise*

ROGAN—*a dummy variable coded 1 for Representative James Rogan and 0 otherwise*

IND98—*individuals' contributions to the incumbent's campaign during the 1997–1998 electoral cycle*

PAC98—*PAC contributions to the incumbent's campaign during the 1997–1998 electoral cycle*

7

ELECTORAL AFTERMATH: THE WAGES OF IMPEACHMENT IN THE HOUSE

Contrary to conventional wisdom, votes on impeachment and subsequent conviction were, to a significant extent, a function of constituency preferences. Although ideology also played a role, we cannot ignore the fact that the majority of representatives and senators simply voted in a manner consistent with the preferences of the voters in their geographic constituencies.

But many legislators clearly did not follow their constituents on the issues of impeachment and conviction. We also know that, at least for Republican House members, efforts were made to respond to this electorally unpopular voting behavior by raising extra campaign funds to enhance their electoral appeal. In this chapter, I examine the electoral impact of impeachment votes and legislators' attempts to preempt or mitigate the negative fallout associated with those votes. What I find is striking. Among House Republicans votes against impeachment were costly in terms of vote margins, but the campaign funds raised in response to the unpopularity of the votes (and the party's general association with the impeachment issue) prevented the party from losing control of the House of Representatives.

Impact of Impeachment Votes on
Election Results: The House

There is no simple way to evaluate the electoral impact of the roll call votes cast on the articles of impeachment. The reason for this is that we must take into account preemptive efforts made by representatives who supported impeachment to offset the voters' negative backlash against them. The especially difficult part of this is estimating the impact of campaign expenditures on vote margins. Although there is a sizable (and constantly growing) literature on the impact of campaign funds on congressional elections, it is not a monolithic (or consistent) literature. I begin by describing the basic development of the research on financial determinants of electoral outcomes, focusing on the most significant recent work. I then explain the method I used to estimate the impact of campaign funds on electoral outcomes for the 2000 election specifically, and the impact of impeachment votes on the 2000 election more generally.

Since Gary Jacobson's widely-cited APSR article in 1978, a consensus has developed around the proposition that challenger expenditures are directly and positively related to the proportion of voters supporting the challenger in House elections. Subsequent research has reinforced this initial finding (see Abramowitz 1991; Erikson and Palfrey 1993, 1998; and Green and Krasno 1988). There is little doubt that challenger success is directly related to campaign expenditures. Incumbents enjoy significant advantages in elections against challengers. Incumbents enjoy a variety of institutional benefits that make competing against them difficult. And their name recognition—an important factor in electoral success—is often significantly greater than the name recognition their challengers enjoy. Challengers unable to raise significant campaign funds are rarely competitive.

However, challengers who are able to match or exceed incumbent campaign receipts can compete with and often defeat incumbents. Challengers who fail to compete in the race for dollars nearly always lose the race for votes.[1] Because the inherent advantages of incumbency are so difficult to overcome, it is often difficult for challengers to raise campaign funds. Challengers rarely win, so investing in their campaigns rarely pays a significant return for the contributor (individual or PAC). The ability of a challenger to raise a significant amount of money is usually a sign that he or she is more competitive vis-à-vis the incumbent than an average challenger. This may be due to the strength of the challenger—for example, extensive experience as an elected official—or the weakness of the incumbent—for example, involvement in a serious scandal—or both (see Herrnson 2000; Jacobson 2001). This interactive effect obscures the impact of challenger campaign spending on vote margins. Do quality challengers win because they are quality challengers, or do they win because they are able to raise significant campaign funds?

Likewise, incumbents who face well-funded challengers generally raise and spend more campaign funds than incumbents who do not face significant opponents. Unfortunately, this perfectly reasonable strategic reaction makes it difficult to separate the independent impact of incumbent campaign spending on vote margins. All else being equal, the incumbents in the tightest races are the most likely to have a poor showing or to lose. Because these are the same candidates who raise and spend the most campaign money, it would appear that—at least in the case of incumbents—the more money raised and spent, the smaller one's electoral margin and the more likely one is to lose. Of course, it seems likely that incumbents in trouble would do even worse if they spent less money.

In methodological terms, conventional procedures for estimating the impact of campaign expenditures on vote margins suffer from *simultaneity bias,* a problem that occurs when one or more factors (such as competitiveness of the race) affect both the independent variable (campaign spending) and the dependent variable (vote margin) at the same time. If this bias is ignored, statistical analysis may produce counter-intuitive and spurious results (such as a negative relationship between incumbent spending and vote margin). As Robert Erikson and Thomas Palfrey explain:

> The obvious reason for the near-zero coefficients for incumbent
> spending using OLS is a simultaneity bias, because incumbents

spend more when they are in electoral trouble. Somewhat less obvious, and less commonly acknowledged, is that the opposite bias
can be present for challengers, who spend more when their
prospects are good. In short, the OLS estimates are biased because one is not controlling for candidates' expectations of the
vote, and these expectations drive spending decisions. (2000:
595)

Statistical solutions to this simultaneity problem involve some
type of procedure for generating prior estimates of race competitiveness from variables that precede the race itself. Some researchers use
two-stage least squares to construct instruments of incumbent
spending in which the simultaneity bias has been removed (Green
and Krasno 1988; Gerber 1998). Erikson and Palfrey (1993, 1998)
set restrictions on the variance-covariance matrix to generate acceptable estimates for the impact of campaign spending, and Alan
Abramowitz (1991) attempts to control for race competitiveness by
including a variable based on the *Congressional Quarterly* estimate
of campaign competitiveness in his regressions of incumbent and
challenger spending on vote margin.

According to Erikson and Palfrey (2000), none of these statistical
solutions fully addresses the simultaneity problem. Using an ingen-
ious application of game theory, Erikson and Palfrey (2000) argue
that both challengers and incumbents react strategically to the likely
competitiveness of their electoral races, and that these strategic reactions indicate that the extent to which the simultaneity bias generates inferential difficulties is a function of the closeness of the race
itself. In races that are expected to be extremely close (prior to accounting for spending effects), the simultaneity bias is likely to approximate zero. In races in which the incumbent has a significant
advantage, the simultaneity bias is likely to be extreme. To accurately estimate the role of campaign fundraising and spending on
electoral outcomes, one must allow for this variance in the simultaneity bias.

Erikson and Palfrey (2000) use conventional OLS analysis to estimate spending effects for House incumbents and challengers, but

they generate these estimates for separate samples of incumbents and challengers. Incumbents and challengers are distributed among the samples (as pairs, obviously) according to the likely competitiveness of their electoral race. Erikson and Palfrey use two different indicators of competitiveness and find comparable results for samples based on either. One indicator of competitiveness is an "expected vote" variable, which is a predictor of actual vote margin created by regressing "pre-spending" variables—district presidential vote for the incumbent's party (by decade), incumbent party, a dummy variable for Southern states, and all of the possible interactive terms—on final vote margin. Using the coefficients from this regression and the actual values for each contest, one can calculate a "pre-spending" vote margin prediction. In election samples divided according to expected vote for the incumbent—less than 52 percent, 52–55 percent, 55–58 percent, and greater than 58 percent—Erikson and Palfrey show that the impact of incumbent and challenger spending is nearly identical for the closest races, and that the relative impact of challenger spending increases as the incumbent's advantage increases.

A second indicator of competitiveness is *Congressional Quarterly's* estimate of the expected election outcome for all House seats, published in October of each election year. *CQ* places each race in one of the following outcome categories: favors the challenger, too close to call, leans for the incumbent, incumbent favored, and safe for the incumbent. After dividing elections into three categories—close (challenger favored or too close to call), leaning (leans toward incumbent or incumbent favored), and safe (safe for incumbent)—Erikson and Palfrey generate results comparable to those based on the quantitative estimates of electoral competitiveness. In close races, incumbent and challenger spending effects are almost identical. In leaning races, incumbent spending still has a positive impact on incumbent vote margin, but the per dollar impact is approximately half the per dollar impact of challenger spending. In safe races, incumbent spending has no statistically significant impact on vote margin, whereas challenger spending is still important. According to Erikson and Palfrey:

... [A]s one moves from competitive to safe districts, the OLS estimate of incumbent spending collapses due to the increased bias plus a possible decline in spending effectiveness when the seat is safe. Meanwhile the OLS estimate of the challenger spending effect stays roughly constant, as the lesser bias may decline only modestly and is offset by the decline in spending effectiveness. (2000: 604)

To estimate the impact of campaign fundraising on electoral outcomes, I modified Erikson and Palfrey's methodology for the particular circumstances associated with the 2000 election. First, because of the nature of the 2000 election, I included several time-specific variables in the model used to generate the "Expected Vote" estimates. Specifically, I replaced the decade-level presidential vote by district with the "Opposition to Impeachment" variable described previously. I also included the "Manager" dummy variable, an "Antiparty" dummy variable (for individuals voting against the majority position in their party), and an "Opposition to Impeachment x Party" interactive term. Because the values for each of these variables were determined prior to the beginning of the 2000 election cycle, there should be no simultaneity bias with campaign fundraising. Although these types of campaign specific variables were not an option for Erikson and Palfrey because of the structure of their analysis (over an extended timeframe), they might reasonably generate more accurate predictions of the final vote margin for elections in 2000. And, after comparing the results from my model of the "Expected Vote" with Erikson and Palfrey's, I have found that to be the case.[2]

I have also chosen to use campaign funds raised rather than campaign funds spent for the challenger and incumbent funding variables. I have done this because campaign expenditures fail to fully capture the electoral impact of money on House elections. When significant gaps exist between funds raised and funds spent (which, according to Federal Election Commission data, is relatively rare), campaign expenditures underestimate the impact of money on House elections. Whereas challengers nearly always spend as much money as they raise, incumbents may sometimes raise huge campaign war chests in the hopes that the size of the campaign bankroll will scare off potential challengers, so incumbents sometimes raise money that they never intend to spend.[3]

Results for the House

To generate spending estimates for members of the House of Representatives, I used the following variables:

VT98—percentage of the two-party vote received by the candidate in 1998

IMPOPP—percentage of constituents opposed to impeachment

SOUTH—a dummy variable coded 1 for each of the Southern states, 0 otherwise[4]

PARTY—a dummy variable coded 1 for each Democrat and 0 for each Republican (Independents were excluded from the analysis)

MANAGER—a dummy variable coded 1 for each of the House impeachment managers, 0 otherwise

ANTIPARTY—a dummy variable coded 1 for all Republicans who voted against all articles of impeachment and for all Democrats who voted for one or more articles of impeachment

I also included the following interactive terms: IMPOPP*PARTY, SOUTH*PARTY, and ANTIPARTY*PARTY to generate separate estimates for Democrats and Republicans.[5] The sample was limited to those individuals who faced competition in both 1998 and 2000.[6]

As expected, previous vote margin (VT98) was positively and significantly associated with current vote margin (see Table 7.1). As previous vote margin increased, so did current vote margin, although the coefficient on VT98 (.59) indicates that there was some significant slippage between the two elections. I also found, as expected, that constituency opposition to impeachment significantly increased the vote percentage for Democrats and significantly de-

TABLE 7.1   Predicting 2000 Vote Margin from Pre-election Cycle Variables

Variable	Parameter Estimate	Standard Error	t Value	Pr>|t|
Intercept	40.40858	6.65095	6.08	<.0001
VT98	0.59116	0.05052	11.7	<.0001
IMPOPP	-0.24576	0.09027	-2.72	0.007
IMPOPP*PARTY	0.51686	0.11959	4.32	<.0001
SOUTH	0.19822	1.19155	0.17	0.868
SOUTH*PARTY	-4.18347	1.74932	-2.39	0.0176
PARTY	-28.2996	6.89147	-4.11	<.0001
ANTIPARTY	-1.10302	2.29064	-0.48	0.6306
ANTIPARTY* PARTY	8.03107	4.37688	1.83	0.0679
MANAGER	-7.00795	1.99537	-3.51	0.0005

$R^2 = .5675$
Adj $R^2 = .55$
$N = 47$

creased the vote percentage for Republicans. All else being equal, Republicans lost over one-quarter of a percentage point for each one point increase in opposition to Clinton's impeachment, whereas the coefficient on the IMPOPP*PARTY variable suggests that Democrats gained votes for each percentage point increase in opposition to Clinton's impeachment. The significant negative co-efficient on the "Party" variable suggests that, all else being equal, Democrats tended to be less successful than their Republican counterparts, but, because of the considerable difference in the impact of opposition to the Clinton impeachment, the raw vote margins do not reflect this baseline advantage.

Region had no effect on Republican vote percentages, but Democrats from the South tended to do slightly worse than fellow partisans from other regions. There is also some evidence suggesting that voting against one's party on the issue of impeachment could be electorally beneficial, at least for Democrats. Democrats who supported one or more of the articles of impeachment tended to receive slightly higher vote percentages than their colleagues. There is no evidence that failing to vote for any of the articles of impeachment (for Republicans) had any negative (or positive) effect on vote percentages.

Finally, serving as a House manager had a significant negative impact on vote percentages. Among all incumbents who won House races in both 1998 and 2000, non-managers received 71.8 percent of their district vote in 1998 and 73.1 percent of their district vote in 2000. The managers who competed for House seats in 2000 received 76.1 percent of their district vote in 1998, doing slightly better than their fellow representatives. However, in 2000, House managers received less than 65.6 percent of their district's vote, more than 10 percentage points less than their colleagues. This figure also does not account for the fact that the manager who attempted to win higher office in 2000—Bill McCollum campaigned for a Senate seat in Florida—lost his election by a considerable margin. Clearly, serving as a House manager was an electorally problematic strategy, an obvious reason for the significant increase in campaign fundraising by House managers documented in Chapter 6.

Because the values for each of the variables included in the model were determined prior to the beginning of the 2000 election cycle (or nearly so, since the House managers would not have been chosen until just after the 1998 election), they can be used to construct predictions of 2000 vote margins that are not affected by campaign fundraising or campaign expenditures (see Erikson and Palfrey 2000). Using the predicted values for 2000 vote percentages and data on both incumbent campaign fundraising and challenger campaign fundraising, one can estimate the impact of fundraising on actual 2000 vote percentages.

As Erikson and Palfrey (2000) argue, the bias introduced into the spending coefficients is a function of the relative likelihood of victory. The closer the likelihood of a dead heat election, the smaller the bias in the funding coefficients. To avoid the problems associated with differential bias levels within the same sample, I divided—as Erikson and Palfrey suggest—the 2000 House elections in which incumbents faced opposition into three categories based on *Congressional Quarterly*'s ranking of race competitiveness. The first category of races includes those incumbents who faced challengers who were favored and those incumbents in races in which there was no clear favorite. This is an exceptionally small category. It includes only five incumbents, and one of these, Michael P. Forbes, was running as an Independent because he failed to win the Democratic Party primary for his congressional district after switching from the Republican Party.[7] This sample is so small it is not possible to generate robust estimates of campaign spending effects or reasonably evaluate the statistical significance of these effects. This is especially unfortunate, because it is in this group that we would expect to see the greatest spending effects. As for incumbents in "safe" seats, I found no evidence of an incumbent spending effect. This is almost certainly because of the considerable variance in bias inherent in the data for this group. The results for incumbents in "safe" seats are consistent with the findings of Erikson and Palfrey (2000).[8]

A list of incumbents in close or competitive races is presented in Table 7.2. Note that both Democrats and Republicans are included, and that some of these races ended up quite one-sided. The results for the fundraising effects model for this sample of incumbents are presented in Table 7.3. As expected, the predicted vote variable is significant and correctly signed. The higher the vote percentage predicted by pre-election cycle variables, the higher the final vote percentage. But even when this prediction variable is included,[9] both challenger spending and incumbent spending matter. As challenger fundraising goes up, challengers' vote percentages increase. As incumbent spending increases, incumbents' vote percentages increase. Interestingly, given the distinctiveness of the sample, the coefficients are quite similar to the coefficient estimates generated by Erikson and Palfrey (2000).

According to the regression coefficients, a 1-point increase in the log of incumbent spending raises the actual vote received by the incumbent approximately 3 percentage points. A comparable increase in the log of challenger spending reduces the incumbent's actual vote by over 2.5 percentage points. Because the incumbent and challenger spending variables are in log terms, change in vote percentage generated by a certain dollar amount expenditure depends on the original funding baseline. For example, a funding increase from just under $200,000 to $500,000 dollars would result in a 1-point increase in the log of funding dollars. If the original baseline were $1,000,000, a 1-point increase in the log of funding dollars would require a funding increase in excess of $1.7 million. As the baseline increases, the dollars required to generate constant changes in vote percentages increase. This reflects the contention that campaign contributions are subject to diminishing marginal returns. The literature on campaign financing and election outcomes clearly indicates that the first $100,000 raised has a much greater impact on vote outcomes than an extra $100,000 added to an already enormous, multi-million-dollar campaign war chest (see Herrnson 2000; Jacobson 2001).

The most important result, for our purposes, is that incumbent fundraising significantly influences electoral outcomes. Results presented in Chapter 6 clearly demonstrate that Republicans in districts in which the Clinton impeachment was unpopular raised extra campaign money to offset the unpopularity of their (and their party's) support for impeachment: As district-level opposition increased, fundraising (both from individuals and from PACS) increased. Likewise, we found that House managers raised hundreds of thousands (in James Rogan's case, millions) of dollars more than their comparably situated Republican colleagues who were not impeachment managers. Now that we have established that incumbent fundraising has a statistically significant and substantively important impact on vote margins, we can reasonably raise the following two important questions:

1. Did the extra fundraising by Republican incumbents actually affect electoral outcomes? It is one thing to alter vote margins; it is something else to actually change who wins and who loses. Incumbents, even those in close or competitive races, start out with such a significant advantage that there is no guarantee that the shift of a few points here or there would make a meaningful difference in determining actual electoral outcomes.

132

TABLE 7.2 Incumbents in Races "that Leaned" Towards the Incumbent or in Races in Which the Incumbent Was "Favored"*

Name	State	District	Party	Actual Vote 2000	Predicted Vote 2000	Total Receipts	Opponent's Total Receipts
DICKEY	AR	4	REP	49	56.8933	1525886	1474113
MINGE	MN	2	DEM	50	60.3996	685601	691081
HORN	CA	38	REP	51	56.54	433336	579940
LUTHER	MN	6	DEM	51	60.3734	1349678	1156004
ROEMER	IN	3	DEM	52	61.4117	578446	884116
BISHOP	GA	2	DEM	53	60.5775	893063	893757
DOOLEY	CA	20	DEM	54	64.5198	1419503	687063
CAPPS	CA	22	DEM	54	59.0092	1506455	686141
BARR	GA	7	REP	54	52.9127	3048115	3781644
NORTHUP	KY	3	REP	54	54.8316	2441164	1593994
SUNUNU	NH	1	REP	54	66.0472	484354	638519
WILSON	NM	1	REP	54	55.0629	1972254	1131914
TAUSCHER	CA	10	DEM	55	59.0753	1425376	946089
EVANS	IL	17	DEM	55	58.6055	1150578	785686
CHABOT	OH	1	REP	55	48.2183	1003536	429054
SESSIONS	TX	5	REP	55	58.7356	1746567	1538286
TIAHRT	KS	4	REP	56	62.8611	653465	264069
TAYLOR	NC	11	REP	56	60.6055	843598	868707
SANDLIN	TX	1	DEM	56	59.5021	1519256	171550
HOOLEY	OR	5	DEM	57	59.4465	817954	162827
SNYDER	AR	2	DEM	58	60.4265	550726	216216
BROWN	FL	3	DEM	58	61.9026	543784	828182

WHITFIELD	KY	1	REP	58	58.8753	1609272	637523
GUTKNECHT	MN	1	REP	58	58.9577	934305	347766
ETHRIDGE	NC	2	DEM	58	58.1534	1030216	237248
BASS	NH	2	REP	58	57.6978	698499	808084
SAXTON	NJ	3	REP	58	62.3427	1616785	1655144
CHAMBLISS	GA	8	REP	59	61.2595	1672237	880413
STUPAK	MI	1	DEM	59	61.7676	891344	621942
STRICKLAND	OH	6	DEM	59	62.2401	695350	173302
WELDON	FL	15	REP	60	64.8028	721458	478155
LUCAS	OK	6	REP	60	65.0957	531596	551448
SPRATT	SC	5	DEM	60	60.0083	1065163	316769
PAUL	TX	14	REP	60	59.7022	2187471	1147629
NETHERCUTT	WA	5	REP	60	61.0241	1474691	459014
McCARTHY	NY	4	DEM	61	61.3186	1842180	224664
ADERHOLT	AL	4	REP	62	60.4951	1598189	1151212
PRICE	NC	4	DEM	62	59.2045	736463	36368
KOLBE	AZ	5	REP	63	57.8058	1314350	450620
GORDON	TN	6	DEM	63	55.5747	1109046	150541
BENTSEN	TX	25	DEM	63	60.394	1064842	2689340
SMITH	WA	9	DEM	64	66.5571	1134014	539360
WATT	NC	12	DEM	66	63.969	278356	23492
NEY	OH	18	REP	66	62.2185	841283	201009
HILLEARY	TN	4	REP	66	62.0805	1283165	985089
QUINN	NY	30	REP	67	63.8578	881834	186931
THORNBERRY	TX	13	REP	68	67.8852	650543	340167

*Note that the campaign finance data for 2000 presented in this table only include contributions through October 18, 2000. Complete data were unavailable at the time of the analysis.

TABLE 7.3   Estimating the Impact of Campaign Fundraising on
Election Outcomes in the House (in Races that Leaned to the Incumbent or
in Which the Incumbent was Favored)[*]

Variable	Parameter Estimate	Standard Error	t Value	Pr>|t|
Intercept	14.97331	23.82303	0.63	0.533
Log of incumbent funds	3.01467	1.44986	2.08	0.0436
Log of challenger funds	-2.54154	0.69604	-3.65	0.0007
PREDICT	0.57828	0.17353	3.33	0.0018

$R^2 = .3739$
Adj $R^2 = .3302$
$N = 47$

[*]Note that the campaign finance data for the 2000 election cycle used to produce the results in this table—and subsequent tables in this chapter—only include contributions through October 18, 2000. Complete data were unavailable at the time of the analysis.

2. If the answer to the first question is affirmative, was the impact on electoral outcomes sufficient to affect the partisan control of the House of Representatives? Even if actual outcomes are effected, it would take more than a couple of seat changes to shift control of the House from the Republicans to the Democrats.

The short answer to both questions is "yes."

From the analysis presented in Chapter 4 we know that district opposition to impeachment positively affected campaign fundraising for Republicans, as did House manager status. Using the coefficients from the individual contribution and PAC contribution models for Republicans, it is possible to estimate the dollar value impact of these factors (constituency opposition to impeachment and manager status) on overall fundraising. To gauge the impact of the "impeachment" funds, first calculate the log of the campaign funds raised by each of the at-risk Republican incumbents. Then calculate the log of remaining campaign funds for each at-risk Republican after the "impeachment" funds have been subtracted (those funds raised because of district-level opposition to impeachment and manager status).[10] Finally, subtract the second number from the first and multiply by the incumbent spending coefficient generated from the results presented in Table 7.3.

To illustrate these calculations, consider the case of George Nethercutt (R.–Wash.). Nethercutt raised $1,474,691. The percentage of his constituents opposed to impeachment was 53.08. If we multiply 53.08 by $12,700 (the estimated amount raised by Republicans for every percentage point of opposition to impeachment), the product is $674,116. The log of 1,474,691 is 14.204, and the log of the difference between 1,474,691 and 674,116 is 13.593. The difference between these two logs is 0.611, and when we multiply this difference by 3.0146 (the spending coefficient from the multivariate model), the product is 1.84. This indicates that Nethercutt's "impeachment" spending resulted in an increase of 1.84 percentage points in his vote margin. We can make similar calculations for Steve Chabot, but we must also add the House manager premium ($431,048). When we do this, Chabot's spending estimate is actually negative. To avoid taking the log of negative numbers, we force all individual spending estimates to be no less than $5,000 (the same amount Erikson and Palfrey add to each candidate's spending total). The electoral impact of Chabot's fundraising was nearly 10 percentage points.[11]

Although a few members' funding estimates may be artificially low—it is highly unlikely that many incumbents would spend as little as $5,000—some members' funding estimates are almost certainly too high. For example, Wilson (R.–N.Mex.) spent less than $65,000 dollars on her 1998 campaign and nearly $2 million on her 2000 campaign. My estimates indicate that significantly less than half of the increase ($727,000) was attributable to the "impeachment" boost. The underestimate here prevents me from moving her to the "loss" category. Likewise, Bob Barr (R.–Ga.) more than doubled his 1998 campaign expenditures in 2000. Even including the manager premium, there is still a sizable gap between his estimated 2000 expenditures and his 1998 expenditures.

TABLE 7.4   Incumbents Saved by Impeachment Funds
(Aggregate Results)

Incumbent	Actual Percent of the Two-Party Vote
HORN	51
HOSTETTLER	53
SUNUNU	54
BARR	54
WILSON	54
NORTHRUP	54
CHABOT	55
SESSIONS	55
TIAHRT	56

Of course, there are some individuals whose impeachment fund estimates are likely to be extremely close to the actual "impeachment" boost. Kolbe (R.–Ariz.) raised just over half a million dollars in 1998 and over $1.3 million in 2000. If we exclude the estimated impeachment premium (just under $680,000), we have a spending estimate of $637,000, still more than a 20 percent increase from one election to the next, but not an unreasonable increase in an unexceptional (i.e., non-impeachment) time period. The gist of the examples presented above is that—as we would expect—some estimates of the "impeachment" premium are probably too high, whereas others are either too low or just about right. There is no evidence, however, that the estimate of the average "impeachment" premium—or the average electoral effect of the impeachment premium—is positively biased. If anything, establishing a positive floor for funding estimates in the thousands of dollars biases the results negatively. These results are likely to underestimate the number of Republicans who owe their current House seats to money they raised to counts the unpopularity of the impeachment saga. Finally, it is worth noting that even after the "impeachment" funds are subtracted, the Republican incumbents in this sample still raised nearly twice as much money as the average Democratic challenger.

TABLE 7.5   Incumbents Saved by Impeachment Funds
(Individual Results)

Incumbent	Actual Percent of the Two-Party Vote
HORN	51
HOSTETTLER	53
SUNUNU	54
CHABOT	55
TIAHRT	56
BASS	58
LUCAS	60

The average spending effect estimate generated from the calculations described here is 6.36 percentage points. If we assume that the aggregate vote reduction affected all candidates equally, then incumbents receiving 56 percent of the two-party vote (or less) would have lost their re-election bids. (See Table 7.4.) Nine Republican incumbents won re-election with 56 percent of the vote or less.[12] Given the partisan distribution of House seats (221 Republicans, 212 Democrats, and 2 Independents) immediately following the election, a shift of nine seats from the Republicans to the Democrats would have given the Democrats outright control of the House (regardless of the voting patterns of the Independent representatives).

If one estimates the individual-level electoral impact of "impeachment" funds, a few of the names change, but the loss pattern is quite similar (see Table 7.5).[13] Note that the members removed from the "loss list" spent considerable sums on their re-election campaigns. Barr spent over $3 million (twice what he spent in 1998). Northup spent over $2 million, which was more than half a million dollars more than she spent in 1998, and Sessions spent just under $1.8 million, more than twice what he spent in 1998. In all likelihood, the "impeachment" funds figures for each of these incumbents have been underestimated. Nevertheless, without the impeachment funds Republicans would have dropped seven seats to the Democrats and these losses would have resulted in an outright shift of House control to the Democrats.

Conclusion

The following general conclusion is unavoidable: The enormous financial advantage enjoyed by Republican incumbents over their Democratic challengers saved them. Given the political fallout from the Republicans' handling of the Clinton impeachment, the "impeachment" funds made the difference between keeping and losing control of the House of Representatives. In a very real sense, Republican money kept them in power. The lesson here is simple. Except in the most extreme cases (read James Rogan),[14] if you can raise enough money, you can safely thwart a sizable majority of your constituency regardless of the prominence of the issue involved. I discuss the implications of these findings in Chapter 9.

In the next chapter I shift my focus to the Senate to examine the impact of constituency pressures on Senate campaign fundraising and the effect of impeachment on Senate elections in 2000.

8

MAKING UP OR LOSING OUT?
FUNDRAISING AND
IMPEACHMENT IN THE SENATE

Just as most of the members of the House did, most (although just barely) Senators voted with their electoral constituencies on the articles of impeachment. All but one of the votes cast by Senate Democrats were consistent with their constituents' preferences,[1] and seven of the 55 Senate Republicans voted in accordance with their constituents' preferences. However, somewhat surprisingly, the pattern for the full Senate does not hold true for the subset of Senate incumbents running for re-election in 2000. Of the senators running for re-election in 2000, over half—all Republicans—voted against the preferences of a majority of their constituents.[2]

I found that Republican legislators who served districts where the opposition to impeachment was high suffered at the polls on election day. I also found that legislators attempted to avert the negative repercussions of unpopular impeachment votes by raising extra campaign funds in the House. As it turns out, a small but significant number of Republican representatives depended on these extra campaign funds—or "impeachment" funds—to retain their seats in the House. I now turn my attention to the Senate to address the following questions (analogous to those I have addressed for the House):

1. Did senators who voted against the preferences of their constituents on the articles of impeachment raise extra campaign funds to offset the potential electoral backlash of the
   unpopular votes?
2. Did those senators who voted against the preferences of
   their constituents on the articles of impeachment suffer at
   the polls because of those votes?

We know that 2000 was a difficult year for incumbent Republicans in the Senate. Although only one incumbent Democrat lost his
Senate seat—Chuck Robb (D.–Va.) lost to the well-financed, popular former governor George F. Allen[3]—five incumbent Republicans
lost their Senate seats.[4] In fact, of the 14 Republican incumbents
running for re-election in 2000 who voted against their constituents'
preferences on one or more of the articles of impeachment, more
than one-third lost their seats. With these results, it will be interesting to see if Senate Republicans made any significant efforts to forestall the potential electoral fallout precipitated by their unpopular
roll call votes on the articles of impeachment. However, before I examine these issues—particularly the fundraising response of Republican senators—it is important to consider the general parameters of
Senate elections, particularly the fundraising context, and it is to
this that I turn now.

Nature of Fundraising and Senate Campaigns

Senate campaigns, particularly competitive Senate campaigns, are
extremely expensive. Data from the Federal Election Commission
show that the 65 Democratic and Republican Senate candidates
spent, collectively, just less than $325 million, a figure that works
out to around $5 million per candidate. This is nearly double the
$173 million spent by the 67 major party Senate candidates just a
decade ago (in 1990). Even if we ignore the $143 million spent for
the five open Senate seats (over $60 million was spent by Jon
Corzinne, D.–N.J., alone), Senate incumbents averaged almost $4

million each. There is no doubt that Senate campaigns are enormously expensive.

Research on campaign financing and the impact of campaign funds on electoral outcomes in the Senate partially reflects the literature on the House. For the last two decades, two general findings have gained considerable support. First, it is generally accepted that campaign spending by challengers has a significant impact on the vote margin received by the challenger and on challenger electoral success. In one of the most thorough examinations of Senate elections, Alan Abramowitz and Jeffrey Segal (1992) found a strong positive relationship between challenger spending and challenger vote share. They concluded that, "[C]hallenger spending was easily the most important single factor influencing the outcome of Senate elections" (1992: 113). In a more recent description of campaign spending and Senate election outcomes, Alan Gerber noted that, "Challenger spending has much greater marginal returns than incumbent spending" (1998: 402). It has traditionally been difficult to show that spending by Senate incumbents has a significant impact on the vote (see Abramowitz 1988), and when a significant impact does exist, it is usually much smaller than the impact for challengers (Abramowitz and Segal 1992).

The rationale behind the greater impact of challenger spending on election outcomes, developed and popularized by Gary Jacobson (1980, 1985, 1990) is straightforward. Incumbents, because of the inherent electoral advantages of the office (franking privilege, staff resources, media opportunities) and the related fact that Senate incumbents are nearly always better known than their challengers, begin elections in a position of distinct advantage relative to their challengers. Because they enjoy this advantage, the marginal electoral return associated with each additional campaign dollar spent is significantly less than the marginal electoral return associated with each extra dollar spent by the challenger.

Although this is a perfectly logical explanation for the traditional result, recent evidence suggests that this result may, in fact, have been an artifact of a methodological obstacle that had yet to be fully appreciated. The most compelling recent work effectively addresses this methodological obstacle and re-examines the spending-outcome relationship in light of this technical breakthrough (Gerber 1998). Gerber's work indicates that incumbent spending is actually strongly and positively related to vote margin and that the impact of dollars spent by incumbents tends to be comparable to—if not greater than—the impact of dollars spent by challengers in Senate races. I consider these results in more detail later in this chapter. For now, we need only realize that, even in the Senate, there is reason to think that campaign spending by incumbents is, in general, strongly and positively related to incumbent vote share. If this is true, then there is reason to expect Senators to respond to a potential electoral backlash from unpopular conviction votes by raising extra campaign money.

Assuming that Republican incumbents attempted to compensate for unpopular conviction votes by raising additional campaign funds, it is important to remember that even incumbents face important constraints on extensive fundraising and that fundraising is a nontrivially costly electoral activity. From the standpoint of constraints, incumbents must compete for campaign funds with other candidates—and not just incumbent senators from their own party. If we assume that there is some upper limit on the available campaign funds in any particular election cycle and that there is at least some nontrivial fungibility of these campaign funds, incumbents compete for campaign funds with other incumbents, open seat candidates, and challengers, as well as House candidates and presidential candidates. During the 2000 electoral cycle, candidates for House seats raised more than $473 million and presidential candidates also raised several hundred million dollars. In the particular case of Republican presidential candidates—especially important for Republican Senate incumbents if we assume campaign funds are more likely to transfer between candidates within a party than transfer between candidates across party lines—George W. Bush raised well over $115 million, making his campaign by far the most expensive major party presidential campaign in U.S. history. That was millions of dollars that was unavailable to Republican senators.

The timetable of a senatorial campaign is also an obstacle for incumbents intent on counteracting the potential negative fallout from unpopular impeachment votes. First, because the conviction votes were not taken until the early part of 1999, well over half of the Senate election cycle (a six-year cycle) had passed before incumbents running for re-election in 2000 could have known that they would need to raise extra campaign funds. Although the great bulk of Senate incumbents' campaign funds are collected during the last two years of their terms, significant portions of funds are gathered prior to that time. Obviously, given the timing of the votes, a significant portion of the fundraising cycle would have passed before Senate incumbents would have known that they needed to raise extra campaign funds.

Finally, raising campaign funds is a time-consuming, labor-intensive task that many senators find unpalatable. According to Abramowitz and Segal:

> The rising cost of Senate campaigns has made fund-raising an increasingly onerous task for Senate candidates. In recent years, a number of incumbents and would-be candidates have cited the time and effort required for fund-raising as reasons for retiring or deciding not to run for the Senate in the first place (1992: 123–24).

As the need to raise ever-larger campaign "war chests" presses in on incumbents, difficult choices must be made. Senators are forced to decide between spending time on policy issues and legislative activities or fundraising. Likewise, personal campaigning and constituency service also suffer when fundraising efforts become a priority. Some legislators may not be willing to make the extra efforts to ensure (or practically ensure) their re-election if those efforts so change their daily responsibilities and opportunities that the job itself is no longer enjoyable. Given the increasingly competitive fundraising environment and the high personal and professional costs of fundraising, did incumbent senators attempt to preempt an electoral backlash associated with unpopular and unrepresentative impeachment votes by raising extra campaign funds? Let us see.

Conviction and Campaign Financing

Initially, I do find some evidence that incumbent senators attempted to proactively prevent or mitigate the electoral fallout from unpopular impeachment votes by raising extra campaign funds. I also find some evidence that suggests that the candidates challenging these incumbents raised extra campaign funds as well. (See Table 8.1.) Senators whose votes on the articles of impeachment were consistent with the preferences of their constituents raised an average of just over $3.3 million dollars. On the other hand, senators whose votes conflicted with the preferences of their constituents raised significantly more money. These senators averaged nearly $5 million each. Senate challengers appear to have also reacted to the opportunity afforded them by the unpopularity of incumbents' impeachment votes by raising significantly more money themselves. Challengers running against candidates who voted with their constituents on the impeachment issue raised an average of $1.4 million per campaign. Challengers running against incumbents who voted against their constituents' preferences raised more than twice as much money (an average of nearly $3 million per campaign). This relationship between incumbent and challenger fundraising is analogous to the relationship between the fundraising of Republican incumbents in the House and their Democratic challengers. As one raises more money, so does the other.

The gross financial averages are reflected, at least initially, in the per constituent fundraising figures. (See Table 8.2.) Here again I find evidence of an effort on the part of senators who crossed their constituents on impeachment to counteract the electoral effects of those unpopular votes through increased fundraising. The data show that incumbents who cast conviction votes consistent with the preferences of their constituents raised approximately $0.25 less per constituent than their colleagues who cast conviction votes that were not consistent with their constituents' preferences. Challengers

TABLE 8.1   Campaign Fundraising by Candidate Type
(Average Dollars)[*]

Candidate Type	Dollars
Incumbent voting with constituency	$3,322,727.36
Challenger of incumbent voting with constituency	$1,403,055.36
Incumbent voting against constituency	$4,980,415.71
Challenger of incumbent voting against constituency	$2,972,800.64

[*]Data gathered from the Federal Election Commisson website
(www.fec.gov). Note that the campaign finance data for the 2000 election cycle used to produce the results presented in this table—and subsequent tables in this chapter—only include contributions through October 8, 2000. Complete data were unavailable at the time of the analysis.

TABLE 8.2   Campaign Fundraising by Candidate Type
(Average Dollars per Constituent)[*]

Candidate Type	Dollars per Constituent
Incumbent voting with constituency	$1.21
Challenger of incumbent voting with constituency	$0.38
Incumbent voting against constituency	$1.46
Challenger of incumbent voting against constituency	$0.79

[*]Data gathered from the Federal Election Commisson website
(www.fec.gov) and the website of the Bureau of the Census (www.census.gov).

of incumbents who voted against their constituents spent twice as much money (again, per constituent) as did the challengers of incumbents who voted with their constituents. We find the same gap between incumbent and challenger spending, and we see that challengers are able to prevent the gap from growing when incumbents raise extra campaign funds. At first glance, whatever advantage may have been gained by incumbents raising extra campaign funds was lost once their challengers modified their own fundraising behavior.

TABLE 8.3   Campaign Fundraising by Candidate Type
(Republican Incumbents)[*]

Candidate Type	Dollars per Constituent
Incumbent voting with constituency	$2.11
Challenger of incumbent voting with constituency	$0.75
Incumbent voting against constituency	$1.46
Challenger of incumbent voting against constituency	$0.79

[*]Data gathered from the Federal Election Commisson website
(www.fec.gov) and the website of the Bureau of the Census (www.cen-
sus.gov).

If we look more closely, however, these relationships begin to disappear. If we eliminate Democratic incumbents from the analysis—
because all of them voted with the majority of their constituencies—
we see that Republican incumbents who voted with their
constituents actually raised more money—per constituent—than
their Republican colleagues who voted against their constituencies.
(See Table 8.3.) The three Senate Republicans running for re-election in 2000 who voted in accordance with their constituencies'
preferences—Hatch (Utah), who voted for conviction on both impeachment articles, and Jeffords (Vt.) and Snowe (Maine), who
voted against conviction on both articles—actually raised more than
$2 per constituent, a figure well in excess of the $1.46 per constituent raised by the remaining Republicans. Likewise, the differences between the fundraising of challengers facing incumbents who
voted with their constituencies and challengers facing uncumbents
who voted against their constituencies disappear.

These results are, to say the least, surprising. One possible explanation is the impact of state population size on Senate campaign
fundraising. We notice that each of the three Republicans in the pro-
constituency category served a relatively small state. The total estimated population (1996) for these three states—Maine, Utah, and
Vermont—was less than 4 million people. Therefore, one of the rea-

sons that the per constituent fundraising for Hatch, Jeffords, and Snowe was surprisingly high—at least relative to the per constituent fundraising of Republican senators whose votes on the articles of impeachment were less popular with their constituents—is that each serves a state with a small population.[5] Whether differences in state population fully explain this anomalous finding requires a more rigorous look at the data. Likewise, to precisely determine the impact of unpopular impeachment votes on fundraising in Senate campaigns requires a more rigorously analytical examination of the data. It is to that analysis that I turn now.

Estimating the Effect of Unpopular Conviction Votes on Campaign Fundraising

To estimate the impact of the unpopularity of senators' votes on the articles of impeachment on campaign fundraising, I modified a technology developed by Gerber (1998) to predict incumbent and challenger spending in Senate races. Gerber's primary objective was to estimate the relative impact of challenger and incumbent spending on Senate election outcomes, and later in this chapter I base my examination of the specific impact of challenger and incumbent fundraising on election outcomes in 2000 on his methodology. Before I introduce his technique for predicting the levels of incumbent and challenger fundraising, I describe the literature on which his analysis is based.

In his article on the electoral effects of candidate spending in Senate races, Gerber summarizes the campaign finance literature in the following manner:

> It is widely believed that challenger spending is very important, but there is surprisingly little evidence in the academic literature that incumbent spending has an important effect on congressional election outcomes. . . . [and evidence supporting an incumbent spending effect suggests that] for given spending levels, incumbent campaign spending appears to have much smaller marginal returns than challenger spending. (1998: 401)

In general, studies of the impact of campaign fundraising on Senate elections find that challenger spending has a much larger marginal impact on vote percentage than incumbent spending, and in some cases, incumbent spending has been found to have no impact at all on vote margins (see Abramowitz 1988; Abramowitz and Segal 1992; Gerber 1998). According to Abramowitz and Segal:

> Although both [the challenger and incumbent spending] coefficients are statistically significant, the estimated coefficient for challenger spending is almost three times as large as the estimated coefficient for incumbent spending. In fact, challenger spending was easily *the most important single factor influencing the outcomes of Senate elections* (1992: 113).

The rationale for the drastic difference in the effectiveness of challenger spending and incumbent spending in Senate elections is straightforward and mirrors that provided for the House. Assuming (as we did for the House) that campaign spending is subject to diminishing marginal returns and that incumbent Senators begin with a significant electoral advantage owing to their position (franking privilege, free media opportunities, etc.), challengers receive significantly more from dollars raised and expended than do incumbents, because they start so much farther down the electoral ladder (see Jacobson 1978 for a fuller explanation of this rationale). Several hundred thousand dollars spent to publicize the campaign of a candidate whom many voters barely recognize prior to the campaign is likely to do significantly more than the same dollars expended on the campaign of an incumbent senator known widely throughout the state.

It is not necessarily the case, however, that incumbent campaign spending will have a smaller marginal effect than challenger spending. Gerber (1998) argues that name recognition is only one of the electoral resources necessary for success in Senate elections. He conjectures that Senate incumbents may also use campaign funds to focus on or promote new issues or positions not raised in previous years and/or inform constituencies about the negative aspects of the opponent. In neither of these cases would the incumbent have the type of preexisting advantage that would lead to campaign spending effects that were significantly different than those faced by challengers.

It is even theoretically possible that incumbent spending could generate a greater marginal electoral return than challenger spending. Incumbents may be better equipped organizationally to make effective use of their financial resources than challengers. As senators and, by definition, highly successful office-seekers, they will have had the opportunity and (probably) the capability to construct a campaign organization that at least rivals that of their challenger and, more likely, is superior to it. Likewise, their knowledge and experience may also provide them with the means to get more out of each dollar of campaign funds than less-experienced challengers. As Gerber argues:

> In theory, incumbent spending may be *more* effective than challenger spending. Incumbents typically have advantages in organization and expertise that make their expenditures more efficient and therefore more effective dollar for dollar than those of challengers. If this is an important consideration, then the marginal effect of spending by the incumbent may be *greater* than the marginal effect of challenger spending. (1998: 402)

Thus, we can have no a priori expectation regarding the relative impact of campaign spending by Senate incumbents and their challengers. As with investigations of the impact of House spending on electoral outcomes, measurement problems are acute. Campaign expenditures, at least intuitively, should have a positive impact on one's vote margin (all else being equal). If not, why would one expend the time and energy to raise the campaign funds in the first place? The key inferential obstacle is that both challenger and incumbent spending are endogenous variables; they depend, at least to some extent, on the context and character of the specific campaign in which they are raised and spent. Unfortunately, the endogeneity of these variables has not been fully recognized or fully incorporated into the analysis of campaign spending on election outcomes. Jacobson (1985), for example, treats both variables as exogenous, as does Abramowitz (1988). Both of these analyses find that, even when statistically significant, incumbent spending has a far smaller marginal effect on vote percentage than challenger spending, but their failure to adequately account for the endogenous character of both incumbent and challenger spending compromises their analyses.

Gerber (1998) develops an innovative methodology for estimating the impact of incumbent and challenger campaign spending on Senate election outcomes. His methodology, described below, is a significant improvement on the existing methods for two reasons. First, he is able to effectively treat both challenger and incumbent spending as endogenous variables. Nearly all previous work treated both incumbent and challenger campaign spending as exogenous variables. However, there is good reason to believe—and empirical evidence to support—the idea that neither incumbent nor challenger spending is completely exogenous. Although certain factors influencing campaign spending levels clearly predate the campaign, others—such as the opponent's spending itself—do not. Failure to adequately account for the endogeneity of these two variables generates severe inferential problems (to the point of biasing the coefficient estimates and the standard errors of the estimates).

Gerber's second (and related) contribution is his development of new instrumental variables—used to deal with the problems associated with variable endogeneity—that are a significant improvement on current instrumental variables. The variables that Gerber includes in his analysis are

- Challenger wealth (CWEALTH),
- State population (POP), and
- Lagged spending (LAGSPEND).

The idea is to identify variables that are likely to be highly correlated with incumbent and challenger spending but do not have a significant influence on the election outcome itself. Challenger wealth is quite likely to influence challenger spending by providing an extra source of campaign funds, and incumbents who face challengers with considerable wealth are more likely to raise extra campaign funds to match challenger spending. In recent elections in particular, a number of exceedingly wealthy challengers have used significant portions of their own wealth to bankroll their campaigns. For example, during the 1998 election cycle, Peter Fitzgerald made personal loans to his campaign fund that added up to more than $13 million, and Darrell Issa's personal loans to his campaign exceeded $10 million. Even these large sums pale in comparison to the more than $60 million in personal loans that Jon Corzine (D–N.J.) contributed to his 2000 campaign for the U.S. Senate. However, aside from influencing funding patterns, there is little or no reason to believe that challenger wealth has an independent impact on electoral outcomes.

The same is true for state population and lagged spending. Both have obvious connections to spending patterns for both incumbents and challengers. As state population increases, per capita campaign fundraising and spending is likely to decrease. There are several reasons for this. First, both individual and PAC contributions are capped (at $1,000 and $5,000, respectively) regardless of the size of state population. Relatively speaking, these contribution restrictions equalize the fundraising environment and make it difficult for Senate incumbents from large states to raise per capita war chests that are comparable to those of Senate incumbents from less-populous states. Similarly, because Senate seats are not allocated according to population, senators from smaller states serve significantly smaller populations. Interest groups have no incentive to court senators from large states because their institutional powers are no greater than those of senators from small states. So, "in per-voter terms, a senator from a small state has much more to sell than a senator from a populous state" (Gerber 1998: 405). Although it is likely to be related to campaign fundraising and spending, there is no evidence that state population is related to electoral outcomes (Westlye 1991; Krasno 1994).

We should also expect lagged spending to have an impact on campaign fundraising and spending but not Senate electoral outcomes. In nearly all cases, spending in the previous Senate election is very unlikely to influence electoral outcomes in the current election because the candidates are different, and there is little reason to think that the level of campaign spending by one of a state's Senate incumbents (and his or her challenger) will have a material influence on the vote margin/electoral outcome of the state's other Senate incumbent (and his or her challenger) in the subsequent election. However, states may have distinctive fundraising characteristics, and this distinctiveness may influence fundraising for both Senate incumbents.

To estimate the extent to which unpopular impeachment votes led to an increase in campaign fundraising, I add two time-specific variables associated with impeachment to Gerber's original set of instrumental variables. The first is the SIMPOPP (or state-level impeachment opposition) variable used in the House analysis. The second is CONVICT, a dummy variable coded "1" if the incumbent voted "yea" for either article of impeachment and "0" otherwise. As in the case of the House analysis, if position taking on impeachment influences fundraising, I would expect both SIMPOPP and CONVICT to be positively related to incumbent campaign fundraising and challenger campaign fundraising. The results from a regression of these variables on Senate incumbents are presented in Table 8.4.[6]

Somewhat surprisingly, I find that neither SIMPOPP nor CONVICT is significantly related to campaign fundraising. For incum-

TABLE 8.4   Predicting Campaign Fundraising by Senate Incumbents

Variable	Parameter Estimate	Standard Error	t Value	Pr>|t|
Intercept	-0.39126	1.48521	-0.26	0.7948
LAGSPEND	0.8924	0.21033	3.28	0.0036
POP	-3.928E-08	1.83E-08	-2.14	0.0442
CWEALTH	-0.35188	0.27834	-1.26	0.2200
CONVICT	0.36939	0.28464	1.57	0.1304
IMPOPP	0.00259	0.02842	0.11	0.9137

$R^2 = .6346$
Adj $R^2 = 5476$
N = 29

bents, the total amount of money spent in the previous Senate election in the state is strongly and positively associated with campaign fundraising. Senators running campaigns in expensive political environments tend to raise more money than those running in relatively less-expensive political environments. Likewise, as we saw in the descriptive data presented previously, population size has a significant dampening effect on campaign fundraising (when calculated in per voter units). But neither of the impeachment-oriented variables appears to have affected fundraising once these other factors are taken into account. In both cases, the impeachment variables are insignificant, and in the case of CONVICT the sign is incorrect. In sharp contrast to my findings for the House, there is no evidence that Senate incumbents responded to the unpopularity of their impeachment votes by raising more campaign funds.

Turning to the determinants of challenger fundraising, I find a pattern similar to the one uncovered for incumbent fundraising. Challengers respond to expensive political environments in much the same way that incumbents do: They raise more money. The relative size of the coefficients of the incumbent LAGSPEND variable and the challenger LAGSPEND variables suggests that challengers are actually more sensitive to the costliness of a state's political context. Again, neither impeachment-oriented variable influenced campaign fundraising. (See Table 8.5.) We have no evidence that challengers at-

TABLE 8.5 Predicting Campaign Fundraising by Senate Challengers

Variable	Parameter Estimate	Standard Error	t Value	Pr>|t|
Intercept	-5.06752	4.33714	-1.17	0.2557
LAGSPEND	1.75546	0.61421	2.86	0.0094
POP	58E-8	35-E08	0.67	0.5105
CWEALTH	-0.02802	0.1282	-0.03	0.9728
CONVICT	0.52847	0.8520	0.77	0.4491
IMPOPP	0.03539	0.839	0.52	0.6103

$R^2 = .3217$
Adj $R^2 = .1602$
N = 27

tempted to take advantage of potentially weakened incumbents by raising more campaign dollars in cases where impeachment was very unpopular and where incumbents voted to convict the president.[7] These results are strikingly different from those for the House. It is important to realize that the insignificance of the impeachment-oriented variables may, at least partially, be a function of the small sample size (n = 27).[8] Nevertheless, I cannot impute the existence of evidence where there is none, and in this case I have no evidence that factors associated with the Senate handling of impeachment affected fundraising patterns for incumbents or challengers.

Failing to account for the potential backlash from impeachment strikes me as a relatively risky electoral strategy. Why did Republicans incumbents, particularly those who were most electorally vulnerable, fail to take the necessary measures to preempt a strong challenge in the wake of impeachment? One possible answer is that the fundraising constraints that senators face are significantly greater than those faced by House members. Obviously, senators are able to raise, on average, far more money than their House counterparts. However, they are also required to raise significantly more money than their House counterparts to remain competitive. It is at least possible that once an incumbent senator realizes that he or she will face a quality challenger (usually a current or former representative or a current or former governor), that incumbent maximizes campaign fundraising. If beleaguered incumbents are already maximizing their campaign fundraising, there will be no room for an extra fundraising bump to compensate for unpopular roll call votes on impeachment.

An alternative (but not necessarily mutually exclusive) explanation is that most incumbent senators did not view impeachment as having a significant electoral downside. Less than two weeks before the election, Emily Pierce and Barbara Murray (2000), writing in *CQ Weekly*, predicted that Democrats would gain only a single seat in the Senate, well short of the five-seat shift that actually occurred. So, very late in the game, two professional political analysts grossly underestimated the strength of Democratic challengers in Senate races nationwide. If this type of prediction could be made this close to the election—by which time it would be far too late to generate a huge influx of new campaign dollars—how much more difficult would it have been to make an accurate prediction a year or more in advance at the very time that the bulk of the incumbents' campaign funds would have been raised. It may be that Senate incumbents agreed with Senator Mitch McConnell's (R.–Ky.) evaluation of the situation: "The election is 22 months away and there is no chance they'll [the constituents] remember this [meaning the Senate votes on impeachment]" (cited in Lowenthal, Keech, and Loewenstein 1999: 1).

In trying to explain why incumbents did not try to inoculate themselves from negative reactions to their own impeachment votes, I am of course assuming that incumbent votes on the articles of impeachment actually mattered in the voting booth. That fact has not yet been established, so it is possible that incumbents did not raise extra campaign funds because they knew that their votes on the articles of impeachment would have no impact on their electoral fortunes. Just because a significant effect could be found in House election results does not mean one existed in Senate races. I now turn to an examination of the impact of impeachment votes on the electoral fortunes of Senate incumbents.

Wages of Conviction

Using the results from our incumbent and challenger regression models, I can construct an instrument for incumbent fundraising and an instrument for challenger fundraising comparable to those described by Gerber (1998). Using the fundraising instruments and the CONVICT variable described previously, I can create a simple explanatory model of Senate election outcomes. (See Table 8.6.)

Each of the variables in the regression model presented in Table 8.6 is statistically significant and signed correctly. As incumbent fundraising increases, the incumbent receives a greater share of the two-party vote. Conversely, as challenger fundraising increases, the incumbent receives a smaller share of the two-party vote. These results are analogous to Gerber's (1998) more general spending results

TABLE 8.6   Estimating the Impact of Campaign Fundraising on
Election Outcomes in the Senate[*]

Variable	Parameter Estimate	Standard Error	t Value	Pr>|t|
Intercept	53.73097	5.03330	10.68	<.0001
Predicted Incumbent Fundraising	8.00683	4.4783	1.80	0.0425
Predicted Challenger Fundraising	-7.35696	2.91273	-2.53	0.0095
Convict	-7.39956	3.62280	-2.04	0.0267

$R^2 = .2811$
Adj $R^2 = .1873$
$N = 27$

[*]The dependent variable is the percentage of the two-party vote received by the incumbent. Note that several variables incorporated in Gerber's (1998) analysis have been excluded from this model (dummy variables for various types of challenger experience, state unemployment level, state partisanship, and state unemployment level/state partisanship). Given the small number of observations in my analysis, multicollinearity beomes problematic when these other variables are added. When one of these variables reached a conventional level of significance, the significance levels of the fundraising and conviction variables decreased, although not drastically, and the conviction variable still outperformed both of the fundraising variables. Significance levels are for one-tailed tests.

in two important ways. First, both challenger fundraising and incumbent fundraising influence electoral outcomes. Second, the electoral impacts of challenger fundraising and incumbent fundraising are comparable. Challenger dollars are not more valuable than incumbent dollars. These results demonstrate that, had Republican incumbents raised extra campaign funds—what I refer to as "impeachment" funds in House elections—they could have increased their vote margins.

The vote margins of those Republicans who supported one or more of the impeachment articles were seriously and negatively affected by this behavior. The results presented in Table 8.6 indicate that the difference between supporting impeachment and opposing

TABLE 8.7   The Impact of Unpopular Impeachment Votes by
Senate Campaign: The Losers

Incumbent Senator	Percentage of Constituents Opposed to Impeachment	Actual Vote Percentage[*]	Predicted Vote Percentage[**]
Abraham (MI)	63.1	49	56
Ashcroft (MO)	59.2	49	56
Gorton (WA)	58.4	49	56
Grams (MN)	58.8	47	54
Roth (DE)	65.0	44	51

[*]This is the two-party vote percentage.
[**]Assuming a "no" vote on both atricles of impeachment. Again, this is the two-party vote percentage.

it was just over 7 percentage points. Simple descriptive statistics support these inferential results. Among Republicans who opposed impeachment—Snowe (Maine) and Jeffords (Vt.)—the average vote percentage was 67.5. Among Republicans who supported impeachment, the average vote percentage was 58.9. If we exclude Hatch (Utah) from the analysis because both he and his constituents supported impeachment, the average vote percentage for Republicans who supported impeachment is even lower (58.4 percent). Impeachment votes made a much bigger difference than expected.[9] Looking at the impact of unpopular impeachment votes at the campaign level, we see that for several senators support for impeachment (against the wishes of their constituents) was exceedingly costly. (See Table 8.7.)

Because Roth (Del.) would have needed the entire 7 percentage points attributable to one or more conviction votes to win his campaign, I am not willing to say that a different choice on the impeachment issue would have made a difference in his case. That implies greater confidence in the precision of the results than is probably warranted. There is little doubt, however, that unpopular impeachment votes made the difference between winning and losing in the cases of Abraham (Mich.), Ashcroft (Mo.), Gorton (Wash.), and Grams (Minn.). The evidence presented here clearly implies that the close losses each of these incumbents suffered—in states where the opponents of impeachment outnumbered its supporters by nearly 3 to 2—could have been avoided if the candidates had either significantly increased their campaign fundraising or cast impeachment votes that represented the preferences of their constituents. During the Senate deliberations on the articles of impeachment, Senator Grams made the following statement:

> It has been said that many have risked their political futures during this process. Perhaps—yet I will not hesitate telling constituents in my state how and why I voted the way I did. With a clear conscience, I will stand in their judgment and I will live with and respect whatever their decision on my political future may be. But remember, those who vote to acquit—that is, to not remove this President—will have the rest of their political lifetimes to explain their votes. They also will be judged. (*Congressional Record*, February 12, 1999)

It appears as if the voters have judged.

Conclusion

In the House of Representatives, Republican incumbents were sensitive to the potential for an electoral backlash engendered by the Clinton impeachment. They prepared accordingly by raising large campaign war chests, and, for the most part, the party avoided significant electoral losses in 2000. Most important, their preparations allowed them to retain control of the House.

In the Senate, I find no evidence that Republican senators made any special efforts to prepare for the post-impeachment backlash. For four (maybe five depending on the classification of the Roth case) Republican senators, this lack of preparation cost them their Senate seats.[10] Exactly why these Republicans failed to prepare—or respond once the threat was evident—is unclear. It may be that they tried and were unable to generate a significant increase in campaign funds. It may be that they did not expect their impeachment votes to matter. It may also be that they did raise extra campaign funds—Abraham (Mich.) alone raised more than $12 million—but that the limitations of the data prevent me from accurately capturing this fundraising dynamic. In any case, impeachment made quite a difference.

9

THE *USUALLY* HIDDEN DANGERS OF POLITICS AS USUAL

The people can never willfully betray their own interests; but they may possibly be betrayed by the representatives of the people.
—*James Madison (Federalist Papers 1982, v. 63)*

It simply was not humanly possible to view the full series of events surrounding the Clinton-Lewinsky scandal without developing a sense of bewildered disillusionment. As low as our expectations of our public officials actually are, plenty of elected officials have failed to meet even those cynical standards.

First, of course, it was not a good time for the former president. There is no way to adequately explain the behavior—in the White House, in hearings, on national television—to which he finally admitted, let alone the alleged behavior to which he has not admitted. At the very least, he had an improper sexual relationship with a young White House intern, lied to his closest associates about that relationship, lied about the existence of the relationship in a deposition in a civil legal proceeding, and lied, on more than one occasion, to the U.S. public. Not Clinton's finest hours by any stretch of the imagination.

However repugnant Clinton's behavior, and I am unaware of any national political figure who characterized his behavior in anything but the most negative terms, reasonable people could certainly disagree about whether any of his actions had risen to the level of impeachable offense. As I noted in Chapter 2, the Constitution's impeachment directives are terse and vague. The phrase "high crimes and misdemeanors" is simply an insufficient foundation for the development of consistent behavioral criteria for situations that arise so rarely. Because the constitutional standard is so imprecise—or open to interpretation, depending on your perspective—a credible argument can be made for either side in the Clinton case. The explanations that some of the more moderate members of the Senate (and to a lesser extent the House) gave for their votes demonstrated this clearly.

Although the behavior to which Clinton admitted was reprehensible, he was finally charged—by independent counsel Starr and the House of Representatives—with a variety of crimes to which he has not admitted and on which the evidence is inconclusive. Therefore, even if some level of agreement existed on the seriousness of the charges, differences of opinion about whether the House managers had satisfied the burden of "reasonable doubt" would lead members to disagree about impeachment and, subsequently, conviction.[1] The final disposition of the charges against Clinton during his early post-presidency—an agreement with the post-Starr independent counsel to provide a partial admission of guilt for a promise of non-prosecution—precludes further legal examination of those charges about which there is still some doubt.

Not surprisingly, average Americans disagreed about whether Clinton should be impeached. Although most thought he had lied in his *Jones* deposition (some even admitting he had committed perjury), a majority of Americans disagreed with the position that Clinton's actions in the *Jones* case were sufficient grounds for impeachment. Likewise, most Americans did not view Clinton's efforts to avoid the public disclosure of his relationship with Monica Lewinsky as sufficiently serious or regime threatening to warrant impeachment. In fact, the general position of Americans on Clinton's impeachment was straightforward and unambiguous: They opposed it.

However, in the case of the Clinton impeachment, the American people failed to carry the day, at least in the House of Representatives.[2] A host of members of Congress also failed their constituents. Many other individuals involved in the whole mess also come out looking rather worse than they would have had their behavior been somewhat different. But the individual human failures are not the main story here. The real story, the one that makes a real difference in the lives of average Americans today and for the foreseeable future, is the institutional story. It is a story about electoral connections and the nature of representation, the advantages of incumbents, the uphill road challengers face, and the power of money. In the following pages I revisit the most disturbing aspects of the politics of the Clinton impeachment and emphasize how the politics of impeachment was, in its basic contours, politics as usual. I conclude with some suggestions for reform that might really change our current system of representation for the better and I explain why other reforms—reforms that appear to have some chance of being enacted—are unlikely to produce significant change.

In textbook treatments of U.S. politics, there are two types of representatives: the delegate and the trustee.[3] In Pitkin's seminal work on the conceptualization of representation, she describes a delegate as a "representative [who] is sent to the central government with explicit instructions, or to do a particular thing" (1967: 134). In somewhat more informal terms, we tend to think of delegates as acting on the expressed wishes of their constituents, basically serving as the agent of the constituency by behaving, in the legislature, as the people would themselves if they were there. A trustee, on the other hand, is expected to act in the interests of his or her constituency rather than on the opinions or preferences of that constituency (at least when the two are in conflict). According to Pitkin:

[The trustee's] duties might not even be to those who elect him, but perhaps to the national interest or to generations yet unborn. Again, the implication is one of freeing the representative from the wishes or opinions of his constituents, while yet regarding him as having an obligation to their welfare. (1967: 128)

Obviously, in the context of the Clinton impeachment, we can view those representatives and senators who sided with their constituents and voted in a manner consistent with their preferences as delegates. Unfortunately, we cannot conclude that those members who did not vote their constituents' preferences necessarily acted as trustees; it is not clear that they acted as representatives at all.

I admit that the language of representation played a large part in the debate over the articles of impeachment in both the House and the Senate. Those members who knew they were going to vote against the wishes of their constituents were especially interested in explaining their behavior in such a way that it appeared to be "representative," but on closer inspection, their behavior was often unrepresentative, and whatever connection between constituent and legislator had existed prior to the impeachment was severed, at least within the context of the impeachment proceedings.

Impeachment's supporters made every effort to describe their behavior in terms that lent a representational air to their motives.[4] They frequently cited the "public interest" and claimed that they were acting in the public interest regardless of the tone of public opinion: straight trustee language. They also frequently dismissed the behavior of those who opposed impeachment as a failure to execute their constitutional duties as servants of the people. This sentiment is clearly stated by David Schippers (lead counsel for the House managers):

... I am, and always have been, of the firm belief that Congress must continue to do its duty even if 99 percent of the American people do not agree. Congressmen are not mere surrogates for their constituents; rather, they are Representatives under a republican form of government. They are expected—indeed required—

to vote their consciences, regardless of the caprices of public
opinion. (Schippers and Henry 2000:302)

It is difficult to see how a representative's "duty" can be inconsistent with "99 percent of the American people"—or 99 percent of
the representative's constituents—in any practical context. Frankly,
it is difficult to see how this type of disjuncture would occur on a
purely theoretical level. The type of representative that Schippers is
talking about is certainly not a delegate, but he or she may have
some claim to being a trustee if at least two criteria are satisfied.
The first criterion is that the representative honestly attempts to further the interests of the constituents. Few representatives or senators
claimed to do otherwise on the issue of impeachment, regardless of
their position on the articles. But it is obviously difficult to assess
the extent to which this criterion was satisfied. Given the prominent
role of individual ideology in explanations of legislative behavior on
the issue of impeachment, it is difficult to see how this criterion
could have been satisfied.

The second criterion is fair and effective elections. By fair and effective elections, I mean that the electoral system is relatively unbiased; perfectly unbiased is probably not a practically useful standard. By unbiased, I mean that no particular group of constituents
or representatives consistently enjoys a privileged place within the
system that is not solely attributable to actual popular support. As
Pitkin writes:

> For the theorist of representative democracy . . . the crucial crite-
> rion [of representation] becomes elections, and these are seen as a
> grant of authority by the voters to the elected officials. Normally
> this grant is limited as to time, so that the officials' status as rep-
> resentatives ends when the time comes for new elections. (1967:
> 43)

However, if elections are not fair and effective, re-election itself cannot be seen as a sufficient grant of representative authority. If our
current electoral system is biased toward incumbents (as it obvi-

ously is), then re-election, in and of itself, is not sufficient grounds to justify the continuation of the representational relationship. More significantly, if representatives do not face a real threat of removal, their claims to serve the public interest when their behavior clearly contradicts expressed public opinion cannot be justified. Claiming that you are serving my interests when you are clearly acting against my preferences is meaningful only to the extent that I can remove you from office. If I cannot, or if it is exceedingly difficult for me to do so, then your claims to representation are meaningless. In fact, if I cannot remove you from office, why would you have any incentive to serve my interests in the first place?

For at least two centuries, students of politics have understood that fair and effective elections are a pillar of representative democracy. James Madison recognized this, and said so, in *Federalist Papers* volume 10. When factions threaten public institutions and the integrity of the political system, elections can serve as a bulwark against their mischief. Specifically, when factions are in the minority—as was the case in the Clinton impeachment—then the majoritarian principle, as it is manifested in our system of electoral institutions, is the primary mechanism by which factions are defeated. Although Madison was primarily concerned with the political threats posed by majority factions, he might have been somewhat more concerned with minority factions had he fully realized the role money would come to play in the U.S. political system.

The importance of elections for the maintenance of a vital representative democracy does not depend on the positive manifestation of public preferences in the behavior of representatives subsequent to the elections. As William Riker (1982) shows in his popularization and extension of Kenneth Arrow's work, given the diversity of choices available to the public, we cannot ensure that preferences will be aggregated in a meaningful manner. Identifying the proper future direction of policy from election results (what Riker refers to as *populism*) is exceedingly difficult (at the limit, foundationally impossible). But democracy (at least from a liberal or Madisonian standpoint) is still a meaningful concept because citizens can protect themselves from tyranny by removing recalcitrant public officials.

Although it may be difficult to tell where the public wants to go, it is not difficult to tell whether the public is happy about where it has been. This, of course, assumes fair and effective elections. Without those, representative democracy ceases to be meaningful.

This obviously overstates the case against many of the supporters of impeachment, but only to a degree. If it were possible for a significant number of representatives to thwart their constituents' clear preferences by raising several fortunes in campaign funds, then any claims to a representational connection between constituent and legislator are lost. On what is widely accepted as the most significant constitutional crisis of the second half of the twentieth century, it is only reasonable to expect citizen preferences to carry the day. In the end, they did, but only because of the founders' foresight in designing the institutional structure of the impeachment process. In a very real sense, the public lost on impeachment. A significant number of representatives and senators—admittedly less than a majority—replaced their constituents' evaluations of the merits of the impeachment case against Clinton with their own. And the data indicate that these evaluations were based mainly on the representatives' and senators' ideological dispositions. Although the public reacted quite negatively to this behavior—more negatively than most experts expected—most representatives were able to bring sufficient financial resources to bear on the election to save their seats (and to keep the Republicans in control of Congress). A few senators were not so lucky (and I will return to this important distinction momentarily). What is important is that a large number of representatives acted in a manner clearly at odds with their local constituencies (and the national constituency) on an issue of historical importance; used their considerable fundraising advantages as incumbents to acquire, in some cases, enormous campaign war chests; and defeated nearly all challengers (often because of the money they raised). This type of thing doesn't—can't—happen in a system of fair and effective elections.

The focus of this book is the legislative politics of the Clinton impeachment, particularly the financial dynamics of the impeachment process. The picture I paint of the state of our current system of representation is not a pretty one. If we cannot expect the public to "win" on a prominent public issue such as a presidential impeachment, what can we expect on "small" political issues that many think are already dominated by special interests? Not much, actually. And this focus on the political pathologies of the role of money in "small" politics—how special interests get what they want in Washington—has obscured the role of money in "big" politics. As we have focused on what contributors receive from legislators to whom they contribute, we have ignored the ability of legislators to raise funds to insulate themselves from the pressures of elections—severing, in some cases, the "electoral connection"—so that they can further their own ideological programs (regardless of their constituents' preferences). Obviously, this doesn't happen every day, but if it can happen on impeachment, it can happen anywhere at any time.

If we hope to strengthen popular government, we must revitalize (or, more accurately, vitalize) the deliberative processes within our current political system and fundamentally reform our current system of campaign financing. The two reforms are not mutually exclusive, and some mixture of both is probably the most effective way to invigorate the representational character of our polity.

As far as the first option is concerned, Lawrence Jacobs and Robert Shapiro (2000) provide the most thorough and thought-provoking argument for the enactment of these types of reforms. From their perspective, politicians have gotten away from their representational responsibilities. Rather than following opinion, politicians are manipulating opinion for their own partisan and ideological purposes. They argue that a variety of "deliberative" reforms (the more extensive use of deliberative polls, the development of "civic journalism," a more careful monitoring of public opinion, and more extensive publicizing of situations in which politicians defy public opinion, for example, the Clinton impeachment) would foster the development of closer ties between representatives and constituents and invigorate our representative democracy. For the most part, these appear to be reasonable suggestions. I won't address their proposals in any detail because I consider campaign finance reform more important.

At the crux of our current representational crisis is the ability of incumbents to insulate themselves, for the most part, from the threat of defeat. If this ability to prevent defeat is a function of an intimate appreciation and respect for their constituents' preferences, then we do not have a problem. But the obvious lesson of the Clinton impeachment is that this insulation is at least partially born of an inherently biased campaign financing system. And the problem is worse than we realized. Money matters in situations where it shouldn't (according to existing theory and conventional wisdom). Money often makes the difference between winning and losing for individual representatives and senators, and it can make the difference between holding or losing control of a chamber of Congress. Money clearly matters a lot. Something needs to change.

In all fairness, there are reasonable people who suggest that changes to the current system of electoral finance would have little or no effect on the extent to which citizens regain some semblance of control over their representatives. Some of these smart people make some reasonably compelling arguments. However, some equally smart people disagree. I believe David Donnelly, Janice Fine, and Ellen Miller drive straight to the point:

> So we have a problem. Simply put, there is too much private money in our political system. Despite the best efforts of a few conservative scholars and columnists, this point is no longer a topic of serious debate. (1999: 10)

Given the increasingly obvious fact that the system is deeply flawed, that it fails in the most obvious and important ways to serve the interests of the general public and the civic society at large, it strikes me that we might at least want to try something different. This is not a book about campaign finance reform, but it is a book about the role of money in modern U.S. electoral politics, and a few specific comments about campaign finance reform are certainly in order.

First, there is no shortage of campaign finance reform proposals. Some focus on enhancing the information available to voters.

Among the proposals in this category are more stringent reporting requirements, increasing public access to contribution disclosure information, a strengthening of the disclosure requirement for political ads (so voters will know who paid for an ad), more widespread publication of campaign finance abuses, and encouraging a more extensive public debate on the role of money in elections.[5] These reforms are consistent with the thrust of Jacobs and Shapiro's deliberatively oriented proposals and are relatively unproblematic. They are also not likely to effect the necessary change.

Somewhat more controversial are proposals that directly affect the amount and/or type of money that contributors can give or candidates can receive. An outright ban on soft money—unregulated contributions made to political parties—and an increase in contributor limits are two of the most prominent examples of this type of reform. Soft money has become an increasingly important part of the electoral process in the United States, and the fact that these funds are unregulated makes it difficult to identify their specific impact on practical politics. However, no one is seriously suggesting that the increasing significance of soft money has strengthened the position of the average citizen relative to wealthier, more concentrated special interests. Current limits on campaign contributions ($1,000 per individual and $5,000 per PAC, per candidate, per election) have not been raised since they were originally set 25 years ago. By raising the limits, so the argument goes, the ability of candidates to raise regulated money will be enhanced, thus limiting the need for and electoral effectiveness of unregulated funds. As I write, it looks as though the Senate will pass campaign finance reform legislation that incorporates, in some fashion, both of these proposals.

Although neither of these proposals is objectionable—Who supports the under-the-table secrecy of soft money in the name of democracy?—they won't get the job done. The central problem—as the case of the Clinton impeachment highlighted—is the fundraising advantage enjoyed by incumbents. Neither the ban on soft money nor an increase in contribution limits will alleviate that problem. I explicitly ignored soft money considerations in the chapters on the impact of fundraising on electoral outcomes. Incumbents simply do not need soft money to maintain their advantage. Similarly, increasing contribution limits will enable individuals and PACs to give more money to challengers, but it will also allow them to increase their contributions to incumbents. Again, it is not at all clear that this proposal gets at the heart of the campaign finance problem.

I am increasingly convinced that the only reform proposals with a realistic chance of re-establishing and reinvigorating the relationship between constituents and their representatives involve public financing (at least for the House). Although mandatory public financing is almost certainly unconstitutional (at least in the current *Buckley* environment), optional public financing (like the current system for presidential elections) is just as certainly constitutionally viable. By providing significant funds for challengers (and incumbents who want them), entrenched incumbents would have to compete—on a regular basis—for their seats. Given an appropriately designed system of public financing, incumbents would have to compete by paying increasingly close attention to what their constituents want and not by raising ever-increasing campaign fund fortunes.

I end by referring the reader to the distinctiveness of the House and the Senate. In the case of the House, representatives can usually raise sufficient campaign funds to avoid serious and persistent electoral challenges. See the case of the Clinton impeachment. The same is not true for the Senate. Failing to pay attention to one's constituents can be electorally problematic, even if you raise a fortune. See the case of the Clinton impeachment. Senators don't react to behavioral slip-ups by raising more money because, in many cases, they are already in the process of raising a fortune. Why? Because they regularly face experienced, well-funded challengers. The competition is usually fierce for seats in the Senate, and quality candidates can find the money to run. In essence, we can see the practical impact of public funding on representational politics by looking at what is already going on in the Senate. Fail to pay attention to your constituents and continually replace their preferences with your own, and you can just plain go home. It isn't all that pretty, but it is representation. If we don't have significant campaign finance reform, don't expect to see much of it (at least not in the House).

NOTES

Notes to Chapter One

1. The article charging the president with obstruction of justice failed on a 50–50 vote and the article charging him with perjury failed on a 45–55 vote. Ironically, these votes were cast on the 190th anniversary of the birth of Abraham Lincoln.

2. Starr is the last independent prosecutor for the foreseeable future, given Congress's unwillingness to renew the enabling legislation that created the office of the independent prosecutor in the first place.

3. Clinton eventually agreed to a monetary settlement of the Jones suit ($850,000) after her legal team appealed the dismissal of the case by U.S. District Court Judge Susan Webber Wright.

4. For comparison, the Republicans lost 5 Senate seats and 48 House seats during the 1974 mid-term elections.

5. The report of the independent counsel to Congress (*The Starr Report* 1998) and the official transcripts of House Judiciary Committee hearings and the floor proceedings in the House and the Senate (McLoughlin 1999) provide the basis for the events chronicled in the following description. I have made every effort to present only the undisputed facts.

6. The resignations took effect at the end of the 2nd session of the 105th Congress.

7. Only five Democrats voted in support of the first three articles of impeachment. None supported the fourth article. There were, however, a sufficient number of Republicans supporting the two successful articles that not a single Democratic vote was required for passage.

8. Senators' explanations were similar to their House colleagues', but the motives they attributed to opponents in their chamber were somewhat different (and more honorable) than the motives representatives attributed to their House opponents. More on this later.

9. During House floor debates on the articles of impeachment, Representative Bilbray (R.–Calif.) made the following comment:

... [A] colleague, Mr. Neal [D-MA], just impugned the moderates who have decided not to vote their way, as if we were somehow being pressured. I would challenge anyone on this floor to name the moderates who have come to you and said we have been pressured. I, for one, and my colleagues I have spoken to have said this is a vote of conscience (McCloughlin 1999: 198).

10. The individualistic orientation of legislators is most aptly characterized in the following passage from Herrnson's recent work on congressional elections:

Members are largely self-recruited, are nominated and elected principally as a result of their own efforts, and know they bear the responsibility for ensuring they get reelected. Local party organizations, Washington-based party committees, PACs, and other groups and individuals may have helped them raise money and win votes, but politicians arrive in Congress with the belief that they owe their tenure to their *own* efforts (1998: 221; emphasis added).

11. Richard Fenno (1966) identifies "good public policy" as one of the three principal objectives all legislators attempt to achieve. The others are re-election and institutional power.

12. For the classic treatment of this issue, see Mayhew (1974).

13. Because Clinton escaped removal, it is possible that future generations will underestimate the significance of this chapter in our political history. What time cannot obscure is the fact that the representatives and senators who made these decisions admitted that only an outright declaration of war, a vote few had ever cast, rivaled in importance the Clinton impeachment.

14. Rep. James Rogan (R.–Calif.), a prominent member of the House management team during the Senate hearings, for example, raised over $1 million during the first six months of the 2000 election cycle; this is approximately the same amount of money that he raised during the *entire* 1998 election cycle. It is more than likely that his role during the impeachment process—as a moderate Republican serving a district opposed to impeachment—greatly aided his ability to generate campaign contributions from traditionally conservative sources (Wicker 1999).

Notes to Chapter Two

1. The report of the independent counsel to Congress (*The Starr Report* 1998) and the official transcripts of House Judiciary Committee

hearings and the floor proceedings in the House and the Senate (McLoughlin 1999) provide the basis for the events chronicled in the following brief outline. I have made every effort to present only the undisputed facts.

2. See Jeffrey Toobin (1999) for an interesting perspective on the legalization of political conflict and the impact of this dynamic on the Clinton-Lewinsky scandal specifically.

3. According to Jeffrey Toobin, one member of this three-judge panel, David Sentelle, lunched with Jesse Helms (R.–N.C.) and Lauch Faircloth (R.–N.C.) shortly before deciding to remove Fiske. Toobin notes that "the timing of the lunch suggested that the senators were lobbying Sentelle to dump Fiske" (1999: 73).

4. Jones attempted to appeal this dismissal to the U.S. Circuit Court of Appeals after the publication of *The Starr Report* (O'Connor and Hermann 2000). Clinton finally settled this case for a financial payment of $850,000. The settlement did not require, and Clinton did not provide, an admission of guilt to any of the allegations on which the suit was based.

5. Thirty-one Democrats supported the inquiry resolution.

6. These witnesses included Harvard law professor Alan Dershowitz and Harvard government professor Samuel Beer.

7. The members of the House Judiciary Committee are listed in Appendix 2-1.

8. The resignations took effect at the end of the 2nd session of the 105th Congress.

9. Members' comments during these closed sessions were subsequently incorporated into the *Congressional Record*.

Notes to Chapter Three

1. In 1997, the year before the public disclosure of Clinton's relationship with Lewinsky, the Gallup Organization polled national opinion on presidential job approval 19 times. In 1998, the Gallup Organization fielded 42 polls that tapped presidential job approval. In 1999, the number was 37, and by 2000, the number had dropped back to 28.

2. See David Schippers and Alan Henry (2000) for a description of the House managers' efforts to wage a full-scale prosecution against the president and their deep disappointment over the Senate's handling of the case and the fact that the president's administration survived.

Notes to Chapter Four

1. See also David Mayhew (1974).

2. The individualistic orientation of legislators is most aptly characterized in the following passage from Herrnson's work on congressional elections:

> Members are largely self-recruited, are nominated and elected principally as a result of their own efforts, and know they bear the responsibility for ensuring they get reelected. Local party organizations, Washington-based party committees, PACs, and other groups and individuals may have helped them raise money and win votes, but politicians arrive in Congress with the belief that they owe their tenure to their own efforts (1998: 221).

3. From a legal standpoint, the impeachment process certainly presented some difficult problems and raised a number of complicated issues. But there is no evidence that the public perceived the issue as complex or complicated, that is, difficult to reach a decision about, and it is the absence of the perception of insurmountable complexity that is important.

4. See Jeffrey Segal and Harold Spaeth (1996) and Lee Epstein and Jack Knight (1998) for an overview of these two perspectives toward judicial decision making.

5. Early attempts to identify the relationship between constituency opinion and representative behavior were actually based on national samples of approximately this size (Miller and Stokes 1963). Subsequent research identified several serious problems with this type of analysis and suggested an alternative methodology (see Erikson 1978). See Robert Erikson, John P. McIver, and Gerald Wright (1987) and Kim Quaile Hill and Patricia Hurley (1999) for critiques of these methodologies.

6. For a recent example of the implementation of this technique, see Quentin Kidd (1998). Note that we are interested in estimating aggregate opinion from individual-level data, not individual opinions from aggregate data, so the relatively new ecological inference technique developed by Gary King (1998) is inappropriate.

7. Respondents indicating no opinion or no knowledge and respondents refusing to answer were coded as missing.

8. The two significant variables in the ordered logistic model were a dummy variable for a Clinton vote in 1996 and a dummy variable for African American. Other demographic variables (e.g., income, a dummy variable for Latino, etc.) were insignificant. In previous studies dealing with district-level opinion on the Clinton impeachment (see Emmert and Lanoue 1999; Jacobson 1999), the district-level Clinton vote in 1996 was used as the indicator of opposition to impeachment. The correlation between the Clinton vote and the district-level indicator is very high (>.95). The main difference is that the Clinton vote variable slightly underestimates opposition to impeachment in districts with sizable African American populations.

9. Although Emmert and Lanoue find multicollinearity a problem for models including both Clinton's vote share in 1996 and member's vote share in 1996, multicollinearity is not a problem when member's 1996 vote share is replaced by member's 1998 vote share. The correlation between Clinton's 1996 vote share and member's 1998 vote share is <0.25.

10. Emmert and Lanoue (1999) argue that the number of Democrats who voted yes on any of the articles of impeachment is so low that it was not possible to estimate individual models for each roll call vote.

11. Because this variable, TOTAL, is an ordinal variable ranging from 0 to 4, the estimation technique is ordered logistic regression. Detailed methodological descriptions of this technique can be found in William Greene (2000) and Peter Kennedy (1997). M.V. Hood and Irwin Morris (1997) also provide a useful description of the technique and the circumstances in which it is most applicable.

12. Emmert and Lanoue also found evidence that seniority and lame duck status affect Democratic votes on impeachment. Lame ducks were eliminated from the sample used in this analysis, and even in Emmert and Lanoue's analysis neither the seniority nor the lame duck variables is significant.

13. It is coded 1 for Democrats and 0 for Republicans.

Notes to Chapter Five

1. Richard Posner notes that "the impeachment of Andrew Johnson was overtly political" (1999: 111).

2. See also Eric Uslaner (1999) for other factors that foster the "shirking" of representational responsibilities in the Senate.

3. Michael Bailey and David Brady (1998) provide an excellent treatment of this issue, demonstrating that the impact of constituency preferences on roll call votes in the Senate (at least on international free trade issues during 1993–1994) is a function of constituency heterogeneity: Senators serving more homogeneous states tended to weight constituency preferences more heavily than senators serving more diverse states. Unfortunately, because of the small number of votes involved in the impeachment case and a somewhat less detailed understanding of the full set of determinants of constituency opinion on impeachment, the structure of their analysis cannot be adequately replicated in this context.

4. Frequently, senators from opposing parties who serve the same state are ideologically distinct. This is true for several Southern states (e.g., North and South Carolina) and several Midwestern states (including Indiana).

5. Recent evidence suggests that Southern Republicans react to sizable, mobilized African American populations by becoming increasingly conservative (to increase support among conservative whites) (see Hood, Kidd, and Morris 1999, 2001). The same type of dynamic may be at work here.

6. See Americans for Democratic Action, "1999 ADA Senate Liberal Quotients (LQs) by State," http://adaction.org/1999senlq.html.

7. Recent work by Tim Groseclose et al. (1998) indicates that ideological indicators such as ADA scores must undergo an adjustment procedure before valid inferences can be drawn over time or across chambers. As I am only concerned with making distinctions between members of the same chamber in the same year, the adjustments are not necessary here.

8. The difference between the ideological scores of senators who supported only one of the articles and the ideological scores of senators who supported both articles is trivial.

9. PARTY and ADA99 are highly collinear. In a regression from which ADA99 has been dropped, PARTY is signed correctly and is significant. However, the explanatory power of a model without ADA99 is somewhat less than the explanatory power of a model without PARTY. By itself, ideology is a better predictor of vote choice and it is not clear that partisanship provides anything beyond ideology. I am not willing to say that partisanship is completely unimportant in this decision-making context, but its real importance remains to be rigorously demonstrated.

Notes to Chapter Six

1. In some of his most recent work, Fenno (2000) demonstrates that the importance of establishing an effective "homestyle" (including the ability to "explain" oneself) has not gone out of style in the nearly 25 years since the original publication of his groundbreaking work on representatives' behavior in their districts and relationships to their constituents.

2. I am not suggesting that the relationship between donor and legislator is any type of simplistic quid pro quo; these relationships are usually far more subtle (see Grenzke 1989b; Stratmann 1991). Nevertheless, whether it is access, time, work in committee, or floor votes, contributors usually expect and receive some consideration (see the following sample of works from an admittedly voluminous literature: Sabato 1984, 1989; Sorauf 1988; West and Loomis 1999; Wright 1985, 1989, 1996).

3. There is, however, some evidence that this advantage may be dissipating (Jacobson 2001).

4. Data gathered from the Federal Election Commission website (www.fec.gov). These figures include contributions made prior to October 18, 2000, the latest data available at the time the analysis was conducted.

5. Given established differences in the structural/institutional determinants of PAC and individual contributions—for example, a much stronger leadership effect for PAC contributions—estimating a model where these two types of contributions are grouped is inappropriate.

6. See Appendix to Chapter 6 for a complete list of the variables used in the analysis. Seniority and ideology (ADA scores) were also included in preliminary versions of the various models. Because these variables were consistently insignificant, they were excluded from the final models.

7. Candidates who refused to accept any PAC funding were excluded from the sample.

8. Results available from the author.

9. This result is not a function of or due to Bill McCollum's large campaign war chest for the 2000 Florida Senate race. House incumbents running for Senate seats, such as McCollum and Richard Lazio (N.Y.), were excluded from the analysis.

10. Data gathered from the Federal Election Commission website (www.fec.gov). Rankings are as of October 18, 2000.

11. The Democratic model includes all of the above variables except MANAGER. Obviously, this variable is excluded because there is no variance on it within the Democratic sample.

12. This is the sum of the IMPOPP coefficients for both the PAC and individual contribution models for Republicans.

Notes to Chapter Seven

1. In 2000, the overwhelming majority of incumbents raised at least twice as much money as their challengers. Not a single incumbent who outspent his or her challenger by a multiple of 2 or more lost.

2. The model with the time-specific variables such as "Manager" and "Antiparty" has a higher R^2 than the general Erikson and Palfrey model. The differences in the PREDICT variables created by the two models are sufficiently small, however, that the spending model results are statistically and substantively comparable regardless of the specific set of variables chosen.

3. Data gathered from the Federal Election Commission website (www.fec.gov).

4. For my purposes, the Southern states are the eleven states of the Confederacy. This operationalization is consistent with the literature on Southern politics (see, in particular, Key 1949).

5. This is consistent with the procedure suggested by Erikson and Palfrey (2000).

6. Candidates receiving more than 80 percent of the two-party vote (a vote percentage more than two standard deviations from the average winning vote total in both the 1998 and 2000 House elections) were excluded from the sample. Increasing this percentage to 85 or 90 percent had no statistically significant impact on the results aside from decreasing the R2 for

the model used to predict vote percentage in 2000. Results available from the author.

7. Most seats in this category are either "open" or are held by representatives who were appointed since the 1998 election. The four other incumbents referenced (those seeking re-election in 2000) are James Rogan (R.–Calif.), Brian P. Bilbray (R.–Calif.), John Hostetler (R.–Ind.), and Jim Maloney (D.–Conn.). Only Hostetler and Maloney won re-election.

8. Limited sample size also prevented me from implementing the alternative analysis—estimates from samples based on predicted 2000 vote—because of the tiny samples associated with the ranges identified by Ericson and Palfrey (2000). It is important to remember that Ericson and Palfrey's (2000) analysis spans a 17-year timeframe that greatly increases the sample size for every relevant category.

9. The challenger and incumbent funding results do not depend on the inclusion of the predicted vote variable. If the predicted vote variable is dropped from the model, no significant statistical or substantive change occurs in the funding variables.

10. In a few cases, the impeachment fund estimates exceeded total campaign receipts. To avoid the problems associated with the undefined log of a negative number, a contribution floor of $5,000 was imposed. Significantly higher floors ($10,000, $20,000, etc.) have only a marginal impact on the aggregate results. Obviously, imposing this contribution floor leads to *underestimation* of impeachment fund effects and makes it more difficult to demonstrate that the impeachment funds made a significant electoral difference.

11. In some cases the high estimate for "impeachment" funds when compared to actual money raised reflects the possibility that a member might not have faced a significant general election opponent absent the impact of impeachment politics. Sununu (R.–N.H.), for example, won two-thirds of the two-party vote in 1998, but barely won re-election in 2000. Had impeachment not been an issue, Sununu might have raised much less money because he might not have faced a significant challenger (or any challenger at all, for that matter).

12. Technically, 56.36 percent of the two-party vote based on the calculations. Because Charles Taylor (R.–N.C.) received 56.48 percent of the two-party vote, he is not included in this table.

13. These results do not depend on the $5000 dollar spending floor. The Republicans would still have lost the House if the floor were significantly higher.

14. And even Rogan's case gives one pause. Rogan was serving a marginal district before the impeachment. His high profile role in the impeachment proceedings was enormously unpopular in his district, and his challenger still had to raise more than $3 million to win a close election.

Notes to Chapter Eight

1. John Kerrey (D.–Neb.) was the only Democrat to vote against a majority of his or her constituents. It is important to note that only the barest majority of voters in Nebraska (less than 53 percent) favored impeachment and conviction, and that Kerrey retired at the end of the 106th Congress.

2. Two senators running for re-election in 2000—Zell Miller (D.–Ga.) and Lincoln Chafee (R.–R.I.) were appointed after the early 1999 conviction votes. Chafee was appointed to the remainder of his father's term (his father died on October 24, 1999), and Miller was appointed to his seat following the death of Republican Senator Paul Coverdell. Chafee completed his father's term, and Miller competed in a special election in 2000 for the balance of Coverdell's term. In a technical sense, both of these individuals were in an election campaign in 2000 as opposed to a re-election campaign. For obvious reasons, both are excluded from the analyses presented in this chapter.

3. It is worth noting that Allen outspent Robb by over $3 million.

4. These senators were Spencer Abraham (Mich.), John Ashcroft (Mo.), Slade Gorton (Wash.), Rod Grams (Minn.), and William V. Roth Jr. (Del.). This does not include the loss of Connie Mack's (Fla.) seat by Bill McCollum.

5. See Gerber (1998) for a detailed explanation of this phenomenon.

6. The dependent variable for the model results presented in Table 8–4 is the log of campaign dollars raised by the incumbent per member of the voting age population.

7. The inclusion of the interactive term IMPOPP*CONVICT has no substantive or statistically significant impact on the results for either the incumbent model or the challenger model. In fact, the extremely high multicollinearity makes this formulation methodologically suspect.

8. The sample size for the House was obviously much larger.

9. At least the impeachment votes made a much bigger difference in the 2000 Senate elections than Senator McConnell expected.

10. It is worth noting that another Senate seat lost by the Republicans was Connie Mack III's Florida seat. Mack retired, and the Republican who tried to replace him, Bill McCollum, was a prominent impeachment supporter and House manager. Although McCollum did not cast a vote for conviction (he was obviously serving in the House at the time), he did lose the election by less than 5 percentage points, so it is not unreasonable to think that his role in the impeachment proceedings made the difference for him also. Admittedly, it is possible he would not even have been able to run for the seat without the publicity that the impeachment proceedings afforded him.

Notes to Chapter Nine

1. As noted in Chapters 2 and 3, the core disagreement between members appears to have been over the extent to which the actions that Clinton could not reasonably deny were impeachable offenses. I have yet to find a statement made by a representative or a senator for which both of the following are true:

1. the member admitted that the charges against the president (made first by the independent counsel and then by the House managers) had been proven beyond a reasonable doubt (i.e., the president had committed perjury, had abused the power of his office, and had obstructed justice) and

2. the member concluded that the charges against the president—although proven beyond a reasonable doubt—were not sufficiently serious to warrant impeachment.

In the case of the Clinton impeachment, disagreements over the constitutional standard for impeachment were also disagreements over claims about Clinton's behavior. Some members spoke of these issues as if they were separable, and theoretically they are separable. But practically speaking, they are not.

2. Obviously, in the final analysis, Clinton and his administration survived the congressional threat, but only by the slimmest of margins. Given the constitutional import of the passage of two articles of impeachment (only the second time in U.S. history that a president has been impeached) and the near majority vote in the Senate for one of these articles, it is stretching credulity to say the public "won" anything that vaguely resembles a "victory." At best, the American people avoided a devastating loss because of the foresight of the drafters of the Constitution (who set the decision rule for removal very high). Grander claims require a blatant disregard for what actually happened.

3. In a few texts there is also a type of representative referred to as a "politico," which is something like an amalgam of the trustee and the delegate. Including the politico in the discussion adds little of substance, so for the sake of brevity and clarity, I focus solely on the trustee and the delegate.

4. For detailed quotes, see the previous chapters, particularly Chapter 4.

5. Darrell West (2000) provides an especially useful look at this set of reforms.

REFERENCES

ABC News polls. Various dates, 1998–2000.

ABC News/*Washington Post* Impeachment Hearing Poll, December 12–13, 1998.

Abramowitz, Alan. 1988. "Explaining Senate Election Outcomes." *American Political Science Review* 82:385–404.

_____. 1991. "Incumbency, Campaign Spending, and the Decline of Competition in U.S. House Elections." *Journal of Politics* 53:34–56.

_____. 1999. "It's Monica, Stupid: Voting Behavior in the 1998 Midterm Election." Paper presented at the Annual Meeting of the American Political Science Association, Atlanta, Georgia.

Abramowitz, Alan I., and Jeffrey A. Segal. 1992. *Senate Elections*. Ann Arbor, MI: University of Michigan Press.

Ackerman, Bruce. 1999. *The Case Against Lameduck Impeachment*. New York: Seven Stories Press.

Aldrich, John. 1995. *Why Parties?* Chicago: University of Chicago Press.

Andolina, Molly W., and Clyde Wilcox. 2000. "Public Opinion: The Paradoxes of Clinton's Popularity." In *The Clinton Scandal and the Future of American Government*, edited by Mark J. Rozell and Clyde Wilcox. Washington, DC: Georgetown University Press.

Apple, R. W., Jr. 1998. "The 1998 Elections: The Congress—News Analysis; New Outlook on 2000 Race." *New York Times*, November 5, sec. A, p. 7.

Arnold, R. Douglas. 1990. *The Logic of Congressional Action*. New Haven, CT: Yale University Press.

Asher, Herbert. 1998. *Polling and the Public: What Every Citizen Should Know*. 4th ed. Washington, DC: CQ Press.

Ayres, B. Drummond, Jr. 1999. "The President's Trial: The Nation; Clinton's Consistent Poll Ratings Show Starr Report Marked Turning Point." *New York Times*, January 26, p. A15.

Bailey, Michael, and David W. Brady. 1998. "Heterogeneity and Representation: The Senate and Free Trade." *American Journal of Political Science* 42:524–44.

Baker, Peter. 2000. *The Breach: Inside the Impeachment Trial of William Jefferson Clinton.* New York: Scribner.

Benedetto, Richard. 1999. "Majority Opinion Hasn't Changed." *USA Today,* January 8, p. 14A.

Berger, Raoul. 1999. *Impeachment: The Constitutional Problems, Enlarged Edition.* Cambridge, MA: Harvard University Press.

Broder, David S. 1998. "Livingston's Resignation Sets an Example and Offers a Challenge." *Star Tribune,* December 23, sec. A, p. 21.

Burnes, Brian. 1998. "Opinion Is Split on Watergate Similarity." *Kansas City Star,* December 12, p. A17.

Campbell, James E. 2000. *The American Campaign: U.S. Presidential Campaigns and the National Vote.* College Station, TX: Texas A&M University Press.

Clawson, Dan, Alan Neustadtl, and Denise Scott. 1992. *Money Talks: Corporate PACs and Political Influence.* New York: Basic Books.

Congressional Record. February 12, 1999, S1478–S1573.

Cox, Gary, and Mathew McCubbins. 1993. *Legislative Leviathan: Party Government in the House.* Berkeley: University of California Press.

Donnelly, David, Janice Fine, and Ellen S. Miller. 1999. *Money and Politics: Financing Our Elections Democratically.* Boston: Beacon Press.

Emmert, Craig J., and David F. Lanoue. 1999. "Voting in the Glare of the Spotlight: Representatives' Votes on the Impeachment of President Clinton." *Polity* 32:253–69.

Epstein, Lee, and Jack Knight. 1998. *The Choices Justices Make.* Washington, DC: CQ Press.

Erikson, Robert S. 1978. "Constituency Opinion and Congressional Behavior: A Reexamination of the the Miller-Stokes Representation Data." *American Journal of Political Science* 22:511–35.

——. 1989. "Economic Conditions and the Presidential Vote." *American Political Science Review.* 83:567–73.

Erikson, Robert S., John P. McIver, and Gerald C. Wright, Jr. 1987. "State Political Culture and Public Opinion." *American Political Science Review* 81:796–813.

Erikson, Robert S., and Thomas R. Palfrey. 1993. "The Spending Game: Money, Votes, and Incumbency in Congressional Elections." Social Science Working Paper No. 806. California Institute of Technology.

——. 1998. "Campaign Spending and Incumbency: An Alternative Simultaneous Equations Approach." *Journal of Politics* 60:355–73.

——. 2000. "Equilibria in Campaign Spending Games: Theory and Data." *American Political Science Review* 94: 595–610.

The Federalist Papers. 1982. By Alexander Hamilton, James Madison, and John Jay. Edited by Garry Wills. New York: Bantam Books.

Fenno, Richard F., Jr. 1966. *The Power of the Purse.* Boston: Little, Brown.

———. 1978. *Home Style: House Members in Their Districts.* Boston: Little, Brown.

———. 1982. *The United States Senate: A Bicameral Perspective.* Washington, DC: American Enterprise Institute.

———. 2000. *Congress at the Grassroots: Representational Change in the South, 1970–1998.* Chapel Hill: University of North Carolina Press.

Flanigan, William H., and Nancy H. Zingale. 1998. *Political Behavior of the American Electorate.* Washington, DC: CQ Press.

Fritz, Sara, and Dwight Morris. 1992. *Gold-Plated Politics: Running for Congress in the 1990s.* Washington, DC: Congressional Quarterly.

Gais, Thomas. 1998. *Improper Influence: Campaign Finance Laws, Political Interest Groups, and the Problem of Equality.* Ann Arbor: University of Michigan Press.

The Gallup Poll Monthly. July 1974

Gallup Polls. Various dates, 1998–1999. By the Gallup Organization.

Gerber, Alan. 1998. "Estimating the Effect of Campaign Spending on Senate Election Outcomes Using Instrumental Variables." *American Political Science Review* 92:401–12.

Gerhardt, Michael J. 2000. "The Impeachment and Acquittal of William Jefferson Clinton." In *The Clinton Scandal and the Future of American Government,* edited by Mark J. Rozell and Clyde Wilcox. Washington, DC: Georgetown University Press.

Gierzynski, Anthony. 2000. *Money Rules: Financing Elections in America.* Boulder, CO: Westview Press.

Ginsberg, Benjamin. and Martin Shefter. 1999. *Politics by Other Means: Politicians, Prosecutors, and Press from Watergate to Whitewater.* New York: W.W. Norton.

Glynn, Carroll J., Susan Herbst, Garrett J. O'Keefe, and Robert Y. Shapiro. 1999. *Public Opinion.* Boulder, CO: Westview Press.

Goidel, Robert K., Donald A. Gross, and Todd G. Shields. 1999. *Money Matters: Consequences of Campaign Finance Reform in U.S. House Elections.* Lanham, MD: Rowman & Littlefield.

Green, Donald P., and Jonathan S. Krasno. 1988. "Salvation for the Spendthrift Incumbent: Reestimating the Effects of Campaign Spending in the House Elections." *American Journal of Political Science* 32:884–907.

Green, John C., and Daniel M. Shea. 1996. *The State of the Parties: The Changing Role of Contemporary American Parties.* 2nd ed. Lanham, MD: Rowman & Littlefield.

Greene, William H. 2000. *Econometric Analysis.* 4th ed. Upper Saddle River, NJ: Prentice Hall.

Grenzke, Janet. 1989a. "Candidate Attributes and PAC Contributions." *Western Political Quarterly* 42:245–64.

Grenzke, Janet. 1989b. "PACs and the Congressional Supermarket: The Currency Is Complex." *American Journal of Political Science* 28:258–81.

Grier, Kevin, Michael Munger, and Gary Torrent. 1990. "Allocation Patterns of PAC Monies: The U.S. Senate." *Public Choice* 67:111–28.

Groseclose, Tim, Steven D. Levitt, and James M. Snyder, Jr. 1999. "Comparing Interest Group Scores Across Time and Chambers: Adjusted ADA Scores for the US Congress." *American Political Science Review* 93:33-50.

Herrnson, Paul S. 1998. *Congressional Elections: Campaigning at Home and in Washington.* 2nd ed. Washington, DC: CQ Press.

———. 2000. *Congressional Elections: Campaigning at Home and in Washington.* 3rd ed. Washington, DC: CQ Press.

Herrnson, Paul S., Robert Biersack, John Green, Lynda Powell, and Clyde Wilcox. 2001. *Investors, Ideologues, and Intimates: The Financiers of Congressional Elections.* New York: Columbia University Press.

Hibbing, John R., and Elizabeth Theiss-Morse. 1995. *Congress as Public Enemy: Public Attitudes Toward American Political Institutions.* Cambridge: Cambridge University Press.

Hill, Kim Quaile, and Patricia A. Hurley. 1999. "Dyadic Representation Reappraised." *American Journal of Political Science* 43:109–37.

Hojnacki, Marie, and David C. Kimball. 1998. "Organized Interests and the Decision of Whom to Lobby in Congress." *American Political Science Review* 92:775–90.

Hood, M.V., III, and Irwin L. Morris. 1997. "*Quedate o Vente*: Analyzing Anglo Opinions on Immigration." *Social Science Quarterly* 50:627–47.

Hood, M.V., III, Quentin Kidd, and Irwin L. Morris. 1999. "From Byrds to Bumpers: Using Southern Senators to Analyze Ideological Change." *American Journal of Political Science* 43:465–87.

———. Forthcoming. "Roll Call Voting in the Senate on Civil Rights Issues." *Legislative Studies Quarterly.*

House Debates. Various dates. Washington, DC: Government Printing Office.

Jacobs, Lawrence R., and Robert Y. Shapiro. 2000. *Politicians Don't Pander: Political Manipulation and the Loss of Democratic Responsiveness.* Chicago: University of Chicago Press.

Jacobson, Gary C. 1978. "The Effects of Campaign Spending in Congressional Elections." *American Political Science Review* 72:469–91.

———. 1980. *Money in Congressional Elections.* New Haven, CT: Yale University Press.

———. 1985. "Money and Votes Reconsidered: Congressional Elections, 1972–1982." *Public Choice* 47:7–62.

_____. 1990. "The Effects of Campaign Spending in House Elections: New Evidence for Old Arguments." *American Journal of Political Science* 34:334–62.

_____. 1997. *The Politics of Congressional Elections.* 4th ed. New York: Longman.

_____. 1999. "Impeachment Politics and the 1998 Congressional Elections." *Political Science Quarterly* 114:31–51.

_____. 2001. *The Politics of Congressional Elections.* 5th ed. New York: Addison Wesley Longman.

"'Justice' Gone Amok Clinton Impeached." 1998. *Miami Herald,* December 20, sec A, p. 15.

Kazee, Thomas A. 2000. "The Congress: The Politics of Impeachment." In *The Clinton Scandal and the Future of American Government,* edited by Mark J. Rozell and Clyde Wilcox. Washington, DC: Georgetown University Press.

Kennedy, Peter. 1997. *A Guide to Econometrics.* 5th ed. Cambridge, MA: MIT Press.

Kernell, Samuel. 1997. *Going Public: New Strategies of Presidential Leadership.* 3rd ed. Washington, DC: CQ Press.

Key, V. O. 1949. *Southern Politics in State and Nation.* New York: A. A. Knopf.

Kidd, Quentin. 1998. "Congressional Foreign and Defense Policy Decision Making: A Comprehensive Examination Across Three Categories of Policy." Ph.D. dissertation, Texas Tech University, Lubbock, Texas.

King, Gary. 1998. *A Solution to the Ecological Inference Problem.* Princeton, NJ: Princeton University Press.

Kingdon, John W. 1989. *Congressmen's Voting Decisions.* 3rd ed. Ann Arbor: Michigan University Press.

Kotok, C. David. 1999. "Gallup Poll Chief Warns of Wary Public." *Omaha World-Herald,* April 23, p. 3.

Krasno, Jonathan S. 1994. *Challengers, Competition, and Reelection: Comparing Senate and House Elections.* New Haven, CT: Yale University Press.

Krasno, Jonathan S., Donald Philip Green, and Jonathan A. Cowden. 1994. "The Dynamics of Campaign Fundraising in House Elections." *Journal of Politics* 56:459–74.

Kuklinski, James H., and Richard Elling. 1977. "Representational Role, Constituency Opinion, and Legislative Roll Call Behavior." *American Journal of Political Science* 21:135–47.

Langer, Gary. 1999. "No Joy at Saga's End: Majority of Americans Feel System Failed Them." *ABCNews.Com,* February 13, http://abcnews. go.com/sections/politics/DailyNews/impeachpoll990213.html.

Lester, Will. 1998. "Like Nixon, Clinton Seeks Solace from Polls." *Buffalo News*, October 11.

Levitt, Steven D. 1996. "How Do Senators Vote? Disentangling the Role of Voter Preferences, Party Affiliation, and Senator Ideology." *American Economic Review* 86(3):425–41.

Loomis, Burdett A. 1998. *The Contemporary Congress*. 2nd ed. New York: St. Martin's Press.

Lowenthal, Diane, William Keech, and George Lowenstein. 1999. "Forgotten, But Not Forgiven: Remembering Congressional Actions on Impeachment." Paper presented at the Annual Convention of the American Political Science Association, Atlanta, GA.

Mayhew, David R. 1974. *Congress: The Electoral Connection*. New Haven, CT: Yale University Press.

McLoughlin, Merrill, ed. 1999. *The Impeachment and Trial of President Clinton: The Official Transcripts, from the House Judiciary Committee Hearings and the Senate Trial*. New York: New York Times Books.

Miller, Warren E., and Donald E. Stokes. 1963. "Constituency Influence in Congress." *American Political Science Review* 57:45–56.

Moore, David W. 1998. "Public Leans Against Impeachment Hearings; Holds Fast Against Removal From Office." *Gallup Poll News Service,* http://www.gallup.com/poll/releases/pr981010.asp.

Morello, Carol, and Robert Saiz Holguin. 1999. "Poll Reflects Disapproval of Bill Clinton, the Man." *USA Today,* January 22, p. 12A.

Moscardelli, Vincent G., Moshe Haspel, and Richard S. Wike. 1998. "Party Building through Campaign Finance Reform: Conditional Party Government in the 104th Congress." *Journal of Politics* 60:691–704.

Nagourney, Adam. 1998. "The Nation: Battles Joined—A Country at War, Both Abroad and at Home; Behind the Urge to Impeach." *New York Times,* December 20, sec. 4, p. 1.

O'Connor, Karen, and John R. Hermann. 2000. "The Courts: The Perils of Paula." In *The Clinton Scandal and the Future of American Government,* edited by Mark J. Rozell and Clyde Wilcox. Washington, DC: Georgetown University Press.

Oleszek, Walter J. 1996. *Congressional Procedures and the Policy Process.* 4th ed. Washington, DC: CQ Press.

Ornstein, Norm. 1999. "Clinton's 'Terminator' Appeal." *USA Today,* January 20, p. 13A.

Ornstein, Norman J., Robert L. Peabody, and David W. Rohde. 1987. "Party Leadership and the Institutional Context: The Senate from Baker to Dole." *Legislative Studies Quarterly* 12:162–63.

Overby, L. Marvin, Beth M. Henschen, Michael H. Walsh, and Julie Strauss. 1992. "Courting Constituents? An Analysis of the Senate Confirmation Vote on Justice Clarence Thomas." *American Political Science Review* 86:997–1003

Page, Susan, and Richard Benedetto. 1999. "Public's Dueling Views: Many Americans Balance Performance vs. Character." *USA Today,* January 19, p. 1A.

Pierce, Emily, and Barbra Murray. 2000. "GOP Likely to Hold Senate." *CQ Weekly,* October 21, p. 2462.

Pitkin, Hannah Fenichel. 1967. *The Concept of Representation.* Berkeley: University of California Press.

"Poll Readings for January 30, 1999." 1999. *National Journal,* January 30, p. 283.

Posner, Richard A. 1999. *An Affair of State: The Investigation, Impeachment, and Trial of President Clinton.* Cambridge, MA: Harvard University Press.

Riker, William. 1982. *Liberalism Against Populism.* San Francisco: W. H. Freeman.

Rohde, David W. 1991. *Parties and Leaders in the Postreform House.* Chicago: University of Chicago Press.

Rozell, Mark J., and Clyde Wilcox. 2000. *The Clinton Scandal and the Future of American Government.* Washington, DC: Georgetown University Press.

Rudolph, Thomas J. 1999. "Corporate and Labor PAC Contributions in House Elections: Measuring the Effects of Majority Party Status." *Journal of Politics* 61:195–206.

Sabato, Larry. 1984. *PAC Power : Inside the World of Political Action Committees.* New York: W. W. Norton.

_____. 1989. *Paying for Elections: The Campaign Finance Thicket.* New York: Priority Press.

Schiller, Wendy J. 2000. *Partners and Rivals: Representation in U.S. Senate Delegations.* Princeton, NJ: Princeton University Press.

Schippers, David P., and Alan P. Henry. 2000. *Sellout: The Inside Story of Clinton's Impeachment.* Washington, DC: Regnery Publishing.

Schmickle, Sharon. 1998. "Now and Then: Mood Was different in '74." *Star Tribune,* December 13, p. 19A.

Segal, Jeffrey A., and Harold Spaeth. 1996. "The Influence of *Stare Decisis* on the Votes of United States Supreme Court Justices." *American Journal of Political Science* 40:971–1003.

Snyder, James M., Jr., and Tim Groseclose. 2000. "Estimating Party Influence in Congressional Roll-Call Voting." *American Journal of Political Science* 44(2):193–211.

Sorauf, Frank J. 1988. *Money in American Elections.* Boston: Scott, Foresman.

Star Tribune. December 23, 1998, p. 21A.

The Starr Report: The Independent Counsel's Complete Report to Congress on the Investigation of President Clinton. 1998. New York: Pocket Books.

Stein, Robert M., and Kenneth Bickers. 1994. "Congressional Elections and the Pork Barrel." *Journal of Politics* 56:377–99.

———. 1995. *Perpetuating the Pork Barrel: Policy Subsystems and American Democracy.* Cambridge: Cambridge University Press.

Steuerle, C. Eugene, Edward M. Gramlich, Hugh Heclo, and Demetra Smith Nightingale. 1998. *The Government We Deserve: Responsive Democracy and Changing Expectations.* Washington, DC: The Urban Institute.

Stimson, James A. 1999. *Public Opinion in America: Moods, Cycles, and Swings.* 2nd ed. Boulder, CO: Westview Press.

Stratmann, Thomas. 1991. "What Do Campaign Contributions Buy? Deciphering Causal Effects of Money and Votes." *Southern Economic Journal* 57:606–20.

———. 2000. "Congressional Voting Over Legislative Careers: Shifting Positions and Changing Constraints." *American Political Science Review* 94:665–76.

Thomas, Martin. 1985. "Election Proximity and Senatorial Roll Call Voting." *American Journal of Political Science* 29:96–111.

Toobin, Jeffrey. 1999. *A Vast Conspiracy: The Real Story of the Sex Scandal That Nearly Brought Down a President.* New York: Random House.

USA Today. January 12, 1999.

USA Today. February 22, 1999.

USA/CNN/Gallup Poll. January 1999.

Uslaner, Eric. 1999. *Movers and Shirkers.* Ann Arbor: University of Michigan Press.

Von Drehle, David. 1998. "Yesterday Was Not a Chapter in a Washington Novel; It Was the Unplotted, Unscripted, Head-Spinning Real Thing." *Washington Post.* December 20, sec. A, p. 37.

Washington Post/ABC News Poll. December 21, 1998.

Washington Post/ABC News Impeachment Hearings Poll. December 12–13, 1998.

Wayne, Stephen J. 2001. *Is This Any Way to Run a Democratic Election?* Boston: Houghton Mifflin.

West, Darrell M. 2000. *Checkbook Democracy: How Money Corrupts Political Campaigns.* Boston: Northeastern University Press.

West, Darrell M., and Burdett A. Loomis. 1999. *The Sound of Money: How Political Interests Get What They Want.* New York: W. W. Norton.

Westlye, Mark. 1991. *Senate Elections and Campaign Intensity.* Baltimore, MD: Johns Hopkins University Press.

Wilcox, Clyde. 1995. *The Latest American Revolution: The 1994 Elections and Their Implications for Governance.* New York: St. Martin's Press.

Wood, B. Dan, and Angela Hinton Andersson. 1998. "The Dynamics of Senatorial Representation, 1952–1991." *Journal of Politics* 60:705–36.

Wright, John R. 1985. "PACs, Contributions, and Roll Calls: An Organizational Perspective." *American Political Science Review* 79:400–14.

———. 1989. "PAC Contributions, Lobbying, and Representation." *Journal of Politics* 51:713–30.

———. 1996. *Interest Groups & Congress: Lobbying, Contributions & Influence.* Boston: Allyn & Bacon.

INDEX

Advertising, 109

Campaign finance
"impeachment" funds, 15,
134–138, 139, 180(n10)
individual contributions,
115–116, 119, 123, 131, 134,
170–171
in House elections, 15, 19,
110–119, 121–127, 129–131,
132 (table), 133 (table),
134–138, 167–171
in Senate elections, 15, 20,
139–159, 167–171
PAC (Political Action
Committee) contributions,
113–116, 119, 123, 131, 134,
170–171
reform, 168–171
role in a democracy 16–17
Clinton, Hillary, 4, 39
Clinton-Lewinsky scandal, xv–xvi,
33, 37–42, 48–52, 54, 161–162
Clinton, William
public opinion of, 2, 18, 38–43
(text and table), 44, 45
(figure), 46 (figure), 47, 49–55
Jones v. Clinton lawsuit, 6, 7,
21–22, 24, 26, 33, 37–38, 52,
162, 173(n3)

and Monica Lewinsky, 6, 7,
22–25, 33, 37–39, 41–42,
162
and Jennifer Flowers, 39
Whitewater investigation, 6,
25–26, 39
Congress
distinctiveness of House and
Senate, 85–92
House Judiciary Committee,
7–8, 27–30, 32–33, 36, 69
House managers of the Senate
trial, 34, 36, 53, 58, 84–85,
115, 117, 119, 129, 131,
134–135
House votes on impeachment, 8,
16, 19, 33, 56–57, 65, 67–69,
72, 75–81, 105–119, 121,
126–128, 163–167
Senate votes on conviction, 8,
19, 34–35, 56–57, 92–95,
97–98 (table), 99, 100 (table),
101 (tables), 102 (tables),
103–104, 139–140, 152–159,
164–167
public opinion of, 44–45
(figure), 46 (figure), 47,
53–56
Credit claiming, 109–110
See also Pork barrel projects.

NAME LIST

Abramowitz, Alan
Ackerman, Bruce
Aldrich, John
Andersson, Angela Hinton
Andolina, Molly W.
Apple, R.W. Jr.
Arnold, R. Douglas
Asher, Herbert

Bailey, Michael
Baker, Peter
Benedetto, Richard
Berger, Raoul
Bickers, Kenneth N.
Biersack, Robert
Brady, David W.
Broder, David

Campbell, James E.
Clawson, Dan,
Cowden, Jonathan A.
Cox, Gary

Donnelly, David

Elling, Richard
Emmert, Craig J.
Epstein, Lee
Erickson, Robert S.

Fenno, Richard F. Jr.

Fine, Janice
Flanigan, William H.
Fritz, Sara

Gais, Thomas
Gerber, Alan
Gerhardt, Michael J.
Gierzynski, Anthony
Ginsberg, Benjamin
Glynn, Carroll J.
Goidel, Robert K.
Gramlich, Edward M.
Green, Donald P.
Green, John C.
Greene, William H.
Grenzke, Janet.
Grier, Kevin,
Groseclose, Tim
Gross, Donald A.

Hamilton, Alexander
Haspel, Moshe
Heclo, Hugh
Hendry, Alan P.
Herbst, Susan
Hermann, John R.
Herrnson, Paul S.
Hibbing, John R.
Hill, Kim Quaile
Hojnacki, Marie
Hood, M.V. III